Further Selections from the Prison Notebooks

Antonio Gramsci

Edited and translated by Derek Boothman

University of Minnesota Press
Minneapolis

Introduction, annotation and selection © Derek Boothman 1995
Translation © Lawrence & Wishart 1995

All rights reserved. No part of this publication may be
reproduced, stored in a retrieval system, or transmitted, in any
form or by any means, electronic, mechanical, photocopying,
recording, or otherwise, without the prior written permission of
the publisher.

First published in 1995 by Lawrence & Wishart Limited

Published simultaneously in the United States in 1995
by the University of Minnesota Press
111 Third Avenue South, Suite 290, Minneapolis, MN 55401-2520

Printed at Redwood Books, Trowbridge, Wiltshire.

Library of Congress Cataloging-in-Publication Data

Gramsci, Antonio, 1891–1937.
   [Selections. English.   19915]
  Further selections from the prison notebooks / Antonio Gramsci :
edited and translated by Derek Boothman.
     p.   cm.
   Originally published: London : Lawrence & Wishart, 1995.
   Includes bibliographical references and index.
   ISBN 0-8166-2658-8
    1. Gramsci, Antonio, 1891–1937.   2. Marxist criticism.
I. Boothman, Derek.   II. Title.
HX288.G69213   1995   94-22165
335'.43'092—dc20   CIP

The University of Minnesota is an equal opportunity educator and
employer.

CONTENTS

Acknowledgements vii
Note on the Translation ix
General Introduction xiii

I	Religion: A Movement and an Ideology	1
II	The Origin of Modern Educational Principles	138
III	The Nature and History of Economic Science	161
IV	Economic Trends and Developments	191
V	Science, Logic and Translatability	278
VI	Reference Points for an Essay on B. Croce	326
VII	The Philosophy of Benedetto Croce	362
	Concordance Table	476
	Notes and References	507
	Index	587

ACKNOWLEDGEMENTS

In a book that ranges as wide in its subject matter as this one any editor and translator would indeed be hard-pressed to follow Gramsci on every single point without expert help and advice. The current translator is no exception and owes a great debt of gratitude to various people who have provided guidance in one way or another. Roger Simon made the initial suggestion of the topics to be dealt with and advised throughout, Jeff Skelley was a great help in the initial stage, while all other members of the staff of Lawrence & Wishart down to the present manager, Sally Davison, have been extremely useful when called on. Any serious work on Gramsci is greatly indebted to previous studies and editions of his writings, in particular to Valentino Gerratana's masterly Critical Edition for the Einaudi publishing house of the *Quaderni del Carcere*. As well as to these people, grateful acknowledgement is here also paid to the encouragement, expert professional opinions and criticism of a number of other friends who were directly or indirectly important, amongst whom the following should be mentioned: Giorgio Baratta; Alberto Burgio; Joseph Buttigieg; Andrea Catone; Tullio De Mauro; Carlo Del Monte; Pat Devine; David Forgacs; Fabio Frosini; Luca Gammaitoni; Nadia Grimaldi; Quintin Hoare; Juha Koivisto; Mikko Lahtinen; Geoffrey Nowell Smith; Cesare Salvi, formerly of the PCI secretariat and currently Senator of the Partito Democratico della Sinistra; Regan Scott; Brian Simon; Aurelio Simone; Anita Weston; the staff of the Gramsci Institute in Rome, its director, Giuseppe Vacca, and especially its (unfortunately) former secretary, Antonio A. Santucci, who both advised and granted exceptionally generous access to the photocopies of the manuscripts of the Notebooks held by the Institute. The Science Faculty at the University of Perugia was kind enough to allow a period of leave for necessary work on the book. Special thanks go to Sandra Giovagnoli and Stefano Boothman for their long-suffering patience, occasional irony and unflagging moral support; to Stephen Hayward, who saw the book through editorially with a mixture of tact, humour, patience, expertise and plain good sense; finally to Sara Sica, who read through the whole of the translation, compared it with the original, and made numerous comments and suggestions which improved the text and helped avoid a number of what, for the translator, would have been embarrassing slips.

It is inevitable that errors and weaknesses, for which the translator alone is responsible, will remain in a text of this complexity. He and the publisher would be glad to hear from readers who find such defects.

A NOTE ON THE TRANSLATION

The translation aims at giving a contemporary wording (avoiding, for instance, too heavy a reliance on masculine forms, like 'mankind' for 'humanity') at the same time as paying attention to the need not to introduce distortions through wordings which would indicate concepts post-dating Gramsci's time. All abbreviations used to refer to previously published translations of Gramsci's writings (e.g. SPN for *Selections from the Prison Notebooks*) are explained at the start of the general introduction. As is conventional, square brackets (i.e. '[...]') indicate editorial interpolations while angle brackets (i.e. '<...>') are used for material that Gramsci added at a later date than the main part of any note (above a line or, very frequently, in the margin). Titles of magazine articles are translated into English but it should be understood that the articles themselves are normally in the language of the magazine. The titles of papal encyclicals, on the other hand, are given in their original language (usually Latin), usually followed by an English translation where a generally accepted one exists; the translated title often bears little resemblance to the original but either uses a phrase from near the start of the document or gives a broad indication of the subject matter. (Modern encyclicals began in the mid-eighteenth century and initially had no official translation; the earliest ones quoted here, from the 1830s, are of this nature. Later on pastoral letters, ecclesiastical reviews and books carried translations and, in more recent times, officially approved translations have appeared under the seal of the Vatican Polyglot Press.)

Gramsci's use of language was highly innovatory; in this he was influenced not only by his studies of linguistics and his journalism but also by the need to get round the prison censorship. In addition, as with any language there exist some concepts that are difficult to translate with precision. A few comments on choices made in the translation may not, then, be out of place.

For 'Marxism' Gramsci normally uses the term 'philosophy of praxis', which has now become a hallmark of his writing; 'historical materialism' usually appears in the abbreviated form 'mat. stor.' while the name 'Marx' (used in this translation) in the notebooks is written 'M.' or, if he is mentioned together with Engels, the two are referred to, in the wording retained here, as the 'founders of the philosophy of praxis'.

The word *ceto* has, in the past, often been translated 'stratum', as indeed it had to be when Gramscian ideas were just being introduced into English in SPN and elsewhere. It is, however, more flexible than this would-be counterpart suggests and may refer to a class fraction or a social grouping or groupings (sometimes cutting across class dividing lines) which have a broadly similar function, e.g. a political or intellectual *ceto*. Given this difficulty, wherever the word occurs, *ceto* has been included in brackets after the translation chosen in that specific context.

Gramsci makes frequent use of the adjective *determinato*, as applied to a set of circumstances, to convey the fact that they happen not just by chance but are brought about by a human agency. The rather awkward-sounding 'determinate' has normally been avoided in favour of the more common 'given', 'particular' or 'specific'; this should be borne in mind when phrases with these words occur. In one special case – although the usage may at first sight seem rather strange – the term 'determinate' will however be used. The contexts in which Gramsci uses the wording *mercato determinato* indicate that this wording can mean the markets for various commodities (i.e. 'specific markets') or, in a stronger form, the market and its conditions for equilibrium (whether in a state of monopoly, perfect or imperfect competition) which are indeed 'determinate' in the sense that they can be described by a set of mathematical equations.[1] (Phrases such as 'a determinate solution' or 'determinate equilibrium' are

General Introduction   xi

found in English in the economic literature of his time and, earlier, 'determinate' in this sense – 'a determinate quantity' – enters the vocabulary of Ricardo himself,[2] to whom Gramsci ascribes the concept – although not necessarily the use of the actual term – 'determinate market'.) At the same time, as he says in 'Ugo Spirito and Co.' (pp.180-1), to say that economics is 'determinate' is a far cry from saying that it is a 'deterministic' science. Again on the subject of economics, while 'command economy' as a term is relatively modern, it has been adopted to translate the expressions *economia secondo un piano* or *economia regolata* ('economy according to a plan' or 'regulated economy').

On the odd occasion Gramsci rescues from literary obsolescence the noun *egemone* (from the Greek ηγεμων, i.e. 'leader') to indicate the person in whom hegemony is embodied; the translation follows him in using the term 'hegemon'. In speaking of the new personality he expects to be created in (and indeed also to create) a new, more advanced socio-economic set-up he has quite frequent recourse (a dozen times in Section F of Chapter IV) to the notion of 'social conformism' in a polemically positive sense; the same notion occurs, especially in the last chapter, to indicate a uniformity of behaviour at the individual and social levels with the intellectual adherence to the philosophy of praxis. The concept thus emerges as a feature of what should be considered his technical political vocabulary; the decision was therefore taken to resurrect the adjective 'conformant' (Italian *conforme*) to describe a feature that actively 'conforms to' a structure.

While not being the knottiest problem as regards translation, the notion of *blocco storico* requires particular attention. This expression is everywhere rendered 'historical bloc', as in the text of SPN, since the emphasis is always on its formation through the historical process. The index in SPN unfortunately however gives 'historic bloc', as if the emphasis were on the momentous nature of such a bloc; this has given rise to some confusion, compounded by the mistaken impression current among some people that by this term Gramsci meant a bloc of social alliances. Really only on one occasion might this be a legitimate reading. The paragraph in question deals with 'certain politico-economic social blocs' (Q9§40, first draft) or 'certain forces' (Q13§23 in the final draft: SPN, p.168) which 'have to be absorbed into a new, homogeneous politico-economic historical bloc' of a hypothetical free communist society of the future; here the notion of social 'homogeneity' might imply an alliance, and thus in this single passage 'historical' might coincide with 'historic'. Elsewhere (and the current volume contains all Gramsci's uses in final drafts of 'historical bloc' not already included in SPN) the expression deals prevalently with a bloc between structure and superstructure or with a social totality. Such a bloc is not merely static as in a 'snapshot-like' depiction, but is rendered dynamic through the introduction of the aspect of hegemony and thus the inclusion of the direction in which a society is moving.[3] Seen in this light the historical bloc represents Gramsci's attempt to transcend the limitations inherent in Marx's description of a complex reality by a means of a two-dimensional base-superstructure metaphor. Hugues Portelli comes to a very similar conclusion: 'A social system becomes integrated only with the emergence and consolidation of a hegemonic system under the direction of a fundamental class, which entrusts its management to the intellectuals: only at this moment does a historical bloc solidify. It follows that the examination of this concept cannot be considered separately from that of hegemony, that of the intellectual bloc. Only this way of conceiving the historical bloc allows us to grasp, in the concrete terms of social reality, the organic linkage between structure and superstructure.'[4]

INTRODUCTION

1 Why 'Further Selections from the Prison Notebooks'?

The publication in 1971 of Quintin Hoare and Geoffrey Nowell Smith's translation *Selections from the Prison Notebooks* (referred to in the present volume as SPN), replacing and greatly extending the 1957 volume *The Modern Prince and Other Writings*, was fundamental to the spread of Gramscian notions (and vocabulary) in the English-speaking world. Since then two other volumes of Gramsci's *Selected Political Writings* have been published covering the years 1910-20 and 1921-26 (SPW 1910-20 and SPW 1921-26 respectively) as well as a volume *Selections from Cultural Writings* (SCW), dealing principally with literary culture (in its 'high' and popular varieties) that draws mainly, but not exclusively, on the Prison Notebooks. In addition a *Gramsci Reader* (GR), which includes key themes from all these Lawrence & Wishart volumes, has appeared, as have two partial selections (containing little overlap) from the prison letters and the beginnings of a series that, rather than grouping together writings on a given subject, will translate the notebooks exactly as they stand from the first through to the last.[1] An idea of the importance attached to Gramsci's ideas may be had from John Cammett's bibliography (going up to 1988) of writings on him.[2] This and its updates by the International Gramsci Society list around 100,000 articles, university theses and books (about one in ten in English) in 32 languages.

Further Selections from the Prison Notebooks is a natural continuation of the 1971 volume in particular but covers a rather different subject area. It was understandable that the first major selections introducing Gramsci to native English speakers should deal mainly with subjects seen as having an immediate relevance to (especially Marxist) political theory and practice, such as his polemic with Bukharin's positivist brand of Marxism, or the 'Modern Prince', alias the political party based on Marxism, or his radically different concept of the intellectual strata (*ceti*) as both the products of 'social groups' (i.e. classes) born on the terrain of the productive process and the agents by which these groups acquire homogeneity and self-awareness of their economic, social and political functions (SPN, p.5). To have left matters like this would however have done a disservice to those who have had their appetites whetted (or indeed to anyone interested in politics and political theory) but who have no access to other writings of Gramsci's. *Further Selections* tries to remedy this situation by bringing together Gramsci's writings on religion, aspects of education not covered in SPN, economics and economic trends, science and the translatability of scientific and philosophical languages, and idealist philosophy (especially in the form given to it by Benedetto Croce, who then enjoyed great prestige particularly in the English- and German-speaking world for his historical, philosophical and aesthetic works). As with Gramsci's other writings this selection shows an original and undogmatic approach, far removed from the mental closure that came to typify the official ideology and authoritarian, bureaucratic political leadership which, appropriating and distorting Marx, later imposed itself in the former Eastern bloc. That the 'open Marxism' associated with Gramsci is no skin-deep cosmetic operation, but part and parcel of his overall stance (that includes his dialectical relationship with European liberal thought, with Croce as his main point of reference, as Hegel was for Marx), is evident everywhere but, in particular, is theorised explicitly in the notes on translatability (see pp.lxii-lxvi and 306-19).

The ever-present theme linking the subjects of this volume is the investigation of ideology at its different levels, and the structures that embody and reproduce it. We meet ideology as philosophical 'high' culture but also as sets of popular and often conflicting ideas, matters treated in their literary – and in part linguistic – aspects in SCW. Subalternity and corporative consciousness, hegemony and the building of the counter-hegemony necessary for the formation of a new historical bloc are thus present throughout the whole of the present volume. As such the area it covers is complementary to the perhaps more overtly political one of the Hoare-Nowell Smith selection; duplication of material found in the body of their text (or in footnote) has however been kept to the absolute minimum indispensable for reasons of continuity. The difference in emphasis between the current volume and that of Hoare and Nowell Smith is also evident from the origin of the material. Their 1971 selection is structured predominantly around the single-theme (or 'monographic') notebooks Q12 on the intellectuals, ('Q' from *Quaderno*, the Italian for 'notebook'), Q13 and other notes on Machiavelli, Q22 on Americanism and Fordism, parts of Q19 on Italian history and those parts of Q11 that deal directly with what were then perceived as immediate philosophical problems of Marxism. In the current volume Chapters III, V, VI and VII (on economics, science and Croce) are structured around Q10 and the rest of Q11, which together play a pivotal role in the whole prison writings; the other chapters also contain material from this same pair of philosophically-oriented notebooks. Chapter I (on religion) includes the whole of Q20 (on trends within the Catholic Church) but goes beyond this incomplete monographic notebook to take in other material, while Chapters II and IV (on education and economic developments) are constructed on the whole from the so-called 'miscellaneous' notebooks.

The writings in the notebooks are fragmentary in the sense that paragraphs, marked off as such by Gramsci with the paragraph sign (§), frequently do not link up one with another to provide an argument of an 'orthodox', linear structure. His analyses, instead, tend to be presented as sets of theses, each firmly rooted in reality. As some have noted, this style of presentation is externally analogous to that of the *Zibaldone*, the 'cultural diary' kept by the early nineteenth-century poet Giacomo Leopardi, but in Gramsci's case it goes much deeper and stems from his method itself: in fact, an early profile depicts him as someone who 'breaks his subject down into a thousand elements ... and dissects, measures and experiences them in a tactile way'.[3] The fragmentation is, however, a purely surface phenomenon: the reassembled elements constitute an integrated whole, while the strict limit posed by the prison regulations on the number of books – including notebooks – he could keep in his cell at any one time[4] (thus leading to subjects often being scattered among whatever notebooks were readily available) merely served to accentuate his already consolidated, 'multi-faceted' approach. Most notebooks are divided into scores of paragraphs, whose numbering here, like that of the notebooks themselves, is that used by Valentino Gerratana for his definitive 1975 Critical Edition.[5] (As an example, Q15§44 means Notebook 15, paragraph 44; large Roman numerals after the notebook number – for Q10 in particular – indicate the part into which Gramsci divided the Notebook, while small Roman numerals after a paragraph number indicate the sub-division he made of that paragraph.) It was his practice, especially in the monographic notebooks, to produce final versions ('C texts') of previously drafted material ('A texts'), often from one of the miscellaneous notebooks, which he then cross-hatched diagonally in such a way as to leave the cancelled paragraphs still easily readable; other paragraphs (the 'B texts'), naturally, exist in only one draft. (Exactly like the drafts of his newspaper articles, written against a strict print deadline, Gramsci's prison writings contain remarkably few corrections and deletions of individual words and phrases.)

It may, then, be appreciated that the nature of the writings can give rise to considerable problems of ordering the material, of which Gramsci was aware. He once explained to his fellow-Communist prisoner Gustavo Trombetti, who had been allotted to his cell to aid him after a breakdown in health, that 'I am writing in ways that I'm not sure others will be able to understand'. Indeed, a doctor (attached, according to Trombetti, to a psychiatric hospital), who had read one of the notebooks in the prison store-room, told Gramsci that it was 'rambling and inconclusive'; Gramsci waited for him to leave then said to Trombetti 'Did

General Introduction   xvii

you hear him? He thinks I'm mad. He really thinks I'm mad. He's read the notebooks and he hasn't understood a thing!'[6] What the apparently 'haphazard' arrangement of material means for editorial purposes is that it is not always easy to provide a smooth transition from one paragraph to the next, to give overall shape to the writings (even at times those in the monographic notebooks), or to bring out the internal consistency or highlight the implications of the subject matter. As in previous selections use has therefore been made of Italian editions (above all the classic six-volume thematic edition, compiled by Felice Platone under Palmiro Togliatti's general guidance, and published between 1948 and 1951). Where appropriate, changes (sometimes radical in nature) have been made as compared with these editions, which regard the ordering of the material and the need to take account both of the interests of a non-Italian readership (by omitting notes judged too specific to Italy) and of the considerable body of analysis of the writings that has appeared over the years, especially since the publication of Gerratana's edition.

What emerges from the Notebooks is a set of overlapping monographs, in which a theme found in one place might unexpectedly take on a new aspect when read in the context of a seemingly quite different argument. Some writings have sometimes remained submerged, only to resurface with fresh relevance and validity when considered in relation to some apparently different topic. In consideration of factors like these (and therefore the consequent necessity to refer to subjects already met with in previous volumes of Gramsci) it has been thought advisable to provide, as well as a short 'technical' introduction to each chapter, a general introduction to the selection itself, arranged in the same order as the main content of each chapter. This general introduction attempts to sketch out where Gramsci's arguments converge with (or sometimes differ from) a number of other major ones developed by people working within (and indeed also outside) a Marxist framework; in addition, taking account of his own (especially) pre-prison positions, the overlap of arguments and the material found in previously published volumes in English, it tries to put the ideas expressed in the wider context of his work through a certain amount of necessary cross-referencing and discussion. It is hoped that readers will find this background useful, and as such is offered as a guide whose parts may be read in conjunction with the appropriate chapter.

A last word of a general nature should be added about the role of Piero Sraffa (1898-1983), mentioned on numerous occasions in the introduction, text and footnotes of the present volume. After years during which his role was shrouded in semi-obscurity, and thus all the more tantalising, three books published in 1990 and 1991 have helped shed light on the relations linking him, Gramsci and Gramsci's sister-in-law, Tatiana (or Tania).[7] Sraffa, winner of the forerunner of the Nobel Prize for Economics and one of the outstanding intellects of the twentieth century, had in 1921 written a series of three articles for Gramsci's journal, *L'Ordine Nuovo*, on the British labour movement, after which the two of them slowly developed what was to become a firm friendship. When Gramsci was imprisoned Sraffa opened an account with a bookshop in Milan to ensure that he received any books and magazines he wanted and could have, and acted as the channel (via Tania) between him and Togliatti, in particular, at the Communist Party centre, then in exile in Paris. He played a role, as circumspect as it was important, in the various attempts to obtain Gramsci's release or at least an improvement of his conditions. (Helped by Angelo Tasca, another of Gramsci's *Ordine Nuovo* group, later however expelled from the Communist Party as a 'rightist', and by his friend and fellow-Marxist economist Maurice Dobb, who saw to the English, Sraffa was the 'Italian in England' who appears as the signatory of the letter, published in the *Manchester Guardian* of 24 October 1927, calling for Gramsci's release from prison on humanitarian grounds.) In the exchanges between Sraffa and Tania, much of it dealing with how best to maintain Gramsci's tenuous link with the outside world, underneath the formal, rather than familiar, modes of address there is a deep appreciation of her role together with a great human warmth, that also came over to Gramsci's sons on the rare occasions he was able to meet them. During the period of prison proper, Gramsci could receive visits only from relations, but on his transfer, after a complete breakdown in health, to a prison-approved clinic in Formia (December 1933) and later (August 1935) to one in Rome, regulations were less rigid and Sraffa was able to make the occasional visit (two in Formia and five in Rome). In Gramsci's final crisis it was, as ever, to him in Cambridge, that Tania turned in her desparate telegram 'Nino sempre gravissimo stop potendo venga' – 'Nino still gravely ill. Come if able': 'an unprecedented tragedy' was his reaction to Gramsci's death. (The story, which has gained wide currency, that he arranged with Raffaele Mattioli, the anti-fascist president of the *Banca Commerciale Italiana*, for the notebooks to be held in a safe place in the bank after Tania, on Gramsci's death, had removed them from under the noses of the police, may quite well be true but it is based only on a remark of Mattioli's, 30 or more years after the events, in conversation with Togliatti's companion, Nilde Iotti, and was neither confirmed by Sraffa nor has subsequently been backed up by hard documentary evidence.)[8]

The advice and stimuli as regards Gramsci's work that Sraffa transmitted through Tania were for various – normally valid – reasons not always followed: the styles and disciplines of the two men were too different for this to happen. Sraffa's work is characterised by a meticulousness and precision that could not be achieved either in a prison cell or, arguably, in the type of intellectual territory that Gramsci was pioneering. In fact, at the end of his introduction to Sraffa's *Letters to Tania for Gramsci*, Gerratana draws attention to the comparison to be made between 'the richness of the analogic thought of the one and the rigour of the analytical thought of the other', although this perhaps understates the type of rigour present in Gramsci's own mode of concept formation and its subsequent application to real situations. Be this as it may, Gerratana is certainly correct in his conclusion that 'we are evidently dealing with two different approaches, which can ... mutually interlock and complete each other only under certain conditions: among these is the requirement that, on one hand, Gramsci should not be read as a closed book and, on the other, one should avoid considering political economy itself as a closed book.'[9]

2   Faith as a Material Force

The current volume opens with a long chapter on religion, the most popular (in the senses of widespread and widely accepted) of all ideological systems. Gramsci, as much as any Marxist, took seriously Marx's dictum that theory (here present as faith) 'becomes a material force as soon as it has gripped the masses';[10] in his own formulation these 'material forces are the content and ideologies are the form' of the historical bloc (SPN, p.377). 'The capacity of faith to mobilise ... indicative of a force that may determine other factors'[11] (for better or for worse) is always present in the notes on religion, whether the subject under discussion is associations of the laity (like Catholic Action), the parliamentary action of political Catholicism, the Reformation and Counter-Reformation, right, centre and left groupings within the Church, popular and, indeed, even messianic trends in Christianity, Church-state relations or the role played by religions (including the great non-Christian ones) in forming popular and/or national consciousness.

The prison notes on religion go beneath the surface of a purely political approach to movements composed of believers, which perhaps characterised his earlier writings, to provide a substantially firmer grounding for analysing such movements. For reasons of space and of overall shape of the presentation some paragraphs dealing with religion have been omitted; these deal mainly with specific national contexts, with aspects of popular religion and folklore, often in any case touched on either here or in SPN, or with Christianity between the fall of the Roman Empire and the rise of the Italian Communes in the Middle Ages (an important topic but perhaps more pertinent to Gramsci's research into the formation of the Italian intellectuals). The selection begins with a working definition of religion as a belief in one or more divinities with a dependence of the believers on it/them and thus a system of believer-deity relationships; this position and a comment on theism as insufficient to be considered a religion (Religion [1], pp.8-9), together with a reference to Kant's position on religion (Religion [2], pp.13-14), set the scene. But for Gramsci the importance of religion and of its intellectuals, in particular the clergy, resided in the role it has assumed as an organising principle of society (that might vary and indeed has varied according to time and place) and not just as a private matter belonging predominantly to the inner realm of the feelings, as in many strands of Protestantism and even some of Catholicism. Even those who subscribe to no religion may find themselves supporting it. In his last years Auguste Comte, the founder of positivism (quoted by Gramsci at second hand in Q5§44, not translated here), wanted the Pope to head 'a religious and social defence league' and viewed 'the papacy as a great conservative element in society'; the atheists who favoured the 1929 concordat between Italy and the Vatican were certainly of this opinion.

Gramsci's view, sharply at variance with old-style anti-clericalism, was that in Italy a socialist government would once and for all 'completely liquidate the Roman question by guaranteeing full liberty to the Church' and that while, as a collaborator on *L'Ordine Nuovo* wrote, only in a future 'international communist society will the [Catholic] Church, and all Churches, have true, absolute freedom', the solution to this problem could not simply be improvised or put off to when the working class took power.[12] 'While Marxist socialists are not religious, neither are they anti-religious' wrote Gramsci and a future workers' state, like the liberal state before it, must find a system of equilibrium' with 'the spiritual power of the Church'; further, while it is essential for the 'revolutionary proletarian vanguard not to have any religious ties ... the religious tie ought not at the same time to constitute an obstacle to working-class unity. All workers – over and above any belief or faith – can and must be united in the struggle against the bourgeoisie.'[13] There is nothing in the *Notebooks* to indicate that he changed his opinion on these pre-prison stances, the last of which was written just six months before his arrest.

On religion as a social phenomenon Gramsci borrows, not for the only time, a concept from the idealist philosopher Benedetto Croce, who (see Chapter VI, p.329 of this volume) took his lead from the 1877 essay 'The *Nerina* of Leopardi' by Francesco De Sanctis, Minister of Public Instruction in the post-1876 government of the left and most famous Italian man of letters of his time. For De Sanctis, Leopardi seems to point the way to the religious conception of an afterlife as a projection of this one: in other words, religion is rooted in the conditions of this world. Croce goes perhaps one step further in his essays 'The Religious Spirit' and 'Religion and Peace of Mind'.[14] In the first of these he rejects religion *but*, as he says, 'only in so far as religion is mythology', elsewhere accepting it, as did other idealists, as the philosophy of humanity in its infancy and hence (despite his personal atheism) suitable for elementary schools; in the latter essay he definitively denies any claim of religion to be superior to philosophy. For Croce, philosophy serves the same purpose as religion but does so from the standpoint of an 'absolute this-worldliness'; in one sense philosophy is a (secular) religion in being a 'conception of the world with a conformant norm of conduct', as Gramsci notes in his treatment of Crocean philosophy (see, e.g., in 'Philosophy, Religion, Ideology', p.384). One important task of the philosophy of praxis (equivalent, in this Crocean definition, to a 'religion') is, therefore, like that of the great religious reformations (see Section B of Chapter I), to attempt to bring about an 'intellectual and moral reform'.

This, then, forms a background for what Gramsci goes on to say about the role of religions in society and, indeed, about philosophies intended to supplant them. His outline history of the Catholic social movement is marked both by its accuracy and, as compared with the work of certain other (Catholic and Marxist) historians, by its lack of tendentiousness. His writings should not be viewed as a mere factual 'chronicle of events' up to the time that Catholic Action remained the sole mass organisation of any type not under the direct control of the totalitarian state and the Fascist Party; if it were so it would be, as Croce was wont to say, 'pseudo-' rather than real historiography. In describing the entry of Catholics into state life, the notes bring out the hierarchy's attempts to ensure conformity between its religious concepts and the conduct of Catholics in social and political life; this is an issue of ongoing concern, which is not the same as saying that the hierarchy uniformly is (or wants to be) in total charge of directing movements in the social or political spheres. The notes do in fact, at least implicitly, examine the conditions for the political autonomy of believers with respect to a religious hierarchy, a theme present in the pre-prison writings. Thus, the hierarchy's response to pressures from below (see e.g., 'Catholic Action's History and Organisation', which opens Section C on Catholic social policy) is at least to guide the activity of Catholics in politics, trade union affairs etc. into safe channels. The question is considered from different angles. If the Church is incapable of being all-embracing (*totalitaria*) in an age of mass apostasy, then it must fight to retain its hegemony through other channels. One of these, discussed in Section D, is that of Church-state concordats, disapproved of in principle by Gramsci, whose stance, it may be noted, was overturned by the practice of the Italian Communist Party after World War II. (A broadly-speaking progressive strand in Catholicism, which has even found some sympathy among members of the hierarchy, also rejects concordats, albeit for different reasons: Giovanni Battista Montini, three decades later to become Pope Paul VI, expressed 'reservations' on the 1929 Concordat, wondering 'whether the freedom of the pope was not better guaranteed by the strong and free faith of the people' while asking 'what territory and treaty will be able to do [the same]'.[15]) Gramsci's objection to concordats was that 'two equal sovereignties are admitted within the same state' ('Nature of the Concordats', pp.59-60); elsewhere he notes that, in such conditions, the state is liable to become a 'theocracy' in which the government 'operates under the impulse of religion and subordinates laws, the relations of civil life, customs to religious dictates' (Q7§97, not translated here). For him the Church continued (as it still in fact does) to wield an influence in other ways, which include associations like Catholic Action, training organisations for the laity, such as those commented on in 'The Workers' Retreats' (pp.47-8), and even separate trade unions and parties.

Naturally tensions emerge that might take the form of a politico-religious utopia ('Davide Lazzaretti', pp.50-5) or, in a more orthodox fashion, of conflicts between left and right wings of parties inspired by Catholicism, such as the Popular Party (PPI). This is implicit in a fleeting reference in Q5§44 (not translated here) to, on one hand, pro-hierarchy conservatives like Filippo Meda, the first Catholic to hold ministerial office (1916) in the Kingdom of Italy, or, on the other, to revolutionaries like Guido Miglioli, expelled from the PPI when he became a leader of the *Krestintern*, set up by the Third (Communist) International to spread revolutionary ideas among the world's peasantry. Sometimes, left-right tensions may be resolved in favour of the progressive forces as in an early case of the hierarchy's approval of Catholic-socialist unity (see 'The Lille Conflict', pp.49-50).

The figure of Miglioli merits further attention. Although appearing on only a handful of occasions in the *Quaderni* (see, in Chapter VII, 'Croce's International Importance', pp.467-9, and footnote 38), he was Gramsci's main point of reference among left-moving Catholics in the pre-prison period and was instrumental in the creation in 1924 of 'farm councils', using as a model the Turin *Ordine Nuovo*-influenced factory council movement. (Later on, in the 1930s, one of his chief organisers, Romano Cocchi – also known as Adami – most unusually for a practising Catholic, was on the Communist Party Central Committee). Gramsci's role in posing the question of religious belief among working people and the material help given Miglioli[16] were acknowledged by the latter in an article in *L'Unità* published on the tenth anniversary (27 April 1947) of Gramsci's death: 'In the Italian proletarian movement [Gramsci] was the first who, starting from a different camp, came to understand and cherish the effort of the Christian and Catholic workers and peasants to unite all the other working people in the necessary and incessant battle for their legitimate demands.' It may be recalled that in the essay 'Some Aspects of the Southern Question' (SPW 1921-26, especially p.443) Gramsci took the stance that 'In Italy the peasant question ... has taken two typical and particular forms – the Southern question and that of the Vatican'. While continuing to uphold the importance of religion as a key to the peasant question, his mature reflection in the *Quaderni* switches the perspective partially to one in which the South-North difference is viewed within the more articulated relationship of the hegemony of the city over the countryside, over a period spanning the age of the free Communes, through Machiavelli, then the Risorgimento, up to his own time; in this process, hegemony became increasingly that of the Northern cities, in particular the industrial ones, over the countryside.[17]

The Miglioli phenomenon is also significant for another important part of the approach Gramsci considered correct for Marxists to adopt towards religious movements. Immediately after the Communist Party's III Congress, held in the French city of Lyon in 1926, he dictated a reappraisal of 'The Party's First Five Years' (SPW 1921-26l, pp.379-99, see especially p.396). He here says that 'the position taken up by the Party ... must in no way lead us to encourage any ideological movements of a strictly religious nature that may emerge ... The party's task consists in explaining the conflicts that arise on the terrain of religion as deriving from class conflicts; and in aiming to bring out with increasing clarity the class features of these conflicts. It does not, by contrast, consist in encouraging religious solutions to class conflicts, even if such solutions appear left-wing in so far as they call into question the authority of the official religious organisation.' (He clarifies elsewhere – see SPN, pp.407-9 – that it would be silly to push this to extremes.)

This position does not however mean that developments within the Church – by which one should, by extension, understand any formally-organised religious structure – are to be ignored: as anyone who cares to follow the debates among theologians can vouch, there exists a complex inter-relationship between positions in the theological and the social fields. (The 'modernist' trend within the Catholic Church, which wanted to update the Church's stance on modern society, stands out as a very direct response to developments in the society of the time.) So it was that alongside, and to be read in conjunction with, the 'Catholic Action' notes, Gramsci wrote another group of paragraphs, the most pertinent of which are included here under the general heading 'Integralist Catholics, Jesuits, Modernists'. These three currents were the 'parties', the right, centre and left, respectively, of that period in the ' "absolute international empire" that is the Church of Rome' ('Luigi Salvatorelli and Fr Turmel', pp.97-9); although changes occur – the time elapsed since the Second Vatican Council has seen the emergence of liberation theology, while many Jesuits now have an advanced position on progressively-oriented social involvement – the categories of analysis themselves remain valid. At the time of the *Quaderni*, the modernists were only just beginning to emerge from their isolation after various papal pronouncements (from Gregory XVI's 1832 *Mirari vos* onwards) against the claimed insidious and anti-religious nature of society. Although, in order to carry on their fight, the modernists in the Catholic Church had to adopt various subterfuges (not without their humorous side – see 'The Rise of the Integralists', pp.76-8, or the sub-sections on the Abbé Turmel, pp.94-9), this in no way detracts from the great human dignity shown by some of their representatives: cases in point are the Irish Jesuit, George Tyrrell, or his Italian translator, Ernesto Buonaiuti (for whom see especially '*Action Française*'s Long Crisis', pp.88-92), who influenced Marxist Church historiography in Italy through his pupil Ambrogio Donini, born into a strict Catholic family but later a Communist leader of the 'old-guard' school.

On the opposite side to the modernists stand the 'integralist Catholics', where 'integralism' may be defined as a trend within religions – and indeed political philosophies, too – that maintains one view as correct to the total denial of the legitimacy of any alternative. Normally, the integralist defence of élitist and reactionary positions in the Church goes hand-in-hand with a similar outlook in society, whether one is dealing with the integralist supporters of *Action Française* in Gramsci's day or others supporting racism and

General Introduction

fascist or other dictatorships in later times. Nevertheless – and this is something which Gramsci, in his striving for understanding and joint action between believers and non-believers, seems to underestimate – there are some integralists who may, on non-religious issues, take a progressive stance and yet, all too often – for reasons of the so-called 'political unity of Catholics' (or of adherents to other religions) – have preferred to remain with co-religionists in parties under the hegemony of conservative forces, rather than unite organisationally with progressive forces: in real life the boundaries between religious and socio-political spheres have often been blurred.

In between the two poles of modernism and integralism comes the mainstream centre of the Church. Its leaders have to maintain a united Church, not solely by keeping together 'right' and 'left' and avoiding schisms, albeit on occasion by a near-complete annihilation of any trace of internal democracy, but also, as Gramsci points out on a number of occasions, by keeping under the same umbrella intellectual and popular, 'folkloristic' forms of religion. Typical of this latter for Gramsci was (see the two parts of 'Religion, the Lottery and the Opium of Poverty', pp.55-9) the attitude adopted towards the lottery in Balzac's *La Rabouilleuse* (written in 1841-2) as the 'opium of poverty', granting a few days' respite from life's hardships; since Balzac was a favourite author of Marx's, this may well have been the source, as Gramsci conjectures, for the famous and often misunderstood comment on religion as 'the opium of the people' (see footnote 67 to Chapter I).

In the task of keeping the body of believers united, the Catholic Church had, for Gramsci, been far more successful than either the Protestant ones or a number of other major religions (e.g. Shinto in the two 'Brief Notes on Japanese Culture', pp.129-32, or perhaps even Islam, 'Brief Notes on Islamic Culture', pp.134-6, and 'The New Evolution of Islam', pp.132-4) where, for differing reasons, the links between official and popular religions may often be rather tenuous. A general point of his is that popular forms of monotheistic religions tend to produce a type of saint, sometimes a thinly disguised divinity from a previous polytheistic religion, who functions as a mediator or mediatrix, on pain of the religion becoming, like Protestantism, overly rationalistic (he sometimes uses the term 'positivist') or intellectualistic. In Islam, in particular, the relative absence of an intellectual stratum, like that comprised by the Catholic 'religious' (i.e. those under vows), meant for him that the intellectuals-people relationship was characterised by a ' "fanaticism" ... which accumulates masses of psychic emotions and impetuses that go on even into normal times' ('Brief Notes on Islamic Culture', cit.).

Lying behind the whole of the writings on non-Christian religions (whether in the body of the Muslim world or the Far East) is the question of nascent nationalism (e.g. 'Italy and the Yemen in the New Politics of the Arab World', pp.210-3 of Chapter IV), the relations with the modern industrialised world, and the entry into it of the peoples of the great non-metropolitan countries. Gramsci takes up the question posed by Marx of 'why does the history of the East *appear* as a history of religions?' but does not pursue his response, agreed by Engels, that 'the basis of all phenomena in the East ... [is] the *absence of private property in land.* This is the real key, even to the Oriental heaven.'[18] His own investigation is at another level and follows quite different directions. In the case of Islam, he underlines the tension between nationalist tendencies and a pan-Islamic cosmopolitanism, like that of the medieval Catholic world, which – it seems implicit in these few paragraphs – may be resolved either way; in any case, as noted above, a major factor is the action of whole masses of people, stimulated by a religious reawakening. The case of India is rather different; given the 'great number of intellectuals of the ecclesiastical type' as well as the 'centuries-old social torpor and the ossified stratification of society' a 'great revolution will be needed just to begin to resolve [the crisis]' ('Religiosity in India', pp.120-1). Nevertheless, as he asks in another context ('The Atlantic and the Pacific', p.196 of Chapter IV), may the axis of the world not shift from the Atlantic (Europe-United States) to where the world's population is most concentrated, i.e. around the Pacific rim, 'if India and

China' (Japan not being mentioned) 'were to become modern nations'?

3 Education

The limited space that Gramsci dedicates explicitly to education should not deceive; the letters to his wife, Julka, on their children's development are eloquent testimony to his interest in the question. Moreover, when his ideas on adult education and his pre-prison undertakings, including his organisation of the Party correspondence course-cum-school, are taken into account, the role of education emerges quite clearly as providing the underpinning to some of the most important themes of the Notebooks – ideology, the formation of consciousness and world outlook, the question of hegemony.

In this light one understands his polemic against romantic, libertarian trends in 'progressive' education, linked for him to the name of Jean-Jacques Rousseau and according to which a child from an early age possesses an innate potential which simply has to be 'unravelled' like a skein of wool, an emotional and intellectual personality that, with the correct handling, will spontaneously blossom: although Gramsci does not say as much, this could, paradoxically, hide an unintentional form of determinism. It is the outlook he criticises in his wife's family on whom 'Geneva and its atmosphere saturated with Rousseau left a great impression' during their exile from tsardom, spent in part there.[19] The conception of his wife and her family was 'too metaphysical, i.e. it presupposes that the child is potentially the whole man and that one must help it develop everything that is already contained in latent form, without any coercion, giving full rein to the spontaneous forces of nature or whatever. I believe, on the contrary, that man is entirely a historical formation obtained by coercion (understood not only in the sense of brutality and external violence) and this is all I believe: otherwise one would fall into a form of transcendence or immanence.'[20]

Gramsci accepted whole-heartedly the principle of the

'active' school, the collaboration between teacher and pupil and the latter's participation in the school, but 'this can only exist if the school is related to life' (SPN, p.37); while he recognised positive aspects in experiments in other countries, doubts still however remained about their practicability on a large scale given that their success seemed to rest on the qualities of individual highly gifted teachers ('Scholastic Questions [1]', p.142). He stressed the necessity, on one hand, for the 'common' school (*scuola unitaria*) that would genuinely unite manual and intellectual work, and, on the other, for a 'formal' content to education; allied to this was the need for a methodology of learning such as once *used to be* inculcated in part by the study of Latin and Greek (SPN, pp.37-8). Gramsci's use of the past tense in the finalised version of this passage leaves no doubt that in the modern school he was thinking not of 'dead' languages but of an updated alternative for mastering methods of study and a modern equivalent to the humanistic culture for which Latin and Greek provided the gateway; they had to be replaced 'as the fulcrum of the formative school and they will be replaced' (SPN, p.39). Pressure had to be applied 'throughout the educational system in order to succeed in creating those thousands or hundreds or even only dozens of scholars of the highest quality which are necessary to every civilisation' (SPN, p.37). In short, hegemony in society would only be achieved through the conquest by the popular, proletarian-led movement of the commanding heights of the adversary's culture.

His stance that the human personality is formed historically rather than genetically also explains his opposition to one aspect of the educational reform brought in by Gentile, typified by the change in name of the Ministry of Public Instruction to that of Education. This may at first glance seem progressive and anti-authoritarian but, for Gramsci, the first steps in a child's development had to be instruction, the instillation of notions into the child, who is then 'educated' – quite literally his or her interpretation of the world is developed (cf. the Latin *educere*, 'to draw out') – only at a second stage, on the basis of the awareness and experience acquired, at school but even more in society at large. (Here, as elsewhere in Gramsci, it would be a mistake, like that committed by the idealist school of educational theorists, to interpret this distinction in rigid terms, implying – wrongly – that pupils were 'mechanical receivers' of notions and purely passive in nature: see SPN, p.35.) In the division between instruction and education the former deals with 'factual' notions – 'the rudiments of science, and the idea of civic rights and duties', the world of things and the introduction into the state and civil society (SPN, pp.33-4) – and only at the later stage do politico-ideological ideas enter the curriculum. This is once more a position at odds with the Gentile reform (based on the proposals of the atheist Croce when he was Minister of Public Instruction in the 1920-21 Giolitti administration) which, after a gap of three generations, reintroduced religious ideology in a strict Roman Catholic form into the elementary schools and was part of a longer-term design on the part of some, that came to fruition with the concordat between the Italian state and the Vatican (see Section D of Chapter I) to weld together the political forces of conservatism, whether of secular or religious origin, into a single hegemonic bloc. (Croce had perhaps not appreciated the longer term implications of his 1920 stance since his was a lone voice in opposition to the agreement with the Church in the fascist-dominated Senate.) Gramsci's view that matters on which there can be dissent should only be dealt with later contrasts sharply with what was to become the norm in countries in the former Soviet sphere of influence, viz. the introduction into schools of the equally 'official' ideology (in a highly debatable and dogmatic form) of Marxism-Leninism. His position is however remarkably similar – although this was probably unknown to him – to that of Marx: 'nothing could be introduced either in primary or higher schools that admitted of party and class interpretation. Only subjects such as the physical sciences, grammar etc., were fit matters for schools ... Subjects that admitted of different conclusions [including religion] must be excluded and left for the adults.'[21]

Gramsci's pre-prison newspaper articles contain frequent references to the need for adult education going well beyond the shoddy version offered by the so-called 'popular' or 'proletarian' universities. British experience in this direction seems to have made an impression on him since he comments favourably on the Fabian Society's projects,[22] while their Italian equivalents paid insufficient attention to the fact that their students did not usually have the mental study habit characteristic of those who had frequented the 'orthodox' university system. Long and patient work was required to be able to reach the methods of research and conclusions of scientific activity (in both the natural and exact and the literary-philological fields); this is echoed later on in the Notebooks by his similar comments on mastering logic, both formal and dialectical (Chapter V, Section C: 'The Logical Instruments of Thought').

His own first serious experiment in adult self-education classes seems to have be the 'Club for Moral Life', launched by the Turin Socialist Party Branch with the aim of building a homogeneous leadership group. In a letter of March 1918, asking advice of the prominent educationalist Giuseppe Lombardo-Radice (admired by him at the time for his fight for the 'spiritual betterment of Italian youth' but, together with Gentile, criticised in 'Some Problems of Modern Pedagogy', p.140 of this volume, for 'curious regressions' in his educational theories), he explained the club's method: a participant would introduce an analysis of some essay by Salvemini or Croce, a part of Marx or a more general topic – in the case raised in the letter a book on education by Lombardo-Radice – and submit it to the others present, who would be expected to comment, with the aim of developing their reasoning powers and reaching the 'intellectual and moral communion of everyone'. Lombardo-Radice's response was cold: his place was 'up here at the front, fighting for the humanity that does not want to serve Germany ... This is not the time for pedagogic academies but for action for the Fatherland and Fatherlands!'[23]

A second attempt at proletarian education was made during the 1919-20 factory occupation period in Turin. This course, run by *Ordine Nuovo*, the justly famous organ that drew Lenin's praise as representing the real revolutionary movement in Italy, was successful and generated a good deal of enthusiasm because, as Gramsci was to write in introducing the project of an internal Communist Party School in 1925, it linked education to 'a movement of an objective nature – the Turin factory and Party movement ... Study and culture for us are none other than the theoretical consciousness of our immediate and supreme goals and the way in which we will succeed in translating them into action.' The paucity of the forces staffing the school was swamped by the breadth and depth of the movement and the programme that had been set was never completed: 'A school adequate to the importance of that movement would have required not the activity of a few people but the ordered, systematic effort of an entire party.'[24] (The high-level type of school was, of course, not the only type that he thought important for the Communist Party; in his six weeks on the prison island of Ustica in 1926-7 he and Amadeo Bordiga, with whom – despite political differences – Gramsci remained on friendly terms, directed a school for fellow political prisoners which, taking into account the fact that 'the pupils, even if sometimes semi-literate, are intellectually well-developed',[25] included all levels of elementary education, not just the more advanced courses.)

It was possible to organise the 1925 school only in the brief period between the 1924 elections that returned Gramsci as a parliamentary deputy and the repression initiated some time before the Communist Party was declared illegal on 5 November 1926. Three multi-part sections of the course were envisaged (on historical materialism, on political questions in general and on the Communist Party itself and organisational questions) but only the first two parts of each section could be sent out to the participants. The first section was to consist mainly of a translation of Bukharin's *Historical Materialism*, of which the *Introduction* and most of the first chapter went out as the first two parts; to judge by the stern critique to which Gramsci subjected the volume in the Notebooks, he must have been horror-struck on analysing and reflecting on it. The second section opened with political economy, and ten of the eighteen parts planned for this section had a strong, explicitly economic, component. There thus seems to be reasonable backing from a source outside the Notebooks for the idea, not openly stated there, that part of Q10 in particular is intended as an outline sketch of the history of economic science; these notes, supplemented by a few others, are editorially ordered in this fashion to form Chapter III of this volume, while some other topics, which were also to form part of the second section of the curriculum, are in Chapter IV. Section F of this latter chapter brings together a number of paragraphs in which the themes of the economic base of a new socialist society and social conformism are linked to the formation of a new social being 'formed essentially from the bottom up, on the basis of the position occupied by the collectivity in the world of production' – and therefore in a positive sense (see, e.g., 'Man as Individual and Man as Mass', pp.275-7) – in a relationship at once pedagogical and hegemonic.

4 Economics and the Economy

The notes on economic science, different in nature from the well-known Notebook 22 on Americanism and Fordism and continuing and far extending what has already been translated on the background to economics in SPN, pp.399-412, may be read, as suggested above, as an attempt, under extremely difficult circumstances, to trace out the main lines of development of the subject. These writings served at least a dual purpose for Gramsci: one, internal to the Notebooks, seems aimed at focusing and organising his own thought, while the other attempts to draw lines of demarcation, especially concerning methodology and the theory of value, between Marxist ('critical') economy and the prevalent 'vulgar' (or, more properly, the marginalist or neo-classical) school and forms part of his project to establish the line of descent and autonomy of Marxism. Taken as a whole, the writings on economics as such amount to an examination – not without its surprises – of the history and also of some of the philosophical presuppositions of political economy, an interpretation supported by the fact that they are, with a few later additions, to be found mainly in the philosophically-oriented Q10.

During the preparation for publication of the *Quaderni* Piero Sraffa expressed reservations about Gramsci's treatment of economics – 'some weakness is due to the fact that Gramsci did not have Marx's text in front of him' – and (perhaps judging by his own standards of perfectionism) considered that 'taken as a whole [the notes] do not come up to the standards of the rest of the volume', i.e. the one containing the twin critiques of Croce – Chapters VI and VII of the present volume – and of Bukharin and other philosophical topics, including (in Sraffa's words) 'the magnificent organic and complete essay' entitled 'Some Preliminary Points of Reference', now in SPN, pp.323-43.[26] He nevertheless went on to say that the notes 'contain many extraordinarily acute observations' and some of his doubts possibly reflect the different interests, emphases and approaches of the two people. A case in point is Gramsci's conception (discussed in this section of the Introduction) of the Ricardo-Marx relationship, which, as noted by Nicola Badaloni, former President of the Gramsci Institute, involves 'not only economics but also philosophy'.[27]

Apart from his preliminary draft of the notes on Americanism and Fordism Gramsci's first systematic writings on political economy (a dozen notes between paragraphs 18 and 42 of Q7) date from late 1930 through 1931. In the first of these paragraphs ('Unity in the Constituent Elements of Marxism', SPN, p.402) he states the view that 'in economics, the unitary centre is value, alias the relationship between the worker and the industrial productive forces'. The stimulus to go on from the reflections in these paragraphs to other problems of political economy came, apparently, from an article he read on Machiavelli's economic notions. In the note 'Machiavelli as an Economist', pp.163-4, written in April 1932 and chosen here to open Chapter III, he asks whether Machiavelli might be regarded as a forerunner of the physiocrats (who maintained that wealth originated from the soil). This was an unorthodox stance since Machiavelli's economic ideas, albeit rudimentary and normally expressed in political rather than directly economic form, were considered more compatible with the earlier – and much more primitive –

mercantilists (see Chapter III, footnote 2). Gramsci's attention had been drawn back to passages in Machiavelli's *Discourses* like those recommending that 'a city should be placed ... in a region where the fertility of the soil affords the means of becoming great' or where, in addition to the role of the land, a decidedly bourgeois ethic is apparent, as in Machiavelli's criticism of the gentry (*gentiluomini*) 'who live idly upon the proceeds of their extensive possessions without devoting themselves to agriculture or any other useful pursuit to gain a living';[28] Gramsci further notes that, for a physiocratic outlook to supersede a mercantilist one, there has to be a relatively well-developed market, and the urban classes have to shed 'certain feudal-corporative privileges' in order to incorporate the rural classes into the state. The paragraph concludes with a brief aside, referring to a suggestion put to him by Piero Sraffa, that Machiavelli's ideas might be compared to those of the Anglo-Irishman William Petty, whom Marx considered the founder of modern economic science, mainly because of his ideas on labour as the source of value.

The next major development in value theory after Petty is ascribed by Gramsci to Petty's fellow-countryman Richard Cantillon, who made a fortune through speculative deals in Paris and who was author of the *Essai sur la nature du commerce en général*, up to recently considered a posthumous publication.[29] Adam Smith, not normally a man to attribute his sources, mentions Cantillon in Book I, Chapter 8 ('Of the Wages of Labour') of the *Wealth of Nations* and there are other fleeting references to him in early nineteenth-century economic literature, but he was really rediscovered by the British economist W.S. Jevons, a major figure in the development of marginalist economics. The *Essai* for him was 'the first treatment on economics', 'more emphatically than any other single work "the cradle of economics" ', a book that contains 'an ingenious theory of value, superior in some respects to the theory of many recent economists'[30], by which statement he seems to have meant that Cantillon's approach prefigured something similar to the marginalist theory he and others were developing. While Gramsci was in prison the *Essai* enjoyed some popularity, going through German and bilingual French-English editions;[31] these were the subject of reviews in two Italian journals that he saw regularly, in one of which Luigi Einaudi quoted a passage – copied in 'The Beginning of Economic Science', p.164 – that sums up Cantillon's position on how wealth comes to be created. Marxist assessments of Cantillon differ in emphasis: Marx himself cites him on piece work rather than on value and, among writers contemporary with Gramsci, Lapidus and Ostrovityanov, harshly criticised for ignoring everything but Soviet achievements, typically do not mention him, I.I. Rubin (in a brilliant and incisive analytical study, unfortunately unknown to Gramsci) adduces textual evidence to class him as still fundamentally physiocratic in outlook[32] and Erich Roll (then a Marxist) judged his theory of value to be eclectic.[33] A decade after Gramsci's death Sraffa, as editorial adviser to Einaudi (publishers of Gramsci's writings), paid tribute to the *Essai*'s value in recommending its publication in a series on key works in the history of economics whereas, as regards better-known authors, 'neither Petty nor Quesnay are authors of any fundamental work that stands by itself'.[34]

Gramsci's interest in Cantillon seems, then, to have some justification. There may be queries about his neglect of Smith (mentioned only once, in passing, in the Notebooks) as a major link in the chain joining Petty to Ricardo (and Marx) but this may simply be due to what appeared in the material to which he had access in prison and, in any case, according to Roll, Smith's theory of value suffers from the same sort of inconsistency as Cantillon's. As a sketch of value theory before Marx, Gramsci's account does not seem compromised by a preference, possibly more apparent than real, for Cantillon over Smith.

Sraffa's own later work raises more serious doubts about the status or perhaps even validity of value theory itself and, indeed, Marx's solution in Vol. III of *Capital* to the transformation of values into prices is manifestly unsatisfactory. The main thrust of Sraffa's work, however, leaves 'orthodox' economics with its logical foundations quite severely shaken while the crucial parts of Marx's theoretical edifice do not stand or fall with his theory of value[36] (which aims at explaining observable facts – class conflict, exploitation and so on);[37] in the worst case, Gramsci's defence of it does not harm other aspects of his argument. Moreover, despite what is stated in 'Unity in the Constituent Elements of Marxism' (see above), human labour – in the form of 'socially necessary labour' and not just as a generic 'activity' – rather than the labour theory of value seems the fundamental concept for him (see 'Classical Economy and Critical Economy' and 'The Beginning of Economic Science', pp.168-70 and 164-5 respectively).

On the question of Ricardo Gramsci shows considerable far-sightedness. He asks whether, in addition to his economic importance, he might also have a significance for the history of philosophy, specifically by 'putting the first theorists of the philosophy of praxis on the road to the supersession of Hegelian philosophy and the construction of their new historicism, purged of any trace of speculative logic? ... My cue comes from the two concepts, "determinate market" (*mercato determinato*) and "law of tendency", fundamental to economic science and in my view to be ascribed to Ricardo'.[38] Sraffa replied in a letter to Tania 'Nino cannot imagine how much his observations have interested me. ... I would however like some explanation of the two concepts of "determinate market" and "law of tendency" ... the second [of which] I have been used, rather, to consider as one of the characteristics of vulgar economy.'[39] Chapters VI and VII of Ricardo's *Principles* are, however, devoted to a discussion of the operation of such laws and, in Sraffa's definitive edition of Ricardo, we read, for example, that 'the natural tendency of profits is to fall', although this fall is 'happily checked at intervals by the improvements in machinery ... as well as by discoveries in the science of agriculture'.[40] Gramsci seems therefore to be correct in ascribing the law to Ricardo while Sraffa, still at the start of his massive task of editing Ricardo's *Works and Correspondence*, perhaps did not as yet appreciate this factor.

Gramsci then proceeds to say that in each moment (economic, political, theoretical) of the new synthesis that

General Introduction

the philosophy of praxis created of the three principal cultural movements of the era (German philosophy, French literature and political practice and British political economy) there were present as a preparatory moment each of these three movements. The 'unitary synthetic moment' was to be identified in the new concept of immanence,[41] purged of its speculative nature thanks to French politics and the 'structural' element introduced by British political economy.[42] This is, then, one way in which Gramsci saw Ricardo's importance as being not simply economic but also philosophical in scope; Ricardo himself was not at all conscious of this and merely regarded his laws as having the same nature as the already known ones of the natural sciences,[43] understood in a mechanical fashion and without any consideration of a dialectical process, such as elucidated by Marx in his discussion of the reasons why the fall in the rate of profit is checked. Rubin adds that while 'Ricardo's method of abstract analysis is precisely what gives his theoretical thinking its consistency and intrepidity ... he forgot that every economic tendency only manifests itself in the *absence* of counteracting tendencies'.[44]

There is also another way in which Ricardo's methodological approach may have been influential philosophically. Roll (who, as a Marxist economic historian of the time, will be cited rather than the non-Marxists Gide and Rist that Gramsci fell back on) observes, as regards the apparent contrast between Ricardo's deductive, abstract method and Smith's inductive and historically descriptive one that if Ricardo 'reverted to the method of "let us suppose" ' (which often introduce his arguments), 'he did so because the essential economic categories, which Smith and his predecessors had laboriously endeavoured to extract from the totality of historical development, were in fact now available in their abstract form. Moreover, with all his apparent abstraction, Ricardo was essentially a concrete thinker: in the sense that his theorising was always about his contemporary world.'[45] His method is, then, analogous to that of Marx, who also took the elementary economic concepts (value, labour, money etc., forged by himself or others) in their most abstract form, and related their validity in practice to the anatomy of the most complex reality known, i.e. the fundamental conditions of production in bourgeois society. This aspect of the Ricardian-Marxist method is also, not surprisingly, a hallmark of Piero Sraffa, whose *Production of Commodities by Means of Commodities* is characterised by a circular motion between abstract and concrete in models of increasing complexity that approach closer and closer to an economic reality grounded in a specific society.

Gramsci's reasoning on Ricardo's philosophical importance in the Marxist tradition is original and seems tenable but can his influence be detected elsewhere? Although indirect, the Ricardian influence (via Sraffa) on the later Wittgenstein seems a case in point. A certain consensus has been forming among people writing from different perspectives about what was meant by the philosopher's tribute to the criticism that Sraffa 'for many years unceasingly practised on my [Wittgenstein's] thoughts'.[46] Rush Rhees, one of Wittgenstein's close collaborators, is cited in Ray Monk's biography as saying that what he gained from his regular talks with Sraffa was an 'anthropological' way of looking at philosophical problems.[47] Brian McGuinness, another biographer of Wittgenstein and himself a distinguished philosopher, expresses this idea more clearly: Sraffa and Wittgenstein's 'manner of thinking is an integral reflection of the character and uses of a community. ... An individual cannot be understood if abstracted from the collectivity to which he or she belongs.'[48] Similarly the philosopher and linguist Ferruccio Rossi-Landi points to the later Wittgenstein's 'return to the real circumstances in which things – including those particular "things" that make up language – take on their meaning'.[49] For Rossi-Landi, Sraffa's formulations – present in their main outline as long ago as 1930 but published only substantially later in the 1960 *Production of Commodities by Means of Commodities* – 'transmitted to Wittgenstein the idea of language use to reveal meaning'.[50] For the Wittgenstein of the *Philosophical Investigations* in 'a *large* class of cases ... the meaning of a word is its use in the language' or, with even more explicit

General Introduction

reference to the social totality, 'an expression has meaning only within the flow of life'; as Rossi-Landi remarks 'commodities and words have in common that values are conferred on them upon them by men in association', i.e. in a social context.[51] While not uncritical of Wittgenstein, Rossi-Landi's highly original essay draws other parallels between his work and Sraffa's, traceable back to the influence of Ricardo on the latter: the increasing complexity of their models or language games, the particular 'method of abstraction that determines its own object as a totality ... discarding what is irrelevant or secondary ... [to avoid] the danger inherent in the generalisation of common properties "by progressive refinement of the analogy" ', 'a return to context, to the relationships between various pieces making up a given totality, to circular rather than unidirectional consideration', just as in Sraffa's rejection of the neo-classical (marginalist) economists' unidirectional flow from the production to the consumption of commodities in favour of a circular 'production of commodities by means of commodities' in his 'explicit return to the classical tradition – *in its Ricardian-Marxist aspects*'.[52]

A circularity factor is also commented on by Gramsci in 'The Dialectic of Distincts' (pp.370-1), noting that this process in Croce's thought (not between abstraction and concrete reality and back but between the categories of the spirit in this dialectic of his – see General Introduction, p.lxxvi) came not only after but because of Croce's study of Marx and 'reflection on the abstract concept of "homo oeconomicus" typical of classical economy'; in Croce's version this man was, however, 'economic man' in the abstract, whom he had, by conscious decision, stripped of reference to any society that has ever existed – a stark contrast with the Ricardian-Marxist line of analysis. This 'genericisation', as Gramsci considered it, may seem strange to anyone influenced in any way at all by Marx, yet it is an aim of some serious economists and represents one of the factors that differentiate Marxist economics from other schools. For example, taking their cue from the French mathematicians who, under the collective pseudonym Nicolas Bourbaki, have since the 1930s been trying to put mathematics on an ahistoric and purely logical basis, Gerard Debreu and Kenneth Arrow have reached a high point in the attempt, through a process of rigorous axiomatisation to avoid Sraffa's type of criticism, to reformulate neo-classical economics so as to 'free the formal content of the theory [of general economic equilibrium] from any reference to an empirical economic content', the 'relations between economic subjects ... [being] mediated solely by the market'. Even then, they have achieved only limited success since there creep in 'specific elements of capitalist economic reality'.[53]

Through a comparison of the various approaches – bearing constantly in mind the 'let us suppose' method of abstraction and its attendant circular movement between abstract and concrete, which was to form an integral part of what Gramsci calls 'historicist' or 'critical', i.e. Marxist, economy – Ricardo's shadow may be seen in places not necessarily foreseeable from inside a 1930s fascist gaol. Behind the concrete-abstract-concrete cycle, that many might now take for granted, there is a principle at stake, whose strength is demonstrated by the fact that even some of its most authoritative opponents in the economic field have not been able to reject it consistently. Thus, Gramsci's insistent return – see Chapter III of the present volume and SPN, pp.399-402 and 410-4 – to certain notions underlying a science (in this case economics), which might at first sight seem to overrate their importance, does in fact acquire a significance and helps distinguish his conception of economic science from the 'pure' or 'vulgar' economics contemporary with him and much more theoretically elaborate and 'refined' economics since.

A pertinent question is indeed raised about the status of economic science. In 'Regarding Pantaleoni's *Pure Economics*' (p.173) Gramsci cites the opinion of Luigi Einaudi, the liberal economist elected President of the Italian Republic in 1948, that economics is a doctrine of the same nature as the mathematical and physical sciences. Lionel Robbins, author of the *Essay on the Nature and Significance of Economic Science* commented on by Gramsci (pp.174-5) the year after the note on Pantaleoni, adopts a similar approach: in so far as economic science is separate from social and political considerations and from any struggle for control over the surplus product, it is reduced to a merely technical study of 'human behaviour as a relationship between ends and scarce means which have alternative uses',[54] where people make 'free choices' totally uninfluenced by mundane issues like class (*sic!*). For the philosopher Ugo Spirito and others ('Ugo Spirito & Co.', pp.180-1 and 'Freedom and "Automatism" or Rationality', pp.179-80) classical economy was 'deterministic', i.e. presumably one of the so-called 'exact' sciences; Gramsci denies this charge since there always exists the human perturbatory element and, as he says, economic laws are laws of tendency only, since changes always set up countervailing forces. The Einaudi-Robbins-Spirito axis (if it may be termed thus) seems to foreshadow the position of Arrow and Debreu (see above), who likewise attempt to exclude what Rush Rhees calls the 'anthropological' (or socio-political) factor and regard economics as a science rather like mathematics. Keynes, while not disdaining mathematics in his own work, puts it at the opposite end of the spectrum by classing it among the moral sciences.[55] Ranchetti places it in an 'intermediate and ambivalent position' between ' "hard and strong" disciplines like in fact mathematics and physics, and "softer and more flexible" ones like the so-called social "sciences" '.[56] In 'The Science of Economics', pp.189-90, written some months later than (and in part going over the same ground as) the rest of his enquiry into economic science, by way of conclusion Gramsci states his view – rejecting the categorisation of economics as a quasi-mathematical science and taking into full account the dialectical element introduced by the human agency – that, by all criteria that could be applied, economics is a science, but of a unique type.

The concept of economic laws as tendential is rejected by some, as may be seen in the half dozen notes of Gramsci's polemic with Croce on value and on the tendency of the rate of profit to fall. In the preface (not available in English) to the second edition of Croce's *Historical Materialism and the Economics of Karl Marx* it is claimed that the consistent application of this law would mean 'neither more nor less than the automatic and imminent end of capitalist society'. Gramsci limits his reply to methodological considerations. The law is only the obverse of the law of relative surplus value, immediately set in motion, by which, starting at the individual factory, constant savings and improvements are made to restore profits; he also points out that by failing to distinguish between what happens at the level of the factory and what happens in an industry in general, Croce's argument loses further validity. In concluding ('Fordism and the Falling Rate of Profit', pp.433-5) this group of notes he makes the explicit link between this facet of his work and 'Americanism and Fordism' as the attempt to escape the tendential fall of the profit rate. At a more empirical level, the theme is taken up again in a later note ('The Crisis', pp.219-23 in Chapter IV) in which he distinguishes between progressive and stationary industries on the international scale in an argument that echoes, albeit maybe distantly, Marx's claim that 'contradictions lead to explosions, cataclysms, crises in which by momentaneous suspension of labour and annihilation of a great portion of capital the latter is violently reduced to the point where it can go on'.[57]

Gramsci's emphasis on the role of the renewal of capital stands out in contrast to his contemporaries among Marxist economists. In a penetrating recent essay on his approach to economics, Jean-Pierre Potier draws attention to the attitude, then prevalent among Marxist economists, to ascribe any increase in the rate of economic exploitation to longer hours, speed-up without the use of new methods and so forth: in other words to the increase of *absolute* rather than *relative* surplus value.[58] The Italian left's general neglect of economics meant that, although Gramsci's argument about the ways in which surplus value could be increased were the first Italian criticism of Croce on territory he had appropriated, they were ignored until after the traumatic defeat of the left trade union confederation (CGIL) at the all-important FIAT factories in the mid-50s; production line workers had a hard time in convincing the union and the left outside the factory that increased production was due to a more rational and advanced, i.e.

Fordist, use of machines, rather than to any considerable increase in the *intensity* of labour. Subsequently these themes were to be developed by the influential magazine *Quaderni Rossi*, which both presaged the explosion in working-class militancy at the end of the 60s and provided top level trade union cadres who in part led it. Raniero Panzieri, a co-editor of the magazine, through his work as translator of Vol. III of Marx's *Capital*, independently explored, far more fully than Gramsci could, the arguments about surplus value.[59] Both stressed that the treatment in Vol. III of *Capital* was not to be understood (as Croce had done) as a mere correction to that outlined in Vol. I, but that the two together illustrated ('Relative Surplus Value and the Falling Rate of Profit', pp.430-3) a different and 'contradictory aspect of the process bound up with technical progress, i.e. the theory of relative surplus value'. In the last part of the twentieth century the topic has again resurfaced, in only a slightly different guise, as production and service industries are decentralised on a world scale in the attempt to reduce costs and counteract the tendential fall in the profit rate.

5 National and International Economic Trends

The whole world underwent a rapid and dramatic change during and after World War I, with upheavals in population and class structure and not merely the technological changes alluded to above. The flux of geo-political events is recorded in a series of paragraphs, mainly in the second notebook, dating almost exclusively from May 1930 through to the end of that year. These notes have been newly edited, bringing together what were considered the most important ones[60] as a backdrop against which, it is hoped, Gramsci's reflections on national and international economic problems and the world crisis may be better seen in context. Oil, for instance, as a domestic U.S. industry or as part of the international nature of U.K. interests, emerges as a theme in 'Oil, Petrol and Petroleum Products', pp.209-10, and briefly in 'Italy and the Yemen in the New Politics of the Arab World', pp.210-3, regarding the Arab peninsula with its interweaving of political, religious and national questions.

The first quarter of the twentieth century saw the United States establish its hegemony over the world after a period in which it had grown in wealth and population ('Geo-political Developments', pp.201-7). It emerged from World War I alone among the Allied nations as solely a lender, with inter-Allied credits of about two billion pounds sterling. By contrast the U.K., on leaving out of the account its difficult-to-recover loan to Russia and its debts to the U.S., was left with credits of only £330 million.[61] Elsewhere in the same paragraph of Q2 (here divided off as 'Britain and the United States after the War', pp.213-4) Gramsci gives an updated breakdown of figures for foreign debt, national income and so on, indicating the nature of the change that had taken place in the post-war period. While liberals – as typified by Keynes – hoped for an altruistic renunciation of war debts, especially by the U.S., Gramsci, in line with orthodox Marxist thinking, regarded foreign credit as a base for imperial or neo-colonial expansion and control ('The Colonies', pp.241-2), although, in the opinion of Keynes in particular, in the short term the U.S. had insufficient capital available for export to aid this process in the 1919-20 period.

Themes dealt with in the notes on the world crisis are also reflected in Section C of Chapter IV, headed 'National Economic Problems and International Relations'. Stress is laid on the upheaval in a country's class structure and place in the international hierarchy caused by ruling-class intervention in such matters as exchange rates, monetary systems and relations between city and countryside or industry and agriculture; on this last aspect Gramsci was once again stimulated by Sraffa.[62] One policy instrument that countries resorted to was duty and excise regulations, by means of which a government could choose which sectors of its population – usually the better-off strata – to cushion against the severest costs of imported goods. Gramsci's argument here is analogous to his well-known one – see 'Some Aspects of the Southern Question' SPW 1921-26, pp.449-50, or here 'Savings, Agricultural Protectionism and

Industry', pp.245-6 and 'On the National Economic Structure', pp.248-53 – about the iniquities of a grain tax that penalised the southern peasantry while favouring a corporative alliance between a reformist working class and their employers under the hegemony of the northern Italian industrialists.

He comes back several times to the fact that Italy in particular was characterised by a parasitic shareholding and rentier middle class that was responsible for an over-consumption of goods. Indeed, in one of his early notes ('Observations on the World Crisis', pp.215-7), written in Summer 1931, he quotes with some approval the thesis of the then prominent Italian economist Pasquale Jannaccone that the economic crisis that became manifest in 1929 was one of over-consumption, in the sense that too little in the way of savings was going to new capital formation in order to reduce the price of mass-consumption goods. What Gramsci contests is the consequence drawn by some that the working class, peasantry and the unemployed were, or even could be, in any way responsible for over-consumption; the finger is pointed at the wealthier stratas' consumption of relatively high-cost semi-luxury items. The capacities existed, if put to proper use, to give everyone a decent standard of living, but what Gramsci in no way foresaw was the staggering post-1945 expansion in consumer goods produced for the advanced world. The ideas of an economic shake-up and a 'savings crisis' are continued in a note headed 'The Crisis', pp.219-23, written some time after the Q10 paragraphs on economic science. Sraffa (called to Cambridge by Keynes in 1927) had sent Gramsci the British Parliament's *Macmillan Report on Finance and Industry*, 'to a great extent written and wholly inspired by Keynes'.[63] In both this report and the 1930 *Treatise on Money*, cited in a letter of Sraffa's whose contents were relayed to Gramsci, Keynes ascribed the crisis to 'an excess of "savings" in the sense of money "set aside" by savers, over "investments" in the sense of new constructions, etc.'; the second part, headed by Gramsci 'Money and Gold', of the sub-section on 'The Crisis' seems to follow the stance Keynes then held.

For some of his ideas on contemporary economic

developments Gramsci seems to have relied, in addition to these sources, on his copy of the 1924 French translation of Keynes's *Tract on Monetary Reform*, a challenge to the then current orthodoxy, although the author was later to modify his views quite radically, considering inadequate even his 1930 *Treatise on Money*.[64] In general, then, Gramsci (partly stimulated by Sraffa) shows both points of contact with and divergences from Keynes. On the United States question Gramsci was more realistic than Keynes who, however, while remaining critical, had a more sanguine appreciation than Gramsci or Sraffa of the prospects for the longer-term stabilisation of capitalist society. In Sraffa's words 'Keynes, who has carried out, without wanting to do so, a critique of the liberal and capitalist economy, concludes with an apology for the capitalist entrepreneur and a quest for "remedies".'[65]

It would be easy, as Jean-Pierre Potier observes, to 'reproach Gramsci with an inadequate knowledge of the Marxist theory of crises, and not to have taken into consideration other functions of the state, such as the economic role it began to assume in the course of the first experiments of the 1930s'.[66] Nevertheless there are points on which he was in advance of many of his conemporaries on the left. One is his emphasis on the process of modernisation and rationalisation both in the industrially-advanced societies of his day and in the the young USSR too ('Reformation and Renaissance. The Present Process of the Molecular Formation of a New Civilisation', pp.270-1, written after he had read Michael Farbman's survey in an *Economist* supplement). Another is his firmly expressed position that the crisis was neither a single event nor – in involving all facets of society (and thus questions of hegemony) – one of a merely economic nature, but a complex process whose roots went back at least to the War ('The Crisis', cited above) and subsequent territorial settlements. And, in later notebooks, e.g. Q19 on the Risorgimento, some aspects of the new types of state economic policy do in fact begin to be touched on.

The national and international economy notes point the way towards reflections on the big victors of World War I,

Britain and the United States. A stimulus to Gramsci's thinking on the USA is to be found in a number of a German magazine dedicated to new American writers: 'Before a people has awoken to itself, found itself and been able to pass judgement on itself, any true literature is impossible. Before the world war, America was not yet mature, had not yet awoken. There had to be a world war for the Americans or, rather, certain far-sighted spirits among them, to discover the face of their own people.'[67] Positions such as this formed the implicit but necessary link between Gramsci's reflections on the different aspects of American intellectual achievement (SCW, pp.278-81 and SPN, pp.20-1 on different aspects of American intellectual life; SPN, pp.277-318 on Americanism and Fordism; and Chapter IV, Section D, of this volume). The phenomenon he called 'Americanism', stemming partly from the experience of founding a new country (Chapter IV, Section A), and the accompanying one of 'Fordism' gave rise to technical intellectuals with an industrially oriented outlook ('Americanism' and 'The Basic Activity of the Age', pp.256-8, both taken from Q15), whose various types, such as Sinclair Lewis's Babbitt (SCW, pp.278-9 and this volume pp.302-3), provided important raw material for American writers to begin the self-reflection up to then conspicuous by its absence. The history of the United States meant that intellectuals there were of necessity different from their European counterparts, considered (in part in their literary-artistic role) as once having provided the ruling classes with their 'cultural self-consciousness [and] self-criticism' (SCW, loc.cit.). In the case of the USA, however, the emergence of a type of traditional intellectual was hard to detect (SPN, pp.20-1). A number of individuals are named (Section D, Chapter IV of this volume) in very brief comments as, by implication, the potential organisers of a culture that could find its popularisers in a numerically slight but culturally well-equipped intelligentsia of a few tens of thousands of people ('Brief Notes on American Culture', pp.259-60).

While Gramsci definitely does see the beginnings of American world hegemony, he does not see (outside

Fordism) any intellectual agents for its international consolidation. In his view Woodrow Wilson – whose famous 'fourteen points' establishing the conditions for peace after World War I are considered by some to have laid the basis for such a hegemony – suffered a defeat ('Geo-Political Developments, pp.204-5) through not having stood up firmly enough to European diplomacy. Only later did Wilson's heirs (Franklin D. Roosevelt, Cordell Hull, George Marshall, George Kennan and so on) once again take up the battle he had lost.[68] The tension between these representatives of the pro-European 'East Coast Establishment' and the more 'isolationist' group within American capital that favoured replacing Europe with Asia as the focus of foreign interest (a constant factor in twentieth-century United States politics) hovers in the background of Gramsci's notes through his comments on Wilson and odd notes such as 'The Atlantic and the Pacific', p.196, on the shift of the world's economic axis towards the Pacific basin, or 'World Politics and European Politics', p.195, with its reference to the growing importance of Japan.

The notes on Britain, too, reflect the changes taking place. As America was developing its international and industrial role, in Britain finance capital was eclipsing its industrial counterpart. Thus in two pieces written within a month of each other ('Britain', pp.262-3, and an 'A' text – Q4§60 – here in its rewritten version, 'London's World Role', pp.266-7, of three or four years later) Gramsci draws attention to now familiar themes like Britain's incipient relative industrial decline, the attempts to retain sterling as an international currency, and the importance of 'invisible earnings', all factors involving the City of London. Britain's already somewhat restricted industrial base and concentration on international trade, which absorbed a comparatively high proportion of the country's population, left countries like Germany in a more advantageous position for recovery from the recession ('Britain and Germany', pp.268-9). The beginning of this decline coincided with the USA's challenge to Britain's position on the world scene, with the greater influence of the Dominions and with stirrings for independence within the Empire or, in the case of Ireland, within the then UK: see 'The British Government', pp.267-8, and 'The Crisis of Parliamentarism', p.268. In these last two sub-sections we read that the domestic response was for the Executive to become an (elective) 'party dictatorship' with a dominant cabinet 'personality who exercises a Bonapartist role' within the parliamentary set-up in what Gramsci calls a 'crisis of the parliamentary regime', already illustrated by the kid-glove treatment of Carson after his quasi-insurrection of 1914.

A crucial (albeit far from fully developed) aspect of Gramsci's concept of hegemony is its economic component, usually completely ignored by those who have written on him. Yet its importance is stated explicitly in 'Some Theoretical and Practical Aspects of Economism'[69]: 'if hegemony is ethico-political, it cannot but also be economic, cannot but have its basis in the decisive function exercised by the leading group in the decisive core of economic activity'. On a dozen or more occasions in the notes here brought together as Section F of Chapter IV, Gramsci uses the word 'conformism' in a sense closely linked to what he terms the 'collective man' and to be understood as referring to the type of uniformity that exists between an economic set-up and the socio-economic behaviour of the individuals comprising it (or, as discussed in Q22 on 'Americanism and Fordism' – SPN, pp.279-318 – their psycho-economic behaviour). Economic rationalisation brings with it a standardisation not only of products but of ways of thinking, of behaviour and of intellectual response to society: in short it helps create a new hegemony. In 'Man as Individual and Man as Mass', pp.275-7, conformism in its negative aspect is stated to be imposed in an authoritarian manner while, positively, it is a freely entered into creation 'from below', the 'collective man' of a future society being 'formed essentially from the bottom up, on the basis of the position occupied by the collectivity in the world of production', while the self-discipline involved is a pre-condition 'for freedom, including freedom of the individual'; the 'struggle between "two conformisms" ' then becomes 'a struggle for hegemony'. Although Section F, as its title says, deals with 'The New Society and the New Economic Individual', equally important is Gramsci's attempt here to sketch out part of the basis for the economic component that hegemony entails. (It may also be noted that if the principal meaning of civil society is the place where hegemony is exercised – as implied in 'Civil Society', pp.75-6 – then, in one important aspect, the economy and its institutions form for Gramsci part of civil society, just as in Marx's 1859 Preface to the *Contribution to the Critique of Political Economy*.[70])

Another key Gramscian notion on the subject of hegemony – that of 'Reformation and Counter-Reformation' – is also present in this same Section of Chapter IV. Allied to conformism, the Gramscian concept of 'reformation' refers to the need to have the philosophy of praxis play a role analogous to that of the great religious reformations of the past which led, despite the deterministic tendency apparent in the existence in Calvinistic Protestantism of an 'elect' destined for salvation, to a 'flowering of individuality' ('Conformism and the Collective Man', pp.269-70). Similarly in the USSR, despite the fact that many critics maintained that from historical materialism there could ' "logically" stem only fatalism and passivity, in actual fact it [gave] rise to a flowering of initiatives and enterprises' ('The Present Process of the Molecular Formation of a New Civilisation', cit.), an interprertation confirmed for Gramsci by Farbman's survey for the *Economist*. Having said that, there is now enough evidence of various types to demonstrate that he had an independent critical stance as regards both the USSR (and its leaders) and the Communist International, while scrupulously observing the type of party discipline then required. In discussions with fellow-prisoners he expressed support as early as 1930 for a transitional Constituent Assembly, in conflict with the International's line between its Sixth and Seventh Congresses of passing immediately to the organisation of soviets;[71] he was of this view right up to the time of his last conversation with Piero Sraffa (26 March 1937).[72] As regards coercion and hegemony in the USSR the famous letter he wrote on behalf of the Political Bureau of the Italian Communist Party to the Central Committee of the CPSU reads: 'Comrades ... on the eve of your XV

Conference we no longer have the confidence of the past. ... In these nine years of world history you have been the organising and driving element of revolutionary forces everywhere ... but today you are destroying your own work.' While in agreement with the political line then upheld by the Stalin-Bukharin axis on the Central Committee, he questioned their treatment of the opposition, arguing that 'firm unity and firm discipline in the party that governs the workers' state, necessary for ensuring proletarian hegemony, cannot be mechanical and imposed by coercion'.[73] Although the rather enigmatic note that closes Chapter IV is a comment on the development of affairs in fascist Italy, it *might* also represent a veiled criticism of the policies being carried out against whole sectors of the Soviet peasantry after Stalin's subsequent break with Bukharin.

The notes, then, that form Chapters III and IV, when considered together with those in Chapter VII on the polemic with Croce over value and the tendency of the rate of profit to fall, show a different Gramsci from the person sometimes depicted as uninterested in economic issues. Since the mid-80s a number of people have looked at these writings again;[74] while 'received wisdom' seems to regard him as *par excellence* the theorist of the 'superstructure', if one is to single out one aspect of his thought it is more correct to consider him the theorist of the historical bloc (and the conditions for its construction), within which the economic strand in his thought ('if hegemony is ethico-political, it cannot but also be economic' – see above) takes its rightful place. This component, which of course includes the analysis of Americanism and Fordism, also forms a necessary backdrop to his other reflections and his detailed, accurate reconnaissance of the social classes and forces present in the society of his time. Indeed, without the integration into an overall picture of factors like these, at both national and international levels, the historical bloc in a given country in a given period, and the nature of hegemony within it, cannot adequately be characterised.

6 Science and Translatability

Gramsci's concept of science or, more precisely, of the foundations of scientific knowledge is developed principally in the parts of Q11 which he numbered III and IV and headed 'Science and "Scientific" Ideologies' and 'The Logical Instruments of Thought', but there are other pertinent comments, especially in the notes on economic science and in part II of Q11 ('Critical Notes on an Attempt at a Popular Sociology', SPN, pp.438-72). Taken as a whole his ideas demonstrate an approach to the subject well ahead of its time. On one hand, the ideas come close to the positions of the young Marx and, on the other, they are anticipatory of some notions of the influential post-1960 realist school of philosophy of science, as typified by Thomas Kuhn.

The context Gramsci was working in was not at all promising. Italian idealist philosophy at the time dismissed science out of hand; for Croce in particular the natural sciences were examples of what he termed 'pseudo-sciences': i.e. once nature as such had been constructed by spirit (for which see 'Empiricism', p.283), the role played by philosophical knowledge (which would have made them 'real' sciences) was supplanted by mere classification. In other words, despite the tremendous upheavals in the philosophical bases of science caused in the first three decades of the twentieth century by quantum theory and Einsteinian relativity, Croce had not progressed far beyond the approach of an Aristotelian-type empirical classification of 'facts', buttressed by conventionalist notions borrowed from idealist philosophers and scientists such as Bergson, Poincaré and (the subject of Lenin's essentially well-founded criticisms) Mach and Avenarius. Piero Sraffa is illuminating on the subject. Shortly after sending Gramsci a copy of *Science at the Cross Roads*, the contributions of the Soviet delegation to the 1931 London *Second International Congress of the History of Science and Technology*, he wrote to Tania: 'All Italians have a great gap in their culture: ignorance of the natural sciences. Croce's case is extreme, but typical. The philosophers think that once they have

General Introduction

shown that scientists deserve to be failed ignominiously in philosophy, their own task is at an end. And so it is that the natural sciences have been handed over to the mercies of the positivists with the effects that we are well aware of.'[75]

Gramsci develops the two-pronged attack on positivist and idealist notions of science suggested by Sraffa's letter. The idea that science was based on an empirical approach, as well as being dear to Croce, was also typical of the positivists, criticised exactly on this score by the influential Frankfurt School. Max Horkheimer parallels Gramsci by taking positivism to task for its empty empiricism, the accumulation of ' "solitary facts", more or less arbitrarily "selected from the infinite number that present themselves" ';[76] scientific activity becomes limited to the 'registration, classification, and generalisation of appearances, without regard to any differentiation of the essential and inessential';[77] the result is that, unlike Marx, positivists made 'no distinction between the surface appearance of things and their core or essence'.[78] In opposition to the mere classification of facts Gramsci emphasised ('Objections to Empiricism', pp.283-4) that finding the 'relationships between them presupposes a 'concept' that allows one to distinguish that series of facts from other possible ones ... a conception whose history must be regarded as complex, a process that must be linked to the whole process of the development of culture'. He also attacked another basic tenet of the positivists: that one sole methodological approach could be applied in all sciences, natural or exact, social or economic: a prejudice to be fought is that one sort of research must of necessity 'be grouped together with [others] into one type and that "type" is "science" ' ('The Science of Economics', pp.189-90). Analogous to this criticism is one of the three main elements of the mature phase of the Frankfurt School, namely the 'epistemological and methodological critique of positivism (or more broadly scientism) in the social sciences'.[79]

Gramsci raises the sort of question that Marcuse tried to deal with 30 years after him: 'Must not the rationality of science and technology, instead of being reducible to unvarying rules of logic and method, have absorbed a substantive, historically derived and therefore transitory a priori structure?'[80] The difference seems to be that Marcuse regards existing science and technology as structures of domination *tout court* and says that nothing short of new ones will do, while Gramsci simply offers the basis for an analysis by recognising that, although science is rooted in the more general notions or predominant ideas (a type of philosophical halo, as he puts it) of its time, it also consists of a hard kernel of fact. One consequence of the former of Gramsci's considerations here is that science, too, is an ideology, a superstructural factor. To suppport this he points to the fact that it has at times suffered an eclipse. It does not however follow, as Mario Missiroli in his ultra-leftist phase claimed ('Science as Ideology', p.293 and its footnote) and as others – in a more or a less extreme form from time to time since – have tried to sustain, that science is a purely 'bourgeois' set of notions; if this were true a class like the proletariat could not appropriate the bourgeoisie's scientific findings without succumbing to bourgeois ideology. Science is a historical category, not in itself self-sufficient as a conception of the world; it is an ideology, albeit of a very particular type since it is the most closely linked of all fields of human knowledge to the observable natural world ('Science as Ideology', loc. cit.). Further, the continual refinement of the instruments used (including mental ones) helps separate what is essential from what is arbitrary, individual and transitory ('Science, Humanity, Objectivity', pp.290-2). It is 'the union of the objective fact with a hypothesis or a system of hypotheses which go beyond the mere objective fact' ('Science as Ideology', cit.).

Here difficulties arise of which Gramsci was only partially conscious. Typical of many philosophers were ideas such as that expressed baldly by Croce's principal English follower, R.G. Collingwood (and, as seen above, shared to a great extent by Gramsci too), that 'natural science ... consists of facts and theories'.[81] Even at the time, however, some scientists had misgivings about such rigid fact-hypothesis distinctions. In discussing atomic structure and radioactivity the 1922 Nobel laureate for chemistry, F.W. Aston, says right at the start of his book *Isotopes*: 'What had been before regarded as a convenient working hypothesis became with remarkable rapidity a definitive statement of fact.'[82] His view is in stark contrast with those of professional philosophers who continued to lag behind the revolutions in physics and chemistry well underway by the turn of the twentieth century. It was not until forty years after Aston that Thomas Kuhn demonstrated in *The Structure of Scentific Revolutions*, a cornerstone of modern realist philosophy of science, that scientific facts and data are *not* separable from theory (or systems of hypotheses) but are 'theory-laden'; two of the main examples he cites are mass in the Einsteinian and Newtonian frameworks and the atom pre- and post-Dalton. He leaves no room for doubt that after such changes in scientific paradigm 'the data themselves had changed' and, quoting 'force, mass, element, compound, cell' as examples, 'the ways in which some [of these terms – or 'signs', for which see below] attach to nature has somehow changed',[83] i.e. 'the datum is such in the light of theoretical interpretations and the reconstruction of facts is guided by theoretical hypotheses'.[84]

In mitigation, the idea that there may not be a completely rigid fact-theory distinction in Gramsci (which, intuitively, would go against his general refusal of such dichotomies), but a convergence or at least compatibility of his concept of scientific fact with the more advanced notions of the realist school comes in 'Philosophy, Religion, Ideology', p.386. He here deals with Croce's criticism that, particularly in the *Theses on Feuerbach*, Marx studied 'in the philosophers exactly what was not philosophical, their practical tendencies and social inclinations'. For Gramsci, as for the realists, an important factor in a new scientific paradigm is the intellectual approach of its proponents which, reflecting implicitly or explicitly an influential philosophical current of the era, can make itself felt in the specific way in which a theory is formulated. If we also consider his answer – in the negative – to the question of whether scientific truths can be considered definitive ('Science, Humanity, Objectivity', cit.) then the avenue is left open to the position that a given fact may always be reinterpreted in the light of a later theory, and hence that 'facts' too may not be quite as rock-solid as at first they seem. (As a particularly striking example of the contribution that philosophy can make in the formulation of a scientific theory one may cite the influence of Søren Kierkegaard and, specifically of his pupil Harald Høffding, over the Danish physicist Niels Bohr in the dominant interpretation of quantum mechanics by the so-called Göttingen-Copenhagen school.[85])

Another position established by Kuhnian realists, but present in embryonic form in Gramsci, relates to how one scientific theory replaces another. In 'Science as Ideology', cit., Gramsci merely notes that rooted within scientific methodology itself is the capacity to distinguish between fact and hypothesis (thereby implying the possibility of discarding false hypotheses) but does not indicate how this happens. One model points to the patient accretion of one fact after another which, at a certain point, can lead to the negation of a hypothesis (i.e. a type of 'falsificationism' found in a sophisticated version in Karl Popper). Kuhn's analysis is now regarded as more convincing: there are from time to time radical changes – revolutions – in scientific outlook. These happen when unexpected observations show up grave deficiencies in the hierarchy of concepts governing a science and a leap, sometimes intuitive, has to be made in order to formulate new fundamental concepts which define a new way of looking at things and of constructing essentially new facts in the ensuing period of 'normal science' laid down by the concepts of the new paradigm. In 'Outlines of Marxist Economics', pp.176-9, Gramsci commits himself to a position similar to the Kuhnian view when he speaks of the 'period of struggle and polemics' in which one outlook tries to establish itself against an older one, followed by (in typically Gramscian terminology) a 'classical period of organic expansion'; this may fruitfully be compared with what Kuhn calls a struggle beween rival paradigms, followed by a period of 'normal science', devoted to solving the problems of reality as posed within the 'winning' paradigm.

The overall tenor and tendency of Gramsci's position, in polemic with the idealists and positivists, is to emphasise a historical, ideological side built into science, which leads to the question of the nature of scientific truth. Here again there is an idea that has a remarkably modern ring to it. Again in 'Science, Humanity, Objectivity', cit., he writes that one asserts as objective reality only what 'is ascertained by everyone ... independent of any merely particular or group standpoint'. The argument is put in slightly different terms in another paragraph from the same notebook, written perhaps only a few weeks earlier: 'objectivity always means "humanly objective" which can be held to correspond exactly to "historically subjective": in other words, objective means "universal subjective" ' ('The So-Called "Reality of the External World" ', SPN, p.445). A key passage ('Some Preliminary Points of Reference', SPN, p.341), although couched in terms of the freedom of research, clarifies this: 'Who is to fix the 'rights of science' and the limits on scientific research? And can these rights and limits indeed be fixed? It seems necessary to leave the task of researching after new truths ... to the free initiative of individual scientists.'[86] The corollary to this is that, within the general constraints posed by society, it is left to scientists to decide what research to follow, that they are the arbiters of the validity of the results and therefore decide what constitutes, at a given time, the truth value of a theory. Kuhn states this explicitly when speaking of 'scientific communities' and a (scientific) 'community structure' that decides on what science – and the scientific truth of a proposition – is, in what he openly declared (to the great scandal of many philosophers at the time) to be a sociological and, indeed, also ideological approach to truth in the natural sciences.[87]

From both approaches then, human elements come into play to disturb any traditional cosy picture of science as a non-historical, totally value-free field of enquiry. With the establishment of this position Gramsci feels able to state ('Science, Humanity, Objectivity', cit.) that 'What is of interest to science is then not so much the objectivity of the real, but humanity forging its methods of research ... that is to say culture, its conception of the world, the relationship between humanity and reality as mediated by technology.' At this point it is useful to recall the views of the young Marx of the *1844 Manuscripts*, first published (in the original German) in 1932 when Gramsci had already formulated his ideas on science. For Marx, as for Gramsci, 'the immediate object of natural science' is man 'for immediate *sensuous nature* for man is, immediately, human sensuousness (the expressions are identical). ... But *nature* is the immediate object of the *science of man*: the first object of man – man – is nature, sensuousness; ... The *social* reality of nature, and *human* natural sciences, or the *natural science of man*, are identical terms.'[88] The positions of the two thinkers are very similar. However, in positing the constitutive role of the ensemble of social relations as the context for the formation of science and the development of the human person ('man is to be conceived as a historical bloc', as he wrote – SPN, p.360 – within a few weeks of the final version of his science notes), Gramsci is in line more with the mature Marx of the 1859 Preface to the *Contribution to a Critique of Political Economy* than with the still Feuerbachian concept of man (*der Mensch*) of the 1844 writings. This approach also goes beyond the idea that scientific advance is due near exclusively to a more or less self-contained scientific community, as Kuhn's early work seems to imply, to the role of society as a whole, a case argued by Soviet scientists in *Science at the Cross Roads* (although Gramsci possibly did not read beyond Bukharin's opening introductory essay to the volume) and later taken up again in a different form by the realists who followed on Kuhn's lead.

Another similarity with Marx lies in the assessment of technology. While Gramsci draws attention to its role as the mediator between humanity and the real world, Marx similarly observes, regarding historiography's neglect of natural science, that industry – in which any technology, however primitive, is a key feature – is 'the *exoteric* revelation of man's *essential powers*' and, by conceiving it thus, 'we also gain an understanding of the *human essence* of nature or the *natural* essence of man. In consequence, natural science will lose its abstractly material – or, rather, its idealistic – tendency, and will become the basis of *human* science.'[89] Elsewhere Marx criticises natural science as practised for its 'abstract materialism, a materialism that excludes history and its processes',[90] a typically Gramscian position which also finds a resonance in some modern

General Introduction

philosophers of science.[91] In the light of all this one sees why the very first study of Gramsci's approach to science underscores the contrast between him and the then dominant Crocean 'systematic devaluation of the epistemological value of scientific activity'.[92]

One other word needs to be added on science. Gramsci picks up the remark of a literary scholar, G.A. Borgese, that 'infinitely small phenomena ... cannot be considered independently of the subject that observes them' ('Modern Science and Misconceptions About It', p.289). This comment received an idealist interpretation when, cited out of context in an article which Gramsci discusses, it was claimed that such phenomena could not be considered 'as existing independently' of the observer, i.e. that in some way matter was 'a creation of the human mind' (loc. cit.), positions which are not a logical consequence of Borgese's statement; a more sophisticated idealism considers such matters non-questions until 'existence' is defined at the quantum level,[93] which might be reinterpreted as asking in what exact way the symbolism used to describe phenomena actually relates to them. Louis de Broglie, one of the philosophically realist minority among the few physicists who enquired into the philosophical foundations of their field, was later to reject the prevalent idealist view that the description of quantum phenomena is a 'representation of a probability which exists only in the mind', arguing that 'a physical reality external to us exists which is independent of our thoughts and of our imperfect means of knowing it'[94] and trusting to the possibility of improving these means. His position may be compared with the stance of Gramsci, as a non-specialist, that science 'poses no form of metaphysical "unknowable", but reduces what man does not know to an empirical "not known" ' ('Science, Humanity, Objectivity', p.292). There continue to be disputes and paradoxes regarding the philosophical foundation and interpretation of quantum mechanics,[95] which can, of course, only be solved by the progress of science as a whole, not by any appeal to philosophical positions. For Gramsci such paradoxes are due, perhaps above all, to the inevitably metaphorical nature of much of – even scientific – language, a viewpoint shared by many modern philosophers of science. Common language is, as he notes, fashioned to fit macroscopic phenomena: the genuine paradoxes of modern science have their counterpart in those of antiquity, on the conception of infinity, which helped 'refine the instruments of thought' ('Modern Science and Misconceptions About It', cit.).

Time after time Gramsci returns to the question of the scientific mentality as a conquest necessary for the intellectual and moral reform of society, and it is perhaps in this perspective that Section C 'The Logical Instruments of Thought' (pp.295-305 of Chapter V) is best understood. While the main emphasis is on the need to raise the cultural level of the masses of the people, judged to be still prevalently at a 'pre-Copernican' stage, he noted some time later that scientists too, while able to understand scientific abstraction in their own fields, are often unable to do so in general: not having mastered abstraction as a 'mental form', they still therefore have a narrow technical or caste mentality ('Formal Logic and the Scientific Mentality', p.305). Over and above the conquest of formal logic, the problem of reasoning dialectically represents a yet higher stage. On this Gramsci seems to indicate, partly through his interest in all points of view on the subject (Croce and Jesuit authors included), that much still remains to be done.

The paragraphs of Q11 devoted to 'The Translation of Philosophical and Scientific Languages', which follow the notes on science and logic, although not as well-known as his 'grand themes', are among the most important of the whole prison writings. His approach to translation follows two convergent paths: one, in various paragraphs scattered among various notebooks, starts from an 'orthodox' standpoint of practical questions of translation, while the other (the Q11 notes) deals with the subject at a high level of abstraction.

It is easier to get to grips with the 'orthodox' path. In studying a foreign language, one notices what at first gives the appearance of identity: the Latin *rosa* is easily understood as referring to a 'rose'. Experience teaches that there is no 'mathematical scheme' linking elements of a language, although some philosophers in the early part of the twentieth century (most notably Russell and Wittgenstein in his first period) were toying with this idea. For Gramsci one increasingly moves away from whatever identity there seems to exist between the same words, either to distinguish between similar, albeit subtly different, usages or to arrive at 'a historical judgement or a judgement of taste in which nuance, "unique and individualised" expressiveness, prevail' (see 'Oratory, Conversation, Culture', SCW, pp.384-5). This allows one to see how the same word, which might appear to denote an object, or concept, can vary – 'identity of terms does not mean identity of concepts' ('Questions of Nomenclature and Content', SPN, p.456) – either across languages or, within the same language, according to time or to its wider context; often Gramscian terms, too – perhaps in particular 'civil society', but also others like 'historical bloc' – do vary in this way, a fact that seems not to have been fully appreciated by all who have written on him.

This flexibility, characteristic of living language, is what was being theorised by Marxist linguists in the Soviet Union in the 1920s (some time before Wittgenstein, revising and largely rejecting his earlier ideas, did the same), particularly by Valentin N. Voloshinov, a pupil and collaborator of the great literary theorist, linguist and philosopher M.M. Bakhtin. Voloshinov distinguishes between 'signal' as a technical instrument for indicating an object or action (and thus a fixed element) and 'sign' which, in representing an aspect of a complex reality by reflecting and refracting the external world, is flexible and belongs *par excellence* to the domain of ideology. In his earlier prison writings on language Gramsci, using Crocean notions, tends to reject such a thing as 'signal' and to accept only the equivalent of the 'sign', when he maintains in an 'A' text (Q7§36) that 'All language is metaphorical – doubly so; it is a metaphor for the "thing" or "material and sensible object" indicated and it is a metaphor for the ideological meanings given to words during previous periods of civilisation'. The first of these positions is modified in the rewritten 'C' text to read that, with respect to these objects or the abstract concept 'it cannot quite be said that all discourse is metaphorical ... so as not to widen the concept of metaphor excessively', while the second one is confirmed and extended: with 'the acquisition of culture by new classes' the words of previous civilisations are taken over in metaphorical form and a 'new "metaphorical" meaning spreads with the spread of the new culture' which also adopts words from other cultures 'without the extensive halo they possessed in the original language' (SPN, pp.450-2). Voloshinov similarly points to the struggle waged (in his case by classes) to appropriate the meaning of words[96] (just as, nearly half a century after him, feminists were to begin a similar battle over the non-neutrality of gender-based language).

Voloshinov uses the word 'sign' not only or even predominantly in a literary context (as the Russian formalists, the target of his criticism, at first tended to do) but to refer to a fragment of reality, 'an entire message ... a whole phrase but not a phrase isolated from the social context or from the ideological field to which it belongs right from the start'.[97] This position fleshes out what Gramsci was saying about metaphor and also, when combined with the clash of class interests (in particular) over the meaning of words, backs up his insistence on the need to *translate* into Marxism terms (i.e. 'signs' in this sense of a complex reference) from other traditions. It further helps understand why, for their full understanding, certain key terms in his vocabulary (historical bloc, hegemony, intellectual and moral reform, Jacobinism, the city-countryside relation, passive revolution and so on) each imply the others; this brings us back, almost full-circle, to the way in which terms in a scientific theory similarly interlock, as seen in Kuhn's analysis and in his notion of 'paradigm'.

It is just this aspect of the reality behind the 'sign' that sets Gramsci off on the more abstract of his convergent paths towards what it means to translate. He asks why the Bolsheviks were 'not able to translate [their] language into the European languages' ('Lenin and Translation', p.306). In countries possessing a similar socio-economic set-up the intellectual responses that reflect or refract this structural element will be analogous, too, and such a ' "basically" identical cultural expression' is a presupposition for translatability ('Translation between Different Civilisations', p.307). Certain riders qualify this statement of his. A sector of intellectual activity in one country may find its most appropriate 'translation' into another sector in a second country: German philosophy expressed fundamentally the same notions as French political practice ('The Mutual Translatability of National Cultures', pp.310-3). An example drawn from the close of the twentieth century might be literature, music, philosophical 'weak thought' or architecture as different national or cultural manifestations of post-modernism.

Through this approach, which roots language firmly in social praxis, Gramsci establishes a fundamental plank in any realist-materialist theory of translation, rejecting the work of the more extreme interpreters of anthropological linguistic theories (typified by the so-called Sapir-Whorf hypothesis) or of philosopher-logicians like W.V.O. Quine who claim that a perception of the world possessed by one social group cannot be translated into the language of a group having a radically different one.[98] For Gramsci the 'exactness' of a translation between cultures or philosophies depends on how similar they are; as regards quite different societies it is to be seen whether 'one can translate between expressions of different stages of civilisation, in so far as each of these stages is a moment in the development of another' (which recalls his comments on metaphor as referring to 'ideological meanings given to words during previous periods of civilisation'). In translating from more to less 'advanced' societies the answer to Quine's question of how to translate into a 'primitive' culture (or, indeed, into that of most members of 'advanced' societies) the statement 'neutrinos have no mass' – or an extremely small one – is presumably that those of a higher degree of civilisation (or knowledge) 'should accelerate the process of education of the more backward peoples and social groups, thereby appropriately universalising and translating its new experience' ('Antonio Labriola [1]', p.158).

Gramsci's condition for translation is an extension of the simple equation ascribed to Marx, namely French politics =

German philosophy: a middle term is introduced representing equivalent stages of civilisation that give rise to similar overall modes of thinking, which are in turn expressed in the cultures of those societies. When wide differences exist between civilisations or cultures, like between the South and the North of the world, or across ethnic groups or the gender gap, in Gramsci's view translation is rendered not impossible, as claimed by some (followers of Quine or Sapir and Whorf or various political intellectuals), but difficult and sometimes inexact ('but what language is exactly translatable into another?' as asks in 'Giovanni Vailati and the Translatability of Scientific Languages', p.309).

In 'Translation between Different Civilisations' (cit.) he says, giving pride of place to Marxism, that 'only in the philosophy of praxis is the 'translation' organic and thoroughgoing'. Marxism is capable of translating into its terms and absorbing relevant contributions from other philosophies, just as Marx did most notably with Hegelianism. It is not at all coincidental that Gramsci wrote the notes on translatability at the same time as the final versions of his notes in Q10 on Croce (which form the backbone of Chapters VI and VII of this volume), for they also constitute the theorisation of his reinterpretation and 'translation' of Crocean idealist propositions, in particular, into the language of the philosophy of praxis: ethico-political history appears, for example, as the expansion of hegemony, while similar operations are carried out on Sorel (the concept of the historical bloc), Renan ('intellectual and moral reform' transposed from the religious to the secular sphere) and so on. Herein lies both a key theoretical underpinning of Gramsci's 'open' Marxism and, it need hardly be added, a guide to understanding better how, in general, Marxism can be renewed through the incorporation into its schema of notions taken from fields that have developed independently of or even in opposition to it.

7 Idealist Philosophy: Gramsci's 'Anti-Croce'

Much of the two parts of Q10 are devoted to Gramsci's

critique of Croce's dialectical form of philosophical idealism, i.e. the current which assigns to spirit a primacy over matter and attempts to absorb all reality into thought. In rebutting with some amusement the criticism, put to him by a fellow-prisoner, that some thought him a Crocean, Gramsci commented, regarding Croce's intellectual stature: 'As a philosopher he represents the highest peak of development reached by Italian thought, while in politics he is the ultimate expression of liberal doctrine in defence of a society now in decline. But our comrades will see how much of a Crocean I am if they read a work I am preparing on him.'[99] Chapters VI and VII of the current volume, presented editorially as explained in the introductions to them, aim at reconstructing this intended essay of Gramsci's. His reflections here are linked to and may be read in conjunction with the sets of notes found mainly in Q11, together with Q10 the first of the 'special' (i.e. non-'miscellaneous' notebooks), and published in SPN under the headings 'The Study of Philosophy' (pp.323-77) and 'Problems of Marxism' (pp.381-472), much of this latter being his critique of Bukharin's Marxism, judged by Gramsci to be mechanistic, undialectical and fundamentally positivist. The importance of the double-pronged attack on positivism and idealism, quite apart from what it has to say about these currents, is that to a large extent it is through this critique that Gramsci defines his own philosophy. Given the status that Croce's philosophy held and the fact that Gramsci does not spell out explicitly a number of key concepts that he takes issue with, the following remarks (while not pretending to go into a detailed reconstruction of Gramsci's overall philosophy, which lies outside the scope of this introduction) may, it is hoped, prove useful as a guide to certain salient aspects of the polemic.

Gramsci applies to Croce the thesis to which he was simultaneously giving final form on the translatability of philosophical languages (Section D, Chapter V of this volume), namely that Marxism is best assimilated into a national culture – and is also enriched – by reinterpreting in Marxist terms and then incorporating the most advanced positions reached by that country's philosophical and cultural schools ('Croce and the Philosophy of Praxis', pp.354-6). While it was Giovanni Gentile, rather than Benedetto Croce, who succeeded in creating a school of followers in the field of philosophy,[100] in the first half of the twentieth century the person responsible more than anyone else for de-provincialising and updating Italy's philosophical and historiographic traditions was, in fact, Croce. Born in 1866 into a wealthy landowning family in the Abruzzo region of southern Italy, he was educated privately and attended Rome University (without however taking a degree) while living in the house of his uncle Silvio Spaventa, minister in the governments of the Historic Right. On moving to Naples – where he lived for the rest of his life – he became thoroughly acquainted with the work of the great eighteenth-century Neapolitan philosopher Giambattista Vico, at the same time as steeping himself in classical German, especially Hegelian, philosophy (though he always denied being a Hegelian in any strict sense). To the end of his long and prodigiously productive life he remained an independent scholar, editing and writing much of the review *La Critica* (from 1945 *Quaderni della 'Critica'*) which he had founded in 1903 and whose last number came out only a year before his death in 1952.

His early prestige on the left dated to the 1890s when, partly influenced by Antonio Labriola, the most important Italian Marxist prior to Gramsci and whose close friend he had become in Rome, he wrote the essays comprising his *Historical Materialism and the Economics of Karl Marx*, which conferred on him the status of a leader, alongside Bernstein in Germany and Sorel in France, of the revisionist current in Marxism. Croce himself found it convenient for many years not to deny publicly this reputation and indeed he did support the socialist press financially while working on this volume; however even during this so-called 'Marxist phase' his relation to Marxism was, to say the least, tenuous and his refusal to state openly his opposition to Marxism (at a time when 'to be Marxist' was fashionable) was due perhaps to factors like intellectual vanity, from which he was not immune. In letters published only relatively recently by Croce's own *Italian Institute for Historical Studies* Labriola wrote to him 'I have never dreamed of thinking that you were a Marxist, or even a socialist' and elsewhere, after saying this in other words, he continues 'in these new studies [i.e. of Marx] you have simply sought a rational complement to your historical-critical-literary culture. ... Your discussion is solely with yourself, just so as to know where to locate Marxism in your culture.'[101] His 'revisionism', if it can be called thus, helped in Labriola's view to weld together the 'reactionary currents' ('Croce's Stance During the First World War', p.334) and also, as Gramsci adds, the various fractions of 'liberal democratic culture' from 1900 to the outbreak of the First World War ('The Party Man', p.463 and SPN, pp.72 and 93); at the end of this period he also contributed to a review run by nationalists who then went over to fascism. A decade after Gramsci's death Croce, curiously, ran together into a single quotation comments on the first and third of these facts, although they were criticisms of him made twenty years apart by different people; he defended himself by emphasising his opposition to the nationalists but in a rare instance of self-criticism ruminated 'Was I unwise? Maybe.'[102]

His standing among left and generally democratic forces rose when he initially adopted a neutralist stance in the Great War. At this time he was just finishing, after fifteen or more years' work, his massive four-volume *Philosophy of the Spirit*, which established the basis for his later historical writings, where philosophy appeared as the methodology of historiography. Although Gramsci does not refer explicitly to this work as much as to other books of Croce's, some of the themes dealt with in Q10 – and even the wording used – leave no doubt that it formed a constant background for him. A more explicit reference point was constituted by Croce's 'minor works', collected essays on moral and ethical problems, critically discussed especially in the 'first part' of Q10 (Chapter VI of this volume) which provided, as Gramsci comments, an influential practical guide to life in particular for non-believers. With Croce's 'Manifesto of the Anti-Fascist Intellectuals' (1925), which attracted several hundred signatures, and his break with his erstwhile close collaborator Gentile – who was to remain the regime's chief philosophical prop (at the same time as he kept channels open with young anti-fascist intellectuals) – his influence reached and remained at a peak among non-Marxist and non-Catholic anti-fascists. Two other Crocean volumes, the histories of Europe and Italy, both published while Gramsci was in prison, furnished raw material, in the form of his concept of 'ethico-political history', for important reflections in particular on the concept of hegemony. The Gramscian and Crocean concepts were related but whereas, for Gramsci, the moment of force implied that of consent and vice versa, Croce (in Gramsci's view) ignored or, at the very least, downrated that of force by *beginning* his histories at the ends (1815 and 1871) of the periods of warfare that defined the lasting form of the two geo-political entities; in any case the political aspect for him was more and more supplanted by a purely moral (and at times moralistic) one, tied to his concept of liberty as a secular religion.[103]

Decades after Croce's death his influence and popularity have waned but, in evaluating his work, account must be taken of historical studies at the time he was active which, according to R.G. Collingwood, the English philosopher-historian close to him, were then progressing at rates 'comparable to those which natural science had achieved about the beginning of the seventeenth century'.[104] In continental Europe this had been due to a great extent to Marx's infuence on historians (see 'Economic History Studies', p.184 of this volume) and Croce, too, in his earlier work acknowledges a debt in this direction. Mirsky, who made a favourable impression on Gramsci for two articles of his in *Labour Monthly* in 1931, noted on the history-philosophy nexus that Croce's philosophy merited attention, among other things because he had been 'a serious student of Marx' and that his later 'uncompromising anti-scientific conception of history was evolved in direct opposition to the Marxist conception. It is chiefly in its Crocean form that the eminently unphilosophical English bourgeois became acquainted with this new aesthetic idealism [of historiography].'[105] Croce thus played an important role, for better or worse (and probably both, successively), in the changes sweeping over his fields and, as Gramsci notes, the positive features of his position, even when he was progressively distancing himself from Marxism, can be traced back to Marx.

Marxist attitudes to Croce were frequently less balanced than those adopted by Mirsky or, for that matter, before him by Plekhanov.[106] In *Marxism and Modern Thought*, which reflected the more or less official Soviet stance of the left sectarian 1928-34 period, the philosopher A.I. Tiumeniev argued that Gentile and Croce expressed 'the will to power of the imperialist and fascist bourgeoisie' and that they had 'passed from criticism of Marxism to fascism and an alliance with religion'.[107] Later on, in the early 1950s, E.Ya. Egermann was perhaps obliged by the intellectual climate of the times to repeat the unjust attack on Croce's alleged pro-fascism in articles that first introduced Gramscian notions to the Soviet public.[108] As against these opinions Vittorio Foa, an outstanding figure of the post-war trade union left, while in gaol in the 1930s for conspiratorial activities, regarded Croce (as did many, liberal-socialist intellectuals like himself or representatives of other strands of anti-fascism) as 'an emblem of liberal and anti-fascist consistency'; in the philosopher's polemic with the free-marketeer Luigi Einaudi 'Croce refused to identify freedom [*libertà*] with free-market economics [*liberismo*] ... In Crocean liberty I then saw a clear opening ... towards possible left, democratic and socialist paths.'[109] Through channels like this, through the literary-aesthetic intellectuals (including the Communist Party's 'Crocio-Gramscians', as they were disparagingly called by some whose Marxism followed a more orthodox trajectory) and, to a lesser extent, through his own leading role in recreating the small Liberal Party during the latter stages of the Second World War, Croce continued to exert an important influence on post-war Italian life and culture.

The one thing on which these commentators and protagonists concur is Croce's stature. The issue at stake is, rather, whether his philosophy is to be rejected *tout court* or whether it contains elements that can be transformed and incorporated into terms within a Marxist paradigm and thus put to more progressive uses. In view of what has been said it should come as no surprise if Gramsci's assessment of him went through various phases. Reflecting in prison on his own development, he could say that still in 1917, influenced in part by Croce's unyielding opposition to positivism and its deformation of Marxism, he himself was 'tendentially somewhat Crocean' ('Croce and the Philosophy of Praxis', p.355). Just before his arrest, however, he had swung round to the opinion that Benedetto Croce and the conservative Southernist 'Giustino Fortunato ... in a certain sense were the two major figures of Italian reaction'. Croce had 'fulfilled an extremely important national function. He had 'detached the radical intellectuals of the South from the peasant masses, forcing them to take part in national and European culture; and through this culture ... secured their absorption by the national bourgeoisie and hence by the agrarian bloc'.[110] The position adopted in the Notebooks is, broadly speaking, an expansion in detail of the later assessment, together with a recognition of the special positive features of Crocean philosophy which, different from other forms of idealism, identified its problems as those springing not so much from previous philosophical thought (i.e. Hegel's formula of the identification of philosophy with the history of philosophy) as from real life, from history as it unfolds ('Croce's Relative Popularity', p.337 and 'Transcendence-Theology-Speculation', p.346); hence the relative absence from his work of grand philosophical systems, as noted in the former of these two sub-sections. Although on a couple of occasions ('Croce and the Philosophy of Praxis', loc.cit., and Q11§51, SPN, p.371) there is mention of the need to carry out an 'Anti-Croce' (and, with it, an 'Anti-Gentile'), i.e. a complete critical destruction such as Engels's *Anti-Dühring* had been, the approach to Croce that prevails is more reminiscent of Marx's complex and mediated position *vis-à-vis* Hegel.

Idealist dialectics stemming from Hegel may be considered as dividing into two main trends: for one of them, exemplified by the English Hegelian J.M.E. MacTaggart, 'the dialectical movement is merely in our mind, being nothing but a series of successive approximations by which we come closer to the timelessly realised "Infinite End", or

General Introduction lxxiii

Absolute Idea', while for the other the dialectic was 'the dynamic historical process (Benedetto Croce, J.N. Findlay)'.[111] This is partially true but Biagio de Giovanni rightly pushes the argument one stage further when he says that 'the scientific form of historical materialism' – and, he might have added, the external world itself – is shifted by Croce 'from the structure to the superstructure';[112] history then 'becomes a formal history, a history of concepts and in the last analysis a history of the intellectuals, indeed an autobiographical history of the thought of Croce' ('The Man Standing on his Head', p.370). The only theory Croce maintained possible in the historical domain was not of *history* but of *historiography* – its conceptualisation and writing – as in the title (*Theory and History of Historiography*) of the last volume of his *Philosophy of the Spirit*.[113] (It may be objected that, even in the later Croce, there is a theory of history in the sense that the outcome of history is seen as liberty; however, rather than being a *theory* of history, liberty for Croce takes on a real form and substance, i.e. is hypostasised, in a more extreme fashion even than in Hegel's speculative idealism, and becomes the *subject* of history, present in every single moment of its development.)

For Croce, then, as for Hegel, 'history is the history of liberty', and thus 'even the history of the oriental satrapies was liberty' and 'liberty, in that case, merely means "movement", unfolding, dialectic' as Gramsci says in 'Liberty as the Identity of History and Mind and Liberty as Ideology'(p.351). Crocean historicism, which – in a weak form – has been defined as the 'tendency to interpret the whole of reality ... in historical, that is to say relative, terms',[114] is – in a stronger form – teleological in so far that, in it, 'metaphysically evil cannot prevail and history is rationality' ('Croce's Relative Popularity', loc.cit., quoting Croce). Both affirmations require there to be laws, and therefore theory, of some kind, but in Crocean idealism these are laws of the mind (which structures the world outside) rather than objective laws of reality. As such, to quote de Giovanni again, the laws are removed 'from the field of historicity' (in the sense of the historical process) 'to the field of historiography'. Historical materialism is then downgraded from a philosophy of history to (in Croce's own phrase) a 'simple canon of historical interpretation'; by the later 1920s he had rejected even this mild form.[115]

Gentile expresses opinions close to Croce's: 'In history, in society, in things, there is neither meaning, nor law; meaning and law are always determinations of the spirit, its subjective development, we may even say; and objectivity is reduced simply to the *certainty* of immediate observation, raised to a necessary and universal cognition ... the things among which we move and understand that we move are nothing but *our* concepts of them: realistic and materialistic concepts but nevertheless concepts.'[116] This may be compared with a key passage from Croce's *Logic*: 'But all the philosophy that we are developing demonstrates that there exists nothing external to the spirit; ... the concepts themselves of the external, mechanical or natural world are not at all formulations imposed externally but formulations of the spirit itself, which fashions that so-called 'exterior', because it is convenient so to do, save to erase it once the spirit no longer finds it convenient.'[117] Whether Croce thought reality lay in the mind or in the world outside is the subject of a query of Gramsci's right at the start of the second part of Q10 ('The Man Standing on his Head', cit.): in 'the process of becoming is it the becoming itself that he sees', i.e. 'real life' and the 'dynamic historical process', or merely 'the concept of becoming'?

While Croce was opposed on one hand to the claims of mechanistic positivism and on the other (in principle if not in practice) to other idealist philosophies that inevitably led to the assertion of some type of absolute idea, he is criticised by Gramsci for his unproblematic vision of 'history as the history of liberty' and for his imposition on reality of a 'preconceptualised idea of history, like all liberal reformist conceptions' ('Croce's Historicism', p.376 and footnote 19 to Chapter VII). Contrary to this outlook, Gramsci's historicism seems to consist ('Identity of History and Philosophy', p.382) in the identity of these two fields 'as the historical prefiguration of a future stage' but, as in his defence against Croce's criticism of Marx's law of the tendency of the rate of profits to fall (see Chapter VII, pp.428-35, and pp.xliii-xlv of this introduction), he saw progressive thrusts in the social sphere bringing into play contrary factors in a dialectical process, the outcome of which could not be foreseen in any given conflict ('Croce and Italian Historiography', p.342); rather than the 'absolute idea', for him the motive force of history, the agency for modifying economic and social relationships, is human praxis, which of course gives his phrase 'philosophy of praxis' a stronger meaning than just a synonym, of use to get round the prison censorship, for Marxism. In Q11§15 ('The Concept of Science', SPN, p.438) he states explicitly 'In reality one can 'scientifically' foresee only the struggle, but not its concrete moments, which cannot but be the results of opposing forces in continuous movement.' For him historicism thus plays a role analogous to that of statistical mechanics in physics; in their respective spheres they are tools for investigating relationships, but experimental data coming from 'opposing forces' or from thermodynamic measurements and models are needed for predictive purposes. To sum up, Gramsci seems to be one of those historicists with whom Karl Popper, a major critic of this current of thought, has 'no quarrel' since they 'see that trends depend on conditions' and 'try to find these conditions and to formulate them explicitly', rather than committing themselves to the 'central mistake' of historicism, viz. that 'its "laws of development" turn out to be absolute trends; trends which, like laws, do not depend on initial conditions' and which thus lead to 'fascist and communist belief in the Inexorable Laws of Human Destiny'.[118] (A conflict between the two does, however, remain on another issue. Gramsci, in ' "Scientific". What is "Scientific"?', Chapter V, pp.281-2 of this volume and 'The Concept of Science', SPN, loc.cit., concludes that each scientific research field must develop 'an appropriate method, its own logic', whereas Popper upholds the old-style positivist 'unity of method' position that 'all theoretical or generalising sciences make use of the same method, whether they are the natural sciences or the social sciences'.[119])

While undoubtedly Gramsci saw potentially positive aspects in Croce's concept of the dialectic, the status of the so-called 'dialectic of distincts' remained an open question; in 'The Man Standing on his Head' (cit.) Gramsci expressed doubt about whether Croce had managed to demonstrate its dialectical nature. The 'distincts', or values characterising the human spirit, divide for Croce into two pairs, the theoretic (thought) and the practical (action). The former pair divides further into the aesthetic (intuitive) and concrete conceptual thought, dealing with the sphere of logic (in philosophy but not in the exact sciences) and presupposing an intuition (a form of direct knowledge prior to the formation of concepts, related to Kant's *Anschauung*) which is the basis for historical judgement and which corresponds ('Definition of Ethico-Political History', p.344) exactly to the 'lyricism' of his theory of aesthetics. The latter pair subdivides into the moral or ethical that presupposes the last category, the useful or utilitarian. (The categories of the four-fold division of the spirit are dealt with principally in the various volumes Croce published in the first decade of the twentieth century that together comprise his *Philosophy of the Spirit*.) Three Crocean categories correspond to the division by philosophers into the traditional ethico-cultural values of the beautiful, the true and the good. This he considered inadequate, hence the addition of the fourth (covering the economic), so wide in its scope that 'even love is an economic factor and the whole of "nature" is reduced to the concept of the economic' ('The Theory of Value as an Elliptical Comparison', p.428 and 'The Dialectic of Distincts', p.371). As he was working out his ideas Gramsci seems to have come round to thinking that the dialectic of distincts might, if translated 'from speculative into historicist language', contain some 'concrete instrumental value' ('Definition of Ethico-Political History', cit.); this also seems to be under his active consideration in Q13§10 (see SPN, p.137). As it stood in Crocean philosophy, however, it represented only 'the purely verbal solution of a real methodological exigency in so far as it is true that there exist not only opposites but also distincts', i.e. processes that are merely just different one from another ('The Autonomy of the Ethico-Political Moment', p.399).

It is not too difficult to see that Croce's additional category, which marked his philosophy off from other brands of idealism, is intimately linked to his study of Marx (confirmed by Gramsci in 'The Dialectic of Distincts', loc.cit.) and represents, as Labriola surmised, the position Marxism came to occupy in his culture, the way in which he claimed he had 'superseded' Marxism and incorporated it into his philosophy. Once Croce had excluded from his eonomic analysis of society 'all goods which cannot be increased by labour, ... all class distinctions, ... all modes of distributing the wealth produced' what remained was 'what is properly economic life ... *economic society in so far as it is a working society*',[120] i.e. an ahistorical generic activity divorced from any real society or, as Gramsci puts it 'the economic principles of man in general, in all places and at all times' ('The Theory of Value in Critical Economy', p.426); the 'new "category" was nothing but a ... mystification of the concrete economic activities undertaken by humanity as it exists historically and operates in historically given circumstances. ... The explanation of phenomena, the main task of science, was assigned, not to the determination of given constant relationships running between them, but to their derivation from an absolute "principle" that transcended, while yet being immanent to, all of them. ... Empirical facts were thus not concretely, i.e. genetically *explained* but *substituted* by their abstract hypostasised definition, which became their "foundation".'[121] This process quite clearly has nothing to do with the abstraction which led to the scientific concept of 'economic man' (*homo oeconomicus*) of Ricardian and Marxist analyses (see Chapter III of this volume). The scientific concepts of Marx and Engels were in fact downrated by Croce; he agreed with the editor of their collected works that they had 'a powerful effectiveness' but this was due to 'the assertion of their practical and political virtue and not at all as the assertion of the scientific value of [their] writings'.[122]

A second important doubt regarding the Crocean dialectic of distincts was the absence of the clash of opposites typical of the Hegelian and the Marxist dialectic. Here Gramsci's view was that Croce followed too closely the dialectic as interpreted by philosophers allied to the Risorgimento 'moderates' such as Gioberti, for whom the historical process was characterised by a myriad of minute steps ('in modern parlance this conception is called reformism' as Gramsci says in 'The National Origins of Crocean Historicism', pp.373-6) that excluded sudden changes or qualitative leaps: 'it is mechanically "presupposed" that the thesis should be "preserved" by the antithesis so as not to destroy the process itself which is thus "foreseen" as a mechanical, arbitrarily preordained repetition *ad infinitum*' ('Croce and Italian Historiography', loc.cit.). Despite the favour bestowed on qualitative changes by Hegel, Croce considered them to be 'anti-history', i.e. 'unnatural' events going against a supposed normal course of history and subject to reversal once history had reverted to type. Allied to Gramsci's criticism of this is the other point he makes that those (including Croce) who viewed the dialectic in this light tried to act as both impartial referee and player for the conservative side (while naturally denying this latter role). In other words they were present on one side (the thesis) at the same time as putting themselves – or their advice and reasonings – forward as the mediating synthesis. This echoes a rather similar comment of Labriola's (unknown to Gramsci) on Croce's distortion of the dialectic: 'Faced with two real moments (*presupposed as data*) you interpose as a third real term (which you call a *thing*), a formal reasoning procedure ... and proceed like one who reasons thus: in nature there exist men and women, plus the principle of gender.'[123]

Followers of Gentilian actualism (or 'actual idealism' or 'philosophy of the pure act', as it is sometimes called) criticised the Crocean dialectic from a different standpoint: namely, that it 'broke up the process of reality' ('Religion, Politics, Philosophy [2], p.414). The basis for this lies in Gentile's fundamental tenet that, unlike in Crocean philosophy, there is no distinction between thought and action ('G. Gentile and the Philosophy of Politics', p.442); so it was that he reached, as the title of one of his most notorious books recites, a *Theory of the Mind as Pure Act*. A corollary of his position was the impossibility of distinguishing between moral and material force; for him 'all force is moral, for it is always directed at the will', thus a government which is so confident that its view is correct as to use any type of force, including thuggery, is already claiming to be the state in the sense of this latter as eternal ideal.[124] This formulation led to the idea, much more extreme than Hegel's claimed glorification of the Prussian state, of the state as it existed (i.e. at that time the Fascist state) as the 'ethical state', no matter – it appears – how distasteful or evil its acts were. (One criticism deserving of attention that has been levelled at Gramsci is that of Norberto Bobbio: although Gramsci deals both with Machiavelli's state-as-force concept – really force *and consent*, as he observes in 'The Autonomy of the Politico-Economic Moment', cit., if one takes into account the *Discourses* as well as *The Prince* – and with the other one, due to Hegel and continued by Croce and in part by Gentile, of the state as the ethical state, like most of the rest of Italian culture of his time, he pays insufficient attention to the liberal idea of the state as rule of law or *Stato di diritto*.[125])

All told, the dialectic was mutilated in the hands of the Risorgimento moderates, the Historic Right (which governed the newly-unified Italian state from 1861 to 1876) and their heirs like Croce and Gentile who often, rather than producing 'philosophy' at least as Croce understood it – viz. speculation not linked to specific class or other group interests – produced 'ideology' in the sense of a practical instrument of government. In fact one of Gramsci's main criticisms of Croce's *History of Europe*, intended by its author as a paradigmatic model of disinterested historiography 'from which every element of class has been exorcised', is that Croce instead describes 'the political masterpiece whereby a particular class manages to present and have the conditions for its existence and development as a class accepted as a universal principle, as a world view, as a religion. In other words he is describing in the very act the development of a practical means of government and of domination' – in other words an early example of a position claiming that the so-called end of ideology has been reached. But, as Gramsci goes on to say, 'Croce is incapable of maintaining that distinction between "philosophy" and "ideology", between "religion" and "superstition" that is essential to his way of thinking' ('Liberty as the Identity of History and Mind and as Ideology', pp.351-4).

That the distinction between ideology as a practical instrument of government and philosophy – the 'methodological element' in historical activity and, indeed, 'history, since history is the reality or consciousness of all that happens'[126] – was one merely of degree and not of kind is something that, from first to last, Croce either never understood or never accepted, and is a point on which the two thinkers were diametrically opposed. After admitting, in his generous review in 1947 of the first Gramscian volume to be published (the *Prison Letters*),[127] that Gramsci's analysis of Croce's shift away from Marxism was correct, praising the fruits of his overall philosophical, historical and aesthetic work and paying tribute to his qualities of great human dignity and complete intellectual honesty, Croce ended by urging communists to use Gramscian notions to raise their philosophical doctrine to the level attained by those thinkers (Thomas Aquinas, Giordano Bruno, Giambattista Vico and the utopian communist monk Tommaso Campanella) whom the Neapolitans had immortalised by erecting statues in their honour; while in one important sense he was right, in wanting to 'immortalise' Gramsci in this way, he also showed his aristocratic disdain for the similarly important task of working on popular consciousness at the more mundane, ideological level.

Croce's initial warmth was soon to cool. He damned with faint praise the selection from the *Quaderni* published as *Historical Materialism and the Philosophy of Benedetto Croce*.[128] On art and poetry Gramsci was claimed to be in line with the new (i.e. Crocean) aesthetic, an assertion that is patently untrue, and, in a volume (*Literature and National Life*) published a couple of years later, Gramsci's highly original and convincing reading of the tenth canto of Dante's *Inferno* (SCW, pp.150-63) departs from precisely this aesthetic on certain key points. On Crocean philosophy Gramsci's writings were judged to be merely the first draft of 'often unfounded' ideas which, since he had not been able to revise them, could not have been meant for publication, despite their author's expressed desire to write something of lasting value (*für ewig*) and despite the interest aroused by the criticisms of Croce – 'the fragments put together mount up to radical critique [of the *History of Europe*]'[129] – when they were first seen by Tania, Sraffa and Togliatti and then published posthumously in the Paris-based review of the Italian Communists in exile. The height of Crocean outrage seemed provoked by the statement in *The Intellectuals and the Organisation of Culture* that 'Croce in particular feels himself closely linked to Aristotle and Plato, but he does not conceal, on the other hand, his links with Senators Agnelli and Benni' (SPN, p.8). This led to Croce's somewhat petulant complaint that he 'had never had the occasion to meet Senators Agnelli and Benni' and, while 'I knew the former was the head of Fiat, I do not even know what the latter was or is the head of'.[130] Gramsci's implicit twofold point here that no hard and fast dividing line exists between philosophy and ideology and (what ought to have been acceptable to Croce) that the philosophical problems he wrestled with sprang in part from real life, met with blank incomprehension. The final comment on Gramsci in Croce's own review was that he was best remembered through 'his noble *Prison Letters*' but 'was unable to create a new thought' – in strange contradiction to the advice he had previously offered to communists – 'because his sole intent was to found in Italy a political party, an office that has nothing to do with the dispassionate search for the truth'.[131] Croce's rigid distinction between philosophy and ideology had once more prevented him from understanding Gramsci's thought.

8 The Gramscian Renewal of Marxism: Living Philology and Translation

There could be no greater disservice to Gramsci than to consider the results of his work as fixed for all time: such an approach would go against his own notion of 'historicity', the transience of the conclusions of the more explicitly *human* sciences in particular. Moreover the limits posed on him in gaol led to what has been called the 'radically provisional' nature of the prison writings. At the start of Q11, repeating what he had written two years earlier in Summer 1930 (in Q4§16), he observes 'The notes contained in this notebook, as in the others, have been dashed off, almost without pausing for the ink to dry, as a rapid *aide-mémoire*. They are all to be revised since they certainly contain inexact formulations, false juxtapositions, anachronisms. Written without having at hand the books that are mentioned it is possible that, on checking, they might have to be corrected radically because just the opposite of what is written turns out to be true.'[132] By general consent this self-estimate is modest to a fault; his expressed hope of writing something of lasting value (*für ewig*) has been amply fulfilled.

When the Notebooks are examined as a whole what emerges, perhaps especially in the present selection, is a picture of Gramsci engaging with themes that have occupied the attention of other leading thinkers of his time and later, both within and outside the Marxist tradition. The historical reconstructions he sketches out, the lines of analysis and solutions he proposes and the conclusions he tends towards or reaches often find a resonance at the highest level attained elsewhere in contemporary thought. It is convergences of this nature that he continually seeks in order to incorporate directly into the Marxist framework the genuine features of other currents or, as he stresses in Q10 and Q11, to purge their approaches and findings of the ideologically unacceptable halo they carry with them and translate them creatively into terms compatible with a Marxist outlook.

Coherent with his position that philosophy stems less from problems posed by previous philosophical thought than from those posed by real life, it is not only the elaboration of conceptual instruments that interests him but also their application to reality through the ability to 'read' the world and its development in what, in polemic with the methods of bookish erudition, he calls a 'living philology' (SPN, p.429). This for him seems to consist of a two-pronged approach: the first one singles out the essential factors of the situation, those which will shape the future and, in a certain sense, be contained within it and hence be regarded in hindsight as real 'history' (see, e.g. Chapter VII, 'Some Causes of Error', p.417), while the second one is seen time and time again in his capacity to weld together the ideas and comments of others into a critical discourse of his own that is, at once, both highly original and, despite its variegated sources, notable for its rigour and consistency.[133] In the analysis of his opponents' positions there is a constant search to find the albeit smallest concession they make to Marxism, to exploit any such chink in their armour as part of the intellectual 'war of position', to reinterpret the more genuine aspects of their underlying concepts and render them valid by transforming and incorporating them in materialist terms. His insistence on detail is typified in one of the most famous passages of the Notebooks – the reasons for the difference between the societies of the East and the West (SPN, p.238) – when he calls for an 'accurate reconnaissance of each individual country' (or, by natural extension, of any field of work). It is this methodology, the stress laid on the circular movement between abstract and concrete which characterises his Marxism as 'a novel framework of inquiry, specifying both the the types of variable to be taken into account and a cluster of concepts to be employed' and separates him off from other brands of 'western Marxism' – due to Lukács, the Frankfurt school and Althusser – that, while rejecting vulgar reductionism, tend towards abstract formulations that sometimes shun concrete reality.[134]

In whatever aspect of his work he was involved with Gramsci was never far away from his concept of translation, whether this referred to individual national cultures, or to rival or different social paradigms, both of which types are forcefully posed as the subject of the 'translatability' notes of Section D of Chapter V. Translation in the sense of translating words is one thing – usually done by individuals – but, in the more serious sense, a translation is done by a community when it decides, on the basis of its own social praxis, on the validity for its purposes of a discourse originating elsewhere. For example the English-speaking world alone can judge by its experience on *whether there can be* a translation into English of Gramsci's ideas, i.e. whether his ideas are relevant and applicable to it. While this yardstick for measuring his value is entirely legitimate what, on the other hand, his work cannot be judged on is some standard of 'orthodoxy' that attempts to measure the validity of his ideas by how near he is to some thinker or other: such a view has more to do with theology – and not particularly advanced or progressive theology at that – than with science. Iring Fetscher put the matter very well when he observed, on the long-running controversy about Gramsci's concept of civil society, that where he departs from 'orthodox' Marxist concepts he enriches Marxism: 'there is something new in Gramsci's thought not to be found in either Marx or Lenin ... the greatness of thinkers never consists in their being close to or distant from another author, but solely in the adherence of their thought to contemporary reality, in the precision and breadth that they give to an image of this reality. And Gramsci's greatness seems to me to consist in the fact that he knew how to interpret the real history of Italy and of the entire world, saying what others had not said before him.'[135]

While this comment of Fetscher's admirably sums up Gramsci's contribution, it is fitting that the last words in the introduction to this volume of the prison writings should be those of Gramsci himself. In a paragraph which he entitled 'Autobiographical Notes' (first published, 25 years after his death, in the February-March 1962 number of the literary magazine *L'Italia letteraria*),[136] different in style and subject matter from anything else in the notebooks, he commented on the life of the political prisoner, on his own state of mind in gaol and, by implication, on why, when General Secretary of the Communist Party of Italy, he did not flee the country in November 1926 to avoid the inevitable, long prison sentence inflicted on him.

Autobiographical Notes

How I began to use greater indulgence in judging the catastrophes afflicting character. Through experience of the process by which such catastrophes come about. No leniency towards those who 'precipitately' carry out an act contrary to their principles where precipitately is meant in the sense of not having thought that to stand firm on certain principles would cause suffering and not having foreseen this. Those who, when suddenly faced with suffering, change their attitude, either without first having suffered or when the pain has just begun, deserve no leniency. But the question presents itself in complex guises. It is strange that normally one is more indulgent toward changes at the 'molecular' level than toward abrupt ones. Now the most dangerous movement is that at the 'molecular' level since, while it demonstrates the subject's will to resist, it allows one (whoever reflects on such things) 'to glimpse' a progressive change in moral personality which at a certain point stops being quantitative and becomes qualitative; in other words one is no longer really dealing with the same person but with two people. (It is understood that 'indulgence' means no more than not adopting a morally philistine position, not at all that one should not take the change [into account] or that it should not be subject to sanction; the absence of sanction would mean 'glorification' or at least 'indifference' to the fact, thus not allowing one to distinguish between necessity and non-necessity, *force majeure* and cowardice.) The principle has developed that the captain must not abandon ship until the last, when all others have been saved; some even go as far as claiming that he 'must' go down with the ship. These assertions are less irrational than they may seem. Certainly it is not excluded that there is anything wrong in the captain saving himself first. But if this observation were to become a principle, what guarantee would there be that the captain had done everything possible: 1) to avoid the shipwreck; 2) to ensure that everything had been done in the event of a shipwreck to reduce damage to persons and things to the minimum? (After all, damage to things means future damage to people.) Only the principle, which has acquired an 'absolute' nature, that in the case of a shipwreck the captain is the last to abandon ship or must even go down with it, gives this guarantee without which the life of the collectivity is imposssible; in other words no one would undertake any measures for their personal safety, and would simply leave it in the hands of others. Modern life is to a great extent made up of these states of mind or 'beliefs' which are as strong as material facts.

To return to the argument, sanction of these changes is a political, not a moral, fact and depends not on a moral judgement but on one of 'necessity' for the future, in the sense that if one did not behave in a certain way, greater damage could come about: in politics it is right to commit a small 'injustice' in order to avoid a greater one, and so it goes on.

What I am saying is that it is 'morally' more justifiable that one should change 'at the molecular level' (where this is understood to be by *force majeure*) than change suddenly, although one usually reasons differently. One hears it said: 'They've resisted for five years, why not six? They could go on another year and come out triumphant.' This, however, is a case of the benefit of hindsight, because in the fifth year the subjects did not know that 'only' another year's suffering lay in store. But, apart from this, the truth is that the person of the fifth year is not the same as in the fourth, the third, the second, the first and so on; one has a new personality, completely new, in which the years that have passed have in fact demolished one's moral braking system, the resistive forces that characterised the person during the first year. A typical example is that of cannibalism. One may say that, at the current level attained by civilisation, cannibalism is so repugnant that normal people are to be believed when they say that faced with the choice, they would kill themselves. In reality, the same people, if faced with exactly the choice 'be a cannibal or kill yourself' would no longer reason like this, because there would have come about such changes in the self that 'killing oneself' would no longer present itself as a necessary alternative: those people would become cannibals without giving suicide the slightest thought. If anyone, in the fullness of their physical and moral strength, is put to the test, there is a probability that they would kill themselves (after persuading themselves that it was not a comedy but a real thing, a serious alternative, they were faced with) but this probability no longer exists (or at least is greatly diminished) if those people are faced with the choice, after having undergone a molecular pressure, in which their physical and moral strength has been destroyed. And so on.

So it is that we see normally peaceful people give vent to unexpected outbursts of anger and ferocity. There is, in actual fact, nothing unexpected about it: there has been an 'invisible' <and molecular> process in which the moral strength that made them 'peaceful' has been dissolved. This fact, relating to the individual, may be considered collective (in which case one speaks of 'the last straw' etc.). The drama of such people consists in this: that a person foresees the process of destruction, in other words they foresee that they will become... cannibals and think that, should this happen, at a certain point I will kill myself. But where does this point come? In reality everyone trusts to their own strength and hopes for new cases that will get them out of the given dilemma. And so it comes about that (the exception proving the rule) the majority of people find themselves with the process of transformation fully underway and beyond the point at which their forces are still able to react, albeit according to the alternative of suicide.

This fact is to be studied in its current manifestations. Not that the fact has not occurred in the past, but it is certain that in the present it has taken on a special and... a voluntary form. That is to say that today one counts on this happening and – something which did not happen in the past – the event is systematically prepared (where systematically means however 'en masse', without of course excluding 'particular' attention paid to individuals). Without doubt an element has crept in today, an element that used not to exist in the past, a 'terroristic' element, an element of material and even moral terrorism, which cannot simply be disregarded. This makes yet more serious the responsibility of those who, although perfectly able, have not – because of inexperience, negligence or even their own perverse will – put a stop to certain matters. <Against this antimoralistic way of seeing things there is the falsely heroic, rhetorical, phrase-mongering conception, against which one cannot fight too hard.>

Q15§9.

I RELIGION: A MOVEMENT AND AN IDEOLOGY

Introduction

A The Church as an Institution and the Clergy as Intellectuals
1 Religion [1], 8; 2 Clergy and Intellectuals [1], 9; 3 Religion as a Principle and the Clergy as Feudal Class-Order, 10; 4 The Clergy as Intellectuals, 11; 5 The Social Origin of the Clergy, 12; 6 The Clergy, Church Property and Analogous Forms of Landed or Non-Landed Property, 12; 7 Religion [2], 13; 8 Past and Present [1]. Fables. Points on Religion, 14; 9 Cultural Questions. Fetishism, 14; 10 The Conception of Organic Centralism and the Priestly Caste, 16; 11 Arms and Religion, 17; 12 Past and Present [2]. *The Spread of Christianity, 18; 13 Conflict between Church and State as Eternal Historical Category, 18; 14 History of the Intellectuals. Struggle between Church and State, 19.

B Reformation and Counter-Reformation
15 Development of the Bourgeois Spirit in Italy, 19; 16 History of the Italian Intellectuals. *Galileo and Giordano Bruno, 20; 17 Catholic Action [1]. *Roberto Bellarmino's Canonisation, 21; 18 Humanism and Renaissance, 21; 19 Reformation and Renaissance. Nicholas of Cusa, 22; 20 *Formation and Reformation, 23; 21 Past and Present [3]. *Lutheran Reformation – British Calvinism – French Rationalism, 24; 22 Notes on Italian Culture. On Protestantism in Italy, 25.

Further Selections from the Prison Notebooks

C Catholic Social Policy, the Hierarchy and Popular Religion in Italy
23 Catholic Action [2]. *Catholic Action's History and Organisation, 28; 24 Catholic Action and the Franciscan Tertiaries, 33; 25 On Poverty, Catholicism and the Church Hierarchy, 34; 26 Catholic Action [3]. *The Pre-History of Catholic Action, 35; 27 Catholic Action [4]. *Catholic Action's Origins, 37; 28 Catholic Action [5]. *Catholic Action and Neo-Guelphism, 38; 29 The Risorgimento. 1848-49, 39; 30 Catholic Action [6]. The Role of the Catholics in Italy, 40; 31 Catholic Action [7]. *Gianforte Suardi, 42; 32 Clergy and Intellectuals [2]. *Leo XIII, 42; 33 Catholic Action [8]. *The Church's Reduced Role in the World, 43; 34 On Catholic 'Social Thought', 45; 35 Catholic Social Thought, 46; 36 Catholic Action [9]. The Workers' Retreats, 47; 37 Catholic Action [10]. *Catholics and Insurrection, 48; 38 Catholic Action [11]. The Lille Conflict, 49; 39 Davide Lazzaretti, 50; 40 Religion, the Lottery and the Opium of Poverty [1], 55; 41 Religion, the Lottery and the Opium of Poverty [2], 58.

D Concordats and Church-State Relations
42 The Concordat [1], 59; 43 Nature of the Concordats, 59; 44 State-Church Relations [1], 60; 45 Concordats and International Treaties, 61; 46 State-Church Relations [2], 70; 47 The State is the Church, 72; 48 Past and Present [4]. Religion in Schools, 73; 49 Catholicism and Secularism. Religion and Science etc., 74; 50 Encyclopaedic Notions [1]. Civil Society, 75.

E Integralist Catholics, Jesuits and Modernists
51 *The Rise of the Integralists, 76; 52 *Action Française and the Integralists, 80; 53 *An Action Française Journalist in Rome, 88; 54 *Action Française's Long Crisis, 88; 55 *Maurras and Paganism, 92; 56 Maurras and 'Organic Centralism', 94; 57 The Turmel Case, 94; 58 The Case of Abbé Turmel of Rennes, 96; 59 *Luigi Salvatorelli and Fr Turmel, 97; 60 Introduction to the Study of Philosophy. *Fr Lippert, 99; 61 *The Encyclicals against Modern Thought, 99; 62 Past and Present [5]. Papal Encyclicals, 100;

63 Roberto Bellarmino, 101.

F Organised Religion in the Metropolitan Countries
64 The Italian Risorgimento. *Jewish Culture and Consciousness in Italy, 102; 65 Integralist Catholics, Jesuits, Modernists. *Spain, 104; 66 Catholic Action [12]. *France, 105; 67 Lucien Romier and French Catholic Action [1], 107; 68 Lucien Romier and French Catholic Action [2], 107; 69 Catholic Action [13]. *Catholic Action in Germany and Austria, 107; 70 Relations between the German Centre and the Vatican, 108; 71 Catholic Action in Germany [1], 109; 72 Catholic Action in Germany [2], 109; 73 Catholic Action in the United States [1], 110; 74 Catholic Action in the United States [2], 110; 75 Catholic Action [14]. *Catholicism and Social Democracy in Britain, 112; 76 British Labourism. The Archbishop of Canterbury and Labourism, 112; 77 The Ecumenical Movement, 113; 78 Ecumenical Movements, 113; 79 Religious Movements. *The Ecumenical Movement and its Subsidiary Organisation, 114; 80 Religion and Politics, 115.

G Religious Culture in Other Major Countries
81 Ecumenicalism and Protestant Propaganda in South America, 115; 82 South American Culture, 116; 83 *Jesuitism in South America, 116; 84 Catholicism in India, 117; 85 *Rebel India, 118; 86 *Non-Resistance and Non-Cooperation, 119; 87 *Religiosity in India, 120; 88 Encyclopaedic Notions [2]. Theopanism, 121; 89 Brief Notes on Indian Culture, 122; 90 Intellectuals. On Indian Culture, 122; 91 The Question of the Intellectuals, 123; 92 Brief Notes on Chinese Culture [1], 124; 93 Brief Notes on Chinese Culture [2], 127; 94 Brief Notes on Japanese Culture [1], 129; 95 Brief Notes on Japanese Culture [2], 132; 96 The New Evolution of Islam, 132; 97 Brief Notes on Islamic Culture, 134; 98 The Influence of Arab Culture on Western Civilisation, 137.

Introduction

There is every reason to suppose that, as with some other major subjects, Gramsci intended his work on religion to be a 'monographic' treatment; indeed, Notebook 20 is headed 'Catholic Action – Integralist Catholics – Jesuits – Modernists'. However, this notebook was broken off after only twenty-odd pages, leaving subsequent editors to collect together his other notes on religion, to be found in half the remaining notebooks. On the whole these writings were well edited for publication, either in *Note sul Machiavelli*, which forms part of the classic six-volume thematic edition of the Notebooks, or in a selection entitled *Gramsci e il Vaticano*. Broadly speaking, the present selection follows these previous editions with relatively minor re-ordering and the addition of two major new sections at the beginning and end of this chapter, that were considered of relevance to the overall reconstruction of his thinking on religion. As is often the case, these sections overlap with another theme – here the question of the formation of the intellectuals.

The opening sub-sections of the chapter sketch out Gramsci's ideas about what constitutes religion, within the narrow purely religious sphere and also within a broader social setting; the role of the clergy, i.e. the main type of religious intellectual, is in clear evidence. Some themes in sections A and B, but also in section D (on Church-state relations), which relate in particular to education and the struggle between secular and religious outlooks, then emerge again under the different guises of hegemony (see especially Chapters VI and VII on Croce) and education itself (Chapter II).

In sections C and E (linked logically and chronologically by section D), which in fact contain the paragraphs to be found in Notebook 20 supplemented with material from elsewhere, Gramsci gives a detailed analysis of social phenomena born on the religious terrain. Their interplay unfolds against a background provided by the battle between an 'orthodox' centre (then represented by the main

Religion: A Movement and an Ideology

body of the Jesuits), the integralist right and the modernist left within the Roman Catholic Church, viewed not at all as the monolithic entity it is sometimes wrongly considered to be. In all this 'modernism' is to be understood as the attempt within Catholicism to come to terms with the trends in society that sprang up after the French Revolution and produced a turmoil in the Church on both socio-political and doctrinal-theological issues as well as on how the Church interpreted its own history. Apart from their intrinsic interest as the analysis of a given historical situation, these notes provide an object lesson, of a level seldom reached by subsequent secular or religious culture, in how to unravel an entangled skein of political, social and purely religious threads. The notes in section E (with the exception of sub-sections 55, 56, 60 and 62) bear Gramsci's heading 'Integralist Catholics, Jesuits, Modernists', which has thus served as a the title of this section and has not been repeated for individual sub-sections.

Section F deals with other aspects of organised religion, including a note on Judaism, in some of the major metropolitan countries. Section G ends the chapter by bringing together a number of notes (all but two of them written in 1930-31 and found in their first or only draft in the preliminary and miscellaneous Notebooks 1 to 8) that deal largely with the religion-intellectuals nexus in the world's great religions outside Europe.

Given the frequent reference to events and personalities within the Roman Catholic Church, and its attitude to the contemporary world, which will be unfamiliar to many English-language readers, there follows a brief guide to where the Popes and their Secretaries of State (the Vatican 'Prime Ministers') stood on issues of relevance, and to various personalities discussed by Gramsci who were representative of the different tendencies within the Church.

Gregory XVI (1831-46) In the encyclicals *Mirari vos* (1832) and *Singulari nos* (1834) on religious indifferentism and on attempts to update the Church's attitude to the people and state he was the first pope to condemn modernism.

Pius IX (1846-78) Though there were hopes that Pius would pursue the reform that seemed to characterise his first two years as Pope, he and his time-serving Secretary of State, Giacomo Antonelli, were responsible for the encyclical *Quanta cura* and its accompanying *Syllabus* (1864) anathematising the 80 major errors of the modern world, that included liberalism, socialism, Protestantism as a legitimate form of Christianity and the separation of Church and state. His promulgation of the dogmas of the Immaculate Conception of Mary (1854) and, at the First Vatican Council (1869-70), of her bodily assumption into heaven and of papal infallibility on doctrinal matters, despite strongish opposition to this latter and decisions to the contrary at the Council of Constance (1414-18), made future relations with Protestants more difficult. He refused to recognise the new unitary Italian state and, through his *non expedit* decree, ruled that Catholics should neither elect nor be elected members of a parliament that had deprived him of what he regarded as divinely granted temporal powers (1870). While perhaps not as extreme as Gregory XVI, he still represented a fairly pure Catholic integralism.

Leo XIII (1878-1903) More flexible than his predecessor, Leo was regarded by Togliatti as 'the first "modern" pontiff' because of the response he produced to the growth of capitalism and the socialist movement, outlined in the 'Leonine corpus', a dozen encyclicals that defined the Church's approach on social issues. He protected and extended Catholic rights and privileges by negotiating with states outside Italy; in Italy the *non expedit* remained in force, though he personally realised that a return to papal temporalism was out of the question. For the Catholic historian, A.C. Jemolo, his papacy was 'half-way between a political and a religious one'.

Pius X (1903-14) Though the *non expedit* remained in use as a tactical weapon, under Pius X Italian Catholics were authorised to vote in general elections in an attempt to forge an alliance between the Catholic and liberal-conservative forces and create a barrier between a radically-inclined Catholic peasantry and working class and the socialist movement; this was fairly successful in the 1913 general election. The first Christian Democrat movement in Italy (and Marc Sangnier's similar *Sillon* in France) were squashed since it was feared they would get out of control. In the religious field modernists were subject to attack and often excommunication, especially after the 1908 encyclical *Pascendi*.

Benedict XV (1914-22) Because of his moderation and implicit opposition to the policies followed by Pius X, Benedict was awarded the cardinal's hat only three months before his election as Pope. His first encyclical (*Ad Beatissimi*) was an appeal for peace and again later he protested against the 'useless carnage' of the First World War; Catholics were however left free to choose how best to operate, and in 1916 Filippo Meda became Italy's first Catholic minister when he accepted a post in the War Cabinet. In 1919 Benedict officially lifted the *non expedit* and allowed the formation of the Popular Party, inspired by Catholicism rather than being directly controlled by the Vatican; it was, as Togliatti was to observe much later, 'less radical than the attempts of a decade before'. Debate and pluralism among Catholics were for him the best methods of reaching the solution that the logic of the situation demanded. Thus some ultra-integralist organisations were suspended and a brake put on attacks on modernists.

Pius XI (1922-39) As compared with Benedict, Pius XI shifted towards the centre and, indeed, was regarded by Gramsci as close to the Jesuits, who then occupied the middle ground. The overtures already apparent towards the Italian state and typified by Pietro Gasparri, Secretary of State to both Pius XI and his predecessor, culminated in the 1929 Treaty, Concordat and financial agreement that regulated relations between state and Holy See and closed once and for all the 'Roman question' that had remained an open sore for the Vatican since the incorporation of Rome into the unitary state. Despite occasional conflicts with fascism, which served to delineate spheres of interest rather than being indicative of deeply rooted differences, Pius showed little love for democracy as such; this also emerges in the attitude shown towards the ecumenical movement.

The modernist tendency discussed by Gramsci had among its first exponents the Abbé Lamennais, subject to Gregory XVI's explicit attack, and Antonio Rosmini, whose *Five Wounds of the Holy Church* was put on the *Index of Banned Books* and who was denied a cardinal's hat by Cardinal Antonelli's machinations. The line continues, fed by the British Cardinal Newman, through the trio of George Tyrrell, Alfred Loisy and Ernesto Buonaiuti, excommunicated more than once and reintegrated thanks to Cardinal Gasparri, to the highly influential figure of Jacques Maritain; Joseph Turmel, whose antics are the subject of Gramsci's amusement, turns out retrospectively to have been a comparatively minor figure. Diametrically opposed to the modernists were integralists such as Umberto Benigni and the French Cardinal Louis Billot; some of them, like Agostino Gemelli in Italy and Charles Maurras, the atheist leader of Action Française, were dyed-in-the-wool fascists. The centre was occupied at Gramsci's time by the group associated with Fr Enrico Rosa of *Civiltà Cattolica*, the principal Jesuit periodical, but as regards the papacy might be said to include Leo XIII and the 'centre-left' Benedict XV.

A THE CHURCH AS AN INSTITUTION AND THE CLERGY AS INTELLECTUALS

1 Religion [1]

'In your travels, you may come upon cities without walls, writing, king, houses (!) or property, doing without currency, having no notion of a theatre or a gymnasium (for physical exercise); but a city without holy places and gods, without any observance of prayers, oaths, oracles, sacrifices

Religion: A Movement and an Ideology

for blessings received or rites to avert evils, no traveller has ever seen or will ever see'. Plutarch, *adv. Col.*, 31.[1]

Turchi's definition of religion (*Storia delle religioni* [*A History of Religions*], Turin 1922): 'The word religion in its broadest sense denotes a relation of dependence that binds man to one or more superior powers on whom he feels he depends and to whom he renders acts of worship of both an individual and a collective nature.' That is to say, the concept of religion presupposes the following constitutive elements:

1. the belief that there exist one or more personal divinities that transcend earthly or temporal conditions;
2. men's feeling of dependence on these higher beings who totally govern the life of the cosmos;
3. the existence of a system of relationships (a cult) between men and gods.

Salomon Reinach in his *Orpheus* defines religion without the presupposition of a belief in higher powers as: 'A sum of scruples (taboos) which impede the free exercise of our faculties.'[2] This definition is too broad and can encompass not only religions but indeed any social ideology that tends to make it possible for people to live together socially and thereby impedes (through scruples) the free (or arbitrary) exercise of our faculties.

It remains to be seen if one can also denote by 'religion' a faith that does not have a personal god as object, but only impersonal and indeterminate forces. In the modern world, the words 'religion' and 'religious' are abused by attributing them to sentiments that have nothing to do with positive religions. Not even pure 'theism' should be considered a religion since within it there is no cult, i.e. no peculiar given relation between man and the divinity.[3]

Q6§41.

2 Clergy and Intellectuals [1]

Is there an organic study of the history of the clergy as

'*class-caste*'? To my mind this would be indispensable as both introduction to and condition of the whole of the rest of the study of the role of religion in the historical and intellectual development of humanity. The Church and clergy's precise *de jure* and *de facto* situation in various countries and eras, its economic functions and conditions, its exact relations with the ruling classes and with the state and so on and so forth.

Q1§154.

3 Religion as a Principle and the Clergy as Feudal Class-Order

When the Church's role in the Middle Ages in favour of the lower classes is held up as an example, one thing simply gets forgotten – that this role was not bound up with the Church as the expression of a moral-religious principle, but with the Church as the organisation of very concrete economic interests, which had to fight against other orders that would have wished to reduce its importance. This role was therefore of a subordinate and incidental nature, but the peasant was no less cheated by the Church than by the feudal lords.[4] One can maybe say this: that the 'Church' as the organisation of the faithful preserved and developed given politico-moral principles in opposition to the Church as a clerical organisation, right up to the French Revolution whose principles were <exactly> those of the community of the faithful against the clergy as a feudal order allied with the king and nobility. On this account, many Catholics regard the French Revolution as a schism <a heresy>, i.e. a complete break between pastor and flock, of the same type as the Reformation,[5] though historically more mature since it took place on the terrain of secularism: not priests against priests, but faithful-infidels against priests. <The real point of rupture between democracy and Church is however to be located in the Counter-Reformation, when the Church needed the secular arm (in the grand style) against the Lutherans and renounced its democratic function.>

Q1§128.

4 The Clergy as Intellectuals

Research into the differing attitudes adopted by the clergy during the Risorgimento, in a dependent relationship with the new religious-ecclesiastic tendencies. Giobertianism, Rosminianism.[6] Episode more characteristic of Jansenism. On the subject of the doctrine of grace and its conversion into a motive force of industrial energy, and of the objection raised by Jemolo to Anzilotti's correct thesis (but where did Anzilotti get it from?), cf. what Kurt Kaser says in *Riforma e Controriforma* [*Reformation and Counter-Reformation*] on the doctrine of grace in Calvinism and Philip's book which cites current documents on this conversion.[7]

These facts document the process of dissolution of the American religious spirit. Calvinism becomes a secular religion, that of the Rotary Club, just like the theism of the Enlightenment was the religion of European freemasonry, but without the comic-symbolic apparatus of the masons and with the difference that the Rotarian religion cannot become universal – it is typical of an aristocracy of the elect (the chosen people, the chosen class) that has been and continues to be successful. It functions by a principle of selection, rather than one of generalisation, by a naive and primitive mysticism typical of those who do not think but work like the American industrialists: a principle which may contain within itself the seeds of even a very rapid dissolution. (The history of the doctrine of grace may be of great interest for illustrating the different ways that Catholicism and Christianity adjust to different historical epochs and different countries.)

American facts reported by Philip from which it turns out that the clergy of all the churches, on certain occasions, has functioned as a public opinion in the absence of a middle-ground party and the press belonging to such a party.

Q1§51.

5 The Social Origin of the Clergy

The social origin of the clergy is important for estimating its political influence. In the North the clergy [is] popular in origin (artisans and peasantry) while in the South it [is] bound more to the 'men of standing' [*galantuomini*] and the upper class. In the South and the islands the clergy, either individually or as representative of the Church, has quite considerable landed property and goes in for usury. As much as a spiritual guide, the clergy often appears to the peasantry in the guise of the landowner weighing in heavily on the rent ('the interest due to the Church') and as usurer having the weapons of the spiritual as well as the temporal power at his disposal. For this reason the southern peasants want priests from their own village (because they are known, less harsh, and because their family – in offering a certain target – comes into play as a conciliatory element) and on occasion they demand the electoral rights of parishioners. Such episodes in Sardinia.[8] (Remember Gennaro Avolio's article in the single issue of *La Voce* on the southern clergy, which mentions the fact that the southern priests live openly with a woman and have demanded the right to marry.) The territorial distribution of the Popular Party indicates the greater or lesser influence of the clergy and its social activity. In the South[9] (on top of this one must bear in mind the weight of the various fractions: in the South, Naples etc.) the prevailing force is that of the right, in other words the old conservative clericalism. Recall the episode of the Oristano elections in 1913.[10]

Q1§52.

6 The Clergy, Church Property and Analogous Forms of Landed or Non-Landed Property

The clergy as a type of social stratification must always be taken into account in analysing the composition of the ruling and possessing classes. In a number of countries, national liberal forces have destroyed Church property, but [have been] powerless to stop similar and even more parasitic types being recreated because their representatives did not and do not carry out even those functions – charity, popular culture, public assistance etc. – that the clergy formerly used to do. The cost of these services certainly used to be a huge one, yet they were not a complete liability. The new stratifications are still more of a liability, since it cannot be said that a function of the following sort is normal: to save 1,000 lire a year, a family of 'savings producers' consumes 10,000 lire, forcing malnutrition on a dozen peasant families from whom ground rent and other usurious profits are extorted. Look at whether these 11,000 lire, if put into the land, might not allow a greater accumulation of savings, on top of an increase in the standard of living of the peasants and thus in their intellectual and productive-technical development.

To what extent in the United States is there being formed Church property in the full sense of the term, as well as property of simply an ecclesiastical type? And this notwithstanding the new forms of saving and accumulation made possible by the new industrial structure.

Q3§77.

7 Religion [2]

The contradiction created by the non-believing intellectuals who have arrived at atheism and 'life without religion' through science or philosophy, but nevertheless maintain that religion is necessary for social organisation – it is said that science is against life, that there is a contradiction between science and life. But how can the people love these intellectuals, consider them elements of its own national personality[?]

This situation is reproduced in Croce, though less scandalously than has happened in the case of some French intellectuals. (Taine is a classic example, creating the various Maurras of integral nationalism.)[11] I think Croce somewhere makes a disdainful reference to Bourget's *Disciple*,[12] but is this not the argument that Bourget is really dealing with, albeit with that rationalistic consequentialism typical of French culture? Kant's position on God and religion between the *Critique of Pure Reason* and the *Critique of Practical Reason*.[13]

Q8§111.

8 Past and Present [1]. Fables. Points on Religion

Current opinion runs thus: religion ought not to be destroyed unless there is something ready to substitute for it in people's minds.[14] But how is one to understand when a substitution has taken place and the old may be destroyed?

Another way of thinking linked to the above. The people, rather the 'common people' as one says in these cases, need religion. Naturally, no one thinks they form part of the 'common herd', but that each of their neighbours is common, and they therefore say that it is necessary for them, too, to pretend to be religious, so as not to perturb the minds of the others and cast them into doubt. Thus it is that many people no longer believe, every one of them being persuaded that they are superior to the others because they no longer need superstition, but every one of them is persuaded that they have to show they 'believe' out of respect for the others.

Q8§155.

9 Cultural Questions. Fetishism

How to describe fetishism. A collective organism is comprised of single individuals who form the organism in so far as they are given and actively accept a hierarchy and a particular leadership. If each one of the single members considers the collective organism to be a body extraneous to themselves, it is obvious that this organism no longer exists in reality but becomes a phantom of the intellect, a fetish. It is to be seen whether this very widespread way of thinking is not a residue of Catholic transcendentalism and the old paternalistic regimes; it is common to a series of organisms –

Religion: A Movement and an Ideology

from the state, to the nation, to the political parties etc. It is natural for this to occur in the Church since, in Italy at least, the toil of centuries that the Vatican has devoted to annihilating any trace of internal democracy and intervention by the faithful in religious activity has been totally successful and this way of thinking has now become second nature to the believer, although it has also, as it happens, determined that special form of Catholicism typical of the Italian people. What is amazing – and characteristic – is that this sort of fetishism is reproduced through 'voluntary' bodies, not of a 'public' or state variety, such as parties and trade unions. One is led to conceiving the relationships between the individual and the organism as a dualism, and to the individual's adopting an external critical attitude towards the organism (if the attitude is not one of enthusiastic and acritical admiration). In any case, the relation is fetishistic. Individuals expect the organism to act, even if they do nothing and do not reflect that, since their attitude is widespread, the organism is of necessity inoperative.

It is further to be recognised that, since a deterministic and mechanical conception of history has wide currency (a common-sense conception bound up with the passivity of the great popular masses), single individuals (seeing that, despite their non-intervention, something nonetheless happens) are led to think that in actual fact there exists above them a phantom entity, the abstraction of the collective organism, a species of autonomous divinity that thinks, not with the head of a specific being, yet nevertheless thinks, that moves, not with the real legs of a person, yet still moves, and so on.

It might seem that some ideologies, such as that of (Ugo Spirito's) actual idealism through which the individual is identified with the state,[15] ought to re-educate the consciousness of single individuals, but it appears that this does not in fact come about since the identification is merely of a verbal and verbalistic nature. Thus it is to be said of any form of 'organic centralism', founded on the presupposition – true only at exceptional moments when popular passions are running high – that the relation between the governors and the governed is given by the fact that the governors work in the interests of the governed and therefore 'must' have their consent, in other words the identification of the individual with the whole must occur, the whole (whatever organism that may be) being represented by the rulers. It may be considered that, just as for the Catholic Church, such a concept is not only useful, but necessary and indispensable, since any form of intervention from below would splinter the Church (which may be seen in churches of a Protestant type), while for other organisms the vital question is not one of passive and indirect but active and direct consent, and hence that of the participation of single individuals, even though this gives an impression of disintegration and chaos. A collective consciousness, which is to say a living organism, is formed only after the unification of the multiplicity through friction on the part of the individuals; nor can one say that 'silence' is not a multiplicity. An orchestra tuning-up, every instrument playing by itself, sounds a most hideous cacophony, yet these warm-ups are the necessary condition for the orchestra to come to life as a single 'instrument'.

Q15§13.

10 The Conception of Organic Centralism and the Priestly Caste

If the constitutive element of an organism is enshrined in a rigidly and rigorously formulated doctrinal system, one has a leadership typical of a caste or priesthood. But is there still a 'guarantee' of immutability? No, there is not. Formulas will be recited by heart without changing an iota, but real activity will be quite different. One must not conceive of 'ideology', of doctrine as something artificial and superposed mechanically (like clothes cover the skin, and not like the skin which is produced organically by the entire biological animal organism), but historically, as an incessant struggle. Organic centralism imagines it can construct once and for all an organism that is objectively perfect right from the start. This illusion can be dangerous, because it makes a movement sink into a quagmire of *personal* academic disputes. (Three elements: doctrine, 'physical' composition of the society of a given historically determined personnel, *real historical movement*. The first and second elements fall under the control of associated and deliberative will. The third element reacts on the other two and determines the incessant theoretical and practical struggle to raise the organism to ever higher and more refined collective consciousnesses.) Constitutionalistic fetishism. (History of the constitutions approved during the French Revolution. The constitution voted in by the Convention in 1793 was deposited in an ark of cedar wood in the precincts of the Assembly and its application suspended until the end of the war; even the most radical constitution could be exploited by the Revolution's enemies and hence the necessity for the dictatorship, i.e. a power not limited by fixed and written laws.)

Q3§56.

11   Arms and Religion

Guicciardini's claim that two things are absolutely necessary for the life of a state: arms and religion. This formula of his can be translated into various other, less drastic, formulas: force and consent, coercion and persuasion, state and Church, political society and civil society, politics and morals (Croce's ethico-political history),[16] law [*diritto*][17] and freedom, order and discipline,[18] or, with an implicit judgement of a libertarian flavour, violence and fraud. In any case, in the political conception of the Renaissance, religion was consent and the Church was civil society,[19] the hegemonic apparatus of the ruling group that did not have an apparatus of its own, in other words did not have a cultural and intellectual organisation of its own, but felt the universal ecclesiastical organisation to be such. The only reason we can consider ourselves out of the Middle Ages is the fact that religion is openly conceived and analysed as '*instrumentum regni*' ['an instrument of the kingdom'].

The Jacobin cult of the 'supreme Being' is to be studied from this point of view. This institution thus appears as an attempt to create an identity between state and civil society, to unify by dictatorial means the constitutive elements of the state in an organic and a wider sense (the state, properly speaking, and civil society) in a desperate search to have the whole of the life of the people and nation in one's grip, but it also appears as the first root of the modern secular state, independent of the Church, which seeks and finds all the elements of its historical personality within itself, within its complex life form.

Q6§87.

12 Past and Present [2]. The Spread of Christianity

A reflection that one often reads is that Christianity spread through the world without the need for arms. It is not in my opinion correct. One can say this up to the moment when Christianity became the state religion (in other words up to Constantine's time) but, from when it became the outward way of thinking of a dominant group, its fortunes and its expansion cannot be distinguished from general history and hence of wars; every war has also been a religious war, without exception.

Q8§97.

13 Conflict between State and Church as Eternal Historical Category

On this subject, cf. the corresponding chapter in Croce's book on politics.[20] One could add that, in a certain sense, the conflict between 'Church and state' symbolises the conflict between any system of crystallised ideas representing a past phase of history and present-day practical necessities. The struggle between conservation and revolution etc., between what has been thought and the new thought, between the old that does not want to die and the new that wants to live, and so on.[21]

Q6§139.

14 History of the Intellectuals. Struggle between Church and State

Different character that this struggle has assumed in different historical periods. In the modern phase, it is the struggle for hegemony in popular education, or at least this is the most salient characteristic to which all others are subordinate. By this token it is the struggle between two categories of intellectuals, the struggle to subordinate the clergy, as a typical category of intellectuals, to state directives, in other words to the dominant class (freedom of teaching – youth organisation – women's organisation – professional organisations).

Q7§104.

B REFORMATION AND COUNTER-REFORMATION

15 Development of the Bourgeois Spirit in Italy

Cf. Manlio Torquato Dazzi's article 'On the Centenary of the Death of Albertino Mussato'[22] in *Nuova Antologia* (16 July 1929). According to Dazzi, Mussato diverged from the tradition of theological history and, more than anyone else of his time, began the study of modern or humanistic history (see the treatises on the history of historiography by B. Croce, Lisio, Fueter, Balzani and so on): it is the utilitarian motives and passions of men that appear as the driving force of history. A contribution to this transformation of the conception of the world came from the fierce factional struggles of the first petty nobility [the *signorotti*] and the Communes. The development can be traced up to Machiavelli, Guicciardini, L.B. Alberti.

The Counter-Reformation suffocated intellectual development. In my view, two main currents are to be singled out in this development. One of them finds its literary culmination in Alberti and turns the attention to what is of a 'private sphere' [*particulare*], to the bourgeois as an individual who develops within civil society and has no conception of political society outside the ambit of his own 'private affairs' [*particulare*]. This individual is tied to Guelphism, which might be termed a theoretical medieval syndicalism. He is federalist without there being a federal centre. For intellectual questions he puts his trust in the Church, which, due to its intellectual hegemony and its political hegemony, too, is the *de facto* federal centre. The real constitution of the Communes is to be studied, i.e. the concrete stances that the representatives adopted towards the government of the Commune; power was held for very short periods (often only two months) and in that time the members of the government were kept encloistered, without female company. They were very rough people, often roused by the immediate interests of their profession (cf. Alfredo Lensi's book on the Palace of the Signorìa as regards the Florentine Republic, where there ought to be numerous anecdotes on these governmental meetings and the life of the petty nobility during their enclosure).

The other current culminated in Machiavelli and in the formulation of the question of the Church as a negative national problem. Dante belonged to this current, as a foe of feudal and communal anarchy, though he sought a semi-medieval solution. In any case he posed the question of the Church as an international one and brought out the need to limit its power and activity. This current is Ghibelline in a broad sense. Dante is really a transition in his affirmation of secularism, albeit in a language that still remains medieval.

Q5§85.

16 History of the Italian Intellectuals. Galileo and Giordano Bruno

The trials of Galileo, Giordano Bruno and so on and the effectiveness of the Counter-Reformation in hindering scientific development in Italy. Advance of the sciences in the Protestant countries or where the Church [was] less immediately strong than in Italy. The Church was to contribute to the de-nationalisation of the Italian intellectuals in two ways: positively, as the universal organ that trained people for the whole of the Catholic world, and negatively, by forcing into exile those intellectuals who did not want to submit to the discipline of the Counter-Reformation.

Q6§152.

17 Catholic Action [1]. Roberto Bellarmino's Canonisation[23]

The canonisation of Roberto Bellarmino as a sign of the times and of an impetus of new power that the Catholic Church is believed to have; strengthening of the Jesuits etc. Bellarmino conducted the trial against Galileo and drew up the eight motivations that sent Giordano Bruno to the stake. Canonised on 29 June 1930; it is not however this date that is of importance but rather when the process of canonisation was begun. Cf. Banfi's *Vita di Galileo* [*Life of Galileo*] (pub. La Cultura) and G. De Ruggiero's review in *La Critica* that documents all the intrigues in which Galileo was ensnared by the Jesuits. Bellarmino is the author of the formula of the *indirect power* of the Church over all civil sovereignties.[24] The feast of Christ the King (instituted in 1925 or 26?) for the last Sunday in October of each year.

Q6§151.

18 Humanism and Renaissance

The complete works of Machiavelli were printed for the last time in Italy in 1554, and the last unexpurgated *Decameron* in 1557; after 1560, the publisher Giolito stopped printing even Petrarch. This marked the beginning of bowdlerised editions of poetry, novellas and romances. Even painters ran up against the ecclesiastical censorship.

In his *History of the Popes*, Pastor writes: 'It may be that in Catholic countries, the general prohibition of all writings in support of the new [Copernican] system of the universe damped ardour for the study of astronomy; however, in France the Gallicans, on the plea of the alleged liberties of the French Church, refused to consider the decrees of the Index and the Inquisition as binding, and if no second Galileo or a Newton or a Bradley arose in Italy, the blame cannot fairly be ascribed to the decree against Copernicus.'[25] Bruers, however, notes that the rigours of the Index caused a frightful panic among scientists and that Galileo himself, in the 26 years that passed between his first trial[26] and his death, was not free to further his inquiry into the Copernican question and have his disciples study it.

Again from Pastor, it appears that cultural reaction was especially efficient in Italy and the great publishers went into decline there; Venice resisted more than anywhere else, but in the end Italian authors and works (by Bruno, Campanella, Vanini and Galileo) were printed without any cuts only in Germany, France and Holland. With the ecclesiastical reaction that culminated in the condemnation of Galileo the Italian Renaissance came to an end even among the intellectuals.

Q17§15.

19 Reformation and Renaissance. Nicholas of Cusa

The *Nuova Antologia* of 16 June 1929 carries a note by L. von Bertalanffy on 'A German Cardinal (Nicolaus Cusanus)' that is curious both in itself and for the brief note that the editors of *Nuova Antologia* add at the end. Bertalanffy succinctly outlines German Protestant opinion on Nicholas of Cusa, without any critical-bibliographical appendix. Rather meanly *Nuova Antologia* draws attention to the fact that Bertalanffy did not mention 'numerous important studies that have been devoted to Cusa in Italy, too, over the last few decades' and gives a list of them right down to Rotta. The only mention of merit is in the last few lines: 'Bertalanffy sees in Cusa a precursor of liberal and modern scientific thought, while Rotta on the other hand is of the opinion that the Bishop of Bressanone "as regards spirit, if not as regards the form of his speculation, is wholly within the orbit of medieval thought". No side ever has a monopoly over truth.' What does this mean?

It is beyond doubt that Cusa was someone who was a reformer of medieval thought and pioneer of modern thought. Proof of this lies in the fact that the Church forgot him and his thought was studied by secular philosophers who discovered in him one of the precursors of modern classical philosophy.

Importance of Nicholas's practical action for the history of the Protestant Reformation. At the Council (of Constance?)[27] he stood up against the Pope and for the rights of the Council but made his peace with him. At the Council of Basel he supported the reform of the Church. He attempted to reconcile Rome and the Hussites, to unite East and West and even thought about preparing the conversion of the Turks, highlighting the common core of the Koran and the Gospels. *Docta ignorantia* and *coincidentia oppositorum*.[28] He was the first to conceive of the idea of infinity, preceding Giordano Bruno and the modern astronomers.

One may say that the Lutheran Reformation broke out because Cusa's reforming activity failed, in other words because the Church was unable to reform itself from within. In favour of religious tolerance etc. (Born in 1401 – died 1464.)

Michele Losacco, 'Cusa's dialectic', a 38-page note presented at an institution meeting on 17 June by Luigi Credaro, one of its members, but *Nuova Antologia* omits to indicate which institute (The *Accademia dei Lincei*?).[29]

Q5§53.

20 Formation and Reformation

To the series of Italian terms '*Rinascimento*' ['Renaissance'], '*Risorgimento*' and so on one may add other corresponding expressions such as the term Restoration, of French origin and indicating a prevalently French fact.[30]

The 'formation and reformation' pairing [may be added] since, according to the meaning assumed historically by the word, something that has been 'formed' may be continually 'reformed' without there being implicit between the formation and the reformation the concept of a catastrophic or a lethargic parenthesis, which is on the other hand implicit for 'renaissance' or 'restoration'. One sees from this that the Catholics hold that the Church of Rome has been reformed on a number of occasions from the inside, while in the Protestant concept of 'Reformation' there is implicit the idea of rebirth and restoration of the primitive Christianity stifled by Romanism. In secular culture one therefore speaks of Reformation and Counter-Reformation, while the Catholics (and especially the Jesuits who are more careful and consistent even in their terminology) do not want to admit that the Council of Trent was solely a reaction to Lutheranism and the whole ensemble of Protestant-like tendencies, but hold that it was a question of an autonomous, positive 'Catholic Reformation' which would have come about in any case. Research into the history of these terms has a non-negligible cultural significance.

Q26§11 (excerpt).

21 Past and Present [3]. Lutheran Reformation – British Calvinism – French Rationalism

Lutheran Reformation – British Calvinism[31] – in France eighteenth-century rationalism and concrete political thought (mass action). In Italy there has never been an intellectual and moral reform that involved the masses of the people. The Renaissance, eighteenth-century French philosophy, nineteenth-century German philosophy are reforms that touch only the upper classes and often only the intellectuals. In its Crocean form, modern idealism is undoubtedly a reform and has had a certain effectiveness, though it has not affected any notably great masses of people and has disintegrated at the first counteroffensive. Historical materialism therefore will have or will be able to have a function that is not only all-embracing[32] as a conception of the world, but all-embracing in that it will involve the whole of society right down to its deepest roots. Recall the polemics (Gobetti, Missiroli and so on) on the need for a reform, conceived of mechanically.

Q4§75.

22 Notes on Italian Culture. On Protestantism in Italy

Reference to the contemporary intellectual current, represented especially by Missiroli, which upheld the principle that the weaknesses of the Italian nation and state were due to the lack of a Protestant reformation. Missiroli, as is apparent, took over this weighty thesis of his from Sorel, who had taken it from Renan (since the latter had argued a similar <and more complex> thesis, adapted to France, in his book *La riforma intellettuale e morale* [*Intellectual and Moral Reform*]). In 1931 *La Critica* printed in instalments an unpublished essay of Sorel's entitled 'The Germanism and Historicism of Ernest Renan' written (dated) May 1915, which should have served as the introduction to the Italian version of Renan's book *Intellectual and Moral Reform* that ought to have been translated by Missiroli and published by Laterza. The Missiroli translation was not published, and one understands why: in May 1915 Italy came into the war and Renan's volume with its preface by Sorel would have seemed utterly pro-German.

At any rate, it seems it can be ascertained that Missiroli's position on the question of 'Protestantism in Italy' is a mechanical deduction from the critical ideas of Renan and Sorel on the formation and intimate nature of French culture. It is not however to be excluded that Missiroli might also have been acquainted with Masaryk's ideas on Russian culture (at least he knew Antonio Labriola's essay on Masaryk;[33] but does Labriola mention the 'religious' thesis? – I think not) and from the *Grido del Popolo* in 1918 he knew the essay on Masaryk with its reference to the religious thesis, which *Kampf*[34] had published in Vienna in 1914 and which I translated, precisely for the *Grido* (Gobetti, too, knew this essay). The criticisms made of Masaryk in this essay are methodologically close to the ones that Croce makes of the supporters of 'Protestant Reformations' and it is strange that this was not noticed by Gobetti (for whom, moreover, one cannot say that, different from Missiroli, he did not understand this problem in a concrete way, as was demonstrated by his politico-practical sympathies). One would on the other hand have to be scathing about Missiroli, who soaks up certain elements of French culture like blotting paper.

From Sorel's essay there also emerges a strange thesis, put forward by Proudhon, on the subject of the intellectual and moral reform of the French people (in his work, Renan is interested in the culturally more sophisticated classes and reserves a particular programme for the people – that of entrusting their education to the country priests), which comes close to that of Renan with respect to the people. Sorel maintains that Renan did actually know this stance of Proudhon's and was influenced by it. Proudhon's theses are to be found in his *La Justice dans la Révolution et dans l'Eglise* [*Justice in the Revolution and in the Church*], Vol. V, pp. 342-4, and according to them an intellectual and moral reform of the French people should be accomplished with the aid of the clergy who, by means of religious symbolism and language, would have given concrete form to and ensured the 'secular' truths of the Revolution. Despite his bizarre features, Proudhon is basically more concrete than he appears; he certainly seems persuaded that an intellectual reform in the secular sense ('philosophical' as he says) is needed but is unable to find any *didactic* means other than the channel offered by the clergy. For Proudhon, too, the model is the Protestant one, in other words, the intellectual and moral reform that Protestantism brought about in Germany, which he would like to see 'reproduced' in France, in the French people, but with a greater historical respect for the French historical tradition contained within the Revolution. (One must of course read Proudhon attentively before using him for this argument.) Sorel's position, too, is strange on this question – his admiration for Renan and for the Germans makes him see the problems as a pure abstract intellectual.

This question of Protestantism must not be confused with

Religion: A Movement and an Ideology 27

the 'political' one that came to the fore in the Risorgimento, when many liberals, as for example those of the 'Perseverance' group, made use of the Protestant bogey to put pressure on the Pope as regards temporal power and Rome.

Thus in any treatment of the religious question in Italy one must in the first place distinguish between two fundamental orders of factors:

1 the real, effective one, by which intellectual and moral reform movements arise within the mass of the people, both in the passage from orthodox and Jesuitic Catholicism to more liberal religious forms, and as an escape from the confessional camp towards a more modern conception of the world;
2 the differing attitudes of the intellectual groups towards a necessary intellectual and moral reform.

Missiroli's current is the least serious of these, the most opportunist, the most dilettante and contemptible because of the person of its leader.

Thus it is necessary to distinguish between various eras for each of these orders of factors: that of the Risorgimento (with secular liberalism on one side, and liberal Catholicism on the other); the one between 1870 and 1900 with positivism and democratic and masonic anti-clericalism; the one going from 1900 to the war, with modernism and idealist philosophism; that up to the Concordat, with the political organisation of Italian Catholics; and the post-Concordat one, with the problem posed afresh both for the intellectuals and for the people. Despite the most powerful Catholic organisation and the reawakening of the religious spirit in this last period, it is undeniable that many things are changing within Catholicism, and that the ecclesiastical hierarchy is alarmed about it, since it is unable to control these molecular transformations. Side by side with a new form of anti-clericalism, more refined and thorough-going than that of the nineteenth century, there is a greater interest in religious affairs on the part of the laity, who bring into their treatment a spirit that is not educated in the hermeneutic rigour of the Jesuits and thus sometimes spills over into heresy, into modernism, into an elegant scepticism. 'It never rains but it pours' for the Jesuits, who would, instead, prefer the laity not to involve themselves in religion except for purposes of worship.

Q14§26.

C CATHOLIC SOCIAL POLICY, THE HIERARCHY AND POPULAR RELIGION IN ITALY

23   Catholic Action [2]. Catholic Action's History and Organisation

Catholic Action, which as a specific form post-dates 1848, used to be very different from the current one, as reorganised by Pius XI. Catholic Action's original position after 1848 (and in part even during the incubation period that lasted from 1789 to 1848, when there arose and took shape both the concept and the fact of the nation and the fatherland, which became the element that introduced an intellectual and moral ordering of the great popular masses in victorious competition with the Church and the Catholic religion) may be characterised as extending to the Catholic religion the observation made by a French historian (check) about the 'legitimist' monarchy and Louis XVIII: it appears that Louis XVIII could not bring himself to accept that, after 1815, the monarchy in France needed to have a specific political party to support it.

All the reasoning of Catholic historians, aimed at explaining the birth of Catholic Action and connecting this formation back to movements and activities that have 'always been in existence' from the time of Christ onward, together with the claims made in papal encyclicals about the incontrovertibility of such reasoning, is extremely fallacious. Throughout Europe after 1848, the historical-political-intellectual crisis, which in Italy assumed the specific and direct nature of anti-clericalism and a struggle – to the point of being a military one – against the Church, was resolved through the clear-cut victory of liberalism (understood as a conception of the world as well as a particular political current) over the cosmopolitan and 'papal-temporal'[35] conception of Catholicism. Before 1848 one saw the formation of more or less ephemeral parties and single individuals who rebelled against Catholicism while, after 1848, Catholicism and the Church 'had' to have a party of their own to defend themselves and lose the least possible amount of ground. They could no longer speak as if they knew they were the necessary and universal premiss of any mode of thought or action (except officially, since the Church will never admit the irrevocability of this state of affairs). Today there are many who can no longer bring themselves to believe that such could once have been the case. To give an idea of this, one can put forward the following model: no one would today seriously think of founding an anti-suicide association (it is not impossible that in some place there does exist some such type of society, but that is quite another thing), since there exists no current of opinion that attempts to persuade people – even with the most limited success – to commit mass suicide (although it seems that single individuals and even small groups who upheld such forms of radical nihilism have existed in Spain). It is obvious that 'life' is the necessary premiss for any manifestation of life.

Catholicism has played this role, traces of which still abound in the language and modes of thought of the peasantry in particular: Christian and man are synonymous, or rather Christian and 'civilised man' are synonymous ('I'm not a Christian!' 'Then what are you, some kind of beast?') The penal colonists still say 'Christians and colonists'. (Amazement at first when the confinees, arriving on the ferry boat at Ustica,[36] were heard to say, 'They're all Christians', 'There's nobody but Christians', 'There's not a single Christian among them.') Those in prison, on the other hand, more normally say 'civilians and detainees', or, in joking fashion, 'soldiers and civilians', although the southerners still say 'Christians and detainees'.

In this same way, it would be interesting to study the whole series of semantic-historical passage that have been gone through in French, starting at 'Christian' and ending up at 'crétin' (whence the Italian 'cretino') or even at 'grédin'. This phenomenon must be similar to that whereby 'villein' has, from 'countryman', ended up meaning 'boor' and even 'lout and scoundrel'. In other words the name 'Christian' used by the peasantry (the peasants of some Alpine regions, it would appear) to refer to themselves as 'men', has, in some cases of local pronunciation, become detached from its religious meaning and has had the same fate as 'manant'.[37] Perhaps the Russian 'krestyanin' = peasant has the same origin, while 'Christian' in the religious sense, the more cultured form, has kept the Greek aspiration χ (in a pejorative sense, 'muzhik' is said). To this conception there is maybe also to be connected the fact that in some countries, where Jews are unknown, it is or was believed that they had a tail or the ears of a swine of some other animal attribute.

A critical historical examination of the Catholic Action movement can give rise, analytically, to a number of studies and lines of research.

The national Congresses. How they are prepared by the central and local press. The official preparatory material: the official and the oppositional reports.

Catholic Action has always been a complex body, even before the formation of the white Confederation of Labour and the Popular Party.[38] The Confederation of Labour used to be considered as being organically a constitutive part of Catholic Action, while the Popular Party on the other hand was not, except that in actual fact it was. In addition to other reasons, the foundation of the Popular Party was advised in the light of a post-war democratic advance, considered to be inevitable, and for which an organ of expression and a brake were deemed necessary without putting at risk the authoritarian structure of Catholic Action, which officially is directed in person by the Pope and the bishops. Without the Popular Party and the democratically-oriented innovations brought about in the trade union Confederation, popularist pressure would have subverted the entire structure of Catholic Action, calling into question the absolute authority of the ecclesiastical hierarchies. The same complexities were, and still are, to be found in the international field; although the Pope represents an international centre *par excellence*, there exist in fact a number of offices which work to co-ordinate and direct Catholic political and trade union action in all countries, examples being the Malines Office which compiled the *Social Code*[39] and the Freiburg Office for trade union activity (a check to be made on how these offices are functioning after the changes that have happened in the German countries, as well as in Italy, in the field of Catholic political and trade union organisation).

The holding of Congresses. Subjects put on the agenda and those left out so as to avoid deep-seated conflicts. The agenda ought to spring from the concrete problems that have compelled attention in between one Congress and the next and from future perspectives, as well as from those points of doctrine around which general currents of opinion are formed and factions come to group themselves.

On what basis and with what criteria do the leaderships get chosen or renewed? On the basis of a generic doctrinal tendency, giving a mandate of confidence to the new Executive in broad general terms, or after the Congress has established a concrete and precise direction for its activity? The internal democracy of a movement (i.e. the greater or lesser degree of internal democracy, that is to say the participation of the rank-and-file members in decision-making and in determining the line of action) can also and perhaps can especially be measured and judged by this criterion.

Another important element is the social composition of the Congresses, the speakers and the leadership elected, as compared to the social composition of the movement as a whole.

Relationship between the adult generations and the youth. Do the actual Congresses concern themselves with the youth movement, which ought to be the main source of recruits and best school for the movement, or are the youth left to fend for themselves?

What is (was) the influence at the Congresses of the subordinate and subsidiary (or what should be subordinate and subsidiary) organisations, the parliamentary group, the trade union organisers, etc.? Is there a special position created at the Congresses for the parliamentary deputies and trade union chiefs in an official and organic way or only *de facto*?

As well as what emerges from the Congress discussions, it is necessary to establish the development undergone both geographically and in time by the most important concrete problems: the trade union question, the relationship between the political centre and the trades unions, the agrarian question, questions of internal organisation, in all their various overlappings. There are two aspects to each question: how it has been treated theoretically and technically, and how it has been confronted practically.

Another question is that of the press in its various aspects – daily, periodical, pamphlets, books, centralisation or autonomy of the press etc.

The parliamentary fraction: when dealing with any given parliamentary activity, a number of criteria regarding research and judgement have to be borne in mind. When a deputy or a senator of a Popularist movement speaks in Parliament there can be three or more versions of his speech:

1) the official version of the *Parliamentary Proceedings*, which usually is revised and corrected, and often made more palatable after the event;

2) the version given by the official papers of the movement to which the deputy officially belongs, this being put together by the deputy in conjunction with the parliamentary correspondent in such a way as not to offend certain susceptibilities, either of the official majority of the party or of the local readership, and so as not to create any premature hindrance to certain current or desired agreements;

3) the version given by the newspapers of other parties or by the so-called organs of public opinion (widely read papers), which is composed by the deputy in agreement with the respective parliamentary correspondents so as to favour certain current agreements: such papers may change from time to time, depending on changes that have come about in respective political leaderships or in the governments.

The same criterion can be extended to the trade union

field, in respect of the interpretation to be placed upon certain events or even upon the general direction taken by the given trade union organisation. For example, *La Stampa, Il Resto del Carlino*, Naldi's *Il Tempo* have in certain years served Catholics, as much as Socialists, as sounding-boards and instruments for the political deals made. A parliamentary speech of a Socialist or Popular Party deputy (or a strike or a declaration made by a trade union leader) would be presented in a certain light by these papers for their public, in a different one by Catholic or Socialist organs. The Popularist and Socialist papers kept their public in the dark about certain statements of their respective deputies that tended to create the possibility of a parliamentary-governmental agreement of the two tendencies and so on and so forth. It is also essential to bear in mind the interviews given by deputies to other papers and the articles published in other papers. The doctrinal and political homogeneity of a party can also be tested by the following criterion: what are the orientations favoured by party members in their collaboration with the papers of another tendency or with the so-called organs of public opinion? Sometimes internal dissent is shown up solely by the dissidents' writing articles, signed or unsigned, in other papers, or giving interviews, or adducing polemical reasons, or letting themselves be provoked in order to be 'forced' to reply, or not denying certain opinions attributed to them etc.

Q20§1.

24 Catholic Action and the Franciscan Tertiaries

Can any comparison be drawn between Catholic Action and institutions such as the Franciscan tertiaries?[40] Certainly not, although it is as well to mention by way of introduction not only the tertiaries, but also the more general phenomenon of the appearance in the Church's historical development of the religious orders so as to be able to define more clearly the nature and limits of Catholic Action itself. The creation of the tertiaries is a most interesting fact of a democratic-popular origin and trend which sheds rather more light on the nature of Franciscanism as a tendential return to the ways of life and belief of primitive Christianity – the community of the faithful and not just of the clergy as it increasingly and constantly became. It would thus be useful to make a thorough study of the outcome of this initiative, which did not really yield a great deal since Franciscanism did not become the whole of religion, as was Francis's intention, but was reduced to one among the many existing religious orders. Catholic Action marked the beginning of a new era in the history of the Catholic religion – the moment when, from an all-embracing[41] conception (in the dual sense – that it was a total world-conception of a society in its entirety) it became partial (that too in the dual sense) and had to have its own party. The various religious orders represent the reaction within the Church (community of the faithful or community of the clergy), either at the top level or among the flock, against the partial disaggregations of the conception of the world (heresies, schisms and so on, and even degeneration of the hierarchies); Catholic Action represents the reaction against the apostasy on an imposing scale of whole masses, that is to say against the mass supersession of the religious conception of the world. It is no longer the Church that determines the battlefield and weapons; it has instead to accept the terrain imposed on it by the adversaries or by general indifference and make use of the arms borrowed from the adversaries' arsenal (the mass political organisation). The Church, in other words, is on the defensive, has lost its autonomy of movement and initiative and is no longer a world ideological force, but merely a subaltern one.

Q20§2.

25 On Poverty, Catholicism and the Church Hierarchy

In a booklet on *Ouvriers et Patrons* [*Workers and Bosses*] (a work that was awarded a prize in 1906 by the Parisian Academy of Moral and Political Sciences), reference is made to the reply given by a French Catholic worker to the person who put to him the objection that, according to the words of Jesus as quoted by one of the Evangelists, there must always be rich and poor – 'Well, let's leave at least a couple of poor so Jesus won't be wrong.' The reply is epigrammatic but worthy of the objection put forward. From the time that the question took on a historical importance for the Church, i.e. when the Church had to face up to the problem of the so-called 'apostasy' of the masses by setting up Catholic unions (workers' unions, because the entrepreneurs were never required to give the organisations that united them a confessional nature), the most widespread opinions on the 'poverty' question to be found in the encylicals and in other authorised documents can be summarised in the following points:

1) private property, especially landed private property, is a 'natural right' that may not be violated even by means of heavy taxation, and from this principle stem the political programmes of the Christian-democrat tendencies for the distribution with compensation of the land to the poor peasants, as well as their financial doctrines;

2) the poor must be content with their lot, since class distinctions and the distribution of wealth are disposed of by God and it would be impious to try and eliminate them;

3) alms-giving is a Christian duty and implies the existence of poverty;

4) the social question is first and foremost moral and religious rather than economic, and must be resolved through Christian charity and through the dictates of morality and the judgement of religion. (This to be compared with the *Social Code* of Malines, in its successive developments.)

Q20§3.

26 Catholic Action [3]. The Pre-History of Catholic Action

For the pre-history of Catholic Action, cf. the article in the *Civiltà Cattolica* of 2 August 1930 entitled 'Cesare D'Azeglio and the Dawn of the Catholic Press in Italy'. By 'Catholic press', one is to understand the 'press of the militant Catholics' among the laity, outside the Catholic 'press' in the strict sense, i.e. as expression of the ecclesisatical organisation.

The *Corriere d'Italia* of 8 July 1926 published a letter from Filippo Crispolti, which is of great interest in the sense that Crispolti 'observed that whoever wanted to bring to light the *first* impulses of that movement from which there sprang in Italy the alignment of the "militant Catholics", i.e. the *innovation* which in our camp gave rise to every other one, should start from those singular Piedmontese societies which went under the name "Friendships" [*Amicizie*] and which were founded or animated by Abbot Pio Brunone Lanteri'. In other words, Crispolti recognises that Catholic Action is an *innovation* and not at all, as the papal encyclicals always say, an activity that has always existed from the apostles onwards. It is an activity closely linked – as a reaction – to the French Enlightenment, to liberalism and so on, and to the action of modern states in separating themselves from the Church, in other words to the secularising intellectual and moral reform which (for the ruling classes) was far more radical than the Protestant Reformation; a Catholic activity that took shape especially after '48, i.e. with the end of the Restoration and the Holy Alliance.

The movement to set up a Catholic press, bound up with the name of Cesare D'Azeglio and under discussion in *Civiltà Cattolica* is also of interest for the stance that Manzoni adopted towards it. One can say that Manzoni understood the reactionary nature of D'Azeglio's initiative and, in elegant terms, turned down the offer of possible collaboration in the venture, frustrating D'Azeglio's hopes by sending his famous letter on *Romanticism*, which, *Civiltà Cattolica* comments, 'given the reason that caused it, may be considered a declaration of principle. Obviously, the literary banner chosen was only a screen for other ideas, other sentiments, which divided them,' in other words their difference stances on the question of the defence of religion. The *Civiltà Cattolica* article is essential for a study of the preparation of the ground for Catholic Action.

Q6§183.

27 Catholic Action [4]. Catholic Action's Origins

On the origins of Catholic Action, look at the article 'The Success of La Mennais's Ideas and the First Manifestations of Catholic Action in Italy' (*Civiltà Cattolica*, 4 October 1930 for the first part of the article, whose continuation will appear at a much later date as we shall have occasion to note), which links up with the previous article on Cesare D'Azeglio etc.[42] *Civiltà Cattolica* speaks of 'that broad movement of ideas and action which showed its face in Italy just as in the other Catholic countries of Europe during the period between the first and second revolutions (1821–1831), a period which witnessed the sowing of some of the seeds (we shall not say whether for better or for worse) which were subsequently to bear fruit in more mature times'. This means that the first Catholic Action movement arose through the impossibility for the Restoration really to be what its name says, viz. the impossibility for it to turn the clock back to the *Ancien Régime*. Catholicism in this respect is just like legitimism: from integralist and all-encompassing [*totalitarie*] positions[43] in the field of culture and politics, they became parties opposed to other parties and, what is more, parties that adopted a position of defence and conservation, and thus forced to make a lot of concessions to their adversaries so as to be better able to sustain themselves. This, moreover, is the significance of the whole of the Restoration as an overall European phenomenon and it is of this that its fundamentally 'liberal' nature consists.

The *Civiltà Cattolica* article poses one essential question: if La Mennais is at the origin of Catholic Action, does this origin not contain the germ of subsequent liberal Catholicism, the germ which, through its successive development, was to give La Mennais Mark II?[44] It is to be noted that all innovations within the Church, when they do not stem from an initiative on the part of the centre, contain within themselves something heretical and end up by explicitly taking on this character until the centre reacts decisively, throwing the innovatory forces into disarray, reabsorbing the waverers and excluding the refractory elements. It is of note that the Church has never had a really well-developed sense of self-criticism as a central function, despite its much vaunted ties with the great masses of the faithful. On this account, innovations have always been imposed rather than proposed, a virtue made of necessity. Historically, the Church has developed by sub-division (the various religious companies being in actual fact fractions that have been absorbed and brought under discipline as 'religious orders'). Another fact about the Restoration: governments made concessions to the liberal currents at the expense of the Church and its privileges, and this is one element that created the need for a Church party, in other words Catholic Action.

A study of the origins of Catholic Action thus brings us to a study of the varying success that La Mennais's ideas have had in different areas.

Q6§188.

28 Catholic Action [5]. Catholic Action and Neo-Guelphism

Cf. the annotations made in another notebook[45] on the two studies published in *Civiltà Cattolica* on 'Cesare D'Azeglio and the Dawn of the Catholic Press in Italy' and 'The Success of La Mennais's Ideas and the First Manifestations of Catholic Action in Italy'. These studies refer in particular to the rich growth of Catholic periodicals in various Italian cities during the Restoration which tried to combat the ideas of the Encylopaedia and the French Revolution, ideas which however were of lasting duration etc. This politico-intellectual movement encapsulated the beginnings of Italian neo-Guelphism, which cannot be viewed separately from that of the Sanfedista Society.[46] (The moving spirit of these reviews was the Prince of Canosa, who lived in Modena, where one of the most important reviews of the group was published.)

There were two main tendencies in Italian Catholicism:
1) a clearly pro-Austrian one, which saw the salvation of the papacy and religion in the imperial gendarmerie as guardian of the Italian political *status quo*:

Religion: A Movement and an Ideology 39

2) the Sanfedista one in the strict sense, which upheld the politico-religious supremacy of the Pope above all in Italy, and was thus a covert adversary of Austrian hegemony in Italy and favourably disposed towards a certain national independence movement (if one can in this case speak of national).

It is to this latter movement that *Civiltà Cattolica* refers when it enters into polemics with the liberals of the Risorgimento and upholds the 'patriotism <and unitary nature>' of the Catholics of the period; but what was the stance adopted by the Jesuits? It appears that they were more pro-Austrian than 'pro-independence' Sanfedistas.

One can thus say that this preparatory period of Catholic Action found its clearest expression in neo-Guelphism, i.e. in a movement of totalitarian return to the political position of the medieval Church, to papal supremacy etc. The catastrophe suffered in '48 by neo-Guelphism reduced Catholic Action to what was then to become its role in the modern world: an essentially defensive one, despite the apocalyptic prophecies of Catholics regarding the catastrophe brought about by liberalism and the triumphal return of the rule of the Church in the wake of the wreckage of the liberal state and its historical antagonist, socialism (thence clerical abstentionism and the creation of the Catholic reserve army).

In this, the Restoration period, militant Catholicism adopted different attitudes according to the state concerned. The most interesting position was that of the Piedmontese Sanfedistas (De Maistre etc.) who supported Piedmontese hegemony and the Italian function of the monarchy and Savoy dynasty.

Q7§98.

29   The Risorgimento. 1848-49

It seems to me that, given their spontaneity, the events of 1848-49 may be regarded as typical for studying the social and political forces of the Italian nation. In those years we can discern a number of basic forces: the moderate reactionaries,[47] municipalists; the neo-Guelphs-Catholic democracy; and the Action Party-national bourgeois left liberal democracy. These three forces fought among themselves and all three were successively defeated in the course of the two years. In the wake of their defeat these tendencies both regrouped their forces and shifted rightwards after a process of clarification and break-aways that all of them underwent. The most serious defeat was that of the neo-Guelphs who disappeared as Catholic democracy and reorganised as bourgeois social elements of the countryside and city alongside the reactionaries, thereby constituting the new force of the conservative liberal right. A parallel may be drawn between the neo-Guelphs and the Popular Party, the new attempt at creating a Catholic democracy, which failed in the same way for similar reasons. Equally, the failure of the Action Party resembles that of the 'subversivism' of 1919-20.

Q8§11.

30 Catholic Action [6]. The Role of the Catholics in Italy

In the *Nuova Antologia* of 1 November 1927 G. Suardi published a note, 'When and How Catholics Could Take Part in General Elections'. The article is very interesting and may be regarded as a documentary record of the activity and role of Catholic Action in Italy.

At the end of September 1904, in the aftermath of the general strike, Tommaso Tittoni, Foreign Minister in the Giolitti government, sent a telegram summoning Suardi to Milan. (Tittoni was in his villa at Desio at the time of the strike and it appears that, given the danger of Milan being cut off by the interruption of communications, he had to assume special and personal responsibilities – this reference of Suardi's would seem to me to mean that the local reactionaries had already dreamed up certain initiatives in agreement with Tittoni.) Tittoni informed him that the Cabinet had decided to call elections immediately and that there was a need to unite all the liberal and conservative

Religion: A Movement and an Ideology   41

forces in an effort to bar the way to the extreme parties. Suardi, a leading liberal from Bergamo, had managed to form a pact with the Catholics in that city for the local elections. It was now necessary to get the same result for the general election by persuading the Catholics that the *non expedit*[48] was of no use to their party, was harmful to religion and of grave damage to the fatherland since it left the way open to the Socialists.

Suardi took on the task. In Bergamo he spoke with the lawyer, Paolo Bonomi, and succeeded in convincing him to go to Rome and obtain a papal audience to add the weight of the Bergamo Catholics to that of Bonomelli and of other authoritative personalities who were pressing for the *non expedit* to be dropped. Pius X at first refused to remove the ban but, terrorised by Bonomi who painted him a catastrophic picture of the consequences that would have been caused at Bergamo by any break between the Catholics and the Suardi group, 'slowly and in grave tones exclaimed "Do then, do what your conscience dictates." (Bonomi): "But have we understood this well, Your Holiness? May we interpret this as a *yes*?" (The Pope): "I repeat: do what is dictated to you by your conscience".' (Immediately afterwards) Suardi had a talk with Cardinal Agliardi (who was of a liberal tendency), who put him in the picture about what was going on in the Vatican after Bonomi's audience with the Pope. (Agliardi [was] in agreement with Bonomi that the *non expedit* should be dropped.) The day after the audience an unofficial Vatican newspaper published an article denying the rumours that were circulating about the audience and about any new position as regards the *non expedit* and asserting strenuously that nothing had changed on this argument. Agliardi immediately asked for an audience at which the Pope, who, in reply to the question put to him, repeated his formula: 'I said (to the people from Bergamo) that they should do what their conscience dictated'. Agliardi then saw to it that a Roman paper printed an article in which it was stated that for an interpretation of the Pope's views on the coming general election, Catholic organisations should address themselves to Bonomi and to Professor Rezzara, as depositaries of this. So it was that Catholic candidatures were put forward (Cornaggia in Milan, Cameroni in Treviglio etc.) and in Bergamo there appeared posters in support of political candidatures on behalf of citizens who up to then had been abstentionist.

For Suardi, this episode marks the end of the *non expedit* and represents the completed moral unity of Italy; he exaggerates somewhat, although the fact is in itself important.

Q3§25.

31 Catholic Action [7]. Gianforte Suardi

Gianforte Suardi, in the *Nuova Antologia* of 1 May 1929 ('Costantino Negri and the XX September 1870')[49] adds a detail to what he had written in the 1 November 1927 issue on the participation by Catholics, with the consent of Pius X, in the 1904 election, a detail which before the conciliation he had omitted for reasons of discretion. Pius X, in welcoming Paolo Bonomi and the others from Bergamo is said to have added: 'Inform Rezzara', who had not taken part in the audience and who, as is known, was one of the most authoritative heads of the Catholic organisation, 'of the nature of the reply I have given you and *tell him that the Pope will remain silent*'. It is the part emphasised here that was omitted in the first article. A detail of rare charm, as may readily be appreciated, and one of the greatest importance morally.

Q5§47.

32 Clergy and Intellectuals [2]. Leo XIII

Commemorative number of *Vita e Pensiero* on the 25th anniversary of the death of Leo XIII. Useful article by Fr Gemelli on 'Leo XIII and the Intellectual Movement'. Pope Leo was linked, in the intellectual field, to the renewal of Christian philosophy, to social studies, to the impetus given to biblical studies. A Thomist[50] himself, his animating idea was to 'bring the world back to a fundamental doctrine thanks to which intelligence will once more be capable of showing man the truth that he must recognise, with this not only preparing the way to faith but giving man the means of safely finding his direction as regards all life's problems. Leo XIII thus presented the Christian people with a philosophy, the scholastic doctrine, not as an immobile and exclusive, narrow framework of knowledge, but as a body of living thought, capable of being enriched by the thought of all the doctors and all the fathers, able to harmonise the speculation of rational theology with the data of positive science, this being a condition for stimulating and harmonising reason and faith, profane and sacred science, philosophy and theology, the real and the ideal, the past and the discoveries of the future, prayer and action, inner life and social life, the duties of the individual and of society, duties towards God and towards one's fellow-men.'

Leo XIII completely renewed Catholic Action. Recall that the encyclical *Rerum Novarum* was almost simultaneous with the Genoa Congress,[51] i.e. with the passage of the Italian working-class movement from primitivism to a realistic and concrete stage, even though still confused and indistinct. (Neo-) scholasticism has allowed the alliance of Catholicism with positivism (Comte, whence Maurras). With Catholic Action, we saw the pure mechanical abstentionism of the post-1870 period being left behind and the beginning of a real activity that led to the dissolution in 1898.[52]

Q1§77.

33 Catholic Action [8]. The Church's Reduced Role in the World

Don Ernesto Vercesi has begun publishing a work *I papi del secolo XIX* [*The Popes of the Nineteenth Century*] whose first volume on Pius VII has now come out. A study of Catholic Action requires one to study the general history of the papacy and its influence on the political and cultural life of the nineteenth century (perhaps even from the era of the enlightened monarchies, of Josephism, etc.,[53] which was the 'preface' to the limitations placed on the Church in civil and political society). Vercesi's book has also been written as a counter to Croce and his *History of Europe*. The gist of Vercesi's book would seem to be summed up in these words: 'The nineteenth century attacked Christianity in its most varied aspects, on the political, religious, social, cultural, historical, philosophical terrains, and so on. The definitive result was that, at the close of the nineteenth century, Christianity in general, and Roman Catholicism in particular, was stronger and more robust than at the beginning of the same century. This is a fact that cannot be called into question by impartial historians.' That it can be 'called into question' is illustrated by this sole fact: that Catholicism has become one party among all others and has passed from the unchallenged enjoyment of certain rights to the defence of the same or to having to claim those that have been lost.

It is certainly unquestionable that the Church, in certain aspects, has strengthened some of its organisations, that it is more concentrated, that it has closed its ranks, that it has proceeded to a better determination of certain principles and directives, but this means just that it has a lesser influence in society, hence the need for struggle and for a more vigorous, militant involvement. It is also true that many states are no longer engaged in active struggle against the Church, but this is because they want to make use of it and subordinate it to their own ends. One could compile a list of specific areas of activity in which the Church counts for very little and has fallen back on secondary positions; in certain respects, i.e. from the standpoint of religious belief, it is, after all, true that Catholicism has been reduced to a large extent to a superstition held by the peasantry, the infirm, the elderly and women. What does the Church count for today in philosophy? In what state is Thomism the predominant philosophy among the intellectuals? And socially speaking, where does the Church use its authority to command and direct social activities? It is exactly the ever greater impetus given to Catholic Action that shows that the Church is losing ground, although it does happen that by retreating it concentrates its forces better,[54] puts up a firmer resistance and 'seems' to be (relatively) stronger.   Q14§55.

34 On Catholic 'Social Thought'

On Catholic 'social thought', it seems to me that one can make the preliminary critical observation that we are not dealing with a political programme that is *compulsory* for all Catholics and towards whose attainment the forces of organised Catholicism are oriented, but purely and simply with a 'bundle of political argumentations', both positive and negative, which are lacking in political concreteness. This may be said without entering into the merit of the questions, i.e. without entering into an examination of the intrinsic value of the measures of a socio-economic nature on which the Catholics base these arguments.

In actual fact, the Church does not want to compromise itself in practical economic life and does not involve itself to the hilt either to put into effect those social principles which it asserts and which have not been put into practice, or to defend, maintain or restore those subsequently destroyed situations in which a part of those principles had already been put into effect. For a good understanding of the position of the Church in modern society, one must understand that it is ready to fight only to defend its own particular corporative freedoms (those of the Church as the Church, as an ecclesiastical organisation), i.e. the privileges which it proclaims are bound up with its divine nature. For this defence no holds are barred for the Church: neither armed insurrection, nor attempts on the life of individuals, nor appeals to foreign invasions. Everything else may, in relative terms, be overlooked, as long as it is not linked to the conditions of existence of the Church. By 'despotism' the Church means the intervention of a secular state authority aimed at limiting or suppressing its privileges, not much more than this. It recognises any *de facto* power and legitimises it, as long as this power does not lay hands on its privileges, but if by chance these are increased, that authority is exalted and proclaimed an arm of providence.[55]

Given these premisses, Catholic 'social thought' has a mere academic value. It has to be studied and analysed not as a directly active element of political and historical life, but in so far as it is a sort of ideological opiate, tending to prolong given states of mind that may be termed a religious type of passive expectancy. Certainly it is a political and historical element, but one that is absolutely particular in kind: a *reserve* rather than a front-line element. As such it may at any moment be therefore 'forgotten' in practice and 'elided', while never being completely given up, since an occasion might present itself when it will be brought to the fore. The Catholics are very wily, but in this case it appears to me they may be *too* wily.

On Catholic 'social thought', the book *Notes d'économie politique* [*Notes on Political Economy*] (Paris 1927) by the Jesuit Fr Albert Muller, who teaches at the St Ignatius commercial high school in Antwerp, should be borne in mind. A. Brucculeri reviews the book in the 1 September 1928 number of *Civiltà Cattolica* ('Thought and Social Action'); Muller, it seems to me, expresses the most radical point of view that the Jesuits can arrive at on this question (family wage, co-participation, control, co-management etc.).

Q5§7.

35 Catholic Social Thought

An article to be kept in mind for an understanding of the Church's attitude when faced with different political-state regimes is 'Authority and "Political Opportunism" ' in the *Civiltà Cattolica* of 1 December 1928. Some ideas could be gleaned for the notes headed *Past and Present*.[56] It should be compared with the corresponding points of the *Social Code*.

The question was posed at the time of Leo XIII and the *ralliement*[57] of one part of French Catholicism to the French Republic. The Pope resolved it by means of these essential points: 1) acceptance, or rather recognition, of the established power; 2) established power to be respected as being representative of an authority stemming from God; 3) obedience to all the just laws promulgated by this authority, but resistance to unjust laws through an agreed effort to amend the legislation and Christianise society.

Religion: A Movement and an Ideology

For *Civiltà Cattolica* this is not 'opportunism', but it would be 'opportunist' to adopt a servile attitude and to exalt *en bloc* those authorities that are such *de facto* and not by right [*diritto*]. (The expression 'right' has a particular value for Catholics.)

Catholics have to distinguish between the 'the role of authority' – an inalienable right of society, which cannot live without an order – and the 'person' who carries out this role and who may be a tyrant, a despot, a usurper etc. Catholics submit to the 'role', not to the person. But Napoleon III was called a man of providence after the *coup d'état* of 2 December,[58] which means that the political vocabulary of the Catholics is different from the common one.

Q5§18.

36 Catholic Action [9]. The 'Workers' Retreats'

See the *Civiltà Cattolica* of 20 July 1929 for 'How the People are Returning to God' and 'The "Workers' Retreats" Organisation'.

The 'Retreats' or 'closed spiritual Exercises' were founded by St Ignatius Loyola (whose most commonly available work is the *Spiritual Exercises*, published by G. Papini in 1929) and from these stem the 'Workers' Retreats', begun in 1882 in Northern France. The Workers' Retreats Organisation began its activity in Italy in 1907 with the first retreat for workers held at Chieri (cf. *Civiltà Cattolica*, 1908, Vol IV, p. 61: 'The "Workers' Retreats" in Italy'). 1929 saw the publication of the volume *Come il popolo ritorna a Dio, 1909–29. L'Opera dei Ritiri e le Leghe di Perseveranza in Roma in 20 anni di vita.* [*How the People are Returning to God, 1909–1929. The Work of the Retreats and the Leagues of Perseverance in Rome in Their Twenty Years of Life*]. From the book, it appears that from 1909 to '29, the organisation itself has brought together more than 20,000 workers, many of them recent converts, in the Leagues of Perseverance in Rome and Lazio. In the years 1928–29 there was a greater success rate <in Lazio and the neighbouring provinces> than there had been in all the previous eighteen years in Rome.

Up to now in Rome, there have been 115 closed Retreats that have seen the participation of about 2,200 workers. *Civiltà Cattolica* writes that 'In every retreat there is always a core of good workers who serve as a positive example and leaven, the others being collected in various ways from ordinary people who may be cold, indifferent or even hostile, and who are persuaded, in part out of curiosity, in part through passive acceptance of their friends' invitation and not infrequently even out of the convenience of having three days' rest and good treatment free.'

The article gives other details regarding the various towns in Lazio: the Rome League of Perseverance has 8,000 members with 34 centres and in Lazio there are 25 branches of the league with 12,000 members. (Monthly communion, while the Church is content with an annual communion.) The organisation is led by the Jesuits. (A section could be put together for the heading *Past and Present*.)

The Leagues of Perseverance tend to keep up the results obtained through the retreats and broaden them out into the masses. They create an active 'public opinion' in favour of religious observance, thereby turning upside down the previous situation in which the climate of public opinion was negative, or at least passive, or sceptical and indifferent.

Q7§78.

37 Catholic Action [10]. Catholics and Insurrection

The article 'A Serious Problem of Christian Education: On the First (Brussels) International Congress on Teaching in the Free Secondary Schools, Held at Brussels (28–31 July 1930)', published in *Civiltà Cattolica*, 20 September 1930, is of interest as regards the measures taken in 1931 against Italian Catholic Action.[59]

The Malines *Social Code*, as we know, does not exclude the possibility of armed insurrection on the part of Catholics. Of course, it restricts the cases in which this is possible, but leaves vague and uncertain the positive conditions under which it becomes possible. It is, however, understood that this possibility regards certain extreme cases of the suppression and limitation of the privileges of the Church and the Vatican. This *Civiltà Cattolica* article, right on the first page and without any additional comment, quotes a passage from Ch. Terlinden's book *Guillaume I, roi des Pays bas, et l'Église Catholique en Belgique (1814–1830)* [*William I, King of the Netherlands, and the Catholic Church in Belgium (1814–1830)*], Brussels, Dewit, 1906, Vol. 2, p. 545: 'If William I had not violated the liberties and rights of the Catholics, they, being faithful to a religion that commands respect for authority, would never have thought of rising up, or of uniting with the liberals, who were their irreconcilable enemies. Neither would the liberals, whose number at that time was small and whose influence over the people weak, have been able by themselves to shake off the foreign yoke. Without the contribution of the Catholics, the Belgian revolution would have been a barren revolt, leading nowhere.' The whole quotation is most striking in each and every one of its three sentences, and in fact the whole article, in which Belgium represents a polemical reference point for the here and now, is of interest.

Q7§78.

38 Catholic Action [11]. The Lille Conflict

The *Civiltà Cattolica* of 7 September 1929 published the full text of the judgement pronounced by the Sacred Congregation of the Council on the conflict between Catholic workers and industrialists in the Roubaix-Tourcoing region. Approval is contained in a letter dated 5 June 1929, sent by Cardinal Sbarretti, Prefect of the Congregation of the Council, to Mons. Achille Liénart, Bishop of Lille.

The document is important in part because it integrates the *Social Code* and in part broadens its framework, as for example where it recognises the right of Catholic workers and unions to form a united front even with socialist workers and unions on economic questions. One must bear in mind

50 *Further Selections from the Prison Notebooks*

that, even though the *Social Code* is a Catholic text, it is however a private or only an unofficial one and could, wholly or in part, be disowned by the Vatican. This document, on the other hand, is official.

The document is certainly linked to the labours of the Vatican in France aimed at the creation of a Catholic political democracy, and the admission of the 'united front', even if susceptible to cavilling and restrictive interpretations, is a 'challenge' to *Action Française* and a sign of *détente* with the radical socialists and the CGT.

In the same number of *Civiltà Cattolica*, there is a wide-ranging and interesting article commenting on the approval by the Vatican. This approval consists of two self-contained parts: in the first, comprising seven short theses, each of them amply accompanied by quotations taken from papal documents, especially those of Leo XIII, a clear summary is given of Catholic trade union doctrine, while the second part deals with the specific conflict under examination, i.e. the theses are applied and interpreted in the real situation.

Q2§131.

39 Davide Lazzaretti

In an article published in the 26 August 1928 number of the *Fiera Letteraria*, Domenico Bulferetti recalls certain facts about the life and cultural background of Davide Lazzaretti. Bibliography: Andrea Verga, *Davide Lazzaretti e la pazzia sensoria* [*Davide Lazzaretti and Sensorial Madness*] (Milan 1880); Cesare Lombroso, *Pazzi e anormali* [*The Mad and the Abnormal*]. (Such was the cultural habit of the time: instead of studying the origins of a collective event and the reasons why it spread, the reasons why it was collective, the protagonist was singled out and one limited oneself to writing a pathological biography, all too often starting off from motives that had not been confirmed or that could be interpreted differently. For a social élite, the members of subaltern groups always have something of a barbaric or a pathological nature about them.) A *Storia di David*

Religion: A Movement and an Ideology

Lazzaretti, Profeta di Arcidosso [*The Story of David Lazzaretti, the Prophet of Arcidosso*] was published in Siena in 1905 by one of the most distinguished disciples of Lazzaretti, the former Oratorian friar[60] Filippo Imperiuzzi; other apologetic pieces exist but according to Bulferetti this is the most noteworthy.

The 'basic' work, however, on Lazzaretti is that of Giacomo Barzellotti, entitled in the 1st and 2nd editions (published by Zanichelli) *Davide Lazzaretti* and then enlarged and in part modified in successive editions (Treves) under the title *Monte Amiata e il suo Profeta* [*Mount Amiata and its Prophet*]. Bulferetti thinks that Barzellotti maintained the causes of the Lazzarettian movement to be of a 'totally special character, due solely to the state of mind and culture of the people living there' and just 'a little through natural love for their own fine native places (!) and a little through the influence of the theories of Hippolyte Taine'. It is instead more obvious to think that Barzellotti's book, which served to mould Italian public opinion about Lazzaretti, is nothing more than a manifestation of literary patriotism (for the love of one's country! – as they say) which led to the attempt to hide the causes of the general discontent that existed in Italy after 1870 by giving explanations for the individual outbursts of this discontent that were restrictive, particularist, folkloristic, pathological, etc. The same thing happened on a bigger scale as regards 'brigandage' in the South and the islands.

Politicians have never bothered about the fact that the killing of Lazzaretti was of a ferocious and coldly premeditated cruelty. (In actual fact Lazzaretti was, quite simply, shot[61] and not killed in combat; it would be interesting to know the secret instructions that the government sent to the authorities.) Neither have the republicans bothered about it (look this up and check on it) despite the fact that Lazzaretti died glorifying the republic (the tendentially republican nature of the movement, which was such as to be able to spread among the peasantry must have contributed especially to making the government decide to exterminate its main leader), perhaps because the tendentially republican strain within the movement contained a bizarre mixture of prophetic and religious elements. But it is just this mix that represents the affair's main characteristic since it shows its popularity and spontaneity. It is further to be sustained that the Lazzarettian movement was bound up with the Vatican's *non-expedit* and showed the government what sort of elementary-popular-subversive tendency could arise amongst the peasantry following on clerical political abstention and the fact that the rural masses, in the absence of regular parties,[62] sought local leaders who came up out of the mass of the people themselves, mixing religion and fanaticism up together with the set of demands that were brewing in an elementary form in the countryside. Another political element to keep in mind is this: that the left had been in government for two years, and its coming to power had caused the people to bubble over with hopes and expectations that were to be deluded. The fact that the left was in power may also explain the lukewarm support for a struggle that led to the criminal slaying of a man who could be depicted as a reactionary, a clerical, a papist and so on.

Bulferetti observes that Barzellotti did no research into Lazzaretti's background culture, despite the references made to it. Otherwise he would have seen that even at Monte Amiata there arrived an abundance of leaflets, pamphlets and popular books printed in Milan. (!? Where does Bulferetti get this from? Further, for who knows peasant life, especially as it used to be, 'abundance' is not necessary for explaining the breadth and depth of a movement.) Lazzaretti was an insatiable reader of them and, as a wagoner, could get hold of them easily. Davide was born in Arcidosso on 6 November 1834 and followed his father's profession up to 1868 when, from being a blasphemer, he became a convert and went into retreat in a grotto in the Sabine Apennines where he 'saw' the vision of a warrior who 'revealed' to him that he was the founder of his line, Manfredo Pallavicino, illegitimate son of a king of France etc. A Danish scholar, Dr Emil Rasmussen, found that Manfredo Pallavicino was the protagonist of a historical novel by Giuseppe Rovani, called in fact *Manfredo Pallavicino*. The plot and adventures of the novel can be seen in just that form in the grotto 'revelation' and it is from this revelation that Lazzaretti's religious propaganda starts off. Barzellotti had, on the other hand, thought that Lazzaretti had been influenced by fourteenth-century legends (the adventures of King Giannino of Siena) and Rasmussen's discovery led him just to introduce in the last edition of his book some vague mention of Lazzaretti's reading, without however referring to Rasmussen and leaving the part of the book on King Giannino quite intact.

However, Barzellotti does study Lazzaretti's subsequent spiritual evolution, his journeys to France, the influence on him of the Milanese priest Onorio Taramelli, 'a man of rare intelligence and wide culture', who was arrested in Milan for having written against the monarchy and then fled to France. It was from Taramelli that Davide received his republican impetus. Davide's red banner bore the words 'The Republic and the Kingdom of God'. In the procession of 18 August in which he was killed, he asked his faithful whether they wanted the Republic. To the resounding 'yes' he answered, 'This day marks the beginning of the Republic in the world. But it will not be that of '48: it will be the Kingdom of God, the Law of Justice [*Diritto*] that follows that of Grace.' There are certain interesting elements in David's reply, which must be linked to his recollections of Taramelli's words – the desire to put a dividing line between himself and '48 which was anything but positive in the memory of the Tuscan peasants, and the distinction between Justice and Grace.

The drama of Lazzaretti must be linked up with the 'exploits' of the so-called Benevento bands, which were near-contemporary happenings. The priests and peasants involved in the Malatesta trial thought in a very similar way to that of the Lazzarettians, as one can see from the judicial proceedings. (Cf., for example, Nitti's book on *Socialismo Cattolico* where mention is quite rightly made of the Benevento bands; see whether there is also a mention of Lazzaretti).[63] At any rate, the drama of Lazzaretti has up to now been seen just from the point of view of literary impressionism, whereas it merits a politico-historical analysis.

Giuseppe Fatini, in the *Illustrazione Toscana* (cf. the *Marzocco* of 31 January 1932) draws attention to present-day survivals of Lazzarettism. It was thought that after Davide's execution by the Carabinieri, all traces of Lazzarettism had been dispersed for ever even on the slopes of Amiata in the Grosseto hinterland. Instead of this, the Lazzarettians or Jurisdavidic Christians, as they like to call themselves, are still very much alive in the Arcidossian village of Zancona for the main part, but with some converts scattered among the neighbouring hamlets. The World War gave them a new motive for drawing closer together around the memory of Lazzaretti, who, according to his followers, had foreseen everything, from the World War to Caporetto, from the victory of the Latin people to the birth of the League of Nations. From time to time the flock of the faithful come out of their little circle distributing propaganda pamphlets addressed to the 'brothers of the Latin people' and containing some of their Master's (even poetic) writings which had not seen the light of day and which had been jealously guarded by his followers.

But what do the Jurisdavidic Christians want? To someone who as yet has not been blessed with the grace of being able to penetrate within the secret of the language of the Saints, it is not easy to understand the essence of their doctrine. This latter is a mixture of religious doctrines from times gone by with a good dose of vaguely socialistic maxims, together with generic references to the moral redemption of man, a redemption that cannot come about except through the complete renewal of the spirit and hierarchy of the Catholic Church. Article XXIV, which closes the 'Symbol of the Holy Spirit' (a sort of 'Creed' of the Lazzarettians), declares that 'Our teacher David Lazzaretti, the anointed of the Lord, judged and condemned by the Roman Curia, is really Christ, Leader [*Duce*] and Judge, in the real and living figure of the second coming of our Lord Jesus Christ on Earth, the Son of Man come to bring to completion the ample Redemption of the whole of mankind by virtue of the third divine law of Justice [*Diritto*] and general Reform of the Holy Spirit, the law which is to reunite all men in the faith of Christ within the Catholic Church in one sole point and one sole law in confirmation of divine promises.' It seemed for a time after the war that the Lazzarettians were taking 'a dangerous road', but they were

Religion: A Movement and an Ideology

able to draw back from it in time and gave their full support to the victors. Certainly not for their divergences with the Catholic Church – 'the sect of papal Idolatry' – but rather for the tenacity with which they defend the Master and Reform, Fatini considers this religious phenomenon from Amiata as worthy of attention and study.[64]

Q25§1.

40 Religion, the Lottery and the Opium of Poverty [1]

In his *Conversazioni Critiche* [*Critical Conversations*], Vol. 2, pp. 300-301, Croce identifies the 'source' of Matilde Serao's *The Land of Cockaygne*,[65] as a thought of Balzac's. In his 1841 novel *La Rabouilleuse*, subsequently entitled *Un ménage de garçon*, in writing of Madame Descoings, who had bet on the same trio of numbers for 21 years, the novelist-philosopher and sociologist comments: 'This mania, so generally condemned, has never been properly studied. No one has realised that it is the opium of the poor. Did not the lottery, the mightiest fairy in the world, work up magical hopes? The roll of the roulette wheel that made the gamblers glimpse masses of gold and delights did not last longer than a lightning flash; whereas the lottery spread the magnificent blaze of lightning over five whole days. Where is the social force today that, for forty sous, can make you happy for five days and bestow on you – at least in fancy – all the delights that civilisation holds?'[66]

Croce had already noted in his essay on Serao (*Letteratura della nuova Italia* [*Literature of the New Italy*], Vol. 3, p. 51) that the idea which gave birth to the *Land of Cockaygne* (1890) was to be found in a passage from Serao's other book *Il ventre di Napoli* [*The Belly of Naples*] (1884), in which 'the lottery is explained as "the great dream of happiness" that the Neapolitans "dream every week anew", living "for six days in a growing hope that invades every corner and transcends the boundaries of real life", the dream "in which there is everything that they are deprived of, a clean house with healthy fresh air, fine warm sunlight shining on the floor, a high white bed, a gleaming chest of drawers, meat and pasta every day, and that litre of wine, and that cradle for the baby together with the wife's linen and the husband's new hat".'

The passage from Balzac might also be linked with the expression 'opium of the people' used in the *Critique of Hegel's Philosophy of Law*, published in 1844 (check the date), whose author was a great admirer of Balzac. 'His admiration for Balzac was so profound that he had planned to write a critique of the *Comédie Humaine*,' writes Lafargue in his memoirs of Karl Marx, published in the note included by Ryazanov (p.114 of the French edition).[67] Latterly (perhaps in 1931) an unpublished letter of Engels has been printed in which he speaks at length of Balzac and the cultural importance to be attached to him.[68]

It is likely that the transition from the expression 'opium of the poor', used by Balzac for the lottery, to the 'opium of the people', for religion, was aided by Pascal's reflection on the 'wager', which brings religion into proximity with games of chance, with betting. It may be recalled that it was just in 1843 that Victor Cousin drew attention to the authentic manuscript of Pascal's *Thoughts*, which had first been printed, with numerous errors, by his friends of Port Royal in 1670 and were then reprinted in 1844 by the publisher Faugère from the manuscript provided by Cousin. The *Thoughts*, in which Pascal develops his argument on the 'wager' are the fragments of an *Apology for the Christian Life* which he never finished. His line of thought (according to G. Lanson, *Histoire de la littérature française* [*History of French Literature*], 19th edn., p.464) is: 'Men despise religion; they hate it, and fear it is true. To remedy this, we must begin by showing that religion is not contrary to reason; that it is venerable, to inspire respect for it, then we must make it lovable, to make good men hope it is true; finally we must prove it is true.'[69]

After the argument against the indifference of the atheists, which serves as a general introduction to the work, Pascal expounds his thesis on the impotence of reason, which is incapable of knowing everything or knowing anything with certainty and which is reduced to judging by the appearances offered by an object in its surroundings.

Religion: A Movement and an Ideology 57

Faith is a superior means of knowing; it is exercised beyond the limits that reason can reach. But even if this were true, and even if there were no means of reaching God, by reason or by any other way, in the absolute impossibility of knowing, one would however have to act as if one did know since, according to probability, there is an advantage in betting that religion is true and in regulating one's life accordingly. By living a Christian life, one is risking an infinitesimal amount, a few years of motley pleasures (*plaisir mêlé*) in order to gain infinity, eternal joy. One can reflect on the fact that Pascal was very shrewd in giving a literary form, logical justification and moral prestige to this gambling argument, which is a common way of considering religion, but a 'shame-faced' mode of thought because at the same time as giving satisfaction, it seems base and unworthy. Pascal confronted this 'shame' (if it may be termed thus, since it could be that the 'wager' argument that is now popular – in popular forms – is derived from Pascal's book and was previously unknown)[70] and sought to cloak a popular way of thinking with some dignity and justification. (How many times has one heard 'What do we lose by going to church and believing in God? If there isn't a God, what does it matter; but if there is, won't it have been useful to have believed?' and so on.) This mode of thought, even in Pascal's 'wager', smacks somewhat of Voltairianism and recalls the way that Heine expressed himself: 'Who knows whether the Eternal Father has not prepared some beautiful surprise for us after our death?'[71] or something of that nature. (See how the students of Pascal explain and provide moral justification for the 'wager' argument. There must be some study of it in P.P. Trompeo's *Rilegature Gianseniste* [*A Jansenist Collection*] where he speaks of the 'wager' in relation to Manzoni; see also Ruffini's study of Manzoni as a believer.)

From an article by Antonio Marescalchi 'Keep on! Even in Silk-worm Cultivation' from the *Corriere della Sera* of 24 April 1932: 'Every half ounce of silk-worm eggs used for cultivation entitles one to compete for prizes that, beginning modestly (400 prizes of 1,000 lire each), include a number from 10 to 20,000 each and go up to five ranging from 50 to

250,000 lire. The Italian people is always ready to take a chance; in the countryside even now, not a single person turns down the "lucky dip" or the tombola. Here, a ticket allowing one to try one's luck is offered gratis.'

There is moreover a close connection between the lottery and religion, wins showing who is among the 'elect' or recipients of a particular grace of a Saint or the Madonna. One could make a comparison between the Protestants' activist conception of grace that provided the spirit of capitalist enterprise with its moral form and the passive and 'good-for-nothing' (*lazzaronesca*) conception of grace typical of the Catholic common people. Look at the role Ireland has had in bringing sweepstakes back into the Anglo-Saxon countries and the protests of papers like the *Manchester Guardian* that represent the spirit of the Reformation.

One should furthermore see whether in the title of his book *Les Paradis Artificiels* (and in his treatment too) Baudelaire drew his inspiration from the expression 'opium of the people'; the formula might have come to him indirectly from political or journalistic literature. It is not in my opinion likely (though it cannot be excluded) that before the book by Balzac there already existed some manner of speaking whereby opium and the other drugs and narcotics were presented as a means for the enjoyment of an artificial paradise. (One must also further bear in mind that up to 1848 Baudelaire was involved in practical activity of some sort, edited political weeklies and took an active part in the Parisian events of 1848.)

Q16§1.

41 Religion, the Lottery and the Opium of Poverty [2]

A French philosopher, Jules Lachelier (on whom see G. De Ruggiero's preface to Lachelier's *Psicologia e Metafisica* [*Psychology and Metaphysics*], Bari 1915) wrote a note (considered 'acute' by De Ruggiero) on Pascal's 'wager' in the volume *Du fondement de l'induction* [*On the Foundations of Induction*] (Paris in the *Bibliothèque de*

Religion: A Movement and an Ideology

philosophie contemporaine series). The main objection to Pascal's formulation of the religious problem of the 'wager' is that of 'intellectual honesty' towards oneself. It would appear that the whole conception of the 'wager', as far as I recall, is closer to Jesuit than to Jansenist ethics, too much the 'merchant's outlook' etc. (cf. other paragraphs on this argument in the preceding notebook).[72]

Q16§10.

D CONCORDATS AND CHURCH-STATE RELATIONS

42 The Concordat

In his book *Esame critico degli ordini rappresentativi* [*A Critical Examination of the Representative Orders*], Fr L. Taparelli defines concordats as '... conventions between two authorities governing the same Catholic nation'.[73] When a convention is agreed, at least equal juridical importance is attached to the interpretations of the convention itself by the two signatories.

Q3§50.

43 Nature of the Concordats

Pius XI writes in his letter to Cardinal Gasparri of 30 May 1930: 'There are present even in the Concordat, *if not two states*, most certainly two totally complete sovereignties, each in other words fully perfect within its own order, which is determined in essence by its respective end, where it is hardly necessary to add that the objective dignity of the ends determines no less objectively and necessarily the absolute superiority of the Church.'

This defines the Church's terrain: in having accepted two separate instruments, the Treaty and the Concordat, for [defining] the relations between state and Church, one has of necessity accepted the terrain that the Treaty defines this relation between two states and the Concordat the relations between two sovereignties within the 'same state'. In other words two equal sovereignties are admitted within the same state since they negotiate on the same footing (each within its own order). Of course even the Church maintains there is no confusion of sovereignties, but does so by arguing that the state is *not competent* to exercise sovereignty in the 'spiritual' and if the state does arrogate this function to itself, it usurps its powers. Moreover, even the Church maintains there can be no dual sovereignty in the same order of ends, doing so exactly because it argues that the ends are distinct and declares itself sole sovereign on the spiritual terrain.

Q5§71.

44 State-Church Relations [1]

The *Vorwaerts* of 14 June 1929, in an article on the concordat between the Vatican City and Prussia, writes that 'Rome has maintained that it (the antecedent legislation which previously constituted a *de facto* concordat) has lapsed in the wake of the political changes that have come about in Germany.' The admission, or rather the assertion, of this principle, on the initiative of the Vatican itself, may be quite far-reaching and contain a considerable number of political consequences.

The Prussian Finance Minister Hoepker-Aschoff, writing in the *Vossische Zeitung* of 18 June 1929, posed the same problem: 'Likewise, it is impossible not to recognise the firm foundation of Rome's argument that, taking into account the many political and territorial changes that have occurred, the agreements entered into should be adapted to meet the new circumstances.' In the same article, Hoepker-Aschoff recalls that 'the Prussian state had always maintained that the agreements of 1821 were still in force'. It appears that, for the Vatican, the war of 1870, with its territorial and political modifications (increases in the size of Prussia, constitution of the German Empire under Prussian hegemony) and the *Kulturkampf*[74] period did not constitute 'modifications' such as to create 'new circumstances', while those modifications brought about after the Great War were essential. Evidently, the juridical thought of the Vatican has undergone change and could still change according to political convenience.

'With 1918, one saw an extremely important innovation in our law, an innovation which, strangely, (but in 1918 there was press censorship!) passed by quite unnoticed – the state once again began to subsidise the Catholic religion, thus abandoning after 63 years Cavour's principle that lay at the base of the Sardinian law of 29 May 1855: the state must not subsidise any religion.' A.C. Jemolo in the article 'State Religion and Permitted Creeds' in *Nuovi Studi di Diritto, Economia, Politica*, 1930, p. 30. The innovation was introduced by the (Delegated) Decree Laws of 17 March 1918, no. 396, and 9 May 1918, no. 655. On this subject, Jemolo refers the reader to the note by D. Schiappoli, 'The Recent Economic Measures in Favour of the Clergy', Naples 1922, from Vol. XLVIII of the *Proceedings of the Royal Academy of Political and Moral Sciences* of Naples.

Q16§11[i].

45 Concordats and International Treaties

The capitulation of the modern state that has happened with the concordats is being masked by a verbal identification of concordats and international treaties. But a concordat is not a common international treaty. In a concordat, a *de facto* interference in sovereignty in *just one* state territory is produced, since all the articles of a concordat refer to the *citizens of only one* of the contracting states, over whom the sovereign power of a foreign state justifies and claims rights and powers of jurisdiction (albeit a special given sort of jurisdiction). What powers has the Reich acquired over the Vatican City by reason of the recent Concordat? And again, the foundation of the Vatican City gives a semblance of legitimacy to the juridical fiction that the concordat is a common bilateral international treaty. Yet concordats were stipulated even before the Vatican City existed, which means that territory is not an essential factor for papal authority (at least from this point of view). It is only a semblance, though, since while the concordat limits the state authority of one of the contracting parties in its own territory, and influences and determines its legislation and administration, no limitation is mentioned in regard to the territory of the other party: if a limitation does exist for this second party, it refers to the activity undertaken within the territory of the first state, both by *citizens* of the Vatican City and by citizens of the other state who have themselves represented by the Vatican City. The concordat is therefore the explicit recognition of a dual sovereignty in just one state territory. Certainly it is not a question of the same form of supranational sovereignty (*suzaineté*), as was formally recognised as the pope's in the Middle Ages and right up to the absolute monarchies and in a different form afterwards, up to 1848, but, as a compromise, it does necessarily derive from this. Moreover, even when the papacy and its supranational power were at their height, things did not always go very smoothly; papal supremacy, even if recognised juridically, in fact was often most bitterly contested and, looking at it in the most favourable light, it was reduced to the political, economic and fiscal privileges of the episcopacy in each single country.

The concordats attack the nature of the autonomy of the modern state's sovereignty in its essence. Does the state get anything in return? Certainly, but it obtains it within its own territory in respect of its own citizens. The state (and in this case it would be better to say the government) maintains that the Church should not hinder the exercise of power but should, rather, favour and support it just like a crutch supports an invalid. In other words, *vis-à-vis* a constituted form of government (constituted externally, as is documented by the concordat itself) the Church pledges itself to promote the consent of one part of the ruled which the state explicitly recognises that it cannot obtain by its own means. Herein lies the capitulation by the state, since it in fact accepts the tutelage of an external sovereignty whose superiority is in practice recognised. The very word 'concordat' is symptomatic. The articles published in *Nuovi*

Religion: A Movement and an Ideology

Studi on the Concordat are among the most interesting and lend themselves most easily to refutation. (Recall the 'treaty' forced upon the Georgian democratic republic after General Denikin's defeat.[75])

But even in the modern world, what is the practical meaning of the situation created in a state by the stipulation of a concordat? It means the public recognition of a caste of citizens of the same state having certain political privileges. The form is no longer the medieval one, but the substance is the same. In the development of modern history, this caste had seen the monopoly of the social role that explained and justified its existence – the monopoly over culture and education – attacked and destroyed. The concordat recognises this monopoly afresh, even though it is attenuated and subject to checks, since it ensures that the caste has preliminary positions and conditions which it could not have and maintain solely through its own strength and through the intrinsic harmony between its conception of the world and actual reality.

One can thus understand the secretive, sordid struggle of the secular and secularising intellectuals against the caste-intellectuals in order to safeguard their autonomy and role. But it cannot be denied that, inwardly, they have given up the struggle and become detached from the state. The ethical nature of a concrete state, of a particular state, is defined by its effective legislation and not by the polemics of the irregular forces of the world of culture. If these latter claim that they are the state, they are only asserting that the so-called unitary state is just that – 'so-called' – because in reality, right at its heart, there is a very serious split, all the more serious in so far as it is tacitly affirmed by the legislators and rulers themselves when they say that this unitary state is in actual fact two states simultaneously: one of these corresponds to the laws as written and applied in practice and the other to those individual consciences which inwardly do not recognise those laws as producing the effect wanted and are thus engaged in a sordid attempt to empty them of their ethical content (or at least try to limit their applicability). This is just the Machiavellianism of small-time political operators; the philosophers of actual idealism, especially the talking-parrot section of *Nuovi Studi* may be said to be the most illustrious victims of Machiavellianism.

It is useful to study the *division of labour* that it is being sought to establish between caste and secular intellectuals.[76] The former have been left the task of the intellectual and moral training of the very young (primary and lower secondary schools) while the latter take charge of the further development of young people at university. But university schooling is not subject to the same monopoly regime which, on the other hand, underlies primary and secondary schools. There exists the University of the Sacred Heart and it will now be possible to create other Catholic universities having equivalent status in everything with the state universities.[77] The consequences are obvious: the primary and secondary schools constitute the schools for the petty bourgeoisie and popular classes – social strata which are monopolised, educationally speaking, by the caste – because the majority of their members do not go on to university, that is to say they will not come into contact with modern education at its higher critical-historical level but will know only a dogmatic education. The university is the school for the ruling class (and personnel) in its own right, the mechanism by which there takes place the selection of individuals of other classes who are to be incorporated into the ruling, administrative and government personnel. But with the existence on equal terms of Catholic universities, even the training of this personnel will no longer be homogeneous or take place in a unified fashion. Not only this, but the caste, within its own universities, will bring about such a concentration of religious and secular culture (*cultura laico-religiosa*) as has not been seen for many a long year and will in fact find itself in much better conditions than the state-secular concentration (*concentrazione laico-statale*), given the fact that the efficiency of the Church, which acts in its entirety as a bloc in support of its own university, far out-distances the organisational efficiency of secular culture. If the state (even in its wider sense of civil society) does not express itself in the form of a cultural organisation according to a centralised plan and if it cannot even do so, because its legislation on religious questions is what it is and its ambiguity cannot but favour the Church, given the massive structure of the latter and the relative and absolute weight which is expressed by such a homogeneous structure, and if, further, the degrees awarded by the two types of university are of equal status, it is obvious that a tendency will be created for the Catholic universities to be the selection mechanism for the insertion of the most intelligent and capable members of the lower classes into the ruling personnel. The factors favouring this tendency are: that there is no educational discontinuity between the secondary schools and the Catholic university, while this discontinuity does exist for the secular-state universities, and that the Church, throughout the whole of its structure, is already equipped for this task of successive elaboration and selection from the grass-roots level. From this standpoint, the Church is a perfectly democratic body (in the paternalistic sense); a peasant's or an artisan's son may in theory become cardinal and pope if he is intelligent and able, and flexible enough to allow himself to be assimilated by the ecclesiastical structure and feel its particular *esprit de corps* and spirit of conservation, as well as the validity of its present and future interests. If, in the higher reaches of the Church's hierarchy, someone of democratic origin is encountered less frequently than he might be, this happens because of complex reasons, in which the pressure of the great families of the Catholic aristocracy or reasons of state (international) are felt only in part. One very influential reason, however, is that many seminaries are really quite badly equipped and cannot give a full, rounded-off education to an intelligent person from the ranks of the people, while the young aristocrat, without any effort on his part directed towards acquiring it, derives from his family environment a series of aptitudes and qualities of utmost importance for his ecclesiastical career: the tranquil security of his own dignity and authority and the art of dealing with and ruling other people.

One reason for the Church's weakness in the past was that religion offered scarce possibilities for any career outside the ecclesiastical one. The clergy itself had deteriorated qualitatively through 'numerically scanty callings' or through response being made only by the intellectually subaltern elements. This crisis was already plain to see before the war and was one aspect of the general crisis of the fixed-income careers with slow turnovers within a large personnel, i.e. it was one aspect of the social unease of the subaltern intellectual stratum (primary and secondary school teachers, priests etc.) which felt the competition from the professions linked to private capitalist organisation in general (e.g. journalism, which absorbs many teachers, and so on). The invasion of the universities or teacher training schools by women and, together with women, priests, had already begun; after the Credaro laws, the Curia could not stop priests obtaining a public diploma allowing them to go in for state jobs, thereby supplementing their individual 'finances'.[78] As soon as they had obtained the diploma, many of these priests left the Church (because of mobilisation and contact with less suffocating and narrow circles than ecclesiastical ones, this phenomenon assumed a certain importance during the war). Ecclesiastical organisation therefore went through a constitutional crisis which could have been fatal to its power had the state, even without the need for an active struggle, maintained its secular position intact. In the battle among different life-forms, the Church was on the point of dying out automatically due to its own exhaustion. The state came to the Church's rescue. The economic conditions of the clergy were improved on a number of occasions, while the general standard of living, especially among the middle strata (*ceti medi*), got worse. The improvement was such that 'callings' were found to have multiplied in a marvellous fashion, impressing even the Pontiff himself, who explained them exactly on the basis of the new economic situation. There was therefore an enlargement of the base from which those judged suitable for the clergy were chosen, thus allowing greater rigour and increased cultural exigencies.

But if the ecclesiastical career remains the most solid foundation of Vatican power, it does not exhaust the possibilities of this latter. The new school structure allows the introduction of Catholic cells into the leading lay personnel, cells which will get progressively stronger, comprising elements which will owe their position solely to the Church. We must consider that clerical infiltration into the state machinery is about to show a progressive increase, since, in the art of selecting individuals and keeping them permanently bound to itself, the Church is almost unbeatable. By controlling the lycées and the other secondary schools through its own trusted personnel, and by using its characteristic tenacity, the Church will follow the worthiest young people of the poorer classes and help them to carry on their studies in the Catholic universities. Study grants, with the additional subsidy of student hostels, organised with the greatest economy, will be the means of this action. In its present-day phase, the Church, with the impetus that the current Pope is giving to Catholic Action, cannot be content just with turning out priests; it wants to permeate the state (remember the theory of indirect government developed by Bellarmino) and, for that, the laity is necessary, as is a concentration of Catholic culture that the laity represents. There are many people who can become more precious auxiliaries of the Church as university professors and as top managers, etc., than as cardinals or bishops.

Once the base of choice for 'callings' has been enlarged, there are great possibilities for extending this type of cultural activity on the part of the laity. The University of the Sacred Heart and the neo-scholastic centre are only the first cells of this work. And in the meantime the 1929 Philosophy Congress was symptomatic: a conflict took place there between actual idealists and neo-scholastics, these latter participants in the Congress going all-out in their quest for victory. After the Concordat the neo-scholastic group wanted in fact to appear combative and sure of itself so as to gain the interest of the young. It has to be borne in mind that one of the strengths of the Catholics consists in the fact that they do not give a fig for the 'decisive refutations' of their non-Catholic adversaries; they just take up the refuted thesis again, unperturbed and as if nothing had happened. They either do not understand intellectual 'disinterest', scientific truthfulness and honesty, or they understand them as other people's weakness and ingenuousness. They count on the power of their world organisation, which is imposed as if it were a proof of truth, and on the fact that the great majority of the population is not as yet 'modern', but still at the Ptolemaic stage as regards its conception of the world and of science.

If the state gives up being an active, a permanently active, centre of its own culture, then to all intents and purposes the Church cannot but triumph. But not only does the state not intervene as an autonomous centre, it destroys any opponent of the Church who is capable of limiting its spiritual dominion over the multitudes.

It can be foreseen that, while the general framework of affairs remains unchanged, the consequences of such a situation in fact may be of the greatest importance. The Church is an even more implacable Shylock than Shakespeare's character: it wants its pound of flesh even at the cost of bleeding its victim dry and, by continually changing its methods, will through its tenacity tend to reach its full programme. As Disraeli remarked, Christians are those more intelligent Jews who have understood what has to be done to conquer the world. The Church cannot be reduced to its 'normal' strength by the philosophical refutation of its theoretical postulates and by platonic assertions of the autonomy of the state (unless it is a militant autonomy) but only by means of practical day-to-day activity, by the exaltation of creative human forces throughout the whole area of social life.

One aspect of the question which it is well worth taking into account is that of the financial resources of the Vatican. The ever-developing organisation of Catholicism in the United States offers the possibility of bringing in much more considerable funds, on top of the normal and by now secure income (which as from 1937, however, will decrease by 15 million lire a year due to the reduction in the interest payable on the public debt from 5 per cent to 3.5 per cent) and on top of Peter's pence. Could there arise questions of an international character on the subject of the Church's intervention in the internal affairs of individual countries, with the state permanently subsidising the Church? A charming question, as they say.

The financial question makes the problem of the so-called

indissolubility between Treaty and Concordat, proclaimed by the Pope, into a very interesting one. Supposing he finds himself having to have recourse to this political means of exerting pressure on the state, would the problem not immediately be posed of returning the monies already received (which are bound up with the Treaty and not the Concordat)?[79] But these sums are so huge, and it is likely that they would, to a great extent, have been spent in the first few years, that their return may be considered, in practice, to be impossible. No state could make such a big loan to the pontiff to help him out of difficulty, much less a private person or a bank. Termination of the Treaty would unleash such a crisis in the practical organisation of the Church that it would, albeit in the long term, find itself insolvent. The financial convention appended to the Treaty must therefore be considered the essential part of the Treaty itself, the guarantee of the near-impossibility of the denunciation of the Treaty, which has been put forward for polemical reasons and to exert political pressure.

Extract from a letter of Leo XIII's to Franz Joseph dated, it seems, June 1892, and quoted on pp.244 et seq. of the book by Francesco Salata, *Per la storia diplomatica della Questione Romana* [*Towards a Diplomatic History of the Roman Question*], 1929; 'And We shall not remain silent that, in the midst of these hardships, We also lack the means of confronting *by Ourself* the incessant and manifold material demands inherent in the government of the Church. It is true that succour comes from the spontaneously offered gifts of charity; but *to Our distress*, there stands always before Us *the thought that they finish by being a burden* to Our children; and, moreover, one must not harbour notions of the inexhaustibility of public charity.' '*By Ourself*' means 'gathered by taxes' from the citizens of a papal state, for whose sacrifices it appears one does not feel *distress*; it seems natural for the populations of Italy to pay the expenses of the universal Church.

In the conflict between Bismarck and the Holy See, one can detect the origins of a series of questions that might be raised on account of the fact that the Vatican is situated in Italy and has certain particular relations with the Italian state. Bismarck 'had his jurists launch the theory of the responsibility of the Italian state for the political activities of the papacy, whom Italy had established in this condition of invulnerability and lack of legal responsibility as regards the damage inflicted on and offences committed against other States' (Salata, op. cit., p. 271).

Q16§11[ii].

46 State-Church Relations [2]

(Cf. p.15a).[80] The Director General of the Fund for Religious Affairs, Raffaele Jacuzio, has published a *Commento della nuova legislazione in materia ecclesiastica*) [*Comment on the New Legislation on Matters Regarding the Church*], with an introduction by Alfredo Rocco (Turin 1932) in which all the acts of the Italian state organs, as well as those of the Vatican, for putting the Concordat into effect are collected together and commented on. In relation to the Catholic Action question, Jacuzio writes (p.203): 'But since there comes into the concept of politics not only the safeguarding of the juridical order of the state, but also everything pertinent to provisions of a socio-economic order, it is very difficult ... to maintain that all political activity is excluded *a priori* from Catholic Action when ... as well as the spiritual education of young people, it also undertakes social and economic activity.'

On the subject of the Concordat, one should also see Vincenzo Morello's book, *Il conflitto dopo il Concordato* [*The Conflict after the Concordat*], 1931, and Egilberto Martire's reply, 'Reasons for the Conciliation', Rome, *Rassegna Romana*, 1932. On this Morello-Martire polemic, see the article 'A Polemic on the Conciliation' signed 'Novus' in the *Critica Fascista* of 1 February 1933. Morello brings out those points in the Concordat on which the state is by its own standards found wanting and has abdicated its sovereignty; not only that, it appears, but he underlines how on certain points the concessions made to the Church are broader than those made by other signatory countries to concordats. There are four main points of controversy:

1) marriage; by article 43 of the Concordat, marriage is regulated by canon law, which is to say that within the state domain, a law extraneous to the state is applied. By that, on the basis of a law extraneous to the state, Catholics can have their marriage annulled, different from non-Catholics, while 'being or not being Catholic should have no importance for civil purposes';

2) by article 5, clause 3, apostate priests or those under censure are banned from certain public offices, i.e. a 'sanction' from the Penal Code is applied to people who have not, in the eyes of the state, committed any punishable offence; article 1 of the Code states, on the other hand, that no citizen should be punished except for a deed expressly considered an offence in penal law;

3) Morello cannot see the advantages in the state wiping the slate clean of the laws on subversion,[81] by recognising the juridical existence of ecclesiastical bodies and religious orders and their faculty for possessing and administering goods of their own;

4) teaching; total and complete exclusion of the state from Church schools, and not at all just those for the technical training of the priesthood (i.e. exclusion of state control over the teaching of theology, etc.) but from those given over to general teaching. Article 39 of the Concordat also refers in fact to the primary and secondary schools held by the clergy in many seminaries, boarding schools and convents, which the clergy make use of to attract boys and youths into the priesthood and into monastic life, but which in themselves are not as yet specialised for this activity. These pupils ought to have the right to state protection.

It seems that in other concordats, account has been taken of certain guarantees *vis-à-vis* the state, by whose terms not even the clergy may be trained in a way that runs contrary to the laws and legal order of the nation, by the precise requirement that a public diploma or certificate (the one giving access to the Universities) is necessary for many ecclesiastical offices.

Q16§14.

47 The State is the Church

The ministerial circular to which 'Ignotus' returns with so much insistence in his booklet *Stato fascista, Chiesa e Scuola* [*Fascist State, Church and the Schools*], Rome 1929, commenting that 'it is not judged by many to be a monument of political prudence, in that expressions of excessive zeal are used, a zeal which Napoleon (which is to say Talleyrand) shunned absolutely, a zeal which might seem excessive were the document issued by the person of the ecclesiastical administration rather than by a civil Ministry'. The circular was signed by the minister, Belluzzo, and sent to the local Education Offices [*Provveditorati*] on 28 March 1929 (Circular no. 54, published in the *Official Bulletin* of the Ministry of National Education on 16 April 1929, and reproduced in its entirety in the *Civiltà Cattolica* of the subsequent 18 May).

For 'Ignotus', this circular provided Catholics with a broad interpretation of article 36 of the Concordat. But after all is said and done, is this true? 'Ignotus' writes that, with article 36 of the Concordat, Italy *would not recognise* but just about (!?) *consider* 'the teaching of Christian Doctrine according to the form received by Catholic tradition as the foundation and crowning-point of public instruction'. But is this restricted and cavilling interpretation of the verb 'to consider' on the part of 'Ignotus' logical? The question is certainly a serious one and the compilers of the documents probably did not at the time think of the importance of their concessions, hence this abrupt regression. (One can only think that the change in name of the Ministry from 'Public Instruction' to 'National Education' is bound up with this need for a restrictive interpretation of article 36 of the Concordat, wishing by this to be able to assert that 'instruction', the 'informative' moment – still the elementary and preparatory stage – is one thing, while 'education', the 'formative' moment, the crowning-point of the educational process, is another, in accordance with Gentile's pedagogy.)

The words 'foundation and crowning-point' used in the Concordat repeat the expression employed in the Royal

Decree of 1 October 1923, no. 2185, on the *Systematisation of the Scholastic Levels and of Educational Curricula in Elementary Instruction*: 'As the foundation and crowning-point of elementary instruction at each of its levels *there is placed* the teaching of Christian doctrine, according to the form received within the Catholic tradition'. In an article, 'Religious teaching in the Secondary Schools', published on 21 March 1929 and regarded as unofficial (but authoritative), *La Tribuna* wrote 'The fascist state has directed that the Catholic religion, the intellectual and moral base of our people, be taught not only in the schools attended by our children, but also in those attended by our young people.'

The Catholics, of course, relate all this to the first article of the Statute, which is reconfirmed in the first article of the Treaty with the Holy See, by the interpretation that the state, as such, *professes the Catholic religion* and not at all just in the sense that the state, in so far as it has need of religious ceremonies in its activity, resolves [variant in the manuscript: *establishes*] that they must be 'Catholic'. On the Catholic stance on public schooling, cf. Fr M. Barbera's article 'Religion and Philosophy in the Secondary Schools' in the *Civiltà Cattolica* of 1 June 1929.

Q5§70.

48 Past and Present [4] Religion in Schools

'This is why, according to the Gentile reform, in the new school curricula art and religion are assigned just to the elementary school and philosophy, by and large, to the secondary schools. In the philosophical intentions of the elementary curricula, the words "the teaching of religion is considered to be the foundation and crowning point of the whole of primary instruction" mean precisely that religion is a necessary but lower category that education must pass through since, according to Hegel's conception, religion is a mythological and lower form of philosophy, corresponding to the childlike mentality not as yet capable of raising itself to pure philosophy, within which religion must subsequently be resolved and absorbed. We may note straight away that, in actual fact, this idealist theory has not succeeded in polluting religious teaching in the elementary school by having it treated there as mythological, *both because the teacher either does not understand or does not bother his head with such theories* and because Catholic religious teaching intrinsically concerns history and dogma, and is *externally watched over and directed by the Church in the curricula, texts, teachings.* Moreover the words "foundation and crowning point" have been accepted by the Church in their obvious meaning and repeated in the Concordat between the Holy See and Italy, according to which (art. 36) religious teaching is extended to the secondary schools. This extension has come to challenge the aims of idealism, which was attempting to exclude religion from the secondary schools to leave the field free for the dominance of philosophy alone, destined to supersede and absorb within itself the religion learned in the elementary schools.' *Civiltà Cattolica*, 7 November 1931 ('The Good and the Bad in the New Pedagogy', author anonymous, but Fr Mario Barbera).

Q7§89.

49 Catholicism and Secularism. Religion and Science, etc.

Read Edmondo Cione's booklet *Il dramma religioso dello spirito moderno e la Rinascenza* [*The Religious Drama of the Modern Spirit and the Renaissance*], Naples 1929. He develops the following concept: 'the Church, strong in its authority, but feeling the void hovering within its head, a head lacking in science and philosophy; Thought, strong in its power, but yearning in vain for popularity and the authority of tradition.' Why 'in vain'? Yet the duality of Church and Thought is not exact, or at least in the imprecision of the language there has taken root a whole mistaken way of thinking and acting in particular. Thought can be opposed to the Religion of which the Church is the organisation militant. Our idealists, secularists, immanentists and so on, have made a pure abstraction of Thought, which the Church has taken easily in its stride by ensuring

Religion: A Movement and an Ideology

that it has state laws on its side and that it controls education. For 'Thought' to be a force (and only as such can it build its own tradition), it must create an organisation, which cannot be the state – since, however much it may proclaim it at the top of its voice, the state has in one way or another given up this ethical role – and which therefore must spring from civil society. These people, who were opposed to the freemasons, will end up by recognising the necessity for the masonry. The 'Reformation and Renaissance' problem mentioned on other occasions. The position of Croce (Cione is a Crocean) who does not know how (and is unable) to become a popular element, in other words a 'new Renaissance' etc.

Q3§140.

50 Encyclopaedic Notions [1]. Civil Society

One must distinguish civil society as understood by Hegel and in the sense in which it is often used in these notes (viz. in the sense of the political and cultural hegemony of a social group over the whole of society, as the ethical content of the state) from the sense given it by the Catholics, for whom civil society is, instead, political society or the state, as compared with the society of the family or the Church. Pius XI writes in his encyclical on education (*Civiltà Cattolica* of 1 February 1930): 'Now there are three necessary societies, distinct from one another and yet harmoniously combined by God, into which man is born; two, namely the family and civil society, belong to the natural order; the third, the Church, to the supernatural order. In the first place comes the family, instituted directly by God for its particular purpose, the generation and formation of offspring; for this reason it has priority of nature and therefore of rights over civil society. Nevertheless, the family is an imperfect society, since it has not in itself all the means for its own complete development; whereas civil society is a perfect society, having in itself all the means for its peculiar end, which is the temporal well-being of the community; and so, in this respect, that is, in view of the common good, it has pre-eminence over the family, which finds its own suitable temporal perfection in civil society. The third society, into which man is born when through baptism he reaches the divine life of grace, is the Church; a perfect society, because it has in itself all the means required for its own end, which is the eternal salvation of mankind; hence it is supreme in its own domain.'[82]

For Catholicism, what is called 'civil society' in Hegelian language is not 'necessary', i.e. it is purely historical or contingent. In the Catholic conception, the state is just the Church and is a universal and supernatural state. The medieval conception is fully adhered to in theory.

Q6§24.

E INTEGRALIST CATHOLICS, JESUITS AND MODERNISTS

51 The Rise of the Integralists

The 'integralist Catholics' enjoyed great fortune under the papacy of Pius X. They represented a European tendency within Catholicism that, politically, was of the extreme right, but they were of course stronger in certain countries such as Italy, France and Belgium where, in one form or another, the left tendencies in the fields of politics and intellectual life made themselves more strongly felt within the sphere of organised Catholicism.

In Belgium, during the war, the Germans seized a large number of confidential and secret documents belonging to the integralists which were then published. There thus came to light abundant proof that the integralists had set up their own secret association for controlling, directing and 'purging' the Catholic movement at all levels within its hierarchy; they had recourse to codes, clandestine correspondence, spies, trusties and so on. The head of the integralists was Mons. Umberto Benigni, and one part of the organisation was constituted by the *Sodalitium Pianum* of

Pius V.[83] Mons. Benigni, who died in 1934, was a man of great practical and theoretical capacity whose activity was truly phenomenal; amongst other things he wrote an enormous work, *La Storia sociale della Chiesa*, [*The Social History of the Church*], of which four large format volumes, of over 600 pages each, have been published by Hoepli. As emerges from *Civiltà Cattolica*, Benigni never for once interrupted his conspiratorial activity within the Church, despite the difficulties the integralists got into because of the policy of Pius XI, a hesitant, faltering and timid policy but one which is however popular-democratic in orientation because of the need to create strong Catholic Action groups. The integralists supported the *Action Française* movement in France and were against the *Sillon*;[84] they are everywhere opposed to political and religious modernism.

In contrast to the Jesuits, they adopted an almost Jansenist stance, that is one of great moral and religious rigour, opposed to any form of laxity, opportunism or centrism. The Jesuits, of course, accuse the integralists of Jansenism (of Jansenistic hypocrisy) and, what is more, of playing into the hands of the (theologising) modernists:

1) through their fight against the Jesuits, and
2) because they have widened the concept of modernism and thus enlarged the target so much that they have offered the modernists the broadest scope for manoeuvre. It has in fact happened that in their common struggle against the Jesuits, integralists and modernists have found themselves objectively on the same terrain and have collaborated with each other (it seems that Buonaiuti has written for Benigni's review).

What now remains of the modernists and integralists? It is difficult to single out and evaluate their objective strength (especially that of the modernists) within the organisation of the Church; the integralists have maintained their forces almost intact, even after the campaign against *Action Française*. In any case, they are always there, working as a continuous 'leaven', in so far as they represent the struggle against the Jesuits and their excessive power, a struggle carried on today by elements of both right and left amidst the apparent indifference of the mass of the clergy, with results that cannot be ignored as regards the mass of the faithful, who know nothing of these battles and their meaning, but exactly because of this find it impossible to attain a unified and homogeneous basic mentality.

These forces of the Church – internal, antagonistic and clandestine or nearly so (for modernism, covert operation indispensable) – find it convenient to have external 'centres', either public or having direct effectiveness where the public is concerned, with their own periodicals or editions of books and pamphlets. Between the clandestine and the public centres, there exist secret links that become the channel for the expression of anger, vendettas, denunciations, base insinuations and gossip in order to fan the flames of the anti-Jesuit struggle. (The Jesuits, too, have an unofficial or even underground organisation, to which there must contribute the so-called 'lay Jesuits', a curious institution which maybe has been copied from the Franciscan tertiaries and which, it would appear, represents numerically about a quarter of all the Jesuit forces. This institution of 'lay Jesuits' deserves closer study). All this shows that the cohesive force of the Church is much less than is commonly thought, not only because of the fact that the growing indifference of the mass of the faithful for purely religious or ecclesiastical questions attaches a very relative value to superficial and apparent ideological homogeneity, but also because of the much more serious fact that the Church centre is impotent to clear the field completely of the organised forces engaged in conscious struggle within the Church itself. It is, above all, the anti-modernist struggle that has demoralised the young clergy, who do not hesitate to swear the anti-modernist oath while continuing to hold to modernist opinions. (Recall the milieux in which young ecclesiastics, Dominicans included, used to congregate in pre-war Turin, and their deviations that went as far as the favourable reception of the modernising tendencies of Islam and Buddhism and the conception of religion as a world-wide syncretism of all the higher religions – God is like the sun, the religions being the rays, each ray leading back to the one sun, etc.)

The following indications have been taken from an article of Fr Rosa ('Reply to "A Baseless and Dishonest

Polemic" ', in the *Civiltà Cattolica* of 21 July 1928). Mons. Benigni continues (in 1928) to have a noteworthy organisation: a series of books under the title *Vérités* is published in Paris with authors signing themselves Récalde, Luc Verus, Simon (Luc Verus being the collective pseudonym of the 'integralists'). Rosa quotes the booklet *Les découvertes du Jésuite Rosa, successeur de Von Gerlach*, Paris 1928, which he ascribes to Benigni at least as regards the material. The Jesuits are accused of being 'friends of the Masons and Jews' (calling to mind Ludendorff's 'doctrine' about the 'Jewish-Masonic-Jesuit International'), are called 'demagogues and revolutionaries' and so on. In Rome, Benigni uses the agency *Urbs* or *Romana* and signs his publications with the name of his nephew Mataloni. His Roman bulletin went under the name *Veritas*. (Is it still coming out or, if not when did it cease publication?) In 1928 or before, he published a pamphlet *Di fronte alla calunnia* [*Faced with Slander*], comprising just a few pages, with documents concerning the so-called *Sodalitium Pianum*; the pamphlet was then reproduced in part and defended by two Catholic periodicals, *Fede e Ragione* [*Faith and Reason*] of Florence and the *Liguria del Popolo* [*The People's Liguria*] of Genoa. He was editor of the periodical *Miscellanea di storia ecclesiastica*.

The pamphlet *Una polemica senza onestà e senza legge* [*A Baseless and Dishonest Polemic*] was written by Prof. E. Buonaiuti against Fr Rosa. Rosa, writing of Buonaiuti's book *Le Modernisme catholique* [*Catholic Modernism*] (a volume in the series edited by P.L. Couchaud and published by Rieder), notes that the author finally admits a series of facts that he had always denied during the modernist polemic (for example that Buonaiuti was the author of 'the modernist campaign run by the *Giornale d'Italia*, something Buonaiuti does not actually say explicitly in his book, but which one may deduce to be very likely, given the tortuous nature of these writers). Benigni concerted the press campaign against the modernists at the time of the Encylical *Pascendi*.[85] In his *Ricerche religiose* [*Religious Researches*] (July 1928) Buonaiuti recounts a typical incident (cited by Fr Rosa together with certain reproachful comments etc.). In

1909, the modernist, Prof. Antonino De Stefano (now a defrocked priest and university history teacher), was to publish an 'International Modernist Review' in Geneva. Buonaiuti sent him a letter. A few weeks later, he was called to the Holy Office.[86] The assessor at that time, the Dominican, Pasqualigo, took him to task word for word on the letter he had written to De Stefano. The letter had been 'appropriated' in Geneva, an emissary from Rome having been 'introduced' into De Stefano's house etc. (For Buonaiuti, of course, Benigni has been an instrument and accomplice of the Jesuits, but it would appear that in 1904 Buonaiuti was a collaborator on Benigni's *Miscellany*.)

On the theme *Integralist Catholics-Jesuits-Modernists* – who represent the three 'organic' tendencies of Catholicism, i.e. they are the forces fighting for hegemony within the Roman Church – a collection should be made of all the useful material and a bibliography constructed. (The numbers of *Civiltà Cattolica*, Buonaiuti's *Religious Researches*, Benigni's *Miscellany*, the polemical pamphlets of the three currents and so on.)

From what emerges from *Civiltà Cattolica* it seems that *Fede e Ragione* is currently the most important review of the integralist Catholics. See who the main collaborators are and on what they differ from the Jesuits – whether on points of faith, morals, politics etc. The 'integralists' are strong in general, having the support of some religious orders (Dominicans, Franciscans) that are rivals of the Jesuits. It should be borne in mind that not even the Jesuits are totally homogeneous – Cardinal Billot, an intransigent integralist until he gave up his cardinal's hat, was a Jesuit, and some of the outstanding modernists, such as Tyrrell,[87] were Jesuits.

Q20§4[i].

52 Action Française and the Integralists

The article 'Truth Balanced Between the Extremes of Error' in the *Civiltà Cattolica* of 3 November 1928 takes as its cue Nicolas Fontaine's publication *Saint-Siège, 'Action Française' et 'Catholiques intégraux'*, [*The Holy See, 'Action Française' and 'Integralist Catholics'*] Paris 1928, of which this judgement is given in one of the notes to the article: 'The author is dominated by political and liberal prejudices, above all when he sees politics in the condemnation of *Action Française*; but the facts and documents that he includes on the famous "Sodality" have never been denied.' Now, Fontaine has written nothing that is completely new (his documents on the 'integralists' had been printed in *Mouvement* in April 1924). Why, then, have the Jesuits not made use of them before? This is an important question and can, I think, be resolved in these terms: the papal action against *Action Française* is the most visible and resolute aspect of a wider action aimed at eliminating a series of consequences of the policy followed by Pius X (in France, but indirectly in other countries, too). In other words, without mounting a frontal attack on them, Pius XI wants to curb the importance of the integralist Catholics, who are openly reactionary and are making it nearly impossible to create a strong Catholic Action and democratic-popular party in France, able to compete with the radicals. The struggle against modernism had unbalanced Catholicism, driving it too far to the right; hence the necessity to 'centre' it afresh on the Jesuits, to re-endow it with a flexible political form, not constrained by doctrinally rigid positions, but allowing a wide-ranging freedom of manoeuvre etc.: Pius XI, without a shadow of doubt, is the Jesuits' Pope.

But the battle against the Catholic integralists on an organic front is much more difficult than the one against the modernists. A more advantageous terrain is offered by the struggle against *Action Française*: here the integralists are fought not so much as integralists but in so far as they are supporters of Maurras. In other words, an 'extended formation' type of battle is being waged,[88] individuals being picked out as not obeying the Pope and as hindering the defence of the faith and morals against a confessed pagan and atheist, while the tendency in its entirety is officially ignored. Herein lies the supreme importance of Fontaine's book, which lays bare the organic link between Maurras and 'integrism'[89] and lends forceful assistance to the action of the Pope and the Jesuits. (It should be noted that Fontaine returns on several occasions to impress upon the French 'secularists' that it is the integralists and not the Jesuits who are 'antidemocratic', and that in actual fact the Jesuits are aiding democracy etc. But who is Fontaine? Is he a specialist in studies on religious policy? Might he not be working under the inspiration of the Jesuits themselves?)

This *Civiltà Cattolica* article, certainly written by Fr Rosa, is very cautious in its use of documents reprinted by Fontaine, avoiding an analysis of those which not only discredit the integralists but show the entire Church in a comic light and reflect discredit on it. (The integralists had organised a veritable secret society, with coded systems in which the Pope is referred to as 'Baroness Micheline' and other personalities by names no whit less extravagant, all of which is ample demonstration of Benigni's mentality *vis-à-vis* his 'hierarchs'.)

On the question of the 'the merits' of Pius XI's policy, it is not easy to draw conclusions, as is shown by the very course of this policy, an uncertain, timid and irresolute policy by reason of the immense difficulties it continually has to run up against. It has been said time and time again that the Catholic Church possesses inexhaustible virtues of adaptation and development. This is not altogether exact. A number of decisive points may be fixed in the life of the Church:

– the first is that defined by the schism between East and West, territorial in nature, between two historical civilisations in conflict, having but few ideological and cultural elements, and which begins with the advent of Charlemagne's Empire, i.e. with a renewed attempt at establishing a political and cultural hegemony of the West over the East; the schism came in a period in which ecclesiastical forces were poorly organised and, automatically, got wider and wider by the very force of events that were impossible to control, as happens when two people who have had no contact for decades, draw further and further away from each other and end up by speaking two different languages;[90]

– the second is that of the Reformation, which came about

in quite different conditions and which, though it resulted in a territorial separation, was most of all cultural in nature, giving rise to the Counter-Reformation and the decisions of the Council of Trent, which puts a very strong curb on the Catholic Church's possibility of adapting itself;

– the third was that of the French Revolution (liberal-democratic Reform) which forced the Church to take up a yet more rigid stance and to assume the mummified shape of a formalistic and absolutist organism whose nominal head is the pope, with theoretically 'autocratic' powers, which in reality are very few because the whole system hangs together only by virtue of the rigidity typical of a paralytic.

The entire society in which the Church moves and is able to evolve has this tendency to become rigid, leaving very few possibilities for the Church to adapt itself, possibilities that were already few because of the current nature of the Church itself.

The irruption of new forms of nationalism, which, after all, are the culmination of the historical process that began with Charlemagne, i.e. with the first renaissance, not only make this adaptation impossible, but also makes the very existence of the Church difficult, as we have seen in Hitlerite Germany. Moreover, the Pope cannot 'excommunicate' Hitlerite Germany, but must sometimes rely on it, and this makes it impossible to follow any positive, vigorous religious policy of an undeviating variety. Faced with phenomena such as Hitlerism, even wide-ranging concession to modernism would now have no meaning, but serve only to increase confusion and disorder. Neither can it be said that things are much brighter in France, because it is just there that the theory of contraposing a 'religion of the fatherland' to the 'Roman' one was created and one can assume an increase of patriotic nationalism, not of Roman cosmopolitanism.

These indications are drawn from the *Civiltà Cattolica* of 3 November 1928. It is argued there that Maurras has found defenders amongst Catholics even in Italy, it being said that there exist 'imitators or supporters, either open or *undercover*, but erring equally from the fullness of the faith and Catholic morality, either in theory or in practice, even when they raise a clamour or, yet again, labour under the deception that they want to defend them *integrally* and better than anyone else'. *Action Française* 'launched a whole series of defamatory claims and incredible libellous material (sic) against the author of these lines (Fr Rosa), right up to those repeatedly suggested libellous claims about the *murders and ruthless executions of fellow brethren*'. (We shall have to see when and where these accusations were made against Fr Rosa. Amongst the Jesuits there was an integralist wing, favourable to Maurras, with front-rank men like Cardinal Billot, who was one of the main people behind the writing of the encyclical *Pascendi* and who gave up the office of cardinal, an extremely rare happening in the history of the Church, which demonstrates Billot's wilful obstinacy, and the resolute will of the Pope to overcome every obstacle in the struggle against Maurras.)

The *Revue internationale des sociétés secrètes*, edited by Abbé Boulin, is 'integralist' and bitterly anti-Jesuit. Boulin is linked to Benigni-Mataloni and makes use of pseudonyms (Roger Duguet). *Action Française* and the integralists attach themselves desperately to Pius X and pretend to remain faithful to his teachings (which in the development of the Church offers a fine precedent, given that the death of any Pope could provide the ground for organising a sect that carries on one particular attitude of his – the 'integralists' want to restore Pius IX's *Syllabus* to a place of honour; in the proposal of *Action Française* to have an ecclesiastic give the course on the *Syllabus* in its schools, one sees a very clever provocation, but Pius XI not only does not want to restore actuality to the *Syllabus*, he is, rather, even seeking to tone down and make the encyclical *Pascendi* more acceptable).

The *Civiltà Cattolica* article is of the highest importance and must be looked at again for further elaboration of this argument. All the nuances in the 'distinctions' drawn on the subject of freemasonry, anti-semitism, nationalism, democracy and so on will have to be considered. Even in regard to the modernists, a distinction is drawn between those who have been deceived etc., and Benigni's anti-modernism is taken to task and so on: 'So much was to be feared and we did not fail to point out to the proper authorities right from the start that such methods would have played into the hands of the real modernists, thereby laying serious dangers up in store for the Church. This was seen subsequently, and may also still be seen, in the negative spirit of reaction not only of liberalism and the old type of modernism but in the new type too, as well as in integralism itself. This latter then wished to be seen as opposing any appearance or form of modernism, and, rather, took it upon itself to be, as is said, more papal than the Pope, while on the other hand, it is now, quite scandalously, either putting up a *hypocritical* resistance to him or fighting him openly, as is happening among the voluble supporters of *Action Française* in France and *their silent accomplices in Italy*.'

The integralists call the Jesuits 'modernisers' and call their tendency 'modernisantism'; they have divided Catholics into integralists and non-integralists, i.e. 'papal' and 'episcopal' Catholics. (It seems that Benedict XV's encyclical *Ad Beatissimi*[91] had, in noting this tendency to introduce these distinctions among Catholics, reproached it for damaging Christian unity and charity.)

The 'Sapinière' (from S.P., the initials of 'Sodalitium Pianum') was the secret society that hid behind the veil of the 'Sodalitium Pianum', and organised the struggle against the modernising Jesuits 'wholly contrary to the first idea and to the official programme put forward by the Supreme Pontiff, and thence approved by the Secretary to the Consistory, certainly not because it served as an outlet for personal passions, for the denunciation and defamation of the most upright and even eminent persons, of Bishops and of whole religious Orders, namely of ours, which had never up to then been prey to any such slanderous attacks not even at the time of its suppression. Last but not least, after the war and a long time after the dissolution of the Sodality – decreed by the Sacred Congregation of the Council, certainly not as an honour to it but rather as a censure and formal ban on it – we witnessed, all *at the expense of a certain well-known and very rich Parisian financier*, Simon, and his cohorts, the publication and lavish free distribution of the most ignominious and critically ignorant libels against the Society of Jesus, its Saints, its doctors and masters, its works and constitutions, albeit solemnly approved by the Church. This is the well known series of the so-called *Récalde*, which has now grown to over a dozen libels, some consisting of more than one volume, in all of which there is the all-too-recognisable – and no less well-paid – hand of accomplices in Rome. It is now being reinforced by the sister publication of defamatory and delirious scandal-sheets, under the general and self-contradictory title *Vérités*, imitations of the twin sheets of the *Urbs* or *Romana* agency, whose articles are later to be seen quoted almost word for word in other "periodical" news sheets.'

The integralists spread 'the worst type of slander' against Benedict XV, as can be seen from the article that appeared on his death in the review *Vieille France* (by Urbain Gohier) and in the *Ronde* (February 1922) 'this (periodical), too, anything but Catholic and moral, honoured though it is by the collaboration of Umberto Benigni, whose name is recorded in the fine company of these more or less dissipated youths'. 'One cannot know how much evil has been wrought in the consciences, how much scandal has been conveyed therein, how great has been the alienation of the mind caused above all in France by this same spirit of defamation, continued under the present Pontificate, that has been propagated right within the very ranks of Catholics, of the religious, and of the clergy. For it is exactly here that political passion has induced people to believe more easily in slanders often having their origin in Rome, after Simon and his other rich confederates had, in a Gallican and journalistic (sic) spirit, bought the services of the authors of these calumnies and procured the free distribution of their libels, mainly those of the aforesaid anti-Jesuits, in the seminaries, presbyteries, ecclesiastical curiae, wherever there was some probability or likelihood that the scurrilous claim could take root; and even among the laity, for the most part young people, and in state-run lycées themselves with an unequalled prodigality'. The already suspect authors write anonymously or make use of pseudonyms. '... It is well-known, especially among journalists, just how little any

Religion: A Movement and an Ideology

appellation of honour is merited by a group of just such a nature, whose moving spirit is the most astute in hiding himself but also bears most guilt and is the most involved in the conspiracy' (is this a reference to Benigni or to some other big name in the Vatican?).

According to Fr Rosa, there was no initial 'agreement' between *Action Française* and the 'integralists', but such a thing did begin to take shape after 1926. This statement, however, was undoubtedly made with the express purpose of excluding any political motive (combating the ultra-reactionaries) from the struggle against *Action Française* and lessening the responsibility of Pius X. The last note of the article says 'One party must not, however, be confused with the other, as some, e.g. Nicolas Fontaine in his previously quoted book *Saint-Siège, 'Action Française' et 'Catholiques integraux'*, have done. This author, as we have remarked, is more than just liberal, but is also *unfortunately* (sic) *extremely well-informed* on the not-at-all edifying cases of the already referred-to secret society that goes under the name *La Sapinière* together with its French and Italian supporters; in this it is ridiculous to taunt him with liberalism – it is instead the facts, to which we shall in due time return, to which the lie must be given'. Fontaine, in actual fact, gives quite an exhaustive proof of the connection between the integralists and *Action Française*, even if it is possible to say that we are dealing with two separate parties, one of which tends to make use of the other, and shows how that connection leads back to Pius X. That *'unfortunately* extremely well-informed' is strange, since Fontaine made use of material that is openly and publicly known, just as it is 'strange' that Fr Rosa has not 'returned' to the subject of *La Sapinière* in the pages of *Civiltà Cattolica* (at least not up to the death of Mons. Benigni, which was not recorded, and it is difficult to think of him speaking of it again unless there is some other strong personality who succeeds Benigni at the top level of the integralists). This silence is significant. The article concludes 'But truth has nothing to fear. And for our part, we are quite resolved to defend it without fear or trepidation or hesitation, even against *internal enemies, be they even ecclesiastics having power and means at their disposal*, who have led the laity astray in order to involve them in their own designs and interests.'

Recall one of Benigni's trips to America (mentioned in *Civiltà Cattolica*; 1927, No. IV, p. 399) to distribute anti-Jesuit libels there; in Rome there must be some place containing tens of thousands of copies of these libels.

Q20§4 [ii].

53   An Action Française Journalist in Rome

Action Française used to have a journalist, Havard de la Montagne, working in Rome, editing a French-language weekly, *Rome*, directed especially at French Catholics, both the religious and the laity, who were either resident in or passing through Rome. It was the voice of the integralists and followers of Maurras, their focal point as well as being the centre of *Action Française*'s news service at the Vatican, not only for religious questions, but above all for French and international political ones of a confidential nature. One must not forget that the Vatican has an information service that sometimes and for some questions is more exact, wider-reaching and more abundant than that of any other government. Being able to use this supply of information was not the least among the reasons for certain of *Action Française*'s journalistic successes, together with lots of its personal and scandal-mongering campaigns. It would appear that after the break in 1926, *Rome* went into decline and then ceased publication.

Q20§4 [iii].

54   Action Française's Long Crisis

Look at the article '*Action Française*'s Long Drawn-Out Crisis' in the number of *Civiltà Cattolica* of 7 September 1929. The reviewer praises the book *La trop longue crise de l'Action Française* [*The Over-Long Crisis of Action Française*] by Mons. Sagot du Vauroux, Bishop of Agen (Paris 1929), a work which 'will prove most useful even to foreigners who are unable to understand the origins, and still less the persistence, combined with such great obstinacy, of [*Action Française*'s] Catholic members, which blinds them right up to the point of making them live and die without the sacraments rather than give up the hateful excesses of their party and its unbelieving leadership'. *Civiltà Cattolica* attempts to justify itself for no longer engaging very often in polemics with *Action Française*, and states among other things 'Beyond this, only an echo of the prolonged crisis reaches Italy, in other words only the distant (!?) association and analogy that it might (!) have with the general paganising tendencies of the modern age.' (This Malthusian polemic constitutes in point of fact the main weakness of the Jesuit position against *Action Française* and is the main cause of the fanatical fury of Maurras and his followers, who, not without reason, are convinced that the Vatican is making a 'whipping boy' of them, that they are playing the role of the boy who once used to accompany the heir to the throne in England and receive the beatings on behalf of his royal master. From this point to that of persuading Maurras's followers that the assault on them is purely a political one, since it is Catholic or universal only in words, is only a short step. The Pope, and *Civiltà Cattolica* likewise, have, as it happens, steered well clear of identifying and 'punishing' with these same sanctions those individual persons or groups which, in other countries, have the same tendencies as Maurras and do not hide them.)

Other indications of 'integralist Catholics': the *Bloc antirévolutionnaire* led by Félix Lacointe, 'worthy friend of the Boulin we have quoted and his associates' (Boulin edits the *Revue Internationale des Sociétés Secrètes*). It seems that Lacointe has written that Cardinal Rampolla was a freemason or something of the kind. (Rampolla was reproached for the policy of *ralliement* followed by Leo XIII. Recall on the subject of Rampolla that the veto put on his election to the papacy came from Austria, but at the request of Zanardelli.[92] On Rampolla and his position towards the Italian state, new elements are offered by Salata in the first (and only) volume of his *Documenti diplomatici sulla questione romana*. [*Diplomatic Documents Relating to the Roman Question*]).

One ideological element that is very significant as regards

the work that the Jesuits are carrying on in France to provide the Catholic-democratic movement with a wide popular base is this historical-political judgement: Who is responsible for the 'apostasy' of the French people? Just the democratic-revolutionary intellectuals whose reference point was Rousseau? No. The ones who bear most responsibility are the aristocrats and the big bourgeoisie who flirted with Voltaire: '... the traditional demands (of the monarchists) for a return to the old ways are as respectable as they are impracticable under present-day conditions. And that they are impracticable is *most of all* the fault of a great part of France's aristocracy and bourgeoisie, since the corruption and the apostasy of the mass of the people originated in the corruption and apostasy of this ruling class, rife up to the eighteenth century, thus confirming that even then *regis ad exemplum totus componitur orbis* [the king sets the example for how the whole world is ordered]. Voltaire was the idol of that part of an aristocracy that was both corrupt and a corrupter of its people and that – through quite scandalous acts of seduction – dug the grave for the people's faith and probity with its own hands. And even though afterwards, with the rise of Rousseau and his subversive democracy in opposition to the Voltairean aristocracy, the two apostate currents, which appeared to start off from contrary errors, were in theory opposed to each other, just like two baleful chorus leaders they then came together in one same practice and ruinous conclusion – that is to say in swelling the revolutionary torrent etc., etc.'

So too today, Maurras & Co. are the adversaries of Rousseauan democracy and the *Sillon*'s 'democratic exaggerations' ('exaggerations', one should take good note, just 'exaggerations'), but the disciples and admirers of Voltaire. (Jacques Bainville edited a *de luxe* version of Voltaire's writings, and the Jesuits have not forgotten this).

On this historical-critical nexus regarding the origins of popular 'apostasy' in France, *Civiltà Cattolica* quotes an article from *La Croix*, 15-16 August 1929, entitled 'The Grievous Apostasy of the Popular Masses in France' which refers to the book *Pour faire l'avenir* [*Constructing the Future*], by P. Croizier of *Action populaire*, published by Spes editions of Paris in 1929.

Amongst the followers of Maurras & Co., as well as the *conservatives and monarchists, Civiltà Cattolica*, following in the path of the Bishop of Agen, detects four other groups: 1) the *snobs* (attracted by, especially, Maurras's literary gifts; 2) the admirers of violence and the strong hand 'with the exaggerations of authority, pushed towards despotism, *under the guise* of resistance to the spirit of insubordination or social subversion of the contemporary era'; 3) the 'false mystics', those 'gullible enough to believe the prophecies of extraordinary restorations, wonderful conversions or providential missions' ascribed to none other than Maurras & Co.; this group, from the time of Pius X, 'undaunted', excuses Maurras's unbelief and attributes it to 'the deficiency of grace', 'almost as if sufficient grace for conversion was not given to all, nor were those who resisted to blame for falling into or persisting in sin'; (it would be this group, therefore, that is semi-heretical since, in order to justify Maurras, it trots out Jansenist or Calvinist positions. On this subject, an explanation is necessary for Maurras's obstinacy in not wishing to be 'converted', this being a fact that cannot be due solely to 'ethical and intellectual integrity and loyalty', and which, exactly on this score, is the cause of the Jesuits' trepidation. These latter understand that if the Maurras group captured state power, the actual situation of French Catholicism would become more difficult than it is at the moment. The Vatican's attitude towards Hitlerism, despite what Rosenberg had written in his *Myth* before the seizure of power, is, on this account, a source of amazement; it is true that Rosenberg is not of the same intellectual stature as Maurras, but the whole of Hitler's movement is of a low and vulgar intellectual calibre, and what afterwards happened to Catholicism and Christianity was predictable.); 4) the fourth group (the most dangerous for *Civiltà Cattolica*) would be that composed of the 'integralists'. (*Civiltà Cattolica* notes that the Bishop of Agen also calls them 'integrists', 'but it is well known that they are not to be confused with the political party called "integrist"[93] in Spain'.) These 'integralists' *Civiltà* writes, 'even in Italy were quite in favour of the positivists and unbelievers of *Action Française*, simply because of their violence against liberalism and other forms of modern error, not realising that they went too far to opposite extremes, extremes of an equally erroneous and pernicious nature etc.' 'Thus, even in Italy, we have seen some of their publications just gloss over, in passing, the condemnation of *Action Française*, instead of publishing the documents relating to it and illustrating the sense of and reason for this condemnation, while on the other hand they halt at length over the republication of and comment on the *Sillon*'s condemnation; almost as though these two movements, opposed to each other and equally opposed to Catholic doctrine, could not be and were not equally blameworthy. This affair is worthy of note since, while in almost every issue of this type of publication, one finds some accusation or fiery outburst against Catholic authors, it appears that either the vigour or the space is lacking for a frank and forceful treatment of the condemnation against the supporters of *Action Française*. There is, rather, a frequent repetition of aspersions, such as that of a claimed leaning to the left, in other words towards liberalism, popularism, false democracy, against whoever does not follow the procedure they adopt.'

(Henri Massis and the 'defenders of the West' group should also be included in the current of the 'integral Catholics'; remember Fr Rosa's gibes against Massis in his reply to Ugo Ojetti's open letter.)

Q20§4 [v].

55 Maurras and Paganism

The *Rivista d'Italia* of 15 January 1927 takes up an article by J. Vialatoux, published in the *Chronique Sociale de France* some weeks before. Vialatoux rejects the thesis upheld by Jacques Maritain in *Une opinion sur Charles Maurras et le devoir des catholiques* [*Charles Maurras and the Duty of Catholics*] (Paris 1926) according to which there is only an incidental relationship between Maurras's pagan philosophy and ethics and his politics, so that if one took his political doctrine, leaving aside the philosophy, one could run into a number of dangers, as in any movement composed of human beings, but the doctrine itself contains nothing deserving of condemnation. For Vialatoux, rightly, the political doctrine springs from (or at least is indivisibly bound up with – G.) the pagan conception of the world. (As regards this paganism, one has to distinguish and clarify the differences between the literary aspect, brimming with references and pagan metaphors, and the essential core which is, after all, naturalistic positivism, taken over from Comte and indirectly from the Saint-Simonians, all of which is tied up with paganism only through its jargon and ecclesiastical nomenclature – G.) The state is humanity's ultimate goal: it brings the human order into being by means of the forces of nature alone, (i.e. 'human' forces as opposed to 'supernatural' ones).

Maurras can be defined by his hatreds even more than by his loves. Primitive Christianity – the conception of the world contained in the Gospels, put forward by the first apologists etc., Christianity, in short, up the Edict of Milan, whose fundamental belief was that the coming of Christ had heralded the end of the world and that it therefore caused the Roman political order to dissolve into a moral anarchy that corroded away every civil and state value – is a Judaic conception for Maurras and an object of his hatred.

It is in this sense that he wants to de-Christianise modern society. For Maurras, the Catholic Church has been and always will be the instrument of this de-Christianisation. He distinguishes between Christianity and Catholicism, exalting this latter as the reaction of Roman order against Judaic anarchy. The Catholic religion, with its superstitious devotions, its feast days, its pomp, its ceremonials, its liturgy, its images, its formulas, its sacramental rites, its majestic hierarchy, acts as a salutary enchantment, taming Christian anarchy and immunising against the Judaic poison of authentic Christianity.

According to Vialatoux, *Action Française*'s nationalism is nothing but an episode of the *religious history* of our time. (In this sense every political movement not controlled by the Vatican is an episode of religious history, in other words all history is religious history. At any rate, it must be added that Maurras's hatred of everything that smacks of Protestantism and is Anglo-Germanic in origin – Romanticism, the French Revolution, capitalism etc. – is just an aspect of that hatred of primitive Christianity. One would have to look in Auguste Comte for the origins of this general attitude towards Catholicism, which is not independent of the bookish rebirth of Thomism[94] and Aristotelianism.)

Q13§37(excerpt).

56 Maurras and 'Organic Centralism'

So-called 'organic centralism' is based on the principle that a political group is chosen by 'co-option' around an 'infallible repository of the truth', someone who has been 'enlightened by reason', who has discovered the infallible natural laws of historical evolution, infallible in the long term even if immediate events 'seem' to give the lie to them. The application of the laws of mechanics and mathematics to social facts, which should have only a metaphorical value, becomes the sole and phantasmagoric intellectual motor (without any purchase on reality). The nexus between organic centralism and Maurras's doctrines is obvious.

Q13§38(excerpt).

57 The Turmel Case[95]

Refer to the article 'The Catastrophe of the Turmel Case and the Methods of Critical Modernism' in the *Civiltà Cattolica* of 6 December 1930. The piece is very important and the Turmel case assumes the greatest interest in the question. Turmel's activity is like something out of a novel. While remaining a priest, he continued for over twenty years, using the most varied pseudonyms, to write articles and books of such a heterodox nature that they ended up by being openly atheistic. In 1930 the Jesuits managed to unmask him and have him declared *excommunicatus vitandus*;[96] the decree of the Holy Office contains the list of his publications and pseudonyms.

It so happens that after the modernist crisis, secret

Religion: A Movement and an Ideology

formations came to be created within the organisation of the Church. As well as that of the Jesuits (who moreover, are not homogeneous and always in agreement, but have a modernist wing – Tyrrell was a Jesuit – and an integralist one – Cardinal Billot was an integralist), there existed and probably still do exist secret integralist and modernist groupings. The identification of Turmel with his pseudonyms has something of the fanciful, too. The Jesuit centre had undoubtedly spread a wide net around him that gradually closed in and finally managed to trap him. It seems that Turmel had protectors within the Roman Congregations, which shows that not all the modernists have been identified, despite the oath taken, and that they are still working in secret. Turmel wrote articles and books under fifteen pseudonyms: Louis Coulange, Henri Delafosse, Armand Dulac, Antoine Dupin, Hippolyte Gallerand, Guillaume Herzog, André Lagard, Robert Lawson, Denys Lenain, Paul Letourneur, Goulven Lézurec, Alphonse Michel, Edmond Perrin, Alexis Vanbeck, Siouville. What happened was that Turmel refuted or praised under one pseudonym articles and books published under another and so on. He was a regular collaborator both for the review *Revue d'histoire des religions* and for the series *Christianisme*, edited by Couchoud and published by Rieder.

Account must also be taken of another article published in the *Civiltà Cattolica* of 20 December 1930: 'The Spirit of "*Action Française*" as Regards "Intelligence" and "Mystique" ', which discusses Jean Héritier's volume *Intelligence et Mystique* (Paris 1930) published as part of the series *Les Cahiers d'Occident* which sets itself the task of disseminating the principles of the *defence of the West*, in the spirit of Henri Massis's well-known book.[97] Massis and his theories are suspect in the eyes of the Jesuits, and, what is more, the contact between Massis and Maurras is public knowledge. The movement led by Massis is to be numbered among those of 'integralist Catholicism' or Catholic reaction. (The *Action Française* movement is also to be counted among those supported by the integralists.)

The birth of integralism in France is to be connected with the *Ralliement* movement championed by Leo XIII; the integralists are those who disobeyed Leo XIII and sabotaged the initiative. Pius X's struggle against *Combisme*[98] seemed to suggest they were right, and he is their pope, as he is the pope of Maurras. Printed as an appendix to Héritier's volume are articles of other authors who deal with the *Ralliement* and who, even on questions of religious history, support Maurras's thesis on the dissolutionary anarchism of Judaic Christianity and the Romanisation of Catholicism.

Q6§195.

58 The Case of Abbé Turmel of Rennes

In his collection of essays *L'Enciclica Pascendi e il modernismo* [*The Encyclical Pascendi and Modernism*], a book published in 1908 or 1909, Fr Rosa devotes a number of 'exceptionally savoury' pages to the 'extraordinary' case of Abbé Turmel; the savour has nothing to do with the elegance and literary merits of the author, a pedestrian scribbler, whose style is even more featureless, flat and dreary than his opponent Buonaiuti, who could himself teach something of the art. Turmel was a modernist who wrote books of a modernist and even totally atheistic nature under various pseudonyms, and then went on to refute them under his own name. Turmel carried on with this game of pseudonyms from 1908 up to 1929, when, by chance, the ecclesiastical authorities stumbled upon quite clear proof of this duplicity. The proofs that led to the abbot being relieved of his duties were not, however, produced straight away, Prof. L. Saltet of the Catholic Institute of Toulouse being, instead, entrusted with the task of providing ample philological-critical-literary proof (see the *Bulletin de Littérature Ecclésiastique* of Toulouse) of Turmel's authorship of a whole series of writings published under as many as fourteen pseudonyms. Turmel was then expelled from the Church. (On this theme, see the other note, further on.)[99] The question of the anonymity and the pseudonyms to which the modernists have had recourse in order to escape immediate measures of repression is dealt with by Buonaiuti in his 1927 book on *Modernismo Cattolico* [*Catholic Modernism*] with a certain degree of sophistry and embarrassed reticence. This 'politicking' tactic undoubtedly harmed Buonaiuti in particular, who was represented by the 'idealists' of *La Voce* as an almost contemptible character. Despite everything, the figure of Buonaiuti is left with a certain aura of moral grandeur and uprightness of character[100] when one thinks that, for more than thirty years, he has been alone in maintaining his position against the Curia and the Jesuits and has been abandoned by his supporters and friends, who either have returned to the fold or have quite decisively opted for the secular camp. Nor is his activity without consequence for the Catholic Church when one bears in mind that his books have had a relatively wide distribution and that the Church has made him repeated offers of compromise.)

Q20§4[iv].

59   Luigi Salvatorelli and Fr Turmel

In the October-December 1932 number of *Cultura* Luigi Salvatorelli writes about Joseph Turmel in his review of the two books *Joseph Turmel, prêtre historien des dogmes* [*Joseph Turmel, Historian Priest of Dogmas*], by Félix Sartiaux, Paris 1931, and *Histoire des dogmes, I, Le péché originel. La rédemption* [*History of Dogmas, I, Original Sin. Redemption.*] by J. Turmel Paris 1931. Sartiaux's book is indispensable for any assessment of the Turmel case.[101] According to Salvatorelli, Turmel never was a modernist in so far as he never 'envisaged the idea of a transformation of the Church and of dogma'. And here is posed the problem, for the purpose of the exact compilation of the notes collected under this heading, of what one should understand by modernist. It is evident that there is no fixed model, lending itself to easy identification, of what comprises 'modernist' and 'modernism', just as no such model exists for any '-ist' or '-ism'. What we have been dealing with is a complex and multi-faceted movement that can stand more than one different reading:
   1) the account the modernists gave of themselves;
   2) that given of them by their adversaries.
The two of these certainly did not coincide.

It may be said that there existed different manifestations of modernism:

1) the politico-social one, which tended to bring the Church back towards the popular classes, thus being favourable to reformist socialism and to democracy, in other words generically to the liberal currents (this manifestation is perhaps the one that has contributed most to spurring on the struggle of the integralist Catholics, who are bound closely to the most reactionary classes, and in particular to the landed aristocracy and the latifundists in general, as is shown by the French example of *Action Française* and the Italian one of the so-called 'Catholic Centre');[102]

2) the 'scientific-religious' one, i.e. one that, as compared with ecclesiastical tradition, favours a new attitude towards 'dogma' and 'historical criticism' and thus represents a tendency towards an intellectual reform of the Church. The struggle between modernists and integralist Catholics was less bitter on this terrain and, indeed, according to the Jesuits, the two forces were often in collusion and alliance, viz. integralist Catholic reviews published articles by modernists (according to *Civiltà Cattolica*, Mons. Benigni's review often published Buonaiuti's anti-Jesuit articles). All this took place behind the scenes, of course, because on stage the struggle had to be presented as especially, rather as solely, a religious one, which does not prevent integralist Catholic support for a self-confessed atheist like Maurras, and does not mean that for Maurras the question could not but be solely political and social.

For the Jesuits, Turmel was <and is> a modernist in the 'scientific' sense (although as regards his conscience he is in fact an atheist, i.e. completely outside the religious field, yet he carries on being a 'priest' for secondary motives, which seems to be a fairly common case among the clergy as the book by Sartiaux and Loisy's *Mémoires*[103] indicate).

What is important to note here is that all three – modernism, Jesuitism and integralism – have meanings that go beyond the narrowly religious definitions: they are 'parties' inside the 'international absolute empire' constituted by the Church of Rome and they cannot avoid posing in religious form problems that are often of a purely worldly nature, problems of 'rule' [*'dominio'*].

Q14§52.

60 Introduction to the Study of Philosophy. Fr Lippert

Cf. Peter Lippert, SJ, *Visione Cattolica del Mondo* (*Die Weltanschauung des Katholizismus*) [*The Catholic View of the World*], trans. Ernesto Peternolli with a preface by M. Bendiscioli ('Modern Catholic Thought'), Brescia 1931.

This book should be read, both for the text by Fr Lippert, one of Germany's leading Jesuit writers, and for the preface by Bendiscioli. The book came out in the series edited by Driesch and Schingnitz, *Metaphysik und Weltanschauung*. Lippert, like the German Jesuits, is concerned with giving a satisfactory answer to the needs that lay at the base of modernism, without being led into those deviations from orthodoxy that characterise modernism, since there is no trace of immanentism in his formulation of the question of Catholicism.[104] Lippert and the German Jesuits do not stray from the dogmas laid down by the Church, with the logical and metaphysical adjuncts of Aristotelian philosophy, nor do they interpret them in any new fashion, but intend rather to *translate* them for modern man into the terminology of modern philosophy, 'to clothe eternal realities in changeable forms' in Lippert's own words.

Q10II§28i.

61 The Encyclicals Against Modern Thought

The first papal encyclical against the political and philosophical manifestations of the modern era (liberalism etc.) was, it seems, Gregory XVI's *Mirari vos* (1832); it was followed by Pius IX's *Quanta Cura*, dated 8 September 1864 and accompanied by the *Syllabus*; the third was Pius X's *Pascendi*, against modernism.

These three are the 'organic' encyclicals against modern thought but they are not in my view the only documents of their kind. For the pre-1864 period the *Syllabus* lists the other encyclicals and various papal documents against modern thought. For the period from '64 to 1907 (8 September, just like the *Syllabus*)[105], I do not recollect if there are any references in *Pascendi* which, moreover, has a particular character of its own, in that modern thought is combated not so much in itself as for the fact that it has managed to penetrate the organisation of the Church and work its way into what, is properly speaking, Catholic scientific activity. But it should not be difficult to find the bibliographical references in the polemical literature. (In *Civiltà Cattolica* the post-1908 manifestations are even more interesting in that they refer to state activities.) At any rate these three encyclicals of 1832, 1864 and 1907 are the most organic and theoretically developed ones and it is to them that reference has to be made in order to define the internal battles between integralists, Jesuits and modernists.

Besides these encyclicals, one must not forget the other 'constructive' ones, of which *On the Condition of the Working Classes* and *On Reconstructing the Social Order*[106] are typical and integrate the great theoretical encyclicals against modern thought, attempting, in their way, to resolve some of the problems bound up with and connected to them. (It must not be forgotten that some of the research for the notes under this heading[107] is linked to that under the heading 'History of Catholic Action'; in other words, in a certain sense the two studies cannot be kept distinct, and it is as such that they must be pursued in detail.)

Q14§20.

62 Past and Present [5]. Papal Encyclicals

A critical-literary examination of the papal encyclicals. Ninety per cent of them consist of a mish-mash of vague, generic quotations whose aim seems to be establish on each and every occasion the continuity of ecclesiastical doctrine from the Gospels down to the current time. The Vatican must keep a formidable file of quotations on all arguments, so when an encyclical has to be compiled, a start is made by

Religion: A Movement and an Ideology

measuring out the necessary doses - so many quotations from the Gospels, so many from the Fathers of the Church, so many from previous encyclicals. The impression one gets is of great coldness. Charity is spoken of, not because such a sentiment is being expressed towards present-day individuals, but because Matthew said so, and Augustine, and 'Our predecessor of blessed memory' and so on. Only when the Pope writes <or speaks> of immediate political issues does one feel a certain warmth.

Q6§163.

63 Roberto Bellarmino

On 13 May 1923 Pius XI conferred the title 'Blessed' on Bellarmino, canonising him later (on the fiftieth anniversary of his entering the priesthood, and thus an especially significant date), together with the Jesuit missionaries who met their death in North America, and finally, in September 1931, declaring him Doctor of the Universal Church.

This particular attention paid to the highest Jesuit authority after Ignatius of Loyola allows us to say that Pius XI, who has been called the Pope of the Missions and the Pope of Catholic Action, must most of all be called the Jesuits' Pope (to say nothing of the Missions and Catholic Action being the twin apples of the Society of Jesus's eye). It may be noted that in the apostolic letter <which exists in translation> declaring Bellarmino Doctor (see the *Civiltà Cattolica* of 7 November 1931), as well as speaking of the Society [*Compagnia*] in general, Bellarmino is called a 'true companion of Jesus'; why 'companion' and not 'soldier' as ought, if one is being precise, to be said? Is the name *Compagnia* [*Company*] just the translation of *Societas* or does it not have a military significance? The Latin word *Societas* cannot have a military meaning (or so it seems to me) but what was Ignatius of Loyola's intention? (Remember Bellarmino's connection with the trial of Galileo).[108] In *Civiltà Cattolica*'s article commenting on the *Apostolic letter* mention is made of the fact that Bellarmino's 'cause' (for beatification and canonisation) had been held up through the 'intrigues and (through) the threats (!) of those ill-advised politicians and adversaries of the papacy, some of them friends of royalist absolutism ("the integralists"), others of demagogic subversion ("the modernists")'. *Civiltà Cattolica* refers to facts dating back to the eighteenth century, but then speaks of 'their wretched successors and present-day imitators'.

(It appears that Bellarmino's beatification in the eighteenth century was one of the elements in the struggle that led to the suppression of the Society by dictate of the Bourbons.)

The Jesuits today see their revenge in the form of the canonisation and conferred 'doctorate' (although the last act of the Pope's coincides with the suppression of the Jesuits in Spain), but caution prevails: 'Certainly no one wishes to exaggerate this event beyond measure, or to over-estimate its importance, significance, opportunity or "actuality" with respect to the present or even more with respect to the unwonted storm – of necessity not only unforeseen but unforeseeable – that blew up when the decree for conferral of the title Doctor was first deliberated and then discussed, etc.'[109]

Q7§88.

F ORGANISED RELIGION IN THE METROPOLITAN COUNTRIES

64 The Italian Risorgimento. Jewish Culture and Consciousness in Italy

In a review in the *Nuova Italia* (20 April 1933) of Cecil Roth's book *Venice* Arnaldo Momigliano makes a number of correct observations on Judaism in Italy. 'The history of the Venetian Jews, like the history of the Jews of any other city in Italy, is in essence precisely the history of the formation of their Italian national consciousness. Neither, should it be noted, did this formation post-date that of Italian national consciousness in general, in such a way that

Religion: A Movement and an Ideology 103

the Jews would have come to insert themselves in an already preconstituted national consciousness. The formation of Italian national consciousness in the Jews runs parallel to the formation of national consciousness in the Piedmontese or the Neapolitans or the Sicilians: it is one moment of the same process and suffices to characterise it. Just as in the period from the seventeenth to the nineteenth century, leaving aside earlier traits, the Piedmontese or the Neapolitans became Italians, so at the same time the Jews living in Italy became Italians. This of course has not stopped them conserving to a greater or a lesser extent Jewish peculiarities within their Italianness, just as becoming Italians for the Piedmontese or Neapolitans did not prevent them from keeping their regional characteristics.'

This thesis, in essence historically correct, is to be compared with that of another Jew, Giacomo Lumbroso, in his book *I moti popolari contro i francesi alla fine del secolo XVIII, 1796-1800* [*The Popular Anti-French Movements at the Close of the Eighteeenth Century, 1796-1800*], Florence 1932, on which subject see *La Critica*, 20 March 1933, pp. 140 *et seq*. Even if the popular movements recorded by Lumbroso are worthy of study and interpretation, to find in them any trace at all of a national spirit is just a joke. In actual fact they were popular only in a manner of speaking and only because of one secondary and petty aspect: the hatred of novelty and the conservative passivism of the backward and barbarised peasant masses. The movements acquired their significance from the clearly reactionary and anti-national or a-national forces that, in full awareness, instigated and more or less openly led them. Only recently have the Jesuits begun to uphold the thesis of the Italianism of the Sanfedistas[110] who simply 'wanted to unify Italy in their own way'.

Attention is drawn in Momigliano's review to another comment worthy of note, namely, that the torment and erratic behaviour of the Jew Leone[111] demonstrated a complex dissatisfaction with Jewish as much as with profane culture which 'is amongst the most important clues that the seventeenth century gives us of the transformation that was taking place in Jewish consciousnesses'.

In Italy there is no anti-semitism exactly for the reasons mentioned by Momigliano:[112] that the national consciousness was and had to be constituted by overcoming the two cultural forms of municipal particularism and Catholic cosmopolitanism, which were closely bound together, and constituted the most characteristic Italian form of a medieval and feudal residue. That the supersession of Catholic cosmopolitanism and thus in reality the birth of a secular spirit, not only distinct from but in conflict with Catholicism, should show itself in the Jews as their becoming a national element, their casting aside their Jewishness [*disebreizzarsi*], seems clear and uncontestable. That is why it may be correct to write, as does Momigliano, that the formation of the Italian national consciousness in the Jews is sufficient to characterise the entire process of formation of Italian national consciousness, as the dissolution of both religious cosmopolitanism and particularism, since, in the Jews, religious cosmopolitanism becomes particularism within the confines of nation states.

Q15§41.

65 Integralist Catholics, Jesuits, Modernists. *Spain

Look at the effect that the religious crisis in Spain has had on the balance of forces within Catholicism. The anti-clerical battle in Spain had the Jesuits as its main target, but it seems to me that it is exactly in Spain that the integralists should have been strong and that the Jesuits ought to have provided a counterweight to these forces. The attempt at an agreement between the Vatican and Alcalá Zamora, thwarted by the Constituent Assembly, ought in fact to have demonstrated the value of the Jesuits' policy by eliminating or sacrificing the integralists (Segura etc.).[113] But the Spanish situation was complicated by the fact that the Jesuits were performing an important capitalist activity through their domination of a number of important tram companies, together with others of a different nature (check the accuracy of these remarks). The Jesuits in Spain have in the past had a particular tradition by way of their struggle against the Inquisition and the Dominicans (look at the significance this struggle had – cf. Lea's book on the Inquisition in Spain).[114]

Q6§164.

66 Catholic Action [12]. France

Special importance attached to French Catholic Action. It is readily apparent that Catholic Action in France can draw upon a much more select and better qualified personnel than in other countries. The Social Weeks focus discussion on themes of a wider-ranging and more topical interest than in other countries. A comparison between the French and Italian Weeks would be interesting. Moreover, the Catholics have an intellectual influence in France like nowhere else, and this influence is better centralised and organised (it is to be understood that this refers to the Catholic sector which, in certain aspects, is restricted in France by the existence of a strong centralisation of secular culture).

On top of this, there has been set up in France the *Union Catholique d'Etudes Internationales* [Catholic Union of International Studies], among whose initiatives is that of a special International Catholic Week. While the annual Assembly of the League of Nations is in session, Catholic personalities from all countries meet in France for a week to discuss international problems, thus contributing to the creation of a concrete unity of thought among Catholics the world over. Under the veil of culture it is evident that we are witnessing a lay Catholic International, separate from the Vatican and constructed on the line of the parliamentary political activity of the popular parties. The 6 May 1933 number of *Civiltà Cattolica* carries a review of the volume containing the main speeches at the third of these International Weeks (*Les grandes activités de la Société des Nations devant la pensée chrétienne* [*The Great Activity of the League of Nations in the Light of Christian Thought*]), the Conference Proceedings of the third International Catholic Week, 14-20 September 1931 (Paris 1932). Note should be taken of the reply given in his lecture by Prof. Halecki of

Warsaw University to the question 'how is it that the Church, after two thousand years of propagating peace, has not yet been able to give us it?' His answer was: 'Christ's teaching and that of His Church is directed individually to the single human being, to each particular soul. It is this truth that explains to us why Christianity can work only slowly on the institutions and on practical collective activity, having to win over one soul after another and beginning this effort anew with every generation.' For *Civiltà Cattolica* this is a 'good response that may be reinforced by the very simple consideration that the pacificatory action of the Church is continually being challenged and annulled by that irreducible (sic) residue of paganism that still survives and inflames the passions of violence. The Church is a good physician and offers healing balm to an infirm society, but this society rejects in whole or in part these medicines.' A very sophisticated reply, not difficult to refute; it is, moreover, in contradiction with other clerical pretensions. When it is to their advantage, the clerical party claim a country is 99 per cent Catholic so it can deduce from this a particular position as regards the right of the Church *vis-à-vis* the state etc. Again, when it is in their interest, they make themselves 'oh, so small' etc. If what Prof. Halecki says were true, the Church's activity over these two thousand years would be a labour of Sisyphus, and would go on being so. But what value ought to be placed on an institution that never builds anything that can carry on from one generation to the next under its own steam, that cannot modify in the slightest the culture and conception of the world of any generation, given that it always has to start again from scratch? The sophism is clear: when it finds it convenient, the Church is identified with society itself (at least with 99 per cent of it), and when not convenient, the Church is solely the ecclesiastical organisation or even just the person of the pope. Then the Church is a 'physician', indicating what medicines society should take, etc. It is thus very curious that the Jesuits should speak of the 'irreducible residue' of paganism: if it is irreducible, it will never disappear, the Church will never be triumphant etc.

Q15§40.

67 Lucien Romier and French Catholic Action [1]

Romier was an invited speaker at the Social Week at Nancy in 1927. There he spoke of the 'deproletarianisation of the multitudes', an argument that was only of indirect relevance to the theme of the Social Week, which was devoted to 'Woman in Society'. On this subject, Fr Danset spoke of the social and moral aspects of 'Rationalisation'.

But is Romier an active member of French Catholic Action, or was it incidental that he took part in this meeting?

The Nancy Social Week of 1927 is of great importance for the history of the politico-social doctrine of Catholic Action. Its conclusions, favourable to the widest participation of women in political life, were approved by Card. Gasparri in the name of Pius XI.[115] The proceedings have been published <Semaines Sociales de France, *La femme dans la société* [*Woman in Society*], Paris 1928>. The volume is indispensable for the study of French political life.

Q5§9.

68 Lucien Romier and French Catholic Action [2]

Recall that in 1925 Romier accepted a seat in Herriot's cabinet of national unity. The head of the recently formed French Catholic parliamentary group also accepted one. Romier was neither deputy nor senator, but political correspondent of *Le Figaro*, a post that he had to give up on agreeing to join Herriot's cabinet. He made his name through his socio-industrial writings; I think he was correspondent for the technical organ of the French industrialists *La Journée industrielle*.

Q5§15.

69 Catholic Action [13]. Catholic Action in Germany and Austria

The weakness of the single national organisations of Catholic Action consists in the fact that their action is limited in scope and continually subject to interference from the internal and international exigencies within each state of the Holy See. To the extent that every national Catholic Action grows and becomes a mass organisation, it tends to become a real and proper party, whose orientations are dictated by the internal necessities of the organisation. This, however, can never become an organic process exactly on account of the intervention of the Holy See. Maybe here is to be sought the reason why Catholic Action has never been particularly welcome in Germany. The Centre[116] was already so well developed as a politico-parliamentary force involved in all the in-fighting going on in Germany that any formation as wide-ranging as Catholic Action and under the strict control of the Episcopate would have compromised the effective power then wielded and the possibilities for development. One should bear in mind the conflict that took place between the Centre and the Vatican when the Vatican wanted the Centre to approve Bismarck's military laws, which were the target of strenuous opposition from the Centre.

A similar development took place in Austria, where clericalism has always been politically strong as a party and has not needed a vast permanent organisation like that of Catholic Action, but simply disorganic electoral flocks under the traditional control of the parish priests.

Q8§129.

70 Relations between the German Centre and the Vatican

For the relationships between the German Centre and the Vatican and therefore for a concrete study of the Vatican's traditional policy in the various countries and the forms it assumes, there is a very interesting article by André Lavedan in the *Revue Hebdomadaire*, summarised in the 15 March 1927 number of the *Rivista d'Italia*. Leo XIII asked the Centre to vote in favour of Bismarck's seven-year law,[117] having had assurances that a satisfactory modification of the politico-ecclesiastical laws would ensue. Franckenstein and

Windthorst did not want to accede to the Vatican request. Of the Centre, only seven voted for the law while 83 abstained.

Q2§20.

71 Catholic Action in Germany [1]

Die Katholische Aktion. Materialen und Akten [*Catholic Action, Materials and Documentation*] by Dr Erhard Schlund, OPM, Munich 1928.

This is a review of Catholic Action in the more important countries together with an exposition of papal doctrine on the subject. A Catholic Action of the common type does not exist in Germany, but it is, rather, the totality of Catholic organisation that is regarded as such. (This means that, in Germany, Catholicism is dominated by Protestantism and does not dare to attack it by means of intense propaganda.) This basis may be used to study how the political base of the 'Centre' is deployed. Cf. also Monsignor Kaller's book, *Unser Laeienapostolat* [*Our Lay Apostolate*], (Leusterdorf am Rhein 1927). Schlund's book tends to introduce and popularise a Catholic Action of the Italian type in Germany, and certainly Pius XI must push in that direction (perhaps cautiously however, since by over-stressing these activities, old struggles and resentments could again come to the fore).

Q5§22.

72 Catholic Action in Germany [2]

On the initiative of the Episcopate, German Catholics founded a 'German Catholic Peace League' in 1919. As regards this League and the successive initiatives undertaken for its development, as well as its programme, see the *Civiltà Cattolica* of 19 January 1929.

In the same number see Pius XI's letter to Cardinal Bertram, the Archbishop of Breslau [Wrocław] on the subject of Catholic Action in Germany, which must be considered a personal intervention by the Pope to give greater impetus to a Catholic Action movement whose organisers, in Germany, are rather lukewarm in their approach. The Pope's letter is a real practico-theoretical programme and is, quite apart from Germany, of general interest. *Civiltà Cattolica* publishes a lengthy commentary on the letter and it is to be understood that this commentary also serves for other countries.

Q5§59.

73 Catholic Action in the United States [1]

The *Civiltà Cattolica* article of 5 January 1929 entitled 'The Electoral Campaign in the United States and its Lessons'. On the Smith candidature for the Presidency.[118]

Civiltà Cattolica records the bitter resistance put up by the Protestant churches against Smith and speaks of a 'war of religion'. There is no mention of the position adopted by Smith in regard to the Pope in his famous letter (cf. Fontaine's book on the Holy See etc.), which constitutes an element of Catholic Americanism. (Catholic stance against prohibition and in favour of the farmers.) One can see that every concentrated action taken by Catholics provokes such a reaction that the results are inferior to the strength they say they possess, hence dangers of any action on a concentrated national scale: has it been a mistake for the Catholics to base themselves on a traditional party, like the Democrats? A mistake to show religion as being bound to one particular party? On the other hand, given the present American system, could they found a party of their own? America is an interesting terrain for studying the current phase of Catholicism both as a cultural and as a political element.

Q5§57.

74 Catholic Action in the United States [2]

Of interest is the correspondence from the United States published in the *Civiltà Cattolica* of 20 September 1930.

Catholics often have recourse to the example of the United States to call to mind their high degree of unity and religious fervour as compared with a Protestant world that is divided up into all sorts of sects and continuously worn away by the tendency to lapse into indifference and an areligious outlook, whence the truly remarkable number of citizens who state in the censuses that they have no religion. It emerges from this correspondence, however, that even among Catholics indifference is not rare. Data are published from a series of articles that have appeared in the 'famous' *Ecclesiastical Review* of Philadelphia over the last few months. One parish priest states that he remained completely in the dark about 44 per cent of his parishioners for a great number of years, despite repeated attempts by him and by his assistants to arrive at an exact census. In all sincerity, he admits that about half his flock remained totally outside his care, and neither did he have any contact apart from that coming from the irregular attendance at mass and the sacraments. These are facts which, according to the parish priests themselves, are confirmed in almost all the parishes in the United States.

At their own expense, the Catholics maintain 7,664 parochial schools attended by 2,201,942 pupils under the guidance of both male and female religious. There remain another 2,275,000 pupils (i.e. more than 50 per cent) who 'either from laziness on the part of the parents or for reasons of distance are forced to attend the non-religious, government schools where never a word is heard of God, of one's duties towards the Creator and not even of the existence of the immortal soul'.

An element of indifferentism comes out of the data on mixed marriages: '20 per cent of families legally joined in mixed marriages neglect Mass if the father does not belong to the Catholic faith; when the mother is not a Catholic, statistics give 40 per cent. Further, these parents totally neglect the Christian education of their offspring.' An attempt was made to restrict the number of these mixed marriages, and even to have them banned, but conditions 'worsened' as the 'recalcitrants' in these cases left the Church (together with their offspring), entering into 'invalid' unions; these cases amount to 61 per cent if the father is 'heretical' and 94 per cent if the mother is a 'heretic'. Generosity was therefore shown: by refusing the dispensation for a mixed marriage <if the woman was a Catholic> the loss was 58 per cent but if dispensation was granted, the loss was 'only' 16 per cent.

It appears, then, that the number of Catholics <in the United States> is just a statistical number that comes from the censuses, i.e. it is harder for people of Catholic origin to state they have no religion than it is for those of Protestant origin. In short, there is more hypocrisy. From this, one can judge how exact and how honest are the statistics of those countries with a Catholic majority.

Q6§187.

75 Catholic Action [14]. Catholicism and Social Democracy in Britain

For the real significance in immediate day-to-day and in more mediated politics of Pio XI's encyclical *Quadragesimo Anno* <written to mark the fortieth anniversary of the encyclical *Rerum Novarum*>[119] as regards the relations between Catholicism and social democracy, one must bear in mind the attitude expressed by the English Cardinal Bourne in the speech he made in Edinburgh (first half of June 1931) on the Labour Party.[120] Cf. British Catholic papers of the time.

Q7§69.

76 British Labourism. The Archbishop of Canterbury and Labourism

During the 1931 British elections, the Labour candidate W.T. Colyer claimed in a meeting that the Archbishop of Canterbury was one of the subscribers to the Labour Party fund. When the Archbishop was asked whether this was true, his secretary replied 'The Archbishop directs me to say that he was a subscribing member of the Labour Party from 1919 to 1925 or 1926 when he found that growing uneasiness with the movement and the party's spirit and temper made a continuance of such membership impossible.' (Cf. the *Manchester Guardian Weekly*, 30 October 1931, p. 357.)

Q7§94.

77 The Ecumenical Movement

The XVth Milan Social Week <September 1928> dealt with the question 'True Religious Unity'; the proceedings of the conference were printed under this title by the *Vita e Pensiero* publishing house (Milan 1928). The argument is dealt with from the Vatican point of view, following the guidelines of the January 1928 encyclical *Mortalium Animos*[121] against the ecumenical movement of the Protestants, who would like to create a type of federation of the different Christian sects, with all of them having the same rights.

This Protestant offensive against Catholicism comprises two essential aspects: 1) the Protestant churches are tending to put a brake on the trend towards disintegration in their own ranks (which continually give rise to new sects); 2) they come together among themselves and, by obtaining a certain consensus from the Orthodox Churches, lay siege to Catholicism in order to try and get it to renounce its primacy and to marshal an imposing Protestant united front in the struggle rather than a multitude of churches, sects and tendencies of differing importance which, if taken singly, would be no great match for the tenacious and unified Catholic missionary initiative. The question of the unity of the Christian churches is a formidable post-war problem worthy of the greatest attention and careful study.

Q5§17.

78 Ecumenical Movements

Nathan Söderblom, the Lutheran Archbishop of Uppsala in Sweden, advocates an *evangelical catholicity*,[122] consisting in a direct adherence to Christ. Prof. Friedrich Heiler, formerly a Roman Catholic, and author of the book *Der Katholizmus, seine Idee und seine Erscheinung* [*The Ideas and Appearance of Catholicism*], Munich 1923, has the same leanings, which means that the ecumenical movements have indeed had some success.

Q3§164 (excerpt).

79 Religious Movements. The Ecumenical Movement and its Subsidiary Organisation

Examination to be made of the *ecumenical movement* and its subsidiary organisation, the 'World Alliance for Promoting International Friendship Through the Churches'. The ecumenical movement is significant for the following reasons:

1) because the Protestant churches tend not only to unite with one another but also, through this union, to acquire a strength for proselytising;
2) of the Protestant churches only the American ones, and to a lesser extent the British ones, were able to expand their proselytism, the force behind it being passed on to the ecumenical movement, even if this latter is under the leadership of Continental European, especially Norwegian and German, elements;
3) union of the Protestant churches may halt the increasing trend to scission present among them;
4) the Orthodox Churches participate in the ecumenical movement as leading centres in their own right.

The movement has had a thoroughly disturbing influence on the Catholic Church, whose massive organisation, centralisation and single command structure put it at an advantage in the slow but sure task of absorbing heretics and schismatics. Ecumenical union has disturbed this monopoly and faces Rome with a united front. The Roman Church furthermore cannot agree to enter the movement on like terms with the other churches and this works in favour of ecumenical propaganda which can reproach Rome with not wanting the union of all Christians because of its own particular interests and so on.

Q5§134.

80 Religion and Politics

An argument worth studying is the following: whether there exists a relationship, and if so what, between the religious unity of a country and the multiplicity of parties and, *vice versa*, between the relative unity of parties and the multiplicity of churches and religious sects. It may be observed that in the United States, where there are only two or at most three political parties with any clout, there exist hundreds of churches and religious sects; in France, where there is a quite remarkable religious unity, there are scores of parties. What makes one pause to think is the case of tsarist Russia, where either political parties normally and legally did not exist or were suppressed, while there tended to be a multiplicity of religious sects of the most dyed-in-the-wool fanatical sort.

This might be explained by noting that both the Party and Religion are forms of world outlook and that religious unity is apparent just as political unity is; religious unity hides a real multiplicity of conceptions of the world that find their expression in the parties, since there exists a religious 'indifferentism', just as political unity hides a multiplicity of tendencies that find their expression in the religious sects and so on. Everyone tends to have a sole organic and systematic world outlook but, since there are many deep-rooted cultural differentiations, society presents a bizarre kaleidoscope of currents that give a religious or a political colouring according to historical tradition.

Q8§131ii.

G RELIGIOUS CULTURE IN OTHER MAJOR COUNTRIES

81 Ecumenicalism and Protestant Propaganda in South America

Cf. the article 'Protestantism in the United States and Latin

America' in the *Civiltà Cattolica* of 1 March, 15 March and 1 April 1930. Very interesting study of the expansionist tendencies of North American Protestants, on the organisational methods of this expansion and on the Catholics' reaction to them.

It is of interest to note that, at the world level, the Catholics find their only – and often victorious – competitors as regards propaganda among American Protestants, despite the fact that there is no strong religious feeling in the United States (the majority of those questioned in the census state they have no religion); the European Protestant churches show little or no tendency to expand. Another noteworthy fact, after the splits that have taken place in the Protestant churches, is that we are now witnessing attempts at unification through the ecumenical movement. (The Salvation Army, English in origin and organisation, must not however be overlooked.)

Q2§135.

82   South American Culture

Cf. the article 'United States Protestantism and Protestant Evangelisation in Latin America' in the *Civiltà Cattolica* of 18 October 1930. The article is interesting and instructive for understanding how Catholics and Protestants are battling it out among themselves. Naturally, the Catholics present Protestant missions as the vanguard of United States economic and political penetration and combat this by stirring up national feeling. Protestants reprove Catholics for the same thing, presenting the Pope and the Church as terrestrial powers cloaking themselves in religion, etc.

Q6§190.

83   Jesuitism in South America

Filippo Meda, *Statisti cattolici* [*Catholic Statesmen*], Naples 1926. Six biographies: Daniel O'Connell, García Moreno, Ludwig Windthorst, Auguste Beernaert, Georg Hertling,

Antonio Maura. Representatives of clerical conservatism (Italian clerico-moderates), i.e. of the pre-history of modern Catholic popularism. Indispensable book for reconstructing the history of Catholic Action. The biography of García Moreno (Venezuela, I think)[123] is also of interest for understanding some aspects of the ideological struggles of the former Spanish and Portuguese American colonies, which are still going through a primitive *Kulturkampf*[124] period, viz. one in which the modern state still has a battle on against the clerical and feudal past.

It is of interest to note the contradiction that exists in South America between the modern world of the big commercial cities of the coast and the primitivism of the interior, a contradiction that gets extended because of the existence on one hand of great masses of native people and on the other of European immigrants who are less easily assimilated than in North America. Though Jesuitism is an advance compared to idolatry, it is a hindrance to the development of modern civilisation as typified by the great coastal cities. It serves as a means of government to keep in power the traditional little oligarchies, who therefore put up only a bland and feeble fight. Freemasonry and the positivist church are the secular religions and ideologies of the urban petty bourgeoisie, which attract the support of that so-called anarcho-syndicalism whose intellectual pasture is found in anti-clerical scientism. (Problem of rousing the native masses to participate in national and political life: did something of this type happen in Mexico through the action of Obregón and Calles?)[125]

Q1§107.

84 Catholicism in India

Upadhyaya Brahmabandhav, the celebrated Catholic *Sannyasi*(?),[126] who wanted to convert India to Catholicism through the Hindus themselves, by Christianising those parts of Hinduism capable of being absorbed; the Vatican disapproved of his nationalist *excesses*. (When did the Upadhyaya carry out his preaching? I think the Vatican would be more tolerant today.) For the question of Christianity in India look at the phenomenon of Sadhu Sundar Singh:[127] cf. the *Civiltà Cattolica* of 7 and 21 July 1928.

Q3§164 (excerpt).

85 Rebel India

Gabriele Gabbrielli, 'Rebel India' in the *Nuova Antologia* of 1 August 1929. (This G.G. is a specialist in writing notes and articles for *Nuova Antologia*, and probably for some daily paper, against the activity of the Ispolcom.[128] He uses material published in Geneva by the *Entente contre la TI*, especially that appearing in its *Monthly Bulletin* and has vague sympathies with Henri Massis's movement for the defence of the West.[129] The sympathies remain generic since, for Massis, the hegemon[130] of Catholic-Latin union cannot be other than France, while for Gabbrielli on the other hand it must be Italy. On the subject of Massis and the defence of the West, one must remember that Fr Rosa gives it short shrift in his reply to Ugo Ojetti, seeing in it the danger of a deviation, to the point of being an out and out deviation, from Roman orthodoxy.)

Four million six hundred and seventy five thousand square kilometres, 319 million inhabitants, 247 million inhabitants in the fifteen enormous provinces, occupying half the total territory, under the direct administration of the British government while the other half is divided into 700 tributary states. Five main religions, an infinite number of sects, 150 dialects and languages all told; castes; illiteracy predominant; peasantry constitutes 80 per cent of the population; <slavery of women, pauperism, endemic famine>. During the war 985,000 Indians mobilised.

Relations between Gandhi and Tolstoy in the 1908-1910 period (cf. Romain Rolland, 'Tolstoy and Gandhi' in the 1928 number of the journal *Europe* wholly devoted to Tolstoy). The entire article is of interest in the absence of other information.

Q5§89.

86 Non-Resistance and Non-Co-operation

... Contemporary history offers a model for understanding Italy's past. There is today a European cultural consciousness and there exists a whole series of declarations by intellectuals and politicians who maintain that a European union is necessary. It may also be said that the historical process tends towards this union and that there are many material forces that will only be able to develop within this union. If this union is brought to fruition in x years, the word 'nationalism' will have the same archeological value as 'municipalism' has at present.

Another contemporary fact that explains the past is Gandhi's 'non-resistance and non-co-operation'. These can help understand the origins of Christianity and the reasons for its development in the Roman Empire. The Tolstoyan movement had the same origins in tsarist Russia, but it did not become a 'popular belief' like Gandhi's. Through Tolstoy, Gandhi too links up with primitive Christianity and in India one again sees a form of primitive Christianity that the Catholic and Protestant world can no longer even manage to comprehend. The relationship between Gandhi's movement and the British Empire is similar to that between Christianity-Hellenism and the Roman Empire. Both are countries of ancient civilisation, disarmed and technically (militarily) inferior, dominated by technically developed countries (the Romans had developed military and governmental technique), though the population of these latter was negligible. That the many who consider themselves civilised should be dominated by the few, regarded as less civilised but materially invincible, defines the relationship primitive Christianity-Gandhianism. The consciousness of the material impotence of a great mass against a small number of oppressors leads to purely spiritual values being upheld etc., to passivity, to non-resistance, to non-co-operation, which however is in fact a dismal and dilute form of resistance, the mattress up against the bullet.

The popular religious movements of the Middle Ages too,

Franciscanism and so on, come into this same relationship of the political impotence of the great masses when faced with numerically fewer but warlike and centralised oppressors: the 'humiliated and offended' dig in behind primitive evangelical pacifism in the naked 'exposure' of their 'human nature', misunderstood and down-trodden despite their affirmations of equality and brotherhood in God the father and so on. In the history of medieval heresies, Francis has his own quite distinct individual position – he does not want to take up the fight, he does not even think in terms of any struggle, different from the other innovators (Waldo, etc. <and the Franciscans themselves>). His position is portrayed in an anecdote recounted in the ancient Franciscan texts. 'To a Dominican theologian who asked him how he should understand the word of Ezekiel "If you do not warn him [the wicked man] to give up his wicked ways, I will hold you responsible for his death," Francis responded thus "the servant of God must behave in his life and his love of virtue so that *through the light of good example and the unction of the word he should succeed in being a reproof to all the unrighteous*; and thus it will happen, I believe, that the splendour of his life and the aura of his good fame will be a testimony to the wrongdoers of their iniquity ..." ' (Cf. Antonio Viscardi, 'Francis of Assisi and the Law of Evangelical Poverty', in the *Nuova Italia* of January 1931.)[131]

Q6§78 (excerpt).

87 Religiosity in India

Giuseppe Tucci's article 'The Religiosity of India' in the *Nuova Antologia* of 16 September 1928. Interesting article, critical of all the commonplaces that one normally hears about India and the Indian 'soul', about mysticism, etc. India is going through a spiritual crisis; the new (critical spirit) is not yet so widely diffused as to form a 'public opinion' that can be opposed to the old – superstition among the popular classes, hypocrisy, characterlessness of the upper, so-called educated, classes. In actual fact in India too, public attention is absorbed in practical questions and interests. (It is obvious that in India, given its centuries-old social torpor and the ossified stratifications of society, and given also, as happens in the great agrarian countries, the great number of middle-level intellectuals, especially of the ecclesiastical type, the crisis is bound to last a long time and a great revolution will be needed just to begin to resolve it.) Many of Tucci's observations on India could also be made about many other countries and other religions. To be borne in mind.

Q2§86.

88 Encyclopaedic Notions [2]. Theopanism

Term used by the Jesuits <for example> to indicate a characteristic of the Hindu religion (but does theopanism not mean pantheism, or is it instead used to indicate a particular religious-mythological conception, in order to distinguish it from the philosophical-superior 'pantheism'?). Cf. the article entitled 'Hinduism' (*Civiltà Cattolica*, 5 July 1930, pp.17-8): 'For Hinduism, there is no substantial difference between God, man, animal and plant: everything is God, not only in the beliefs of the lower classes, amongst whom such a pantheism is conceived of animistically, but also in the higher classes and people of good education, in whose way of thinking the divine essence is revealed in the theopanistic sense, as the world of souls and of visible objects. Although in essence the error is the same, none the less, in the way of conceiving and expressing it, one may distinguish *pantheism*, which imagines the world as an absolute being, an object of religious worship ("everything is God"), from *theopanism*, which conceives of God as the true-spiritual reality from which everything emanates: "God becomes everything", necessarily, incessantly, without beginning and without end. Theopanism is (with only a few other dualistic systems) the most common way in which Hindu philosophy conceives God and the world.'

Q6§178.

89 Brief Notes on Indian Culture

From the interview that Aldous Huxley gave to F. Lefèvre (*Nouvelles Littéraires*, 1 November 1930[132]): '*What is your opinion of the revolts and all the events in India?* – I think that they've got civilisation off on the wrong foot there. Top class universities have been created but no elementary schools. They thought it was enough to educate a caste which would then be able to raise the standard of the masses, but I don't see that the results obtained have been very happy ones. Those who have benefited from western civilisation are all Kshatriyas or Brahmins.[133] Once they have been educated, they no longer work for a living and become dangerous. These are the people who want to take over the government. It's after visiting India that I got a better understanding of the difference you could have in the Middle Ages between a *villein* and a *cardinal*. India is a country where the superiority of divine right is still accepted by the *untouchables* who themselves recognise their own unworthiness.'

There is a measure of truth here, but very little. How can elementary schools be created for the masses in India unless the appropriate personnel has first been trained? And to do this, is it not necessary first of all to turn to the already existent intellectual classes? And again, can the sole fact that intellectual groupings are unemployed create a situation like that in India? (Recall Loria's notorious theory about unemployed intellectuals.[134]) Are these intellectuals 'isolated' or have they not rather become the expression of the middle and industrialist classes that India's economic development has produced?

Q6§32.

90 Intellectuals. On Indian Culture

Cf. the series of articles 'Hindu Philosophical Systems and Sects' published in *Civiltà Cattolica* in July 1930 and the following months. The Jesuits pose this problem: Catholicism in India manages to make converts only, and even so to a limited extent, among the lower castes. Indian intellectuals are very resistant to propaganda and the Pope has said that work has to be done among them too, the more so in that the masses of the people would convert if important nuclei of intellectuals converted. (The Pope knows the mechanism of cultural reform of the popular-peasant masses better than many secular left elements: he knows that one cannot convert a great mass in molecular fashion but that, to hasten the process, it is necessary either to conquer the natural leaders of the great masses, in other words the intellectuals, or to form groups of intellectuals of a new type, hence the creation of native bishops.) From this stems the need for an exact knowledge of the ideologies and ways of thinking of these intellectuals so as to have a better understanding of the organisation of cultural and moral hegemony in order to destroy or assimilate it. These studies by the Jesuits have therefore their particular objective importance, in that they they are not 'abstract' and academic, but aimed at concrete practical goals. They are of great use for a knowledge of the moral and cultural hegemony exercised in great Asiatic countries such as India and China.

Q7§71.

91 The Question of the Intellectuals

When did cultural life begin in the various countries of the world and of Europe? How can what we divide into 'ancient', 'medieval' and 'modern history' be applied to the various countries? Yet these different phases of world history have been absorbed by modern intellectuals, even by those coming from countries that have only recently become part of cultural life. This fact is however a source of other friction. The civilisations of China and India are resisting the introduction of western civilisation, which in one form or another is still going to end up by winning. Is it possible that, at a stroke, these will decay to the condition of folklore? Of superstition? May this fact however not hasten the rupture between people and intellectuals and the expression by the people of new intellectuals formed in the sphere of historical materialism?

Q7§62.

92 Brief Notes on Chinese Culture [1][135]

In the 23 October 1927 number of *Marzocco* Alberto Castellani draws attention to a book *Die Gedankenwelt des chinesischen Kulturkreises* [*The Conceptual World of Chinese Cultural Groupings*], Munich-Berlin 1927 (*Chinese Philosophy in European – and Japanese – Guise*) by Alfred Forke. Forke is professor of Chinese language and civilisation at the University of Hamburg and is well-known as a specialist in the study of Chinese philosophy.

Chinese philosophy is difficult for a westerner to study for several reasons:
1) Chinese philosophers did not write down their thought as systematic treatises; it was the disciples who collected the teachings of their masters, rather than the masters who wrote for their eventual disciples;
2) philosophy in the proper sense was intertwined with and almost suffocated in the three great religious currents – Confucianism, Taoism, Buddhism; thus to the eyes of a western non-specialist the Chinese often appeared either not to have a real and proper philosophy or to have three philosophical religions (however this fact that philosophy was intertwined with religion has its significance from the cultural point of view and characterises the historical position of the Chinese intellectuals).

Forke has in fact attempted to present Chinese thought in European form, in other words he has liberated what really constitutes philosophy from combinations and heterogeneous associations with other matters, thus making it possible to draw parallels between European and Chinese thought. Ethics is the most flourishing part of this construction while Logic is less important 'because even the Chinese themselves have always had more an instinctive and

Religion: A Movement and an Ideology 125

intuitive sense than an exact concept of it as a science'. (For the cultural aspect, this point is very important.) Only a few years ago, a Chinese author, Prof. Hu Shih,[136] in his *Storia della Filosofia Cinese* [*History of Chinese Philosophy*], Shanghai 1919, assigned a pre-eminent position to Logic, bringing it once more to the surface from ancient texts whose teachings he attempted, not without some effort, to reveal. Perhaps the rapid invasion of Confucianism, Taoism and Buddhism, which have no interest for the problems of logic, may have hindered its future as a science. 'The fact is that the Chinese have never had a work like the Gautama's *Nyàya* or Aristotle's *Organon*.' China thus lacks a philosophical discipline of 'knowledge' as such (*Erkenntnistheorie*), of which Forke finds only tendencies.

Forke further goes on to examine Chinese philosophy as it has branched out abroad, especially in Japan. Together with other cultural forms, Japan has also taken philosophy from China, at the same time as giving it a certain character of its own. The Japanese do not have metaphysical and speculative tendencies like the Chinese (they are 'pragmatist' and empiricist). When, however, Chinese philosophers are translated into Japanese, they acquire a greater perspicuity. (This means that the Japanese have taken from Chinese thought what was useful for their culture, somewhat like the Romans did with the Greeks.)[137]

Castellani has just published *La dottrina del Tao ricostruita sui testi ed esposta integralmente* [*The Doctrine of Taoism: a Global Outline as Reconstructed from the Texts*], Bologna 1927, and *La regola celeste di Lao-Tse* [*The Celestial Rule of Lao-Tzu*], Florence 1927. Castellani compares Lao-Tzu and Confucius (though I do not know in which of these books): 'Confucius is the Northern Chinese, noble, cultured, speculative; Lao-Tzu, fifty years his elder, is the Southerner, popular, bold, imaginative. Confucius is the statesman; Lao-Tzu advises against public involvement. The former cannot live if he is not in contact with the government, the latter flees from any civil association and takes no part in its affairs. Confucius is content to call the rulers and the people to the example of the good old days: Lao-Tzu undoubtedly dreams of the age of universal innocence and the virginal state of nature. The former is the courtier for whom etiquette is important; the latter is the solitary person to whom the *sharp word* comes readily. For Confucius, full to the brim with forms, rules, rituals, the human will enters in an essential way into the production and determination of *political affairs*. Lao-Tzu on the other hand believes that all affairs, without exception, are self-constructions, outside and without reference to our will and that, in themselves, they all have a rhythm that is unaltered and unalterable by any intervention of ours. Nothing for him is more ridiculous than the typical Confucian, a nosey little busybody believing in the importance and almost the specific weight of every gesture he makes; nothing for him is meaner than this short-sighted and presumptuous little animal, so far from Taoism, who thinks he is a leader and is instead being led, who thinks he has things in the palm of his hand while it is instead himself who is being held.' (This passage is taken from an article 'Chinese Knowledge' by A. Faggi in the 12 June 1927 number of *Marzocco*.) 'Not to do' is the principle of Taoism; it is precisely the 'Tao', the 'way'.

The Chinese state form. The absolute monarchy was founded in China in 221 BC and lasted until 1912, notwithstanding changes of dynasty, foreign invasions, etc. This is the point of interest; every new master found a ready-made organism waiting, which he took over by taking power at the centre. Continuity is thus a phenomenon of death and passivity in the Chinese people. Evidently, even after 1912, the situation has still remained relatively stationary in the sense that the general apparatus has remained almost intact. The mandarins have been substituted by the tu-chun[138] military and every so often one of these attempts the formal reunification of the country by seizing central power. The importance of the Kuomintang would have been much greater if they really had posed the question of an All-China Convention. But now the movement has been unleashed it is difficult to my way of thinking for a lasting order to be reconstituted without a thorough-going national mass revolution.

Q5§23 (excerpt).

93 Brief Notes on Chinese Culture [2]

From the article 'The Chinese Reformer Suen Wen and his Political and Social Theories' in the *Civiltà Cattolica* of 4 May and 18 May 1929. 'The nationalist party has promulgated decree upon decree to honour Suen Wen, the most important of these being the one prescribing the "Monday ceremony". In all schools, offices, military posts, in any institution that in some way or other belongs to the nationalist party, everyone assembles each Monday in front of the portrait of the "Father of the Country" and, all together, bow their heads three times. Then they proceed to the reading of his "political Testament" containing the quintessence of his doctrines, and there follow three minutes of silence for meditating over its great principles. This ceremony is carried out in every important gathering.' In all schools it is obligatory to study the *Sen Min-chu-i* (triple demism),[139] even in Catholic or any religious denominational schools, as a *sine qua non* for their legal existence. The apostolic delegate to China, Mons. Celso Costantini, adopted a position on these legal obligations in a letter to Fr Pasquale D'Elia, SJ, an Italian missionary and member of the Sinological Office of Zi-Ka-Wei. The letter was published at the beginning of the book *Le triple démisme de Sun Wen* [*Sun Wen's Triple Demism*], translated, annotated and introduced by Pascal M. D'Elia, SJ, Shanghai 1929.

Costantini does not believe that Sun has been 'deified'. 'As for bowing the head before the portrait of Sun Yat-Sen, Christian pupils have nothing to worry about. In itself and by its nature, bowing the head has no superstitious significance. The government's intentions are that this ceremony is nothing other than the merely civil respect paid to a man considered the Father of his Country. It may be that it is excessive, but it is in no way idolatrous (the government itself being atheist) and no sacrifice is connected with it. If, somewhere, unauthorised sacrifices take place, this is to be regarded as superstition and Christians are not to take part in any way whatsoever. Our function is in no way to create an erroneous consciousness, but to shed light on where our pupils might have some doubt about the meaning of such civil ceremonies.' As to the obligatory teaching of triple demism, Costantini continues: 'In my own personal view it is legitimate, if not to teach, then at least to explain the principles of Dr Sun Yat Sen's triple demism in the public schools. It is a question not of an optional subject but one imposed by the government as a *sine qua non*. There are a number of things that are good, or at least not bad, about triple demism which correspond to or at least can be reconciled with Catholic sociology (*Rerum novarum* [*On the Condition of the Working Classes*], *Immortale Dei* [*On the Christian Constitution of States*], *Social Code*).[140] In our schools we must see to having the explanation of this question put in the hands of Catholic teachers who have had an adequate training in Christian sociology and doctrine. Certain things are to be explained and corrected ...'

The *Civiltà Cattolica* article summarises the Catholic position as regards the doctrines of Chinese nationalism, a position that, as may be seen, is active because it tends to the creation of a 'Catholic nationalistic' trend through a particular interpretation of the doctrines themselves. From the political historical point of view it would be useful to see how the Jesuits have arrived at this result by looking at all the *Civiltà Cattolica* publications regarding Chinese events from 1925 onwards. In his book, by foreseeing the objection that could be made against him by those of his readers who would have preferred to keep quiet about these new ideas, rather than giving them publicity, Fr D'Elia 'correctly (...) replies: "Not to speak of these questions does not mean resolving them. Whether one wishes it or not, our Chinese Catholic brethren will know of them through hostile and tendentious commentaries. It seems that there is less danger in instructing them ourselves by directly proposing Sun Wen's doctrine to them. Let us make the effort to show that the Chinese can be good Catholics, not only by remaining Chinese but also by taking account of some of the theories of Sun Wen".'

Q5§51.

94 Brief notes on Japanese Culture [1]

The 1 June 1929 number of *Nuova Antologia* contains the introduction ('The National Religion of Japan and the Religious Policy of the Japanese State') to Raffaele Pettazzoni's volume *La mitologia giapponese* [*Japanese Mythology*] in the series 'Texts and Documents for a History of Religions' that Zanichelli are publishing in Bologna. Why has Pettazzoni given his book the title *Mythology*? There is a certain difference between 'Religion' and 'Mythology' and it would be advisable to keep the two words quite separate. Has religion in Japan become a simple 'mythology', i.e. a purely 'artistic' or 'folkloristic' element, or does it rather still have the value of a conception of the world that is still alive and operative? Since it appears from the introduction that it is this latter value that Pettazzoni attaches to Japanese religion, the title is ambiguous. I am noting from the introduction a number of elements that will be of use for the study of a 'Japanese' paragraph among those collected together under the heading 'intellectuals'.

Buddhism was introduced into Japan in 552 AD. Until then Japan had known just one religion, its own national religion. From 552 to the present day, Japanese religious history has been defined by the relations and the interference between this national religion and Buddhism (a type of extra-national and supra-national religion like Christianity and Islam). Christianity, introduced into Japan by the Jesuits in 1549 (Francis Xavier), was eradicated by violence in the first decades of the seventeenth century and then reintroduced by Protestant and Catholic missionaries in the second half of the nineteenth century, but has not on the whole had any great importance. After the introduction of Buddhism, the national religion adopted the Sino-Japanese name Shinto from 'way (Chinese: *tao*) of the gods (Chinese: *Shen*)' while *butsu-do* indicated Buddhism (*do*-way, *butsu*-Buddha). In Japanese one says *Kami-no-michi* (Kami-divinity) for *Shinto*. Kami does not mean 'god' in the western sense, but more generally 'divine beings' who also include deified ancestors. (Not only Buddhism but also ancestor-worship was introduced from China and this latter seems to have been more intimately incorporated into the national religion.) Shintoism is, however, basically a religion of nature, a cult of the divinity (Kami) of nature, in which pride of place is given to the goddess of the sun *Amaterasu*, the god of hurricanes *Susanowo*, the couple Heaven and Earth, namely *Izanagi* and *Izanami*, etc. It is of interest that Shintoism represents a type of religion which has completely disappeared from the modern western world, but which used to be common amongst the civilised peoples of antiquity (the national and polytheistic religions of the Egyptians, Babylonians, Indians, Greeks, Romans and so on). *Amaterasu* is a divinity like Osiris or Apollo or Artemis and it is of interest that a civilised modern people like the Japanese believe and adore such a divinity. (Perhaps things are not however quite as simple as they may appear.) Yet Buddhism, a type of supra-national religion, exists side by side with this national religion, and for this reason one can say that in Japan, too, there has been fundamentally the same religious history as in the West (with Christianity). Indeed it is the case that the expansions of Christianity and Buddhism took place at the same time in their respective zones and, again, the Christianity that spread throughout Europe was not that of Palestine but that of Rome or Byzantium (with Latin or Greek for the liturgy), just like the Buddhism that spread throughout Japan was not that of India but that of China, with Chinese for the liturgy. But, contrary to Christianity, Buddhism let other pre-existing national religions continue (in Europe national tendencies showed themselves within Christianity).

Buddhism was initially accepted by the educated classes in Japan together with Chinese civilisation (but did Chinese civilisation bring just Buddhism?). A religious syncretism (Buddhism-Shintoism) took place. Elements of Confucianism. In the eighteenth century, there was a reaction against this syncretism in the name of national religion which culminated in 1868 in the advent of modern Japan. [Shintoism was] declared the state religion. Persecution of Buddhism. But only for a short time. In 1872 Buddhism was recognised officially and given equal status with Shintoism as

Religion: A Movement and an Ideology 131

much in the roles they played – principally the pedagogical one of educating the people in the feelings and principles of patriotism, civic spirit and loyalty – as in law, with the suppression of the 'Shinto Office' and the institution of a ministry for religion, having jurisdiction as much over Shintoism as over Buddhism. But in 1875, the government changed its policy yet again. The two religions were separated and [Shintoism] came to take on a special and unique position. Various bureaucratic provisions, coming one after another, culminated in the elevation of Shintoism to a patriotic and national institution, with the official renunciation of its religious character (it became – it seems – an institution similar to the Roman cult of the Emperor, but without a religious character in the strict sense, so even a Christian can practise it). The Japanese can belong to any religion, but they must bow before an image of the Emperor. State Shinto thus became separate from the Shinto of the religious sects. Bureaucratically, too, there was a sanction. There exists today an 'Office for religions' within the Ministry of Education for the various churches of popular Shintoism, for the various Buddhist and Christian churches and an 'Office for shrines' for state Shintoism in the Ministry of the Interior. According to Pettazzoni this reform was due to the mechanical application of western constitutions to Japan: in other words it was to assert the principle of religious freedom and the equality of all religions in the eyes of the state and to raise Japan from the position of inferiority and backwardness that Shintoism, as a religion, conferred on it as compared with the type of religion current in the West.

It seems to me that Pettazzoni's criticism is artificial (look at what is happening in China regarding Sun Yat Sen and the three principles: a type of areligious state cult is being created with – it seems to me – Sun's picture being the subject of a cult similar to that of the Emperor of Japan). Among the people and among persons of culture, too, the consciousness and feeling of Shinto as a religion lives on, however (and this is natural, but to me the importance of the Reform[141] seems undeniable, tending consciously or otherwise to the formation of a new secular consciousness in forms as paradoxical as may be). (This discussion on whether state Shintoism is a religion or not is in my opinion the most important part of the cultural problem in Japan, but such a discussion certainly cannot be carried on for Christianity.)

Q5§50.

95 Brief Notes on Japanese Culture [2]

Cf. the other note on religions in Japan *vis-à-via* the state,[142] on the reforms brought about in Shintoism that, while on one hand, has been reduced to a popular religion (or superstition), on the other, has been deprived of the element constituted by the 'cult of the Emperor', which has become an element in itself and ordained a civic duty, a moral coefficient of state unity. Look at how this reform was created, given its great importance and ties with the birth and development of parliamentarism and democracy in Japan. After the extension of the suffrage (when and in what form?) every election, with the shifts in the political forces of the parties, and with the changes that the results can bring about in the government, works actively towards dissolving the 'theocratic' and absolutist mental form of the great masses of the Japanese people. The conviction that authority and sovereignty do not rest in the person of the Emperor, but in the people, leads to a veritable moral and intellectual reform corresponding to the one that occurred in Europe through the Enlightenment and classical German philosophy, thereby bringing the people of Japan up to the level of its modern economic structure and removing them from the political and ideological influence of the barons and the feudal bureaucracy.

Q8§87.

96 The New Evolution of Islam

1) Michelangelo Guidi, 2) Sirdar Ikbal Ali Shah. The *Nuova Antologia* of 1 October 1928 contains a mediocre article by the pro-British Afghan diplomat Ikbal Ali Shah and a brief

introductory note by Prof. Michelangelo Guidi. While not providing an answer, Guidi's note poses the questions of whether Islam as a religion can be reconciled with modern progress and whether it is susceptible to evolution. Reference is made to *Die Krisis des Islams* [*The Crisis of Islam*], a recent short book by Prof. R. Hartmann, 'a profound and diligent German scholar of oriental languages and civilisations'. The book, published after the author had spent some time in Ankara, answers the question in the affirmative and quotes Prof. Kampffmeyer's judgement in a review of Hartmann's booklet in *Oriente Moderno* (August 1928) that a brief stay in Anatolia is insufficient for judging such live issues and so on, and that too many of Hartmann's sources are literary in origin and, in the Orient more than elsewhere, appearances deceive, etc. Guidi (in this note at least) draws no conclusion, recording simply that the opinion of the orientals themselves can help us (but, considered singly, are they not deceptive 'appearances', etc.?), though at the start he writes that it would be utopian to think of Islam remaining in its splendid isolation, utopian to think that during this waiting period new formidable religious agents may mature within it and the force lodged in the oriental conception of life may prevail over western materialism and reconquer the world. The problem is in my opinion much simpler than is wished to make it appear since implicitly 'Christianity' is considered inherent to modern civilisation, or at least the courage to pose the question of the relations between Christianity and modern civilisation is not there. Why could Islam not do the same as Christianity? It seems to me rather that the absence of a massive ecclesiastical organisation of the Christian-Catholic type ought to make this adaptation easier. If it is admitted that modern civilisation in its industrial-economic-political manifestation will end up by triumphing in the East (and everything demonstrates that this is happening and indeed that these discussions on Islam are taking place because there is a crisis brought about by just this diffusion of modern elements), why not therefore conclude that Islam will necessarily evolve? Will it be able to remain just as it is? No – it is already no longer what it was before the war. Is it possible that it will fall at a stroke? Absurd hypothesis. Possible that a Christian religion will take its place? Absurd so to think for the masses of the people. The Vatican itself realises how contradictory it would be to want to introduce Christianity in the eastern countries into which capitalism is being introduced; the orientals see an antagonism in it, not noticed in our countries because it has been adapted in a molecular fashion and has become Jesuitism, viz. a great social hypocrisy. From this stem the difficulties of missionary work and the scanty value attached to conversions, which, moreover, are very few.

In actual fact the most tragic difficulty for Islam is given by the fact that a society in a state of torpor through centuries of isolation and a rotten feudal regime (feudal lords not of course being materialist!) has been put into too brusque a contact with a frenetic civilisation already in its phase of dissolution. Christianity has taken nine centuries to evolve and adapt, doing so a little at a time and so on, while Islam has been forced to run at break-neck speed. But in reality it is reacting just like Christianity: the great heresy on which heresies in the proper sense of the word will be founded is the 'feeling of nationhood' as against theocratic cosmopolitanism. Herein lies the reason for the return to 'origins' pure and simple, just as in Christianity; the return to the purity of the first religious texts as opposed to the corruption of the official hierarchy. The Wahabites[143] represent just this and, by means of this principle, Sirdar Ikbal Ali Shah explains Kemal Pasha's reforms in Turkey; we are not witnessing a 'novelty' but a return to the old ways, to purity and so on and so forth. This Sirdar Ikbal Ali Shah seems to me to demonstrate exactly how there exists a Jesuitism and a series of elements among Muslims that is just as developed as in Catholicism.

Q2§90.

97 Brief Notes on Islamic Culture

Absence of a regular clergy serving as a link between theoretical Islam and popular beliefs. A thorough study

Religion: A Movement and an Ideology 135

would have to be made of the Islamic type of ecclesiastical organisation and the cultural importance of its theological universities (like the one in Cairo) and learned men. The gap between the intellectuals and the people must be very wide, especially in some parts of the Muslim world; this would explain why the polytheistic tendencies of folklore keep appearing and try to adapt to the general framework of Mohammedan monotheism. Cf. the article 'Saints in Islam' by Bruno Ducati in the *Nuova Antologia* of 1 August 1929. The phenomenon of saints is specific to North Africa, but is also to be found in other regions. It has its *raison d'être* in the popular need (which exists in Christianity too) to find intermediaries between the self and the divinity. Mohammed, like Christ, was proclaimed – proclaimed himself – the last of the prophets, i.e. the last living link between the divinity and mankind. The intellectuals (priests and learned men) should have maintained this link through the sacred books but such a form of religious organisation tends to become rationalistic and intellectualistic (cf. Protestantism which has had this line of development), while the primitive people tend towards a mysticism of their own, represented by union with the divinity through the mediation of the saints (Protestantism does not and cannot have saints and miracles). The bond between the intellectuals of Islam and the people became just 'fanaticism', which can only be momentary and limited, but which accumulates masses of psychic emotions and impetuses that go on even into normal times. (Catholicism is in agony since it cannot, as in the past, periodically create waves of fanaticism; in the post-war years it has found substitutes, collective eucharistic ceremonies, celebrated in fairytale-like splendour which, relatively speaking, stimulate a certain fanaticism; before the war, too, the so-called missions, whose activities culminated in the erection of a huge cross and tumultuous scenes of penitence etc., excited something similar though on a small and very local scale.) This new movement in Islam is *Sufism*.[144] The Muslim saints are privileged beings who, by special favour, can enter into contact with God, acquiring a perennial miraculous virtue and the capacity to resolve the theological problems and doubts of reason and conscience. Sufism, organised into a system and manifested in Sufic schools and religious confraternities, developed a real theory of sainthood and established a veritable hierarchy of saints. Popular hagiography is simpler than that of the Sufis. For the people, the saints are the most celebrated founders or heads of religious confraternities, but even someone unknown, a wayfarer who pauses in some locality to carry out acts of asceticism and wonderful deeds for the surrounding population, can be proclaimed a saint by public opinion. Many saints recall the old gods of the religions conquered by Islam.

Maraboutism depends on a source of Muslim sainthood different from Sufism: *Murabit* (marabout) means what is in the *ribat*, i.e. in the fortified frontier place from which raids were made in the holy war against the infidels. In the *ribat* the cult had to be more austere because of the role of the garrison, comprised of more fanatical and often volunteer soldiers (the shock troops[145] of Islam). When the military purpose lost its importance, there remained a particular form of religious dress and the 'saints' were more popular even than those of Sufism. The centre of Maraboutism is Morocco; in going Eastward, Marabouti tombs get few and far between.

Ducati devotes a minute analysis to this African phenomenon, insisting on the political importance of the Marabouts, who find themselves at the head of insurrections against the Europeans, play the role of judges of the peace and were on occasion the vehicle for a superior civilisation. He concludes as follows: 'For the social, civilising and political consequences which stem from it, this cult (of the saints) deserves to be subjected to ever closer study and more attentive scrutiny, since the saints constitute a power, an extraordinary force, which may act as the biggest obstacle to the spread of western civilisation, as – if ably exploited – it may also become a precious auxiliary of European expansion.'

Q5§90.

98 The Influence of Arab Culture on Western Civilisation

Ezio Levi has collected together in the volume *Castelli di Spagna* [*Spanish Castles*], Milan 1932, a series of articles published in various journals regarding the cultural relations that developed, through Spain in particular, between European civilisation and the Arabs.[146] Almost all his inspiration is drawn from the numerous works on this subject by the many specialist Spanish Arabists. In his review of the introduction to Angel Gonzales Palencia's book *L'eredità dell'Islam* [*The Heritage of Islam*] in the *Marzocco* of 29 May 1932 (this introduction having been issued separately in pamphlet form under the name *El Islam y Occidente* [*Islam and the West*], Madrid 1931), Levi lists a whole number of loans that eastern culture has made to Europe in cooking, medicine, chemistry and so on. Gonzales Palencia's complete book will be of great interest for a study of the Arab contribution to European civilisation, an evaluation of the role played by Spain in medieval times and a more precise characterisation than we have at present of the Middle Ages themselves.

Q16§5.

II THE ORIGIN OF MODERN EDUCATIONAL PRINCIPLES

Introduction

1 *Some Problems of Modern Pedagogy, 139; 2 Scholastic Questions [1], 140; 3 The Professional School, 143; 4 Professional Orientation, 144; 5 Universities and Academies, 145; 6 The Academies, 147; 7 Italian and French Culture and Academies, 147; 8 The Italian Universities, 148; 9 Scholastic Questions [2], 150; 10 Intel-;ectual and Moral Order, 151; 11 The Organisation of Cultural Life, 152; 12 Types of Periodical, 153; 13 Italian Culture, 153; 14 *The Popular Libraries, 154; 15 Ideological Material, 155; 16 Introduction to the Study of Philosophy. *Pedagogy and Hegemony, 156; 17 Antonio Labriola [1], 157; 18 Antonio Labriola [2], 160.

Introduction

The material collected under this heading includes some key ideas of Gramsci's on the educational process. The chapter opens with comments on the development of young children (for which see also his various letters to his wife about their own two sons, available in English in the two partial selections *Gramsci's Prison Letters*, London and Edinburgh 1988 and *Letters from Prison*, London 1975) and on progressive schools, also dealt with elsewhere, before going on to deal with universities and adult education in the broad sense. The eighteen sub-sections chosen are taken from all

The Origin of Modern Educational Principles

but two of the notebooks now numbered from 1 through to 15. The earliest note, from near the start of Notebook 1, dates from mid-to-late 1929; for the others, up to that from Notebook 5 (end of 1930), the numbering of the notebooks and their paragraphs more or less reflects the chronological order of writing. This is somewhat coincidental and is not the case for the rest of the notes included here, all of which – with the exception of that, dating from May 1933, on Cardinal Newman's ideas of the university – were written between the turn of 1931-32 (paragraphs from Notebooks 6 and 8) and the autumn of 1932; the two notes on Antonio Labriola have not been dated more precisely than 1932. The paragraphs thus split (by chance) into two series with a gap of about a year between them, the order of presentation jumping back and forth between the two groups.

Superficially these writings may seem less systematic than those on other themes Gramsci deals with. Such an idea is more apparent than real: for him education is part and parcel of the overall questions of hegemony and the formation of intellectuals. This linkage must be constantly borne in mind, under pain of distorting and doing violence to the arguments themselves.

1 Some Problems of Modern Pedagogy

Look for the precise historical origin of certain modern educational principles: the active school, in other words the friendly collaboration between teacher and pupil; the open-air school; the necessity to allow the pupil's spontaneous faculties to develop freely under the watchful eye, but not obvious control, of the teacher.

Switzerland has made a great contribution to modern education (Pestalozzi etc.) through the tradition of Rousseau in Geneva, but in actual fact this pedagogy is a confused form of philosophy connected [to] a series of empirical rules. It has not been taken into account that Rousseau's ideas were a violent reaction against the school and the teaching methods of the Jesuits and, as such, represented a step forward. But subsequently, a sort of church was set up that paralysed educational studies and gave rise to curious regressions (in Gentile's and Lombardo-Radice's doctrines). 'Spontaneity' is one of these regressions: a child's mind is imagined to be like a skein that the teacher helps to unravel. In reality, each generation educates the succeeding one, in other words forms it, education being a struggle against the instincts bound up with elementary biological functions, a struggle against nature in order to dominate her and create a person 'actual' to the era. No account has been taken of the fact that from when children begin to 'see and touch', perhaps when only a few days old, they accumulate sensations and images which increase and gain in complexity as language is acquired. On analysis, 'spontaneity' becomes more and more problematical. Moreover 'school', i.e. direct educational activity, is only a fraction of the life of a pupil who comes into contact with both human society and the *societas rerum* [the world of things] and forms much more important criteria from these 'extra-scholastic' sources than is popularly supposed. The common school, comprising the manual and the intellectual, has this advantage, too, that it puts the child simultaneously into contact with both human history and the history of 'things' under the control of the teacher.

Q1§123.

2 Scholastic Questions [1]

In the 13 September 1931 number of *Marzocco* G. Ferrando takes a look at a work by Carleton Washburne, an American educationalist who came to Europe specifically to see the workings of the new progressive schools which draw their inspiration from the principle of the pupils' own autonomy and the necessity, in so far as is possible, to satisfy their intellectual needs (*New Schools in the Old World* by Carleton Washburne, New York 1930). Washburne describes twelve schools, all different from one another, but all animated by a spirit of reform, which in some schools is moderated and grafted onto the old stock of the traditional school, while in others it assumes even a revolutionary

The Origin of Modern Educational Principles 141

nature. Five of these schools are in Britain, one in Belgium, one in Holland, one in France, one in Switzerland, one in Germany and two in Czechoslovakia, each one of them showing us a different aspect of the complex educative process.

Oundle public school,[1] one of the oldest English schools, is different from the other schools of the same type only in that, side by side with the theoretical courses in classical subjects, it has instituted manual and practical courses. All students have to choose between a machine shop and a science laboratory. Manual work is accompanied by intellectual work and although there is no direct relation between the two, the pupils still learn to apply their knowledge and develop their practical abilities. (This example shows how necessary it is to give a correct definition of the concept of the common school in which work and theory are closely bound one to the other – the mechanical juxtaposition of the two activities can be simply snobbery. One hears it said that some great intellectuals amuse themselves by operating lathes, doing woodwork, binding books and so on, but one would not say that these are examples of the unity of mental and manual labour. Many of these modern schools in fact adopt a snobbish style which has nothing – except superficially – to do with the problem of creating a type of school that will educate the instrumental and subordinate classes to a leading role in society, in their entirety and not as single individuals.)

The Streatham Hill girls' secondary school applies the Dalton system (which Ferrando calls 'a development of the Montessori method').[2] The girls are free to follow the practical and theoretical lessons they want as long as, at the end of each month, they have carried out the programme assigned to them; class discipline is in the hands of the pupils. The system has one great defect – in general the students leave doing their work until the last few days of the month, which does harm to the seriousness of the school and constitutes a serious inconvenience to the teachers, who have to help them and are overwhelmed with work, while in the first weeks they have little or nothing to do. (The Dalton system is nothing more than the extension to the secondary schools of the method of study followed in the Italian universities, which leaves the student with every liberty for study. In some faculties they take twenty exams in the fourth year at university, then get their degree and the professor does not so much as know them.)

In the little village of Kearsley E.F. O'Neill has founded a primary school in which any 'fixed curriculum ... [and] fixed program' have been abolished.[3] The teacher tries to grasp what the children need to learn and then begins to talk on that given subject, with the aim of arousing their curiosity and interest; as soon as he has succeeded, he leaves them to get on by themselves, limiting himself to answering their questions and guiding them in their research. This school, which represents a reaction against all types of formula, against dogmatic teaching, against the tendency to make education into something mechanical, 'has given surprising results'. The children are so enthusiastic about the lessons that they sometimes stay at school until on into the evening, become attached to and are morally influenced by their teachers, who become their companions instead of being autocratic pedagogues. On the intellectual plane, too, their progress is substantially greater than that of pupils from ordinary schools. (As an experiment it is very interesting, but could it be generalised? Could a sufficient number of teachers be found to achieve the end? And will there not be undesirable happenings not referred to here, like, for example, children who have to leave school, etc.? It could be an elite school or an 'after school' system, substituting for family life.)

A group of primary schools in Hamburg – absolute freedom is given to the children, who are not divided into classes and have no subjects to study, nor any teaching in the proper sense of the word. The children's education comes solely from the questions they ask of the teachers and from the interest that they show in a given fact. The head of this school, Herr Gläser, maintains that the teacher does not even have the right to determine what the children must learn. He is not to know what they will do in life, just as he does not know what sort of society to prepare them for. The one thing he does know is that they 'have living souls to be

The Origin of Modern Educational Principles   143

developed and that he wishes to give them every opportunity possible to express fully what is within them'. For Gläser education consists in 'the freeing of each person's individuality, the natural opening and expanding of each person's soul.'[4] In eight years the pupils of these schools have achieved good results.

The other schools that Washburne speaks of are interesting because they develop certain aspects of the educational problem, such as for example the 'progressive' school in Belgium founded on the principle that children learn by coming into contact with the world and by teaching the others. The Cousinet school in France develops the habit of collective effort, of collaboration. That of Glarisegg in Switzerland puts special emphasis on developing each pupil's sense of freedom and moral responsibility etc. (It would be of use to follow up all these experiments, which are nothing other than 'exceptional', more than anything else to see what should not be done.)

Q9§119.

3   The Professional School

In November 1931 there was a wide-ranging debate in the Chamber of Deputies on professional teaching in the course of which all the theoretical and practical elements for a study of the problem emerged in quite a lucid and organic fashion. Three types of school: professional, technical junior and classical. The first is for the workers and peasants, the second for the petty bourgeoisie and the third for the ruling class.

The question hinged on the argument as to whether the professional schools are to be strictly practical and an end in themselves, so as not to allow a passage either to the classical or even to the technical school. The breadth of viewpoints consisted in the demand that the possibility of passage to the technical school must be allowed (passage to the classical school was *a priori* excluded by everyone). (The problem [is] connected to that of military rank – can a private soldier become a non-commissioned officer and, if so, can he become a junior officer and so on? This holds for any staff, taken generally, e.g. in the state bureaucracy.)

It would be interesting to reconstruct the history of the professional and technical schools through the debates in parliament and the principal municipal councils, given that some of the main professional schools were either of municipal foundation or the result of private bequests, administered or controlled or supplemented through local council budgets. The study of professional schools linked to consciousness of the necessities of production [and] its developments. Professional schools for agriculture – a very important chapter because of the many private initiatives (recall the Faina schools in the Abruzzo region and in Central Italy). Specialised agricultural schools (for viticulture etc.). Agricultural schools for the small and middle peasantry, to create in other words managers and heads for farming enterprises. But has there existed a type of professional agricultural school, i.e. one aiming at creating the specialised agricultural worker?

Q6§179.

4 Professional Orientation

Cf. Fr Brucculeri's study in the *Civiltà Cattolica* of 6 October, 3 November and 17 November 1928. In these articles is to be found the first material for an initial formulation of research into this topic. The study of the question is complex since:

1) in the present situation as regards the social division of roles, certain groups are limited in their professional choice (understood in the broad sense) by different conditions, be they economic (they cannot wait) or technical (every additional year at school modifies the general directions prevailing for the choice of their profession);

2) one must always bear in mind the danger of institutes which are called on to pronounce on the natural bent of individuals then suggesting that these latter are capable of doing a certain job even when they have no wish to accept it. (This case is to be borne in mind now that rationalisation

etc. has been introduced; the question is not merely technical, but concerns wages, too. American industry has made use of high wage levels to 'select' workers in rationalised industry, at least to a certain extent; other industries, instead, by putting forward these scientific or pseudo-scientific schemes, may tend to 'force' all traditional crafts to let themselves be rationalised without having attained a wage that would allow them an appropriate way of life such as to permit them to make up for the greater amount of nervous energy they use. One may find oneself faced with a real social danger: the current wage scales are based especially on the need to recover muscular strength. The introduction of rationalisation without a change in the way of life may lead to the rapid wear and tear of one's nerves and cause a health crisis of unheard-of dimensions.)

The study of this question must be carried out from the point of view of the common work-oriented school.

Q5§41.

5 Universities and Academies[5]

The problem of the new role that the universities and academies will be able to undertake. Today these two institutions are independent of each other, the academies being the symbol, often justly derided, of the gap that exists between high culture and everyday life, between the intellectuals and the people (and hence the certain amount of success the futurists enjoyed in their first anti-academic, anti-traditionalist etc. period of *Sturm und Drang* [Storm and Stress]). In a new system of relations between life and culture, between intellectual and industrial labour, the academies ought to become the cultural organisation (for finding the right intellectual slot and for the intellectual creation and expansion) of those who, after the common school, will go on to a professional job, as well as becoming a meeting ground between them and university people. The professionally employed members of society must not fall into intellectual passivity but must have specialised institutes available (through collective rather than individual initiative, as an organic social function recognised as a public necessity and utility). These institutes, with which they will be able to collaborate, should include every branch of research and scientific work, and will have all the necessary facilities for any form of cultural activity they might intend to take part in. Academic organisation [will have to be] reorganised and livened up from top to bottom. There will be centralisation of expertise and specialisation on a territorial basis: national centres to bring together the large existing institutes, regional and provincial sections and local groups in the towns and countryside. This organisation will be divided into fields of scientific-cultural expertise, all represented in the higher centres but only partially in the local groups. Unify the various existing types of cultural organisation: academies, cultural institutes, philological societies and so forth, by integrating traditional academic work, which is predominantly carried out through the ordering of past knowledge or through seeking to establish a mean of national thought as a guide to intellectual activity, with activities linked to collective life, with the world of production and of labour. Check will be kept over industrial conferences, the activity of the scientific organisation of labour, experimental laboratories in factories and so on. A mechanism will be set up to select and advance the intellectual capacities of the masses of the people that are today being sacrificed and are losing their way in a maze of errors and blind alleys. Every local group should as a matter of course have its moral and political science section, and will come to organise other special sections to discuss the technical aspects of industrial and agricultural questions, problems of the organisation and rationalisation of work, the factory, farm and office and so on. Periodic congresses at different levels will bring the most capable people to general notice.

It would be useful to have a complete list of the academies and other cultural organisations currently in existence and the arguments that form the main subject of their work and are published in their proceedings. To a large extent they are cultural cemeteries, though they continue to play a role in the psychology of the ruling class.

There should be close collaboration between these bodies and the universities, just as there should with all the higher specialised schools of all sorts (military, naval and so on). The aim is to obtain a centralisation of and impetus from national culture superior to that of the Catholic Church.

(This scheme for the organisation of cultural work according to the general principles of the common school should be carefully developed in each of its single parts and serve as a guide for the constitution of even the most elementary and primitive cultural centre, which ought to be conceived of as an embryonic and molecular form of the whole of the more massive structure. Even initiatives that are known to be transitory and experimental should be considered capable of being absorbed within the general scheme and, at the same time, as vital elements that help create the entire framework itself. Attentive study to be made of the organisation and development of the Rotary Club.[6])

Q12§1 (excerpt).

6 The Academies

Their role in the development of culture in Italy, in crystallising it and making it into a museum piece, far from national-popular life. (But were the academies cause or effect? Were they perhaps not multiplied to give partial satisfaction to activity that did not find an outlet in public life etc.?) The *Encyclopaedia* (1778 edition) clearly states that Italy could then boast 550 academies.

Q6§211.

7 Italian and French Culture and the Academies

A comparison between Italian and French culture may be made by comparing the *Accademia della Crusca* to the *Académie des Immortelles*. The study of language lies at the basis of both, but the Crusca stance is that of the 'pedant', the person constantly examining the language as such. The

French take as their standpoint that of the 'language' as conception of the world, as the basic – national-popular – foundation of the unity of French civilisation. For this reason the *Académie Française* has a national role in the organisation of high culture, while the *Crusca* ... (What is the current position of the *Crusca*? It has certainly changed its nature – it publishes critical texts etc., but as regards the Dictionary, what stage has been reached in work on it?)

Q3§145.

8 The Italian Universities

Why do universities in this country not exert the same influence as regulators of cultural life as they do elsewhere?

One of the reasons is to be sought in the fact that there is no organised contact between students and the teaching staff in the Italian universities. The professor teaches from the dais in front of a mass of listeners, that is to say he delivers his lecture and leaves. Only when the students get to the stage of the degree dissertation do they approach the professor and ask for a suitable topic and specific advice about scientific research methods. For the mass of students the courses are nothing but a series of lectures, all or only a part of them followed with greater or lesser attention; the student relies on the duplicated notes, the work that the teacher himself has written on the subject or the bibliography he has suggested. Closer contact exists between individual teachers and individual students who want to specialize in a given discipline. For the most part contact is formed by chance, for example for religious or political motives or through family friendship, and has an enormous importance for academic continuity and the fruitful development of the various disciplines. A student begins to strike up a relationship with a professor, who meets him in the library, invites him home, advises him which books to read and what research to go in for. Every teacher tends to form his own 'school', has his own given points of view (called 'theories') on given parts of his science, which he would like to see supported by 'his followers or disciples'. In competition with other universities, every professor wants his university to turn out 'eminent' young people who will make 'serious' contributions to his science. As a result, the same faculty sees competition among professors of similar subject matters to attract certain students who have already distinguished themselves through some review or short article or in discussions of the subject matter (where these are held). The professor then really does guide his pupil; he suggests a subject, advises him on how to carry it forward, facilitates his research, accelerates his formation as a scientist through the diligence of their conversations, has him publish his first essays in specialist journals, puts him in contact with other specialists and, to all intents and purposes, grabs hold of him.

This custom, apart from the occasional case of a *mafia* operation,[7] is beneficial since it supplements the function of the university. From being a personal affair, a private initiative, it ought to become an organic function. I am not sure to what extent, but it seems to me that the German-type seminars represent this function or attempt to carry it out. Grouped around certain professors is a throng of hopefuls, all trying to find an easier way of procuring a university post for themselves. Many young people, on the other hand, especially those from the lycées out in the sticks, find themselves totally at sea both in the academic environment and in that of university social life. The first six months of the course serve to get the student used to the specific nature of university studies and timidity in the relationship between teacher and student is a perennial feature. This is not the case in the seminars, or at least not to the same degree.

In any case this general structure of university life does not create, certainly not in the university, any permanent intellectual hierarchy between the professor and the mass of students. After the period at university the few links formed are dissolved and in the country at large there is a lack of any cultural structure centred around the university. This went to make up one of the elements in the fortune of the Croce-Gentile duo before the war, in constituting a great centre in the intellectual life of the nation. Amongst other things they also fought against the inadequacy of university life and against the scientific and pedagogical (and often the moral) mediocrity of the official teachers.

Q1§15.

9 Scholastic Questions [2]

Cf. Metron's article 'The Easy and the Difficult' in the *Corriere della Sera* of 7 January 1932. Metron makes two interesting observations as regards the engineering courses and the examinations taken by engineers at university: 1) that for every hundred things said by the lecturer, the student absorbs only one or two; 2) that in examinations for access to their profession, candidates know how to answer the 'difficult' questions but stumble over the 'easy' ones.

However Metron's analysis of the reasons underlying these two problems is not very precise and he does not point to any 'tendential' remedy. In my opinion the two deficiencies are linked to the school-type system of lesson-lectures without any 'seminars' and to the traditional nature of the examinations that has created a traditional exam psychology. Notes and duplicated hand-outs. The notes and hand-outs deal especially with the 'difficult' questions; the teaching itself pays attention to the 'difficult' on the assumption that the student on his own account will cope with the 'easy stuff'. The nearer the exams get, the more condensed the revision becomes until on the eve of the exam the student just goes over the most difficult questions; it is as if he were mesmerised by the difficult, all his faculty for memorisation and intellectual capacities being concentrated on the difficult arguments and so on. As for the low level of absorption – the lesson-lecture system leads the teacher not to repeat himself, or to reduce repetition to the minimum possible. It is in this way that the arguments are presented, within a certain defined framework, which give them a totally one-sided aspect as far as the student is concerned. The student absorbs one or two of every hundred things said by the teacher; but if the hundred is made up of a hundred different unilateral aspects, the absorption cannot but be very low. A university course is conceived as being like a book on the topic, but can one become cultured through the reading of just one book? One is, then, dealing with the question of the method of university teaching: does one go to University *to study* or *to study in order to know how to study*? Is one to study 'facts' or the method used to study the 'facts'? The practice of the 'seminar' should in fact round out the oral teaching and breathe life into it.

Q6§206.

10 Intellectual and Moral Order

Extracts from Cardinal Newman's book *Lectures and Essays on University Subjects*.[8] First, and in the most general terms, the human task of the university is to educate minds to think in a clear, sure and individual manner, by lifting them out of the fog and chaos in which an inorganic, pretentious and disorienting culture threatened to engulf them, thanks to badly assorted reading, to lectures having more sparkle than substance, to conversations and discussions without any meaning: 'A young man of sharp and active intellect, who has had no other training, has little to show for it besides a litter of ideas heaped up into his mind anyhow. He can utter a number of truths or sophisms as the case may be, and one is as good to him as another. He is up with a number of doctrines and a number of facts, but they are all loose and straggling, for he has no principles set up in his mind round which to aggregate and locate them. He says one thing now and does another thing presently; and when he attempts to write down distinctly what he holds upon a point in dispute, or what he understands by its terms, he breaks down. He sees objections more clearly than truths, and can ask a thousand questions which the wisest of men cannot answer; and withal, he has a very good opinion of himself and he declares against others who do not happen to adopt his ways of furthering it [the spread of knowledge].'

The method that university discipline prescribes for all forms of research is quite different, and quite different too is the result: 'a formation of mind – that is a habit of order and systems, a habit of referring every accession of knowledge to what we already know, and of adjusting the one with the other; and, moreover, as such a habit implies, the actual acceptance and use of certain principles as centres of thought ... Where this critical faculty exists, history is no longer a story book, or biography a romance; orators and publications of the day are no longer infallible authorities; eloquent diction is no longer a substitute for matter, nor bold statements, or lively descriptions, a substitute for proof.' University discipline must be considered as a type of discipline for intellectual training capable of bearing fruit in institutions that are not 'university' ones in the official sense.

Q15§46.

11 The Organisation of Cultural Life

Study the history of the formation and of the activity of the Italian Society for the Advancement of Science. A study also to be made of the history of the British Association,[9] which seems to me to have been the prototype for this sort of private organisation. The most fruitful characteristic of the Italian Society lies in the fact that it brings together all the 'friends of science', whether clerics or the laity, so to speak, specialists and 'amateurs'. This body represents the embryonic type of that organ that I have sketched out elsewhere, and in which the work of the academies and universities must meet and join together with the need the national-popular masses have for scientific culture, thus uniting theory and practice, intellectual and industrial labour: an organ which could find its root in the Common School.

The same thing could be said of the Touring Club, which is in essence a broad association of friends of geography and travel, in so far as certain sporting activities are brought under one roof (tourism = geography + sport), i.e. the most popular and amateur form of the love of goegraphy and the sciences connected with it (geology, mineralogy, botany, speleology, crystallogaaphy etc.). Why then should the Touring Club not be organically linked with the geo-

The Origin of Modern Educational Principles

graphical institutes and the geographical societies? There is the international question – the Touring Club works within an essentially national framework, while the geographical societies are concerned with the whole geographical world. Connection of tourism with sports societies, with rock-climbing, canoeing etc., excursion activities in general; connection with the figurative arts and with the history of art in general. In actual fact it could link up with all practical activities, if the national and international excursions were organised at holiday periods (bonus) for work in industry and agriculture.

Q8§188.

12 Types of Periodical

A permanent column on scientific tendencies. Not to popularise scientific notions but rather to expound, criticise and fit 'scientific ideas' and their repercussions on ideologies and conceptions of the world into a framework, and to further the educational-didactic principle of the 'history of science and technology as the basis for historical-formative education in the new school'.

Q4§77.

13 Italian Culture

Public intellectual services: over and above schooling at its various levels, what other services cannot be left to private initiative, but in a modern society *must* be ensured by the state and local authorities (town councils and provinces)? The theatre, libraries and museums of different types, the art galleries, zoological and botanical gardens, etc. A list should be made of institutions which are to be considered useful for public education and culture and which are indeed considered such in a series of nations, institutions which could not be accessible to the public (and which it is maintained must, for national reasons, be accessible) without intervention by the state. It may be observed that it is just these services that are almost completely neglected by us, the libraries and theatres being typical examples. The theatres exist in so far as they are a business undertaking – they are not considered a public service. Given the small theatre-going public and the mediocrity of the cities, in decadence.

On the other hand Italy abounds in charitable institutions and legacies to charity, maybe more so than any other country. All due to private initiative. It is true that they are administered and distributed badly. (These elements [are] to be studied as national nexuses between governors and governed, as factors of hegemony. Charity as element of 'paternalism'; intellectual services as elements of hegemony, in other words of democracy in the modern sense.)

Q14§56.

14 The Popular Libraries

Ettore Fabietti, 'The First 25 Years of the Popular Libraries in Milan', *Nuova Antologia*, 1 October 1928. Very useful article for the information it gives about the origin and development of this institution which has been the most conspicuous initiative in the field of popular culture in modern times. The article is quite serious, even though Fabietti has shown himself not to be very serious; however one has to recognise his many merits and his indisputable organisational ability as regards working-class culture in the democratic sense. Fabietti brings out the fact that the workers were the best 'customers' of the popular libraries – they take care of the books, do not lose them (contrary to other categories of readers – students, clerical employees, professional workers, housewives, the well-to-do (?), and so on). The reading of *'belles lettres'* represents a relatively low percentage, lower than that in other countries. There are workers who have offered to pay half the cost of expensive books just so as to be able to read them, workers who have made donations of up to a hundred lire to the popular libraries, a dyer who became a 'writer' and translator from the French as a result of his reading and studies carried out

The Origin of Modern Educational Principles

in the popular libraries, but who has gone on being a worker.

The literature of the Milanese popular libraries will have to be studied for the 'real' insights it gives into popular culture – what the most widely read books are as regards subject and author etc., publications by the popular libraries, their nature, tendencies etc. Why should this initiative be found on the grand scale only in Milan? Why not in Turin or in other big cities? Nature and history of Milanese 'reformism' – the Popular University, the Humanitarian, etc.[10] Very interesting and essential argument.

Q2§88.

15 Ideological Material

A study of how in actual fact the ideological structure of a dominant class is organised, in other words the material organisation intended to maintain, defend and develop the theoretical or ideological 'front'. The quantitatively biggest and most dynamic part is printed matter in general: publishing houses (which either explicitly or implicitly have a programme and are linked to a given tendency), political newspapers, journals of all sorts – scientific, literary, philological and so on, periodicals down as far as the parish newsletter. Such a study made on the national scale would be gargantuan, so a series of studies could be carried out for a city or series of cities. An expert local staff writer should have this study as a general outline for his work, or should rather do it on his own initiative: what superb articles could be written on these cities on this subject!

The printed word is the most dynamic part of this ideological structure, but not the only one. Everything that influences or may influence public opinion directly or indirectly belongs to it: libraries, schools, groups and clubs of different kinds, right up to architecture, street lay-out and street names. One would not be able to explain the position the Church has maintained in modern society if one were not aware of its continuous patient and persistent efforts to develop its particular section of this material structure of ideology. There would be a certain importance in making a serious study of this. As well as providing a living historical model of this type of structure, it would get people into the habit of a more cautious and precise calculation of the forces acting in society. What can an innovatory class oppose to this formidable complex of trenches and fortifications of the dominant class? The spirit of cleavage, in other words the progressive acquisition of the consciousness of its own historical personality, a spirit of cleavage that must aim at an extension from the protagonist class to the potential allied classes. All this demands complex ideological work, the first condition of which is an exact knowledge of the field that has to be cleared of its human mass element.

Q3§49.

16 Introduction to the Study of Philosophy. Pedagogy and Hegemony[11]

Every historical act cannot but be performed by the 'collective man'. In other words this presupposes the attainment of a 'socio-cultural' unity through which a multiplicity of dispersed individual wills, heterogeneous in their aims, are welded together for the same goal on the basis of an (equal) and common conception of the world (general and particular, operating in temporary bursts – in an emotional way – or permanently so that the intellectual basis gets so well rooted, assimilated, experienced, that it can become passion).[12] Since this is what does happen, great importance is assumed by the overall question of language, i.e. the collective attainment of a single cultural 'climate'.

This problem can and must be seen alongside the modern way of considering educational doctrine and practice, according to which the relationship between teacher and pupil is active and reciprocal, so every teacher is always a pupil and every pupil a teacher. But the educational relationship cannot be limited to strictly 'scholastic' relationships, by means of which the younger generations come into contact with the older ones, absorbing the historically necessary values and experiences of the latter in

The Origin of Modern Educational Principles

the process of 'maturing' and developing their own historically and culturally superior personality. This relationship exists throughout all society considered as a whole as well as for each individual relative to other individuals, between intellectual and non-intellectual sections of the population, between governors and the governed, between elites and their followers, between leaders and led, between vanguards and the body of the army. Every relationship of 'hegemony' is necessarily an educational relationship and occurs not only within a nation, between the various forces that comprise it, but in the entire international and world field, between complexes of national and continental civilisations.

Q10II§44 (excerpt).

17   Antonio Labriola [1]

If one wants to carry out a full and detailed analysis of Antonio Labriola, one must take account of the bits and pieces of his conversation that have come down to us by way of his friends and pupils (for his fame is that of having been an exceptionally gifted 'talker') as well as his writings, which are often only allusive or extremely succinct. Scattered here and there in B. Croce's books, one can glean quite a number of these odd fragments. So it is that we read in the Second Series of *Conversazioni Critiche* (*Critical Conversations*), pp. 60-61: ' "How would you go about the moral education of a Papuan?" one of us asked Prof. Labriola years ago when we were scholars attending one of his lectures in Pedagogy, objecting as we were to the effectiveness of Pedagogy. "Provisionally," (our Herbartian professor[13] replied with the harshness of a Vico or a Hegel), "provisionally I would make a slave of him, and this would be the pedagogy in his case, except to see whether a start could be made on using something of our pedagogy with his grandsons and great-grandsons." ' Comparison may be made between this reply of Labriola's and the interview he gave on the colonial question (Libya) around 1903, reprinted in the volume *Scritti vari di filosofia e politica*

[*Miscellaneous Writings on Philosophy and Politics*][14]. A similar juxtaposition may also be carried out as regards Gentile's way of considering religious education in the primary schools. We would seem to be dealing with a pseudo-historicism, with a mechanicism that is rather empirical and very close to the most vulgar evolutionism. One might recall what Bertrando Spaventa says about those who would like to confine men for ever to the cradle (i.e. under the sway of authority, which, when all is said, does educate the immature peoples to liberty) and who consider the whole of life (of other people's lives) as like the cradle.

It seems to me that historically the problem ought to be posed differently: whether, that is, a nation or a social group which has reached a higher degree of civilisation should not (and therefore should) 'accelerate' the process of education of the more backward peoples and social groups, thereby appropriately universalising and translating its new experience. Thus when the British enrol recruits from amongst primitive peoples who have never seen a modern rifle they do not instruct these recruits in the use of the bow, boomerang or blow-pipe, but actually train them to handle a gun, even if the norms of instruction are, of necessity, adapted to the 'mentality' of that given primitive people. The mode of thought implicit in Labriola's reply does not in consequence seem dialectical and progressive but, rather, mechanical and backward, like Gentile's 'pedagogical-religious' one, which is nothing more than a derivation of the concept that 'religion is good for the people' (people = youth = primitive stage of thought to which corresponds religion etc.) in other words the (tendentious) dereliction of the education of the people. In the interview on the colonial question the mechanicism implicit in Labriola's thought comes out even more obviously. For it may quite well be that it is 'necessary to reduce the Papuans to slavery' in order to educate them, but it is none the less necessary for someone to say that it is only incidentally necessary since there exist certain given conditions, that – in other words – this is a 'historical' and not an absolute necessity: it is necessary, rather, that there should be a struggle over the issue, and this struggle is exactly the condition by means of

The Origin of Modern Educational Principles

which the grandsons or great-grandsons of the Papuan will be freed from slavery and educated by modern pedagogy. That there are people who assert most vigorously that the slavery of the Papuans is but a necessity of the moment and who rebel against this necessity is also a philosophical-historical fact: 1) since it will contribute to reducing the period of slavery to the time necessary; 2) since it will cause the Papuans themselves to reflect on themselves and educate themselves, in so far as they will feel they have the support of people of a superior civilisation; 3) since only this resistance shows that one really is in a higher epoch of civilisation and thought etc.

Labriola and Gentile's historicism is of a very shoddy type. It is the historicism of the jurists for whom the knout is not a knout when it is a 'historical' knout.[15] We are, moreover, dealing with a most nebulous and confused manner of thinking. That a 'dogmatic' explanation of scientific notions may be necessary in the primary schools or that a 'mythology' is necessary does not mean that the dogma should be religious dogma and the mythology that particular mythological one. That a backward people or social group may need a coercive external discipline so as to be educated in the ways of civilisation does not mean that they should be reduced to slavery, unless one considers all state coercion to be slavery. There is a coercion of a military type for work, too,[16] which can also be applied to the dominant class, and which is not 'slavery' but the appropriate expression of modern pedagogy directed towards the education of an immature element (which, certainly, is immature, but is so close to elements that are already mature, while, organically, slavery is the expression of universally immature conditions). Spaventa, who looked at things from the standpoint of the liberal bourgeoisie against the historicist 'sophisms' of the reactionary classes, expressed in sarcastic form a conception that was much more progressive and dialectical than Labriola and Gentile's.[17]

Q11§1.

18 Antonio Labriola [2]

(Cf.§ on p.3).[18] Hegel claimed that slavery is the cradle of liberty. For Hegel, as for Machiavelli, the 'new princedom' (i.e. the dictatorial period that characterises the beginnings of any new type of state) and the related slavery are justified only as education and discipline for not-as-yet-free man. B. Spaventa however, in the appendix to his *Principi di Etica* (*Principles of Ethics*), Naples 1904, makes the apposite comment 'But the cradle is not life. Some would like to see us confined for ever to the cradle.'

(A typical example of the cradle that turns into a life-time is that offered by customs protectionism, which is always put forward as justified as a 'cradle', but tends to become an eternal cradle.)[19]

Q11§5.

III THE NATURE AND HISTORY OF ECONOMIC SCIENCE

Introduction

1 *Machiavelli as an Economist, 163; 2 Points to Reflect on for a Study of Economics [1]. *The Beginning of Economic Science, 164; 3 Points to Reflect on for a Study of Economics [2]. *The Method of Economic Research, 165; 4 Brief Notes on Economics [1]. *The Concept of 'Homo Oeconomicus' , 166; 5 Points to Reflect on for a Study of Economics [3]. *On the Subject of the So-Called Homo Oeconomicus, 167; 6 Points to Reflect on for a Study of Economics [4]. *Classical Economy and Critical Economy, 168; 7 Points to Reflect on for a Study of Economics [5]. *Observations on Pantaleoni's *Pure Economics*, 170; 8 Points to Reflect on for a Study of Economics [6]. *Regarding Pantaleoni's *Pure Economics*, 171; 9 Brief Notes on Economics [2]. *Lionel Robbins, 174; 10 Brief Notes on Economics [3]. *Political Economy and Critical Economy, 176; 11 *Outlines of Marxist Economics, 176; 12 Freedom and 'Automatism' or Rationality, 179; 13 Brief Notes on Economics [4]. Ugo Spirito & Co., 180; 14 Encyclopaedic Notions. Conjuncture [1], 181; 15 Encyclopaedic Notions. Conjuncture [2], 182; 16 Points for a Study of Economics. *The Einaudi-Spirito Polemic over the State, 182; 17 Economic History Studies, 184; 18 Graziadei's Land of Cokaygne, 185; 19 Graziadei and the Land of Cokaygne, 186; 20 Graziadei, 186; 21 On Graziadei, 187; 22 Points to Reflect on in Economics. *The Science of Economics, 189.

Introduction

The backbone of this chapter is formed by all the notes on economic science from Notebook 10, written principally in the second half of 1932, apart from two which deal with the world crisis and appear in Chapter IV and half a dozen others in Chapter VII which take to task Croce's interpretation of Marxist economics. Gramsci himself gave most of these notes merely general headings with no precise indication of their contents, so these have been provided editorially. A paragraph from Notebook 8, 'Machiavelli as an Economist' (April 1932), whose conclusion is restated in Notebook 13 on Machiavelli (see SPN p.143), has been chosen to begin the chapter, both since it refers to an earlier period than those of classical and post-classical political economy with which Marxist economics is contrasted in the rest of the chapter, and also because it appears to have provided Gramsci with the initial stimulus to formulate his ideas about economic science.

Paragraph 23 of Notebook 10 was, (note 26, p.510) not included in the first thematic Italian editions of the Notebooks, being first published only in the 1975 Critical Edition. Since it raises basic questions which are then developed in later notes, it has been located immediately after Gramsci's comments on the early phase of modern economic thought. A few notes near the end of the chapter, criticising Antonio Graziadei, an economist on the right of the Communist movement, and Ugo Spirito, then the theorist of a would-be 'left' form of a corporativist economy, are taken from Notebooks 7 and 8; these were written in February 1931 and March 1932 respectively. Gramsci's main reflections on economic theory were completed by the end of 1932 and, though they informed later work of his, he returned to the theme only rarely, as in two notes of May 1933, stimulated by a review of Lionel Robbins's *Essay on the Nature and Significance of Economic Science*, and in one of the last paragraphs of Notebook 10 (from about the same period). This latter note, in going over ground previously touched on regarding the status of economics as a science, is here interpreted as

Gramsci's tentative conclusion to his work in this field.

Other comments of his on economics, if not mentioned above or cited in the General Introduction (or pp.xliii-xlv) in footnotes to this chapter, may be found in SPN, especially pp.401, 402-3 and 410-12 and pp.279-318 (which consists of all but one minor paragraph of Notebook 22 on 'Americanism and Fordism', dating to 1934 but little changed from the first drafts written prevalently in 1930).

1 Machiavelli as an Economist

Specific studies on Machiavelli as an 'economist': Gino Arias in the *Annali di Economia della Università Bocconi* [has published] a study in which certain indications [are to be found]. (Study by Vincenzo Tangorra.)[1] It appears that, in one of his writings on Machiavelli, Chabod finds the Florentine somewhat lacking when compared, for example, to Botero in that there is an almost total absence of economic references in his works. (On Botero's importance for the study of the history of economic thought, cf. Mario De Bernardi and L. Einaudi's review in *La Riforma Sociale*, March-April 1932.)

Some general observations are necessary as regards Machiavelli's political thought and its relevance to the present in contrast with that of Botero whose approach is more overall and systematic, albeit less lively and original. The nature of the economic thought of the time must also be borne in mind (hints of this to be found in the article of Einaudi's referred to above) together with a discussion of the nature of mercantilism (economic science or economic policy?). If it is true that mercantilism is <mere> economic policy, in that it cannot presuppose a 'determinate market' and the existence of a preformed 'economic automatism' whose elements, historically speaking, are formed only at a certain stage of development of the world market, it is obvious that economic thought cannot merge into general political thought, i.e. into the concept of the state and the forces which it is thought should come together to constitute it. If one can show that Machiavelli aimed at creating links between city and countryside and at extending the role of the urban classes up to the point of asking them to forgo certain feudal-corporative privileges with respect to the countryside, so as to incorporate the rural classes into the state, one will also have shown that, implicitly, Machiavelli had in theory overcome the mercantilist stage and already had some traits of a 'physiocratic' nature[2] – that he was thinking, in other words, of a politico-social environment which is the same as that presupposed by classical economy.

Prof. Sraffa draws attention to a possible comparison between Machiavelli and William Petty, a seventeenth-century English economist whom Marx calls the 'founder of classical economy' and whose <complete> works have also been translated into French. (Marx was to speak of him in the volumes on *Mehrwert, History of Economic Doctrines*.)[3]

Q8§162.

2 Points to Reflect on for a Study of Economics [1]. The Beginning of Economic Science

When can one speak of a beginning to economic science? (Cf. Luigi Einaudi, 'On a Query Regarding the Birth of Economic Science' in *La Riforma Sociale*, March-April 1932, about certain publications of Mario De Bernardi's on Giovanni Botero.) One can speak of it from the time that the discovery was made that it is not gold that constitutes wealth (and thus even less so the possession of gold), but labour. William Petty (*A Treatise of Taxes and Contributions*, 1662, and *Verbum Sapienti*, 1666)[4] had an insight and then Cantillon (1730) stated explicitly that wealth does not consist of gold: '... Wealth in itself is nothing but the Maintenance, Conveniences, and Superfluities of Life ... To all this the Labour of man gives the form of Wealth'.[5] Botero came close to a very similar statement in a passage from his book *Delle cause della grandezza della città*, printed in 1588 (and now reprinted by De Bernardi from this first edition in the series *Testi inediti e rari* [*Unpublished and Rare Texts*], published under the editorship of the Juridical Institute of the Royal University of Turin, 1930): 'And, forasmuch as Art doth contend and strive with nature, a man may here well aske me, which of these twoo do most import to increase a place with multitude of people; the fruitfulnes of the Land, or the Industrie of man? The Industrie of man without all doubt. First, for that such things as are wrought by the cuning hand of man, are of much more, and of far greater price and estimation, then such things as nature doth produce. Forasmuch as nature giveth the matter and the subject, but the Art and Cuning of man, giveth an unspeakable variety of formes and fashions.'[6]

According to Einaudi, however, one cannot ascribe to Botero either the labour theory of wealth or the paternity of economic science, as against Cantillon on the other hand, for whom 'it is no longer solely a question of a fit comparison for having us understand which of two factors – nature or labour – gives things a *greater* price, as in Botero's investigation, but theoretical research on *what* in fact *wealth* is.'

If this is the starting point of economic science, and if it is in this way that the fundamental concept of economics was established, then any further research cannot but enrich theoretically the concept of 'labour'. This concept, in the meantime, cannot be submerged into the more generic one of industry and activity but must instead be placed firmly in that human activity which is equally necessary in any social form. This enrichment has been accomplished by critical economy.

One will have to look at *The History of Economic Doctrines* (*Der Mehrwert*); Cannan's *A Review of Economic Theory*.[7]

Q10II§25.

3 Points to Reflect on for a Study of Economics [2]. The Method of Economic Research

In examining the question of the method adopted in economic research and the concept of abstraction, it has to be considered whether the criticism that Croce makes of critical economy – that it proceeds by 'a continuous medley of theoretical deductions and historical descriptions of logical and of material connections' (*Materialismo storico ed economia marxistica*, p.160[8]) – is not, rather, one of the features characteristic of the superiority of critical economy over pure economics and one of the forces that make it most fruitful as regards scientific progress. Moreover, one may note the signs of dissatisfaction and irritation that Croce himself shows for the most common procedures of pure economics, with its byzantine ways and scholastic mania for dressing up the most trivial banalities of common sense and the most empty generalities in some pompous scientific cloak. Critical economy has sought the right tempering between the deductive and the inductive methods, viz. the construction of abstract hypotheses not on the indeterminate basis of a generalised, historically indeterminate man who cannot from any standpoint be recognised as an abstraction from a concrete reality, but on that of actual reality, 'historical description', which provides the real premiss for constructing scientific hypotheses – the abstraction of the economic element or of those from amongst the aspects of the economic element on which attention is to be focused and scientific examination carried out. In this way, generic 'homo oeconomicus' cannot exist, but one can abstract the type of each one of the agents or protagonists of economic activity who have followed one on another in history: the capitalist, the worker, the slave, the slaveowner, the feudal baron, the glebe serf. It is not for nothing that economic science was born in the modern era when the extension of the capitalist system made a relatively homogeneous type of economic man widespread, i.e. when it created the real conditions by reasons of which a scientific abstraction became relatively less arbitrary and less generically devoid of substance than had hitherto been possible.

Q10II§37i.

4   Brief Notes on Economics [1]. The Concept of 'Homo Oeconomicus'

The discussion about the concept of 'homo oeconomicus'

has become one of the many discussions on so-called 'human nature'. Each of the disputants has his 'faith' and maintains it with arguments of a prevalently moralistic nature. 'Homo oeconomicus' is the abstraction of the economic activity of a given form of society, i.e. of a particular economic structure. Every social form has its 'homo oeconomicus', i.e. its own economic activity. To maintain that the concept of homo oeconomicus has no value scientifically is just a way of saying that the economic structure and the activity conformant to it have undergone radical change, or that the economic structure has been so changed that the mode of economic behaviour must of necessity change in order to conform to the new structure. But it is exactly here that dissent lies, and not so much objective scientific as political dissent. What, moreover, would be the meaning of a scientific recognition that the economic structure has undergone radical change and that economic behaviour must change to conform to the new structure? Its meaning would be one of political stimulus, no more than that. Between the economic structure and the state with its legislation and its coercion stands civil society, and it is this latter which has to be radically transformed, in concrete terms and not just in the written word as it appears in statutes and learned books. The state is the instrument for bringing civil society into line with the economic structure, but the state has to 'want' to do that, i.e. the representatives of the change that has already come about in the economic structure have to be in control of the state. To expect civil society, through the work of propaganda and persuasion, to come into line with the new structure, to expect the old 'homo oeconomicus' to disappear without being buried with all the honours he deserves, is to fall into a new form of economic rhetoric, a new form of vacuous and inconclusive economic moralism.

Q10II§15.

5 Points to Reflect on for a Study of Economics [3]. On the Subject of the So-Called Homo Oeconomicus

On the subject of the so-called 'homo oeconomicus', i.e. of

the abstraction made of man's needs, one may say that such an abstraction is not at all ahistorical, and although it appears in the guise of mathematical formulations, it is nowhere near being of the same nature as mathematical abstractions. 'Homo oeconomicus' is the abstraction of the needs and economic operations of a given form of society, just as the ensemble of hypotheses put forward by the economists in the development of their scientific arguments is nothing other than the ensemble of premises that underlie a given form of society. One could do something useful by systematically bringing together the 'hypotheses' of some great 'pure' economist such as M. Pantaleoni,[9] and correlating them so as to show that they are in fact the 'description' of a given form of society.

Q10II§27.

6 Points to Reflect on for a Study of Economics [4]. Classical Economy and Critical Economy

Where in particular does the emphasis lie in scientific research in classical economy and where, as against that, does it lie in critical economy?[10] Why is this the case, i.e. with a view to reaching what practical goals or resolving what given theoretical and practical problems? For critical economy, it would seem sufficient to define the concept of 'socially necessary labour' in order to arrive at the concept of value, since one must take as one's starting point the labour of all working people to arrive at definitions both of their role in economic production and of the abstract, scientific concept of value and surplus value, as well as one of the role of all capitalists considered as an ensemble. For classical economy, on the other hand, the important thing is not the abstract, scientific concept of value (which it attempts to reach by other means, but only for the formal reasons of having a logically and verbally consistent system, arriving there – or thinking it has arrived there – using marginal utility by way of psychological research), but the more concrete and more immediate concept of the profit of the individual or the firm. What is therefore of importance is a study of the dynamic of 'socially necessary labour', a dynamic that assumes various theoretical formulations – the theory of comparative costs, of static and dynamic economic equilibrium.[11] For critical economy, the interesting problem begins once 'socially necessary labour' has already been established in a mathematical formula; for classical economy, on the other hand, the whole interest lies in the dynamic phase of the formation of 'socially necessary labour' at the local, national and international levels, and in the problems posed by the differences in the divisions of the work processes in the various stages of this labour process. It is the comparative cost, i.e. the comparison of the 'particular' labour embodied in the various goods, that is of interest to classical economy.

But is not also this research of interest to critical economy? And is it 'scientific', in a work like the *Précis*,[12] not to deal with these nexuses of problems, too? Critical economy passes through different historical stages and it is natural in each one of them for the emphasis to be placed on what the historically prevalent theoretical and practical nexus is at a particular time. When it is property that is in command of the economy, emphasis is placed on the 'ensemble' of socially necessary labour, as a scientific and mathematical synthesis, since in practice one wants labour to become aware of itself as a whole, of the fact that it is first and foremost an 'ensemble' and that as an 'ensemble' it determines the fundamental process of economic motion (whereas property is very little interested in socially necessary labour even for the purposes of knowing how property itself is scientifically constituted – the important thing is specific labour under conditions determined by given technical equipment and by a given immediate market of provisions, as well by a given immediate political and ideological environment; taking all these into account, one will, when faced with setting up a firm, seek to identify those conditions that most closely conform to the goal of the maximum 'particular' profit and not reason on the basis of socially necessary 'averages'). When it is labour itself however that has taken command of the economy, it too, because of the fundamental change in its position, will have to worry about questions of specific utilities and comparisons between them in order to draw from them initiatives as regards movement forwards.[13] What after all are the 'competitions', if not one particular way of becoming involved in this nexus of problems and of understanding that forward progress comes about through individual 'thrusts'? That is to say by 'comparing' costs and insisting on continuously reducing them through singling out and even bringing about the objective and subjective conditions in which such becomes possible.

Q10II§23.

7 Points to Reflect on for a Study of Economics [5]. Observations on Pantaleoni's 'Pure Economics'

Observations on the *Principî di Economia Pura* by M. Pantaleoni (new edition 1931).[14]

1) On re-reading Pantaleoni's book one can better understand the reasons for Ugo Spirito's copious outpourings.

2) The first part of the book, which deals with the hedonistic postulate, might more properly serve as the introduction to a refined text book on the culinary art or an even more refined manual of love-making positions. It's a pity that writers on the art of cookery don't study pure economics since, with the benefit of help from the experimental psychologist's couch and from statistical methods, they would be able to arrive at much more complete and systematic treatments than those commonly available. The same may be said of the more clandestine and esoteric scientific activity that strives to further the art of sexual pleasure.

3) Pantaleoni's philosophy is eighteenth-century sensationalism developed within nineteenth-century positivism. Its 'man' is man in general, taken in the abstract, i.e. biological man, an ensemble of painful and pleasurable sensations, who however becomes the man of a particular social formation each time that one passes from the abstract to the concrete, that is to say each time one speaks of

economics and not of natural science in general. Pantaleoni's book is what one may call a 'materialistic work' in the 'orthodox' and scientific sense!

4) These 'pure' economists locate the origin of economic science in Cantillon's discovery that wealth is labour, wealth is human industry. However when they themselves try to get down to producing science, they forget these origins and smother in the ideology that, in the light of its own methods, first developed the initial discovery. It is not the positive core of the origins they develop but rather the philosophical halo adorning the cultural world of the time, however much this world has been criticised and superseded by the culture that came after it.

5) What has to be substituted for the so-called 'hedonistic postulate' of 'pure economics' in a critical and historicist economy? The description of a 'determinate market', viz. the description of the determinate social form, of the whole as opposed to the part, of the whole which determines – to a determinate extent – that automatism and ensemble of uniformities and regularities that economic science attempts to describe with the greatest exactness, precision and completeness. Can it be demonstrated that such a formulation of economic science is superior to that of 'pure' economics? One can say that the hedonistic postulate is not abstract but generic, since it can be made the premiss not just to economics but to a whole range of human activities that may be termed 'economic' only if the notion of economics is extended and made generic to such an enormous extent as to <empirically> empty it of all meaning and make it coincide with a philosophical category, as in fact Croce has sought to do.[15]

Q10II§30.

8 Points to Reflect on for a Study of Economics [6]. Regarding Pantaleoni's 'Pure Economics'

I) Fix with precision the point at which 'abstracting' is distinguished from 'making generic'. Economic agents cannot be subjected to a process of abstraction by which the hypothesis of homogeneity becomes biological man. This is not abstracting but, rather, making generic or making 'indeterminate'. Abstraction will always be the abstraction of a historically determined category, seen in fact as a category and not as multiple individuality. Homo oeconomicus, too, is historically determined, albeit as an ensemble remaining indeterminate: he is a specific abstraction. In critical economy this process takes place when value is equated to exchange value rather than use value, thereby potentially reducing use value to exchange value in the sense that an economy based on exchange modifies even physiological habits and the psychological scale of both tastes and the final degrees of utility, which thus appear as 'superstructures' and not primary economic data, the object of economic science.[16]

II) The concept of determinate market to be established. How it is conceived in 'pure' economics and how in critical economy. A determinate market in pure economics is an arbitrary abstraction, having a purely conventional value for the scope of pedantic and scholastic analysis. A determinate market for critical economy, on the other hand, will be the ensemble of the concrete economic activities of a particular social form, assumed according to the laws governing their uniformity, i.e. 'abstracted' but without this abstraction ceasing to be historically determined. One abstracts the individual multiplicity of the economic agents of modern society when one speaks of capitalists, but in point of fact the abstraction lies within the historical domain of a capitalist economy and not of a generic economic activity that in its categories abstracts all the economic agents who have ever appeared in world history, reducing them generically and indeterminately to biological man.

III) One may ask whether pure economics is a science or whether it is 'something else' which, however, proceeds by a method which, in so far as it is a method, has a scientific rigour all of its own. That activities of this sort do exist is shown by theology. Theology, too, sets off from a series of hypotheses and thence constructs a massive, solidly consistent and rigorously deduced, doctrinal edifice thereon. But is theology a science on this account? Einaudi (cf. 'Once More on the Way of Writing the History of Economic Dogma' in *La Riforma Sociale* of May-June 1932) writes that economics is 'a doctrine having the same nature as the mathematical and physical sciences (this assertion, one may observe, being one which is not necessarily linked with the other one that employing the instrument of mathematics is either necessary or useful for studying it)', but it would be difficult to furnish a consistent and rigorous proof of this claim. The same concept has been expressed by Croce (*Critica*, January 1931) in the words: 'Economics does not change its nature whatever the nature – capitalist or communist – of the social set-up, whatever the course of history, in the same way that arithmetic does not change its nature with the objects to be counted.' While on the subject, mathematics and physics are not in my view to be confused. Mathematics may be called a purely 'instrumental' science, the complement of a whole series of 'quantitative' natural sciences, whilst physics is an immediately 'natural' science. Mathematics may be compared with formal logic, with which, moreover, higher mathematics is, in many aspects, unified. Can the same be said of pure economics? Discussion on this is still lively and, it seems, is showing no signs of abating. Furthermore, one can see no great unity among the so-called pure economists. For some, the only pure economics is hypothetical economics, which formulates its proofs by means of a 'let us suppose that', i.e. pure economics is also that economics which makes abstract or generalises all economic problems that have historically ever been posed. For others, instead, the only pure economics is that economics which can be deduced from the economic principle or hedonistic postulate, that is to say an economics which abstracts completely from any historical reality and presupposes only a generic 'human nature' which remains the same throughout all time and space. But if one bears in mind Einaudi's open letter to Rodolfo Benini, published in *Nuovi Studi* some time ago, one sees that the position of the pure economists is wavering and hardly a secure one.

Q10II§32.

9 Brief Notes on Economics [2]. Lionel Robbins

In *La Riforma Sociale* of March-April 1933 there appears a review signed by three stars of *An Essay on the Nature and Significance of Economic Science* by Lionel Robbins, professor of Economics at the University of London (London 1932). The reviewer, too, asks himself 'what is economic science?', in part accepting and in part correcting or integrating the concepts that Robbins expounds. It appears that the book corresponds to Croce's requirement in his pre-1900 essays that economic treatises ought, of necessity, to be prefaced by a theoretical introduction outlining the distinguishing concepts and methods of economics itself, but a certain amount of discretion must be used in understanding this correspondence. Robbins does not appear to have that philosophical rigour which Croce was demanding, and is more the 'empiricist' and formal logician. The book may be of interest as the most recent monograph in this line of research, which depends on the dissatisfaction that one often notes among economists about definitions of their science and the limits they are wont to place upon it. For Robbins, too, 'economics' ends up by having an extremely broad and extremely generic meaning, which hardly coincides with the concrete problems that economists really study, but coincides, rather, with what Croce calls a 'category of the spirit', the economic or 'practical moment', i.e. the rational relationships between the means and the end. Robbins 'examines the conditions that characterise the human activity studied by economists and arrives at the conclusion that these are: 1) the diversity of the ends; 2) the insufficiency of the means; 3) the possibility of alternative uses. Consequently, he defines economics as that science which studies human behaviour as a relationship between ends and scarce means which have alternative uses.'

It appears that Robbins wishes to free economics from the so-called 'pleasure' principle and make a clear distinction between economics and psychology 'rejecting the last vestiges of the historical association between utilitarianism

The Nature and History of Economic Science

and economics'.[17] (This probably means that Robbins has developed a new concept of utility, different from and more comprehensive than the traditional one.)

Leaving on one side any judgement on the merits of the question, one may draw attention to what careful studies modern economists devote to their science in order continually to perfect the logical instruments of their science, so much so that one can say that a great deal of the prestige enjoyed by economists is due to their formal rigour, their exactness of expression etc. The same tendency is not present in critical economy, which all too often makes use of stereotyped expressions and expresses itself in superior tones that are not warranted by the exposition: it gives the impression of tiresome arrogance and nothing else. For this reason, it seems useful to stress this aspect of economic studies and economic literature. In *La Riforma Sociale* attention is always drawn to publications of Robbins's type and there is no difficulty in obtaining a bibliography in respect of them.

It remains to be seen whether Robbins's formulation of the economic problem is, generally speaking, a demolition of marginalist theory, although it appears that he says it is possible to build, on the basis of a marginalist analysis, 'a completely unitary economic theory' (that is by abandoning the dualism still held by Marshall in the criteria for explaining value, i.e. the duality of marginal utility and the cost of production).[18] For, if individual valuation is the sole source for explaining economic phenomena, what is the meaning of the statement that the field of economics has been separated off from that of psychology and utilitarianism?

As regards the need for a methodological-philosophical introduction to treatises in economics, one might call to mind the examples of the prefaces to the first volume of *Critical Economy* and to the volume *The Critique of Political Economy*:[19] they are all perhaps too short and bald, but this principle is adhered to, and elsewhere in the body of the text there are numerous references to method and philosophy.

Q15§43.

10 Brief Notes on Economics [3]. Political Economy and Critical Economy

(cf. p.26.)[20] Keeping the relationship between political economy and critical economy in its organic and historically current forms has proved to be beyond our scholars. In what do the two currents of thought differ in their formulation of the economic problem? Do they differ from each other now, in present-day cultural terms, rather than – and no longer in – those of eighty years ago? This does not come out in the text books of critical economy (e.g. the *Précis*),[21] yet it is the point of immediate interest to beginners and is one which defines the general orientation for all further research. In general this point not only is assumed as known but is taken for granted without any need for discussion, whereas neither of these things is true. Thus it comes about that only those possessed of the herd instinct, who basically could not care less about the question, are launched on the study of economic problems, any scientific development thus being made impossible. What strikes one is how a critical standpoint that requires the greatest intelligence, open-mindedness, mental freshness and scientific inventiveness has become the monopoly of narrow-minded, jabbering wretches who, only by reason of the dogmatism of their position, manage to maintain a place not in science itself but in the marginal bibliography of science. In these matters the greatest danger is represented by an ossified form of thought: better a certain disorderly refractoriness than the philistine defence of preconceived cultural positions.

Q15§45.

11 Outlines of Marxist Economics

Consideration should be given to the following point. How, in present-day terms, could and should one write an outline of critical economic science that would fulfil the same role as that occupied for previous generations by the abridgements of Cafiero, Deville, Kautsky, Aveling, or Fabietti, or, more recently, that of Borchardt?[22] The same question may be posed for a separate series of works, viz. the instructive type of popularisation of economic literature such as is represented in the western languages by Lapidus and Ostrovityanov's *Précis d'Economie Politique*, but which in the original language must now be represented by a substantial number of text books, differing in type and quite widely in bulk, according to the readership for whom they are intended.

One may observe:
1) that today, after publication of the critical edition of the various works of critical economy, we again have the onus and scientific obligation placed upon us to find a solution to the problem of once more producing works of this type;
2) that Borchardt's abridgement, in so far as it is not compiled solely from Vol.I of the *Critique of Political Economy*, but from the three volumes, is obviously superior to those of Deville, Kautsky etc. (leaving aside for the moment the intrinsic merits of the different treatments);
3) that a modern type of digest ought to be yet more extensive than that of Borchardt, in that it should take into account the entire economic treatment carried out by the author himself and be presented as a compendium and exposition of the whole doctrinal corpus of critical economy rather than just a summary of certain works, however fundamental these may be;
4) that the method of exposition adopted ought not to be determined by given literary sources, but originate from and be dictated by the critical and cultural requirements of current interest to which one wants to provide a scientific and organic solution;
5) that unimaginative and slavish summaries are on this account to be avoided, the whole material, instead, being of necessity recast and reorganised in an 'original' and preferably systematic fashion following a scheme that is a 'didactic' aid to study and learning;
6) that the entire set of examples and concrete facts must be brought up to date, reference to those in the original text being made only as and when, and to the extent to which,

the economic history and legislation of the country for which the text book is being prepared either do not offer corresponding ones for a different development of the historical process or are nowhere near as important or vivid;
7) that the exposition must be critical and polemical, in the sense that it has to respond, as implicitly and tacitly as may be, to the formulation given to economic problems in the given country by the most accepted economic culture and by the official and respected economists. From this standpoint, Lapidus and Ostrovityanov's manual is 'dogmatic', puts forward its claims and develops its themes as if no one radically 'challenged' and rejected them, rather as if they were the expression of a science which, from the period of struggle and polemics to become established and triumph, has now entered its classical phase of organic expansion. Obviously, however, this is not the case. The text book must be strongly polemical and forcefully argued and must not leave any essential question – or any question that vulgar economics considers essential – without an answer (implicit and understood according to its own autonomous method of presentation, if this perhaps is preferable), in such a way as to drive vulgar economics out of its lairs and strongholds and destroy its credentials in the sight of the younger generation of students;
8) that any text book of economic science cannot be divorced from a course in the history of economic doctrines. The so-called fourth volume of the *Critique of Political Economy* is in fact a history of economic doctrines, and it is exactly with this title that it has been translated into French. The whole conception of critical economy is historicist (which does not mean that it should be confused with the so-called historical school of economics) and its theoretical treatment cannot be disentangled from a history of economic science, whose central core may be partially reconstructed from the fourth volume referred to, as well as from indications scattered throughout the entire work of the original authors;
9) that one cannot therefore do without a general introduction – brief though it may be – which, following the lines of the preface to the second edition of Volume I, should

give in summary an exposition of the philosophy of praxis and the more important and essential methodological principles, drawing them from the entire corpus of the economic works, where they are incorporated into the treatment or scattered here and there and mentioned only when the concrete opportunity arises.

Q10II§37ii.

12 Freedom and 'Automatism' <or Rationality>

Is freedom in conflict with so-called automatism? Automatism is in conflict with free will, not with freedom. Automatism is a group freedom, in opposition to individualistic free will. When Ricardo said 'given these conditions'[23] we shall have these economic consequences, he did not make economics itself 'deterministic' and neither was his conception 'naturalistic'. He observed that, given the collaborative and co-ordinated activity of a social group that, following certain principles accepted (freely) out of conviction, works towards certain goals, a development then occurs which may be called automatic and which may be considered as the development of certain recognisable laws that can be isolated using the methods of the exact sciences. At any moment a free choice is made according to certain basic orientations that are identical for a great mass of individuals or single wills, in so far as these latter have become homogeneous in a determined ethico-political climate. Nor is it the case that everyone acts in the same way; individual free wills are, rather, manifold, but the homogeneous part predominates and 'dictates law'. For if free will becomes generalised, it is no longer free will, but a shift in the basis of 'automatism', a new rationality. Automatism is nothing other than rationality, but contained in the word 'automatism' is the attempt to present a concept shorn of any speculative halo: it is possible that the word rationality may end up by being attributed to automatism in human operations, while 'automatism' will go back to indicating the movement of machines, which become 'automatic' after human intervention and whose automatism is merely a verbal metaphor, as it is when applied to human operations.

Q10II§8.

13 Brief Notes on Economics [4]. Ugo Spirito & Co.

The charge that traditional political economy is conceived of in a 'naturalistic' and 'deterministic' fashion. A baseless accusation, since classical economists do not have to worry much about the 'metaphysical' question of determinism, and all their deductions and calculations are based on the premiss *'let us suppose that'*. But what is this 'suppose that'? Jannaccone, in reviewing Spirito's book[24] in *La Riforma Sociale*, defines the 'let us suppose' as a 'determinate market' and this is correct in the terms of the language of the classical economists. But what is the 'determinate market' and what in fact is it determined by? It will be determined by the basic structure of the society in question and it is therefore this structure that one must analyse, identifying those of its <relatively> constant elements which determine the market etc., and the other 'variable and developing' ones which determine conjunctural crises up to the point when even its <relatively> constant elements get modified and the crisis then becomes an organic one.

Classical economy is the only 'historicist' one under the appearance of its abstractions and its mathematical language, while it is actually Spirito who dissolves the historicism and drowns economic reality in a flood of words and abstractions. However the tendency represented by Spirito and by others of his group is a 'sign of the times'. The demand for an 'economy based on a plan', not only on a national scale but on a world one, is interesting in itself, even if the justification for it is purely verbal: it is a 'sign of the times'-it is the still 'utopian' expression of the developing conditions that, as such, pose the need for an 'economy based on a plan'.

The current interest of writers like Spirito stands out even more because of their approach towards certain classical economists such as Einaudi. Einaudi's articles on the crisis, especially those in the January-February 1932 number of *La Riforma Sociale* are often characterised by all the discernment of a mere child. He reprints passages from economists of a hundred years ago, not realising that the 'market' has changed, that the 'let us suppose that's' are no longer what they once were. International production has developed to such a pitch and the market become so complex that certain reasonings now appear literally childlike. Maybe over the last few years no new industries have been born? Suffice it to mention those of artificial silk and aluminium. What Einaudi says is generically right, because its meaning is that past crises have been overcome by 1) an extension of the circle of capitalist production throughout the world; 2) a rise in standard of living for certain strata of the population or a more contained rise in that of all of them. But Einaudi does not take into account that economic life has been ever more pivoted around the principle of a series of big mass productions and it is these which are in crisis. Control over this crisis is impossible just by reason of its size and depth, which have reached such a scale that quantity becomes quality, i.e. the crisis has become *organic* and no longer *conjunctural*. Einaudi's reasonings are appropriate for conjunctural crises because he wants to deny the existence of an organic crisis, but this is the 'politics of the immediate', not scientific analysis: it is the 'will to believe', 'medicine for the soul' practised, moreover, in a puerile and comic fashion.

Q8§216.

14 Encyclopaedic Notions. Conjuncture [1]

A conjuncture may be defined as the set of circumstances which determine the market in a given phase if these circumstances, however, are conceived of as in movement, in other words as an ensemble that gives rise to a process of ever new combinations, i.e. the process of the economic cycle. The conjuncture is studied to predict and thus also, within certain limits, to determine the economic cycle in such a way as to favour business. On that account, the conjuncture has also been defined as the oscillation of the economic situation, or as the set of oscillations.

Q15§16ii.

15 Encyclopaedic Notions. Conjuncture [2]

The origin of the expression helps towards a better understanding of the concept. In Italian = economic fluctuation. Bound up with very rapidly changing post-war phenomena. (In Italian, the meaning of 'favourable or unfavourable <economic> opportunity' remains attached to the word 'conjuncture'. The difference between 'situation' and 'conjuncture': conjuncture is the whole of the immediate and transitory characteristics of the economic situation, and by this concept one must therefore understand the more fundamental and permanent characteristics of the situation itself. A study of the conjuncture is thus intimately bound up with immediate politics, with 'tactics' <and 'agitation'>, while the 'situation' refers to 'strategy' and to propaganda, etc.)[25]

Q6§130.

16 Points for a Study of Economics: The Einaudi-Spirito Polemic over the State

The Einaudi-Spirito polemic over the state is to be linked to the Einaudi-Benini polemic (cf. *La Riforma Sociale* of September-October 1931). But both sides in the Einaudi-Spirito polemic are in the wrong – they refer to different things and use different languages. The Benini-Einaudi polemic sheds light on the previous one. In both cases Einaudi assumes the same position as when, in polemic with Croce, he attempts to fix a limit to any scientific function of the philosophy of praxis. The consistency of Einaudi's position is 'intellectually' admirable; he understands that any theoretical concession to the enemy, even if only an intellectual one, may bring his whole edifice tumbling down.

In his conception of the state Einaudi considers

governmental intervention in economic affairs to act as an interference with free competition in favour of certain groups, whether this comes about through its 'juridical' regulation of the market (i.e. through giving the determinate market a legal form in which all economic agents operate under 'like juridical conditions') or through governmental intervention creating economic privileges. Spirito, on the other hand, was referring to his speculative conception of the state, in which the individual is identified with the state.[26] But there is a third aspect of the question that is implicit in both these writers, and it is that by which, in identifying the state with a social group, state intervention takes place not only in the way mentioned by Einaudi, or in the way that Spirito wants, but is a preliminary condition for any collective economic activity, an element of the determinate market, if not even the determinate market itself, since it is the very political-juridical expression of the fact by which a given commodity (labour) is, first of all, undervalued, then placed in a condition of competitive inferiority, and finally made to shoulder the cost for the whole of the given system. This point is brought out by Benini, and certainly it is not a fresh discovery, but the interest lies in the fact that Benini has got to this position and in the route he has taken to get there, since he arrived there by setting off from the principles of classical economy, and it is this which Einaudi finds irritating.

Einaudi had, however, in a letter of his published in *Nuovi Studi*, mentioned Giovanni Vailati's 'marvellous ability' to present a theorem in economics (or even in philosophy), together with its solution, in the various scientific languages that have arisen from the historical process of development of the sciences; that is to say he implicitly admits the mutual translatability of these languages.[27] Benini has done exactly that: he has utilised the language of liberal economics to describe an economic fact that had already been described in the language of the philosophy of praxis, albeit with all the limitations and due caution pertaining to the case (the Benini episode finds a close comparison in the Spirito episode at the Ferrara convention). On this subject, one should bear in mind what Engels said about the possibility, even if one starts from the marginalist conception of value, of reaching the same conclusions (even though in a vulgar form) as those arrived at by critical economy.[28] An analysis should be made of all the consequences of Engels's statement. One of them seems to me to be that if one wishes to defend the critical conception of economics, one must systematically insist on the fact that orthodox economics does deal with the same problems, albeit in another language, demonstrating this identity of the problems being treated and demonstrating that the critical solution is the superior one. In short, the texts must be 'bilingual' – the authentic text and its vulgar or liberal economics translation as the parallel or interlinear text.

Q10II§20.

17 Economic History Studies

Recall the polemic between Einaudi and Croce (Einaudi in *La Riforma Sociale*) when the fourth edition of the volume *Historical Materialism and the Economics of Karl Marx* came out with its new preface in 1917. It may be of interest to study how the various currents of study and research into socio-economic history have been formed in each separate country, what their leanings are, etc. That a school of economic history, linked to classical economy, existed in Britain is certain, but have its subsequent developments been influenced by historical materialism or not? (See to what extent Seligman's book both can be located within this trend and in fact expresses this trend's need to measure itself against historical materialism.[29]) In the same way there existed a juridico-economic current in France that worked along historical materialist lines (Guizot, Thierry, Mignet) but was then influenced in its turn (Henri Pirenne and the modern French historians, Hauser and so on).[30] In Germany, the current is more closely tied to economics (with List), but Sombart has been influenced by historical materialism etc. In Italy, more closely linked to historical materialism (but influence of Romagnosi and Cattaneo).

Q8§212.

18 Graziadei's Land of Cokaygne

In his slim volume *Sindacati e Salari* [*Unions and Wages*] Graziadei finally remembers, 35 years later, to refer to the note on the Land of Cokaygne that Croce devoted to him in the essay 'Recent Interpretations of the Marxian Theory of Value' (p.140 of the volume *Historical Materialism etc.*) and terms 'somewhat rough-and-ready' the example of his that Croce analyses. In fact, Graziadei's case of 'a society in which profits exist, not indeed with surplus labour, but with no labour' is typical of Graziadei's recent output, and Rudas has done well to quote it at the beginning of his essay on 'Price and Surplus Price' published in *Unter dem Banner* in 1926.[31] (I no longer remember if Rudas attributed this to him.) Graziadei's whole conception is based on this ramshackle principle that machines and material organisation (by themselves) produce profit, i.e. value. In 1894 (the *Critica Sociale* article analysed by Croce) his hypothesis was total (the whole of profit exists without any labour); now his hypothesis is partial (not all profit exists through labour) but the 'rough-and-ready' nature (to call the primitive hypothesis only 'rough-and-ready' is a delicate euphemism) is still there partially. His whole way of thinking is 'rough-and-ready', like any cheap-jack hectoring lawyer, not like an economist. Regarding Graziadei, one has really to go back to the basic principles of economics, to the logic of this science: Graziadei is a past master in petty logic, in the art of cavilling and the casuistry of sophism, but not in that of grand logic, whether in economics or in any other science of thought.

Graziadei's same Land of Cokaygne principle emerges from the introduction of tariff barriers as the element which 'creates' profit and salary margins. It is demonstrated (compare with the anti-protectionist literature) that without producing any 'value' and without making a single worker actually work (the only people who do anything are the typists who copy out non-existent share certificates) one can obtain lavish 'profits' and distribute high 'dividends' (cf., for example, L. Einaudi and E. Giretti, 'Chains of Interlocking

Limited Companies', *Riforma Sociale*, January-February 1931). It remains to be seen whether it should be economic science that deals with this 'economic' activity (although it is 'economic' in the Crocean sense, like brigandage, the *mafia* etc.) or the judiciary. Recall a polemic in *Critica Sociale* between Graziadei and Luigi Negro (before 1900, I think) in which Negro observed that Graziadei is given to accept industrialists' public statements about their activity as 'correct' and as a basis for scientific speculation.

Q7§23.

19 Graziadei and the Land of Cokaygne

See Papini's *Gog* (interview with Ford, p.24) for the words attributed to Ford: 'Using no workers, manufacture an ever greater number of objects costing hardly anything.'

Q7§27.

20 Graziadei

As well as Loria's theories, see if the questions raised by Graziadei[32] do not perhaps stem from Rodbertus's theories. In their *Histoire des Doctrines Économiques* (5th edition, 1929 reprint), Gide and Rist write on p.504: 'The difference between his (Rodbertus's) attitude and Marx's is also of interest. Marx, thoroughly well versed in political economy and English socialism, sets off from the theory of *exchange* and makes labour the source of all *value*. Rodbertus, who drew his inspiration from the Saint-Simonians, sets off from *production* and makes labour the sole source of the whole *product*, a simpler and truer proposition than the former, but still an incomplete one. Not only does Rodbertus not say that labour alone creates value, but he expressly denies it on more than one occasion and adduces the reasons for his opinion.'[33] In a footnote Rist cites the bibliographical references on this argument and quotes a letter of Rodbertus's to R. Meyer of 7 January 1872, where mention is made of the fact that the 'demonstration might in case of need be used against Marx'.

Q8§166.

21 On Graziadei

To get the better of Graziadei, one has to go back to the basic concepts of economic science. Firstly, it has to be established that economic science starts from the hypothesis of a determinate market, purely competitive or purely monopolistic as may be, except that one then ascertains what variations may be introduced into this constant by one element or the other of the real, never 'pure' situation. Secondly, that the object of study is the production of real new wealth and not the redistribution of existing wealth (unless one really does want to study this redistribution), i.e. the production of value and not the redistribution of value already distributed on the basis of a determined production. Careful research will then have to be carried out into Graziadei's political and scientific biography. His book on Chilean nitrates in which he was incapable of envisaging the possibility of the synthetic production of nitrogen, which opened up a breach in Chile's monopoly; it would be interesting to look again at the dogmatic statements he made about this monopoly. As regards his political position, Graziadei's reply to the enquiry carried out by *Viandante* in 1908–9;[34] Graziadei was one of the most right-wing and opportunist. His pamphlet on trade unionism: his model was British labourism, with him as a liquidationist of the party. His post-war position was a curious phenomenon of the psychology of an intellectual who [was] persuaded 'intellectually' of the inanity of political reformism and thus split off from it and opposed it. But the realm of abstract intelligence is one thing and the practical one of action quite another. After 1922 he found the terrain of withdrawal and of retreat to his pre-war position in the field of science. One may pose the question of whether it is in good faith to look back into a man's past for all the mistakes he has made in order then to upbraid him for the ends of a current polemic.

Is it not human to err? Is it not rather through one's mistakes that today's scientific personalities have been formed? And is not everyone's biography to a great extent the struggle against the past and the fight to overcome the past? If someone today is an atheist, is it legitimate to remind him that he was baptised and, up to a certain age, obeyed religious observances? But Graziadei's case is quite different. He has been very careful not to criticise his past and put it behind him. In the field of economics, he limited himself, for a certain period, to keeping silent, or rather he maintained, on the subject of the rate of centralisation of capital in the countryside, that 'current practice' supported his theories. (For the conclusion he came to regarding the superiority of the share-cropping system over the centralised capitalist undertaking, which is the same as speaking of the superiority of artisan production over the factory system, he based himself not just on the Romagna but even on Imola. He did not take into consideration the fact that the *obbligato*[35] had almost disappeared over the 1901-10 period, as is shown by the 1911 census, and in particular he took no account of the politico-protectionist factors that determined conditions in the Po Valley – Italy was so short of capital that its large scale use in agriculture would have been a real miracle.)

In politics he got away by claiming, in a sophist fashion, to be a 'historicist' or that he 'kept up with the times' <if it's the hangman who's in charge, you have to be his assistant – that's Graziadei's historicism>, that is to say never to have been bound by any principles. In the 1895-1914 period one 'had to be' a labourite, in the post-war period anti-labourite and so on. Recall his tedious insistence over the claim that 'military expenditure is non-productive', a claim which he boasted always to have opposed as silly and demagogic – see how he then opposed it when he was in favour of joining the government. In the same way, one may note his pessimistic-gossipy view of 'Italians' *en bloc*, all of them characterless, cowardly, civilly inferior beings and so on and so forth, a stupid and trivially defeatist conception, a form of anti-rhetoric which is, in actual fact, the depressing real rhetoric of a false artfulness of the Stenterello-Machiavelli type. It is beyond doubt that there is in Italy a particularly repugnant petty-bourgeois stratum, but is this stratum the whole of Italy? A silly generalisation. Moreover, even this phenomenon has its historical origin and is not at all an inevitable quality of Italians as such: Graziadei's historical materialism is like that of Ferri, Niceforo, Lombroso or Sergi, and it is known what historical function this biological conception of the 'barbarity' attributed to Southerners (rather, to filthy Southerners)[36] has had in the politics of Italy's ruling class.

Q7§30.

22 Points to Reflect on in Economics. The Science of Economics

The question to pose is whether there exists a science of economics and in what sense. It may be that economic science is a science *sui generis* unique in point of fact of its kind. What might be done is look at how many ways the word science is used by the various philosophical currents, and see whether one of these senses may be applied to economic research. It seems to me that economic science stands by itself, i.e. it is a unique science, since it cannot be denied that it is science and not only in the 'methodological' sense, that is to say not only in the sense that its procedures are scientific and rigorous. It also seems to me that economics cannot be compared to mathematics, although mathematics, among all the various sciences is perhaps the one most closely comparable to economics. In any case, economics cannot be considered a natural science (whatever way one conceives of nature or the external world – subjectivist or objectivist), and neither can it be considered a 'historical' science in the common meaning of the word, etc. One of the prejudices against which it is perhaps still necessary to fight is that, in order to be a 'science', a certain research should be grouped together with other researches in one type and that 'type' is 'science'. It can instead happen not only that such a grouping is impossible, but that a research is 'science' in one given historical period and not in another, for another prejudice is that if a research is 'science', it would always have been and will always be science. (That it was not science was because there were no scientists, not that there was no subject of science.) It is expressly for economics that these critical elements must be examined; there was a period in which there could not be a 'science' not only because there were no scientists but also because there did not yet exist those certain premisses which created that certain 'regularity' or that certain 'automatism', whose study is exactly what gives rise to scientific research, but regularity or automatism can be of different types at different times and this will create different types of 'sciences'. It must not be thought that since an 'economic life' has always existed the possibility of there being an 'economic science' ought always to have existed, in the same way that since the stars have always been in motion the 'possibility' of there being an astronomy has always existed, even though the astronomers were called astrologers etc. In the economy the element of 'interference' is the human will, the collective will, differently oriented according to the general conditions of life of men, i.e. 'tending' or organised differently.

Q10II§57.

IV ECONOMIC TRENDS AND DEVELOPMENTS

Introduction

A The Geo-political Situation
1 Geo-Politics, 195; 2 World Politics and European Politics, 195; 3 The Atlantic and the Pacific, 196; 4 America and the Mediterranean, 196; 5 *Great Britain and the United States, 196; 6 *Britain, Russia, Germany, 197; 7 Encyclopaedic Notions [1]. *The Four Pillars of Europe, 198; 8 A Policy for Peace in Europe, 199; 9 Augur, 200; 10 *Geo-Political Developments, 201; 11 America, 207; 12 Past and Present [1]. Otto Kahn, 208; 13 Oil, Petrol and Petroleum Products, 209; 14 Italy and the Yemen in the New Politics of the Arab World, 210; 15 Britain and the United States after the War, 213; 16 The American Negroes, 214.

B The World Economic Crisis
17 Past and Present [2]. Observations on the World Crisis, 215; 18 Past and Present [3]. *The Standard of Living, 217; 19 Psychology and Politics, 218; 20 Past and Present [4]. The Crisis, 219; 21 Past and Present [5]. Elements of the Economic Crisis, 223; 22 Brief Notes on Political Economy, 225; 23 Points to Reflect on in Economics [1]. *Agnelli's Ideas, 226; 24 Points to Reflect on in Economics [2]. *Labour and Consumption, 229.

C National Economic Problems and International Relations
25 *Post-War Contradictions, 230; 26 *Inflation and the Domestic Economy, 231; 27 *International Tariffs and

Trade, 231; 28 The National Economy, 233; 29 Relations Between City and Countryside, 234; 30 City and Countryside, 235; 31 *Colonies, Capital Flow and the Demographic Question, 237; 32 *Questions of Hegemony, 240; 33 The Colonies, 241; 34 Robert Michels, 242; 35 Past and Present [6]. Studies on the National Economic Structure, 243; 36 Nationalisations and State Takeovers, 244; 37 Past and Present [7]. Nationalisations, 245; 38 The Italian Risorgimento. *Savings, Agricultural Protectionism and Industry, 245; 39 Past and Present [8]. The Error of the Anti-Protectionist Left, 246; 40 Past and Present [9]. The Individual and the State, 247; 41 On the National Economic Structure, 248; 42 *Humanity-as-Labour and Modern Internationalism, 253.

D American Industrial Culture
43 America and Europe, 254; 44 *American Industry, 254; 45 Past and Present [10]. Fordism, 256; 46 Americanism, 256; 47 *The Basic Activity of the Age, 257; 48 American Pragmatism, 258; 49 American Philosophy, 258; 50 Vittorio Macchioro and America, 259; 51 Brief Notes on American Culture, 259.

E Britain's Role in the World Economy
52 Cultural Questions. Disraeli, 261; 53 The British Empire, 261; 54 Constitution of the British Empire, 262; 55 Britain, 262; 56 Paying off the National Debt, 263; 57 London's World Role, 266; 58 Past and Present [11]. The British Government, 267; 59 *The Crisis of Parliamentarism, 268; 60 Past and Present [12]. Britain and Germany, 268.

F The New Society and the New Economic Individual
61 Cultural Topics. *Conformism and the Collective Man, 269; 62 Reformation and Renaissance. *The Present Process of the Molecular Formation of a New Civilisation, 270; 63 *The Modern Prince and the Collective Man, 272; 64 *Economic Activity and the Law, 272; 65 Freud and the Collective Man, 273; 66 Encyclopaedic Notions [2]. *Liberty-Discipline, 274; 67 Man as Individual and Man as

Mass, 275; 68 *Passive Revolution and the Planned Economy, 277.

Introduction

The arrangement of material in this chapter is, for the most part, new. In the first Italian editions of the Notebooks much of it was initially included in various notes, especially on international topics, in the volume 'Machiavelli' or in the miscellany 'Past and Present'. Other paragraphs have, however, been taken from the volumes on 'Historical Materialism', the 'Risorgimento' and 'The Intellectuals', while sub-sections 5, 6, 7, 26, 56 and 62 were published for the first time only in Gerratana's 1975 Critical Edition.

Section A – which brings together Gramsci's reflections on geo-political developments – consists, with the exception of one later sub-section, of paragraphs from the first half-dozen notebooks that were written between spring 1930 and the end of that year. To avoid jumping back and forth in the themes dealt with, the long Q2§16 has been broken up into three shorter sub-sections, two of which are to be found in Section A and one in Section E. The notes in Section A take into account many of the major post-war strategic changes agreed at international conferences in the 1920s and, as such, they give an insight into Gramsci's thinking on how the world had emerged from the First World War and was still developing.

Section A thus functions as a background against which he formulated his ideas (to be found in Section B) on the world economic crisis that had, in his view, been building up since the war. These crisis notes fall into two distinct sets. The first group, to be found in Notebook 6, dates from spring and summer 1931 while the second group, consisting of the last five sub-sections of Section B, was written between February and May 1933. The latter group, partly under the influence of the Keynes-inspired 'Macmillan Report', which Gramsci had read in the meantime (see sub-section 20 and footnote 25), returns to the subject in greater detail.

Although the notes comprising Section C are largely

about Italy, they have a wider relevance to the question of the economic relationships between the industrialised world and either the countries on its economic fringes or the developing countries. A greater overall depth is evident in the five sub-sections taken from the 'miscellaneous' Notebook 15 (first half of 1933) and from the first few paragraphs (1934) of Notebook 19 on 'The Risorgimento', to which the comments from earlier notebooks serve as a counterpoint. The more convincing integration of economic with other aspects of the argument in the later notes is probably due to Gramsci's intervening study, principally in Notebook 10, of economic topics (see in this volume Chapter III, the two sub-sections at the end of Section B of this chapter and the last dozen or so sub-sections of Chapter VII, Section C). Some brief notes, on different modes of land tenure and use among the peasantry, were considered of strictly specialist interest and therefore not included.

The last three sections of this chapter are constructed from notes that Gramsci wrote at widely separate times during his imprisonment. Sections D and E discuss two of the major industrialised groupings of the 1930s. Britain and its empire are considered predominantly from an industrial and politico-institutional standpoint, while the United States is treated as a case-study in the culture of industrialism, though without neglecting the potential future contribution of American intellectuals to the cultural sphere in general. These American notes thus form a useful adjunct to the celebrated Notebook 22 on 'Americanism and Fordism' (SPN, pp. 279-318).

In the eight notes comprising Section F Gramsci sketches out some ideas about how he thought a new human personality might evolve during the transition towards a free communistic society. Of particular interest is his recurrent polemical and unorthodox use of the notion of social conformism as a phenomenon springing up from below rather than being imposed from above. In a certain sense, then, these notes lead back to the more general discussion in the so-called second part of Notebook 10 (see Chapter III) of the *homo oeconomicus*, but this time as such a person might take shape in the future.

A THE GEO-POLITICAL SITUATION

1 Geo-Politics

Before the war, Rudolf Kjellén, a Swedish sociologist, was already trying to construct a science of the state and of politics on a new basis, taking as his starting point the territorial unit as organised politically (development of the geographical sciences – physical geography, anthropography, geo-politics) and the mass of human beings living in society on that territory (geo-politics and demopolitics). Note that two of his books in particular – *The State as a Life Form* and *The Great Powers of Today* (*Die Grossmächte der Gegenwart* of 1912, then revised by the author to become *Die Grossmächte und die Weltkrise* [*The Great Powers and the World Crisis*], published in 1921; Kjellén died in 1922) – had a wide sale in Germany, giving rise to a branch of research. There exists a *Zeitschrift für Geopolitik* [*Journal of Geo-politics*] and there are voluminous works of economic geography and of political geography (one of which, *Weltpolitisches Handbuch* [*Manual of World Politics*], has designs on becoming the statesmen's manual). In Britain as well as in America and in France, too.

Q2§39.

2 World Politics and European Politics

These two are not the same thing. In a duel between Berlin and Paris or between Paris and Rome, the winner is not master of the world. Europe has lost its importance and world politics depends more on London, Washington, Moscow, Tokyo than it does on the Continent.

Q2§24.

3 The Atlantic and the Pacific

Role of the Atlantic in civilisation and the modern economy. Will this axis shift over to the Pacific? The largest masses of the world's population are in the Pacific. If China and India were to become modern nations with great volumes of industrial production, their consequent detachment from a dependency on Europe would in fact rupture the current equilibrium: transformation of the American continent, shift in the axis of American life from the Atlantic to the Pacific seaboard, etc. Look at all these problems in economic and political terms (trading etc.).

Q2§78.

4 America and the Mediterranean

Book by Prof. G. Frisella Vella, *Il traffico fra l'America e l'Oriente attraverso il Mediterraneo* [*Trade between America and the East through the Mediterranean*], Palermo 1928. Frisella's starting point is the 'Sicilian' one. Since the most appropriate part of the world for American economic expansion is Asia, and since America's channels of communication with Asia are the Pacific and the Mediterranean, Europe must not put up any resistance to the Mediterranean's becoming a great trading route between America and Asia. Sicily stands to benefit greatly from this traffic, becoming the intermediary for American-Asiatic trade and so on. Frisella Vella is convinced of the inevitability of American world hegemony etc.

Q5§8.

5 Great Britain and the United States

Augur, 'The New Aspect of the Relations Between Great Britain and the United States of America', *Nuova Antologia*, 16 December 1928. (Augur puts forward the hypothesis that the United States is trying to become the hegemonic political force of the British Empire, in other words the USA is trying to conquer the British Empire from within and not from the outside by means of war.)

In the same number of *Nuova Antologia* see also the article by Oscar di Giamberardino, 'United States Naval Policy'; this article is of great interest and should be borne in mind.

Q2§97.

6 Britain, Russia, Germany

Britain as a sea power in opposition to the Russo-German block (the author[1] foresees the resurgence of German might that will restructure Russia under its own control and unite with it territorially). In this situation traditional (British) naval supremacy over the continent would come to lose its effectiveness given the territorial size of the Russo-German bloc. Britain on the defensive through being saturated with the territories it dominates and having its fleet reduced as a hegemonic factor. The Russo-Germanic bloc would then represent the anti-British revolt. There would come into being an uninterrupted continuity from the Arctic to the Mediterranean and from the Rhine to the Pacific: Turkey would here be the next lower factor in this hierarchy with the adhesion of Bulgaria and Hungary not being improbable in the case of a conflict. (Lithuania already links Germany and Russia [diplomatically].)

The British threat to force the straits of Denmark (exception being made for the German role of the Kiel canal) is neutralised by possible minefields at German disposal around the southern borders of Denmark and Sweden. French influence in the North is of no importance. Sweden and Finland are loath to make enemies of Britain but at the same time are tending ever more towards Germany.

Resurgence of Germanism. Germany is still 'potentially' the strongest Continental nation. National unity is being strengthened and the state set-up is intact. She is at the moment manoeuvring adroitly between West and East while waiting to regain her political freedom faced with an England that is trying in vain to divide her from Russia in order to get the better of both.

Russia: the author's conceptions about Russia are very hazy and superficial. 'The amorphism typical of Russia is incapable of structuring the state or even of conceiving what the state is. Every single founder of the Russian state was a foreigner or of foreign origin (Rurik, the Romanovs). For historical, geographical and political reasons the organising power cannot but come from Germany. It will not be a military conquest but just economic, political and cultural subordination. It would be anti-historical to break Russia up and subject her to colonial experiments as certain political theorists would have wanted to do. The Russian people are mystical, not religious, and they are, *par excellence*, feminine in nature and lacking in substance,' and so on and so forth. (The question is much less verbally complex. Russia is too much a peasant country, with too primitive an agriculture, to be able to organize a modern state with 'facility' – her industrialisation is her modernisation process.)

Q2§40

7 Encyclopaedic Notions [1]. The Four Pillars of Europe

Paul Bourget's assertion at the outbreak of war (I think, although it might even have been before) that the four pillars of Europe were the Vatican, the Prussian General Staff, the British House of Lords and the French Académie. Bourget forgot Russian tsarism which was the strongest pillar, the only one that survived the French Revolution and Napoleon and 1848.

A careful search would have to be made for where, when and in what precise terms Bourget made this claim. Maybe he himself was ashamed of including Russian tsarism. One could set off from this proposition of his to deal with the role played by Russia in the history of Europe. It defended western Europe from the Tartar invasions, it was European civilisation's bulwark against Asiatic nomadism, but this role quickly became conservative and reactionary. With its endless multinational population, it was always possible for Russia to put huge armies, absolutely insulated from liberal propaganda, into the field against the peoples of Europe; such was the case in 1848, leaving an ideological sub-stratum that was still operative in 1914 (the steamroller being the Cossacks who were to destroy the University of Berlin, etc.). There are many still incapable of appreciating what a historic change was brought about in Europe in 1917 and what freedom was conquered by the peoples of the West.

Q6§39.

8   A Policy for Peace in Europe

'A Policy for Peace in Europe' by Argus, *Nuova Antologia*, 1 June 1927. The article speaks of the frequent visits to Britain by representatives of the German worlds of politics and letters. When these German intellectuals are asked, they say that every time they manage to make contact with influential personalities in the English-speaking world, they are asked the following question: 'What is Germany's stance *vis-à-vis* Russia?' And in desperation (!) they answer 'But we cannot take sides in a dispute between London and Moscow!' At the root of the British conception of foreign policy lies the conviction that a conflict with Russia is not only inevitable but already under way, albeit in strange and unusual forms that make it invisible to the eyes of the great mass of the people. The article is completely pro-British (in the same period I remember an article by Manfredi Gravina in the *Corriere della Sera* that was so outrageously Anglophile – preaching the explicit subordination of Italy to Britain – that it took one's breath away): the British want peace, but they have shown they know how to make war. They are sentimental and altruistic, they think about European interests; if Chamberlain has not broken with Russia, this is because that could harm other states finding themselves in less favourable conditions than Britain.

Détente with France forms the basis of British policy, but

the government may also favour other states: Britain wants to be on good terms with everybody. Hence closer ties with Italy and Poland. In Britain, certain people are not favourably disposed towards the regime in Italy. But Britain's policy is one of loyalty and friendship and will continue to be so even if the regime changes since, among other things, Italian policies are courageous, and so on and so forth.

Q2§18.

9 Augur

Augur is a frequent writer for *Nuova Antologia* on matters of world politics, especially the role of the British Empire and the relations between Britain and Russia; he must be a Russian émigré. His collaboration with *Nuova Antologia* must be an indirect one – articles published in journals in Britain and then translated for *Nuova Antologia*. His journalistic activity aims at the moral isolation of Russia (breaking off diplomatic relations), together with the creation of a united anti-Russian front as a preparation for war. Linked to the right wing of the British Conservatives as regards Russian policy but differing from them as regards the United States; supports close Anglo-American unity and insists on Britain giving up the islands in its possession in the Caribbean (Bahamas etc.) to America, or at least disarming them. His articles are highly presumptuous (maybe stemming from the assumed great authoritativeness of his sources); he is attempting to instil into his readers the certainty and inevitability of a war of extermination between Britain and Russia in which Russia cannot but succumb. The official relations between the two countries are like the waves on the surface of the ocean, forever changeable, but deep down is a powerful historical current that leads to war.

Q2§32.

10 Geo-Political Developments

Francesco Tommasini, 'World Politics and European Politics', *La Nuova Antologia*, 1 May-16 May 1927.[2]

Political hegemony of Europe before the World War
Tommasini [says] that world politics was under European leadership from the Battle of Marathon (490 BC) right up to the World War. (Until a short time ago, however, the 'world' did not exist and neither did world politics; moreover, Chinese and Indian civilisations have also counted for something.) At the turn of the century there were three European world powers, *world* ones by reason of the size of their territories, their economic and financial power and the possibility they had of channelling their activity in an *absolutely* autonomous direction so that, whether they liked it or not, all other powers, greater or lesser as may be, were subject to their influence. These powers were Britain, Russia and Germany. (Tommasini does not consider France a great power!) *Britain*: had beaten three great colonial powers (Spain, the Netherlands, France) and subjugated another (Portugal), had won the Napoleonic Wars and for a century had been the master of the whole world. *Two powers standard*.[3] Strategic points of the world in its hands (Gibraltar, Malta, Suez, Aden, the Bahrein Islands, Singapore, Hong Kong). Industries, trade, finance. *Russia*: was threatening India and stretching out towards Constantinople. Big army. *Germany*: intellectual activity, in competition industrially with Britain, large-sized army, fleet a threat to the *two powers standard*.

The formation of United States power
Independence in 1783 recognised by Britain through the Treaty of Versailles; it then consisted of thirteen states, of which ten were originally colonised by the British and three (New York, New Jersey and Delaware) ceded by the Netherlands to Britain in 1667, and amounted to 2 million square kilometres, but the populated part was in effect only the eastern Atlantic seaboard. According to the 1790 census,

the population was less than 4 million, including 700,000 slaves. The exact same territory in 1920 comprised twenty states with 71 million inhabitants. At that time, the United States bordered on Canada in the North, yielded to Britain by France in 1763 after a war lasting seven years; in the West there was Louisiana, a French colony that was bought in 1803 for 15 million dollars (a territory of 1,750,000 square kilometres), so the whole Mississippi basin came under its domination. The western border was then the Sabine River, with the Spanish colony of Mexico on the other side, while along the southern border was Spanish Florida, acquired in 1819.

Mexico, which was then double its present size, rose against Spain in 1810 and had its independence recognised by the Treaty of Cordoba in 1821. From that moment United States policy was aimed at the appropriation of Mexico; Britain supported the Emperor Iturbide while the United States favoured a republican movement that triumphed in 1823. French intervention in Spain. British and United States opposition to the Holy Alliance in aid of the Spanish attempt to regain the American colonies. From this stemmed President Monroe's message to Congress (2 December 1823) in which the famous doctrine was set out. Request not to intervene against the ex-colonies which had proclaimed their independence, kept it and had it recognised by the United States, which could not remain indifferent on the sidelines were there such an intervention under whatever form.

In 1835 Texas (690,000 square kilometres) declared its independence from Mexico and a decade later joined the United States. War between the United States and Mexico. Through the Treaty of Guadalupe Hidalgo (1848), Mexico was forced to give up the territory constituting the present-day states of California, Arizona, Nevada, Utah and New Mexico (about 1,700,000 square kilometres). The United States thus arrived at the shores of the Pacific, which was then occupied right up to the Canadian frontier, and reached its present dimensions.

The War of Secession from '60 to '65. France and Britain encouraged the Southern separatist movement and

Economic Trends and Developments 203

Napoleon III tried to profit from the crisis by strengthening Mexico with Maximilian. After the Civil War the United States remembered the Monroe Doctrine in Paris and demanded the withdrawal of French troops from Mexico. In 1867 purchase of Alaska. United States expansion as a great world power began at the end of the nineteenth century.

Principal American problems: 1) regulation of immigration in order to ensure a greater homogeneity among the population (this problem was really posed after the World War and, over and above the national question, was also and especially bound up with the industrial revolution); 2) hegemony over the Caribbean and the Antilles; 3) dominion over Central America, especially the Canal Zone; 4) expansion in the Far East.

World War. The Central Empires blocked; the Entente ruler of the seas: the US supplied the Entente, exploiting all the opportunities that presented themselves. The colossal cost of the war and the thoroughgoing upheaval of production in Europe (the Russian Revolution) made the United States the supreme arbiter of world finance. Hence its assertion in the political sphere.

Population of the United States
Its national composition given by immigration. Government policy. In 1882 Chinese workers were forbidden entry. At first, certain considerations made with respect to Japan but through the so-called Root-Takahira *Gentlemen's agreement*[4] of 1907, Japanese immigration, though not ruled out as such, was greatly curtailed by invoking clauses regarding the culture, health and possessions of the immigrants. But the great change in immigration policy came only after the war. The law of 19 May 1921, which remained in force until 1 July 1924, prescribed that each single nation's annual immigration quota should be limited to 3 per cent of the American citizens of that respective nation as determined by the 1910 census. (With successive modifications.) Yellow immigration excluded once and for all.

The United States in the Caribbean
Spanish-American war. Through the Paris peace treaty (10 December 1898) Spain renounced all rights on Cuba and yielded Puerto Rico and its other minor islands to the United States. The island of Cuba, which dominates the entrance to the Gulf of Mexico, was to become independent, its constitution being promulgated on 12 February 1901, but in exchange for recognising this independence and withdrawing its troops, the United States had its right to intervene guaranteed. With the bilateral treaty of 2 July 1903, the United States obtained commercial privileges and rent of the naval base in Guantanamo Bay.

The United States intervened in Haiti in 1914; on 16 September 1915 an agreement gave the United States the right to have a High Commission at Port-au-Prince in charge of customs administration. The Dominican Republic was placed under American financial control in 1907 and troops land there during the war, being withdrawn in 1924. In 1917 the United States bought the Virgin Islands from Denmark. In this way, the Gulf of Mexico and the Caribbean are dominated by the United States.

The United States and Central America
The Panama Canal and other possible canals. The Panamanian republic pledged itself through the Washington Treaty of 15 December 1926 to take the side of the United States in case of war. The treaty is not yet ratified since it is incompatible with the Statute of the League of Nations, of which Panama is a member, but ratification is not necessary. Question of Nicaragua.

Wilson
Wilson's world-scale policy. His conflict with the prevailing political forces in the United States. Failure of his world policy. Warren G. Harding became president on 4 March 1921. Regarding the question of the island of Yap, Harding made it clear in his note of 4 April that the United States had no intention of intervening in the relations between the Allies and Germany and neither was it asking for a revision of the Treaty of Versailles, but it would keep all the rights

due to it through its intervention in the war. These principles [were] explicated in the message of 12 April and led to the Washington Conference which lasted from 12 November 1921 to 6 February 1922 and dealt with China, the balance of power in the Far Eastern seas and limits on naval armaments.

China
In 1899 America came out in favour of Chinese territorial integrity and an open doors policy. In 1908, through the exchange of notes between Root and Takahira, the United States and Japan renewed their solemn declarations regarding the integrity and political independence of China. After China had accepted the so-called '21 demands' of Japan (the 1915 ultimatum), the United States declared (notes to Peking and Tokyo of 13 May 1915) that it did not recognise the agreements reached. At the Washington Conference the United States got the European powers and Japan to renounce a good part of the special advantages and privileges that they had previously acquired. Japan undertook to withdraw from Kiaochow. Only in Manchuria did Japan retain its position. As from 1908 the United States had already given up the indemnities due to it after the Boxer Rebellion and devoted the relative sums to cultural ends in China. In 1917 China suspended the payments. Agreements: Japan and Britain made the same type of renunciation as the United States; France made use of the funds to compensate for damages those who had lost out when the Industrial Bank of China went bust. Italy and Belgium have decided to set aside about four-fifths of the sum still due to them for cultural ends.

The Far East
United States possessions: the Philippines and the island of Guam (Marianne); Hawaii; the island of Tutuila in the Samoan group. Before the Washington Treaty the situation in the Far East was dominated by the Anglo-Japanese alliance agreed through the Defence Treaty of 30 January 1902 at London which was based on the independence of China and Korea, with British interests prevailing in China

and Japanese in Korea. After the defeat of Russia it was substituted by the Treaty of 12 August 1905; the integrity of China was confirmed as was the equality in economic and trading rights of all foreigners, the signatories mutually guaranteeing their territorial rights and special interests in East Asia and India: Japanese supremacy in Korea and Britain's right to defend India in the neighbouring Chinese regions, i.e. Tibet. This alliance was viewed negatively by the United States. Friction during the war. In the session of the Washington Conference held on 10 December 1921 Lord Balfour announced the end of the alliance, which was substituted by the treaty of 13 December 1921 through which France, Britain, the United States and Japan for a period of ten years pledged:
1) to respect one another's possessions and insular dominions in the Pacific and to refer any controversy that could arise among any of them about the Pacific and possessions and dominions in question to a Conference of the states themselves;
2) to act in concert in the case of aggressive attitudes taken up by any other power.

The treaty was limited to island possessions and, as regards Japan, was applied to Karafuto (Southern Sakhalin), Formosa and the Pescadores, but not to Korea or Port Arthur. A separate declaration specified that the treaty was also to apply to the islands held under mandate in the Pacific, but this did not imply that the United States was in agreement with the mandates. Reciprocal guarantee of the *status quo* is of special importance for the Philippines since it stops Japan stirring up the discontent of the indigenous population.

In the treaty to limit naval armaments there is a very important clause (article 19) in which France, Britain, the United States and Japan pledged to respect up to 31 December 1936 the *status quo* as regards fortifications and naval bases in the possessions and dominions to the East of latitude 110° from Greenwich, passing through the island of Hai-Nan. Japan has been sacrificed because it has its hands tied even in the case of the small archipelagos in the neighbourhood of the big metropolitan islands. Britain can fortify Singapore and the United States Hawaii, thereby dominating both points of access to the Pacific. Limitations on passenger shipping lines. Naval parity obtained between Britain and the United States.

United States hegemony. Tommasini foresees an alliance between the United States and Britain and that a reawakening will take place against this alliance and in favour of a coalition that may comprise China, Japan and Russia with the technical-industrial help of Germany. He is still basing himself on the first stage of the Chinese nationalist movement.

Q2§16 (excerpt).

11 America

May South and Central America be considered Latin? If so, in what does this Latinity consist? It is not due to chance that there has been a large scale sub-division. In order to maintain this state of disaggregation, great pressure is applied by the United States, which as a nation is concentrated and which attempts, by way of its immigration policy, not only to maintain but to increase this concentration (which is an economic and political necessity, as has been demonstrated by the internal struggle between the various nationalities to influence the government's war policy and as is demonstrated by the influence of the national element in working-class political and trade union organisation, etc.). The US is trying to superpose a network of organisations and movements under its leadership on this fragmented situation, comprising: 1) a pan-American union (state policy); 2) a missionary movement to substitute Catholicism with Protestantism; 3) opposition to the Amsterdam trade union federation and attempt to create a pan-American Union of labour (see whether other movements and initiatives of this type exist); 4) a banking, industrial and credit organisation extending over the whole of America. <This is the first element>.

Southern and Central America is characterised by: 1) a considerable number of Indians who, even if only in a passive way, have an influence on the state – it would be useful to have information regarding the social position of these Indians, on their importance in the economy, on how they come into the land ownership question, on how they take part in industrial production; 2) the dominant white races in Central and Southern America who cannot relate back to European fatherlands that may have played some important historical and economic role, such as Portugal, Spain <Italy>, comparable to that of the United States.

These white races represent a semi-feudal and Jesuitic stage in many states, and so one may say that all the states in Central and South America (with the possible exception of Argentina) still have to go through the stage of *Kulturkampf* and the advent of the modern secular state (Mexico's struggle against clericalism being an example of this phase).[5]

Q3§5 (excerpt).

12 Past and Present [1]. Otto Kahn

His trip to Europe in 1924. His statements about the regime in Italy and MacDonald's in Britain. Similar statements by Paul Warburg (Otto Kahn and Paul Warburg both belong to the big American company Kuhn-Loeb and Co.), by Judge Gary, by the delegates of the American Chamber of Trade and by other big financiers. Sympathies shown by big international finance for the regimes in Britain and Italy. How this may be explained in the light of United States world expansionism. The security of American capital abroad: not so much shares as debentures. Other guarantees political rather than purely commercial through the debt treaty signed by Volpi (look at the parliamentary proceedings since certain 'details' were not published in the newspapers) and through the J.P. Morgan loan. Caillaux's and France's attitude towards the debt problem and why Caillaux refused to sign the agreement.[6] However Caillaux, too, represents high finance, but French high finance, which is also aiming at hegemony or at least a certain position of superiority (in any case it does not want to be subordinate). Caillaux's book *Dove va la France? Dove va l'Europa?* [*Whither France? Whither Europe?*], where the politico-social programme of big finance [is] clearly set forth and where the sympathy for labourism is explained. Real similarities between the political regimes of the United States and Italy, already referred to in another note.

Q3§55.

13 Oil, Petrol and Petroleum Products

'Oil, Petrol and Petroleum Products' by Manfredi Gravina in the 16 December 1927 number of *La Nuova Antologia* (continued in the 1 January 1928 number and of interest for whoever wants a general briefing on the oil question). The article is a summary of recent publications on the oil question. Here I quote some bibliographical references and make a few observations: Karl Hoffmann, *Oelpolitik und angelsächsischer Imperialismus* [*The Politics of Oil and Anglo-Saxon Imperialism*], Berlin 1927, which Gravina calls a masterly treatment, an excellent synopsis of the great oil problems in the world today that is indispensable for whoever wants to study the question in depth with exact data at hand (with the reservation that 'oil' is all too often seen in each and every international action). The 'Federal Oil Conservation Board' was created in America in 1924 with the aim of looking at every appropriate means for rationalising the excessive exploitation of America's oil wealth and using it to the greatest and best effectiveness (Hoffmann defines this Board as a 'great corporation dealing with the industrial preparation side for the possible future war in the Pacific'). On this Board, Senator Hughes,[7] ex-Secretary of State, represents the direct interests of two companies of the Standard Oil group ('Standard Oil' of New York and 'Vacuum Oil'). The 'Standard Oil Trust' that John D. Rockefeller set up in 1882 had to fall into line with anti-trust legislation. The 'Standard' of New Jersey is still considered to be a real and proper centre for Rockefeller's petrol activities, controlling 20-25 per cent of world output, 40-45 per cent of the refineries and 50-60 per cent of the oil pipelines from the wells to the pumping stations. As well as Standard Oil and its affiliated companies, other companies have grown up among whom the so-called Big Independents[8] must be borne in mind.

Standard Oil is linked to the Harriman Consortium (rail and sea transportation, eight shipping companies) and to the Kuhn Loeb & Co. banking group of New York, headed by Otto Kahn. In the British field the most important two groups are Royal Dutch Shell and Anglo-Persian Burmah. The managing director of Shell is the Dutchman, Sir Henry Deterding. Shell is subservient to the British Empire despite Holland's great financial and political interests. Anglo-Persian Burmah may be considered an agent of the British government and more especially of the Admiralty which has three trustees on the Board. The Chairman of Anglo-Persian is Sir Charles Greenway, flanked by a technical advisor, Sir John Cadman, who headed the government oil service during the war. Greenway, Cadman, Deterding and the Samuel brothers (the founders of the British Shell company which then amalgamated with Royal Dutch) are in fact considered the top men in British oil politics.

Q2§54.

14 Italy and the Yemen in the New Politics of the Arab World

Article signed with 'three stars' in the *Rivista d'Italia* of 15 July 1927. Treaty of Sana signed on 2 September 1926 between Italy and the Yemen. Yemen is the most fertile part of Arabia (*Arabia felix*).[9] It has always been *de facto* autonomous, under a dynasty of Imams descending from el-Hussein, second son of the Caliph Ali and Fatimah, the daughter of Mohammed. Only in 1872 did the Turks establish their dominion over the Yemen. In 1903 an insurrection, which in 1904 found its leader in the new Imam, the 28-year-old Yahya ibn-Mohammed Hamid.[10] Defeated in 1905, Yahya took up the fight once more in 1911, aided by Italy, then at war with Turkey, and

Economic Trends and Developments 211

consolidated its independence. In the European war, Yahya took the side of Turkey so as to oppose British policy which hinged on increasing the power of Sherif Hussein[11] (proclaimed King of Arabia on 6 November 1916) and on the independence of Asir.

After the peace and the failure of Hussein's unitary policy, resulting in his abdication in '24 and his exile to Cyprus in '25, there remained the question of the Asir, an emirate created during the Italo-Turkish war. The famous Moroccan holy man, Ahmed ibn-Idris el-Hasani el-Idrisi had established himself in the Asir, and his descendent Mohammed Ali, known during the Libyan war as Sheikh Idris,[12] fomented a rebellion, with Italian support, among the tribes of the Asir.[13] After his recognition by the British as an independent Emir in 1914, Mohammed [Idris] collaborated with Hussein and received the Tihamah together with Hodeida[14] from the British; he granted an oil field concession in the Farasan islands to a British company. Squeezed between Hussein in the North and Yahya in the South, in 1920 the Emir formed an alliance with the Sultan of the Najd[15] (Ibn Saud) and, in return for his protection, ceded him Abha, Muhail and Beni Shahr, i.e. the extreme part of northern Asir, thus assuring him an outlet to the Red Sea. The Wahabites[16] occupied those territories and used them so as better to fight [in] the Hejaz (Hussein). On 8 January 1926, the victorious Wahabites proclaimed Ibn Saud King of the Hejaz.[17] The Wahabites showed themselves the most capable in unifying Arabia; through a proclamation of 18 June 1923, Yahya posed his candidature for the caliphate and leadership of the Arab nation. He managed, with some luck, to ensure effective control of the numerous Sultanates and tribes of the so-called Hadramawt[18] and to reduce quite notably the Adeni hinterland, without hiding his designs on Aden itself. He then threw himself against the Emir of Asir (who in his view was a usurper) and conquered the whole southern part up to Loheiya [al-Luhayyah], Hodeida included, coming into contact with the Wahabites who had, at the request of the Emir, extended their occupation of the Asir. The Emir of Asir let himself be persuaded by the ex-Sanusi[19] to engage in acts of hostility against Italy (the ex-Sanusi was a guest of Ibn Saud's at Mecca after his expulsion from Damascus in December 1924).

The Italo-Yemeni treaty recognised Yahya's royal title as well as full absolute independence. The Yemen was to import all its necessities from Italy, etc. (Ibn Saud signed a treaty with the UK on 26 December 1915 and took possession not only of the Najd but also of al-Hasa, al-Qatif and al-Jubail[20] in exchange for giving up any claim to Kuwait, al-Bahrain and Oman which, as is well-known, are British protectorates. In a debate in the House of Commons on 28 November 1922 it was officially stated that Ibn Saud was receiving a regular stipend from the UK government. With the treaties of 1 and 2 November 1925, after the conquest of the Hejaz, Ibn Saud accepted very adverse frontiers with Iraq and Transjordan that Hussein had not wanted to accept, which proved the close nature of the understanding he had with Britain.) The Italo-Yemeni treaty caused quite a stir – there was talk of a secret political and military alliance: in any case the Wahabites did not attack the Yemen (talk of Italo-British friction and so on). Rivalry between Ibn Saud and Yahya, both of whom aspired to promote and dominate Arab unity.

The Wahabites: a Muslim sect founded by Abd-el-Wahhab which sought to expand through the use of arms. It obtained many victories but was driven back into the desert by the famous Mohammed Ali and his son Ibrahim Pasha. Sultan Abdullah was captured and executed at Constantinople (December 1818) and his son Turki managed only with some difficulty to hold on to a statelet in the Najd. The Wahabites want to return to the pure letter of the Koran, getting rid of all the traditional superstructures (cult of the saints, rich decoration of mosques, religious pomp). As soon as they had conquered Mecca, they demolished domes and minarets, destroyed the tombs of famous saints, including that of Khadija, Mohammed's first wife, etc. Ibn Saud promulgated decrees against wine and tobacco, forbade people to kiss the 'black stone'[21] and to invoke the name of Mohammed in the formula of the profession of faith and in prayer.

The puritan initiatives of the Wahabites provoked protests

in the Muslim world; the governments of Persia and Egypt complained bitterly. Ibn Saud adopted a more moderate position. Yahya is attempting to capitalise on this religious reaction. He and the majority of the Yemenis follow the Zeidi[22] rite, in other words they are heretics for the Sunni Arabs. Religion is against him, so he tries to play on nationality and the fact of his descent from the prophet which allows him to claim the title of Caliph. (In the *thaler* that he had coined, there is written 'minted in the See of the Caliphate of Sana'.) His region, as one of the most fertile of Arabia, together with its geographic position give him certain economic possibilities.

It seems that the Yemen has an area of 170,000 square kilometres with a population of one to two million. On the plateau the population is pure Arab and white, while on the coast the people are predominantly dark-skinned. There is a certain administrative apparatus, embryonic schooling, an army with compulsory military service. Yahya himself is enterprising and of modern tendencies, though jealous of his independence. For Italy, the Yemen is the pawn in the Arab world.

Q2§30.

15 Britain and the United States after the War

Britain came out of the war as victor. Germany deprived of its fleet and colonies. Russia, which could again become a rival, reduced to secondary status for at least a number of decades (this opinion is extremely debatable: the British would perhaps have preferred tsarist Russia – even a victorious tsarist Russia – as a rival rather than present-day Russia, which has its influence not only on imperial policy but also on British domestic politics).[23] Britain has acquired about another 10 million square kilometres of possessions with about 35 million inhabitants, but has however had to tacitly recognise United States supremacy, for economic reasons as well as for the transformation of the Empire. The wealth of the United States, which in 1912 was calculated to be 925 thousand million gold francs, rose to 1,600 thousand million in 1922. The merchant navy: 7,928,688 tons in 1914 rose to 12,500,000 in 1919. Exports: 15 thousand million gold francs in 1913; 37,500 million in 1919, going down again to about 24 in 1924-5. Imports: about 10,000 million [gold francs] in 1913, 16 in 1919 and 19 in 1924-25.

Britain's wealth over the decade 1912-1922 rose only from 387 to 445 thousand million gold francs. Merchant navy: 1912, 13,850,000 tons; 1922, 11,800,000. Exports: 1913, 15,000 million gold francs; 1919, 17,000 million; 1924, 20,000 million. Imports: 1913, 19,000 million [gold francs], 1919 about 28,5000 million and 1924 27,500 million. Public debt: 31 March 1915, £1,162 million; 1919, £7,481 million; 1924, £8,482 million; on the asset side there were after the war Credit Loans to allied powers, colonies and dominions, the new East European states etc. that in 1919 amounted to £2,541 million and in 1924 to £2,162 million, but it was not sure whether they could be entirely recovered. For example, in 1924 the Italian debt was £553 million and in 1925 £584 million, but by the agreement of 27 January 1926 Italy is to pay only £276,750,000 over a 62-year period, including interest. In 1922 Britain, on the other hand, consolidated its debt to the United States in $4,600 million, repayable over 62 years at 3 per cent until 1932 and 3½ per cent thereafter.

Q2§16 (excerpt).

16 The American Negroes

Beniamino De Ritis's correspondence from New York, 'Colonies for Cash?', in the *Corriere della Sera* of 18 February 1932. American tendencies to link the problem of European debt with United States political strategy needs in the Caribbean; demand that Europe give up its possessions in the Antilles and its African colonies too. The *Herald Tribune* has published an article by the economist Stephen Leacock in which he says that cession of the Congo would suffice to pay the entire war debt: '... a great dream would come true. Six generations ago the Congo natives were driven on board the slave ships to America – six generations of toil and tears and history; and now they would come back, millions of workers equipped with the white man's arts and sciences ... All that is needed is ... adjustment of debts and reparations on a basis of territorial rewards'.[24]

Q8§47.

B THE WORLD ECONOMIC CRISIS

17 Past and Present [2]. Observations on the World Crisis

Cf. the two articles by P. Jannaccone and G. Arias in the March 1931 number of *Economia*, devoted to 'The World Economic Depression'. Jannaccone observes that 'the primary cause' (sic!) of the crisis 'is over-, not under-consumption'; that is to say, we are faced with a deep and, very probably, by no means transient perturbation in the *dynamic* equilibrium between the share of the national income going to consumption and that going to savings and the rate of production necessary for maintaining an unchanged or increasing standard of living for a population that is rising at a given rate of net growth. A breakdown of this equilibrium can happen in different ways: an expansion of the share of income consumed at the expense of that saved and reinvested for future production, a fall in the rate of the productivity of capital or an increase in the rate of net growth of the population. At a certain point, in other words, average individual income, instead of growing, remains constant and then from constant begins to fall progressively: at this point crises break out, the decrease in average income leads to a contraction even in absolute terms in consumption, this being reflected in further reductions in production etc. The world crisis, therefore, for Jannaccone is a *savings crisis* and 'the sovereign remedy for stemming it, without lowering the rate of [net] population increase, lies in increasing the share of income earmarked for saving and new capital formation. This is the warning of high moral value that flows from the reasoning of economic science'.

Jannaccone's observations are undoubtedly acute. The

conclusions however, that Arias draws from them are purely tendentious and in part imbecile. Admitting Jannaccone's thesis for the sake of argument, one might ask to what is the excess of consumption to be attributed? Can it be shown that the masses of the working people have seen their standard of living rise to such an extent as to represent an excess of consumption? In other words, has the wages to profits ratio become catastrophic for profits? A statistical analysis could not demonstrate this even for America. Arias 'ignores' a 'historical' element of some importance: is it not the case that, especially through trade and the stock exchange, a category of people who merely 'take their money out' has been introduced into the national income distribution in the post-war era (or at least has grown with respect to the previous period) and that this category does not represent any necessary, indispensable function while, at the same time, it does absorb a substantial share of income? No notice is taken of the fact that 'wages' are always, of necessity, tied to a job (though one would have to separate out the wages or recompense absorbed by the category of workers employed in the service of the socially unproductive and absolutely parasitic categories) – there are [moreover] disabled or unemployed workers who live on public charity or benefit – and that the income absorbed by the wages sector is identifiable almost to the last penny. It is, on the other hand, difficult to identify the income absorbed by the non-wages sector that has no necessary and indispensable function in trade and industry. The ratio between 'employed' workers and the rest of the population would provide a snapshot of the weight of 'parasitism' incident on production. Unemployment of the non-waged sector: this group is not shown up in the official statistics because in some way it 'lives' by its own means, etc. In the post-war period the unproductive parasitic sector has grown enormously both relatively and absolutely, and it is this which is eating up savings. In the European countries it is even higher than in America etc. The causes of the crisis are, then, not 'moral' (enjoyment, etc.) and neither are they political, but they are, rather, socio-economic, that is to say the same nature as the crisis itself: society creates its own toxins in having to provide a living for those masses (not only of unemployed wage-earners) of the population who hinder saving and thus break the dynamic equilibrium.

Q6§123.

18 Past and Present [3]. The Standard of Living

To try and raise the material standard of living of the people above a certain level ought to be a principle of good government. There is no special 'humanitarian' reason and not even any 'democratic' tendency to be sought here: even the most oligarchic and reactionary government should recognise the 'objective' validity of this maxim, i.e. its essentially political value (a universal one in the political sphere, in the art of maintaining and increasing state power). No government can leave the idea of an economic crisis out of the reckoning and still less so the hypothesis of being forced to declare war, that is to say having to overcome the greatest crisis that a state and social set-up can be subjected to. And since every crisis means a decline in the people's standard of living, it is obvious that a fall-back zone has already to be in existence that is sufficient to ensure that the 'biological' and hence psychological resistance of the people does not crumble away at the first impact with the new reality. The degree of real power of a state has therefore also to be measured in the light of this element, which is then related to the other elements that judge the structural solidity of a country. For if the dominant classes of a nation have not succeeded in overcoming the economic-corporative stage that leads them to exploiting the popular masses right up the extreme limits that conditions of strength allow, i.e. to reducing them to a mere vegetative biological existence, it is clear that one cannot speak of the power of the state but only of the camouflaging of power. In this examination of an essential point of the art of politics it is essential in my view to avoid quite systematically any extra-political reference (in the technical sense, i.e. outside the technically political sphere), i.e. a humanitarian one or one of a given political ideology (and not because 'humanitarianism' is not itself also a politics, etc.). It is necessary, for this paragraph, to go back to the article by Prof. Mario Camis, published in the January–February 1926 number of *Riforma Sociale*.

Q6§75.

19 Psychology and Politics

It is especially in times of financial crisis that 'psychology' is bandied about as the efficient cause of given marginal phenomena. Psychology (lack of confidence), panic, etc. But what does 'psychology' mean in this case? It is a fig leaf lending some modesty to 'politics', i.e. a particular political situation. Since by 'politics' one normally understands the action of parliamentary groupings, or parties, or newspapers or, in general, any action carried out according to a predetermined and express directive, the name 'psychology' is given to those elementary, non-predetermined, unorganised and not explicitly directed mass phenomena that are indicative of a rent in the social unity between governors and governed. Through these 'psychological pressures' the governed express a lack of confidence in their leaders, demanding the introduction of changes in both personnel and the overall directions of financial and hence economic activity. Savers do not invest savings and withdraw investments from given activities that appear particularly risky, etc. They are content with minimal – indeed with zero – interest and sometimes even prefer to sacrifice part of their capital so as to safeguard the rest.

Is 'education' sufficient for avoiding these crises of generic confidence? They are symptomatic just because they are 'generic' and it is difficult to educate a new confidence against 'genericity'. The frequent succession of such psychological crises indicates that an organism is sick, in other words that the social ensemble is no longer able to produce capable leaders. What we are dealing with, then, are political – or rather socio-political – crises of the leadership group.

Q6§90.

20 Past and Present [4]. The Crisis

Special consideration must be devoted to a study of the events which may be subsumed under the name of crisis and which have been prolonged catastrophically from 1929 right down to today.

1) Whoever wants to give one sole definition of these events or, what is the same thing, find a single cause or origin, must be rebutted. We are dealing with a process that shows itself in many ways, and in which causes and effects become intertwined and mutually entangled. To simplify means to misrepresent and falsify. Thus, a complex process, as in many other phenomena, and not a unique 'fact' repeated in various forms through a cause having one single origin.

2) When did the crisis begin? This question is bound up with the first one. Since we are dealing with a process and not an event, this is an important question. We may say that there is no starting date as such to the crisis, but simply the date of certain of the more striking 'manifestations' that have erroneously and tendentiously become identified with the crisis. The autumn of 1929, with the Wall Street crash, is the beginning of the crisis for some people, and this is understandable for those who wish to seek the origin and cause of the crisis in 'Americanism'. But the events of the autumn of 1929 in America represent just one of the striking manifestations of the critical development, nothing more. The whole post-war period is one of crisis, accompanied by attempts to obviate it that from time to time have had some success in this or that country, nothing more. For some (and perhaps they are not mistaken) the war itself is a manifestation of the crisis, even its first manifestation; the war was in fact the political and organisational reply of those who were responsible for the crisis. (This shows that it is difficult in real terms to separate the economic crisis from the political and ideological ones etc., even though this is possible scientifically, i.e. through a process of abstraction.)

3) Does the crisis have its origins in technical relationships, i.e. in the position of the relative classes, or in

other factors? Legislation, disorders etc.? It certainly seems demonstrable that the crisis has 'technical' origins, i.e. in the respective class relationships, but also that at its beginning the first manifestations or predictions gave rise to various types of conflict and to legislative intervention which showed up the 'crisis' itself or increased some factors, but did not determine it.

These three factors – 1) that the crisis is a complicated process, 2) that it began at least with the war, even if this was not its first manifestations, and 3) that the crisis has internal origins, in the modes of production and thus of exchange, and not in political or juridical factors – appear to be the first three points to clear up with precision.

Another point is that the simple facts – that is, the fundamental contradictions of present-day society – get forgotten because of apparently complex (but it would be better to say 'far-fetched') ones. One of the fundamental contradictions is this: that whereas economic life has internationalism, or better still cosmopolitanism, as a necessary premiss, state life has developed ever more in the direction of 'nationalism', of 'self-sufficiency' and so on. One of the most apparent features of the 'present crisis' is nothing other than the intensification of the nationalistic element (nationalistic state element) in the economy: quota systems, clearings, trading currency restrictions, balanced trading between two single states etc. We might, then, say – and this would be more exact – that the 'crisis' is none other than the quantitative intensification of certain elements, neither new nor original, but in particular the intensification of certain phenomena, while others that were there before and operated simultaneously with the first, sterilising them, have now become inoperative or have completely disappeared. In brief, the development of capitalism has been a 'continual crisis', if one can say that, i.e. an extremely rapid movement of elements that mutually balanced and sterilised one another. At a certain point in this movement, some elements have gained predominance and others have disappeared or have become irrelevant within the general framework. Events that go under the specific name of 'crisis' have then burst onto the scene, events that are more or less serious according to whether more or less important elements of equilibrium come into play. Given this general framework, one can study the different levels and aspects of the phenomenon – monetary, financial, productive, national and international trade etc. – and it is not to be excluded that each of these aspects, given the international division of labour and of roles, has in one country or another appeared as the prevalent one or the one that has manifested itself most obviously. But the basic problem is that of production and, within production, the imbalance between progressive industries (for which constant capital has been increasing) and stationary industries (where the immediate workforce counts for a great deal). It is understandable that even in the international field there has been a stratification between progressive and stationary industries and that the countries where there is an over-abundance of progressive industries have felt the crisis more etc. Hence the various illusions depending on the fact that it has not been understood that the world is a unit, whether one likes it or not, and that all countries, when they remain in certain structural conditions, will pass through certain 'crises'. (For all these arguments, we shall have to look at the literature produced by the League of Nations, by its experts and by its financial commission, which will at least serve to have above all else all the material on the question, and so too for the publications in the most important international journals, together with those of the various Lower Houses.)[25]

Money and gold. The gold monetary standard is made necessary by international trade and by the existence of national divisions and the role they play (which leads to particular technical factors in this field that cannot be left out of consideration, among them the velocity of circulation, which is no small economic factor). Given that goods are exchanged against goods in all fields, the question is whether this fact, which is undeniable, takes place in a short or a long time and whether this time difference is of importance. Given that goods are exchanged against goods (services being understood as included among goods) the importance of 'credit' emerges quite clearly, viz. the fact that a quantity of goods or basic services, which thus indicate a complete trade cycle, produce bills of exchange and that equality of these bills (in terms of powers of exchange) should be maintained at any one time so as not to halt the exchange process. It is true that goods are exchanged against goods, but this takes place 'in the abstract', in the sense that the agents in the exchange are different (there being no individual 'barter', so to speak, and this in fact accelerates the movement). If, then, it is necessary to have monetary stability within a state, it is even more necessary to have a stable currency that serves for international exchange, in which 'the real agents' disappear behind the phenomenon. When money varies within a state (inflation or deflation) a new class stratification comes into being in the country itself, but when an international currency varies (sterling, for example, or – to a lesser extent – the dollar) a new hierarchy among states is created, which is more complex and leads to a halt in trade (and often to wars), i.e. there is a passage of goods and services 'free of charge' between one country and another and not only between one class and another in the population. Internal currency stability is a demand of certain classes and external stability (for international currencies for which undertakings have already been entered into) for all traders. But why do these currencies vary? The reasons, without doubt, are manifold: 1) because the state is spending too much, i.e. it does not want to make certain classes bear the expenses directly, but passes them on indirectly to other classes and, if possible, to foreign countries, and 2) because it does not wish to lower a cost 'directly' (wages for example) but only indirectly and over a long period, thereby avoiding dangerous friction etc. In any case, even monetary effects are caused by the opposition of social groups, which must be understood in the sense not always of the same country in which the fact happens but of a rival country.

This is a principle that has not been explored very deeply, yet it is of utmost importance for an understanding of history: the fact that a country has been destroyed by 'foreign' or barbarian invasions does not mean to say that the history of that country is not included in the struggle between social groups. Why did the invasion take place? Why that movement of population etc.? Just as, in a certain sense, in a given state history is the history of the ruling classes, so, on a world scale, history is the history of the hegemonic states. The history of subaltern states is explained by the history of hegemonic states. The fall of the Roman Empire is explained by how life developed in the Roman Empire itself, but this tells us why certain forces 'were lacking'; in other words it is a negative history and, as such, it leaves us dissatisfied. The history of the fall of the Roman Empire is to be sought in the development of the 'barbarian' populations and even further, since the movements of the barbarian were often 'mechanical' [consequences] (i.e. ones that are not well-known) of another, entirely unknown movement. This is why the fall of the Roman Empire gives rise to 'flights of oratory' and is presented as an enigma – first, because no one wants to admit that the decisive forces of world history were not then within the Roman Empire (primitive though they were) and, second, because there are no historical documents of those forces. If there is an enigma, we are not dealing with the 'unknowable' but simply with the 'unknown' because of lack of documentation. The negative part – why did the Empire allow itself to be beaten? – remains to be seen, but it is just the study of the negative forces that is the least satisfying, and quite rightly so, since such a study in itself presupposes the existence of positive forces and no one ever wants to confess they do not know these. There are also ideological elements – of arrogance – which are anything but negligible and which come into play in the question <of the historical formulation of the fall> of the Roman Empire.[26]

Q15§5.

21 Past and Present [5]. Elements of the Economic Crises

In an advertisement for the review *Riforma Sociale*, 'the most serious and characteristic' causes of the crisis are listed as follows: 1) high taxation; 2) industrial consortia; 3) workers' trades unions; 4) salvage operations; 5) external conditionings; 6) battles for the national product;[27]; 7) quota systems; 8) inter-allied debts; 9) armaments; 10) protectionism.

It appears that some elements are similar, although listed separately, as specific causes. Others are not listed, as for example the bans on emigration. It seems to me that one should, in making an analysis, begin by listing the barriers that national (or nationalistic) policies have imposed on the circulation 1) of goods; 2) of capital; 3) of people (workers and founders of new industries and commercial companies).

That the liberals do not speak of the obstacles put on the circulation of people is symptomatic, since in a regime of a liberal character everything holds together and one obstacle creates a series of others. If it is maintained that the obstacles placed on the circulation of men are 'normal', i.e. justifiable, i.e. due to *'force majeure'*, this means that the whole crisis is 'due to *force majeure*', that it is 'structural' and not just due to the conjuncture, and that it cannot be overcome except by creating a new structure that will take account of the tendencies built into the old structure and dominate these through the new premisses it is based on. The major premiss in this case is nationalism, which does not consist solely in the attempt to produce on one's own territory everything that is consumed there (which means that all forces are oriented in the expectation of a state of war) – since this is expressed in traditional-style protectionism – but in an attempt to determine the main trading currents with given countries either because they are allies (since then the aim is to buttress them and get them in a more suitable cast for a state of war), or because it is wanted to cut them down to size even before a military war (and this new type of economic policy is that of the 'quota system' that starts off from the absurd concept that there ought to be an 'equal balance' of trade between two countries, and not that each country can reach an equal balance only by trading without distinction with all other countries).

Among the elements of crisis adduced by *Riforma Sociale*, not all can be accepted uncritically, as for example ... 'high taxation'. This is damaging when aimed at maintaining a population out of all proportion to the administrative needs, not when it serves to provide capital that only the state can provide, even though this capital is not immediately productive (and *Riforma Sociale* does not mention military defence). The so-called 'public works' policy is not in itself open to criticism except in given conditions; that is to say, the public works programmes that may be criticised are those which are useless or of a luxury nature, not those which create the conditions for a future increase in trade or which avoid certain but avoidable damage (e.g. the case of floods), there being no possibility of anyone's being driven to (gaining from) substituting the state in this activity. This may also be said of the 'industrial consortia': the consortia open to criticism are the 'artificial' ones, not those created by the force of events; if every 'consortium' is to be condemned, then so too is the system since the system, even without any artificial pressure – i.e. without recompense provided by law – drives towards the creation of consortia, in other words towards a diminution of general expenses.

Thus it is for the 'workers' unions' which do not spring up artificially, but rather are or were born despite all the adversities and legal obstacles (not only legal ones but private criminal activity that goes unpunished by the law). The elements listed by *Riforma Sociale* thus show up the weakness of the liberal economists when face to face with the crisis: 1) they keep quiet about some elements, and 2) they arbitrarily mix together the elements considered, not distinguishing the 'necessary' ones from the others etc.

Q14§57.

22 Brief Notes on Political Economy

Luigi Einaudi has collected together in one volume the essays he has published in these years of crisis. One of the themes to which he has returned most often is this: that we will get out of the crisis when people's inventiveness has once again taken on a certain impetus. This statement does not seem correct from any point of view. Without a doubt, the period of development of economic forces has among other things been characterised by inventions, but is it correct to say that inventions have been less essential and even less numerous over this most recent period? It would not appear so. At the most, one can say that they have captured the imagination less, just because they were preceded by a period of a similar, but more original, type. The whole rationalisation process is nothing but a process of 'inventiveness', of the application of new technical and organisational discoveries. It seems that by inventions, Einaudi means only those inventions which lead to the introduction of new types of commodity, but even from this standpoint the statement is perhaps not exact. In actual fact, however, essential inventions are those which bring about a diminution of costs, thereby enlarging the markets for consumption and unifying ever vaster masses of people and so on; from this point of view, what period has been more 'inventive' than that of rationalisation? It might seem to have been even too inventive, right up to 'inventing' hire purchase and the artificial creation of new needs for mass consumption. The truth is that it seems almost impossible to create new essential 'needs' to be satisfied, with new totally original industries, such as would lead to a new period of economic civilisation corresponding to that of the development of big industry. Or rather, it is the case that these 'needs' belong to socially non-essential strata of the population and their diffusion would be unhealthy (cf. the invention of 'artificial silk', satisfying the need for an apparent luxury of the middle bourgeois strata [ceti]).

Q15§26.

23 Points to Reflect on in Economics [1]. Agnelli's Ideas

See the January-February 1933 number of *Riforma Sociale*. Some preliminary remarks on Agnelli's as much as on Einaudi's way of posing the question:
1) On the one hand, technical progress does not come about 'in an evolutionary fashion', a little at a time, so that we can predict what will happen beyond certain limits: progress comes about through specific thrusts in given fields. If it went according to the reasoning of, in particular, Einaudi, we should arrive at what is hypothesised in the Land of

Cokaygne, where goods are obtained without any work being done.

2) On the other hand, the most important question is that of the production of foodstuffs: we do not think that, given the multiplicity of levels of more or less technically advanced work, wages have 'up to now' been 'elastic'[28] just because, within certain limits, a redistribution of foodstuffs – in particular those types which give life a certain style – has been allowed (together with foodstuffs, we must here include clothing and housing). Now the limits on labour productivity are much more marked in the production of foodstuffs than in the production of manufactured goods (here, the 'global quantity' of foodstuffs is understood, not their modification into the final marketable product, which does not increase their quantity). The possibilities of 'leisure' (in Einaudi's sense) beyond certain limits are given by the possibility of increasing foodstuffs as a quantity and not by labour productivity; the 'land area', together with seasonal climatic variations etc., pose iron limits, although it must be admitted that there is still a long way to go before these are reached.

Polemics like those between Agnelli and Einaudi make one think of the psychological phenomenon that during famine one's mind turns more towards the abundance of food: there is, to say the least, an ironic side to these polemics. The discussion is in fact mistaken in a psychological sense, because it tends to make one believe that present unemployment is 'technical', but this is a false idea. 'Technical' unemployment is of little account when compared with the general unemployment. Further. The reasoning goes as if society were made up of 'workers' and 'industrialists' (employers in the strict, technical sense), which is false and leads to illusory reasoning. If this were so, given that the industrialist has limited needs, the question would be simple really: the question of giving industrialists a higher salary or a reward for their talent would be irrelevant and no reasonable person would refuse to take it into account – the fanaticism of equality is not born of 'bonuses' given to worthy industrialists. The fact is this: that, given general conditions, the greater profit created through technical progress in the work process creates new parasites, that is people who consume without producing, who do not 'exchange' labour against labour, but exchange other people's labour against their own 'leisure' (leisure in the worse sense, i.e. idleness).[29] Given the relationship noted above on technical progress in the production of foodstuffs, a selection of foodstuff consumers is made, in which the 'parasites' come into the reckoning before the actual workers and most of all before the potential workers (i.e. those currently unemployed). It is from this phenomenon that the 'fanaticism of equality' is born, and it will stay 'fanaticism' – that is an extreme and irrational tendency – as long as this situation lasts. One can see that it is already disappearing where it is apparent that at least people are working to get rid of or ease this general situation.

The fact that 'industrial society' is not composed just of 'workers' and 'entrepreneurs', but of intinerant 'shareholders' (speculators) upsets the whole of Agnelli's reasoning: if technical progress gives rise to a bigger profit margin, the outcome is that this is distributed not rationally, but 'always' irrationally to shareholders and their like. Neither can it be said that there are any 'healthy firms' at the present time; they have all fallen ill, and this is said not out of moralistic or polemical prejudices, but objectively. It is the very 'size' of the market for shares that has created this unhealthiness: the mass of shareholders is so big that they now obey the laws of the 'crowd' (panic, etc., having its special technical terms in 'boom', 'run'[30] and so on) and speculation has become a technical necessity, more important than the work of professional engineers or workers.

Observation of the 1929 crisis in America has spotlighted exactly this point: that there exist unstoppable speculatory phenomena which have brought down even the 'healthy' firms, on account of which one can say that 'healthy firms' do not exist any more. In consequence, one can use the word 'healthy' coupling it with a historical reference – 'in the sense it once had', viz. when certain general conditions did exist that allowed certain general phenomena not only in a relative but also in an absolute sense. (On many notes of this paragraph see the book by Sir Arthur Salter, *Ricostruzione: come finirà la crisi*, Milan 1932).[31]

Q10 II§55.

24 Points to Reflect on in Economics [2]. Labour and Consumption

Distribution of the human forces of labour and consumption. Compared with the forces of production, one may observe how those of consumption are always on the increase. The economically passive and parasitic population. But the concept of 'parasitic' must be spelled out in detail. It may turn out that one can show that an intrinsically parasitic function is necessary given the existing conditions: this makes the parasitism even more serious. It is exactly when a parasitism is 'necessary' that the system which creates such necessities stands condemned out of its own mouth. But it is not that the consumers pure and simple grow just in number; it is also their standard of living that increases, thereby increasing the share of goods that are consumed (or destroyed) by them. If one looks carefully, one must reach the conclusion that the ideal of all members of the ruling class is that of creating the conditions in which their heirs may live without working, off unearned income: how can such a society possibly be healthy when its members work just in order not to have to work any more? Since this idea is impossible and unhealthy, the result is that the whole organism is degraded and ill. A society that tells one to work in order to create parasites, to live on so-called past labour (a metaphor to indicate the present labour of others) in actual fact destroys itself.

Q10 II§53.

C NATIONAL ECONOMIC PROBLEMS AND INTERNATIONAL RELATIONS

25   Post-War Contradictions

Giuseppe Paratore, 'Italy's Economy, Finance and Money at the End of 1928', *La Nuova Antologia*, 1 March 1929.

An interesting article, but too hasty and too conformist. To be kept in mind for reconstructing the situation in 1926 up to the passing of the special laws.[32] Paratore draws up a list of the main contradictions of the post-war years: 1) territorial divisions have multiplied tariff barriers; 2) everywhere, the response to an overall reduction in consumption capacity has been an increase in industrial plant; 3) the response to a tendential economic depression has been an accentuated spirit of economic nationalism (every nation wants to produce everything and wants to sell without buying); 4) to an overall impoverishment there has corresponded a tendency towards a real increase in state expenditure; 5) higher unemployment has gone along with less emigration (before the war about 1,300,000 workers used to leave Europe every year, while nowadays there are only 600-700 thousand emigrants); 6) a capital value has been placed on part of the war damage and this gives rise to interest that, for quite a long time, has been payed off through debt conversion; 7) there is an indebtedness to the United States of America (for political and trading debts) which, should it give rise to real transfers, would jeopardise any monetary stability.

Paratore draws attention to the following elements in Italy's post-war situation: 1) a considerable dimunition in its human capital; 2) a debt of about 100 thousand million lire; 3) a fluctuating volume of debt that is causing some anxiety; 4) a national budget in disarray; 5) a monetary order out of kilter, as is seen from the large reduction in and dangerous instability of both the domestic and international values of the currency; 6) a particularly negative balance of trade, aggravated by a complete aimlessness as regards foreign trade relations; 7) many outdated financial legal provisions relating to the private and public economic spheres.

Q2§122.

26 Inflation and the Domestic Economy

In his article 'Italy's Economy, Finance and Money' in the 1 March 1929 number of the *Nuova Antologia*, Giuseppe Paratore writes that Italy has a 'twofold economic constitution (an industrial capitalist one in the North and an agrarian savings-based one in the South)', noting that this situation made it difficult to stabilise the lira in 1926-27. The most direct and simple method, that of quickly consolidating monetary devaluation thereby immediately creating a new parity (along the lines prescribed by Kemmerer, Keynes and Cassel), was inadvisable etc.

It would be of interest to know which factor turned out in the end to be best defended: the Northern or the Southern economy and this because, in actual fact, stabilisation was brought about in the midst of a precipitous fall after a great deal of hesitation (in 1926 the dollar went from 477.93 in January through 479.93 in February, 480.03 in March, 479.63 in April, 500.28 in May, 527.72 in June to 575.41 in July).[33] It should, moreover, be borne in mind that the South was more homogeneous than the North in its demands and had the solidarity of all the nation's savers while in the North the capitalists were divided – exporters favouring inflation, others looking to the domestic market and so on and so forth. Furthermore, a low level of stabilisation would have created not just an economic but a socio-political crisis because the social position of millions of citizens would have been altered.

Q3§160.

27 International Tariffs and Trade

Lodovico Luciolli, 'The USA's Customs Policy', *La Nuova Antologia*, 16 August 1929.

A very useful and interesting article to consult since it summarises the history of tariffs in the United States together with the special role that customs duties have always played in the United States. It would be interesting to have a *historical* review of the various forms that customs policies have assumed or are assuming in the various countries, and especially in the economically and politically more important ones; what this in essence means is the various attempts at organising the world market and establishing the most favourable position in it from the point of view either of the national economy or of the industries that are basic to the economic activities of the nation. A new tendency in present-day economic nationalism to be followed up is this: a number of states are trying to make sure that their imports from a given country are kept 'under control' *en bloc*, the 'exports' that correspond to them being equally well controlled. It is obvious that this type of measure is to the advantage of those nations whose (visible) balance of trade is in the red, but how can one explain the fact that this principle is beginning to get established in France, a country which exports more than it imports? To begin with, we are dealing with a trading policy aimed at boycotting imports from a given country, but from that beginning a general policy may develop, to be located within a wider framework of a positive nature that may develop in Europe, as a consequence of American tariff policies, in order to try and stabilise certain national economies. In other words, every important nation may tend to equip its own political hegemony over the nations that are subordinate to it with an organised economic substratum. Regional political agreements might become regional economic agreements, in which levels of imports and exports would be 'agreed', no longer between just two states but between a group of states, thereby getting rid of many very evident and by no means small drawbacks. In this tendency it seems to me may be included the policy of Empire free-trade and protectionism towards the non-imperial countries of the group that has recently been formed in Britain around Lord Beaverbrook (or some such name), as well as the agricultural agreement reached in Sinaia and then extended in Warsaw.[34]

This political tendency could be the modern form of the *Zollverein* [customs union] that led to the federal German Empire, or of the attempts at a tariffs league among the Italian states before 1848, or, further back, eighteenth-century mercantilism. It could become the intermediate stage of Briand's pan-European attempts[35] in that it corresponds to the need for the national economies to go beyond a national framework without, at the same time, losing their national nature.

By following this tendency the world market would come to be constituted no longer of a series of national but of international (interstate) markets which would, internally, have organised a certain stability of essential economic activities and which could enter into reciprocal relationships on the basis of the same system. This system would take account more of politics than of economics in the sense that, in the economic field, it would place more importance on finished goods than on heavy industry. This is in the first stage of organisation. For we have in fact seen how the attempts at forming international cartels based on raw materials (iron, coal, potash, etc.) have set hegemonic states such as France and Germany against one another; neither the one nor the other can yield any of its position and world role. There are too many difficulties and obstacles. What, on the other hand, would be simpler is an agreement between France and its vassal states on an organised economic market along the lines of the British Empire, which could cause the German position to collapse and force her to come within the system, but under French hegemony.

These are all still very vague hypotheses, but they should be borne in mind when studying the above-mentioned tendencies.

Q2§125.

28 The National Economy

The whole economic activity of a country can only be judged in relationship to the international market; it 'exists' and is to be evaluated in so far as it is inserted into an international unit. From this stems the importance of the principle of comparative costs[36] and the solidity shown by the fundamental theorems of classical economy in the face of the verbalistic criticisms levelled at it by every new form of mercantilism (protectionism, economies subject to central controls, corporativism etc.). There does not exist any purely national economic 'balance', either overall or even for a particular activity. The whole national economic complex is projected into the surplus that gets exported in exchange for corresponding imports, and if, within this national economic complex, there is some good or service that costs too much and is produced non-economically, this loss is reflected in the surplus exported and becomes a 'present' the country gives to other countries, or at least – since one cannot always speak of a 'present' – a net loss to the country with respect to those countries in any evaluation of the country's relative and absolute status in the international economic world.

If, within a country, grain is dear to produce, the industrial goods exported and produced by workers fed on that grain, on an equal price footing with the equivalent foreign good, contain a greater quantity of national labour embodied in them and a greater quantity of sacrifices than does the same foreign good. One's work is a sacrifice for the 'other country'; sacrifices are made for the 'other country', not one's own. The classes which, domestically, make use of these sacrifices are not the 'nation', but represent an exploitation exercised by 'foreigners' over the truly national forces etc.

Q9§32.

29 Relations Between City and Countryside

In order to have data on the relations between the industrial nations and the agrarian ones, and thus have indications as to the question of the situation of the semi-colonies of the agrarian countries (as well as the internal colonies in the capitalist countries), see the book by <Mihail> Manoilesco, *La teoria del protezionismo e dello scambio internazionale*

[*The Theory of Protectionism and International Exchange*], Milan 1931. Manoilesco writes that 'the product of the labour of an industrial worker is in general always exchanged against the product of the labour of several agricultural workers, on average in the ratio one to five.' Manoilesco, on this account, speaks of an 'invisible exploitation' by the industrial countries of the agricultural countries. Manoilesco is the current governor of the National Bank of Romania and his book expresses the ultra-protectionist tendencies of the Romanian bourgeoisie.

Q8§193.

30 City and Countryside

Giuseppe De Michelis, 'Premisses and Contribution to a Study of the Drift from the Countryside', *La Nuova Antologia*, 16 January 1930. An interesting article from many points of view. De Michelis poses the question in a fairly realistic fashion. But what is the drift from the countryside? Though the problem has been talked about for 200 years, it has never yet been posed in precise economic terms.

(Even De Michelis forgets two fundamental aspects to the question: 1) one of the reasons for the complaints over the drift away from the countryside lies with the landowning interests, since the landowners see wages rising due both to competition from urban industry and to a more 'legal' way of life that is less open to those whims and abuses that are part and parcel of rural life; 2) as regards Italy, he makes no mention of emigration among the peasantry – the international form of drift from the countryside towards the industrial nations; this is really a criticism of the Italian agrarian set-up in so far as the peasant goes off to be a peasant somewhere else, increasing his standard of living in the process.)

De Michelis is right in his observation that agriculture has not suffered through this exodus: 1) because the agricultural population *on the international scale* has not gone down; 2) because production has not fallen – there has in fact been surplus production, as is shown by the crisis in the prices of agricultural produce.

(The above was true in the previous crisis, in other words when population and production corresponded to phases of industrial prosperity; now, however, that the crisis in agriculture is going hand in hand with that in industry, one can no longer speak of over-production but of under-consumption.)

The article quotes statistics that demonstrate the progressive extension of the area under cereal cultivation and, even more, that given over to industrial crops (hemp, cotton etc.) as well as a rise in production. The problem is looked at from an international stance (for a group of 21 countries), i.e. from the standpoint of the international division of labour. (From the point of view of individual countries, the problem is subject to variation and herein lies the current crisis: it is a reactionary resistance to new world relations, to the increased importance of the world market.)

The article quotes a number of bibliographical references, which will have to be looked at, but it finishes with a gigantic error. De Michelis says: 'The formation of the city in ancient times was nothing other than the slow and progressive separation of trades from the agricultural activity with which they had previously been confounded, so that they could assume an independent life. Thanks above all to the increase in electrical power, progress over the forthcoming decades will consist in bringing trades back to the countryside so that, under forms that have been changed and perfected procedures, they can again be linked up with what is properly speaking agricultural labour. In this redeeming function of rural artisan production, Italy is once again preparing itself to assume the role of standard-bearer and master.'

De Michelis perpetrates confusion on a number of scores: 1) linking the city up with the countryside cannot come about on the basis of artisan production, but only on the basis of rationalised and standardised big industry. His 'artisan' utopia is based on the textile industry, for which it was thought that, through the possibility (which has come true) of electrical energy being distributed over long distances, it would have been possible to give the peasant family back its electrically-powered modern mechanical loom. But today one sole worker can already (so it seems) oversee up to 24 looms, which poses new problems as regards large scale capital investment and competition, as well as insoluble ones of the general organisation of the peasant family; 2) the time that the peasant has to remain unemployed (the fundamental problem of modern agriculture which puts a peasant in an economically inferior position with respect to the city that 'can' work the year round) can only be put to good industrial use in a planned, well-developed economy which can make itself independent of time fluctuations in sales that already happen and that lead to dead seasons in industry, too; 3) the great concentration of industry and production-line manufacture of interchangeable pieces allow factory departments to be taken out to the countryside, thereby relieving congestion in the big cities and making industrial life more salubrious. It is not the artisan who will go back to the countryside, but, vice versa, the more modern and standardised worker.

Q2§137.

31 Colonies, Capital Flow and the Demographic Question

See the speeches made in parliament by the Foreign Minister, Dino Grandi, in 1932 and the discussions stemming from them in the Italian and international press. Grandi posed the Italian question as a world one that had, of necessity, to be solved alongside the others that constitute the political expression of the general post-war crisis, which in 1929 deepened to the point of near catastrophe. These questions were: the French security problem, the German equal rights problem and the problem of a new set-up for the Danube and Balkan states. The way that Grandi posed the question was an able attempt to force any eventual world congress convened to resolve these problems (as well as any attempt by normal diplomatic activity) to deal with the 'Italian question' as a fundamental element of European and world reconstruction and pacification. What, according to this way of putting it, does the Italian question consist of? It consists in the fact that the country's demographic increase is in conflict with its relative poverty, i.e. in the existence of over-population. Italy ought, therefore, to be given the chance to expand, economically as well as demographically etc. But if the question is posed in this way, it does not seem easy to resolve without giving rise to fundamental objections. If it is true that general international relations, in the way that they have taken on an ever more rigid aspect since 1929, are most unfavourable to Italy (especially economic nationalism and the 'racism' that hinders the free circulation not only of goods and capital, but above all human labour), it might also be asked whether Italy's own policy has not contributed and is still not contributing to creating these new relations and making them more rigid. It would appear that the main research to be done should be along these lines: is the individual low level of national income due to the 'natural' poverty of the country or rather to socio-historical conditions that have been created and kept in being by a particular choice of political direction and that make the national economy as leaky as a sieve? In other words, does the state not cost too much, where by state we mean, as is necessarily the case, not only the administration of state services, but also the ensemble of classes which comprise it in the strict sense and dominate it? Is it therefore possible to think that without a change in these internal relations the situation could change for the better even though internationally the relations were to improve? It may also be observed that that the projection of the question onto the international field can represent a political alibi to demonstrate to the masses.

It may be conceded that the national income is low, but does it not then get destroyed (devoured) by too great a passive population, thereby making any progressive capitalisation, albeit at a reduced rate, impossible? The demographic question must therefore be analysed in its turn, and it must be established whether the demographic composition is a 'healthy' one, even for a capitalist, private property regime. The 'natural' relative poverty of individual countries in the modern civilised world (and in normal times) has an importance that in its turn, too, is relative; at most, it will prevent certain marginal profits that stem from a geographic 'position'. National wealth is conditioned by the international division of labour and by having known how, within the possibilities offered by this division, to choose the most rational and profitable one for each given country. We are therefore dealing essentially with the 'directive capacity' of the dominant economic class, with its spirit of initiative and organisation. If these qualities are lacking, and the economic undertaking is essentially based on sheer exploitation of the productive and working classes, no international agreement can heal this situation.

There is no example in modern history of colonies being created by merely 'peopling' a region; these colonies have never existed. Emigration and colonisation follow the flow of capital invested in the various countries and not vice versa. The current crisis that is manifesting itself especially as a fall in raw material and cereal prices demonstrates that the problem is in fact not only of the 'natural' wealth of the various countries of the world, but one of social organisation and of the transformation of raw materials for certain ends and not for others. That we are dealing with organisation and politico-economic policy direction is also to be seen in the fact that every country in the modern civilised world has had its 'emigration' during certain stages of its economic development, but that this emigration has stopped and often has been reabsorbed.

That there is no desire (or no ability) to change internal relations (and not even to correct them in a rational fashion) can be seen from the policy towards the national debt, which continually increases the weight of 'demographic' passivity, just when the active sector of the population is being forced to contract due to unemployment and the crisis. The national income is falling, the number of parasites rising, savings are being reduced and disinvested from the productive process in order to be reinvested in the public debt, i.e. being made the cause of a new relative and absolute parasitism.

Q19§6.

32 Questions of Hegemony

North and South. Northern hegemony would have been 'normal' and historically beneficial if industrialism had had the ability to expand its cadre force rapidly enough to incorporate ever new economically comparable zones. Had this been the case hegemony would have been the expression of a struggle between old and new, between progress and backwardness, between the more and the less productive. The economic revolution would then have been national in nature (and taken place over the entire national territory), even though its motive force would have been temporarily and functionally regional. All economic forces would have received a stimulus and their consequent contraposition would have resulted in a higher level of unity. This, however, was not the course taken by events. The ensuing hegemony had a permanent guise and the rivalry took on the appearance of a condition for the existence of Northern industry that was historically necessary for an indeterminate – and therefore seemingly 'perpetual' – length of time.

Emigration. A comparison of Italy and Germany. It is true that, at first, industrial development caused a wave of emigration from Germany but, later on, it not only put a halt to this but also gave rise to a sizeable immigration. It may be said, for a purely mechanical comparison between the phenomena of emigration in the two countries, that when such a comparison is made in depth other essential differences emerge. In Germany industrialism at first produced a surplus of the 'industrial cadre force' itself and it was this force which emigrated, in well-defined economic conditions: a trained and gifted quantity of human capital left the country, together with a certain stock of finance capital. This emigration from Germany was the reflection of a surplus of active capitalist energies that were helping the development of the economies of other countries which themselves were either more backward or at the same level but lacking in labour-power and management cadres. In Italy the phenomenon was more elementary and passive; the basics never reached a point of resolution but are, rather, still continuing up to this day. Although emigration has in effect diminished and undergone qualitative changes, it is important to note that this has not come about through an absorption of the remaining forces into a broader industrial cadre force with a standard of living at the same level as 'normal' countries. The change is an effect of the world crisis, in other words of the existence in all the industrialised countries of reserve armies of labour superior to the economic norm. The Italian role as provider of a reserve army for the whole world has come to an end, not because the demographic equilibrium of Italy has been normalised but because that of the entire world has been upset.

Intellectuals and workers. Another fundamental difference lies in the fact that German emigration was organic; that is to say, alongside ordinary workers there also emigrated specialists in industrial organisation. In Italy it was just the working mass, as yet predominantly formless both industrially and intellectually, that emigrated. The corresponding intellectual elements stayed behind; they too were similarly inchoate, i.e. not at all modified by industrialism and its attendant civilisation. A formidable level of intellectual unemployment was thus created, which caused a whole series of phenomena of corruption and political and moral decomposition, with quite material economic consequences. The state apparatus itself, in all its various facets, was prey to this and so assumed its current particular character. Thus the conflicts, which each single one of these facets contributed to deepening, worsened rather than disappeared.

Q1§149.

33 The Colonies

Study whether and to what extent the colonies have served for populating purposes in the sense of colonialism being linked to a population surplus within the colonising nations. Certainly more British went to the United States after American independence than when the country [was] still a

British colony etc.; there were more British in the independent United States than in the British colonies etc. The colonies have allowed an expansion of productive forces and have thus absorbed the population surplus of a number of countries, but the 'direct dominion' factor has had no influence in this. Emigration follows its own laws of an economic nature, viz. migratory currents spring up in the various countries according to the different types of workforce or technical expertise needed in those same countries. A state is a coloniser not because of a high birth rate but because it is rich in capital that it wants to invest abroad etc. This being the case, see which countries the migratory currents of states with no colonies are directed towards and which of these countries 'could' (in the abstract) themselves become colonies. German, Italian and Japanese emigration is overwhelmingly in the direction of the non-'colonisable' countries.

Q8§80.

34 Robert Michels

In Alberto Giaccardi's article 'A Colonial Greater Germanism as One Cause of the World Conflict' in the 16 May 1930 issue of *La Nuova Antologia*, we find on p.238 'The "place in the sun" demanded by Germany too soon began to expand so much that it would have put everyone else in the shade, or very nearly so. A learned German, Robert Michels, denied any right to demand colonies even to the Italians, whose situation was analogous to that of the German people, on the grounds that "Italy, although demographically strong, is poor in capital".' Giaccardi does not quote his bibliographical source for this.

In the number that came out on the succeeding 1 July Giaccardi published a 'correction' of this statement of his, evidently at Michels's request. He cites Michels's *L'Imperialismo italiano* [*Italian Imperialism*], Milan 1914, and his 1912 article 'Factors in the Historical Origin of Italian Imperialism' in the *Archiv für Sozialwissenschaft*, January-February 1912, pp.91-2, concluding: 'This corresponds perfectly to the Italian sentiments constantly (!) demonstrated by the distinguished professor from Perugia University who, although hailing from the Rhineland, has chosen Italy as his adopted homeland, and has always carried out intense and effective activity in our favour.'

Q7§64.

35 Past and Present [6]. Studies on the National Economic Structure

Exact significance of the three initiatives on which there has been so much discussion: 1) obligatory consortia; 2) *Istituto Mobiliare Italiano* (IMI); 3) powers of the state to prevent new industries being created and to extend those already in existence (in other words the need to have a state licence *from a given date* for an industrial initiative); 4) *Istituto per la Ricostruzione Industriale* (IRI), divided into two juridically autonomous sections – a) the industrial finance division and b) the industrial restructuring division.[37]

In the meantime we need to have an exact 'history' of the legal stages that each institute has gone through and to be able to identify the immediate causes that led to its foundation. As regards the general prospects of these institutes, one must bear in mind the particular role the Italian state has always played in the economy in substituting for so-called private enterprise, either because this latter is absent or because the investors do not 'trust' it. The 'economic' question might be posed as follows: whether or not these institutes represent an onerous expenditure compared with what would be the case if the self-same role were played by private enterprise. This may seem a false way of putting it, but in fact it isn't: in so far as there is no private agent for some role that is necessary for the modernisation of the life of the country, it is without doubt better for the state to assume the responsibility. But it is best to say this openly, i.e. to say that we are not talking about actual progress so much as recognising a backwardness that has to be overcome 'at all costs' and paying the price for it. Nor is it at all true to say the price will be paid once and for all: paying today will not avoid our having to pay another price when we go from nationalisation to counteract backwardness to nationalisation as a historical stage, organic and necessary to the development of the economy towards its programmatic construction stage. The current stage is that which, in a certain sense, corresponds to the enlightened monarchies of the eighteenth century. It has the outward and mechanical terminology of modernity, borrowed from other countries where this stage really is modern and progressive.

Q15§1.

36 Nationalisations and State Takeovers

Cf. M. Saitzew, *Die öffentliche Unternehmung der Gegenwart*, [*Public Enterprise Today*] Tübingen 1930. Saitzew is a professor at Zurich University. According to him the area over which public enterprises act, in certain branches especially, is much greater than is thought; in Germany public enterprise capital is a fifth of the total national wealth (public enterprise expanded during the war and the immediate post-war years). In Saitzew's opinion, public enterprises are not a form of socialism but part and parcel of capitalism. The objections to public enterprise could also be made in relation to limited companies; one hears arguments repeated that held when private firms were individual ones, whereas nowadays it is the limited company that is prevalent etc.

The booklet will be of use to see how far public undertakings have spread in some countries. The nature of the public undertaking, according to Saitzew, is not so much that of having income for the state as its main aim as that of stopping the formation in certain branches of the economy, in which competition is technically impossible, of a private monopoly that would be dangerous for the community.

Q7§40.

37 Past and Present [7]. Nationalisations

Cf. A. De Stefani's article 'Covering Losses' in the *Corriere* of 16 March 1932: 'In the present protectionist regimes, even in normal times it is the whole of the nation that contributes to balancing the books of firms and creating their profits ... The problem of covering a firm's losses is precisely that of sharing them out beyond the circle of those who, in terms of common law, ought to bear them: owners (shareholders), creditors (lenders, contractors and suppliers). This process could, in the cases in which the state sees to covering a firm's losses, be called a process of nationalising losses, an extension of the principle of compensation for damage due to war or acts of God.' De Stefani does not see the irony of nationalising losses but not profits, of compensating for the damage created by speculation (which they *will* have) but not by unemployment (which no one willingly accepts).

Q8§92.

38 The Italian Risorgimento. Savings, Agricultural Protectionism and Industry

Cf. the article by Salvatore Valitutti, 'Big Industry in Italy', in the February 1933 number of *Educazione Fascista*, an article which consists of allusions and fleeting references but which all the same is quite interesting and to be looked at again when the opportunity arises.

It is not however correct to pose the question as he does: 'It was true (...) that the southern Italian economy was agricultural and feudal and that that of the rest of Italy was more modern and industrial.' In southern Italy there was and there still is a particular type of agricultural activity, and agricultural protectionism benefited the North more than the South because it was cereals that were protected and here the North, more so than the South, was the great producer. The difference between North and South lay also and especially in their social compositions, in the different positions occupied by the masses of the peasantry who, in the South, had to maintain through their labour too great a sector of the economically passive population, of those living 'on unearned income' etc. Nor can one say that 'the practice consisting of modesty of means and silent meditation' that characterised the first thirty years of the Kingdom of Italy – a modesty more honoured in the breach than the keeping – 'halted the progress of those economic activities which were more needful of dynamism and wealth and which, if carried out in the interests of the South, would have produced the effect of refounding and reorganising Italian life on the basis of the Kingdom of Naples'. Why ever should it have been carried out in the interests of the South? In the interests of all the new forces of the nation, in their just proportions and not in a hierarchy of privilege. The backward structure of the South was, instead, exploited and made permanent – even made more extreme – in order to drain the savings of its parasitic classes off towards the North.

In addition, the role of the socialist movement in the formation of modern Italy is not presented very exactly in quite a number of ways even though it is praised and highly commended. Bonomi's position was a caricature of what Engels envisaged in the first few years' numbers of *Critica Sociale*, and in this sense the syndicalist reaction that took its inspiration from Engels was quite natural and was in fact a pro-Southern one and so on (Valitutti must here be referring to my article on the Southern question).[38] For Bonomi's position, one would have to look at his book on the *New Roads*,[39] in which the whole question must be developed much more organically.

Q15§44.

39 Past and Present [8]. The Error of the Anti-Protectionist Left

Writers on *La Voce, Unità*, syndicalists etc).[40] These individuals formulated the questions as ones of principle (a scientific principle), as the choice of the general direction of the state – or rather, even the national – policy of governments. They divided free-trade industrialists off from protectionists etc., inviting the people to choose between these two categories. But could they be so divided, or were rather their interests not already closely linked through the banks, and did this link not tend to become ever stronger through financial groupings and industrial cartels? If the aim was that of creating an efficient 'free-trade' force it was therefore necessary not so much to set oneself unattainable goals, such as that of creating a division in the industrial camp and giving hegemony over the popular masses (above all over the peasantry) to one part of it, as to tend towards the creation of a bloc amongst the popular classes under the hegemony of what, from a historical perspective, represented the most advanced of them. (Rerum Scriptor's book on the *Tendenze vecchie e bisogni nuovi del movimento operaio italiano* [*Old Tendencies and New Needs of the Italian Working-Class Movement*] could be reviewed in this sense.) For, in fact, Rerum Scriptor and his friends just attained the shabby goal of deflecting peasant bitterness in the direction of relatively 'innocent' social groups etc.

Q8§72.

40 Past and Present [9]. The Individual and the State

The way in which the economic situation has changed at the 'expense' of old-style liberalism. Is it true that individual citizens know their rights better than anyone else in present-day conditions? Is it true that in present-day conditions there is selection by merit? 'Individual citizens in so far as they cannot know (and above all cannot control) the general conditions in which affairs develop, given the size of the world market and its complexity, in actual fact do not even know their own affairs – the need for big industrial organisations etc. Moreover, the state with its ever more heavy tax burden strikes at its own citizens but cannot harm the citizens of other nations (who are taxed less heavily or have taxation systems that distribute the burden differently); big states that have to incur great expenditure for comprehensive public services (including the army, navy etc.), hit their own citizens harder (unemployment pay and so on being added to the bill). But does state intervention through customs duties create a new base? Through its customs policy, the state 'chooses' which of its citizens to protect even though they may not 'warrant' such protection etc., and thus provokes a fight among the various groups over the division of the national income etc.

Q6§109.

41 On the National Economic Structure

The May-June 1932 number of *Riforma Sociale* carries a review of Rodolfo Morandi's book *Storia della grande industria in Italia* [*A History of Large-Scale Industry in Italy*], Bari 1931.[41] The review contains a number of points of a certain methodological interest (while the review's author remains anonymous, he may be traceable to Prof. De Viti De Marco).

The first objection to Morandi is that he does not take into account what Italian industry has cost: 'It is not enough for an economist to be shown factories that give work to thousands of workers, reclamation projects that create cultivable land and other such similar facts which the public is generally satisfied with for its general judgement on a country, on a historical era. The economist is well aware that the same result may represent a bettering or worsening of a certain economic situation, depending on whether it has been obtained through a package of lesser or of greater sacrifices.'

(The general criterion is correct that one must examine the cost of introducing a certain industry into the country, who has borne the cost for it, who has gained advantage from it and whether the sacrifices made could not have been more usefully made in another direction, but the whole of this examination has to be made not so much in an immediate as a wide-ranging perspective. Furthermore, it is not enough to use the sole criterion of economic utility for examining the passage from one form of economic organisation to another; one must also consider the political criterion, viz. whether the passage was objectively necessary and corresponded to a certain general interest, even if this were a long-term one. Admitted that, for the indispensable requisites of a great modern state, unification of the peninsula had, of necessity, to cost sacrifices to one part of the population, one must still examine whether these sacrifices were shared out equitably, to what extent they could have been spared and whether the direction followed in exacting them was the right one. It is more than certain that capitalism was not introduced into Italy and developed from a national point of view, but from the standpoint of narrow regionalism and restricted groups and that it has to a great extent failed in its tasks, thus giving rise to an unhealthy emigration. The emigrants themselves have not been reabsorbed and the need to emigrate has never ceased, thereby causing the economic ruin of entire regions. Indeed, emigration has to be considered, on one hand, as a phenomenon of absolute unemployment and, on the other, as a manifestation of the fact that the domestic economic regime has not guaranteed a standard of living approaching that found at the international level, such as to make it pointless for people already in work to prefer the risks and sacrifice connected with leaving their own villages behind.)

Morandi fails to grasp the real significance of protectionism in the development of Italian big industry. He thus reproaches the bourgeoisie absurdly for its 'deliberate and totally ruinous policy of not having attempted the salutary Southern *adventure*, given that there agricultural production can hardly pay man back for the great efforts that have to be put in'. He does not ask himself whether the South's poverty was caused by the protectionist legislation which allowed the North's industrial development, and how a domestic market could exist that could be exploited by means of excise duties and other privileges, if the protectionist system was extended to the whole peninsula thereby transforming the rural economy of the South into an industrial one (though one can conceive of such a pan-Italian protectionist regime as a system for ensuring that certain social groups receive a given income – in other words as a 'wages regime'; and one can see something of this kind in cereals protection, linked to industrial protection, which works only in favour of the big landowners and the grain-milling industry etc.). Morandi may be taken to task for the excessive severity with which he judges and condemns people and events of the past, since it is enough to compare conditions before and after independence to see that something has nevertheless been done.

It seems dubious whether one can write a history of big industry abstracting from the main factors (population growth, financial and tariff policy, railways etc.) that have contributed to defining the economic characteristics of the period under consideration. (This criticism is quite right; a good deal of the activity of the Historic Right from Cavour to 1876 was in fact devoted to creating the general technical conditions whereby big industry was made possible and large scale capitalism could spread and flourish. It was only with the advent of the left, and especially with Crispi, that the 'manufacturers were manufactured' through protectionism and privileges of all sorts. The financial policy of the right, aimed at balancing the budget, made the subsequent 'productivist' policy possible.) 'In this way, for example, it is impossible to understand why ever such an abundance of the workforce came about in Lombardy in the first decades after unification, and hence why the level of wages remained so low if capitalism is represented as an octopus stretching out its tentacles to grab more and more prey from the countryside, instead of taking into account the transformation that was going on at the same time as regards agricultural tenancies and the rural economy in general. And it is easy to come to a simplistic conclusion regarding the narrow-mindedness and obstinacy of the boss classes by noting the resistance they put up to any demand for an improvement in the conditions of the working classes, if one does not also bear in mind what the increase in population has been compared to new capital formation.' (The question, however, is not quite as simple as that. The savings or capitalisation rate was low because the capitalists wanted to maintain the whole legacy of parasitism of the previous period so as not to see the political clout of their class and their allies seriously weakened.)

Criticism of Morandi's definition of 'big industry'; it is not clear why he has excluded from his study made of the most important industrial activities (transport, food industries etc.). He shows excessive sympathy for colossal industrial bodies, which are too often considered, without a shadow of a doubt, as superior forms of economic activity, despite the fact that he recalls the disastrous collapses of Ilva, Ansaldo, the Banca di Sconto, Snia Viscosa, Italgas.[42] 'Another point of disagreement which deserves to be brought out, since it stems from a very widespread error, is that the author considers that a country must of necessity remain suffocated by competition from other countries if it starts its own industrial organisation after them. This economic inferiority, which, according to him, Italy is condemned to, does not seem to be at all proven, because conditions in the market, in technology, in political set-ups are all in continual movement and thus the goals to be reached and the roads to be taken are very often shifted quite suddenly so that individuals and nations who were left behind or who had hardly made a move may find themselves out in front. If this were not so, it would be difficult to explain how new industries can rise up and flourish side by side with the very oldest ones in the same country, and how that enormous industrial development came to be achieved in Japan at the end of the last century.' (In this respect, one should see whether many Italian industries, rather than being created on the basis of the most advanced technology of the most advanced country, as would be rational, were not instead created through the cast-off machinery of other countries, doubtless acquired cheaply but already outmoded, and whether this fact was not 'more useful and profitable' for the industrialists who gambled on the low cost of the workforce and on government privileges more than on a technically perfected production.)

In his analysis of the statement presented to the Banca Commerciale Italian at the Annual General Meeting for the financial year 1931, Attilio Cabiati (*Riforma Sociale*, July-August 1932, p.464) writes: 'From these considerations there emerges the fundamental vice with which Italian economic life has always been afflicted: the creation and maintenance of an industrial apparatus that is too great with respect both to the rate of accumulation of savings in the country and to the capacity of absorption of domestic consumption. The country thus lives to a great extent through the force of protectionism and state aid of various kinds. But state protectionism, which in some cases reaches and goes beyond a hundred per cent of the product's value on the international market, thereby making life more expensive, at the same time acted as a brake on savings formation, which moreover was competed for by the state itself, often hard pressed by needs of its own which were out of proportion to our apparatus. The war, by enlarging this apparatus out of all proportion, forced our banks, as is said in the above-mentioned statement, "to (adopt) a courageous and resolute treasury policy" which consisted in borrowing "in rotation" abroad, in order to lend at longer term at home. "This type of treasury policy" the statement goes on to say "came up against its natural limit, however, in the banks' need to preserve at all costs sufficient either liquid or easily realisable reserves". When the world crisis broke the "liquid investments" could only be realised at an exceptionally high discount rate, foreign savings stopped short and national industries were unable to repay. The result was, *exceptis excipiendis*,[43] that the Italian banking system found itself in a situation that in certain ways was identical to that of the financial market in Britain in the middle of 1931 ... the old (error) consisted in having wanted to create an industrial organism, out of all proportion to our forces, with the sole aim of making us "independent of other countries", without stopping to think that while we ceased "to depend" on other countries for products, we remained ever more dependent on them for capital.'

We may pose the problem of whether, given another state of affairs, the industrial base of the country could be enlarged without having to turn to other countries for capital. The example of other countries (Japan, for example) shows that this is possible; every form of society has its own law of accumulation of savings and it may be maintained that in Italy, too, a more rapid accumulation may be achieved. Italy is the country that, in the conditions created by the Risorgimento and the way in which it developed, bears the highest weight of parasitic population (i.e. one which lives without in the least being involved in productive life) and is the country that has the largest number of rural and urban petty and middle bourgeois who consume a great proportion of the national income and who, out of this, do not save enough for national necessities.

Q19§7.

42 Humanity-as-Labour and Modern Internationalism[44]

Modern expansion is of a capitalist-financial order. In present-day Italy 'humanity' as an element is either 'humanity-as-capital' or 'humanity-as-labour'. Italian expansion can only be that of humanity-as-labour and the intellectual who represents this humanity-as-labour is no longer of the traditional type, a rhetorical windbag recounting yesteryear's yellowing pages. Traditional Italian cosmopolitanism has to become a modern type of cosmopolitanism such, that is, as to ensure the best conditions for the development of Italian humanity-as-labour in whatever part of the world it is to be found. Not the citizen of the world in as much as *civis romanus* [a citizen of Rome] or a Catholic, but as a producer of civilisation.

One can therefore say that the Italian tradition is carried on dialectically in the working people and their intellectuals, not in the traditional citizen and the traditional intellectual. The Italian people is that people which is 'nationally' more interested in a modern form of cosmopolitanism. Not only the worker but the peasant and in particular the southern peasant. To collaborate in the economic reconstruction of the world in a unitary fashion is in the tradition of the Italian people and of Italian history, not in order to dominate it hegemonically and appropriate the fruit of other people's labour for itself, but in order to exist and in fact to develop as the Italian people. It may be demonstrated that Caesar is at the source of this tradition. Nationalism of the French variety is an anachronistic excrescence in Italian history, typical of those who turn their heads to look back, like the damned in Dante. The 'mission' of the Italian people lies in taking up once again Roman and medieval cosmopolitanism, but in its more modern and advanced form. Let it even be a proletarian nation, as Pascoli wanted: proletarian as a nation since it has constituted the reserve army for foreign capital, since it, together with the Slavonic peoples, has given the rest of the world a labour force. Exactly on this account must it take its place in the modern front of the fight to reorganise the world, including the non-Italian world, which through its labour it has contributed to create, etc.

Q19§5 (excerpt).

D AMERICAN INDUSTRIAL CULTURE

43 America and Europe

In 1927 the International Labour Office in Geneva published the results of a survey carried out on the relationships between employers and the workforce in the United States, *Les rélations industrielles aux Etats Unis*. According to Gompers the final goal of American trade unionism consists in progressively acquiring joint control starting off from the individual factory and going on to industry as a whole, the culmination being a sort of overall parliament. (See what form the workers' tendency towards industrial autonomy takes on in the words of Gompers & Co.)

Q3§26.

44 American Industry

In the 16 February 1930 number of *La Nuova Antologia* there are two articles. The first, not worth a great deal, is by Professor J.P. Rice, and is entitled 'Viewpoints on America: Intellect and American Tradition'. (Rice was nominated by the Italy-America Society in 1930 to give the annual series of lectures sponsored by the Westinghouse Foundation to strengthen the links between America and Italy.) The second article, 'The United States' Industrial Revolution', by Pietro Lanino, a professional engineer, is of interest because it shows how this highly-regarded writer on and theorist of Italian industry has not understood the first thing about the American industrial capitalist system. (In 1930 Lanino also wrote a series of articles on American industry in the organ of the association of limited companies, the *Rivista di politica economica*.)

Right from the first paragraph Lanino claims that in America there has been 'a complete overthrow of what up to now have been the basic economic criteria of industrial production. As regards pay, the law of supply and demand has been jettisoned. Despite pay rises, production costs have fallen.' Nothing, in fact, has been jettisoned. Lanino has not understood that new technology and techniques based on rationalisation and Taylorism have created a new and original psycho-technical skill and that skilled workers of this type are not only few in number but still being trained, so high wages are the bait for attracting workers of the 'right disposition'; this is the confirmation of the 'law of supply and demand' as regards pay. If Lanino's claim were true, one would not be able to explain the high rate of *turnover*[45] among trained workers, i.e. the fact that many workers give up the high wage rates of some firms for lower wages in others. In other words the law of supply and demand would be jettisoned not only by the industrialists but also by the workers, who sometimes remain unemployed by giving up high wages. This is a riddle that Lanino has steered clear of solving. The whole article is based on this initial incomprehension. There is nothing to wonder at in the American industrialists' attempts, with Ford foremost among them, to argue that we are witnessing a new form of relations. Over and above the economic effects of high wages they have also tried to obtain the social effects of intellectual hegemony, and this is quite normal.

Q2§138.

45 Past and Present [10]. Fordism

High wages do not, in Ford's industrial practice, represent what he himself in theory wants them to mean (cf. the notes on what in essence high wages mean as a method of selecting a skilled labour force of the type appropriate for Fordism, considered both as a work and production method and as a commercial and financial system: the necessity of avoiding any interruption in the work process, hence the open shop, etc.). Apart from this fact it should be noted that in a number of countries in which capitalism is still backward and whose economic composition shows a balance between big modern industry, artisan production, small and medium agricultural holdings and latifundia, the masses of the workers and peasants are not considered as a 'market'. The industrial market is conceived as the export one, principally to backward foreign countries, where political penetration aimed at creating colonies and zones of influence is a more real possibility. Industry, with its domestic protectionism and low wages, procures its markets abroad through a veritable permanent dumping.[46]

Countries where nationalism exists, but the situation cannot be considered a 'national-popular' one: the great popular masses are in other words put on a par with cattle. Is the perpetuation of such a large industrial artisan stratums [*ceto*][47] in some countries not bound up with the fact that the great masses of the peasantry are not regarded as a market for big industry, whose market is predominantly the foreign one? And does the so-called rebirth or defence of the artisan workers not in fact express the desire to maintain this situation at the expense of the poorer peasants, who are debarred from any type of progress?

Q6§135.

46 Americanism[48]

Duhamel has expressed the idea that a country at a high level of civilisation should flourish artistically, too. This was said of the United States, and the concept is correct: but is it so at every single moment of a country's development? Bear in mind the American theory that in every period of civilisation its great people express the fundamental activity of the era, which itself is also one-sided. In my opinion these two ideas may be reconciled in the distinction between the economic-corporative phase of a state and the ethico-political one. For the United States artistic flowering may be conceived as being the same as in Europe, given the homogeneity in the forms of civil life; so it was that in a certain period Italy produced artists for the whole of Europe etc. The countries that were at that time 'tributaries' of Italy were developing 'economically' and on this development there followed a veritable artistic flowering, while Italy lapsed into decadence. This happened after the Renaissance in the cases of France, Germany, Britain. A very important historical element in the study of these 'artistic flowerings' is the factor of the continuity of the intellectual groups, i.e. the existence of a strong cultural tradition which is, in point of fact, lacking in America. Another negative element, from this standpoint, is certainly represented by the fact that the American population has not developed organically on a national basis but is rather the product of the continual juxtaposition of nuclei of immigrants, albeit immigrants from the Anglo-Saxon countries.

Q15§30.

47 The Basic Activity of the Age

Carlyle in his *On Heroes, Hero Worship and the Heroic in History* is the source of the American theory (mentioned by Cambon in his preface to a book of Ford's) that the great people of an age are great in the basic activity of the age itself. Thus it would be absurd to 'reprove' the Americans for having no great artists when they have great 'technicians', just as it would be to reprove the Renaissance for having had great painters and sculptors but not great technical minds. [...]

It is not to be excluded that where tradition has left a

broad stratum of intellectuals, and a lively or a prevalent interest for certain activities, 'geniuses' develop who correspond not to the times in which they live concretely, but to those in which they live 'ideally' and culturally. Machiavelli might be one of these. Furthermore, it gets overlooked that every age or environment is contradictory and that one <expresses or> corresponds to one's time or environment by combating them strenuously as well as by collaborating with the forms that official life takes. It seems that in this argument, too, one has to take account of the question of the intellectuals and the way they are selected in the various epochs of development of civilisation. And from this point of view there may be a good deal of truth in the statement about America. Progressive epochs in the practical field may still not have had the time to come to the fore in the creative aesthetic and intellectual field, or may be backward, philistine etc. in this.

Q15§53 (excerpt).

48 American Pragmatism

Could one say of American pragmatism (James) what Engels said of British agnosticism? (I think in the preface to the English edition of *Socialism: Utopian and Scientific*.)[49]

Q1§34.

49 American Philosophy

Study Josiah Royce's position within the framework of the American conception of life. What importance and role has Hegelianism played in this conception? Can modern thought become widespread in America, by going beyond empiricism-pragmatism without going through a Hegelian phase?[50]

Q1§105.

50 Vittorio Macchioro and America

Vittorio Macchioro has written a book: *Roma capta. Saggio intorno alla religione romana* [*Rome Captured. An Essay on Roman Religion*], published by G. Principato, Messina, whose whole construction is founded on the 'poverty of the imagination of the Roman people'. In 1930 he went to America as correspondent for the Neapolitan paper *Il Mattino* and his first despatch (7 March) had the following theme (cf. *L'Italia Letteraria* of 16 March 1930): 'The Americans have no vision and do not know how to create images. Away from the influence of Europe <!>, there will never in my opinion be any great American poets or painters. The American mentality is essentially practical and technical, whence a particular sensitivity for quantity, i.e. for figures. Just as a poet has a sensitivity for images or a musician for sounds, so the American is sensitive to figures. This tendency to conceive of life as a technical fact explains American philosophy itself. Pragmatism stems precisely from this mentality which sets no store by and fails to grasp the abstract. James, and even more so Dewey, are the most genuine products of this unconscious need for technicism, through which education gets mistaken for philosophy, abstract ideas having no value in themselves but only in so far as they can be translated into action. ("The poverty of imagination of the Roman people made the Romans begin to conceive of the divinity as an abstract force which became exteriorised only in action"; cf. *Roma capta*). And it is for this reason that America is the country *par excellence* of churches and schools, where theoreticalness is grafted onto life.'

To my way of thinking, the cloth from which Macchioro's thesis is fashioned may be cut for any coat.

Q4§76.

51 Brief Notes on American Culture[51]

G.A. Borgese in 'Strange Interlude' (*Corriere della Sera*, 15

March 1932) divides the population of the United States into four strata: the financier class, the political class, the intelligentsia, the common people. The intelligentsia is minute in the extreme compared with the first two, some tens of thousands – of whom a few thousand are writers – concentrated mainly in the East. 'One should not go simply on numbers. It is intellectually among the best equipped in the world. One person who forms part of it compares it to what the Encyclopaedia represented in seventeenth-century France. For the moment, for those who prefer not to exaggerate, it seems like a mind without a body, a soul deprived of its motive force; its influence on public affairs is near zero.' He goes on to note that after the crisis, the financier class, which formerly overshadowed the political one, has in the last few months been 'succoured' and virtually controlled by it. 'Congress is propping up the banks and the stock exchange while in Washington the White House is shoring up Wall Street. The old equilibrium on which the American state is based is being threatened without a new order springing up.' Since in actual fact the financier and political classes in America are one and the same, or two aspects of the same, the sole significance of this would be that a real differentiation has taken place, in other words that the economic-corporative stage of American history has entered into crisis and we are about to pass into a new phase; this will be seen clearly only if a crisis of the historic parties (Republicans and Democrats) comes about and a powerful new party is created that permanently organises the masses of the common people. The germs of such a development were already in existence (in the Progressive Party)[52] but the economic-corporative structure has up to now always reacted effectively against them.

The observation that the American intelligentsia occupies a historical position like that of the Encyclopaedia is most acute and is capable of being developed.

Q8§89.

E BRITAIN'S ROLE IN THE WORLD ECONOMY

52 Cultural Questions. Disraeli

Why is it that Disraeli understood imperial necessities better than any other British head of government? Comparison may be made between Disraeli and Caesar. But Disraeli did not successfully pose the question of the British Empire's transformation and had no one to continue his work: Englishness prevented the fusion into a single unified imperial class of the national groups that of necessity were being formed throughout the Empire. It is self-evident that the British Empire could not be founded on a bureaucratic-military structure, as happened in the Roman case; fruitfulness of the programme of an 'imperial parliament' as conceived by Disraeli. That imperial parliament would however have had to legislate for Britain too, which for a Briton is an absurdity: only a semite, free of preconceptions like Disraeli, could be the expression of organic British imperialism. Analogous modern historical phenomena.

Q17§53.

53 The British Empire

From the United Kingdom of Great Britain and Ireland, it has become the 'Unione britannica di Nazioni' (British Commonwealth of Nations). Particularist tendencies.[53] Canada, Australia and New Zealand in an intermediate position between Britain and the United States. Relationship between United States and Canada is ever more intimate. Canada has special plenipotentiary minister in Washington. In the case of a serious conflict between the United States and Britain, the British Empire would crumble.

Q2§16 (excerpt).

54 Constitution of the British Empire

Article in the 16 September 1927 number of *La Nuova Antologia*, under the signature 'Junius': 'Prospects for the British Empire after the Recent Imperial Conference'.[54]

Quest for an equilibrium between the Dominions' need for autonomy and the Empire's need for unity. (Within the Commonwealth, Britain shoulders the political weight that comes from her industrial and financial power, from her fleet, her Crown colonies or dominions or possessions under some other name – India, Gibraltar, Suez, Malta, Singapore, Hong Kong etc. – or from her political experience and so on. Since the war, phenomena of disintegration: power of the United States, which is also an Anglo-Saxon country and which exerts influence over certain dominions, and national and nationalistic movements which in part are a reaction to the workers' movement – in the advanced capitalist countries – and in part a movement against capitalism led by the workers' movement itself: India, negroes, Chinese etc. The British are finding a solution to the national problem for the advanced capitalist dominions, and this aspect [is] of great interest: remember that Ilyich [Lenin] maintained that it was not impossible for the national questions to find a peaceful solution even in a bourgeois regime – the classical example being the peaceful separation of Norway from Sweden.[55] The British, however, have been hit especially by the national movements in the colonies and semi-colonies: India, the African negroes etc.)

Q2§48 (excerpt).

55 Britain

The composition of the British balance of trade was subject to constant modification for about fifty years prior to the war. The part constituted by the export of goods declined in relative importance and equilibrium was reached more and more thanks to so-called invisible exports, i.e. the interest accruing on capital invested abroad, freight charges for British merchant shipping and the profits made by London as an international financial centre. In the post-war period, as a result of competition from other countries, the importance of invisible exports has grown further. From this stems the care which successive Chancellors of the Exchequer and the Bank of England have taken to keep sterling on a par with gold, thus restoring it to its position as an international currency. This goal has been reached but at the expense of increasing the cost price of industrial production, which in turn has led to a loss of foreign markets.

But has this been the cause (at least the most important element) of Britain's industrial crisis? To what extent has the government sacrificed the interests of the industrialists to those of the financiers who organise foreign loans and are in charge of the London world financial market? Going on further, it may be that sterling's return to its former value preceded rather than brought about the crisis, since all countries, even those which stayed on a fluctuating exchange rate for a time and have now stabilised on a lower rate than at the start, went into and are still going through a crisis. It might be said that Britain's having been first into the crisis could have encouraged its industry to run for shelter first and thus to recover before other countries, thereby regaining world hegemony. Moreover, immediate return to the gold standard avoided in Britain the social crises brought about by transfers of ownership and by the sudden collapse of the petty bourgeois classes. In a country like Britain – traditionalist, conservative, ossified in its social structure – what would have been the effects of phenomena of inflation, oscillation, stabilisation of the currency at a lower level? Certainly much more serious than in other countries.

In any case the precise relationship should be established between the export of goods and invisible exports, between the industrial and the financial factor. This would help explain the relatively scanty political importance of the workers, as well as the ambiguous character of the Labour Party and the slightness of the pressure on it to develop and differentiate itself.[56]

Q5§86.

56 Paying off the National Debt

For over a century Britain, the United States and the Netherlands have been paying off their National Debts. Hamilton in 1814 was the first to show that a real reduction in the National Debt could only be brought about by using the surplus of revenue over expenditure and posited the principle that the creation of a debt had to go hand-in-hand with a plan for its gradual extinction. Between 1919 and 1924, Britain brought its National Debt down by £650 million, i.e. by an amount equal to the entire pre-war debt. The debt can be redeemed: 1) through a special fund; 2) through a budget surplus; 3) through allotting a fixed sum.

Figures are given[57] for the sums set aside in the budget for redemption purposes and for the budget surpluses from 1921 to 1926-27. It is significant and noteworthy that, though there was a *deficit* of £36,694,000 in '26-27, £60 million were however allotted in that budget for redemption. This sum was not only higher but much higher than those of previous years: £25 million in '21-22, £24 million in '22-23, £40 million in '23-24, £45 million in '24-25, £50 million in '25-26 (with a budget deficit of £14 million). There is a drop in the budget surplus that begins in '24-25; in '26-27 the deficit of £36 millions is arrived at by an increase in the fixed amount devoted to propaganda against the miners, i.e. by an increase in the capitalists' share of the budget at the expense of the working class.

On the history of British finance bear in mind that at the end of the eighteenth century, Pitt adopted Price's *sinking fund*[58] mechanism, which then had to be abandoned. Hamilton. Up to 1857 budgetary surpluses were devoted preferentially to alleviating the tax burden. After that date debt reduction recommenced and became the cornerstone of Britain's financial policy. Suspended during the war, it was taken up again after the armistice. As regards the budgetary record recall that the sums devoted to debt reduction from 1921 onwards – taken from the *Financial Statement* – were as follows (the first figure referring to the reduction set aside in the budget and the second to a further surplus, also used for

Economic Trends and Developments

debt reduction): 1921-22 – £25,010,000 and £45,693,000; 1922-23 – £24,711,000 and £101,516,000; 1923-24 – £40,000,000 and £48,329,000; 1924-25 – £45,000,000 and £3,659,000; 1925-26 – £50,000,000 together with a deficit of £14,038,000; 1926-27 – £60,000,000 with a £36,694,000 deficit. Summing these figures to obtain the real surplus, we obtain these figures: £70,703,000; £126,227,000; £88,329,000; £48,659,000; £35,962,000; £23,306,000. There is a drop in the surplus, but not a real deficit.

The parliamentary commission on the public debt, chaired by Lord Colwyn, concluded a recent report by recommending a faster rate of debt redemption through increasing the amount set aside for this purpose from £75 million to £100 million annually. One can well understand the political significance of this proposal, given Britain's industrial crisis. They want to avoid any effective state intervention, thereby putting all the ample budgetary possibilities into the private sector which, in all probability, instead of investing these enormous capital sums in crisis-stricken domestic industry, will invest them abroad, whereas the state could use these same sums to reorganise basic industries in favour of the workers.

In the United States the administrative system is founded on the conversion of the consolidated debt into debts redeemable through interest reduction.

In France the fund is constitutionally autonomous and independent of the Treasury, through mistrust of this latter which could put its hands on the sums allotted to debt reduction if it found itself short.

In Belgium Francqui (the minister) increased the sinking fund. [...]

(This article of Tittoni's ought to be regarded as outlining the desiderata of the governmental sector of the bourgeoisie after the events of November 1926;[59] the language is very cautious and convoluted, but the substance is very strong. The criticism comes especially in the comparison between what has been done in other countries and in Italy.)

Q2§6 (excerpt).

57 London's World Role

How, historically, did London develop its world economic role? American and French attempts to supplant London. London's role is one aspect of Britain's economic hegemony that is still continuing even after British trade and industry have lost the position they used to have. What is the financial yield to the British bourgeoisie of London's role? (In some of Einaudi's pre-war writings this argument is touched on broadly. Mario Borsa's book on London. Angelo Crespi's book on the British Empire. Guido De Ruggiero's book.)

This theme has been dealt with in part by the Chairman of the Westminster Bank. In his statement to the Annual General Meeting in 1929,[60] he drew attention to the complaints that the efforts made to preserve London's position as an international financial centre impose excessive sacrifices on industry and trade, but he went on to note that London's financial market produces an income that contributes to a great extent to correcting the *deficit*[61] in the balance of payments. A Board of Trade enquiry reported that in 1928 this contribution amounted to £65 million, in '27 £63 million and in '26 £60 million: this activity must therefore be considered as one of the biggest British 'export' industries. One must bear in mind the important role that London plays in exporting capital, which produces an annual yield of £285 million and which makes the export of British goods easier, given that these investments increase the purchasing power of overseas markets. British traders then find it easier than their opposite numbers in all other countries to obtain credit facilities, bills of exchange etc., from the banks because of the mechanism that international finance has created in London. It is therefore obvious that the sacrifices made to preserve London's supremacy in the field of international finance are amply justified by the benefits that accrue. But it was believed that to preserve this supremacy the British monetary system had to be based on the free movement of gold and that any measure that impeded this freedom would be to London's detriment as an international centre for short-term money transactions. The overseas deposits in London represented very substantial sums placed at the disposal of the market there. It was thought that if these funds had ceased to come in the interest rate would perhaps have been more stable but undoubtedly higher.

What has happened to all these points of view after the collapse of sterling?[62] (It would be of interest to know what terms in the language of trade have become international because of London's world role, terms that occur frequently not only in the technical press, but also in the newspapers and general political periodicals.)

Q16§7.

58 Past and Present [11]. The British Government

An interesting article by Ramsay Muir on the system of government in Britain was published in the November 1930 number of *Nineteenth Century* (quoted in the *Rassegna settimanale della Stampa Estera* [*Weekly Review of the Foreign Press*] of 9 December 1930). Muir holds that one cannot speak of a parliamentary regime in Britain, since parliamentary control over government and the bureaucracy is non-existent, but only of a party dictatorship and an inorganic one at that since power oscillates between extreme parties. In parliament, debate is not what it ought to be, viz. the debate of a council of state, but is instead debate between parties contending for the body of the electorate at the next election, with promises from the government and discredit heaped on the government by the opposition. The deficiencies of the British system of government were laid bare after the war through the great problems of reconstruction and adaptation to the new situation. (But this was also true on the eve of war – cf. the case in Northern Ireland of Carson, whose audacity and sense of impunity came from this self-same governmental system through which his subversive actions were to be cancelled on the return to power of the Conservatives.) Muir isolates the origin of party dictatorship in an electoral system where there is no run-off and, in particular, no proportional representation. This makes compromise and middle-of-the-road opinions difficult (or at least forces the parties into an internal opportunism that is worse than parliamentary compromise). Muir does not notice other phenomena: within the government itself there is a small group that dominates the whole cabinet and, even further, there is a personality who exercises a Bonapartist role.

Q6§40.

59 The Crisis of Parliamentarism

[...] Maybe one should say something of Lord Carson, mentioning the fact that the crisis of the parliamentary regime already existed before the world war and existed in fact even in Britain, i.e. in the country where this regime seemed most firmly-rooted and efficient. This does not mean that one has to write an entire biography of Lord Carson. To someone of an average culture there are only two biographical data of interest: a) in 1914, on the eve of war, Lord Carson enrolled an enormous armed corps in Ulster for the purpose of insurrectionary opposition to the enforcement of the Irish Home Rule Bill, approved by a parliament which, according to the English saying, 'can do anything but make a man of a woman'; b) Lord Carson was not only not punished for 'high treason' but, shortly afterwards, became a minister on the outbreak of war.

Q24§3 (excerpt).

60 Past and Present [12]. Britain and Germany

Comparison between the two countries regarding their behaviour when faced with the crisis of the depression of 1929 and after. From this study there should emerge the real structure of both the one and the other together with their mutual functional position within the world economic set-up, a structural element that is not usually subjected to close scrutiny. One may begin the analysis from the

Economic Trends and Developments

phenomenon of unemployment. Is the same significance attached to the masses of the unemployed in Britain and Germany? Does the theorem of 'definite proportions' in the internal division of labour hold in the same way in the two countries? One can say that British unemployment, while being numerically lower than that of Germany, indicates that the coefficient of 'organic crisis' is greater in Britain than in Germany, where on the other hand the 'cyclical crisis' coefficient is more important. In other words in the event of a 'cyclical' upswing, absorption of unemployment would be easier in Germany than in Britain. This difference depends on the following structural element: commerce has a greater weight in Britain as compared with industrial production, i.e. there exists in Britain a mass of 'proletarians' linked to a trading function that is greater than the German equivalent, where on the other hand the industrial mass is more numerous. Composition of the active population and its distribution among the various activities. A large number engaged in commerce (bankers, stockbrokers, salespeople etc.) gives rise to the widespread employment of personnel for their daily services: the aristocracy is richer and more powerful than in Germany. There is a greater number of 'ritual parasites', i.e. of social elements employed not directly in production but in distribution and in the (personal) services of the propertied classes.

Q9§61.

F   THE NEW SOCIETY AND THE NEW ECONOMIC INDIVIDUAL

61   Cultural Topics. Conformism and the Collective Man[63]

Individualism and individuality (consciousness of individual responsibility) or personality. It remains to be seen how much is justified and how much wrong or dangerous in the tendency against individualism. A necessarily contradictory attitude. Two aspects, positive and negative, of individualism. The question therefore has to be posed historically and not abstractly and schematically. Reformation and Counter-Reformation. The question is posed in a different manner in the countries that have had a Reformation or have been paralysed by the Counter-Reformation. The collective man or imposed conformism and the collective man or proposed conformism. (But can one any longer call it conformism in that case?) A critical consciousness cannot be born without breaking down Catholic or authoritarian conformism and thus without a flowering of individuality: must the relationship between man and reality be direct or pass through the agency of a priesthood? (In other words, like the relationship between man and God in Catholicism? This is, after all, a metaphor for the relationship between man and the real world.) The struggle against individualism is one against a particular type of individualism with a particular social content, and, to be precise, against economic individualism in a period in which this has become anachronistic and anti-historical (though it is not to be forgotten that it was historically necessary and was a stage of progressive development). To fight to destroy an authoritarian conformism that has now become backward and an encumbrance and, through a stage comprising the development of individuality and critical personality, reach the collective man is a dialectical conception that schematic and abstract mentalities find it difficult to grasp. Just as it is difficult to understand our maintaining that through the destruction of one state machinery we arrive at the creation of another stronger and more complex one.

Q9§23

62 Reformation and Renaissance. The Present Process of the Molecular Formation of a New Civilisation

It can be demonstrated that the present process of the molecular formation of a new civilisation may be compared to the movement of the Reformation by studying partial aspects of the two phenomena. The historico-cultural question to resolve in the study of the Reformation is that of the transformation of the conception of grace, which 'logically' ought to lead to the greatest amount of fatalism and passivity, into a real practice of enterprise and initiative on a world scale that was <instead> its dialectical consequence and formed the nascent ideology of capitalism. But we are now seeing the same thing happen as regards the conception of historical materialism; while for many critics there can 'logically' stem from it only fatalism and passivity, in reality, on the other hand, it gives rise to a flowering of initiatives and enterprises that leaves many observers astounded (cf. the *Economist* supplement[64] by Michael Farbman). If one were to carry out a study of the Union,[65] the first chapter or even, rather, the first section of the book ought really to develop the material brought together under this heading of 'Reformation and Renaissance'. One may call to mind Masaryk's book on Dostoevsky[66] and his thesis about the need for a Protestant Reformation in Russia, together with Leo Davidovich's criticisms in the review *Kampf* of August 1914.[67] It is noteworthy that in his memoirs (*La Résurrection d'un Etat. Souvenirs et réflexions, 1914-18* [*The Resurrection of a State. Memoirs and Reflections, 1914-18*], Paris), exactly in the field in which the Reformation should have operated – that is to say as the factor determining a new attitude towards life, an active attitude of enterprise and initiative – Masaryk recognises the positive contribution of historical materialism through the work of the group that embodies it. (On the subject of Catholicism and Protestantism and their reciprocal stance towards the doctrines of grace and 'good works', recall that such 'works' in the language of Catholicism bear little resemblance to the activity and initiatives that entail labour and toil, but have a restricted and 'corporative' meaning.)

Q7§44.

63 The Modern Prince and the Collective Man[68]

In the modern Prince the question of the collective man, i.e. that of 'social conformism' or of the aim of creating a new level of civilisation by educating a 'political class' which in idea already incarnates this level. Thus it is a question of the role and stance adopted by every physical individual in the collective man and also a question of what is the 'nature' of law in a new, realistic and positive conception of the state.

The question of the 'political class' (cf. Gaetano Mosca's books). But Mosca poses the question in an unsatisfactory manner. One cannot understand even what Mosca's precise understanding of a political class is, given that the notion is hazy and elastic. It would seem to embrace all the owning classes and the whole of the middle class; but what is then the role of the upper class? On other occasions reference is made solely to a political aristocracy, to the 'political personnel' of a state and yet again to that part that acts 'freely' within the representative system, i.e. excluding even the upper reaches of the bureaucracy which, according to Mosca, must be controlled and guided by the political class. Mosca's deficiency is apparent in the fact that he does not confront the overall problem of the 'political party'; this is to be understood given the nature of his books and, above all, that of the *Elementi di scienza politica*.[69]

Q8§52 (excerpt).

64 Economic Activity and the Law[70]

A conception of penal law that, being tendentially innovatory, is not to be found in a complete form in any pre-existing doctrines, even if many of them contain it tacitly (though there is, in point of fact, no way it can be implicit in the so-called positive school, particularly not in Ferri's conceptions).[71] In what sense can this be said? In the sense that penal law has its role to play in the life of the state, is related in such a way to other aspects of that life that, if the content changes, the relationship or relative form remains unaltered. If every state tends to create or maintain a certain type of civilisation and therefore of collective life, justice (the law) will be an instrument to this end and must be developed accordingly so as to be most effective and produce the greatest positive results.

Law will have to be freed of any residue of transcendentalism and every absolute; in practice, of any moralistic fanaticism. It will not, however, be able to take as its starting point the notion that the state has no right to 'punish', if this term is reduced to its human meaning, maintaining as its sole viewpoint that its task is to fight the socially 'dangerous'. The state must, in reality, be conceived of as 'educator' in so far as it does in fact tend to create a new type or level of civilisation. How does this come about? Though it is essentially on the economic forces that one operates, though it is the apparatus of economic production that gets reorganised and developed, and though it is the structure into which innovations are introduced, one must not draw the conclusion that superstructural factors should fend for themselves, should be left to develop spontaneously, putting up sporadic shoots at random. The state, in this field too, is a 'rationalisation', an instrument of acceleration and Taylorisation, operating according to a plan, pushing, encouraging, stimulating, etc. The negative or repressive aspect of this activity is precisely penal justice, penal law, which cannot be detached from the whole complex of positive or civilising activities. Moreover, if one does not start off from an abstract stance, one sees that 'penal law' has been broadened, taken on original forms and been integrated by activity which rewards (by a type of 'pillory of virtue', that is not the philistine institution described by Eugène Sue).

Q8§62.

65 Freud and the Collective Man

The most salutary and immediately acceptable nucleus of Freudianism is the need to study the unwholesome repercussions entailed in the construction of any 'collective man', any 'social conformism', any level of civilisation especially in those classes who 'fanatically' make a 'religion', a mystique and so on of the new type of person that we must work towards. It remains to be seen whether Freudianism must not, of necessity, mark the end of the liberal period, a period that is in point of fact characterised by a greater responsibility (and sense of this responsibility) on the part of selected groups in the construction of non-authoritarian, spontaneous, libertarian 'religions'. A conscript will not feel the same degree of remorse as a volunteer for the possible killings committed in wartime and so on (but will say 'I was ordered to do it, I could not do otherwise' etc.). The same thing may be noted for the various classes: the subaltern classes have less moral 'remorse' because what they do does not regard them in the broad sense, etc. On this account, Freudianism is more a 'science' to be applied to the upper classes and it might be said, paraphrasing Bourget[72] (or an epigram about him), that the 'sub-conscious' only begins at an income level of some tens of thousands of lire. Religion, too, is less strongly felt as a cause of remorse by the popular classes who are perhaps not too averse from thinking that Jesus Christ was in any case crucified for the sins of the rich. The question is posed of whether it may be possible to create a 'conformism', a collective man without unleashing a certain amount of fanaticism, without creating 'taboos': in short, critically, as the consciousness of necessity, freely accepted because it is recognised 'in practice' as such, through an accurate estimation of the means and ends to be brought into line with each other, etc.

Q15§74.

66   Encyclopaedic Notions [2]. Liberty-Discipline

The concept of liberty should go hand in hand, not immediately with discipline understood as externally-imposed discipline, as the enforced limitation of liberty, but with that of a responsibility that generates discipline. Responsibility as against individual free will. The only liberty is 'responsible' or 'universal' liberty in so far as it puts itself forward as the individual aspect of a collective or group 'liberty', as the individual expression of a law.

Q6§11.

67 Man as Individual and Man as Mass

The Latin proverb 'Senatores boni viri, senatus mala bestia' ['Though the Senators are good as men, the Senate is a vicious beast'] has become a commonplace. What is the meaning of this proverb and what meaning has it assumed? That a crowd of people, dominated by immediate interests or in prey to a passion aroused by the impressions of the moment transmitted acritically from mouth to mouth, unites around the worst collective decision corresponding to the lowest animal instincts. The observation is just and realistic in so far as one is referring to a crowd that happens by chance, like one that gathers 'under a roof during a downpour' and is composed of people not bound together by relations of responsibility towards other people or groups of people or towards a concrete economic reality whose collapse would involve individuals in disaster. One can therefore say that in such crowds individualism not only is not overcome but is driven to an extreme through the certainty of impunity and irresponsibility.

It is, however, also a common observation that an assembly of intractable and unruly members 'kept in good order' reaches collective decisions of a level above that of the individual mean: quantity becomes quality. If this were not so, it would be impossible to have either an army or, for example, those unheard-of sacrifices that well-disciplined groups of people know how to make on certain occasions when their sense of social responsibility is strongly aroused by the immediate sense of common danger and when the future seems more important than the present. One may quote the example of an open-air rally which is different from an indoor meeting or from the mass-meeting of a trade union and so on. A General Staff officers' meeting is different from one of the soldiers of a platoon etc.

The tendency towards conformism in the contemporary

world is more widespread and deeper than in the past, the standardisation of ways of thinking and acting having taken on a national or even a continental dimension. The economic base of the collective man: the big factories, Taylorisation, rationalisation etc. But, in the past, did the collective man exist or not? He existed, in Michels's terms, under the form of charismatic leadership. In other words, a collective will was attained under the impetus and immediate suggestion of a 'hero', of a representative personality, but this collective will was due to extrinsic factors, being created and then disintegrating continuously. Today's collective man is, on the other hand, formed essentially from the bottom up, on the basis of the position occupied by the collectivity in the world of production: the representative personality today has a role in the formation of the collective man, but one that is far less important than in the past, so much so that this person could disappear without the collective cement disintegrating and the whole edifice tumbling down.

It is said that 'western scientists maintain that the mass psyche is nothing more than the resurgence of the old instincts of the primordial herd and is therefore a regression to a cultural stage that has already been overcome.'[73] This is to be read as a reference to so-called 'crowd psychology', i.e. crowds that happen by chance; the statement is pseudo-scientific and bound up with positivist sociology.

On social 'conformism' it should be noted that the question is not a new one and that the alarm launched by certain intellectuals is simply comical. Conformism has always existed. We are now dealing with a struggle between 'two conformisms', i.e. with a struggle for hegemony, with a crisis of civil society. The old intellectual and moral leaders of society are feeling the ground give way under their feet and realising that their 'preaching' has become just that – 'preaching', i.e. something extraneous to the real world, pure form without any content, an empty, mindless shell. Hence their desperation, their conservative and reactionary tendencies. Since the particular form of civilisation, of culture, of morality that they represented is decomposing, they bewail the death of every civilisation, of every culture, of every morality and are calling for repressive measures by the state or forming groups isolated from and in resistance to the the real historical process, thereby prolonging the duration of the crisis, given that the eclipse of a way of living and thinking cannot take place without crisis. The representatives of the new order wanting to be born, moreover, through their 'rationalistic' hatred of the old, are coming out with utopias and hare-brained schemes. What is the reference point for the new world coming into being? The world of production, of labour. The maximum degree of utilitarianism must underlie every analysis of the moral and intellectual institutions to be created and of the principles to be upheld; collective and individual life must be organised to maximise the yield from the productive apparatus. The development of economic forces on new bases and the progressive establishment of the new structure will heal the inevitable contradictions and, having created a new 'conformism' from below, will allow new possibilities for self-discipline, in other words for freedom, including that of the individual.

Q7§12.

68 Passive Revolution and the Planned Economy[74]

One could conceive things as follows. Passive revolution would be brought about through the fact of transforming the economic structure in a 'reformist' fashion from an individualistic to a planned economy (a command economy). The creation of an economy 'mid-way' between one of the pure individualist type and one that, in the full sense, functions according to a plan would allow the passage to more advanced political and cultural forms without radical and destructive cataclysms of an exterminatory kind. 'Corporativism', through its internal development, could either be or become this middle-ground economic form of a 'passive' character.

Q8§236 (excerpt).

V SCIENCE, LOGIC AND TRANSLATABILITY

Introduction

A Preliminary Notions
1 Encyclopaedic Notions[1]. 'Scientific': What is 'Scientific'?, 281; 2 Encyclopaedic Notions[2]. Science and Scientific, 282; 3 Encyclopaedic Notions[3]. Empiricism, 283; 4 Popular Manual of Sociology. *Objection to Empiricism, 283; 5 Methodological Criteria[1], 284; 6 Methodological Criteria[2], 285; 7 Philosophers-Literati and Philosophers-Scientists, 285.

B Science and Scientific Ideologies
8 *Modern Science and Misconceptions About It, 286; 9 *Science, Humanity, Objectivity, 290; 10 *Science as Ideology, 293; 11 Philosophy-Ideology, Science-Doctrine, 293; 12 *Popular Ignorance about Science, 294.

C The Logical Instruments of Thought
13 *Methodology, Logic, Epistemology, 295; 14 Dialectics as Part of Formal Logic and Rhetoric, 297; 15 The Purely Instrumental Value of Formal Logic and Methodology, 298; 16 Bibliography. *Tobias Dantzig, 298; 17 The Technique of Thought, 298; 18 Past and Present[1]. Don Ferrante's Logic, 303; 19 Philosophical and Scientific Esperanto, 303; 20 Cultural Topics. Formal Logic and Scientific Mentality, 305.

Science, Logic and Translatability

D The Translatability of Scientific and Philosophical Languages
21 Introduction to the Study of Philosophy[1]. The Translatability of Scientific Languages, 306; 22 Introduction to the Study of Philosophy[2]. The Subjective Conception of Reality and the Philosophy of Praxis, 306; 23 *Lenin and Translation, 306; 24 *Translation between Different Civilisations, 307; 25 Giovanni Vailati and the Translatability of Scientific Languages, 307; 26 *The Mutual Translatability of National Cultures, 310; 27 Introduction to the Study of Philosophy[3]. *Gioberti on French and German Philosophy, 313; 28 The Translatability of Different National Cultures, 314; 29 Miscellaneous Notes. The History of Terminology and Metaphors, 315; 30 The Proposition that One Must 'Put Man Back on his Feet', 318.

E Machines and Technology
31 On Ancient Capitalism, 319; 32 Encyclopaedic Notions[4]. The Machine, 320; 33 Political Nomenclature. Artisans; Small, Medium and Big Industry, 321; 34 Introduction to the Study of Philosophy[4]. *Technology as the Mediator Between Science and Reality, 323; 35 On the Development of Military Technology, 323; 36 Past and Present[2]. *War, 324.

Introduction

The bulk of this chapter is composed of three groups of notes (the main part of Sections B, C and D), which include all of Parts III, IV and V of the eleventh notebook, written in the autumn of 1932, which Gramsci, somewhat unusually, marked off as self-contained units with the headings seen here; the longer Parts I and II of Q11 have already been published in SPN pp.323-43 ('Some Preliminary Points of Reference') and 419-72 ('Critical Notes on an Attempt at Popular Sociology', his critique of Bukharin's positivist Marxism), respectively. The fact that Gramsci gave to Q11 (including the 'miscellaneous' paragraphs 50 to 70 comprising Part VI and excluding only the 'Notes and References of a Critical-Historical Nature' of paragraphs 1 to 11) the major title 'Notes for an Introduction and an Initiation to the Study of Philosophy and the History of Culture' indicates that Parts I to V were to be regarded as a set of inter-related individual essays. As none of Parts III, IV or V add up to more than half a dozen sub-sections, there seemed no valid editorial reason to modify the order either of the Parts or of the material within them; minor insertions were merely introduced (as in SPN pp.419-72, cited above) that readers will note by the attribution at the end of each sub-section.

The sections of this chapter based on Q11 have been prefaced by a brief series of general notes outlining Gramsci's general ideas on the sciences and their methods (Section A), of which 'Objections to Empiricism' and 'Methodological Criteria [1]' have previously been published in SPN pp.461-2 and SCW pp.134-5 respectively but are repeated here as a necessary premiss to the main argument. Section B, dealing specifically with science and its epistemological bases and showing a notable affinity with the approach of the young Marx, represents a double-pronged attack on philosophical idealism's ignorance of science and positivism's pretensions to provide a universal methodological approach for all sciences, in the context of the philosophical problems that were rearing up as a consequence of the revolution in physics that had begun at the turn of the twentieth century. The discussion of positivism leads directly into general questions of the relationships between formal and dialectical logic in Section C, the philosophical as well as the merely 'formal' aspect of logic and the need for the ordinary 'man in the street' to master the techniques involved as a precondition for the intellectual and moral reform dealt with in great detail in Chapters VI and VII. In Section D Gramsci outlines his highly innovatory notion of the translatability of scientific and philosophical languages, an approach that provides the intellectual underpinning to the exercise he frequently carries out in 'translating' concepts taken from other philosophies into forms compatible with Marxism; he thus sketches out for future generations some of the conditions

Science, Logic and Translatability 281

and methods necessary for renewing and overhauling Marxism itself through the incorporation of the advances made in other fields. (To avoid duplication with work already published reference may be made to other discussions of science or technology and their popularisation in SPN pp.341, 433-4, 437-40, 457-8 and 458-61 and SCW pp.422-3, where in the first of these places the choice of wording 'knowledge' and 'specialists' – though not wrong – corresponds to Gramsci's more precise 'science' and 'scientists' respectively; remaining paragraphs of consequence from Q11 may be read in this Chapter or in Chapters II and VII of this volume or in SPN, especially pp.371, 375-7, 403-7 and 410-4. Sub-sections 7 and, more surprisingly, 26 were not included in the first Italian editions of the Notebooks, appearing only in the 1975 Critical Edition; on the subject – the mutual translatability between national cultures – of the latter of these two notes see also 'The Philosophy of Praxis and Modern Culture' in SPN pp.388-99, especially pp.393-5.)

Section E (like Section A comprising writings from different Notebooks that all date to within a year either side of the Q11 notes) includes a number of reflections on technology, previously indicated in sub-section 9 and repeated here in sub-section 34, as providing the mediation between the real world and science, considered (in polemical opposition to Croce's crude and dismissive approach) as involving a form of thought in its own right.

A PRELIMINARY NOTIONS

1 Encyclopaedic Notions [1]. 'Scientific': What is 'Scientific'?

The ambiguity about the terms 'science' and 'scientific' stems from the fact that they took on this meaning from a certain group of sciences, the natural and physical sciences to be precise. Any method that was similar to the method of research and investigation current in the natural sciences – which became the sciences *par excellence*, sciences-as-fetish – was called 'scientific'. There do not exist sciences *par excellence* and there does not exist a method *par excellence*, 'a method in itself'. Every type of scientific research creates an appropriate method for itself, its own logic, whose generality and universality consist solely in being 'in conformity with the end'. The most generic and universal methodology is nothing other than formal or mathematical logic, i.e. the ensemble of those abstract instruments of thought that have continuously been discovered, improved and refined throughout the history of philosophy and culture. This abstract methodology, i.e. formal logic, is – wrongly – despised by the idealist philosophers: the study of it corresponds to the study of grammar, i.e. it corresponds not only to an enrichment of the past experiences of the methodology of thought (of the technique of thought), to the absorption of past science, but is also one condition for the further development of science itself.

A study to be made of the fact by which formal 'logic' has to an ever increasing degree become a discipline linked to the mathematical sciences – Russell in Britain, Peano in Italy – right up to the point of being elevated, as in Russell's case, to the pretension of being the 'only real philosophy'. One could take as a starting point Engels's assertion that 'scientific' is contraposed to 'utopian'; does the subtitle of Turati's *Critica Sociale* have the same meaning as in Engels? Certainly not; for Turati, 'scientific' comes close to the meaning of 'the method belonging to the physical sciences' (the subtitle disappeared at a certain point: find out when – it had certainly disappeared by 1917) and even then the sense is a very generic and tendentious one.[1]

Q6§180.

2 Encyclopaedic Notions [2]. Science and Scientific

Dubreuil in his book *Standards* correctly notes that the adjective 'scientific' that is used so much as an accessory to words – scientific management, scientific organisation, etc. –

does not have the pedantic and threatening meaning attributed to it by many people, but he does not then explain exactly how it should be used. In actual fact, scientific means 'rational' and, more precisely, 'that which conforms rationally to the end' to be attained, i.e. obtaining the maximum yield from the minimum effort, obtaining the maximum economic efficiency etc. by a rational <choice and> definition of all the operations and actions that lead towards the end.

The adjective 'scientific' is now extensively used, but its meaning can always be reduced to that of 'conforming to the end' in that this 'conformity' is rationally (methodically) sought after the most minute analysis of all the elements (right down to the tiniest details) that are both constitutive and necessarily constitutive ones (including in the calculation the elimination of the emotive elements).

Q6§165.

3 Encyclopaedic Notions [3]. Empiricism

Ambiguous meaning of the term. The term empiricism is commonly used in the sense of non-scientific. But it is also used in the sense of non-categorical (characteristic of philosophical categories) and therefore of 'concrete' and real in the 'bodily' sense of the word. Empirical reality and categorical reality etc. For Croce, for example, the philosophical sciences are the sole true sciences, while the physical or exact sciences are 'empirical' and abstract, since for idealism nature is a conventional and 'convenient' abstraction etc.

Q9§59.

4 Popular Manual of Sociology. Objection to Empiricism

The investigation of a series of facts to find the relationships between them presupposes a 'concept' that allows one to distinguish that series of facts from other possible ones: how does the choice of the facts to be adduced as proof of the truth of one's assumption come about, if the criterion of choice is not already in existence? But what will this criterion of choice be, if it is not something that is at a higher level than each individual fact investigated? An intuition, a conception, whose history must be regarded as complex, a process that must be linked to the whole process of the development of culture etc. (This observation is to be linked to the other on the 'sociological law' by which one does nothing other than repeat the same fact twice, the first time as a fact, the second as a law – this is sophism of the double fact, not a law.[2])

Q17§23.

5 Methodological Criteria [1]

A critical examination of a 'dissertation' may consist of these questions:
 1) judging whether a given author has, from the premisses assumed as the starting point (or standpoint), been able to draw *all* the consequences rigorously and coherently – it may be that there is a lack of rigour, a lack of consistency, that there are tendentious omissions, that scientific 'imagination' is lacking (i.e. that the author has not been able to see all the implications of the principle assumed etc.); 2) evaluating the starting points (or standpoints), the premisses, that can be summarily denied, limited, or shown to be no longer historically valid; 3) seeing whether the premisses are mutually homogeneous, or whether, through the author's inability or insufficiency (or ignorance of the historical state of the problem), there has been some contamination between premisses or principles that are mutually contradictory or heterogeneous or historically incompatible.

Thus a critical evaluation may have different cultural (or politico-polemical) goals. It may aim at demonstrating someone's incapability and worthlessness as an individual; that the cultural group to which they belong is scientifically unimportant; that those who 'think' or claim they belong to a certain cultural grouping are either deceiving themselves

Science, Logic and Translatability 285

or want to deceive others; or that they are making use of the theoretical premises of a respectable group in order to draw conclusions that are tendentious, extremely limited in scope, etc.

Q14§5.

6 Methodological Criteria [2]

A typical manifestation of intellectual dilettantism (and of the intellectual activity of dilettantes) is as follows: in dealing with a question there is a tendency to expound everything one knows rather than just what is necessary and important to an argument. Every opportunity is taken to flaunt what has laboriously been learnt, to put on display the rags and ribbons of one's market-stall. Every insignificant little fact is elevated to one of world-shattering importance so as to give unbridled rein to one's Weltansschauung, etc. It thus happens that, since one wants to be original and not repeat what has already been said, one has to maintain on every occasion that there has been a great change in the fundamental 'factors' of the situation, and one hence falls into all kinds of stupidities.

Q14§36.

7 Philosophers-Literati and Philosophers-Scientists

Is there any value in the fact of a philosopher's having started off from a scientific experiment or from a 'literary' experience?[3] That is to say, which philosophy is more 'realistic' – that which starts from the 'exact' sciences or that which starts from 'literature', i.e. from the observation of man in so far as he is intellectually active and not just a 'mechanical part of nature'?

Q11§61.

B SCIENCE AND SCIENTIFIC IDEOLOGIES

8 Modern Science and Misconceptions About It

Eddington's assertion: 'If we eliminated all the unfilled space in a man's body and collected his protons and electrons into one mass, the man would be reduced to a speck just visible with a magnifying glass' (cf. *La nature du monde physique*, French edition, p. 20)[4] has seized G.A. Borgese's imagination and sent him on a flight of fancy (cf. his booklet).[5] But what does Eddington's statement mean in concrete terms? If we pause to reflect on it for a moment, we see that there is no meaning to it at all over and above the literal one. Even if the above reduction were to be carried out (by whom?) and were then, however, to be extended to the whole world, there would be no change in ratios and relationships,[6] things would stay just as they are. Things would change if men, or certain men, were the only ones to undergo this reduction so that, hypothetically, we would have a realisation of some chapters from Gulliver's Travels, with the Lilliputians, the giants and Borgese-Gulliver in among them.

In actual fact we are dealing with mere word-play, with science fiction, not with a new scientific or philosophical thought. It is a way of posing the question that is fit only for creating fantasies in empty heads. Perhaps matter seen under the microscope is no longer really objective matter, but is, rather, a creation of the human mind having no objective or empirical existence? On this question one might recall the Jewish short story about the girl who felt a teeny, weeny sting...just like a light flick from a finger nail. In Eddington's physics and in many other manifestations of modern science the surprise of the ingenuous reader depends on the fact that the words used to indicate certain facts are bent to denote arbitrarily quite different facts. A body remains 'massive' in the traditional sense even if the 'new' physics demonstrates that it is comprised of one part in a million of matter and 999,999 parts vacuum. A body is 'porous' in the traditional sense and does not become so in the sense of the 'new' physics even after Eddington's claim. Humanity's position stays the same, none of the fundamental concepts of life are shaken in the slightest, let alone overturned. The glosses of the various Borgeses in the long run will serve only to reduce the subjectivistic conceptions that allow trivial playing around with words in this way to a state of ridicule.[7]

Prof. Mario Camis (*Nuova Antologia*, 1 November 1931, in the column 'Biological and Medical Science') writes: 'In considering the unsurpassed minuteness of these methods of investigation there came to mind the expression used by a participant at the last Philosophy Congress at Oxford. From what Borgese says, this person, in speaking of the infinitely small phenomena to which everyone's attention is now being drawn, observed that "they cannot be considered independently of the subject that observes them".[8] These are words which give rise to quite a number of reflections and, from completely new standpoints, bring back into play the great problems of the subjective existence of the universe and the meaning of sensorial information in scientific thought.' It appears that this is one of the few examples that has filtered through to Italian scientists of a way, prevalent among British scientists in particular, of thinking about the 'new' physics which attempts to do a balancing act. Prof. Camis ought to have reflected that if the observation quoted by Borgese makes one reflect, the first reflection ought to be this: that science can no longer exist as it has been conceived of until now, but must be transformed into a series of acts of faith in the assertions of individual experimenters since observed facts do not exist independently of their mind. Has the whole progress of science not up to now been manifested in the fact that new experiments and observations have corrected and extended previous experiments and observations? How could this happen if a given experiment were not reproducible, and if, with another observer, it could not be checked and extended, thereby giving rise to new and original connections? But the superficiality of Camis's observation comes straight out of the context of the article from which the above quotation is taken since, in this article, Camis explains how the expression that gave rise to Borgese's inanities might and should be understood in a merely empirical and not a philosophical sense.

Camis's article is a review of the book *On the Principles of Renal Function* by Gösta Ekehorn (Stockholm 1931). In it, there is a discussion of experiments on elements which are so small that they cannot be described (and this, too, is meant in a relative sense) in words having cogency and meaning for other people: elements which, therefore, the researcher has still not yet succeeded in abstracting from his own subjective personality in order to objectivise them. All engaged in research have to arrive at a perception by their own means, directly, by following the whole process through in the minutest detail. Let us make this hypothesis: that microscopes do not exist and that only certain people have a natural visual capacity equal to that of the normal eye aided by a microscope. On this hypothesis it is obvious that the experiments of observers who have this exceptional vision cannot be abstracted from their physical and psychical personality, and cannot be 'repeated'. Only the invention of the microscope would here equalise physical conditions of observation and allow all scientists to reproduce the experiment and extend it collectively. But this hypothesis allows us to observe and identify only one part of the difficulties; in scientific experiments one does not deal only with visual capability. As Camis says: Ekehorn pierces a glomerulus of frog's kidney with a puncture pipette 'whose preparation is the work of such fineness and is so much *bound up with the indefinable and inimitable manual intuitions*[9] of the research worker that Ekehorn himself, in describing the skew cut of the glass capillary tube, says that he is unable to give instructions in words but that he has to content himself with a vague indication'.[10] The mistake is to think that such phenomena happen only in scientific experiments. In actual fact, in any factory for certain high-precision industrial operations, there exist individual specialists whose ability is based solely and exactly on the extreme sensitivity of their sight, touch and manual dexterity. In Ford's books one may see examples to this effect: in order, in the fight against friction, to obtain surfaces without the least granularity or unevenness (which leads to a notable saving of material), incredible steps forward have been taken with the aid of electrical machinery that tests the perfect adherence of material in a way that no individual ever could. One may call to mind the fact that Ford refers to: a Scandinavian technician who managed to give steel such a surface uniformity that a force of several hundredweight had to be used to detach one surface from another to which it had been made to adhere.

What Camis, therefore, notes is not at all consistent with the imaginative fantasies of Borgese and his sources. If it were true that the infinitely small phenomena in question cannot be considered as existing independently of the subject who observes them, they would in fact not even be 'observed', but 'created' and would fall into the same domain as the pure imaginative intuition of the individual. The question of whether the same individual can create (observe) the same fact 'twice' would also have to be posed. One would not even be dealing with 'solipsism' but with witchcraft, with demiurgic powers.[11] It would not be these (non-existent) phenomena but rather these imaginative intuitions that would, like works of art, be the subject of science. The scientific herd, which does not enjoy any demiurgic faculties, would devote itself to a scientific study of these great miracle-working scientists. But if, on the other hand, despite all the practical difficulties inherent in different individual sensitivities, the phenomenon did repeat itself and could be objectively *observed* by various scientists independently of one another, what would the assertion quoted by Borgese mean except that a metaphor was being used to indicate the difficulties inherent in giving a description and an objective representation of observed phenomena? It does not seem difficult to explain this difficulty: 1) because of the lack of literary ability of scientists who, up to now, have been *didactically* trained to describe and represent only macroscopic phenomena; 2) because of the insufficiency of common language, which has also been fashioned for macroscopic phenomena; 3) because of the relatively slight development of these sub-microscopic sciences, which are awaiting a further development of their methods and criteria in order to be understood by the *many* through the channels of literary communication (and not only by direct experimental observation, which is the privilege of very few); 4) one must always bear in mind that many sub-microscopic experiments are indirect, chain ones whose result 'is seen' in the results and not in the act itself (as in the experiments of Rutherford).[12]

One is, in any case, dealing with the initial and transitory phase of a new scientific era, which – together with a great intellectual and moral crisis – has produced a new form of 'sophistry' that recalls the classic sophisms of Achilles and the tortoise, the heap and the grain, the arrow shot from the bow that cannot but be at rest etc.[13] These are all, however, sophisms that have represented a phase in the development of philosophy and logic and have served to refine the instruments of thought.

Q11§36.

9 Science, Humanity, Objectivity

Bring together the principal definitions that have been given of science (in the sense of natural science). 'Study of phenomena and of their laws of similarity (regularity), coexistence (coordination), succession (causality).' Other tendencies, taking into account the most convenient order that science establishes between phenomena, in such a way as to be better able to master them through thought and dominate them for the purposes of action, define science as 'the most economic description of reality'. The most important question to be resolved about the concept of science is this: whether science can give us, and if so in what way, the 'certainty' of the objective existence of so-called external reality. For common sense the question does not even exist; but from what has the certainty of common sense originated? Essentially from religion (at least from Christianity in the West); but religion is an ideology, the best-rooted and most widespread ideology, not a proof or a demonstration. One may maintain it is an error to ask of science as such the proof of the objectivity of reality, since this objectivity is a conception of the world, a philosophy and thus cannot be a scientific datum. What has science to offer in this direction? Science makes a selection of sensations, the primordial elements of knowledge: it considers certain sensations as transitory, as apparent, as fallacious because they depend on special individual conditions and certain others as lasting, as permanent, as superior to those special individual conditions. Scientific work has two main aspects: the first constantly corrects our way of knowing, corrects and reinforces our sensory organs, formulates new and complex principles of induction and deduction, that is to say refines the very instruments of experiment and experimental control; the second one applies this ensemble of instruments (of a material and a mental variety) to draw a dividing line between what is essential in the sensations and what is arbitrary, individual, transitory. One thus establishes what is common to everyone, what everyone can control in the same way, one independently of another, as long as each has observed to an equal degree the technical conditions of ascertainment. 'Objective' means this and only this: that one asserts to be objective, to be objective reality, that reality which is ascertained by all, which is independent of any merely particular or group standpoint. But, basically, this too is a particular conception of the world, an ideology. However, this conception, when taken in its entirety, can be accepted by the philosophy of praxis because of the direction it indicates.

The philosophy of praxis rejects, however, the common sense conception,[14] although that too concludes, materially, in the same way. Common sense asserts the objectivity of the real in so far as reality, the world, has been created by God independently of and before humanity; reality is, therefore, an expression of the mythological conception of the world. On top of this, in describing this objectivity, common sense falls into the crudest errors – it is still to a great extent at the Ptolemaic astronomy stage, not knowing how to determine the real connections of cause and effect etc.: that is, it calls 'objective' a certain anachronistic 'subjectivity' since it is not even able to conceive that a subjective conception of the world might exist and what that could or might mean.

But is everything asserted by science 'objectively' true? Conclusively so? If scientific truths were conclusive, science would have ceased to exist as such, as research, as new experiments, and scientific activity would be reduced to popularising what has already been discovered. Fortunately for science this is not true. But if scientific truths themselves are not conclusive and unchallengeable, then science too is a historical category, a movement in continual development. Only that science does not lay down any form of metaphysical 'unknowable', but reduces what humanity does not know to an empirical 'not knowledge' which does not exclude the possibility of its being known, but makes it conditional on the development of physical instrumental elements and on the development of the historical understanding of single scientists.

If this is so, what is of interest to science is then not so much the objectivity of the real, but humanity forging its methods of research, continually correcting those of its material instruments which reinforce sensory organs and logical instruments of discrimination and ascertainment (which include mathematics): in other words culture, the conception of the world, the relationship between humanity and reality as mediated by technology. In science, too, to seek reality outside of humanity, understood in a religious or metaphorical sense, seems nothing other than paradoxical. Without humanity what would the reality of the universe mean? The whole of science is bound to needs, to life, to the activity of humanity. Without humanity's activity, which creates all, even scientific, values, what would 'objectivity' be? A chaos, i.e. nothing, a void, if one can indeed say that, because in reality, if one imagines that humanity does not exist, one cannot imagine language and thought. For the philosophy of praxis, being cannot be separated from thinking, humanity from nature, activity from matter, subject from object; if one carries out this separation, one falls into one of the many forms of religion or into senseless abstraction.

Q11§37.

10 Science as Ideology

To make science the basis of life, to make science into the conception of the world *par excellence*, which lifts the veil formed by ideological illusion and leaves humanity face to face with reality as it actually is, means falling back into the concept that the philosophy of praxis needs philosophical supports outside of itself. But in actual fact science too is a superstructure, an ideology. Can it not, however, be said that, in the study of superstructures, science occupies a privileged position since its reaction on the structure is of a particular kind, being greater in extension and continuity of development, especially from the eighteenth century onwards, when science obtained a position on its own in the public esteem? That science is a superstructure is also demonstrated by the fact that it has had whole periods of eclipse, obscured as it was by another dominant ideology, religion, which claimed that it had absorbed science itself; thus the science and technology of the Arabs seemed pure witchcraft to the Christians. Further, and notwithstanding all the efforts of scientists, science never appears as a bare objective notion – it always appears in the trappings of an ideology; in concrete terms, science is the union of the objective fact with a hypothesis or system of hypotheses which go beyond the mere objective fact. It is true however that in this field it is relatively easy to distinguish the objective notion from the system of hypotheses by means of a process of abstraction that is inherent in scientific methodology itself, in such a way that one can appropriate the one while rejecting the other. This is why one social grouip can appropriate the science of another group without accepting its ideology (the ideology of vulgar evolution, for example), so the observations in this respect of Missiroli (and of Sorel) are wide of the mark.[15]

Q11§38.

11 Philosophy-Ideology, Science-Doctrine

Cf. Gaëtan Pirou, *Doctrines sociales et science économique*,

Paris. The author distinguishes between theories aimed at explaining economic behaviour (economic science) and those aimed at modifying economic and social behaviour (which he calls social doctrines). He then investigates the relations connecting social doctrines and economic science, paying particular attention to the claim put forward every so often by liberalism or Marxism to be in agreement with science, whereas two different things are in question. 'The truth is, it seems to us, that science and doctrine move at different levels and that doctrines are never a simple extrapolation into the future of the evolutionary curve or an obligatory deduction of the teachings of science.' Linking up with Sorel the author also states that 'doctrines must be studied not as truths put into formulae, but as forces set in motion'. Alfonso De Pietri-Tonelli, from whose bibliographical review (in the *Rivista di Politica Economica*, 31 March 1930) I have taken the lines above, refers the reader back to his political economy course, in which he says he makes the same distinctions, even that of the 'forces set in motion' which would, it seems, correspond to his theory of impulses.

Question of the relationships between science and life. Marxism is no mere social doctrine, in Pirou's distinction, since it even 'puts forward the claim' to be able to explain 'science', in other words to be more science than 'science'. Into the question of ideology-philosophy = doctrine-science, there also comes the question of the 'primitiveness' or 'irreducibility' of the political or practical moment. Ideology = scientific hypothesis capable of educating and of mobilising energies, verified <and criticised> by the real development of history, i.e. made to become science (real hypothesis), systematised.

Q4§61.

12 Popular Ignorance about Science

It is to be noted that, together with the most superficial infatuation for the sciences, there exists in reality the greatest ignorance about scientific facts and methods, things that are very difficult and are becoming all the more difficult because of the progressive specialisation of new branches of research. Scientific superstitition carries such ridiculous illusions and such infantile conceptions that religious superstition finds itself ennobled by them. Scientific progress has given birth to belief in and the expectation of a new Messiah who will bring about the Land of Cokaygne on this earth. The forces of nature, without any intervention from human toil but through the action of ever more perfected mechanisms, will give society an abundance of everything necessary for satisfying its needs and living at ease. This infatuation – the abstract superficial faith in humanity's miracle-working ability – leads paradoxically to the sterilisation of the very bases of this ability and to the destruction of all love for concrete and necessary work in order to indulge in fantasies, as if one has been smoking a new type of opium. Its dangers are quite obvious and must be fought by various means, of which the most important must be a better knowledge of the essential notions of science through the popularisation of science on the part of scientists and serious students, and no longer by all-knowing journalists and the self-opinionated self-taught of this world. In actual fact, since too much is expected of science, it is conceived of as a superior form of witchcraft, and because of this one cannot realistically evaluate what science has to offer of a concrete nature.

Q11§39.

C THE LOGICAL INSTRUMENTS OF THOUGHT

13 Methodology, Logic, Epistemology

Cf. Mario Govi, *Fondazione della Metodologia. Logica ed Epistemologia* [*Foundation of Methodology. Logic and Epistemology*], Turin 1929. Govi is a positivist and his book aims at bringing the old, classical positivism up to date and creating a neopositivism. Basically, 'methodology' has a very restricted 'small-calibre logic' meaning for Govi: for him it is a question of constructing a new formal logic, divorced from any content even where he speaks of the various sciences (classified according to a general methodology, but always done so from the outside), which are presented in their particular abstract (specialised, but abstract) logic, called Epistemology by Govi.[16] Govi in fact divides methodology into two parts: general methodology – logic in the proper sense of the term – and special methodology, or epistemology. The principal and primary aim of epistemology is the exact knowledge of that special cognitive goal towards which each different inquiry is directed so that one is then better able to determine the means and the procedure for attaining it. Govi reduces the number of different legitimate cognitive goals of human inquiry to three. These three constitute what is knowable to mankind and cannot be reduced to just one; in other words they are different in their essentials. Two of them are final cognitive goals: theoretical knowledge, or knowledge of reality, and practical knowledge or knowledge of what one has or has not to do; the third consists of the various parts of knowledge that are the means for acquiring the preceding two. Epistemology is thus composed of three parts: theoretical science or the science of reality, practical science and instrumentational science. From this flows a whole analytical classification of the sciences. The concept of *legitimate* occupies a place of great importance in Govi's sytem (being part of general methodology or the science of judgement). Every judgement, considered by itself, is either true or false; considered subjectively, that is as the product of the thought activity of the person making it, the judgement is legitimate or illegitimate. A judgement can be known to be true or false only in so far as it is recognised to be legitimate or illegitimate. Those judgements which are common to everyone (whether they are innate to or are made by everyone), and which are formed in the same way by everyone, are legitimate judgements. Thus primitive concepts, formed *naturally*, without which one cannot think, are legitimate, as are methodologically formed scientific concepts, primitive judgements and judgements derived methodologically from legitimate judgements.

These comments are drawn from the article 'Methodology or Agnosticism' in the *Civiltà Cattolica* of 15 November 1930. It appears that Govi's book is of interest for the historical material that he has collected especially about general and special logic, the problem of knowledge and the theories concerning the origin of ideas, the classification of the sciences and the various divisions of human knowledge, the various conceptions and divisions of theoretical, practical Science etc. Govi calls his philosophy 'empiricist-integralist', distinguishing it from the religious conception and from the rationalist one in which Kantian philosophy has pride of place. He also distinguishes it, although in a subordinate way, from that 'empiricist-particularist' conception which is positivism. He differentiates himself from positivism in so far as he rebuts some of its excesses, that is to say the negation not only of any religious or rationalist metaphysics, but also any possibility and legitimacy of a metaphysics. Govi does instead admit the legitimacy of a metaphysics, but one whose foundations are purely empirical (!) and which is constructed, in part, after and on the basis of particular real sciences. (Cf. What proportion of Govi's theories have been taken from the British neo-realists, especially from Bertrand Russell.)

Q11§40.

14 Dialectics as Part of Formal Logic and Rhetoric

Cf. the booklet *Dialectica* by Fathers Liberatore and Corsi of the Society of Jesus (Naples 1930) for the way in which the dialectic is conceived by the neo-Thomists. Father Liberatore has been one of the most noted Jesuit polemicists and editor of *Civiltà Cattolica*.

Compare also the two volumes on *Dialettica* by B. Labanca, a Catholic. Furthermore, in his chapter on 'Dialectics and Logic' in *Fundamental Problems*, Plekhanov conceives of dialectics as a branch of formal logic, as the logic of motion as compared with the logic of stasis.[17] The link between dialectics and rhetoric carries over into common everyday language in the higher sense when one wants to indicate a cogent piece of oratory, in which the deduction or connection made linking cause and effect is of a particularly convincing nature, and in a degenerate sense for the barrack-room lawyer type of oratory which leaves rustics gaping.[18]

Q11§41.

15 The Purely Instrumental Value of Formal Logic and Methodology[19]

Formal logic and abstract methodology may be juxtaposed to 'philology'. Philology, too, has an openly instrumental value, as also has erudition. The mathematical sciences have an analogous function. Conceived of as an instrumental value, formal logic has its own meaning and content (the content is in its function) just as the instruments and tools of labour have their own value and their own meaning. The fact that a 'file' can be used indifferently to file iron, copper, wood, different metal alloys etc., does not mean that it is 'without content', purely formal etc. Thus, formal logic has a development of its own, its own history, etc.; it can be taught, enriched etc.

Q11§42.

16 Bibliography. Tobias Dantzig

See the book by Tobias Dantzig, mathematics professor at the University of Maryland, entitled *Le Nombre* [*Number*], (Paris, 1931 or 32?): history of number and the successive formation of methods and the notions of and research into mathematics.[20]

Q11§43.

17 The Technique of Thought

Compare on this theme the assertion contained in the preface to *Anti-Dühring* that 'the art of working with concepts is not something inborn or given with ordinary consciousness but is a technical work of thought which has a long history, not more and not less than experimental research in the natural sciences' (quoted by Croce in *Historical Materialism and the Economics of Karl Marx*, 1921, p. 31).[21] This concept is referred to in several notes.[22] Engels's original text should be seen in order to put the extract in its general context. Croce, in quoting it, notes in parenthesis that we are not dealing with a 'strange' concept, but one which had already become part of common sense before Engels. But it is not a question of a greater or lesser originality or strangeness of the concept in this case and for this treatment; it is a question of its importance and status within a system of philosophy of praxis, and of seeing if it has that 'practical and cultural' recognition due to it. One must use this concept as a reference point for understanding what Engels means when he writes that, after the innovations brought in by the philosophy of praxis, of the old philosophy there remains, among other things, *formal logic*, a claim that Croce quotes in his essay on Hegel and after which he adds an *exclamation* mark.[23] Croce's amazement at the 'rehabilitation' of formal logic that seems implicit in Engels's claim must be linked to his theory of the *technique* of art, for example, and to a whole series of other opinions of his that constitute the sum total of his effective 'anti-historicism' and methodic abstraction (the 'distincts', whose 'methodic' principle Croce boasts of having introduced into the 'dialectical' tradition, from being a scientific principle go on to being a cause of 'abstractness' and of anti-historicism in their formalistic application).[24] But the analogy between artistic *technique* and the *technique* of thought is, at least in a certain sense, superficial and fallacious. An artist may exist who 'knowingly' or 'on reflection' knows nothing of past technical developments (naïvely borrowing his technique from common sense), but this cannot happen in the sphere of science in which progress has to and does exist, and in which the furtherance of knowledge is closely connected with instrumentational, technical and methodological developments and progress and is conditioned by them, exactly as in the experimental sciences defined in a narrow sense.

The question must, indeed, be posed as to whether modern idealism, and Croceanism in particular, with its reduction of philosophy to a methodology of history is not essentially a 'technique'; whether the very concept of 'speculation' is not, in essence, a 'technical' research, to be understood – certainly – in a higher, less extrinsic and material, sense than the research that culminated in the construction of scholastic formal logic. It seems that Adolfo Omodeo is not far from this point of view when he writes (*Critica*, 20 July 1932): (Loisy)[25] 'who has had experience of theological systems, distrusts those of philosophy. He is afraid that a formula imposed by a system will kill all interest in concrete history, that a more or less dialectical deduction will destroy the human fullness of effective spiritual formation. And in actual fact all post-Kantian philosophies, besides directing one towards a pan-historical vision, contain an active metahistorical tendency which would in itself like to provide a metaphysical concept of the spirit. Loisy cautions against the same exigency that in Italy has led to the attempt to reduce philosophy to a mere abstract methodology of history, as against the metaphysical conceit that looks down on the "gross materialities of history" with contempt. He makes this concept of his quite clear in the problem of ethics. He puts philosophical formulae to one side since, through a consideration of ethics, they nullify the problem of life and of moral action, of the formation of the personality and of conscience, things which we are used to calling the historicity of the spirit, which is not a corollary of abstract philosophy. But perhaps the requirement has been pushed too far, to the point of refusing to recognise the role of philosophy as the methodic control over our concepts.'

Even though expressed in non-rigorous terms, the methodological requirement in Engels's statement should be considered. It is all the more pertinent in that the implicit reference is made not for intellectuals and the so-called educated classes but for the popular uneducated masses, for whom the conquest of formal logic, the conquest of the most elementary grammar of thought and language, is still to be attained. The question might arise as to what status this technique is to have within the different domains of philosophical science: namely, whether it should form part of the very science, as already developed, or of the preparatory study to the science, i.e. of the process of construction as such of the science. (Similarly no one can deny the importance, in chemistry, of catalysts just because no trace remains of them in the final result.) The same problem is presented for the dialectic too: it is a new way of thinking, a new philosophy, but through that it is also a new technique. The principle of distinction, maintained by Croce, and consequently all his polemics with Gentile's actualism, are they too not technical questions? Can one detach the technical fact from the philosophiocal one? One can do so, however, for practical didactic ends. And in fact one should note the importance that the technique of thought has in constructing didactic programmes. Nor can one make a comparison between the technique of thought and the old rhetoric. This latter produced neither artists nor taste, nor did it provide any criteria for the appreciation of beauty: it was useful only for the creation of a cultural 'conformism' and a language of conversation among the *literati*. The technique of thought, developed as such, will certainly not produce great philosophers, but it will provide people with criteria that enable them to carry out checks and make judgements and it will correct distortions in common sense ways of thinking.

A comparative examination of the technique of common sense, i.e. the philosophy of the man in the street, and that of considered and coherent thought, would be of interest. With regard to this, Macaulay's observation on the logical weaknesses of a culture formed through declamation and oratory holds once again.[26]

The whole of this argument ought to be studied in depth after all possible relevant material has been collected. The question raised by the pragmatists (Prezzolini, Pareto etc.)[27] on language as a cause of error is to be linked to this argument. The question of the study of the technique of thought as an introductory study, as a process of elaboration, is to be worked out in detail, but one must proceed with caution since the image of a technical 'instrument' may lead to mistake. Between 'technique' and 'thought in action', there exist more identities than exist in the experimental sciences between the 'material instruments' and science in the strict sense of the term. Maybe one can conceive of an astronomer who does not know how to use his instruments (the research material to be subjected to mathematical treatment may be obtained from others) since the relationships between 'astronomy' and 'astronomical instruments' are exterior and mechanical, and in astronomy too there exists a technique of thought over and above the technique of material instruments. It is possible for a poet not to know how to read and write: in a certain sense even a thinker may have everything that interests him in other people's work read to him, or have what he has already thought written down for him. It is because reading and writing refer to the process of memory that they are an aid to memory. The technique of thought cannot be compared to these operations and, on this account, one might say that it is as important to teach this technique as it is to teach reading and writing, without this involving philosophy, just as knowing how to read and write does not have a bearing on the poet as such.

'The mental and manual instruments at man's disposal are always the same (?): observation, experiment, inductive and deductive reasoning, manual dexterity (?) and an inventive imagination. According to the method followed in using these means, one gives an empirical or a scientific direction to human activity, with this difference between the two: that the latter is much faster and has a much greater output.' Mario Camis, 'Aeronautics and the Biological Sciences', in the *Nuova Antologia* of 16 March 1928.)

Examples of a simplistic way of reasoning which, according to popular opinion, is the way in which the vast majority of people reason (those who subject themselves to no sort of control and do not therefore realise how much feeling and immediate interest disturb the logical process).[28] Babbitt's reasoning on trade union organisations (in Sinclair Lewis's novel): 'A good labor union is of value because it keeps out radical unions, which would destroy property. No one ought to be forced to join a union, however. All labor agitators who try to force men to join a union should be hanged. In fact, just between ourselves, there oughtn't to be any unions allowed at all; and as it's the best way of fighting the unions, every business man ought to belong to an employers' association and to the Chamber of Commerce. In union there is strength. So any selfish hog who doesn't join the Chamber of Commerce ought to be forced to.'

Don Ferrante's reasoning is formally impeccable, but wrong in its factual premises and the presumptuousness of the reasoner, whence the piece's humour. Ilyich's manner of reasoning in Tolstoy's novella *The Death of Ivan Ilyich* (' "Caius is a man, all men are mortal; therefore Caius is mortal" ... but *he* was not Caius').[29]

Q11§44.

18 Past and Present [1]. Don Ferrante's Logic

One could juxtapose Don Ferrante's mental form and that contained in the so-called Rome 'theses' (recall the discussions on the 'coup d'état' and so on).[30] This latter was just like Don Ferrante's denying the 'plague' and the 'contagion' and thus dying of it 'stoically' (if indeed it is not a case of using another, more appropriate adverb). But in Don Ferrante, in effect, there was at least more 'formal' reasoning in that he reflected his own era's way of thinking (and Manzoni satirises this by personifying it in Don Ferrante), while in the more modern case we are dealing with an anachronism, as if Don Ferrante had risen from the dead, together with his entire mentality, right in the middle of the twentieth century.

Q14§25.

19 Philosophical and Scientific Esperanto

From an incomprehension of the historicity[31] of languages and therefore of philosophies, ideologies and scientific opinions, there stems a tendency that is characteristic of all forms of thought (including idealist-historicist ones) to build themselves up as an Esperanto or Volapük[32] of philosophy and science. One can say that, although it appears in forms which always differ one from another and are more or less attenuated, the state of mind of primitive peoples towards the other peoples with whom they entered into relations has been perpetuated. Every primitive people used to (or still does) refer to itself by a word which also means 'man' and to the others by words which mean 'dumb' or 'stammerers' (barbarians) in so far as they do not know the 'language of men' (from this has come the beautiful paradox that 'cannibal' or people-eater has the original – etymological – meaning of 'man *par excellence*' or 'real man'). For the Esperantists of philosophy and science, everything that is not expressed in their language is a delirium, a prejudice, a superstition, etc.; making use of an analogous process to what is found in a sectarian mentality, they transform what should be a mere historical judgement into a moral one or into a diagnosis of a psychiatric order. Many traces of this tendency are to be found in the *Popular Manual*. Philosophical Esperantism is especially rooted in positivist and naturalistic conceptions, 'sociology' perhaps being the principal product of such a mentality. Hence the tendencies towards abstract 'classification', methodologism and formal logic. Logic and general methodology are conceived of as existing in and for themselves, like mathematical formulae, abstracted from concrete thought and from particular concrete sciences (just as one might suppose language to exist in dictionaries and grammar, technique outside work and concrete activity etc.). Moreover, it should not be thought that the 'anti-Esperantist' form of thought means scepticism or agnosticism or eclecticism. Every form of thought must certainly consider itself to be 'exact' and 'true' and combat other forms of thought, but it must do so 'critically'. The question, then, is one of the amounts of 'criticism' and 'historicism' contained in any form of thought. The philosophy of praxis, by reducing 'speculativity' to its just proportions (i.e. by denying that 'speculativity', as even the historicists of idealism understand it, is the essential nature of philosophy), seems to be the historical methodology that adheres most closely to reality and truth.

Q11§45.

20 Cultural Topics. Formal Logic and Scientific Mentality

In order to understand the superficiality and weakness of the foundations of the modern scientific mentality (although a distinction must, perhaps, be made between one country and another), it is enough to recall the recent polemic over the so-called 'homo oeconomicus',[33] one of the basic concepts of economic science that is as plausible and necessary as all the abstractions on which the natural sciences are based (and, albeit in a different form, the historical or humanistic sciences, too). If, because of its abstract nature, we were not justified in using the distinctive concept of homo oeconomicus then we would be equally unjustified in using the symbol H_2O for water, given that in actual fact there exists no single H_2O-water but an infinite quantity of individual 'waters'. The vulgar nominalist objection would be back with us in all its force etc.

Scientific mentality is weak as an element of popular culture, but it is also weak within the scientific community, which has the scientific mentality of a technical group, i.e. one that understands abstraction in its own particular science but not as a 'mental form'. Again, such a group understands its own particular 'abstraction', its own particular method of abstraction, but not that of the other sciences (whereas one must take the position that there exist various types of abstraction and that the scientific mentality is the one that is capable of understanding every type of abstraction and justifying it). The most serious conflict of 'mentality' is, however, that between the so-called exact or mathematical sciences, which moreover are not the whole of the natural sciences, and the 'humanistic' or 'historical' sciences, i.e. those which deal with humanity's activity in history, with its active intervention in the life process in the universe. (One should analyse the judgement that Hegel gives of political economy, in particular the ability demonstrated by economists to 'abstract' in this field.[34])

Q17§52.

D THE TRANSLATABILITY OF SCIENTIFIC AND PHILOSOPHICAL LANGUAGES

21 Introduction to the Study of Philosophy [1]. The Translatability of Scientific Languages

The notes written under this heading are in fact to be brought together in the general section on the relationships between speculative philosophies and the philosophy of praxis and their reduction to this latter as a political moment that the philosophy of praxis explains 'politically'. Reduction of all speculative philosophies to 'politics', to a moment of historico-political life; the philosophy of praxis conceives the reality of human relationships of knowledge as an element of political 'hegemony'.

Q10II§6iv.

22 Introduction to the Study of Philosophy [2]. The Subjective Conception of Reality and the Philosophy of Praxis

The philosophy of praxis 'absorbs' the subjective conception of reality (idealism) into the theory of the superstructures; it absorbs and explains it historically, that is to say it 'goes beyond' it reducing it to one of its own 'moments'. The theory of the superstructures is the translation in terms of realist historicism of the subjective conception of reality.

Q10II§6ii.

23 Lenin and Translation

In 1921 Vilich [Lenin], in dealing with organisational questions, wrote and said (more or less) this: we have not been able to 'translate' our language into those of Europe.[35]

Q11§46.

24 Translation Between Different Civilisations

The following problem must be resolved: whether the mutual translatability of the various philosophical and scientific languages is a 'critical' element that belongs to every conception of the world or whether it belongs (in an organic way) just to the philosophy of praxis, being appropriable only in part by other philosophies? Translatability presupposes that a given stage of civilisation has a 'basically' identical cultural expression, even if its language is historically different, being determined by the particular tradition of each national culture and each philosophical system, by the prevalence of an intellectual or practical activity etc. Thus it is to be seen whether one can translate between expressions of different stages of civilisation, in so far as each of these stages is a moment of the development of another, one thus mutually integrating the other, or whether a given expression may be translated using the terms of a previous stage of the same civilisation, a previous stage which however is more comprehensible than the given language etc. It seems that one may in fact say that only in the philosophy of praxis is the 'translation' organic and thoroughgoing, whilst from other standpoints it is often a simple game of generic 'schematisms'.

Q11§47.

25 Giovanni Vailati[36] and the Translatability of Scientific Languages

Passage in *The Holy Family*, where it is claimed that Proudhon's French political language corresponds to and can be translated into the language of classical German philosophy.[37] This claim is very important for understanding certain aspects of the philosophy of praxis, for finding the solution to many apparent contradictions in historical development, and for responding to some superficial objections to this historiographical theory (as well as being useful for combating certain mechanistic abstractions).

It is to be seen whether this critical principle can be juxtaposed to or merged with analogous statements. In the September-October 1930 number of *Nuovi Studi di Diritto, Economia e Politica* we read in a note on page 303 contained in an open letter ('Whether there exists, historically, the alleged repugnance of economists towards the concept of the state as producer') written by Luigi Einaudi to Rodolfo Benini: 'If I possessed the whole wonderful faculty which our late lamented friend Vailati had to the greatest degree – that of being able to translate any theory whatsoever from a geometrical language into an algebraic one, from a hedonistic one to that of Kantian ethics, from the pure normative terminology of economics into the applied one of rule formation, I might attempt to retranslate Spirito's page into your formalism, in other words, that of classical economics. It would be a fruitful exercise, similar to those which Loria tells of having undertaken in his youth – the successive expression of a given economic proof first of all in the language of Adam Smith, then of Ricardo, then Marx, John Stuart Mill and Cairnes. But these are exercises which must, just as Loria did with his, be consigned to the drawer once they have been carried out. They are of use in teaching every one of us the lesson of humility, when for a moment we labour under the illusion of having seen something new, since if this novelty could have been expressed in the words and fitted into the conceptual framework of these representatives of old, this would tell us that what we had seen was already contained in their thought. But these exercises cannot and must not prevent each generation from using that language which is most apt to its way of thinking and of understanding the world. History is rewritten, so why should economic science also not be rewritten, first in terms of costs of production, then in terms of utility, thence of static equilibrium and on to dynamic equilibrium?'

Einaudi's critical-methodological starting point is very limited and refers not so much to the languages of different national cultures as to particular languages of different scientific personalities. Einaudi links up here to the current represented by certain Italian pragmatists, such as Pareto and Prezzolini. In his letter he sets himself quite limited critical and methodological goals: he wants to teach a little lesson to Ugo Spirito, in whom the novelty of ideas, of methods, of the statement of problems is very often purely and simply a verbal question, one of terminology, of personal or of group 'jargon'. It is however to be seen if this is not the first step of the vaster and deeper problem implicit in the assertion contained in the *Holy Family*. Just as two 'scientists', who owe their cultural formation to the same background, think they are upholding different 'truths' just because they employ a different scientific language (and we do not say that there is not a difference between them or that this difference is not without significance), so too two national cultures, the expressions of fundamentally similar civilisations, think that they too are different, antagonistic, one opposed to the other, one superior to the other because they use languages that come from different traditions, formed through activities characteristic of and particular to each: a politico-juridical language in France, a philosophical, doctrinal and theoretical one in Germany. For the historian, in actual fact, these civilisations can be mutually translated, the one reduced to the other. Certainly, this translatability is not 'perfect' in every respect, even in important ones (but what language is exactly translatable into another? what single word is exactly translatable into another language?), but it is so in its 'basic' essentials. It is also possible that one really is superior to the other, but hardly ever in what their representatives and their fanatical supporters claim, and especially hardly ever when taken as a whole: the real progress of civilisation comes about through the collaboration of all peoples, through national 'thrusts', but such thrusts are almost always in respect of given cultural activities or groups of problems.

Gentile's philosophy is the one today which makes most issue of questions of 'words', of 'terminology', of 'jargon', which puts forward as new 'creations' (those which are in fact new) what are new verbal expressions, themselves not always fortunate and adequate. Einaudi's note has, in consequence, somewhat put out Ugo Spirito who cannot however manage to reply with anything conclusive. (See the whole polemic in the review quoted.)

Q11§48.

26 The Mutual Translatability of National Cultures

The observation in *The Holy Family* to the effect that French political language is equivalent to the language of classical German philosophy has been expressed 'poetically' by Carducci in the expression 'Immanuel Kant cut off the head of God/And Maximilien Robespierre that of the King.'[38] On the subject of this comparison of Carducci's between the practical politics of M. Robespierre and the speculative thought of I. Kant, B. Croce records a series of very interesting philological 'sources' but these, for Croce, are of purely philological and cultural importance, without any theoretical or 'speculative' significance. Carducci derives this motif from Heinrich Heine (third book of *Zur Geschichte der Religion und Philosophie in Deutschland*, [*On the History of Religion and Philosophy in Germany*], 1834).[39] But Heine's comparison of Robespierre with Kant is not original. Croce, who has sought out the origins of the comparison, writes of having found a distant reference to it in a letter of 21 July 1795 that Hegel wrote to Schelling which Hegel then developed in the lectures he gave on the history of philosophy and the philosophy of history. In his first lectures in the history of philosophy Hegel says that 'Kant, Fichte and Schelling's philosophy contains, in the form of thought, the revolution' towards which spirit had latterly progressed in Germany, that is to say during a great era in universal history in which 'only two peoples have taken part, the Germans and, although they are opposite, rather in fact because they are opposite, also the French'; the result being that, whereas the new principle 'has burst onto the scene in the form of the spirit and concept' in Germany, in France on the other hand, it has been developed 'in the form of actuality' (cf. *Vorles. über die Gesch. d. Philos.*, Berlin 1844).[40] In his lectures on the philosophy of history, Hegel explains that the principle of formal will, of abstract freedom, in whose terms 'the simple unity of Self-consciousness, the Ego, constitutes the absolutely independent Freedom, and is the fountain of all general conceptions', 'among the Germans ... assumed no other form than that of *tranquil theory* but the French wished to give it practical effect' (*Vorlesungen über die Philosophie der Geschichte*, Berlin 1848, pp. 531-32).[41] (This passage from Hegel is in fact paraphrased in *The Holy Family*, it seems, where a statement of Proudhon's is defended against the Bauers, or, if it is not defended, it is explained in accordance with this Hegelian hermeneutical canon). But the passage from Hegel appears much more important as the 'source' of the thought expressed in the *Theses on Feuerbach* that 'the philosophers have explained the world and the point is now to change it';[42] that is to say, that philosophy must become politics in order to realise itself, in order to go on being philosophy, that 'tranquil theory' must be 'put into practical effect', must become the 'form of actuality' as the source of Engels's claim that the legitimate heir of classical German philosophy is the German 'people' and, lastly, as an element that goes to make up the theory of the unity of theory and practice.[43]

A. Ravà, in his book *Introduzione allo studio della filosofia di Fichte* [*Introduction to the Study of Fichte's Philosophy*] (Modena 1909) informs Croce that as early as 1791 Baggesen, in a letter to Reinhold, juxtaposed the two revolutions, that Fichte's 1792 piece on the French Revolution is animated by this sense of affinity between the product of philosophy and the political event, and that in 1794 Schaumann paid special attention to developing this comparison, pointing out that France's political revolution 'makes the need for a fundamental determination of the rights of man felt from the *outside*' and that the philosophiocal reform in Germany 'shows from the *inside* the sole means and way by which this need may be satisfied'; Indeed, Ravà notes, this same comparison gave rise to a satire against Kantian philosophy in 1797. His conclusion is that 'comparison was in the air'.

The comparison came to be repeated lots of times in the course of the nineteenth century (by Marx, for example, in his *Critique of Hegel's Philosophy of Law*[44]) and 'passed into general currency' thanks to Heine. In Italy, some years before Carducci, it is to be found in a letter of Bertrando Spaventa's, entitled 'Bigotry, Positivism and Rationalism', published in the *Rivista Bolognese* of May 1868, and reprinted in his *Scritti filosofici* [*Philosophical Writings*]. Croce concludes by expressing his reserves on the comparison, in that it is a 'statement of a logical and historical relationship'. 'Since if it is true that the French Revolution responded quite well to the theorist of natural law in Kant in so far as regards the facts, it is also true that that same Kant belongs to the philosophy of the eighteenth century which preceded and informed that political upheaval; while the Kant who opened up the future, the Kant of the *synthesis a priori*,[45] is the first link in a new philosophy, which goes beyond the philosophy that was incarnated in the French Revolution.' One understands this reserve of Croce's. It is, however, inappropriate and out of place, since the very quotations that Croce cites from Hegel show that we are not dealing with the particular comparison between Kant and Robespierre, but with something more extended and comprehensive, with the political upheaval in France in its entirety and the philosophical reform in Germany in its entirety. That Croce is favourable to 'tranquil theories' and not to 'the forms of actuality', that a reform 'in ideas' rather than the one in course seems to him the fundamental one is understandable. It is in this sense that German philosophy was influential in Italy in the period of the Risorgimento, through liberal 'moderatism' (in the strictest sense of 'national liberty'), although in De Sanctis one may detect an intolerance of this 'intellectualist' position, witness his passage to the 'Left' and in some of his writings, especially *Scienza e vita* [*Science and Life*] and his articles on *verismo*, etc.[46]

The whole question should be looked at again, studying the references given by Croce and Ravà, and tracking down others in order to fit them into the context of the question dealt with under the current heading, namely that two fundamentally similar structures have 'equivalent' superstructures that are mutually translatable, whatever the particular national language. Contemporaries of the French Revolution were conscious of this fact, and this is of the greatest interest. (Croce's notes on Carducci's comparison between Robespierre and Kant are published in the 2nd

Series of *Conversazioni Criticihe*, pp. 292 *et seq.*).

Q11§49.

27 Introduction to the Study of Philosophy [3]. Gioberti on French and German Philosophy

The following extract relating to the history of philosophy is taken from Chapter XI of Part II of Gioberti's *Rinnovamento* [*Renewal*]: 'Humanism is linked to previous philosophical doctrines and represents the last span of Cartesian psychologism, which, *although following different trajectories in France and Germany*, still reached the same outcome. Transformed, however, by Locke and Kant into *empirical and speculative sensationalism*, the force of logic caused it in the short term to give birth to the gross atheism of the later followers of Condillac and the refined atheism of the new Hegelians. Gottlieb Fichte, setting off from the principles of the critical school, had already identified God with man, as subsequently Friedrich Schelling equated him with nature; Hegel, bringing together and interlocking these, their dictates, regarded the human spirit as the peak of the absolute. This latter, descending from the abstract zone of the idea into the concrete one of nature and passing on into that of the spirit, acquires here the consciousness of its own self and becomes God. The new Hegelians accept the conclusion while rejecting the non-existent hypothesis of the pantheistic absolute and the imaginary edifice of the premisses, whence, instead of asserting together with the maestro himself that the spirit is God, they teach that the concept of God is a vain image and a fanciful mask of the spirit.'[47]

Gioberti's note to the effect that classical German philosophy is the same thing in a different language as French materialism etc. seems of interest. The passage should be compared with the one from *The Holy Family* which speaks of French materialism. (Recall that in *The Holy Family*, in fact, the expression 'humanism' is used in the same sense as in Gioberti – something that is not transcendent – and that the author wanted to call his philosophy 'neo-humanism'.)[48]

Q17§18 iii.

28 The Translatability of Different National Cultures

Parallel between the civilisations of Greece and Rome and importance that the Greek and the Roman world had in the humanist and the Renaissance periods respectively. Current day publications on the old problem of the 'superiority' and 'originality' of Greek art compared with that of Rome: see the study by Augusto Rostagni 'Autonomy of Latin Literature' in the *Italia Letteraria* of 21 May 1933 and following numbers. As regards Humanism and the Renaissance, Rostagni makes no distinction between the different aspects of Italian culture: 1) the erudite-humanist study of Greco-Roman classicity that becomes exemplary, a model of life and so on; 2) the fact that this reference to the classical world is none other than the cultural shell within which there was developed the new conception of life and of the world in competition with and often (later becoming ever more) in opposition to the medieval-religious conception; 3) the original movement which the 'new man' realises as such, and which is new and original despite the humanistic shell modelled on the ancient world.

In relation to this one may observe that spontaneity and artistic vigour were present before humanism became 'organised', hence the proposition suggested elsewhere that humanism was to a great extent reactionary as a phenomenon; it represented, in other words, the detachment of the intellectuals from the masses, who were then beginning to assume a national form, and was thus an interruption in the politico-national formation of Italy in order to return (in another form) to the position of imperial and medieval cosmopolitanism.

The parallel between Greeks and Romans is a false and unrewarding problem, political in nature and origin. Did the Romans have a philosophy? They had their own 'way of thinking' and of conceiving man and life, and this was their real 'philosophy', embodied in juridical doctrines and political practice. One can (in a certain sense) say for the Romans and the Greeks what Hegel has to say about French politics and German philosophy.[49]

Q15§64.

29 Miscellaneous Notes. The History of Terminology and Metaphors

The traditional expression that the 'anatomy' of a society is constituted by its 'economy'[50] is a simple metaphor derived from discussions that developed around the natural sciences and classification that entered its 'scientific' stage just when it began to take anatomy as its starting point rather than secondary and incidental characteristics. The metaphor was also justified by its 'popularity', i.e. by the fact that even an intellectually unrefined audience was offered a scheme it could easily understand (due account is hardly ever taken of the fact that the philosophy of praxis, in setting itself the task of the intellectual and moral reform of culturally backward social strata, has recourse to metaphors that at times are 'crude and violent' in their popularity). A study of the cultural-linguistic origin of a metaphor used to indicate a concept or a newly discovered relationship can help towards the better understanding of the concept itself, in as much as it gets related back to the historically determined cultural world from which it sprang, just as such a study is useful to define the limit of the metaphor itself, stopping it in other words from becoming prosaic and mechanical. In a certain era the experimental and natural sciences were a 'model', a 'type',[51] and given that the social sciences (politics and historiography) were trying to find a foundation that was objective and scientifically appropriate for giving them the same self-assurance and vigour as the natural sciences, it is easy to understand that they had recourse to these sciences to create their language.

Furthermore, from this standpoint, one must distinguish between the two founders of the philosophy of praxis, whose language does not have the same cultural origin and whose metaphors reflect different interests.

Another 'linguistic' indicator is bound up with the development of the juridical sciences: it is stated in the Preface to the *Critique of Political Economy* that 'One cannot judge a historical epoch by what it thinks of itself,'[52] that is by the sum total of its ideologies. This principle should be linked to the almost contemporaneous one by which a judge cannot judge the accused by what the accused thinks of himself and of his own acts of omission (although this does not mean that the new historiography[53] is conceived of as being akin to court proceedings). It was this principle that led to the radical reform in procedural methods, contributed to having torture abolished and provided judiciary and penal activity with a modern basis.[54]

Another question belongs to the same order [of] observations, concerning the fact that superstructures are considered as mere labile 'appearances'. One should, in this 'judgement' too, see more a reflection of discussions born in the field of the natural sciences (zoology and the classification of species, the discovery that 'anatomy' must form the basis of classifications) than a consistent derivation from metaphysical materialism, for which mental facts are a mere semblance, *unreal* and *illusory*, of material facts. Onto this historically ascertainable origin of 'judgement' we are seeing a partial superimpostition, and even in part a substitution, of what one may call a mere 'psychological attitude' of no 'cognitive or philosophical' importance, which is not difficult to demonstrate. Its theoretical content is very scanty (or indirect, and perhaps is limited to an act of will that has an implicit cognitive or philosophical value in so far as it is universal) and immediate polemical passion predominates not only over an exaggerated and deformed assertion in the opposite sense (viz. that only the 'spiritual' is real) but over the political-cultural 'organisation' of which this theory is the expression. One can see that the affirmation that superstructures are 'appearances' is not a philosophical act, one of knowledge, but solely a practical act, one of political polemic, from the fact that it is posited not as being 'universal' but as holding only for certain given superstructures. Putting the question in terms of individuals, one may observe that those who are sceptical as regards the 'disinterestedness' of others, but not as regards their own 'disinterestedness', are not philosophically 'sceptical', but turn the question into one of one's 'concrete individual history'. Scepticism would be this, i.e. a philosophical act, if the 'sceptics' doubted themselves or their own philosophical capacities in consequence, for it is an obvious observation that the sceptic, in philosophising in order to negate philosophy, in reality exalts and affirms it. In the case given, the assertion that the superstructures are an 'appearance' means only the assertion that a given 'structure' is condemned to perish, has to be destroyed, and the problem posed is whether this assertion is of the few or of the many, whether it is already or is about to become a decisive historical force or whether it is purely an isolated (or isolatable) opinion of some fanatical individual obsessed with a fixed idea.

The 'psychological' attitude providing substance to the assertion of the 'appearance' of the superstructures might be compared with the attitude current in certain periods (these too being 'materialistic' and 'naturalistic' ages!) towards 'women' and 'love'. Take the case of a graceful young women, gifted with all those physical attributes that traditionally give rise to the judgement that this woman is 'lovable'. The 'practical' man would evaluate her 'skeletal' structure, the width of her pelvic girdle, then try and get to know her mother and grandmother to see what probable process of hereditary deformation the young woman of today would undergo as the years went by, so as to see what sort of 'wife' he would have in ten, twenty or thirty years' time. This 'satanic' youth, basing his attitude on an ultra-realistic pessimism, would have observed the girl with the eyes of a Stecchetti,[55] would have judged her to be 'in reality' a mere sack full of putrefaction, would have imagined her already dead and buried, with 'eye-sockets empty and fetid' and so on and so forth. It seems that this psychological attitude is characteristic of the age just after puberty and is bound up with the first experiences, with the first reflections, with when one is first disabused, etc. However, life helps one overcome this and a 'given' woman no longer excites such thoughts as these.

In judging the superstructures to be an 'appearance' there

is a fact of the same kind: a 'disabusal', a pseudo-pessimism that suddenly disappears when the state has been 'conquered' and the superstructures are those of one's own moral and intellectual world. And in fact these deviations from the philosophy of praxis are to a great extent connected to groups of intellectuals who are socially 'vagabond', disenchanted etc., groups that are adrift, but ready to drop anchor when they chance on some decent port.

Q11§50.

30 The Proposition that One Must 'Put Man Back on his Feet'

In examining the influence of Hegelianism on the founder of the philosophy of praxis, one must recall (bearing especially in mind Marx's eminently practical-critical nature) that Marx was part of German university life shortly after the death of Hegel, when there must still have been a most vivid recollection of Hegel's lectures and of the impassioned discussions relating to recent actual history that this teaching gave rise to, discussions in which the historical concreteness of Hegel's thought must have come over in a much more obvious fashion than is apparent in his systematic writings. Some propositions of the philosophy of praxis are, it seems, to be considered as especially tied up with the liveliness of these conversations: the statement that Hegel makes men walk on their heads, for example.[56] Hegel uses this expression in speaking of the French Revolution when he says that, at a certain moment, it seemed that the world was walking on its head (the correct quote to be checked here). Croce wonders (check where and how) where Marx had picked up this image, as if it had not been used by Hegel in his writings. The image is so little 'bookish' that it gives the impression of having arisen in the course of conversation.

Antonio Labriola, in his essay 'From One Century to the Next' writes, 'It's exactly that *pig-tailed reactionary* Hegel who noted that those men (of the Convention) were the first, after Anaxagoras, to have attempted to turn the notion of the world upside down, basing it on reason.'

This proposition, both in the use that Hegel makes of it and in that of the philosophy of praxis, should be compared with the parallel, drawn again by Hegel and mention of which is to be found in *The Holy Family*, between French practical-juridical thought and German speculative thought (on this subject, see the notebook on the 'Introduction to the Study of Philosophy', p. 59).[57]

Q10II§60.

E MACHINES AND TECHNOLOGY

31 On Ancient Capitalism

On ancient capitalism, or rather on ancient industrialism, one should read G.C. Speziale's article 'On Nemi's Galleys and Naval Archeology' in the *Nuova Antologia* of 1 November 1930 (polemic with Prof. Giuseppe Lugli who wrote in *Pègaso*; articles in daily newspapers at the same time). Speziale's article is of great interest, but he seems to me to exaggerate the importance attributed to the possibilities for industrialism in antiquity (cf. the question of ancient capitalism discussed in the *Nuova Rivista Storica*). In my opinion Speziale does not have any precise notion of what the 'machine' was in the classical world and what it is today (this observation holds especially for Barbagallo and Co.).[58] The 'innovations' Speziale insists on were not yet to be seen in Vitruvius's definition of 'machine', i.e. devices suitable for facilitating the movement and transport of heavy bodies (see exactly what Vitruvius's definition was), and are thus only relative novelties. The modern machine is quite a different thing in that it not only 'helps' but 'substitutes' the worker; it may be that Vitruvius's 'machines' continue to exist alongside 'modern' ones and that the Romans might have reached a certain, as yet unknown perfection in this direction, and this is no wonder, but in all this there is nothing 'modern' in the proper sense of the word that has been established by the industrial 'revolution', i.e. by the invention and widespread adoption of machines that 'substitute' the human labour used previously.

Q6§156.

32 Encyclopaedic Notions [4]. The Machine

Article by Metron, 'The Spread of the Machine', in the *Corriere della Sera* of 15 March 1932. Extended meaning of the concept of machine. In the East the safety razor and the car are both machines; in the West a machine is the name for the 'device' for sewing and for writing, as well as the electric motor and the steam engine. For Metron they are different things; as far as he is concerned the machine real and proper consists of one 'which allows the utilisation of natural energies' (an ambiguous formulation, since even the safety razor and the Archimedean lever allow us to use previously unused natural energies), while the others, if one wishes to be exact, are only 'tools or transmissions'. 'The tool types of machine improve and perfect human labour; machines producing motion are a complete substitute for it. The real revolution in the world is not due to machines like the sewing machine or typewriter which still constantly require the human motor, but to those machines which completely eliminate muscular effort.'

Metron goes on to observe that 'According to the calculations contained in a study published on the occasions of the world energy conference, held in Berlin in 1930, the mechanical energy from all sources (coal, mineral oils, waterfalls etc.) used up each year by the whole of the human race can be estimated at about one trillion 700 billion kilowatt-hours, i.e. 900 kilowatt-hours a head. Now 900 kilowatt-hours represent almost ten times the work that a strong man can do in a year. In essence, each man of flesh and blood has had ten other metallic men working for him and his benefit. If this process were to continue, it could not lead to other than an ideal form of leisure which, rather than lowering to the animal level, is ennobling: in other words, muscular force is left at man's complete disposal so that he should work only with his brain, i.e. the noblest and most coveted form of work.'

This is written in 1932, that is to say when, just in those countries in which the 'metallic men' work for other men in a proportion way above the world average, there exists the most appalling crisis of enforced leisure and degrading poverty. This, too, is an opium of poverty!

In actual fact, the distinction Metron draws between machines as motive forces and machines as tools, the former having revolutionary prevalence, is not a precise one. The machines that produce motion have 'enlarged' the field of work and production, have made some things possible that, before their discovery, were either impossible or nearly so. It is machines as tools, however, that have really taken the place of human labour, and have turned the whole human organisation of production upside down. A correct observation: from 1919 onwards the innovation of greatest importance has been the introduction into the factory of the mechnical transport of materials, of men and of conveyors.

The question, moreover, of the prevalence of machines that produce motion or of machines as tools is, beyond certain limits, an idle one. It is of importance for establishing the distance that separates antiquity from modernity. On top of all this, there are differentiations even in tool-type machines and so on.

Q8§90.

33 Political Nomenclature. Artisans: Small, Medium and Big Industry

Quantitative concepts and qualitative concepts. From the quantitative standpoint, one can start from the number of workers employed in each firm, establishing average figures for each class: from 1 to 5 artisan workshop, from 5 to 50 small industry, from 50 to 100 medium-sized industry, 100 upwards big industry. We are here dealing with types or very relative generalisations that may change from country to country. The qualitative concept would be more scientific and precise, but it is much more complex and presents a lot of difficulties. Qualitatively speaking, the classes should be established by a combination of various elements: besides the number of workers, the type of machinery and how one machine meshes in with another, the degree of division of labour, the ratio between different types of worker (manual, specialised manual or machine minder, semi-skilled and skilled) and the degree of rationalisation (as well as of industrialisation) of the productive and administrative apparatus as a whole. A rationalised firm has fewer workers than one that has not been rationalised, and thus one with 50 workers may be more a 'big industry' that one that has 200 (which happens when certain firms, for certain parts of their production, make use of an outside firm that is like the specialised department of a whole group of firms that are not linked organically etc.). These single elements have different relative weights according to the branch of industry. In the building industry, for example, mechanisation will never reach the levels it does in engineering. The type of machinery in textiles develops quite differently from that in engineering, etc.

To this concept of the size of an industry is linked the concept of 'machine'. And there is also linked the notion of the 'extended factory', which is one aspect of artisan production, out-work and small industry. But cannot even a <big> building enterprise, in a certain sense, be considered an extended factory? And what about the tramway or railway? (From the point of view of territorial organisation, or in other words of technical concentration, these undertakings are dispersed, and this has its importance for the psychology of the workers employed. A railway signalman will never have the same psychology as the manual worker in a big factory, etc.) Another important element is the motive power used: is an artisan who makes use of electrical energy any longer an artisan in the traditional sense? The modern fact of the ease of distribution of electrical motive power, even in the case of small productive units, transforms and renews all types of industry and firm.

Q7§96.

34 Introduction to the Study of Philosophy [4]. Technology as the Mediator Between Science and Reality

Here is how the point of view of 'Saggiatore' ('Essayist') is summarised in the *Critica Fascista* of 1 May 1933: 'We are ... in the field of *absolute objectivism*. The sole criterion of truth is experiment, the immanence of thought in what is really known. (1) The sole mediation between thought and reality is science. (2) And what is really desired is solely that which man can do and does in his historical life, which is associative, circumstantiated life as defined by the concrete tasks which emerge from its unfolding. The state (3) is there as the control and measure of this human activity made real in history. It distinguishes in practice between what are the roaming, wishful thoughts of scattered individuals and the real positions of a will in action that history sanctions by unifying them and making something lasting of them in what is collectively created.' (1. or in the really experienced? i.e. in the identity of theory and practice? 2. but is not science, too, thought? instead of science, technology, and thence, between science and reality, technology is the sole mediation; 3. but what does state mean? Only the state apparatus or the whole of organised civil society? Or the dialectical unity between government power and civil society?)

The standpoints of the 'Saggiatore' group are of interest in that they show an intolerance of verbalistic philosophical systems, but this group too is something indistinct and confused. The document is however testimony of how much modern culture is permeated with the realist concepts of the philosophy of praxis.

Q15§33 (excerpt).

35 On the Development of Military Technology

The most characteristic and significant trait of the current stage of military technology and thus of the direction taken by scientific research in so far as it is connected with the development of military technology (or tends towards this end) would seem to be found in the following: that in some of its aspects military technology tends to make itself independent of general technology considered as a whole and to become an activity on its own, autonomous of the rest. Until the world war military technology was a simple, specialised application of general technology and on that account the military might of a state or group of states (allied for purposes of mutual integration) could be calculated with almost mathematical precision on the basis of economic (industrial, agricultural, financial, technologico-cultural) power. After the world war this calculation has no longer been possible, at least to the same degree of precision or approximation, and this factor constitutes the most formidable unknown in the present politico-military situation. Suffice it to list a number of elements as a reference point: the submarine, the bomber, gas and chemical and bacteriological means applied to warfare. Taking the case to its limit, the *reductio ad absurdum*, one may say that Andorra is able to produce enough gas and bacteriological weapons to exterminate the whole of France.

This military technology situation is one of the most 'silently' working elements in that transformation of the art of politics that has brought us to the passage, even in politics, from the war of manoeuvre to that of position or siege.[59]

Q13§28.

36 Past and Present [2]. War

From the *Enciclopedia Italiana* (article on 'War'): 'Too many Second Empire writers seem convinced that rhetoric – and the great martial episodes of the Revolution and First Empire lend facile support to this notion – is enough to keep military morale high and that a high military morale is enough by itself to neutralise any possible technical superiority on the other side.'

If this assertion is right as regards military criticism it is even more authoritative when applied to the criticism of political action. Perhaps only in one sole aspect of political action, i.e. in that of elections in ultra-democratic liberal regimes, may it be true that rhetoric and a 'high fighting morale' (on paper) can substitute for a minute and organic determination in advance and thus yield 'astonishing' victories. This judgement could be transferred to the series of notes on Machiavelli, in that part which contains an analysis of the different moments of a situation and especially the most immediate one in which each situation comes to a climax and is, in effect, resolved, i.e. becomes history.

Q17§36.

VI REFERENCE POINTS FOR AN ESSAY ON B. CROCE

Introduction

*Summary, 328; 1 *Croce's Stance during the World War, 332; 2 *Croce as Intellectual Leader of Revisionism, 335; 3 *Development of the Theory of Ethico-Political History, 335; 4 *Croce's Relative Popularity, 337; 5 *Croce and Religion, 338; 6 *Croce and Italian Historiography, 341; 7 *Definition of Ethico-Political History, 343; 8 *Transcendence-Theology-Speculation, 346; 9 *Paradigms of Ethico-Political History, 348; 10 *Liberty as Identity of History and Mind and as Ideology, 351; 11 *Croce and the Philosophy of Praxis, 354; 12 *Ethico-Political History and Hegemony, 357; 13 Notes, 358;

Introduction

In early spring 1932 Gramsci began work on the tenth Notebook, immediately dividing it into two parts. The first 80 pages were, with the exception of the very first few paragraphs, written later than the last 20; for this reason it is the first 80 pages that are now known as the second part (Q10II) and the last 20 as the first part (Q10I). It is Q10I that is reproduced here, under the name that Gramsci himself gave it, as Chapter VI. Although he does not say so explicitly he seems principally to follow the key themes of the volume *Etica e politica* (*Ethics and Politics*), one of the ' "minor" writings, that is to say the collections of articles,

Reference Points for an Essay on B. Croce

of occasional pieces, of short essays which have a greater and more obvious link with life, with the concrete movement of history' in which Croce outlines much of his moral stance and of the methodology that underlies his major historical work of the 1930s, the *History of Europe*. Nearly all the material of these two books is available in four separate volumes in English, for which see this Chapter and its footnotes. At times, e.g. when critically dissecting in §10 the Crocean concepts of ideology, philosophy and liberty and their interconnections, Gramsci's incisive style of polemical prose reaches an exceptional level of analytical and literary clarity.

Gramsci drafted a few preliminary notes (about half the last 20 or so paragraphs of Q8), again in early spring 1932, and then immediately began to give them their near-final shape, taking the unique step of first writing a somewhat extended and slightly re-ordered form of them in twelve paragraphs (numbered by himself – an unusual practice for him), of which the last two, acting as a sort of conclusion, are first drafts; these twelve paragraphs occupy the first two manuscript pages of Q10I and are here presented under the editorial title 'Summary'. He then proceeded to develop the ideas as paragraphs 1 to 12 of the main body of Q10I, each one corresponding to the same number of the 'Summary'. As a postscript he added a series headed 'Notes' numbered 1 to 8 (see §13, the only sub-section in this Chapter that bears an editorially added number); half these notes – like other parts of Q10I – are based on the Q8 paragraphs mentioned above while points 1, 6, 7 and 8 seem, however, not to be based on previous drafts. The final phase was to integrate the notes with other comments. It is probably an indication of the value that Gramsci put on his work on Croce that these later additions (included in the text or in the wide margin down the right hand side of the page) are among the last things he wrote, three years later, when his strength was already giving out. As elsewhere in this volume such later additions are in angular brackets, viz. <...>.

The first Italian editions of the Notebooks and some subsequent translations are based on an edited-down version of the 'Summary', each part of which then runs directly into the text of its corresponding sub-section with no indication of any distinction. In the interests of the accuracy demanded by a modern thematic anthology Q10I appears here just as in the manuscript, albeit at the cost of a little repetition; it is thus absolutely unchanged in order even though an alternative choice might, for example, have grouped together sub-sections 3, 7, 9 and 12 *en bloc* since they all deal explicitly with the Crocean notion of 'ethico-political history', a key concept which, on reinterpretation by Gramsci, becomes fundamental to his notion of hegemony (also dealt with at length, if not always explicitly, in Chapter VII) and, as he notes in passing, of the historical bloc.

Summary

<Introduction. General notes: 1) Remarks on method (cf. first note); 2) The party man; the party as the practical resolution of particular problems, as an organic political programme (collaboration on the conservative *Giornale d'Italia*, *La Stampa*, etc., *Politica*); the party as a general ideological tendency, as a cultural form (p.37a); 3) Croce and G. Fortunato more as the 'leaven' in than as the leaders of the 1900-1914 cultural movements in Italy (*La Voce*, *L'Unità*, etc., up to *La Rivoluzione Liberale*).>[1]

1. Croce's stance during the world war as the guideline for understanding the reasons underlying his subsequent activity as a philosopher and leader of European culture.

2. Croce as intellectual leader of the revisionist tendencies in the 1890s. Bernstein in Germany, Sorel in France, the economic-juridical school in Italy.

3. Croce from 1912 to 1932 (development of the ethico-political theory of history) tends to remain the leader of the revisionist tendencies with the aim of piloting them as far as the radical critique and (politico-ideological) liquidation both of historical materialism – even in a watered-down form – and of the economic-juridical school <cf. the marginal note on the next page>.[2]

4. Elements of Croce's relative popularity: α) the stylistic-literary element <absence of pedantry and abstruseness>; ß) the philosophic-methodological element

(unity of philosophy and common sense); γ) the ethical element (Olympian calm).

5. Croce and religion: α) the Crocean concept of religion <the starting point for the essay 'Religion and Peace of Mind' is to be found in De Sanctis's 1877 essay on Leopardi's 'Nerina' (*Nuova Antologia*, January 1877)>;[3] ß) Croce and Christianity; γ) the varying fortunes of Croceanism among Italian Catholics (the Italian neo-scholastics and the various stages of their philosophical manifestations – leaning first towards positivism, then idealism and now set to return towards 'pure' Thomism; the eminently 'practical' character of Father Gemelli's activity and his philosophical agnosticism);[4] δ) Papini and Ferrabino's articles in *La Nuova Antologia* as prominent manifestations of the Catholic laity <four articles in *La Civiltà Cattolica* (in 1932 and '33), all devoted solely to the introduction to the *History of Europe*; after the third of them, the book was put on the Index>; ε) is Croce a 'religious' reformer? <cf. a number of short essays published in *La Critica* in which some points of Catholic theology (grace etc.) are translated into 'speculative' language and the essay on the Caracciolo[5] of Calvinist theological fame etc.; 'translations' and interpretations of a similar kind are to be found *en passant* in many of Croce's writings.>

6. Croce and the Italian tradition <or a certain current within the Italian tradition>:[6] the historical theories of the Restoration; the moderate school; from 'prefiguring' an ethico-national dynamic, Cuoco's passive revolution transformed into a formula for 'action'; the 'speculative' dialectic of history and its arbitrary mechanicism (cf. Proudhon's position, criticised in *The Poverty of Philosophy*); the dialectic of the 'intellectuals' who conceive of themselves as embodying the thesis and antithesis and thus as elaborators of the synthesis; is, then, this less than total 'engagement' in the historical process not a form of scepticism? <Or of laziness? Or at least is it not in itself a political 'act'?>

7. Real meaning of the formula 'ethico-political history'. It is an arbitrary and mechanical hypostasisation of the moment of 'hegemony'. The philosophy of praxis does not exclude ethico-political history. The opposition between

Crocean historical doctrines and the philosophy of praxis lies in the speculative nature of Croce's conception. Croce's conception of the state.

8. Transcendence-theology-speculation. Speculative historicism and realist historicism. Idealist subjectivism and conception of the superstructures in the philosophy of praxis. A polemical sleight of hand on the part of Croce who 'today' gives a speculative <metaphysical, transcendental> meaning to the terms of the philosophy of praxis, hence the 'identification' of the 'structure' with a 'hidden god'. <Look at Croce's successive judgements on the importance and philosophical stature of the founders of the philosophy of praxis, as found in the different editions of his books and essays, where they are constantly subject to mutation without any specific justification.>

9. The history of Europe considered as 'passive revolution'. Can one write a history of nineteenth-century Europe without an organic treatment of the French Revolution and the Napoleonic wars? And can one write a modern history of Italy without the struggles of the Risorgimento? For extrinsic and tendentious reasons Croce in both cases leaves out the moment of struggle, in which the structure is formed and modified, and placidly assumes history to be the moment of cultural expansion, i.e. the ethico-political moment. Does the conception of 'passive revolution' have any 'current' significance? Are we now living through a period of 'revolution-restoration' to be put in order permanently, to be organised ideologically, to be extolled lyrically? Is Italy to have the same relationship to the USSR as the Germany <and Europe> of Kant and Hegel had with the France of Robespierre and Napoleon?

10. 'Liberty' as the identity of history and mind and 'liberty' as unmediated, detailed ideology, as 'superstition', as a practical instrument of government. <If one says that the 'nature of man is mind', one is saying that this nature is 'history', i.e. the ensemble of social relations as they are developing, i.e. once again the ensemble of nature and history, of material and mental or cultural forces etc.>

11. Can one, however, say that there is no trace of the philosophy of praxis in Croce's conception, even after the

development it has undergone over the last few years? Does his historicism not show any influence of his intellectual experience during the decade 1890-1900? Croce's position in this respect is to be seen in the preface to the 1917 edition of *Historical Materialism*: he would like to have us believe that the value of this experience was essentially negative in the sense that it played a part in destroying prejudices etc. But the persistent animosity that Croce has lately shown towards any element of the philosophy of praxis is suspect (above all his presentation of De Man's extremely mediocre book); one gets the impression that Croce is protesting too much so as not to be brought to account. The traces of a philosophy of praxis are to be found in the solution *of particular problems* <it remains to be seen whether these problems, if taken altogether, might not implicitly contain a total elaboration of the philosophy of praxis, i.e. Croce's whole methodology or philosophy, that is to say whether those problems not directly relatable to the corresponding ones of the philosophy of praxis may however be directly relatable to the others>: the doctrine of error seems to me to be the most typical example of this. In general one can say that the polemic against the philosophy of the pure act has forced Croce to adopt a greater realism and to feel a certain distaste at least as regards exaggerations in the speculative language used by the actualists.

<A certain literature is already being built up regarding the 'residues' or survivals (though in actual fact they are developments possessing their own peculiar organic nature) in Croce's philosophy of the doctrine of the philosophy of praxis; cf. for example Enzo Tagliacozzo's 'In Memory of Antonio Labriola' (*Nuova Italia*, 20 December 1934-20 January 1935, especially the second part of his article) and Edmondo Cione's essay 'The Logic of Historicism', Naples 1933 (perhaps an extract from the proceedings of the Royal Academy of Moral and Political Sciences). (From a review of this essay published in the January-February 1935 issue of the *Nuova Rivista Storica*, it appears that for Cione it was only with the *History of Europe* that Croce completely freed himself of the survivals of the philosophy of praxis. This and other essays by Cione should be looked at.) *Note*: In his

review of a number of articles by Guido Calogero (*Critica*, May 1935), Croce draws attention to the fact that Calogero uses 'philosophy of praxis' to refer to an interpretation of his own of Gentilian actualism. These are questions of terminology (but maybe not only terminology) that have to be cleared up.>

12. Would it, then, be futile to conceive of history as ethico-political history? It must be established that careful study and reflection has to be devoted even to the most recent phase of Croce's historiographical thought. In essence it represents a reaction against 'economism' and fatalistic mechanicism, even though it is presented as the supersession of the philosophy of praxis. The criterion holds for Croce, too, that one's thought must be criticised and evaluated not for what it professes to be, but for what it really is and for how it manifests itself in concrete historical writings. For the philosophy of praxis this self-same speculative method is not futile but has, rather, been rich in 'instrumental' values of thought, then incorporated into the philosophy of praxis (e.g. the dialectic). Credit must therefore be given to Croce's thought for its instrumental value and in this respect it may be said that it has forcefully drawn attention to the study of the factors of culture and ideas as elements of political domination, to the function of the great intellectuals in state life, to the moment of hegemony and consent as the necessary form of the concrete historical bloc. Ethico-political history is therefore one of the canons of historical interpretation that must always be borne in mind in the study and detailed analysis of history as it unfolds if the intention is to construct an integral history rather than partial or extrinsic histories.

1 Croce's Stance during the World War

Croce's stance during the world war. His writings on the subject collected together in *Pagine sulla guerra* [*Pages on the War*]. It would, however, be interesting to see them again in their first draft, as they were published in *La Critica* or other periodicals, and take into account the other questions of a cultural and moral nature which interested Croce at the time and which show to what other developments, more or less directly connected to the war situation, he considered it necessary to react. His attitude during the period of neutrality and then during the war indicates what intellectual and moral (and thus social) interests prevail even today in his literary and philosophical activity. Croce reacts against the popular view of the war (with its consequent propaganda) as a war of civilisation and therefore of a religious nature, a concept which in theory ought to lead to the annihilation of the enemy. In the moment of peace he sees that of war, and in the moment of war that of peace; he fights to ensure that the possibilities of mediating between the two aspects should never be destroyed. Peace must follow war and may bring about quite different groupings from those of war, but how would it be possible for different states to collaborate after they had unleashed the religious fanaticisms of war? It follows from this that no immediate necessity of politics may or must be elevated to the status of a universal criterion. But these terms do not exactly encompass Croce's position, since one cannot say that he is against the 'religious' conception of war in so far as this is politically necessary in order to convince the great masses of conscripts to sacrifice themselves in the trenches and die. This is a problem of political technique which it is up to the technicians of politics to solve.

What matters to Croce is that the intellectuals should not stoop to the level of the masses, but understand that ideology, as a practical instrument of government, is one thing and philosophy and religion quite another, not to be prostituted in the conscience of the priestly caste itself. Intellectuals must be the governors and not the governed, those who construct ideologies to govern others and not charlatans who let themselves get bitten and poisoned by their own vipers. Croce thus represents politics on the grand scale as against small-time politics, the Machiavellianism of Machiavelli as against the Machiavellianism of Stenterello. He adopts a very high vantage point and is solid in his belief that even violent criticism and the most savage personal attacks have their 'political' necessity and utility in order for him to be able to maintain this detached position. Croce's attitude during the war may be compared only with that of the Pope, who was head both of those bishops who blessed the weapons of the Austrians and Germans and of those who did likewise for Italian and French arms without there being any contradiction in this. (Cf. *Politics and Morals*: 'The term Churchmen must be understood, as in the term Church etc.')[7]

<This same stance, which is not without its drawbacks, is to be found in Croce's approach to modernism.[8] In point of fact, since it is not possible to conceive of the popular masses passing from the religious to the 'philosophical' stage, and since modernism was in practice gnawing away at the Church's massive practical-ideological structure, Croce's attitude served to consolidate the Church's positions. In just this way his 'revisionist' stance served to consolidate the reactionary currents (to Labriola, who pointed this out to him, Croce responded 'as to politics and the attempts of the reactionaries, *provideant consules*').[9] The same may also be said for his convergence with *Politica* in 1920 and for the practical stances he actually did adopt in Naples (speeches etc., participation in the Giolitti government and so on). This position of the 'pure intellectual' becomes either a real and proper deleterious form of 'Jacobinism' (and in this sense Amadeo can be compared with Croce in a way that perhaps did not cross Jacques Mesnil's mind)[10] or a despicable 'Pontius Pilatism' or first one, then the other, or even both of them simultaneously.>

<On war, Lyautey's comment may be applied to Croce:[11] in actual fact, national feeling among the self-styled nationalists is 'tempered' by such a pronounced cosmopolitanism, of a caste, cultural etc. nature that it may be regarded as a veritable instrument of government and its 'passions' as not immediate, but subordinate to the possession of power.>

Q10I§1.

2 Croce as Intellectual Leader of Revisionism

Croce as intellectual leader of the revisionist tendencies at the end of the nineteenth century. In Georges Sorel's letter to Croce of 9 September 1899 we read: 'Bernstein has just written to me that he has indicated in *Neue Zeit*, no. 46, that to a certain extent he took his inspiration from your writings. This is interesting since the Germans are not cut out to admit foreign sources for their ideas.'[12] Sorel's letters to Croce, which form a very important documentation testifying to the intellectual relationship between them, have now been printed in *La Critica* (1927 onwards). It would appear that Sorel's intellectual dependence on Croce was greater than might previously have been thought. Croce published his revisionist essays in the book *Historical Materialism*, but one must add to these Chapter XI of the first volume of *Conversazioni critiche* [*Critical Conversations*]. The boundaries of Crocean revisionism still have to be drawn; it seems to me that the limit of this first phase may be seen in the interview with Prof. Castellano, published in *La Voce* and reproduced in *Cultura e Vita Morale*.[13] Croce's reduction of historical materialism to an interpretative canon of history gave rise to <critically strengthened> the economic-juridical direction taken by the Italian school.

Q10I§2.

3 Development of the Theory of Ethico-Political History

Development of the theory of ethico-political history. Croce systematically 'enriches' his studies in the theory of history, this new phase being represented by the volume *Theory and History of Historiography*.[14] But the most significant factor in Croce's scientific biography is that he continues to consider himself the intellectual leader of the revisionists, his intention in further developing historiographical theory consisting in wanting to arrive at the liquidation of historical materialism but wanting this development to come about in such a way as to be identified with a cultural movement at the European level.

The assertion, made during the war, that the war itself could be termed a 'historical materialist war'[15] and the historical and cultural developments in Eastern Europe from 1917 onwards – these two elements made Croce determined to develop with greater precision his historiographical theory that aimed at the liquidation of any, even watered down, form of the philosophy of praxis (already before the war 'activistic' theories founded on irrationalist conceptions – their development in the post-war period – Croce's reaction: cf. *History of Italy* and then the speeches and writings on *History and Anti-History*).[16] That his historiographical theories are directed against the philosophy of praxis is stated explicitly by Croce in a brief polemic with Corrado Barbagallo published in the *Nuova Rivista Storica* in 1928-29. (Prof. Luigi Einaudi's attitude towards some of Croce's publications that define this 'liquidationist' phase should be noted. According to Einaudi Croce still makes too many concessions to the philosophy of praxis, recognising certain scientific merits in this cultural movement.) Documentation of the fact that Croce feels himself very strongly to be the leader of a great intellectual current in Europe, and that he considers this position, together with the obligations stemming from it, to be of great import, may be seen especially in his *History of Italy* but also in a series of occasional writings and reviews published in *La Critica*. One has also to recall certain recognitions of this leading role that are documented: the most curious is that of Bonomi in his book on Bissolati (it would be of interest to know if Bonomi made any reference to Croce in his *Vie Nuove* [*New Roads*]. Schiavi's preface to De Man's book. For the period 1890-1900, Orazio Raimondo's letter, printed by Prof. Castellano in his book on the fortune of Crocean ideas (*Introduzione allo studio delle opere di B. Croce* [*Introduction to the Study of Croce's Works*], Bari).[17]

Q10I§3.

4 Croce's Relative Popularity

Elements of the relative popularity of Croce's thought, a popularity the more notable in that there is nothing in Croce that might capture the imagination and excite strong passions or give rise to movements of a romantic character. (On this point, we are leaving aside the popularity of Croce's ideas on aesthetics, which have provided the fuel for journalistic excursions by dilettantes.) One of these elements is the stylistic-literary one. Benjamin Crémieux has written that Croce is the greatest Italian prose writer since Manzoni, but this comment is liable to lead to misconceptions; in my view it is more exact to place Croce's writings in the line of Italian scientific prose that includes authors like Galileo. Another element is the ethical one, to be found in the strength of character that he has demonstrated in a number of moments of national and European life, such as the position – that one may term Goethe-like – which he adopted during and after the war. While many intellectuals were losing their heads, did not know what direction to take in the general chaos, were reneging on their own past and drifting whiningly from side to side in their doubt as to who would prove the stronger, Croce remained imperturbably calm in stating his belief that 'metaphysically evil cannot prevail and that history is rationality'. But it must be said that the most important element in Croce's popularity is inherent in his very thought and method of thinking, and is to be sought in the greater adherence to real life of Crocean as compared with other speculative philosophies. Of interest from this standpoint is Croce's piece entitled 'The Philosopher' – reprinted in *Eternità e storicità della filosofia* [*Eternity and Historicity of Philosophy*], Rieti 1930, as well as all the other essays brought together in this slim volume – in which the main characteristics that distinguish Croce's activity from that of the traditional 'philosophers' are brilliantly distinguished. Dissolution of the concept of any delimited and closed – and thus pedantic and abstruse – philosophical 'system'; affirmation that philosophy must resolve the problems that from time to time are presented as the historical process unfolds. Systematicity is to be sought not in an external architectural structure but in the internal consistency and the productive sweep of each particular solution. Philosophical thought is not therefore conceived as a progression – thought giving rise to other thought – but as thought originating in historical reality. This approach explains Croce's popularity in the English-speaking countries, which stands higher than in the Germanic ones since the former have always preferred, as the solution to moral and practical problems, conceptions of the world put forward not in terms of grand, cumbersome systems, but rather in common sense terms, integrated by criticism and reflection. Croce has written hundreds upon hundreds of short essays (reviews, rejoinders and other occasional notes) in which his idealist thought circulates intimately, unhindered by scholastic pedantry; every solution seems self-sufficient, acceptable independently of other solutions, in so far as each one is in fact presented as the expression of sound common sense. Again, Croce's activity is presented essentially as criticism, starting with the destruction of a series of traditional prejudices, with the demonstration of the falsity and inconclusiveness of a series of problems that comprise the comic 'dada' of previous philosophers and so on, and by so doing it identifies itself with the attitude that sound common sense has always adopted towards this arrant nonsense.

Q10I§4.

5 Croce and Religion

Croce and religion. Croce's position on religion is one of the most important points to be analysed if one wants to understand the historical significance of Croceanism in the history of Italian culture. For him religion is a conception of reality, presented in mythological form, together with an ethic that conforms to this conception. Every philosophy, that is to say every conception of the world, in so far as it has become a 'faith', i.e. is considered not as a theoretical activity (the creation of new thought) but as a spur to action (concrete ethico-political activity, the creation of new history) is therefore a religion.

Croce is however very cautious in his relationship to traditional religion. His most 'advanced' writing is 'Religion and Peace of Mind', forming Chapter IV of the *Frammenti di Etica*,[18] first published during the war, towards the end of 1916 or the beginning of 1917. Although Croce appears not to want to make any intellectual concession either to religion (not even of the very ambiguous type made by Gentile) or to any form of mysticism, his attitude is however anything but militant and combative. This position of his is, indeed, most significant and ought to be brought clearly out into the open. A conception of the world cannot prove itself worthy of permeating the whole of society and becoming a 'faith' unless it shows itself capable of substituting previous conceptions and faiths at all levels of state life. To have recourse to the Hegelian theory of mythological religion as the philosophy of primitive societies <of the infancy of humanity> so as to justify confessional teaching even if only in primary schools, means nothing other than the reintroduction of a sophisticated version of a 'religion that is good for the people' whilst in reality abdicating and capitulating before clerical organisation. Moreover, one cannot but emphasise that a faith that cannot be translated into 'popular' terms shows for this very reason that it is characteristic of a given social group.

Despite this position *vis-à-vis* religion Croce's philosophy has been the object of much study by the neo-scholastic group of Catholics, and his solutions to individual problems accepted by Olgiati and Chiocchetti. (Olgiati uses the materials of Crocean criticism for his book on Marx while Chiocchetti, in his volume *La Filosofia di B. Croce* [*The Philosophy of B. Croce*], defends the adoption of some Crocean doctrines like that of the practical origin of error.) There was a period in which the neo-scholastics, who had represented an attempt to incorporate modern scientific doctrines and nineteenth-century positivism into Thomism, tried – when faced with the discredit that positivism was held in among intellectual circles and with the rising fortunes of neo-idealism – to find common ground between Thomism and idealism, thus explaining why Crocean and Gentilian philosophies enjoyed a certain success among this group.[19] For some time the neo-scholastics have been concentrating their efforts on a more restricted terrain that is more properly their own, and fighting any infiltration of idealism into their doctrines; they certainly believe they can inherit everything that can be salvaged from positivism and appropriate it for themselves, thereby becoming the sole theoretical opposition to idealism.

Catholic opposition to Croce is now on the increase for especially practical reasons. (*Civiltà Cattolica*'s critical stance towards Croce is quite different from the one they adopt towards Gentile.) The Catholics understand very clearly that Croce's significance and intellectual role are not comparable with those of the traditional philosophers, but are those of a real religious reformer, who at least manages to keep the intellectuals detached from Catholicism and who thus also makes a strong clerical revival among the popular masses quite difficult. For Croce, 'after Christ we are all Christians', i.e. the essence of Christianity has been absorbed by modern civilisation and one can thus live without 'mythological religion'.

The anti-Crocean polemic on the part of the Catholic laity is of little account. Giovanni Papini's 'Croce and the Cross' in the *Nuova Antologia* of 1 March 1932 and Aldo Ferrabino's 'Europe in Utopia' in the *Nuova Antologia* of 1 April 1932 should be borne in mind.

First Note. Papini's most important observation – and one that is not out of place – on the *History of Europe* regards the religious orders.[20] But his remark does not hold, since it is beyond all doubt that after the Council of Trent and the foundation of the Society of Jesus there has sprung up no religiously active order producing new or renewed currents of Christian sentiment. It is of course true that new orders have come into being but these have, so to speak, been of a predominantly administrative and corporative nature. Jansenism and modernism, the two great religious and renovatory movements that have arisen within the Church in this period, have neither given birth to new orders nor renewed the old ones.

Second Note. Ferrabino's article is more worthy of note for a certain claim it lays to historical realism as against speculative abstractions. But it too is abstract and puts forward a very disjointed, extemporised interpretation of nineteenth-century history, of a Catholic-rhetorical nature, with the accent on the rhetorical side. The reference to Marx on p.348 is anachronistic since Marx's theories of the state were all worked out prior to the foundation of the German Empire and were in fact jettisoned by Social Democracy during the very era of expansion of the imperial principle. This shows, contrary to what Ferrabino writes, that the Empire was capable of influencing and assimilating all the social forces present in Germany.

Q10I§5.

6 Croce and Italian Historiography

Croce and the Italian historiographic tradition. It may be said that Croce's historiography is that of the Restoration[21] reborn and adapted to the needs and interests of the present period. Croce carries on the historiography of the pre-1848 neo-Guelph tendency,[22] as invigorated by the Hegelianism of the moderates who represented the continuation of that current after 1848. This historiography is a degenerate and mutilated form of Hegelianism, for its basic preoccupation is a blind fear of Jacobin movements, of any active intervention by the great popular masses as a factor of social progress.

When Vincenzo Cuoco's formula regarding 'passive revolutions' was put forward (after the tragic experiment of the Parthenopean Republic of 1799),[23] it foreshadowed events and was intended to create a national ethic of greater forcefulness and popular revolutionary initiative. Examination should be made of how it was transformed, through the mind and social panic characteristic of the neo-Guelph-moderates, into a positive conception, into a political programme and an ethic that, behind the glittering rhetorical and nationalistic tinsel of 'primacy' and 'Italian initiative', of 'Italy will go it alone', hid the unease of the 'sorcerer's apprentice' and the intention of abdicating and capitulating at the first serious threat of a thoroughly popular Italian, i.e. radically national, revolution.

A cultural phenomenon comparable to that of the neo-Guelph-moderates, albeit in a more advanced historical-political position, is that of Proudhon's ideological system in France. Although this statement may appear paradoxical, it seems to me that Proudhon might be termed the Gioberti of the French situation since, with respect to the French working-class movement, Proudhon's position is the same as that of Gioberti as regards the Italian liberal-national one. Proudhon mutilates Hegelianism and the dialectic in the same way as the Italian moderates and, for this reason, the critique of their politico-historiographical conception is the same, still live and actual, as that contained in the *Poverty of Philosophy*. Edgar Quinet defined this conception 'revolution-restoration', which is just the translation into French of the concept of 'passive revolution', interpreted 'positively' by the Italian moderates. The philosophical error (of practical origin!) of this conception consists in this: it is 'mechanically' presupposed that, in the dialectical process, the thesis should be 'preserved' by the antithesis so as not to destroy the process itself which is therefore 'foreseen' as a mechanical, arbitrarily preordained repetition *ad infinitum*. In actual fact this is simply one of the many ways of 'forcing the world into line', one of the many forms of anti-historicist rationalism. Even in its speculative formulation the Hegelian conception does not allow one to tame and put reality into a strait-jacket, while not giving rise with this to forms of arbitrariness and irrationalism such as are found in the Bergsonian conception. In history as it really is the antithesis tends to destroy the thesis, the synthesis that emerges being a supersession, without one being able to tell in advance what of the thesis will be 'preserved' in the synthesis, without one being able to 'award' points in advance according to Queensberry Rules. That this may then happen in practice is a question of immediate 'politics', since in real history the dialectical process is separated out into innumerable partial moments; the error lies in elevating what is pure immediacy to the methodological plane, raising what is just ideology to the rank of philosophy. (This is just as if the following fable were to be considered an element of mathematics. A child is asked, 'If you have one apple and you give half of it to your brother, how much have you left?' The child replies, 'One apple'. 'How come? Didn't you give half to your brother?' 'No, I didn't give him any,' and so on. The element of immediate passion is introduced into the logical system, and one then expects the instrumental value of the system to remain valid.)

That such a way of conceiving the dialectic was wrong and 'politically' dangerous was realised by the self-same Hegelian moderates of the Risorgimento such as Spaventa: suffice it to recall his comments on those who, with the excuse that the moment of authority is necessary and indispensable, would like to keep humanity forever in its 'cradle' and enslaved.[24] But they could not go beyond certain limits, the limits of their social group which had to be made to leave its 'cradle' behind in concrete terms; the composition was found in the 'revolution-restoration' conception, in other words in a tempered reformist conservatism. It may be observed that such a way of conceiving the Hegelian dialectic is typical of the intellectuals, who conceive of themselves as the arbiters and mediators of real political struggles, as personifying the 'catharsis' – the passage from the economic aspect to the ethico-political one[25] – i.e. the synthesis of the dialectical process itself, a synthesis that they 'manipulate' in a speculative fashion in their mind, measuring out the elements 'arbitrarily' (that is to say passionately). This position justifies their less than total 'engagement' in the real historical process and is, without doubt, very convenient. It is the position that Erasmus took with respect to the Reformation.

Q10I§6.

7 Definition of Ethico-Political History[26]

Definition of the concept of ethico-political history. It may be observed that ethico-political history is an arbitrary and mechanical hypostasis of the moment of hegemony, of political leadership, of consent in the life and development of the activity of the state and civil society. This formulation of Croce's of the problem of historiography reproduces his formulation of the problem of aesthetics: the ethico-political moment in history is what the moment of form is in art; it is the 'lyricism' of history, the 'catharsis' of history. But things are not so simple in history as they are in art. In art the production of 'lyricism' is perfectly located in a personalised cultural world, where one can admit the identification of content and form and the so-called dialectic of distincts in the unity of the spirit. (It is only a question of translating speculative language into historicist language, i.e. of seeing whether this speculative language has a concrete instrumental value, superior to previous instrumental values.) But in history and the production of history the 'individualised' representation of states and nations is merely metaphorical. The 'distinctions' that have to be made in such representations are not 'speculative' and cannot be so presented on pain of falling into a new form of rhetoric and a new species of 'sociology' which, for all its 'speculative' nature, would not be any the less an abstract and mechanical sociology. They exist as distinctions of 'vertical' groups and 'horizontal' stratifications, i.e. as a co-existence and juxtaposition of different civilisations and cultures, bound to one another by state coercion and culturally organised in a contradictory and, at the same time, 'syncretistic' 'moral consciousness'.

At this point a critique must be made of the Crocean conception of the political moment as the moment of 'passion' (a permanent and systematic 'passion' being inconceivable), of his denial of 'political parties' (which are precisely the concrete manifestation of this inconceivable permanent passion, the proof of the internal contradiction of the 'politics-as-passion' concept) and therefore of the inexplicability of standing armies and of the organised existence of the civil and military bureaucracy, and the necessity for Croce and Crocean philosophy to act as the matrix for Gentile's 'actualism'. For it is only in an ultra-speculative philosophy such as actualism that these contradictions and insufficiencies of Crocean philosophy find their formal and verbal composition; at the same time, however, actualism shows up more obviously the far from concrete nature of Croce's philosophy, just as 'solipsism' is testimony to the internal weakness of the subjective-speculative conception of reality. That ethico-political history is the history of the moment of hegemony may be seen from a whole series of Croce's theoretical writings (and not just those contained in the volumes *The Conduct of Life* and *Politics and Morals*),[27] all of which should be subjected to concrete analysis. This may also – indeed especially – be seen from some scattered references to the concept of the state. For example Croce has somewhere claimed that it is not always the case that the 'state' must be sought where the official institutions would seem to indicate, since it might sometimes be found instead in revolutionary parties.[28] In the light of the state-hegemony-moral consciousness conception, this assertion is not paradoxical since it may indeed happen that the political and moral leadership of the country in a given critical situation is not exercised by the legal government but by a 'private' organisation and even by a revolutionary party. But it is not difficult to demonstrate how arbitrary is Croce's generalisation of this common sense observation.

The most important problem to discuss in this paragraph is this: whether the philosophy of praxis excludes ethico-political history, whether it fails to recognise the reality of a moment of hegemony, treats cultural and moral leadership as unimportant and really does consider superstructural factors to be 'appearances'. One can say that not only does the philosophy of praxis not exclude ethico-political history, but that, indeed, in its most recent stage of development it consists precisely in asserting the moment of hegemony as essential to its conception of the state and in attaching 'full weight' to the cultural factor, to cultural activity, to the necessity for a cultural front alongside the merely economic and merely political ones. Croce commits the serious error of not applying to his criticism of the philosophy of praxis the methodological criteria that he applies to the study of much less important and significant philosophical currents. If he were to employ these criteria, he would be able to see that the judgement contained in his attribution of the term 'appearance' to the superstructures is none other than the judgement of their 'historicity' expressed in opposition to popular dogmatic conceptions and therefore couched in a 'metaphorical' language appropriate to the public for whom it is destined. The philosophy of praxis thus judges the reduction of history to ethico-political history alone as improper and arbitrary, but does not exclude the latter. The opposition between Croceanism and the philosophy of praxis is to be sought in the speculative character of Croceanism.

<Relations between Croce's theories of ethico-political history or 'religious' history[29] and Fustel de Coulanges's historiographical theories as found in his book on *The Ancient City*.[30] Note that *The Ancient City* was published by Laterza very recently (maybe in 1928), more than forty years after it was written (Fustel de Coulanges died in 1889) and immediately after the translation published by Vallecchi. One can only think that the French book attracted Croce's attention while he was working on his theories and preparing his books. One may bring to mind the fact that in the last lines of his 1915 *Autobiography*[31] Croce announced that he intended to write a *History of Europe*. What directed him towards these problems of historiography and political science were his reflections on the war.>

Q10I§7.

8 Transcendence-Theology-Speculation

Croce takes every opportunity to underline how, in his activity as a thinker, he has studiously tried to eradicate from his philosophy any residual trace of transcendence and theology and hence of metaphysics as understood in the traditional sense. Thus, in contrast with the concept of 'system', he has stressed the value of the philosophical problem. In this way he has denied that thought produces other thought in the abstract, and has asserted that the problems that philosophers have to resolve are not an abstract derivation from previous philosophical thought, but are suggested by history as it is currently unfolding and so on. Croce has even gone so far as to claim that his recent, latest criticism of the philosophy of praxis is in fact linked to this anti-metaphysical, anti-theological preoccupation of his, in so far as the philosophy of praxis, in his view, tends towards theology and the concept of 'structure' is no more than the ingenuous reproposition of the concept of a 'hidden god'.

One must recognise Croce's efforts to make idealist philosophy remain faithful to life, and among his positive contributions to the development of science has to be numbered his struggle against transcendence and theology in the particular forms assumed in religious-confessional thought. But one cannot accept that he has consistently succeeded in his aims. His philosophy remains a 'speculative' philosophy, its essence containing not merely a trace of transcendence and theology but transcendence and theology in their entirety, with the crudest, mythological outer skin only just sloughed off. That Croce, it seems, finds it equally impossible to comprehend the basic assumptions of the philosophy of praxis (so much so that one is left with the impression of witnessing not a crude *ignorantia elenchi* [ignorance of the arguments] but ignoble hair-splitting polemical sophistry) shows how he has been blinded by speculative prejudice and sent careering off along the wrong track. The philosophy of praxis certainly derives from the immanentist conception of reality, but only in so far as this latter is stripped of its speculative halo and reduced to pure history or historicity or to pure humanism. If the notion of structure is conceived 'speculatively', it assuredly does become a 'hidden god' but, for that very reason, it must be conceived not 'speculatively' but historically, as the ensemble of social relations in which real people move and act, as an ensemble of objective conditions which can and must be studied with the methods of 'philology' and not of 'speculation'. It must be studied as something 'certain' that may also be 'true', but it must be studied first of all in its 'certainty' in order for it to be studied as 'truth'.[32] The philosophy of praxis is bound up not only with immanentism but also with the subjective conception of reality in so far as it turns this latter upside down, explaining it as a historical fact, as the 'historical subjectivity of a social group', as a real fact which presents itself as a phenomenon of philosophical 'speculation' while it is simply a practical act, the form assumed by a concrete social content and the way that the whole of society is led to fashion a moral unity for itself. The claim that we are dealing with 'appearance' has no transcendental and metaphysical significance whatsoever, but is the simple statement of its 'historicity', of its 'death-life' status, of its taking on a transient nature because a new, higher and more comprehensive, social and moral consciousness is being developed and is emerging as the sole 'life', the sole 'reality' as compared to a dead past that is, at the same time, a long time dying. The philosophy of praxis is the historicist conception of reality, liberated from any residue of transcendence and theology even in their latest speculative incarnation; idealist Crocean historicism is still at the theological speculative stage.

Q10I§8.

9 Paradigms of Ethico-Political History[33]

It seems that the *History of Europe in the Nineteenth Century* is the work of ethico-political history destined to become the paradigm of Crocean historiography offered to European culture. However one must also take into account his other studies such as the *History of the Kingdom of Naples*, *History of Italy 1871-1915*, and also *La rivoluzione napoletana del 1799* [*The Neapolitan Revolution of 1799*] and the *Storia dell'età barocca in Italia* [*History of the Baroque Era in Italy*].[34] The most tendentious and revealing however are the *History of Europe* and the *History of Italy*. These two works immediately pose the question of whether it is possible to write (conceive of) a history of Europe in the nineteenth century without an organic treatment of the French Revolution and the Napoleonic wars. And is it possible to write a history of Italy in the modern era without dealing with the struggles of the Risorgimento? In other words is it by chance, or for some more tendentious reason, that Croce begins his narratives in 1815 and 1871? By chance that he leaves out the moment of struggle, the moment in which the conflicting forces are formed, assemble and take up their positions? By chance that he leaves out the moment in which one ethico-political system is dissolved and another one is forged by iron and fire? By chance that he leaves out the moment in which one system of social relations disintegrates and falls apart while another one arises and establishes itself? By chance that instead he placidly assumes history to be the moment of cultural or ethico-political expansion? For these reasons, one may say that *History of Europe* is nothing more than a fragment of history, the 'passive' aspect of the great revolution which began in France in 1789, and then spilled over into the rest of Europe with the republican and Napoleonic armies, dealing a hefty blow to the old regimes and resulting, not in their immediate downfall as in France, but in a 'reformist' corrosion that lasted until 1870.

The problem arises of whether, because of its tendentiousness, this approach of Croce's has some contemporary and immediate reference, whether it aims at creating an ideological movement corresponding to that of the period he is dealing with, an era of restoration-revolution in which the needs that found a Jacobin-Napoleonic expression in France were satisfied in small doses, legally, in a reformist manner, thereby managing to safeguard the political and economic positions of the old feudal classes, avoiding agrarian reform and making especially sure that the popular masses did not go through a period of political experience such as occurred in France in the Jacobin era, in 1831 and in 1848. But under present conditions would it not be more precisely the fascist movement that corresponds to moderate and conservative liberalism?

It is perhaps not without significance that in the early years of its development fascism claimed kinship with the tradition of the old right, the Historic Right. It might be one of the numerous paradoxical manifestations of history (a ruse of nature, as Vico would have said) that Croce, stimulated by his particular preoccupations, should have contributed to strengthening fascism by indirectly providing it with an intellectual justification, after having helped to purge it of a number of secondary features, of a superficially romantic nature but nevertheless irritating to his classical, Goethe-like composure. The ideological hypothesis could be presented in the following terms: a passive revolution would be constituted by the fact that, through the legislative intervention of the state and through organisation in corporations, more or less far-reaching modifications would be introduced into the economic structure of the country to accentuate the 'production plan' element; in other words stress would be laid on the socialisation of and co-operation in production without thereby affecting (or at least not going beyond regulating and controlling) the individual and group appropriation of profit. In the concrete framework of Italian social relations this could be the sole solution for developing the productive forces of industry under the leadership of the traditional ruling classes, in competition with the more advanced industrial formations of countries which have a monopoly over raw materials and have accumulated huge amounts of capital.

Whether or not such a scheme might be put into practice, and if so in what forms and to what extent, is only of relative importance. What does matter from the political and ideological point of view is that it can and really does have the virtue of lending itself to the creation of a period of hope and expectation, especially among certain Italian social groups, such as the great mass of the urban and rural petty bourgeoisie. The hegemonic system is thus maintained and the forces of military and civil coercion kept at the disposal of the traditional ruling classes.

This ideology would serve as an element in a 'war of position' in the international economic field (whereas free competition and free trade would here correspond to a war of manoeuvre), just as 'passive revolution' does in the political field. In the Europe of 1789 to 1870 there was a (political) war of manoeuvre during the French Revolution and a long war of position from 1815 to 1870. In the present era the war of manoeuvre took place politically from March 1917 to March 1921, to be followed by a war of position whose ideological representative for Europe, as well as its practical one (for Italy), is fascism.

Q10I§9.

10 Liberty as the Identity of History and Mind and as Ideology[35]

Liberty as the identity of history [and mind][36] and liberty as religion-superstition, as unmediated, detailed ideology, as a practical instrument of government. If history is the history of liberty – according to Hegel's proposition – the formula holds for the history of the whole human race at all times and in all places; even the history of the oriental satrapies is liberty. Liberty, in that case, merely means 'movement', unfolding, dialectic. Even the history of the oriental satrapies was liberty, because it was movement and a process of unfolding, so much so that those satrapies did in fact fall. Once again, history is liberty in so far as it is the struggle between liberty and authority, between revolution and conservation, a struggle in which liberty and revolution continually prevail over authority and conservation. But in this case are not all currents and parties expressions of freedom, dialectical moments of the process of liberty? What is then the main feature of the nineteenth century in Europe? It is not that of being the history of liberty but that of being the history of liberty aware of itself as such. In nineteenth-century Europe there sprang up a previously non-existent critical consciousness; history was made in the knowledge that it was being made, in the knowledge that history is the history of liberty, etc.

The term 'liberal' in Italy, for example, was in this period very wide-ranging and comprehensive in its meanings. In Pietro Vigo's *Annali d'Italia* [*Annals of Italy*], the liberals comprise all the non-clericals, all the opponents of the Syllabus,[37] and thus also number the supporters of the International. But a current and party, going under the specific name of liberal, were created and they used the speculative and contemplative position of Hegelian philosophy to construct an unmediated political ideology, a practical instrument of domination and social hegemony, a means for conserving particular political and economic institutions founded, first, in the course of the French Revolution and, then, during the ebbing away of the revolutionary tide in Europe. A new position of authority was constituted and a new conservative party born which quite clearly tended to fuse with that of the Syllabus. And this coalition still called itself the party of liberty.

A number of problems thus arise: 1) what, in concrete terms, does 'liberty' mean for each of the various tendencies in nineteenth-century Europe? 2) were these movements animated by the concept of liberty or, rather, by the specific content with which they filled the formal concept of liberty?[38]

And did the fact that no party centralised peasant aspirations for agrarian reform not then actually stop these great masses from becoming faithful followers of the religion of liberty? Did liberty, on the other hand, not mean for them just the freedom and right to maintain their barbaric superstitions, their primitivism, thereby making of them a reserve army for the party of the Syllabus? Is it not that a concept like liberty – which lends itself to use even by the Jesuits against the liberals, who then become the libertines as opposed to the 'true' partisans of real liberty – is really just a conceptual shell, of value only for the real kernel that each social group fills it with? Can one therefore speak of a 'religion of liberty'? And just what then does 'religion' mean in this case? For Croce a religion is any conception of the world that puts itself forward as an ethic. But has this happened for 'liberty'? Liberty was a religion for a limited number of intellectuals but amongst the masses it took on the appearance of one of the elements constituting an ideological meld or amalgam, whose main constituent was the old-style Catholic religion and of which another important – if not decisive – element, from the secular point of view, was one's 'fatherland'. Nor should it be said that 'fatherland' was synonymous with 'liberty'; 'fatherland' certainly was a synonym, but of state, i.e. of authority and not of 'liberty', an element of 'conservation', a source of persecutions and of a new Holy Office.

Even from his own standpoint it seems to me that Croce is incapable of maintaining that distinction between 'philosophy' and 'ideology', between 'religion' and 'superstition' that is essential to his way of thinking and to his polemic against the philosophy of praxis. He thinks he is dealing with a philosophy and he is instead dealing with an ideology; he thinks he is dealing with a religion and it is instead a superstition; he thinks he is writing a history from which every element of class has been exorcised and he is, instead, producing a highly accurate and praiseworthy description of the political masterpiece whereby a particular class manages to present and have the conditions for its existence and development as a class accepted as a universal principle, as a world view, as a religion. In other words he is describing in the very act the development of a practical means of government and of domination. The error of a practical origin has not in this case been committed by the nineteenth-century liberals – who, on the contrary, triumphed in practice and reached the goal they set themselves – but by their historian, Croce. After first distinguishing philosophy from ideology, he has finished up by confusing a political ideology with a world view, thereby demonstrating in practice that the distinction is impossible and that it is not two categories that are being dealt with but the same historical one, the distinction in it being solely one of degree. One can call philosophy the world view that represents the moral and intellectual life (the catharsis of a particular practical life) of an entire social group, considered dynamically and thus seen not only in its current and unmediated interests but also in its future and mediated ones; while one can call ideology each particular conception of the class's internal groupings, who aim at aiding the resolution of immediate and restricted problems. But for the great masses of the population who are governed and ruled the philosophy or religion of the ruling group and its intellectuals continually takes on the appearance, as the ideological motif typical of a servile mass, of fanaticism and superstition. And does the ruling group perhaps not set itself the aim of perpetuating this state of affairs? Croce ought to explain why on earth the Weltanschauung of liberty cannot become one of the educational elements in primary school teaching and why he himself, as Minister,[39] introduced the teaching of confessional religion into these schools. This lack of 'expansivity' among the great masses testifies to the restricted, immediately practical nature of the philosophy of liberty.

Note 1. On the subject of the concept of authority and liberty, one should reflect on the chapter 'The Unending Struggle between "State" and "Church" ' in *Politics and Morals*. This chapter is of exceptional interest since there the critique of and opposition to the philosophy of praxis are implicitly mitigated while the 'economic' and practical element finds some consideration in the historical dialectic.

Q10I§10.

11 Croce and the Philosophy of Praxis

Can one however say that there is no longer any trace of the philosophy of praxis in Croce's conception, even after the development this latter has gone through over the last few years? Does Croce's historicism really no longer show any influence of his intellectual experience in the decade up to 1900? His position in this respect emerges from various of his writings. Of especial interest are the 1917 preface to the new edition of *Historical Materialism*, the section devoted to historical materialism in his *Storia della storiografia italiana nel secolo XIX* [*History of Nineteenth-Century Italian Historiography*] and his *Autobiography*. But if the point of interest is what Croce thinks of himself, this is neither sufficient nor exhaustive of the question. Croce's position as regards the philosophy of praxis is not, according to him, that of a further elaboration (a supersession) by means of which the philosophy of praxis became a moment of a more developed conception; for him the value of the experience was solely negative in the sense of having contributed to destroying prejudices, residuals of passions and so on. To use a metaphor drawn from the language of physics, the philosophy of praxis worked in Croce's mentality like a catalyst, which is necessary for obtaining the new product, but which leaves no trace in the product itself. But is this, after all, true? It seems to me that inside its form and its speculative language it is possible to trace more than one element of the philosophy of praxis in Croce's conception.

One could maybe go further and indeed there would be immense historical and intellectual significance at the present time in pursuing the following line of research: that just as the philosophy of praxis was the translation of Hegelianism into historicist language, so Croce's philosophy is to a quite notable extent the retranslation into speculative language of the realist historicism of the philosophy of praxis.

In February 1917 in a brief introduction to a republication of an essay of Croce's, 'Religion and Peace of Mind' (cf. *The Conduct of Life*, pp. 27-33), which had then only recently come out in *La Critica*, I wrote that just as Hegelianism had provided the premiss for the philosophy of praxis in the nineteenth century, at the origins of present-day civilisation, so Crocean philosophy could offer the premiss for a renewal of the philosophy of praxis in our times, for our generations. The question was just touched on in passing, and even then in certainly a primitive and most certainly an inadequate way, since at the time the concept of the unity of theory and practice, of philosophy and politics, was still unclear to me and I was tendentially somewhat Crocean. But now, even though the maturity and capacity necessary for the undertaking may be lacking, it is in my view worthwhile looking afresh at the position and putting it forward in a critically more developed form. In other words Croce's philosophical conception has to be adapted in the way that Hegel's was by the first theorists of the philosophy of praxis. This is the sole historically fruitful way of carrying through an adequate renewal of the philosophy of praxis, of raising this conception – which due to the necessities of day-to-day practical life has been getting 'vulgarised' – to the heights it must reach for the solution of the more complex tasks demanded by the current development of the struggle. That is to say it must be elevated to the level of creating a new integral culture, having the mass characteristics of the Protestant Reformation and the French Enlightenment at the same time as having the classicism of Greek and Italian Renaissance culture: in the words of Carducci, a culture which synthesises Maximilien Robespierre and Immanuel Kant,[40] politics and philosophy in a dialectical unity intrinsic to a social group that is not just French or German but European and world-wide. We must not only draw up an inventory of what we have inherited from classical German philosophy but bring it back into operative life, to do which we have to come to terms with Crocean philosophy. Putting it in other words, for us as Italians to be the heirs of classical German philosophy means that we must be the heirs to Crocean philosophy, which at the present time represents the world-wide moment of classical German philosophy.

Croce is too obdurate in his fight against the philosophy of praxis and has recourse to paradoxical allies such as the extremely mediocre De Man.[41] This stubbornness is suspect and may represent an alibi for a refusal to settle accounts. This reckoning however has to take place in the widest-ranging and most thoroughgoing way possible. It would be worth the trouble of a whole group of people dedicating ten years of their life to a work of this type, an *Anti-Croce* that in today's cultural climate could have the same significance that *Anti-Dühring* had for the pre-war generation.

Note 1. The traces left by the philosophy of praxis are to be found above all in the solution Croce has given to particular problems. A typical example is, in my view, the doctrine of the practical origin of error. In general it may be said that the polemic against Giovanni Gentile's philosophy of the pure act has forced Croce into adopting a greater realism and into feeling a certain distaste and intolerance at least for the exaggerations of speculative language, a language that has become a jargon and an 'Open, Sesame' for the minor actualist brethren.

Note 2. But Croce's philosophy cannot, however, be examined independently of Gentile's. An *Anti-Croce* must also be an *Anti-Gentile*. Gentilian actualism will add the chiaroscuro effects necessary to throw the features of the picture into greater relief.

Q10I§11.

12 Ethico-Political History and Hegemony[42]

From everything that has been said previously it emerges that Croce's historiographical conception of history as ethico-political history must not be judged as futile, as something to be rejected out of hand. On the contrary, it needs to be forcefully established that Croce's historiographical thought, even in its most recent phase, must be studied and reflected upon with the greatest attention. Essentially, it represents a reaction against 'economism' and fatalistic mechanicism, even though it is put forward as the destructive supersession of the philosophy of praxis. The criterion that a philosophical current must be criticised and evaluated not for what it professes to be but for what it really is and shows itself to be in concrete historical works applies to Croce's thought too. For the philosophy of praxis the speculative method itself is not futile but has generated 'instrumental' values of thought in the development of culture which the philosophy of praxis has incorporated (the dialectic for example). Credit must therefore, at the very least, be given to Croce's thought as an instrumental value, and in this respect it may be said that it has forcefully drawn attention to the importance of cultural and intellectual factors in the development of history, to the function of great intellectuals in the organic life of civil society and the state, to the moment of hegemony and consent as the necessary form of the concrete historical bloc. That this is not futile is demonstrated by the fact that, in the same period as Croce, the greatest modern theoretician of the philosophy of praxis [i.e. Lenin] has – on the terrain of political organisation and struggle and with political terminology – in opposition to the various tendencies of 'economism', reappraised the front of cultural struggle and constructed the doctrine of hegemony as a complement to the theory of the state-as-force and as a contemporary form of the 1848 doctrine of 'permanent revolution'. For the philosophy of praxis the conception of ethico-political history, in that it is independent of any realist conception, may be adopted as an 'empirical canon' of historical research which needs constantly to be borne in mind in examining and understanding historical development, if the aim is that of producing integral history and not partial and extrinsic history (history of economic forces as such, etc.).

Q10I§12.

13 Notes

1. Elements of ethico-political history in the philosophy of praxis: concept of hegemony, reappraisal of the philosophical front, systematic study of the function of intellectuals in historical and state life, doctrine of the political party as the vanguard of every progressive historical movement.

2. Croce-Loria. It can be shown that there is not, after all, such a great difference between Croce's and Loria's ways of interpreting the philosophy of praxis. In his reduction of the philosophy of praxis to an empirical canon of historical interpretation, by which the attention of historians is drawn to the importance of economic factors, Croce has done nothing other than reduce it to a form of 'economism'. If Loria is stripped of all his stylistic quirks and wild fantasies (certainly losing much of what is characteristic of him in the process), it is seen that he comes close to Croce as regards the more serious core of his interpretation (cf. on this subject *Conversazioni Critiche*, I, pp. 291 et seq.).

3. Speculative history and the need to use less sophisticated instruments. Leon Battista Alberti wrote of mathematicians: 'They measure the shapes and forms of things in the mind alone and divorced entirely from matter. We, on the other hand, who wish to talk of things that are visible, will express ourselves in cruder terms.'[43]

4. If, in such a generic way, it were true that the history of nineteenth-century Europe were the history of liberty, the whole of preceding history would, equally generically, have been the history of authority. All previous centuries would have been the same indistinct, dun colour, without any development, without any struggle. Moreover, a hegemonic (ethico-political) principle triumphs after having defeated another principle (and having assumed this latter as its

moment, as Croce would in fact put it). But why does one win out over the other? Due to its intrinsic qualities of a 'logical' and abstract rational nature? Not to enquire into the reasons for this victory means writing an externally descriptive history, without bringing to the fore the necessary and causal links. Even the Bourbon regime represented an ethico-political principle, personified a 'religion' whose flock was found among the peasants and the lower depths of society. There has therefore always been a struggle between two hegemonic principles, between two 'religions', and the triumphal expansion of the one has not merely to be described, but justified historically. It must be explained why, in 1848, the Croatian peasants fought against the Milanese liberals and the Venetian-Lombard peasants against the Viennese liberals.[44] At that time the real ethico-political nexus between governors and governed was the person of the emperor or king ('It's written for you all to read, King Frankie's the one that we need'),[45] as later the nexus was to be the concept not of liberty but of fatherland and nation. The popular 'religion' taking the place of Catholicism (or, better, combined with it) was that of 'patriotism' and nationalism. I have read that during the Dreyfus case a French scientist, who was a Minister and freemason, stated explicitly that his party wanted to destroy the Church's influence in France, and since the mob needed a fanaticism (the French use the term 'mystique' in politics) an upsurge in patriotic feeling had to be organised. One must further bear in mind the meaning assumed by the term 'patriot' in the French Revolution (it certainly did mean 'liberal', but with a concrete national significance), and how, through the course of the struggles of the nineteenth century, its place was taken by that of 'republican' because of the new meaning attached to the term patriot, which had become monopolised by the nationalists and the right in general. That the concrete content of popular liberalism was the concept of fatherland and nation may be seen from its process of unfolding in nationalism and from the fight against nationalism both by Croce, representing the religion of liberty, and by the Pope, representing Catholicism. (In a folklorist form Pascarella's sonnets on 'La Scoperta dell'America' ['The Discovery of America'] provide documentation of this popular religion of the fatherland.)

5. Speculative history may be considered a return, in literary forms made more astute or less ingenuous by the development of the critical faculty, to historical methods already discredited as empty and rhetorical, and acknowledged as such by Croce himself. Ethico-political history, in so far as it is divorced from the concept of historical bloc, in which there is a concrete correspondence of socio-economic content to ethico-political form in the reconstruction of the various historical periods, is nothing more than a polemical presentation of more or less interesting philosophical propositions, but it is not history. In the natural sciences this would be like a return to classifications based on the colour of the skin, plumage, or fur of animals rather than on anatomical structure. Reference to the natural sciences in historical materialism and discussion of the 'anatomy' of society was only a metaphor to provide an encouragement to further methodological and philosophical research. In the history of humankind, which does not have the task of classifying facts in a naturalistic fashion, the 'skin colouring' forms a 'bloc' with the anatomical structure and with all the physiological functions; one cannot consider an individual who has been 'flayed' to be a real 'individual', and likewise for someone 'boned' and left without skeleton. A sculptor, Rodin, has observed (cf. Maurice Barrès, *Mes Cahiers* [*My Notebooks*]): 'If we were not prejudiced against the skeleton, we would see how beautiful it is.' In a painting or a sculpture of Michelangelo's we 'see' the skeleton of the figure portrayed, we feel the solidity of the structure underneath the colours or the marble relief. Croce's history represents filleted, skeletonless 'figures' whose flesh droops and sags even under the cosmetics of the writer's literary elegance.

6. Transformism as a form of the passive revolution in the post-1870 period.

7. To appreciate Croce's role in Italian life, note that both Giolitti and Salandra[46] conclude their memoirs with a letter of his.

8. In Crocean language one can say that the religion of

liberty is opposed to the religion of the Syllabus, which refuses modern civilisation *tout court*; the philosophy of praxis is a 'heresy' of the religion of liberty since it was born on the self-same terrain of modern civilisation.

Q10I§13.

VII THE PHILOSOPHY OF BENEDETTO CROCE

Introduction

A Premiss
1 Some General Methodological Criteria for the Critique of Croce's Philosophy, 366; 2 *The Central Nucleus of the Essay, 367; 3* South and North, 368; 4 *The Man Standing on his Head, 369.

B Crocean Philosophy
5 *The Dialectic of Distincts, 370; 6 Croce and Hegel, 371; 7 *Ethics and Politics, 372; 8 Science of Politics, 373; 9 The 'National' Origins of Crocean Historicism, 373; 10 *Croce's Historicism, 376; 11 *The Histories of Italy and Europe, 377; 12 Introduction to the Study of Philosophy[1]. History and Anti-History, 378; 13 *History, Anti-History and Hegel, 379; 14 Past and Present[1]. *Giolitti and Croce, 379; 15 Past and Present[2] *The World is Moving Towards ..., 380; 16 Identity of History and Philosophy, 382; 17 *Philosophy, Religion, Ideology, 383; 18 *Crocean Passion and Sorelian Myth, 389; 19 *Passion and Politics[1], 392; 20 *Passion and Politics[2], 393; 21 *Political Ideologies, 394; 22 *The Autonomy of the Politico-Economic Moment, 399; 23 Appendix. Philosophical Knowledge as a Practical Act, an Act of the Will, 402; 24 Introduction to the Study of Philosophy[2]. Reality of the External World, 402.

C Croce and Historical Materialism
25 *Religion, Philosophy, Politics[1], 403; 26 *A Philosophy

The Philosophy of Benedetto Croce

for Barbarians, 404; 27*Originality and Popularisation, 405; 28 *Religion, Philosophy, Politics[2], 406; 29 *Croce and Deceptive Appearances, 415; 30 The Real Development of History, 416; 31 Some Causes of Error, 417; 32 *Croce in the Second Post-War Period, 417; 33 *The War of Historical Materialism, 418; 34 *Croce's Four Criticisms of Marxism, 419; 35 *The Immediate Practical Element, 420; 36 *Croce, Einaudi, Loria, 421; 37 *Note on Luigi Einaudi, 422; 38 Cultural Topics. *Philosophy of Praxis and Historical Economism, 423; 39 *The Crocean Critique of Marxism, 424; 40 *The Theory of Value in Critical Economy, 425; 41 *The Theory of Value as an Elliptical Comparison, 426; 42 *Croce and the Falling Rate of Profit, 428; 43 *Relative Surplus Value and the Falling Rate of Profit, 430; 44 *Fordism and the Falling Rate of Profit, 433.

D Croce, Actualism and Reformism
45 Past and Present[3] *Political and Civil Society, 435; 46 Identification of Individual and State, 439; 47 Notes on Italian Culture[1]. Science and Culture, 439; 48 Notes on Italian Culture[2]. Science, 440; 49 Giovanni Gentile, 441; 50 G. Gentile and the Philosophy of Politics, 441; 51 Past and Present[4]. *Gentile-Gioberti, 442; 52 A Judgement on Gentile's 'Actual Idealism', 443; 53 Past and Present[5]. Gentile's Philosophy, 443; 54 Past and Present[6]. The Crocean Utopia, 444; 55 *The Theoretical Affirmation, 445; 56 *Actualism, Ideology and Philosophy, 446; 57 *Croce on De Man, 447; 58 Henri De Man, 448; 59 Sorel, Proudhon, De Man[1], 449; 60 Sorel, Proudhon, De Man[2], 454; 61 Sorel, Proudhon, De Man[3], 460; 62 The Movement and the End, 461.

E Croce's Position in the Intellectual World
63 *The Party Man, 462; 64 *Croce in the Intellectual Hierarchy, 464; 65 Croce's International Importance, 467; 66 *Croce as a Renaissance Man[1], 469; 67 Croce and Julien Benda, 470; 68 *Croce as a Renaissance Man[2], 470; 69 Croce and Modernism, 472; 70 *Croce as a Renaissance Man[3], 473.

Introduction

Whoever has read the 'second part' of Gramsci's tenth notebook (Q10II) realises the headache it poses for any editor. Although it seems that Gramsci initially intended Q10II to be entirely devoted to 'The Philosophy of Benedetto Croce' – the title with which the manuscript notebook opens – after its 'Preface' and the first five paragraphs (which contain a notable similarity with some of the subject matter of Q10I) other material begins to make its appearance. Some of the later paragraphs, entitled 'Introduction to the Study of Philosophy', together with the similarly-headed notes from Q11, on which he worked more or less simultaneously, are published in English in SPN pp.321-472; others dealing with economic science and economic crises are to be found in Chapters III and IV (Section B) of this volume. Once these paragraphs have been taken out the remainder consists of the notes relating specifically to Crocean philosophy.

To attempt to introduce a logical sequencing into the notes on Croce the approach adopted was to divide them into different detailed subject groups. About ten or a dozen such groupings emerged, some of which could then be aggregated into bigger sections on the basis of affinity of subject matter. At this point comparison was made with the tasks Gramsci set himself in Q10II§1 of examining '1) Croce's historicism, ... his conception of the world, of life, i.e. his philosophy *tout court*; 2) his dissent from Gentile and from actualism; 3) his incomprehension of historical materialism, hand in hand with his obsession with it.' (An additional aim of giving 'a full outline of the intellectual tradition of the South' is mentioned in Q10II§38ii – 'South and North' – but it is arguable that, rather than being treated in Q10, this is found in Q19, editorially entitled 'The Risorgimento', contained to a large extent in SPN, pp.52-120.)

Two of the sections constructed (Sections B and C of this Chapter) were seen to correspond fairly exactly to Gramsci's points 1 and 3 while other material (now the notes in Section

The Philosophy of Benedetto Croce

D coming from Q10II) that corresponded to point 2 was much more scanty. The editorial decision was therefore taken to supplement this material with notes from elsewhere. The main sources turned out to be the notes on Gentile in Q11 (the 'Anti-Croce' hypothesised by Gramsci also being of necessity an 'Anti-Gentile' – see Note 2 of Q10I§11), the notes on leading exponents of revisionism (in particular those on Sorel, Proudhon and De Man from the end of Q11) and other notes he was able to write later on when he had access to, e.g., articles on Bernstein (mentioned alongside Sorel and Croce in Q10I§2 and Q10II§3 as the main turn-of-the-century revisionists in their respective countries).

Two other sets of notes remained at this point. One was of a rather general nature, preliminary to a study of Croce, so appears as the introductory Section A to this Chapter; the other, not easily classifiable in terms of Gramsci's stated aims, deals in an overall way with the status of Croce and Crocean philosophy and has therefore been taken as representing Gramsci's provisional summing-up of this phase of his work (Section E).

Given that the whole of this Chapter is devoted to Croce, it seemed superfluous to include the headings ('Notes/Points/Reference Points for an Essay on Croce') that Gramsci appended to the Q10 paragraphs in particular, merely in order to separate them off from other material contained there. Most of the sub-sections forming this Chapter were first published in Italian in the thematic volume *Historical Materialism and the Philosophy of Benedetto Croce* with the exception of sub-sections 6 and 29 of this Chapter (Q10II §4 and §34), unpublished until the 1975 Critical Edition. The inclusion in this Chapter of material from Q11 together with that from Q10 means that, in the main text or in footnote in this volume or in SPN, all major writings from these two key Notebooks are now available in English.

One more, rather vexed, question still remains – the problem raised by some commentators of whether, given the fact that Q10II is evidently not, contrary to the initial stated intention, devoted entirely to Croce, Gramsci's critique of

Croce may be considered complete. In one sense it obviously is incomplete since Gramsci himself notes in Q10I§11 that 'it would be worth the trouble of a whole group of people dedicating ten years of their life' to such a project, whereas the instruments at his disposal in prison were meagre and inadequate to the task. Nevertheless, within the Notebooks, nearly two-thirds of the over 300 finalised 'B' and 'C' text references to Croce are in the two parts of Q10 and about one in 20 in Q11 while the others (an eighth before Q10 and about a sixth after it, when Gramsci had outlined his aim *vis-à-vis* Croce), with certain exceptions in part noted here, are generally either of a minor nature or not directly pertinent to the points listed in Q10II§1. The conclusion that emerges, taking into account the physical limitations in which he was constrained to work, is that the critique is as complete as was possible at the time for a single essay, as opposed to a multi-volume work.

A PREMISS

1 Some General Methodological Criteria for the Critique of Croce's Philosophy[1]

Initially it would be of advantage to study Croce's philosophy in the light of some criteria that he himself affirms <criteria which, in their turn, form part of the general conception itself>:
1) Do not seek a 'general philosophical problem' in Croce but rather see in his philosophy that problem or that series of problems which are of most interest at a given time, i.e. those which are of most relevance to present-day life and are like a reflection of it. This problem or series of problems seems to me that of historiography on one hand and that of the philosophy of practice, of political science, of ethics on the other.
2) As well as the systematic and organic works a careful

study to be made of Croce's 'minor' writings, that is to say the collections of articles, of occasional pieces, of short essays which have a greater and more obvious link with life, with the concrete movement of history.
3) Define the terms of a 'philosophical biography' of Croce, i.e. identify the different expressions assumed in his thought, the different formulations and resolution of certain problems, the new problems that have emerged from his labours and been forced on his attention. For this research, in fact, it is of use to study his minor writings in the back numbers of *La Critica* and the other publications that contain them; the basis for this research can be provided by *An Autobiography* and by the writings, certainly authorised, of Francesco Flora and Giovanni Castellano.[2]
4) Critics of Croce: positivists, neo-scholastics, actualists and their objections.[3]

Q10II [Preface].

2 The Central Nucleus of the Essay

As its central nucleus the essay could undertake an examination of the concept of ethico-political historiography, which is the real crowning achievement of Croce's whole philosophical work. One could thus examine his activity, in the various attitudes adopted towards the philosophy of praxis, as all leading to this outcome and, indeed, reach the conclusion that these self-same labours of Croce's have been carried out in parallel with those of the best theoreticians of the philosophy of praxis. Thus his claim to have 'definitively superseded' this philosophy is mere critical boastfulness, which should be taken together with the analytical demonstration that whatever there is of a 'healthy' and progressive nature in Croce's work is none other than the philosophy of praxis presented in speculative language.

Q10II§29ii.

3 South and North

Taking account of the scope of the essay, it would perhaps be opportune to give an outline of the intellectual tradition of the South (especially as regards political and philosophical thought) as opposed to the rest of Italy, especially Tuscany, as this has been reflected up to Croce's (and Giustino Fortunato's) generation. Great use may be made of Luigi Russo's book on De Sanctis and the University of Naples, among other things for seeing how the southern tradition reached such a degree of theoretical-practical development with De Sanctis that, in comparison, Croce's stance represents a step back without, for other reasons, one being able to consider that of Gentile – who more than Croce has been involved in practical action – as a continuation of De Sanctis's activity. On the cultural contrast between Tuscany and the South one might out of curiosity recall Ardengo Soffici's epigram (I think in his column 'Giornale di Bordo' ['Log-book']) on the 'artichoke'. Soffici says, more or less, that the Tuscan artichoke does not at first sight seem as attractive a prospect as the Neapolitan one. It is tough, shaggy, all spiny and sharp, but once you begin to strip off the inedible woody outer leaves and throw them away, you get more and more flavour from the edible part until, when you get to the choke itself, you find it compact, fleshy and with an exquisite flavour. Take the Neapolitan artichoke on the other hand, and right from the start there is something you can eat, but what wateriness and poor flavour; you go on peeling off the leaves but it doesn't improve and at the centre you find nothing but an inedible, disgusting mass of fibre.

Opposition of the scientific and experimental culture of the Tuscans to the speculative culture of the Neapolitans. Only that Tuscany now occupies no particular role in national culture and has only the conceit of past memories to live on.

Q10II§38ii.

4 The Man Standing on his Head[4]

How is one to formulate, for Croce's philosophy, the problem of 'putting man the right way up', of getting him to stand on his feet instead of his head? The problem is that of the residues of 'transcendence, of metaphysics, of theology' in Croce, the problem of the quality of his 'historicism'. He is quite forthcoming in his frequent claims to have made every effort to rid his thought of any residual trace of transcendence, theology and metaphysics, right up to the point of rejecting any idea of 'system' and 'fundamental problem' in philosophy. But is it however exact to say he has succeeded?

He claims to be dialectical (although, over and above the dialectic of opposites, he introduces into the dialectic a 'dialectic of distincts', which he has not succeeded in demonstrating is dialectical or, indeed, just what it is),[5] but the point to be clarified is the following: in the process of becoming, does he see the becoming itself or the 'concept' of becoming? To my way of thinking this seems the essential starting point for a detailed assessment of: 1) his historicism and, in the last analysis, his conception of reality, of the world, of life, in other words his philosophy *tout court*; 2) his dissent from Gentile and from actualism; 3) his incomprehension of historical materialism, hand in hand with his obsession with this very same historical materialism.

That Croce has always been and – now even more acutely than in the past – still is obsessed by historical materialism is not difficult to show. That an obsession of this type has become violent over the last few years is proved by the references contained in his *Politics and Morals*,[6] by his intervention on the subject of the aesthetics of historical materialism at the Oxford Congress[7] (cf. the note published in *La Nuova Italia*), by the review of the complete works of Marx and Engels published in *La Critica* in 1930,[8] by the references contained in the *Capitoli introduttivi di una Storia dell'Europa nel secolo XIX* [*Introductory Chapters to a History of Europe in the Nineteenth Century*],[9] by the letters to Barbagallo published in the *Nuova Rivista Storica* in

1928-29 and especially by the importance afforded the book by Fülöp-Miller,[10] as appears from some notes published in *La Critica* in 1925 (I think).

If, in the perennial flux of events, it is necessary to establish concepts without which reality cannot be understood, it is also necessary, in fact it is indispensable, to establish and remember that reality in motion and the concept of reality, though they may be logically distinct, must be conceived historically as an inseparable unit. Otherwise there happens what is happening to Croce, that history becomes a formal history, a history of concepts, and in the last analysis a history of the intellectuals, rather an autobiographical history of Croce's thought, a history of those who have an exaggerated view of their own importance. Croce is falling into a new and strange form of 'idealistic' sociologism, no less quaint and no less inconclusive than positivist sociologism.

Q10II§1.

B CROCEAN PHILOSOPHY

5 The Dialectic of Distincts

Examine whether the principle of 'distinction', i.e. what Croce calls the 'dialectic of distincts', has been determined by reflection on classical economy's abstract concept of 'homo oeconomicus'. Assuming that this abstraction is of a purely 'methodological' value and significance, or even that it concerns the technique of science (i.e. immediate and empirical), one must look at how Croce has elaborated the whole system of 'distincts'. At any rate such an elaboration, like, moreover, other parts of the Crocean system, would seem to have originated in the study of political economy and more precisely in that of the philosophy of praxis, which however cannot but mean that the Crocean system had an immediate 'economic' determination and origin. The same difficulty that many actualist philosophers encounter in understanding the concept of 'homo oeconomicus' they also find in understanding the significance and import of the 'dialectic of distincts'. This line of research has a dual aspect: both logical and historical. To my way of thinking, Croce's first 'distinction' was 'historically' exactly that of the 'moment of the economy or of utility' which does not and cannot coincide with that of the economists in the strict sense since Croce brings into the economic moment or moment of utility a series of human activities (e.g. love) that are irrelevant to the ends of economic science.

Q10II§59iii.

6 Croce and Hegel

From Guido Calogero's article 'Neo-Hegelianism in Contemporary Italian Thought' in the 16 August 1930 number of *Nuova Antologia* (which is the text of Calogero's speech in German at the 1st International Hegel Congress at The Hague, 21-24 April 1930):

'For Croce (...) the merit of Hegel's doctrine is above all that of its "logic of philosophy", i.e. of its theory of the dialectic as the sole form of thought through which thought might, by unifying them, really overcome all those dualisms that on the plane of classical intellectualistic logic can only be noted, losing with this the sense of the unity of the real. Hegel's immortal conquest is the affirmation of the unity of opposites, conceived not in the sense of a static and mystic *coincidentia oppositorum* [*unity of opposites*] but in that of a dynamic *concordia discors* [*discordant concord*], which is absolutely necessary to reality because it can be thought of as life, development, value, in which every positivity is forced to realise itself asserting and simultaneously eternally overcoming its negativity. At the same time the dialectical conciliation of the essential dualisms of the real (good and evil, true and false, finite and infinite etc.) leads to the categorical exclusion of all those other forms of dualism that are based on the fundamental antithesis of a world of reality and a world of the appearance, of a sphere of transcendence or of the noumenon and of a sphere of immanence or of the phenomenon; antitheses which are all eliminated by the rigorous dissolution of their transcendental or noumenal element, which represents the sheer necessity, incapable of satisfaction in this way and now satisfied by other means, of rising above the world of antinomies and contradictions to that of unmoved and peaceful reality. It is thus Hegel who really instituted immanentism: in the doctrine of the identity of the rational and the actual[11] there is sanctioned the concept of the unitary value of the world in its concrete development, just as in the critique of the abstract *sollen*[12] there is typically expressed the antithesis of every negation of that unity, and the antithesis of every hypostasisation of the ideal in a sphere transcendent to that of its effective realisation. And from this point of view, for the first time the value of actuality is identified absolutely with that of its history: in Hegelian immanence there is simultaneously, then, the supreme foundation of all modern historicism.

'Dialectic, immanentism, historicism: in these one could summarise the essential merits of Hegelianism from the viewpoint of Crocean thought, which, in this sense, may truly regard itself as the follower and continuer.'

Q10II§4.

7 Ethics and Politics

The juxtaposition, in order to indicate Croce's most recent historiography, of the two terms *ethical* and *political* expresses the exigencies that define the contours of his historical thought. While *ethical* refers to the activity of civil society, to hegemony, *political* refers to state-governmental initiative and coercion. When there is conflict between the ethical and the political, between the exigencies of liberty and those of force, between civil society and state-government, a crisis develops and Croce goes as far as asserting that sometimes the real 'state', i.e. the directive force of the historical impetus, is to be sought not where one would think, in the state as understood juridically, but in 'private' forces and even among the so-called 'revolutionaries'.[13] This proposition of Croce's is highly important for a full understanding of his conception of history and politics. In so far as these theses are concretely incorporated into his historical writings, it would be useful to subject them to a concrete analysis.

Q10II§41iii.

8 Science of Politics

What meaning is to be attached to the often-repeated accusation of 'materialism' that Croce levels against certain political tendencies? Is it a judgement of a theoretical and scientific order, or a manifestation of a political polemic now in course? It seems that in these polemics materialism means 'material force', 'coercion', 'economic factor' etc. But might it be that 'material force', 'coercion', 'economic factor' are indeed 'materialistic'? What would 'materialism' mean in this case? Cf. *Politics and Morals*, pp.129-30: 'There are times in which etc.'[14]

Q10II§5.

9 The 'National' Origins of Crocean Historicism

Look in Edgar Quinet for the exact meaning and justification he gives of the formula of the equivalence revolution-restoration in Italian history.[15] According to Daniele Mattalia ('Gioberti in Carducci' in the *Nuova Italia* of 20 November 1931), Carducci adopted Quinet's formula by way of the Giobertian concept of 'national classicism' (*Rinnovamento* [*Renewal*], III, 88; *Primato* [*Primacy*], nos. 1,5,6,7 ...). See whether Quinet's formula may be brought into line with that of Cuoco's 'passive revolution'; they perhaps express the historical fact that a unitary popular initiative was missing from the development of Italian history together with the other fact that this development took place as the reaction of the dominant classes to the sporadic, elementary and non-organic rebelliousness[16] of the popular masses together with 'restorations' that accepted a certain part of the demands expressed from below, and were thus 'progressive restorations' or 'revolutions-restorations' or even 'passive revolutions'. One could say that it has always been a question of the revolutions of 'Guicciardinian man' (in the sense meant here by De Sanctis), in which the leaders have always looked to their 'own interests':[17] Cavour in fact 'diplomatised' the revolution of Guicciardini's man and he himself as a type approximated to Guicciardini.

Croce's historicism would therefore be no more than a form of political moderatism,[18] whose only method of political action is posited to be that in which progress, historical development, stems from the dialectic of conservation and innovation. In modern parlance this conception is called reformism. The tempering of conservation and moderation constitutes in fact the 'national classicism' of Gioberti, just as it does the literary and artistic classicism of the latest Crocean aesthetic. But this historicism of the moderate and reformist variety is nothing like a scientific theory, nothing like 'real' historicism; it is only the reflection of a practico-political tendency, an ideology in the negative sense. For why must 'conservation' be just that given 'conservation', that given element of the past? And why must one be 'irrational' and 'anti-historicist' if it is not just that specific element that one is conserving? In reality, if it is true that progress is the dialectic of conservation and innovation, and innovation conserves the past by superseding it, it is also true that the past is a complex thing, a complex of the living and the dead, in which a choice cannot be made arbitrarily, *a priori*, by an individual or by a political current. If a choice is made in such a way (on paper) it is not historicism that one is dealing with but an arbitrary act of will, the manifestation of a practico-political, unilateral tendency, which cannot provide the basis for a science but only for an immediate political ideology. What will be conserved of the past in the dialectical process cannot be determined *a priori*, but will be a result of the process itself, and will be characterised by historical necessity, and not by arbitrary choice on the part of so-called scientists and philosophers. And one can meanwhile observe that the innovatory force, in so far as it is not itself an arbitrary fact, cannot but be already immanent in the past, cannot but itself in a certain sense be the past, an element of the past, whatever of the past is alive and developing; the innovatory force is itself conservation-innovation and contains within itself all the past worth developing and perpetuating. For this species of moderate historicists (and moderate is to be understood in the political, class sense, i.e. referring to those classes which were at work in the restoration after 1815 and 1848) Jacobinism was irrational, and anti-history equalled Jacobinism. But who will ever be able to prove historically that it was only an act of will that led the Jacobins? And is it not now a banal historical statement that neither Napoleon nor the Restoration destroyed the Jacobins' *faits accomplis*? Or maybe the anti-historicism of the Jacobins would consist in what of their initiatives was not 100 per cent 'conserved' but only a lesser fraction. It does not seem plausible to sustain this argument since one cannot reconstruct history through mathematical calculations and no innovatory force, moreover, achieves immediate realisation; this force, rather, is always rationality and irrationality, free will and necessity, i.e. it is 'life' with all the weaknesses and strengths of life, with all its contradictions and its antitheses.

Establish firmly this relationship that Croce's historicism has with the moderate tradition of the Risorgimento and with the reactionary thought of the Restoration. Note how his conception of the Hegelian 'dialectic' has deprived this latter of all its vigour and stature, turning it into a scholastic question of words. Croce's function today is a repetition of that of Gioberti, of whom one can make the same criticism as that contained in the *Poverty of Philosophy* regarding the way in which he has not understood Hegelianism. And it is this 'historicism', however, which is one of the points and the permanent motifs in Croce's whole intellectual and philosophical activity and one of the reasons for the fortunes and the influence exerted by his activity over the last thirty years.

In fact Croce fits into the cultural tradition of the new Italian state, bringing national culture back to its deprovincialised origins and purging it of all the grandiloquent and grotesque dross of the Risorgimento. Establishing with precision the political and historical significance of Crocean historicism means precisely cutting it down to its real import as immediate political ideology, stripping it of the resplendent greatness that is attributed to it as if it were the manifestation of an objective science, of serene, impartial thought above all the miseries and contingencies of the everyday struggle, of a disinterested contemplation of the eternal becoming of human history.

Q10II§41xiv.

10 Croce's Historicism

It remains to be seen whether Crocean historicism is not, in its own way, an ably disguised form of preconceptualised history,[19] like all liberal reformist conceptions. If one can generically assert that the synthesis preserves what is still vital in the thesis, superseded by the antithesis, one cannot – without being arbitrary – assert what will be conserved, what one regards *a priori* as vital, without falling into ideologism, without falling into a preconceptualised idea of history. What does Croce maintain there is to conserve of the thesis on account of its vital nature? Since he is only rarely a practical politician, Croce is very wary of drawing up lists of principles to be put into practice and programmatic conceptions, to be declared 'non-modifiable', but they can however be deduced from the entire corpus of his work. But if even that were not feasible, there would always remain the assertion that what is 'vital' and inviolable is the liberal form of the state, i.e. the form that guarantees every political force the right to move and campaign freely. But how can this empirical fact be confused with the concept of liberty, that is to say of history? How can the contending forces be asked to 'contain' the struggle within certain limits (the limits of conservation of the liberal state) without becoming arbitrary and falling into the preconceived pattern? In the struggle 'blows are not exchanged by agreement' and every antithesis must of necessity present itself as the radical antagonist of the thesis, up to the point of proposing its complete destruction and complete substitution. To conceive historical development as a game with its referee and its pre-established norms to be respected loyally is a form of preconceptualised history, in which ideology has not political 'content' but the form and method of struggle as its foundation. This is an ideology that tends to enervate the antithesis, to break it up into a long series of moments, i.e. to reduce the dialectic to a process of reformist 'revolution-restoration' evolution, in which only the second term has any validity, since it is a question of continually patching up <from outside> an organism which internally is unable to keep itself healthy. One could, moreover, say that a similar reformist stance is a 'ruse of providence' to hasten the ripening of the internal forces that have been kept reined in by reformist practice.

Q10§41xvi.

11 The Histories of Italy and Europe

Knowing that Croce's two most recent histories, of Italy and of Europe, were conceived at the start of the world war to conclude a process of meditation on and reflection over the causes of the events of 1914 and 1915, one may ask what precise 'educative' aim they have. Precise, especially precise. And one concludes that they haven't one, that they are even to be included in that literature on the 'Risorgimento' of a manifestly literary and ideological nature which in actual fact succeeded in interesting only restricted circles of intellectuals: a typical example is Oriani's book on *Lotta politica* [*Political Struggle*].[20] Croce's current interests and thus the practical aims they give rise to have been noted. One observes that they are in fact 'generic', of an abstract and 'methodological' educational character so to speak; in a nutshell they 'preach'. The one precise point is the 'religious' question, but can even that be said to be 'precise'? The position adopted even on the problem of religion remains that of the intellectual and although it cannot be denied that this position, too, is important, one must say that it is not enough.[21]

Q10II§29i.

12 Introduction to the Study of Philosophy[1]. History and Anti-History[22]

If the discussion between history and anti-history is the same as whether nature and history may proceed only in an 'evolutionary' fashion or may do so by 'leaps', it would be salutary to remind Croce that even the tradition of modern idealism is not against 'leaps', i.e. against 'anti-history'. (See Hegel's references to this in Plekhanov's article.)[23] We are then dealing with the discussion between reformists and revolutionaries about the concept and the fact of historical development and progress. The whole of historical materialism is a reply to this question.

The question is posed badly. We are in fact dealing with distinguishing between what is 'arbitrary' and what is 'necessary', between what is 'individual' and what 'social' or collective. Should all those movements which, to assume some mantle of justification and respectability, themselves adopt the name 'revolutions' be accepted as such? Conceptions and revolutionary phraseology are becoming inflated. In his essay on 'The Jew of Verona' De Sanctis had already noted and poured scorn on the belief that clothes make the man and the habit the monk. One should look at whether the phraseology of 'revolution' was wanted 'on purpose' to create the 'will to believe', a 'creation' shored up by quite solid 'supportive' arguments (courts, police and so on). It is undoubtedly true that all those Nietzschean charlatans in revolt against the existing state of affairs, against social conventions, etc., have ended up by retching up everything and thus ridding certain attitudes of all seriousness, but one must not let oneself be led in one's judgements by these charlatans. The warning that one must be 'sober' in one's words and outward attitudes is given so as to ensure greater substantial strength of character and concrete will. It is not just a 'theoretical' question to be against 'wish fulfilment', abstract stances, or a fake heroism, but one involving overall attitude and style.

Q8§210.

13 History, Anti-History and Hegel

For a better understanding of Croce's theory of 'History and Anti-History', as he expounded it at the Oxford Congress (and which at another point came close to the possibility of 'leaps' in nature and history), one must examine Croce's study 'Historical Interpretations of Philosophical Propositions'[24] in which, as well as the argument from which the title is derived, very interesting in itself and not observed by Croce in his latest polemic against the philosophy of praxis, there is a restrictive and cavilling interpretation of the Hegelian proposition 'what is actual is rational and what is rational is actual' exactly in the anti-historical sense.[25]

Q10II§41ix.

14 Past and Present[1]. Giolitti and Croce

It may be noted, and will have to be documented chronologically how Giolitti and Croce, one in the present-day political sphere and the other in that of cultural and intellectual politics, have committed exactly the same errors. Neither of them understood where the current of history was going and in practice helped what they would have wished to avoid and tried to combat. In reality, just as Giolitti did not understand what change was brought about in the mechanism of Italian public life by the entry onto the scene of the great popular masses, so Croce did not understand in practice what a powerful cultural influence the immediate passions of these masses would have had (in the sense of modifying the leading intellectual cadre force). From this point of view, note Croce's collaboration with F. Coppola's *Politica*[26] (De Ruggiero was one of its collaborators in the same period too). Why ever was it that Croce, who through his articles in *Italia Nostra* and *Critica* had taken up a given position towards Coppola & Co. in the 1914-15 period (Coppola was a special target of the brief notes penned by De Lollis, I think, in *Italia Nostra*), could in 1919-20 lend support to this group by collaborating precisely through articles criticising and posing limits on the liberal system? And so it goes on ...

Q6§107.

15 Past and Present[2]. The World is Moving Towards...

La Critica of 20 March 1933 carries one of Croce's 'occasional pieces' entitled 'The World is Moving Towards...'. It seems however that Croce has not mentioned all the aspects of the formula, which in essence is political, a formula for political action. To succeed in convincing people that 'the world is moving ...' in a certain direction means nothing more than managing to convince them of the ineluctable nature of one's own action and obtaining passive consent for its realisation. It is certainly of interest to look at how this conviction is formed: that 'cowardice' and other forms of moral baseness play their part is beyond doubt but the fact that there is so much 'cowardice' and baseness around is a political fact that should be analysed and its concrete origins sought out. From such an analysis it would perhaps turn out that Croce's attitude to life is one reason why these attitudes are so current. Not wanting to involve oneself to the hilt, the distinction between on one hand what an intellectual and on the other what a politician has to do (as if the intellectual was not a politician too, and not only a politician of the ... intellectual strata) and, fundamentally, the whole of the Crocean conception of history lies at the origin of this currency. One sees that being a partisan of freedom in the abstract counts for nothing, it is just the position of someone sitting at a desk and studying the facts of the past, but not that of a real participant in the struggle of the times.

This formula of the 'world that is moving' to the left or the right or towards a compromise etc. started to gain popularity in Italy in 1921 and was an evident sign of the demoralisation that was sweeping across vast strata of the population. One could reconstruct this intellectual movement with an almost exact date. It is true that the formula itself is of no significance, but the expression of the 'world' bodily shifting somewhere is however a convenient one. One is dealing with a 'prediction' that is nothing but a judgement on the present, interpreted in the most facile way, in order to strengthen a particular programme of action, with the acquiescence of imbeciles and the fearful. But if the task of the intellectual is seen as that of a mediator between two extreme positions and this task of mediation is not given over to historical development itself, what is the intellectual doing if not collaborating with the actor in the historical drama who has least scruples and least sense of responsibility? This, it seems, has been Croce's stance. Would it not have been more intellectually honest to come onto the scene in his real role, as the ally of one of the two sides 'with some reservation', instead of wanting to appear above the poverty that characterises the passions of the sides themselves and as the incarnation of 'history'? As has been observed on other occasions, this arbitrary dialectical mediation 'part' has a long and unfortunate history – Proudhon in France, for whom Napoleon III did not hide his sympathies (Saint-Beuve's book),[27] Gioberti in Italy, who may be rightly taken as symbol of the political and intellectual disorder of 1848, and so on.

On this nexus of problems see Ugo Spirito's article 'Revolutionary Historicism and Anti-Historical Historicism' in the *Italia Letteraria* of 13 November 1932. It is noteworthy that Spirito too links the current polemic on 'historicism' to the polemic in the last century around the formula 'natura non facit saltus' ['history does not proceed by leaps']. But Spirito is incapable of getting under the surface of the facts and ideas and if he states like the 'Anti-Proudhon'[28] that it is necessary for the terms of the dialectic to be employed in all their power as contraposed 'extremisms', he cannot see that his own position is a mediation or arbitrary supersession in so far as it is based on the antithesis being violently suppressed and, instead, what is put forward as the antithesis is in fact a completely intellectualistic attempt at mediation that lives in the mind of just a few third rate intellectuals. Spirito too is to be numbered among the theorists (of a more or less unconscious nature since in his writings, especially those in *Critica Fascista*, there appears a preoccupation of his to 'concede something so as not to lose everything' – here see especially an article written straight after the Corporative Congress at Ferrara[29] and his exposition of the thesis of a 'proprietary corporation') of 'passive revolution or revolution-restoration' and not, as he would have it, among the 'extremists' of some form of ideal or real dialectic. If Croce's fault is that of wanting to seem different from what he really is, Spirito too, together with his group, is guilty of the same thing and fundamentally the two errors are in practice identical. We are eye witnesses of Siamese twins battling it out because they are too united.

Q15§36.

16 Identity of History and Philosophy

The identity of history and philosophy is immanent in historical materialism (but, in a certain sense, as the historical prefiguration of a future stage). Did Croce derive his impetus from the philosophy of praxis of Antonio Labriola? This identity has, in any case, become something quite different in Croce's conception from what is immanent in historical materialism; his own most recent ethico-political historical writings are testimony to this. The proposition that the German proletariat is the heir to classical German philosophy does in fact contain this identity between history and philosophy; so also does the proposition that up to now the philosophers have only explained the world and that the point is now to transform it.

Croce's proposition regarding the identity of history and philosophy is richer than any other in critical consequences: 1) it remains incomplete if it does not also arrive at the identity of history and politics (and by politics one has to understand what is actually brought to fruition and not only the different and repeated attempts at this <some of which, taken singly, come to nothing>), and 2) thus also at the identity of politics and philosophy.

But if it is necessary to admit of this identity, how can one any longer distinguish ideologies (equivalent, according to

Croce, to instruments of political action) from philosophy? That is to say, the distinction is possible, but it is only of degree (a quantitative distinction) and not qualitative. Ideologies, rather, are the 'true' philosophy since they are then those philosophical 'popularisations' that lead the masses to concrete action, to the transformation of reality. In other words, they are the mass aspect of every philosophical conception, which in the 'philosopher' assumes the characteristics of an abstract universality, divorced from time and space, the characteristics peculiar to a literary and anti-historical origin.

It is essential to carry out a critique of Croce's concept of history: is it not purely bookish and erudite? Only the identification of history and politics rids history of this peculiar characteristic. If politicians are historians (not only in the sense of creating history, but in the sense that by operating in the present they interpret the past), historians are also politicians and in this sense (which moreover is also present in Croce) history is always contemporary history, i.e. politics, but Croce cannot arrive at this necessary conclusion, exactly because it leads to the identification of history and politics, and thus of ideology and philosophy.

Q10II§2.

17 Philosophy, Religion, Ideology

Nexus between philosophy, religion, ideology (in the Crocean sense). If, by religion, one is to understand a conception of the world (a philosophy) with a conformant norm of conduct,[30] what difference can there exist between religion and ideology (or instrument of action) and in the last analysis, between ideology and philosophy? Does there or can there exist philosophy without a conformant moral will? Can the two aspects of the religious outlook, of religiosity – philosophy and the norm of conduct – be conceived as being separate from each other and, if so, how? And if philosophy and morals are always unitary, why must philosophy logically precede practice and not vice-versa? Or is not such a formulation absurd and must one not conclude that philosophy's 'historicity' means nothing other than its 'practical nature'? One can perhaps say that Croce has touched upon the problem in *Conversazioni critiche*, I, pp. 298-300, where, in analysing some of the *Glosses on Feuerbach* he reaches the conclusion that in them 'faced with pre-existing philosophy', those who speak are 'not, assuredly, other philosophers, as one would have expected, but the practical revolutionaries', that Marx 'did not so much turn Hegelian philosophy upside down as philosophy in general, every sort of philosophy; and supplanted philosophical by practical activity'. But is one not instead dealing with the demand – opposed to 'scholastic', purely theoretical or contemplative, philosophy – for a philosophy that produces an ethic conformant to it, a will capable of becoming reality, and that is in the last analysis identified in it? The XI thesis – 'Philosophers have only interpreted the world differently, the point is now to change it' – cannot be interpreted as a gesture repudiating every type of philosophy, but only one of irritation towards philosophers and their parrot-like utterances and as the vigorous affirmation of a unity between theory and practice. Even if we admit the absurd hypothesis that Marx wanted to 'supplant' philosophy in general by practical activity, just from what would be shown by the peremptory argument that philosophy cannot be negated except by engaging in it, i.e. by reaffirming what one wished to deny, it may be observed that this solution of Croce's is ineffective from a critical standpoint. Indeed Croce himself in a note to the volume *Materialismo Storico e l'Economia Marxistica* explicitly recognises (had recognised) as justified the need, advanced by Antonio Labriola, to construct a philosophy of praxis.[31]

This interpretation of the *Glosses on Feuerbach* as the demand for the unity of theory and practice, and thus as the identification of philosophy with what Croce now calls religion (conception of the world with a conformant mode of conduct) – which, after all, is only the assertion of the 'historicity' of philosophy made in terms of an absolute immanence, of an 'absolute this-worldliness' – can still be justified by the famous proposition that 'the German workers' movement is the heir to classical German philosophy', which does not at all mean, as Croce writes, 'heir who certainly would, rather than carrying on the work of its predecessor, undertake another, *different and opposite in nature*' but means that the 'heir' continues its predecessor's activity, but does so 'in practice' since it has deduced from mere contemplation an active will capable of transforming the world[32] and, in this practical activity, there is also contained the 'knowledge' that it is only rather in practical activity that there lies 'real knowledge' and not 'scholasticism'. From this it can also be deduced that the nature of the philosophy of praxis is in particular that of being a mass conception, a mass culture, that of a mass which operates in a unitary fashion, i.e. one that has norms of conduct that are not only universal in idea but 'generalised' in social reality. And the activity of the 'individual' philosopher cannot therefore be conceived except in terms of this social unity, i.e. also as political activity, in terms of political leadership.

From this point of view, too, it appears that Croce has known how to put his study of the philosophy of praxis to good use. For what is the Crocean thesis of the identity of philosophy and history if not one way, the Crocean way, of presenting the same problem posed by the glosses on Feuerbach and confirmed by Engels in his pamphlet on Feuerbach? For Engels, 'history' is practice (experiment, industry); for Croce history is still a speculative concept. In other words, Croce has gone back over the same path but in the opposite direction – from speculative philosophy a 'concrete and historical' philosophy, the philosophy of praxis, had been arrived at, whereas Croce has translated the progressive acquisitions of the philosophy of praxis back into speculative language, and in this retranslation lies the best of his thought.

One may see with greater exactness and precision the meaning that the philosophy of praxis has given to the Hegelian thesis that philosophy is converted into the history of philosophy, i.e. the historicity of philosophy. This leads to the consequence that one has to negate abstract or speculative 'absolute philosophy' i.e. the philosophy born of the preceding philosophy and heir to its 'supreme problems', so-called, or even only the 'philosophical problem' which becomes, on this account, a problem of history, of how the particular problems of philosophy are born and develop. Precedence passes to practice, to the real history of the changes in social relations; from these therefore (and therefore, in the last analysis, from the economy) there arise (or are suggested) the problems that philosophers set themselves and elaborate on.

For the broader concept of the historicity of philosophy, i.e. that a philosophy is 'historical' in so far as it gets disseminated, in so far as it becomes the conception of reality of a social mass (with a conformant ethic), it is understandable that the philosophy of praxis, notwithstanding the 'surprise' and 'scandal' expressed by Croce, should study 'exactly (!) what in philosophers is not philosophical, namely the practical tendencies and the social and class sentiments that they represent. Hence in eighteenth-century materialism they perceived the French life of the time, completely taken up with the immediate present, with the convenient and the useful; in Hegel, the Prussian state; in Feuerbach, the ideals of modern life, to which Germanic society had not yet risen; in Stirner, the soul of the village draper; in Schopenhauer, that of the petty bourgeois; and so it goes on.'

But was this not exactly a 'historicisation' of the respective philosophies, a search for the historical nexus between philosophers and the historical reality that they took as their staring point? One will be able to say and does in fact say: but is not philosophy instead just what 'is left' after this analysis by which one identifies what is 'social' in the work of the philosopher? In the meantime this demand must be posed and justified mentally. After having distinguished what is social or 'historical' in a particular philosophy, what corresponds to a need of practical life, one that is neither arbitrary nor hare-brained (and it is certainly not easy to make this distinction, especially if it is attempted straight away, i.e. without an adequate perspective), an evaluation then has to be made of this 'residue' which will not after all be as big as would appear at first sight, if the question were posed starting from the Croce's partisan judgement as regards its futile or scandalous nature. That a historical exigency is conceived by an 'individual' philosopher in an individual and personal fashion and that the philosopher's own particular personality has a deep influence on the concrete expressive form of that philosophy is, without doubt, evident. That these individual characteristics are important is also, undoubtedly, to be conceded. But what significance is this importance to have? It will not be merely instrumental and functional, given that if it is true that philosophy does not develop from other philosophy but is a continuous solution of problems proposed by historical development, it is also true that philosophers cannot ignore the philosophers who went before and, in fact, they usually operate just as if their philosophy were a polemic or a development of preceding philosophies, of the concrete individual works of previous philosophers. Sometimes it is even 'useful' to propose one's own discovery of truth as if it were the development of a previous thesis of another philosopher, since it is a strength to graft oneself onto a particular process of development of the particular science to which one contributes.

At any rate, the theoretical nexus is apparent by which the philosophy of praxis, while continuing Hegelianism, 'turns it upside down' without on this account wanting, as Croce believes, to 'supplant' every sort of philosophy. If philosophy is the history of philosophy, if philosophy is 'history', if philosophy develops because the general history of the world (and thus the social relations in which men live) develops, and not at all because a great philosopher is succeeded by a greater one and so on, it is clear that the practical work of creating history also creates 'implicit' philosophy, which then becomes 'explicit'. This will be the case in so far as philosophers elaborate it coherently, in so far as problems of knowledge ensue which, over and above the 'practical' form of solution, sooner or later find theoretical form through the work of specialists, after having immediately found their naïve form in popular common sense, i.e. among the practical agents of historical transformations. One sees how the Croceans are unable to understand this way of posing the question from their wonderment (cf. De Ruggiero's review of Arthur Feiler's book[33] in *La Critica* of 20 March 1932) when faced with certain happenings ('... the paradoxical fact comes about that a narrowly and barrenly materialistic ideology gives rise, in practice, to a passion for the ideal, to a burning desire for renewal, which cannot be denied a certain (!) sincerity') and the abstract explanation they have recourse to ('All this is true in principle (!) and is also providential, since it shows that humanity has great internal resources which come into play at the very moment when a superficial reason would profess to deny them') through formal dialectical tricks in current usage ('The religion of materialism, by the very fact that it is religion, is no longer material (!?); economic interest, when raised to ethics, is no longer merely economic.') This verbiage of De Ruggiero's is either vain or to be traced back to one of Croce's propositions that every philosophy, as such, is nothing other than idealism; but having stated this thesis, why the great battle of words? Would it be just over a question of terminology?

<In his memoirs (*La Résurrection d'un Etat. Souvenirs et réflexions. 1914-1918* [*The Resurrection of a State. Memoirs and Reflections*]),[34] Masaryk recognises the positive contribution of historical materialism, through the work of the group that incarnates it, for bringing about a new attitude towards life, characterised by its activeness, enterprise and initiative, i.e. in the field where he had previously theorised the need for a religious reform.>

Other critical comments, not out of place in these notes on Croce, may be made in respect of this remark of De Ruggiero's (this particular section could be reduced to a note): 1) that when these speculative philosophers are unable to explain a fact, they have immediate recourse to the usual ruse of providence, which of course explains everything; 2) of a superficial nature there is only the 'philological' information of De Ruggiero who would be ashamed not to know all the documents about some minute fact in the history of philosophy but neglects to inform himself much more thoroughly on really momentous events such as those touched upon in his review.

The Philosophy of Benedetto Croce

The position discussed by De Ruggiero, by which an ideology 'basely etc.' gives rise in practice to a passion for the ideal etc. is not after all so new in history. Suffice it to mention the theory of predestination and grace characteristic of Calvinism and its giving rise to a vast expansion of the spirit of initiative. In terms of religion it is the same fact to which De Ruggiero refers, and which he is incapable of penetrating maybe because of his still fundamentally Catholic and anti-dialectical mentality (cf. how the Catholic Jemolo, in his history *Jansenism in Italy*, is incapable of understanding this activist conversion of the theory of grace, is unaware of the literature on the subject and wonders where Anzilotti has derived such nonsense from).

Q10II§31i.

18 Crocean Passion and Sorelian Myth

A critique must be made of Croce's formulation of political science. Politics, according to Croce, is the expression of 'passion'. On Sorel, Croce (*Cultura e vita morale*, 2nd edition, p.158) has written: 'The "spirit of cleavage" was insufficient guarantee for it (syndicalism), perhaps among other things because a theorised cleavage is one that has been superseded, nor did the "myth" provide it with sufficient fervour, perhaps because Sorel, in the very act of creating it, dissipated it by giving a doctrinal explanation of it.' But has Croce not realised that the observations he makes about Sorel can be turned against himself: is it not that the theorised passion is superseded too? The passion, for which a doctrinal explanation is given, is it, too, not 'dissipated'? Nor can one say that Croce's 'passion' is something different from the Sorelian 'myth', that passion means the category, the spiritual moment of practice, while myth is a specific passion which, being historically specific, can be superseded and dissipated without in so doing annihilating the category, which remains a perennial moment of the spirit; the objection is true only in the sense that Croce is not Sorel, a trivial and obvious statement. Meanwhile one may note how intellectualistic and illuministic is Croce's formulation. Since not even the myth concretely studied by Sorel existed just on paper, an arbitrary construction of his own intellect, it could not be dissipated by a page here and there of doctrine known only within restricted intellectual circles who then put out the theory as scientific proof of the scientific truth of the myth that, in a naïve way, impassioned the great popular masses. If Croce's theory were true, political science ought to be nothing more than a new 'medicine' for the passions, and it is not to be denied that a large part of Croce's political, articles are just that – an intellectualistic and illuministic medicine for the passions. Thus his certainty that he has in reality killed off vast historical movements, because he thinks he has 'superseded and dissolved' them in the realm of ideas, ends up by being comic. But in actual fact it is not even true that Sorel has only theorised a particular myth and explained it doctrinally; for Sorel the theory of myths is the scientific principle of political science, it is Croce's 'passion' studied in a more concrete manner, it is what Croce calls 'religion', i.e. a conception of the world with a conformant ethic, it is an attempt to reduce the conception of ideologies in the philosophy of praxis, exactly as seen through the eyes of Crocean revisionism, to scientific language. In this study of the myth as the substance of political action Sorel has also made a wide-ranging study of the specific myth which lay at the base of a certain social reality and which was the mainspring of its progress.[35] In consequence his treatment has two aspects: one that is properly theoretical, belonging to political science, and an immediate, programmatic political aspect. It is possible, though very debatable, that the political and programmatic aspect of Sorel's thought has been superseded and dissipated; today one can say it has been overtaken in the sense that it has been integrated and purged of all intellectualistic and literary elements, but even today it must be recognised that Sorel worked on actual reality and that this reality has not been superseded and dissipated.

That Croce has not escaped from these contradictions and that in part he is aware of this can be understood from his attitude towards 'political parties' as it emerges from the chapter 'The Party as Judge and as Prejudice' in the volume *Cultura e vita morale* and from what, even more significantly, is said about parties in *Politics and Morals*. Croce reduces the political act to the activity of the individual 'party leaders'. So they can satisfy their own passion they construct for themselves, in the parties, the instruments appropriate to ensuring victory (it is therefore enough to administer the medicine for the passions to just a few individuals). But even this does not explain anything. The issue at stake is this: parties have always existed, permanently, even if in other shapes and under other names, and it is self-contradictory to speak of a permanent passion (only in metaphorical terms can one speak of madmen who reason etc.), and, even more so, a permanently military organisation has always been in existence to train men to carry out, in cold blood without any passion, what constitutes the most extreme practical action – the killing of other men who, as individuals, are not hated individually and so on. Furthermore, even in peace time the army is the political actor *par excellence*: how is passion to be reconciled with permanence, with order and systematic discipline etc.? Political will must have some other mainspring as well as passion, a mainspring which itself must also be of a permanent, ordered, disciplined nature and so on. It is not always the case that political struggle, like military struggle, is always resolved in bloodshed, with personal sacrifices that go even as far as the supreme sacrifice of life. Diplomacy is in fact that form of international political struggle (and it is not to be ruled out that a diplomacy might exist for national struggles between parties) which exerts its influence for winning victories (not always of little consequence) without bloodshed, without war. Just the 'abstract' comparison between the military and political forces (alliances etc.) of two rival states convinces the weaker to make concessions. This is a case, here, of a tamed and reasonable 'passion'. In the case of leaders and their followers it is the leaders and the leading groups who use their cunning to inflame the passions of the crowd and lead it on to struggle and to wage war, but in this case it is not passion which is the cause and substance of politics but the conduct of the leaders whose cold reasoning is kept intact. The last war, after all, has shown that it is not passion that keeps the masses of the soldiery in the trenches, but either terror of the court martial or a coldly reasoned out and reflected on sense of duty.

Q10II§41v.

19 Passion and Politics [1]

That Croce has identified politics with passion can be explained by the fact that he came into politics in a serious way by becoming interested in the political action of the subaltern classes who, 'being forced', being 'on the defensive' by finding themselves in circumstances beyond their control and attempting to free themselves of some injury present (albeit imaginary etc.) or whatever, really do confuse politics with passion (even in the etymological sense). But political science must, according to Croce, not only explain one side, the actions of one side, but also the other side, the action of the other side. What has to be explained is political initiative, whether it is 'defensive' and thus 'impassioned' but also whether it is 'offensive' i.e. not directed at avoiding an injury present (albeit an imaginary one since even an imagined wrong causes suffering and, in so far as one suffers, it is real). If one makes a careful examination of this Crocean concept of 'passion' devised in order to provide politics with a theoretical justification, one sees that in its turn it can only be justified by the concept of permanent struggle, for which 'initiative' is always 'impassioned' since the struggle is uncertain and one is continually on the attack not only to avoid being beaten but also to hold down the adversary who 'could win' if not continually persuaded that he is the weaker, i.e. continually defeated. In short, there cannot be 'passion' without antagonism, and antagonism among groups of men, since, in the struggle between man and nature, passion is called 'science' and not 'politics'. In consequence, one can say that, in Croce, the term 'passion' is a pseudonym for social struggle.

Q10II§56.

20 Passion and Politics [2]

Can passion be born from worry over the future price of lard? Can an old lady with twenty servants feel passion at the thought of having to reduce them to nineteen? Passion can be a synonym for economics, not in the sense of economic production or the quest for ophelimity[36] but in the sense of continuous study to prevent a given relationship changing unfavourably, even if the unfavourable change may be one of 'general utility', of general freedom, but in that case 'passion' and 'economics' mean 'human personality' historically determined in a certain 'hierarchical' society. What is the 'point of honour' of criminal elements if not an economic pact? But is it not also a form of demonstrating one's personality (polemics, struggle etc.)? To 'be undervalued' (disparaged) is the pathological fear afflicting everyone in those forms of society in which hierarchy is present in 'refined' ways (stretching into every nook and cranny) in all the minute details etc. Among the criminal elements hierarchy is based on physical force and on cunning: to be 'taken for a ride', to be made to look silly, to let an insult go unpunished etc. is degrading. In consequence there exists a whole protocol and conventional ceremonial with its richness of nuances and implications that is observed in the mutual relationships of the members of the fraternity and to fail to observe the protocol counts as an insult. But this does not happen only among criminals: questions of rank are present in all forms of relationship from that between states to that among members of a family. If someone has a duty to do for a certain length of time and is not relieved at the proper time he gets angry and even reacts with extreme (to the point of criminal) violence; this can happen even if after duty the person has nothing to do or does not have complete freedom of movement (e.g. a soldier who has to do sentry duty, but who, after his watch, must however stay in barracks). That in these episodes there is a manifestation of 'personality' means only that the personality of a lot of men is mean and narrow but it is still personality. And it is undeniable that there are forces existing that tend to keep personality at this level and make it even meaner; for too many people being 'something' means just that others have to 'go without' (be something less). However, that even these little things, these trifling stupidities are 'everything' or 'a great deal' to some people emerges from the fact that such episodes actually provoke reactions in which life and personal liberty are put in jeopardy.

Q10II§58.

21 Political Ideologies[37]

One of the most interesting points to look into further is Croce's doctrine of political ideologies. It is not therefore enough to read his *Politics and Morals* and its appendix [*An Autobiography*]: one must also make a study of the reviews published in *La Critica* (which include that of Malagodi's slim volume *Ideologie Politiche* [*Political Ideologies*], one of whose chapters was devoted to Croce – these occasional writings will perhaps be collected together in the third or fourth volumes of *Conversazioni Critiche*). After maintaining in *Historical Materialism and the Economics of Karl Marx* that the philosophy of praxis was only a way of speaking and that Lange had done well not to discuss it in his history of materialism (on the relations between Lange and the philosophy of praxis, which oscillated considerably and were very uncertain, see R. Ambrosio's essay 'Dialectics in Nature' in the *Nuova Rivista Storica*, 1932, pp.223-52), Croce changed his ideas radically at a certain point and built his new revision around exactly that definition which Prof. Stammler gave, basing himself on Lange, and to which Croce himself refers in *Historical Materialism* (p.31) as follows: 'Just as philosophical materialism does not consist in the assertion that material facts have an influence over spiritual ones, but rather in the making of these latter a mere appearance, without reality, of the former: so the "philosophy of praxis" must consist in asserting that the economy is the true reality and that law is a deceptive appearance.'[38] For Croce too superstructures are now merely appearances and illusions, but has Croce thought through this change in his position and in particular does it correspond to his activity as a philosopher? Croce's doctrine on political ideologies very evidently derives from the philosophy of praxis: they are practical constructions, instruments of political leadership. In other words one might say that ideologies for the governed are mere illusions, a deception they are subject to, whereas for the governors they constitute a willed and conscious deception. For the philosophy of praxis ideologies are anything but arbitrary; they are real historical facts which must be combated and their nature as instruments of domination exposed, not for reasons of morality and so on, but precisely for reasons of political struggle so as to make the governed intellectually independent of the governors, in order to destroy one hegemony and create another as a necessary moment of the overturning of praxis. It appears that, as compared to the philosophy of praxis, Croce is much nearer the vulgar materialist interpretation. For the philosophy of praxis the superstructures are an objective and operative reality (or they become such when they are not pure individual machinations). It explicitly affirms that men become conscious of their social position and therefore of their tasks on the terrain of ideologies, which is no small affirmation of reality; the philosophy of praxis is itself a superstructure, the terrain on which specific social groups become conscious of their own social being, their own strength, their own tasks, their own becoming. In this sense what Croce asserts is correct (p.31 of *Historical Materialism*), namely that the philosophy of praxis is 'history made or in the making'.

There is however a fundamental difference between the philosophy of praxis and other philosophies: other ideologies are non-organic creations because they are contradictory, because they aim at reconciling opposing and contradictory interests; their 'historicity' will be brief because contradiction appears after each event of which they have been the instrument. The philosophy of praxis, on the other hand, does not aim at the peaceful resolution of existing contradictions in history and society but is rather the very theory of these contradictions. It is not the instrument of government of the dominant groups in order to gain the consent of and exercise hegemony over the subaltern classes; it is the expression of these subaltern classes who want to educate themselves in the art of government and who have an interest in knowing all truths, even the unpleasant ones, and in avoiding the (impossible) deceptions of the upper class and – even more – their own. The critique of ideologies, in the philosophy of praxis, involves the ensemble of the superstructures and affirms their rapid transience in that they tend to hide reality – namely struggle and contradiction – even when they are 'formally' dialectic (like Croceanism), in other words they deploy a speculative and conceptual dialectic and do not see the dialectic in historical becoming itself.

An aspect of Croce's position may be seen in the 1917 preface to *Materialismo Storico*, in which he writes that it is to the founder of the philosophy of praxis that 'we shall reserve ... likewise our gratitude for having contributed to the enchantress-like seductions ... of the Goddess of Justice and the Goddess of Humanity' – but why not to those of the Goddess of Liberty? Liberty, in fact, has been deified by Croce and he has become the high priest of a religion of Liberty. It is to be observed that the meaning of ideology is not the same in Croce as it is in the philosophy of praxis. In Croce the meaning is restricted in a somewhat indefinable way, although, through his concept of 'historicity', philosophy too acquires the value of an ideology. One can say that for Croce there are three degrees of liberty: economic liberalism and political liberalism – which are neither economic science nor political science (although Croce is less explicit in the case of political liberalism) but, in point of fact, immediate 'political ideologies'; the religion of liberty; and idealism. Even the religion of liberty, since it too, like any conception of the world, is of necessity bound up with a conformant ethics, ought not to be science but ideology. For Croce only idealism is pure science, since he claims that all philosophers, in as much as they are philosophers, cannot but be idealists, whether they will or no.

The concept of the concrete (historical) value of the superstructures in the philosophy of praxis needs to be developed further, by juxtaposing it with Sorel's concept of the 'historical bloc'. If people become conscious of their social position and their tasks on the terrain of the superstructures, this means that there exists a necessary and vital nexus between structure and superstructure. A study should be made of what currents of historiography the philosophy of praxis was reacting against at the time of its foundation and what the most widespread contemporary opinions were regarding the other sciences too. The very images and metaphors on which the founders of the philosophy of praxis frequently draw give some clues in this direction: the claim that the economy is to society what the anatomy is in the biological sciences – one must remember the struggle that went on in the natural sciences to expel from the scientific terrain the principles of classification that were based on external and mutable elements. If animals were classified according to the colour of their skin, or of their hair or their plumage, these days there would be a general protest. In the human body one certainly cannot say that the skin (and even the historically prevalent type of physical beauty) are mere illusions and that the skeleton and the anatomy are the only reality: yet for a long time something similar was said. By highlighting the anatomy and the function of the skeleton no one was trying to assert that man (and still less woman) can live without the skin. Continuing the same metaphor, one can say that it is not the skeleton (strictly speaking) that makes one fall in love with a woman, but that one nevertheless realises how much the skeleton contributes to the grace of her movements and so on and so forth.

Another element contained in the preface to *Zur Kritik* [*A Contribution to the Critique of Political Economy*] is certainly to be connected with the reform of judicial and criminal legislation. The preface says that just as one does not judge individuals by what they think of themselves, so one cannot judge a society by its ideologies. This assertion is perhaps connected to the reform in penal law whereby material proof and the evidence of witnesses have ended up by replacing the statements of the accused extracted through torture etc.

Referring to so-called natural laws and the concept of nature (natural right, state of nature etc.) 'which, proceeding from the philosophy of the seventeenth century was predominant in the eighteenth century', Croce comments on pp.94-5 of *Historical Materialism* that 'this conception is in fact only obliquely attacked by a criticism like that of Marx who, when analysing the concept of nature, showed that it was the ideological complement of the historical development of the bourgeoisie, an extremely powerful weapon of which this class availed itself against the privileges and oppressions which it intended to overthrow'. The comment serves Croce for the following statement regarding method: 'This concept may indeed have originated as a weapon made occasional use of for practical ends and nevertheless be intrinsically true. "Natural laws" in this case is equivalent to "rational laws"; and it is necessary to deny both the rationality and the excellence of these laws. Now, just because of its metaphysical origin, this concept can be rejected altogether – but it cannot be refuted in any one particular case. It disappears with the metaphysic of which it was a part, and it now seems to have disappeared completely. Peace be unto the "sublime goodness" of natural laws.'[39] Taken as a whole the passage is not very clear or lucid. One should reflect on the fact that in general (i.e. sometimes) a concept may arise as an instrument for a practical and occasional end and none the less be intrinsically true. But I do not think that many people would argue that, once a structure has been changed, all the elements of the corresponding superstructure must of necessity collapse. What happens, instead, is that out of an ideology which arose to guide the popular masses – and which therefore cannot but take account of certain of their interests – several elements survive: natural law itself, which may have waned for the educated classes, is preserved by the Catholic religion and is more alive in the people than one thinks. Besides, in his criticism of the founder of the philosophy of praxis, the historicity of the concept, its transience, is affirmed and its intrinsic value was limited to this historicity, but not denied.

Note I. The phenomena of the breakdown of parliamentarism that we are now witnessing can offer many examples of the function and concrete value of ideologies. How this decomposition is presented so as to hide the reactionary tendencies of certain social groups is of the greatest interest. Many scattered notes have been written on these arguments in various notebooks (e.g. on the question of the crisis of the principle of authority etc.) which, collected together, are to be read in the context of these notes on Croce.

Q10II§41xii.

22 The Autonomy of the Politico-Economic Moment

The importance that Machiavellianism and anti-Machiavellianism have had in Italy for the development of political science and the significance within this development taken on recently by Croce's proposition on the autonomy of the politico-economic moment and the pages he has devoted to Machiavelli. Can one say that Croce would not have reached this point without the cultural contribution of the philosophy of praxis? Bear in mind on this subject that Croce has written that he cannot understand how no one has ever thought of developing the concept that the founder of the philosophy of praxis fulfilled for a modern social group the same work that Machiavelli accomplished in his time.[40] From this comparison of Croce's one could deduce the total injustice of his current cultural stance, not only because the founder of the philosophy of praxis had much wider interests than Machiavelli or Botero (who, according to Croce, fleshes out Machiavelli's work in the development of political science, although this is not very exact, if one considers not only the *Prince* but the *Discourses* too) but also because in him [i.e. in Marx] there is contained in a nutshell the ethico-political aspect of politics or theory of hegemony and consent, as well as the aspect of force and of economics.[41]

The question is this: given the Crocean principle of the dialectic of distincts (which is to be criticised as the merely verbal solution to a real methodological exigency, in so far as it is true that there exist not only opposites but also distincts), what relationship, which is not that of 'implication in the unity of the spirit',[42] will there exist between the politico-economic moment and other historical activities? Is a speculative solution of these problems possible, or only a historical one, given the concept of 'historical bloc' presupposed by Sorel? Meanwhile one can say that while the politico-economic (practical, didactic) obsession destroys art, morals, philosophy, on the other hand these activities are also 'politics'. In other words, economic-political passion is destructive when it is external, imposed by force, according to a pre-established plan (and even that it is thus may be politically necessary, there being periods when art, philosophy etc. go to sleep, while practical activity is always lively) but it can become implicit in art etc. when the process is normal and non-violent, i.e. when there is homogeneity between structure and superstructure and the state has overcome its economic-corporative phase. Croce himself (in the volume *Politics and Morals*) mentions these various phases, one of violence, of misery, of inexorable struggle, which cannot be the subject of ethico-political history (in the strict sense of the term) and one of cultural expansion which, for him, is 'true' history.[43] In two recent books of his, the *History of Italy* and the *History of Europe*, it is precisely the moments of force, of struggle, of misery that are omitted, and history begins in one book after 1870 and in the other after 1815. According to these schematic criteria one can say that Croce himself implicitly recognises the priority of the economic factor, i.e. of the structure as point of reference and of dialectical impetus for the superstructures, in other words the 'distinct moments of the spirit'. It seems that the point of Crocean philosophy which one must insist on has to be the so-called dialectic of distincts. There is a real need to distinguish opposites from distincts, but there is also a contradiction in terms because the dialectic has only opposites.

In considering the non-verbalistic objects that Gentile's school make of this theory of Croce's, should one not go back to Hegel? Examine whether the movement from Hegel to Croce-Gentile has not been a step backwards, a 'reactionary' reform. Have they not made Hegel more abstract? Have they not amputated the most realistic, most historicist part? And is it not, instead, exactly of this part that only the philosophy of praxis, to a certain extent, represents a reform and supersession? And is it not precisely the entirety of the philosophy of praxis that has turned Croce and Gentile off down this track, even though they have made use of this philosophy for particular doctrines? (i.e. for implicitly political reasons?) Between Croce-Gentile and Hegel a linking tradition Vico-Spaventa (-Gioberti) has been formed.[44] But did this not mean a step backwards with respect to Hegel? Can Hegel be considered outside the context of the French Revolution and Napoleon with his wars, i.e. outside the vital and immediate experiences of a most intense historical period of struggles, miseries, when the external world crushed individuals, bringing them down to the ground, flattening them against the ground, when all past philosophies were criticised by reality in such an absolute way? Could Vico and Spaventa offer anything of the like? (Even Spaventa who took part in historical events of regional and provincial importance, as compared with those of '89 to 1815 which turned the civilised world of the day upside down, and forced people to think 'in world terms'? Events which set social 'totality', the whole conceivable human kind, the whole 'spirit' in motion? This is why Napoleon could appear to Hegel as the 'spirit of the world' on horseback!)[45] What historical movement of great importance did Vico take part in? Though his genius consists in fact in having conceived a vast world from a backwater of 'history' aided by the unitary and cosmopolitan conception of Catholicism... Herein lies the essential difference between Vico and Hegel, between God and providence and Napoleon-the spirit of the world, between a remote abstraction and the history of philosophy conceived as only philosophy, that was to lead to the identification, albeit the speculative identification between history and philosophy, between doing and thinking, right up to the German proletariat as the sole heir to classical German philosophy.

Q10II§41x.

23 Appendix. Philosophical Knowledge as a Practical Act, an Act of the Will

This problem may be studied most of all in Croce but in the idealist philosophers in general since they lay particular stress on the inner life of man-as-individual, on spiritual activity and facts.[46] This is the case in Croce because of the great importance in his system assumed by the theory of art, of aesthetics. In spiritual activity and, to give a clear example, in the theory of art (but also in economic science; the starting point for the formulation of this problem may be regarded as the essay 'The Wordly Pair of Sciences: Aesthetics and Economics' that appeared in *La Critica*, 20 November 1931),[47] do the theories of the philosophers *discover* truths up to then unknown, or 'invent', 'create' mental schema, logical connections that *change* the spiritual reality that existed up to then and was historically concrete as the *culture* current in an intellectual grouping, in a class, in a civilisation? This is one of the many ways of posing the question of the so-called 'reality of the external world', of reality and nothing else. External to the individual thinker does there exist a 'reality' (the standpoint of solipsism may be useful for didactic purposes, and philosophical Robinsonades[48] may, if used with discretion and caution, be as useful in practice as economic ones) which in the historical sense is unknown (i.e. not yet known but not on account of that 'unknowable', a noumenon), and which gets 'discovered' (in the etymological sense), or is it rather that in the spiritual world one 'discovers' nothing (i.e. nothing is revealed) but one rather 'invents' and *'imposes'* this on the world of culture?

Q10II§42.

24 Introduction to the Study of Philosophy[2]. Reality of the External World

As well as the example of Tolstoy,[49] one may also recall the facetious form in which a journalist portrayed the 'professional or traditional' philosopher (represented by

Croce in the chapter 'The "Philosopher"') who for years and years had been sitting at his desk, rapt in concentration, wondering 'But this inkwell – *is it within me or without?*'[50]

Q10II§6iii.

C CROCE AND HISTORICAL MATERIALISM

25 Religion, Philosophy, Politics [1]

Croce's speech at the aesthetics section of the Oxford Philosophical Congress (summarised in the *Nuova Italia* of 20 October 1930):[51] here he develops in extreme form the theses on the philosophy of praxis expounded in his *Storia della storiografia italiana nel secolo XIX* [*History of Italian Historiography in the Nineteenth Century*]. In what way is a critical assessment to be made of this most recent critical position of Croce's *vis-à-vis* the philosophy of praxis (a stance that completely overturns the one he maintained in his *Historical Materialism and the Economics of Karl Marx*)? It must be assessed not as the judgement of a philosopher but as a political act of immediate practical import. It is undeniable that within the philosophy of praxis there has sprung up a current of inferior quality that may be considered in relation to the conception of the founders of the doctrine like popular Catholicism in relation to that of the theologians or the intellectuals: just as popular Catholicism can be translated into the terms of paganism, or of religions that, because of the superstitions and the witchcraft by which they are or were dominated, are inferior to Catholicism, so this inferior quality philosophy of praxis can be translated into 'theological' or transcendental terms, i.e. those of pre-Kantian or pre-Cartesian philosophies. Croce is behaving like the masonic anti-clericals and vulgar rationalists who combat Catholicism exactly by means of these comparisons and translations of vulgar Catholicism into 'fetishistic' language. He is falling into the same intellectualistic position as that for which Sorel reproaches

Clémenceau, namely judging a historical movement by its propaganda literature and not appreciating that even banal pamphlets may be the expression of extremely important and vital movements.

Q10II§41i (excerpt).

26 A Philosophy for Barbarians

In an article on 'Clémenceau' published in the *Nuova Antologia* of 16 December 1929 and in another in the *Italia Letteraria* of 15 December (the former signed 'Spectator' and the latter with his full name), Mario Missiroli reproduces two important extracts from letters that Sorel sent him on Clémenceau. In the *Nuova Antologia* the two extracts are printed as forming a whole while in *L'Italia Letteraria* they are, instead, separate and, between the two, Missiroli introduces an 'elsewhere' which helps stylistically towards a better understanding of the context:

1) 'In his (Clémenceau's) estimation, Marx's philosophy, which forms the backbone of contemporary socialism, is an obscure doctrine – good for German barbarians – as it always has seemed to those ready and brilliant intelligences used to easy reading. Lightweight minds like his do not understand what Renan understood so well, namely that historical values of great importance may emerge linked with a literary production of obvious mediocrity, i.e. exactly the type of socialist literature offered to the people.' 2) 'I believe that if for many years Clémenceau took little account of socialism, he ought to have taken even less when Jaurès became the idol of the socialist parties. Jaurès's flights of oratory irritated him. As an "extreme lightweight" – the definition is that of Joseph Reinach – he judged that there could be no serious content in socialism, given that a university professor and recognised leader of the new doctrine could derive only empty rhetoric from it. He did not bother to find out if the masses, once aroused by the vacuous declamations of their chiefs, could find leaders from their own ranks able to take them into regions not even dreamt of by the chieftains of democracy. Clémenceau does

not believe in the existence of a class that is working away to fashion the consciousness of a great historic mission that it has to fulfil, a mission whose aim is the total renewal of our civilisation. He thinks that the duty of the democracies is to bring succour to the disinherited who ensure the production of material wealth, which no one can do without. In times of difficulty an intelligent power should make laws to impose such sacrifices on the rich as would safeguard national solidarity. A well-ordered evolution, leading to a relatively easy life, is what the people would demand in the name of science if they had good counsellors. In his eyes the socialists are anything but good shepherds when they introduce the notion of revolution into the politics of a democratic country. Like all his generation, Clémenceau still has a vivid recollection of the Commune. I firmly believe that he has not yet forgiven the Parisian people for the brutality with which the insurgent National Guard drove him from the Commune of Montmartre.'

Q10II§41xiii.

27 Originality and Popularisation

Croce's judgement on Giovanni Botero in the volume *Storia dell'età barocca in Italia* [*History of the Baroque Era in Italy*] should be borne in mind. Croce recognises that the seventeenth-century moralists, however much smaller in stature they were when measured against Machiavelli, 'represented, in political philosophy, a further and higher stage'. This judgement should be compared to Sorel's on Clémenceau, who could not see – even 'through' a mediocre literature – the needs that such a literature represented and that these were not mediocre. It is a prejudice of intellectuals to measure historical and political movements with the yardstick of intellectualism, originality, 'genius', i.e. that of impeccable literary style and great, brilliant personalities, rather than instead that of historical necessity and political science,[52] that is to say the concrete and effective capacity to make the means conform to the end. This is also a popular prejudice at certain stages of political organisation (the stage of the charismatic man) and is often confused with the prejudice for the 'orator': the politician must be a great orator or great intellectual, must have the 'consecration' of genius etc., etc. One next arrives at the lower stage of some regions populated by peasants or negroes, in which you get followed if you have a beard.

Q10II§41ii.

28 Religion, Philosophy, Politics [2]

For a philosophy, is it a strength or a weakness to have gone beyond the usual limits of restricted intellectual groupings [*ceti*] and been disseminated widely among the great masses, albeit adapting itself to their mentality and losing some part, small or large, of its vigour? And what significance is there in the fact that a conception of the world spreads and takes root in this way and continually has moments of renewal and fresh intellectual splendour? It is a superstitious fear of fossilised intellectuals to believe that a world outlook can be destroyed by criticisms of a rational kind. How many times has there been talk of a 'crisis' of the philosophy of praxis? And what does this permanent crisis mean? Does it not perhaps mean life itself, which proceeds by negations of the negations? Now, by what has the strength of the successive theoretical renewals been conserved if not by the loyalty of the popular masses who had made the conception their own, albeit in superstitious and primitive forms? It is often said that in certain countries the fact that there was no religious reform is the cause of regression in all fields of civil life and it is not noted that the geographical expansion of the philosophy of praxis is, indeed, the great reform of modern times, it is an intellectual and moral reform which carries out on a national scale what liberalism only managed to do for restricted strata [*ceti*] of the population. Exactly the analysis that Croce made in his *History of Europe* of religions and the concept that he developed of religion serve for a better understanding of the historical significance of the philosophy of praxis and the reasons why it has stood up so well to all the attacks and all the desertions.

Croce's position is that of the Renaissance man *vis-à-vis* the Protestant Reformation with the difference that Croce is reliving a position that has historically been shown to be false and reactionary and that he himself (and his pupils: cf. De Ruggiero's volume on *Rinascimento e Riforma*[53]) has contributed to demonstrate as false and reactionary. That Erasmus could say of Luther: 'where Luther appears, culture dies' is understandable.[54] That Croce should today reproduce Erasmus's position is not at all understandable since Croce has seen how, from the primitive intellectual crudeness of Reformation man, there did however spring classical German philosophy and the vast cultural movement from which the modern world was born. Again: Croce's whole treatment of the concept of religion in the *History of Europe* is an implicit critique of petty bourgeois ideologies (Oriani, Missiroli, Gobetti, Dorso etc.) that explain the weaknesses in the national and state organism in Italy by the absence of a religious Reformation, understood in a narrowly confessional sense. Broadening and clarifying his concept of religion, Croce demonstrates the mechanistic nature and abstract schematism of these ideologies, which were nothing more than the constructions of literary-inclined intellectuals. But just on this score – and this is in fact a more serious criticism of him – he has not understood that it is precisely the philosophy of praxis, with its vast mass movement, that has represented and does represent a historical process similar to the Reformation, in contrast with liberalism, which reproduces a Renaissance, narrowly restricted to a small number of intellectual groups, and which at a certain point capitulated in front of Catholicism, right up to the point that the sole effective liberal party was the Popular Party, i.e. a new form of liberal Catholicism.

Croce reproaches the philosophy of praxis for its 'scientism', its 'materialistic' superstitition, its presumed return to the 'intellectual Middle Ages'. These are the reproaches that Erasmus, in the language of the time, directed at Lutheranism. Renaissance man and the man created by the development of the Reformation have been fused together in the modern intellectual of the Crocean type, but this type, though incomprehensible without the

Reformation, is himself no longer able to understand the historical process through which, setting off from the 'medieval' Luther, one had of necessity to arrive at Hegel and therefore – when faced with the great intellectual and moral reform represented by the dissemination of the philosophy of praxis – mechanically reproduces the stance adopted by Erasmus. This position of Croce's can be studied with great precision in his practical attitude towards confessional religion. Croce is, in essence, anti-confessional (we cannot say anti-religious given his definition of what constitutes religion), and for a large group of Italian and European intellectuals his philosophy, especially in its less systematic manifestations (such as reviews, occasional pieces and so on, brought together in volumes like *Cultura e vita morale* [*Culture and Moral Life*], *Conversazioni critiche* [*Critical Conversations*], *The Conduct of Life* etc.) has constituted a real and proper intellectual and moral reform of a 'Renaissance' type. 'To live without religion' (and here without confessional religion is meant) was the pith that Sorel elicited from his reading of Croce (cf. 'Letters of G. Sorel to B. Croce', published in the *Critica* of 1927 and subsequently). But Croce has not 'gone to the people', has not wanted to become a 'national' element (just as the Renaissance men were not, unlike the Lutherans and Calvinists), has not wanted to create a group of disciples who (given that he personally might have wanted to save his energy for the creation of a high culture) could popularise his philosophy in his place and try to make it into an educational element right from the primary school stage (and thus educational for the simple worker and peasant, that is to say for the simple man in the street). Perhaps this was not possible, but it was worth the trouble of trying to do it, and not having tried is also significant. In one of his books Croce has written something to the effect that 'One cannot deprive the man in the street of religion without immediately substituting it with something that satisfies the same needs for which religion was born and still persists.'[55] There is some truth in this assertion, but does it not contain a confession of the impotence of idealist philosophy for becoming an integral (and national) world outlook? For how could one destroy religion in the consciousness of the ordinary person without at the same time replacing it? Is it possible in this case only to destroy without creating? It is impossible. Even vulgar-masonic anti-clericalism substitutes a new conception for the religion which it destroys (in so far as it actually does destroy it) and if this new conception is crude and at a low level, this means that the religion that was substituted was in reality even cruder and at an even lower level. Croce's assertion, for this reason, can only be a hypocritical way of once again putting forward the old principle that religion is necessary for the people. Gentile, less hypocritically, and more consistently, has put the teaching [of religion] back into the primary schools (they have even gone further than Gentile wanted and extended religious teaching to the secondary schools). His justification for this action was the Hegelian conception of religion as the philosophy of the childhood of humanity (see Croce's programme for school reform, which fell because of what happened in parliament to Giolitti's 1920-21 government but which, in respect of religion, was not a great deal different from what became the Gentile programme if memory serves me right), a justification that has become pure sophism when applied to the present day and is just a way of doing clericalism a good turn. Bear in mind the *Ethical Fragment* on religion;[56] why was it not developed? Maybe it was impossible to do so. The dualistic and 'objectivity of the external world' conception, as it has taken root in the people through the traditional religions and philosophies that have become 'common sense', can only be uprooted and substituted by a new conception intimately fused with a political programme and a conception of history that the people recognises as the expression of its absolute necessities. It is impossible to conceive of life and the dissemination of a philosophy which, at one and the same time, is not actual politics, closely bound to the predominant activity in the life of the popular classes, i.e. labour, and which does not therefore manifest itself, within certain limits, as necessarily connected to science. This, albeit new conception, will initially take on superstitious and primitive forms like those of mythological religion, but will find in itself, and in the intellectual forces that the people will express from deep down within, the elements necessary for overcoming this primitive phase. This conception connects man to nature through the means of technology maintaining the superiority of man and exalting this superiority in creative work, and in so doing exalts the spirit and history. (See M. Missiroli's article on science published by *L'Ordine Nuovo* with a rejoinder by P.T.)[57]

On the subject of the relations between idealism and the people, this extract from Missiroli is of interest (cf. *L'Italia Letteraria*, 23 March 1930, 'Calendar: Religion and Philosophy'): 'It is on occasion probable, when faced with the logic of the philosophy teacher especially if this person is a follower of absolute idealism, that the common sense of the scholars and the good sense of the teachers of other subjects will come together in support of the theologian rather than the philosopher. I should not like, in any eventual debate in front of an audience of tyros, to find myself having to plead the case of modern philosophy. Humanity is still wholly Aristotelian and common opinion still follows the dualism typical of Graeco-Christian realism. That knowing is a "seeing" rather than a "doing", that truth lies outside us, existing in itself and for itself, and is not a creation of ours, that "nature" and the "world" are intangible realities, are not doubted by anybody and one runs the risk of being taken for mad if one asserts to the contrary. The defenders of the objectivity of knowledge, the most unbending defenders of positive science, of the science and method of Galileo against the gnoseology[58] of absolute idealism are today to be found among the Catholics. What Croce calls pseudo-concepts and what Gentile defines as abstract thought constitute the last ditch of objectivism. Whence the ever more visible tendency of Catholic culture to set store by positive science and experiment against the new metaphysics of the absolute. It is not to be excluded that Catholic thought might be rejuvenated by taking refuge inside the citadel of experimental science. For thirty years the Jesuits have been working to eliminate the conflicts – in actual fact based on misunderstandings – between religion and science and it is not by chance that Georges Sorel in

The Philosophy of Benedetto Croce

what is now an extremely hard to come by piece, noted that among all scientists the mathematicians are the only ones for whom there is nothing miraculous about the miracle.'

This way of seeing the relations between experimental science and Catholicism is not very constant in Missiroli and, furthermore, his hypothesis is not well founded on real facts. In the volume *Date a Cesare* [*Render unto Caesar*] the picture Missiroli paints of the culture of those who have taken religious vows is not very brilliant and promising for any development posing a threat for secular culture. In a recent reply to a referendum carried out by *Il Saggiatore* Missiroli sees for the future in Italy a general dissemination of the natural sciences at the expense of speculative thought and at the same time a wave of anti-clericalism, i.e. he foresees a conflict between the development of the experimental sciences and religious currents. That the Jesuits have been at work for thirty years to reconcile science and religion does not seem very exact, at least in Italy. In Italy neo-scholastic philosophy, which had taken on this mission, is represented more by the Franciscans (who have surrounded themselves at the University of the Sacred Heart[59] with a good number of the laity) than by the Jesuits, who abound most of all, it seems, in students of experimental psychology and of erudite method (biblical science etc.). In fact one has the impression that the Jesuits (at least those on *Civiltà Cattolica*) look somewhat suspiciously on scientific studies and even on the University of the Sacred Heart by reason of the fact that its teachers flirt with modern ideas a little too much. (*Civiltà Cattolica* never stops censuring any too forceful support for Darwinism etc. Moreover, the neo-scholastics of the Gemelli group have flirted not a little with Croce and Gentile and have accepted particular theories of theirs: Monsignor Olgiati's 1920 book on Karl Marx is constituted wholly on the basis of Crocean critical materials and Fr Chiocchetti, who has written a book on Croce, accepts Croce's theory of the practical origin of error, which cannot be seen in isolation from the whole Crocean system.)

Croce's attitude towards Catholicism has from 1925 onwards been assuming clearer shape, and took on its new, most conspicuous manifestation in his *History of Europe in the Nineteenth Century* which has been put on the Index. Some years ago Croce was surprised that his books had not been put on the Index: but why should they have been? The Congregation of the Index (which is after all the Holy Office of the Inquisition) follows a shrewd and prudent policy. It puts rubbishy, valueless books on the Index, but avoids as much as possible drawing public attention to the works of great intellectuals as being contrary to the faith. It digs in behind the very convenient excuse that all books contrary to certain principles listed in the introductions to the different editions of the Indices are <must be understood to be> automatically on the Index. In this way it was decided to put D'Annunzio on the Index only when the government decided to publish a national edition of his works and to put Croce on it for his *History of Europe*. In actual fact, the *History of Europe* is the first book of Croce's in which the writer's anti-religious opinions took on active political significance and were subject to an unprecedented diffusion.

In his recent attitude towards the philosophy of praxis (whose most conspicuous manifestation up to now was the speech at the aesthetics section of the Oxford congress), Croce reneges on (or rather overturns) his first, pre-1900 position (when he wrote that the name 'materialism' was only a manner of speaking and entered into polemics with Plekhanov by stating that Lange was right not to have discussed the philosophy of praxis in his *History of Materialism*).[60] Not only was he not justified logically in this reversal, but he also reneged, again unjustifiably, on his own past philosophy (or at least a notable part of it) in so far as he was a philosopher of praxis 'without knowing it'. (See Gentile's essay on the subject in the volume *Saggi Critici* [*Critical Essays*], Florence.)

Some of the questions posed by Croce are purely verbal. When he writes that superstructures are conceived of as appearances, does he not think that this may simply mean something similar to his assertion of the non-'definitive' nature, i.e. the 'historicity', of every philosophy? When one speaks of 'illusion' for practical, 'political' reasons, in order to make a social group independent of the hegemony of another group, how can one, in good faith, confuse a polemical language with a gnoseological principle? And how does Croce explain the non-definitive nature of philosophies? On the one hand he makes this assertion gratuitously, without justifying it except by means of the general principle of 'becoming', and on the other he reasserts the principle (already asserted by others) that philosophy is not an abstract thing but the resolution of problems that are constantly being posed by the ongoing development of reality. The intention of the philosophy of praxis, in contrast, is to justify, not by generic principles but through concrete history, the historicity of philosophies, a historicity which is dialectical because it gives rise to struggles between systems, to struggles between ways of seeing reality, and it would be strange if those who are convinced of their own philosophy maintained that opposing beliefs were concrete and not illusory (and it is this we are dealing with, since otherwise philosophers of praxis would have to consider their own conceptions to be illusory or be sceptics and agnostics). But the most interesting point is this: that Croce's doctrine of the practical origin of error is nothing but the philosophy of praxis reduced to a particular doctrine. In this case, *error* for Croce corresponds to *illusion* for the philosophers of praxis. Only that *error* and *illusion* must, in the case of this latter philosophy, mean nothing other than 'historical category' transient in nature because of changes in practice, i.e. the affirmation not only of the historicity of philosophies, but also a realistic explanation of all subjectivist conceptions of reality. The theory of the superstructures is no other than the philosophical and historical solution to subjectivist idealism. Beside the doctrine of the practical origin of error there must be placed the theory of political ideologies, explained by Croce in their meaning of practical instruments of action: but where is the boundary located between what is to be understood as ideology in the strict Crocean sense and ideology in the sense used in the philosophy of praxis, i.e. the whole ensemble of the superstructures? In this case, too, the philosophy of praxis has proved useful to Croce for constructing a particular doctrine. Furthermore, both 'error' and 'ideology as the practical instrument of action' can be represented for Croce, too, by entire philosophical systems that are, all of them, erroneous because they have their origin in practical needs and social necessities. Although he has not yet written it explicitly, it would not be wondered at if Croce were to uphold the practical origin of mythological religions, thus explaining their erroneous nature on the one hand and their tenacious resistance to the critiques of secular philosophies on the other, given that some hint in this sense could be found in his writings. (Machiavelli, with his conception of religion as instrument of domination, might already have stated the thesis of the practical origin of religions.)

Croce's assertion that the philosophy of praxis 'detaches' the structure from the superstructures, thus bringing back theological dualism and positing the 'structure as hidden god'[61] is not correct and not even a particularly profound invention. The accusation of theological dualism and of a breaking up of the process of reality is vacuous and superficial. It is strange that such an accusation should have come from Croce, who introduced the concept of the dialectic of distincts and for this is continually being accused by the followers of Gentile of having himself broken up the process of reality. But, leaving this aside, it is not true that the philosophy of praxis 'detaches' the structure from the superstructures when, instead, it conceives their development as intimately bound together and necessarily interrelated and reciprocal. Nor can the structure be likened to a 'hidden god' even metaphorically. It is conceived in an ultra-realistic way, such that it can be studied using the methods of the natural and exact sciences. Indeed, it is precisely because of this objectively verifiable 'consistency' that one may maintain that the conception of history is 'scientific'. Is it perhaps the case that the structure has been conceived as something immobile and absolute rather than as reality in motion? Does not the statement in the *Feuerbach Theses* about the 'educator who must be educated' posit a necessary relation of active reaction by humanity on the structure, thereby asserting the unity of the process of reality? Sorel's construction of the concept of 'historical bloc' grasped precisely in full this unity upheld by the philosophy of praxis.

It should be noted how cautious and prudent Croce was in the first essays collected in *Historical Materialism and the Economics of Karl Marx* and how many reservations he put forward in stating his criticisms and interpretations (it would be of interest to record these cautionary reservations), and how by contrast the method apparent in his recent writings is so different. If, moreover, these writings were on target, they would demonstrate how he wasted his time in the first period and how extraordinarily simple and superficial was his approach. Only that in this first period Croce at least attempted to justify his cautious assertions logically while he has now become dogmatic and thinks that no justification is warranted. One could find the practical origin of his current error by recalling the fact that before 1900 he considered it an honour to pass even politically as a follower of the philosophy of praxis, since the historical situation of the time made this movement an ally of liberalism, while today things have undergone a big change and certain manoeuvres would prove dangerous.

Q10II§41i (excerpt).

29 Croce and Deceptive Appearances

How big the change is that has come about in Croce's critical position *vis-à-vis* the philosophy of praxis can be gauged by comparing this extract from his essay 'Prof. Stammler's Book' with the final chapters from the *Storia della storiografia italiana nel secolo XIX* [*History of Italian Historiography in the Nineteenth Century*]. Whereas in the first of these writings Croce states, 'According to him (Stammler), however, Marx's work does not deal with such trifling matters: as, for instance, that so-called economic life influences ideas, the sciences, the arts and so on – old lumber of little consequence. Just as philosophical materialism does not consist in the assertion that material facts have an influence over spiritual ones, but rather in the making of these latter a mere appearance, without reality, of the former: so historical materialism *must consist* in asserting that the economy is the true reality and that law is a deceptive appearance,'[62] in the later work he assumes exactly this position of Stammler's without even trying to justify it by some principle or hint of a proof.

What in 1898 was simply Stammler's arbitrary forced interpretation, in 1915 became such an obvious truth that it was not even worth the trouble of further explication.

Q10II§34.

30 The Real Development of History

How is one to understand the expression 'material conditions' and the 'ensemble' of these conditions? As the 'past', as 'tradition', understood concretely, objectively establishable and 'measurable' by means of 'universally' subjective methods of ascertainment, in other words just 'objective'. The working out of the present cannot but continue the past by developing it, cannot but graft itself onto 'tradition'. But how is one to recognise 'true' tradition, the 'true' past and so on? In other words real, effective history and not the vain hope of creating new history that seeks its tendentious 'superstructural' justification in the past? The real past is precisely the structure, because the structure is the evidence, the incontrovertible 'document' of what has been done and continues to exist in reality as the condition for the present and the future. It is to be observed that in examining the 'structure' individual critics can err by claiming that what is dead or what is not a germ of new life to be developed is actually alive, but the method itself cannot be refuted peremptorily. That the possibility of error may exist is undoubtedly to be admitted, but this will be the error of individual critics (politicians, statesmen) and not a flaw in the method. Every social group has a 'tradition', a 'past' and puts this forward as the only past and the total past. The group that, in understanding and justifying all these 'pasts', is best able to identify the line of real development (and hence a contradictory line, but which, in that contradiction, is open to supersession) will make 'fewer mistakes', will identify more 'positive' elements to act as a fulcrum for creating new history.

Q10II§59ii.

31 Some Causes of Error

A government, politician or social group puts a political or economic measure into operation. It then too easily draws general conclusions for interpreting present-day reality and predictions regarding the development of that reality. Insufficient account is taken of the fact that when the measure is put into practice, the initiative promoted etc. may be due to an error of calculation and thus not represent any 'concrete historical activity'. In historical life, just as in biological life, besides children born alive there are also stillbirths. History and politics are closely bound up, indeed they are the same thing, yet it is necessary to draw a distinction in evaluating historical facts and political facts and actions. In history, given its broad perspective on the past and given that the very results of initiatives are a document of historical vitality, fewer errors are committed than in the evaluation of political facts and actions currently taking place. Great politicians cannot therefore but be 'highly cultured' people, in other words they must 'know' the greatest number of elements of real life, not just as 'erudition', 'from books', but in a 'living' way, as the concrete substance of political 'intuition' (for these elements to become the living substance of a politician's 'intuition', however, they must also be learned 'from books').

Q3§33.

32 Croce in the Second Post-War Period[63]

To understand Croce's attitude in the second post-war period it is of use to bear in mind Mario Missiroli's reply, published in 1932, to an inquiry carried out by the review *Il Saggiatore* (it would be of interest to know all the replies to the inquiry). Missiroli wrote (cf. *Critica Fascista*, 15 May 1932); 'I do not as yet see anything that has taken clear shape, but only states of mind, tendencies that are, above all, of a moral nature. It is difficult to foresee what orientation culture may come to assume but I do not hesitate to formulate the hypothesis that we are moving towards an absolute positivism, that restores honour to science and rationalism in the old sense of the term. Experimental research may turn out to have pride of place for this new generation, which does not know and does not want to know the verbalisms of the most recent philosophies. It does not seem to me rash to predict a renewal of anti-clericalism, which, personally, I am far from wanting to see.'

What meaning is to be attached to 'absolute positivism'? Missiroli's 'prediction' coincides with the assertion made on various occasions in these notes that the whole of Croce's recent theoretical activity is explained by his foreseeing a renewal of the philosophy of praxis in grand style with tendentially hegemonic characteristics, a renewal capable of reconciling popular culture and experimental science with a vision of the world that is neither crude positivism, nor distilled actualism nor bookish neo-Thomism.

Q10II§11.

33 The War of Historical Materialism

Croce's political-intellectual biography is not to be found in its entirety in his *Autobiography*. For that part dealing with his relationship to the philosophy of praxis many essential elements and suggestions are to be found scattered throughout the whole of his work. In the volume *Cultura e vita morale* [*Culture and Moral Life*] (2nd edition, p. 45, but also elsewhere in the volume, where he explains the origin of his sympathy for Sorel) he states that, his tendencies of a democratic nature notwithstanding (since a philosopher cannot but be democratic), his stomach refused to digest democracy until it had taken on some of the flavour of the philosophy of praxis, which 'as is quite well known, has been steeped in classical German philosophy'.[64] During the war he claimed that it was in fact the war of the philosophy of praxis (cf. De Ruggiero's interview with Croce, quoted in the *Revue de métaphysique et de morale*, the *Pagine di guerra* [*Pages on the War*], and the preface to the 1917 edition of *Historical Materialism*[65]).

Q10II§41xi.

34 Croce's Four Criticisms of Marxism

The most important place in which Croce summarises the criticisms that, according to him, are decisive and representative of a historical era, is the *History of Italy 1871 to 1915* in the chapter where he mentions the fortunes of the philosophy of praxis and of critical economy. In the preface to the second edition of the volume *Historical Materialism and the Economics of Karl Marx* he defines the principal theses of his revisionism to be the following four points. The first is that the philosophy of praxis should hold as a simple canon of interpretation, and the second that the labour theory of value is nothing but the result of an elliptical comparison between two different types of society, theses which, he claims have 'been generally accepted', 'have become normal, and one now hears them repeated almost without recalling who was the first to put them into circulation'. The third thesis, critical of the law regarding the falling rate of profit (a 'law which, if it were established exactly ... would mean no more or less than the automatic and imminent (!?) end of capitalist society') 'is perhaps harder to accept', but Croce rejoices in the support of the 'economist and philosopher' Charles Andler (in the *Notes critiques de science sociale*, 10 March 1900). The fourth thesis, that of a philosophical economics, 'is more properly offered to the reflection of philosophers' and Croce refers readers to his forthcoming volume on practice. For the relations between the philosophy of praxis and Hegelianism, he refers readers to his essay on Hegel.[66]

In the 'Conclusion' to his essay 'Concerning the Interpretation and Criticism of Some Concepts' (*Historical Materialism*, pp.48-119, the conclusion being on pp. 115-9) Croce summarises in four points the positive results of his inquiry: 1) in regard to economic science, the justification of critical economy, understood not as general economic science, but as comparative sociological economics, dealing with the conditions of labour in society; 2) in regard to the science of history, the liberation of the philosophy of praxis from any *a priori* concept (whether inherited from

Hegelianism or a vulgar evolutionist contagion) and the understanding of the doctrine certainly as a fruitful, but as a simple canon of historical interpretation; 3) in regard to practical matters, the impossibility of inferring the social programme of the movement (or indeed any other social programme) from propositions of pure science, since a judgement on social programmes must be brought into the field of empirical observation and practical persuasions; 4) in regard to ethics, the denial of the intrinsic amorality or the intrinsic anti-ethical character of the philosophy of praxis.[67] (It would be useful to derive other points of discussion and criticism from all Croce's writings on the argument, carefully summarising them, together with all the relevant bibliographical references, while continuing to keep a special place for those points indicated by Croce himself as the ones to which his interest [and] his more methodical and systematic reflection have been drawn.)

Q10II§41viii.

35 The Immediate Practical Element

May there be some importance for Croce in L. Einaudi's friendly warnings regarding his stance as a 'disinterested' critic of the philosophy of praxis? The same question emerges in another guise: how much of what is pushing Croce into his present 'liquidationist' position is due to the immediate practical element? In this respect, one may observe that Croce does not at all intend to enter into polemics with the philosophers of praxis, and that this polemic is of such little interest to him that he is not even driven to seek somewhat fuller and more exact information than that which, evidently, is at his disposal. One can say that Croce is not so much interested in combating the philosophy of praxis as historical economism, i.e. the element of the philosophy of praxis that has penetrated the traditional conception of the world, creating splits within it and thereby making it 'politically' less resistant; he is not so much interested in 'converting' his adversaries as in reinforcing his own camp. In other words, Croce presents as 'offensive' an action which is merely 'defensive'. If such were not the case, Croce ought to make (ought to have made) a 'systematic' revision of his specialised work on the philosophy of praxis, confess that he was completely mistaken then, demonstrate these past errors in contrast with his current convictions etc. In such a careful and scrupulous man as Croce, the lack of interest shown towards the objective need to justify logically this latest passage of his ways of thinking is at least strange and can find no explanation other than that of immediate practical interests.

Q10II§16.

36 Croce, Einaudi, Loria

On the subject of the note under this heading that immediately precedes this one, viz. on the relations between Croce and Einaudi, one might add an observation to the effect that Einaudi is not always a very careful and attentive reader of Croce. On p.277 of *La Riforma Sociale* of 1929 Einaudi writes: 'A theory must not be attributed to whoever *perceived it by intuition* or who stated it incidentally or expounded a principle from which it could be deduced or gave a disjointed account of the *different notions* which *aspired* towards a united *re*composition.' The positive part of the proposition is then mentioned in this way: 'in what other book was the following proposition assumed as the "desired" object of "particular" treatment, etc.'?

Croce, in *Materialismo Storico*, IV, p.6., had in fact written: 'It is one thing to throw out an observation in passing, which is then let fall without its being developed, and it is another to establish a principle from which fruitful consequences emerge; it is one thing to state a generic and abstract thought and another to think it in real and concrete terms; finally, it is one thing to invent and another to repeat at second or third hand.'[68] Einaudi's statement is derived from Croce with additional curious linguistic improprieties and theoretical awkwardness. Why did Einaudi not just simply quote Croce? Perhaps because the extract from Croce is contained in a piece directed against Prof. Loria.

Another example of Einaudi's superficiality can be found in a subsequent number of *La Riforma Sociale*, in the long review of R. Rigola's *Autobiografia*.

Q10II§18.

37 Note on Luigi Einaudi

It does not appear that Einaudi has studied the works of critical economy and the philosophy of praxis directly; rather, one can say that he speaks of them, especially of the philosophy of praxis, like someone who has been eavesdropping, someone who has heard them talked about often at third or fourth hand. He has picked up the main ideas from Croce (*Historical Materialism*), but in a superficial and often disjointed way (compare with a previous paragraph).[69] What is of greater interest is the fact that someone who has always been a highly esteemed writer on *Riforma Sociale* (and for a certain length of time, I believe, also one of the editorial committee) is that very same Achille Loria who has popularised an inferior version of the philosophy of praxis. One can in fact say that what in Italy passes under the banner of the philosophy of praxis is nothing but Loria's idea of scientific goods, and shoddy, smuggled goods they are, too. Recently, in this very *Riforma Sociale*, Loria has published a notebook of his jottings in a near-random order, to which he has given the title 'New Confirmations of Historical Economism'. In the November-December 1930 number of *Riforma Sociale*, Einaudi published a note, 'The Myth (!) of the Technical Instrument', on the subject of Rinaldo Rigola's autobiography that reinforces the opinion mentioned above. Croce, in fact, had already shown in his essay on Loria (in *Historical Materialism*) that the 'myth (!) of the technical instrument' was one of Loria's own inventions, something that Einaudi does not mention, persuaded as he is that we are instead talking about a doctrine of the philosophy of praxis. Einaudi further goes on to make a whole series of mistakes through his ignorance of the subject: 1) He confuses the development of the technical instrument with the development of the economic forces; to speak of the development of the forces of production for him means speaking only of the development of the technical instrument; 2) he maintains that, for critical economy, the forces of production are simply material things and not social – and thus human – forces and relations, which are incorporated into material things and whose juridical expression is the property right; 3) in this article too, we can see the usual typical economistic 'cretinism' of Einaudi and many of his free-marketeer friends who really are enlightened propagandists. It would be interesting to see Einaudi's collected works of journalistic propaganda again; it would appear from these that the capitalists have never understood their real interests and that they have always gone against their economic interests.

Given Einaudi's undeniable intellectual influence over a wide stratum of intellectuals, it would be worth the trouble of searching through all the notes in which he refers to the philosophy of praxis. One should further bear in mind the obituary of Piero Gobetti that Einaudi published in *Il Baretti*, which explains the attention that Einaudi devotes to refuting every article of liberal origin that recognises the importance and influence that the philosophy of praxis has had in the development of modern culture. In this respect, one should also bear in mind the article on Gobetti in Giuseppe Prato's *Piemonte*.

Q10II§39.

38 Cultural Topics. Philosophy of Praxis and 'Historical Economism'

Philosophy of praxis and 'historical economism'. Confusion between the two concepts. However the problem to be posed is: what importance must be attached to 'economism' in the development of the methods of historiographical research, granted that economism cannot be confused with the philosophy of praxis? It is beyond doubt that a group of financiers, who have interests in a given country, may steer the politics of that country, push it into war or keep it out of one. But the ascertainment of this fact is not 'philosophy of praxis', it is 'historical economism', namely the affirmation that 'immediately', as a 'chance' occurrence, factors have been influenced by specific interest groups. That the 'smell of petrol' might heap serious problems down on a country is also beyond doubt etc., etc. But these statements, checked up on, demonstrated true etc., are still not philosophy of praxis, indeed they may be accepted and made by someone who rejects the whole of the philosophy of praxis. One may say that the economic factor (understood in the immediate and Jewish sense[70] of historical economism) is only one of the many ways in which the more far reaching historical process is presented (factors of race, religion etc.), but it is this farther reaching process that the philosophy of praxis wishes to explain and exactly on this score it is a philosophy, an 'anthropology', and not a simple canon of historical research.

Q17§12.

39 The Crocean Critique of Marxism

The starting point for Croce's critique of the philosophy of praxis may be taken as the dogmatic assertions he makes on this score in the *History of Italy* and the *History of Europe*. He claims in these volumes that his conclusions are definitive and by now commonly accepted, but says that the critique will be expounded systematically. In the meantime it should be noted that his assertions are much less axiomatic and formally decisive than he would have us believe. The theory of value is anything but intrinsically denied in his main work where he states that the only scientific 'theory of value' is that of the final degree of utility[71] and that the Marxist theory of value is 'something else' but he recognises the solidity and effectiveness of that 'something else' and asks economists to refute it with quite different arguments from the ones normally employed by Böhm-Bawerk and Co. His subsidiary thesis that this theory is an elliptical comparison, as well as being unjustified, is in actual fact immediately challenged by the observation that we are dealing with a logical continuation of the Ricardian theory of value and

Ricardo, for one, did not make 'elliptical comparisons'. The reduction of the philosophy of praxis to an empirical canon of interpretation is merely asserted by the indirect method of exclusion, i.e. one that is still not intrinsic. For Croce, the question certainly is 'something' important, but since it can't be this and it can't be that etc., it must be a canon of interpretation. The proof does not seem conclusive. The same formal prudence appears in his paper on the fall in the rate of profit. What is it that the author of the theory wanted to say? If he wanted to say this, he was not precise, but did he want to say this? Then we'll have to give more thought to this, etc. It really must be stressed how this cautious attitude has undergone a complete change over the last few years, and his whole position has become definitive and dogmatic just at the moment when it is much more markedly acritical and unjustified.

Q10II§31ii.

40 The Theory of Value in Critical Economy

That the theory of value in critical economy is not a theory of value, but 'something else' founded on an elliptical comparison, i.e. with reference to a hypothetical future society etc. But the proof is unsuccessful and its refutation is contained implicitly in Croce himself (cf. the first part of the essay 'Concerning the Interpretation and Criticism etc.'[72]). One has to say that this discovery of the elliptical comparison is purely literary, since the labour theory of value has a whole history that culminates in the doctrines of Ricardo and the historical representatives of this doctrine certainly did not intend to make elliptical comparisons. (This objection is stated by Prof. Graziadei in his booklet *Capitale e Salari* [*Capital and Wages*][73] – one should look at whether it had been presented previously and by whom; it is so obvious that it ought to come at once to the pen-nib.) It should also be seen whether Croce was familiar with the volume *Der Mehrwert* [*Theories of Surplus Value*], which contains the exposition of the historical development of the labour theory of value. (Chronological comparisons between the publication of *Der Mehrwert*, which was posthumous and after volumes 2 and 3 of the *Critique of Political Economy*, and Croce's essay.[74]) The question, therefore, is this: can one say that the type of scientific hypothesis that characterises critical economy, which abstracts not the economic principles of man in general, in all places and at all times, but those of the laws of a specific form of society, is an arbitrary one or is it, on the other hand, not more concrete than the type of hypothesis of pure economics? And, granted that a type of society presents itself full of contradictions, is it correct to abstract only one of the terms of this contradiction? Moreover, every theory is an elliptical comparison, since there is continually a comparison being made between the real facts and the 'hypothesis' purged of these facts. When Croce says that the theory of value is not the 'theory of value' but something else, he does not in actual fact destroy the theory itself but poses a formal question of nomenclature. This is why the orthodox economists were not happy with his essay (cf. the chapter in the book *Historical Materialism* in polemic with Prof. Racca).[75] Thus there is no validity in the observation made in regard to the term 'surplus value', which, instead, expresses with great clarity what one in fact wants to say for the reasons for which Croce criticises that term. One is dealing with the discovery of a new fact, which is expressed by a term whose novelty consists in the formation,[76] contradictory in actual fact as compared with traditional science. That 'surplus values' might not exist in a strict literal sense may be true, but the neologism has a metaphorical, not a literal, meaning, i.e. it is a new word that cannot be resolved into the literal value of the original etymological forms.

Q10II§38i.

41 The Theory of Value as an Elliptical Comparison

The theory of value as elliptical comparison. As well as the objection that the theory of value has its origins in Ricardo, who assuredly did not intend to make an elliptical comparison in the sense Croce thinks, there are certain other series of reasonings to be added. Was Ricardo's theory arbitrary and is the more precise solution of critical economy arbitrary? And at what point in the reasoning would the arbitrariness or sophism lie? One would need to make a careful study of Ricardo's theory, and in particular of his theory of the state as an economic agent, as the force which safeguards the property right, i.e. the monopoly of the means of production. It is certain that the state as such does not produce but is the expression of the economic situation, but one can however speak of the state as economic agent in so far as the state is in actual fact synonymous with this situation. For if one studies the hypothesis of pure economics, as Ricardo meant to do, must one not abstract from this situation of force represented by states and by the legal monopoly of property? That this is not an idle question is shown by the changes brought about in the situation of force existing in civil society by the birth of the trade unions,[77] although the state did not change in nature. We are not dealing at all, therefore, with an elliptical comparison made in the light of a future social form different from the one studied, but with a theory that came out of the reduction of economic society to its pure 'economic nature', i.e. to the maximum determination of the 'free play of economic forces', in which since the hypothesis is that of homo oeconomicus, the theory could not but abstract from the given force of the whole of a class organised in the state, of a class which had its trade union in parliament, while the wage earners could not coalesce and bring to bear the force given by the collectivity to each single individual. Ricardo, like the other classical economists, moreover, was extremely open minded and his labour theory of value did not raise any eyebrows when it was put forward (cf. Gide and Rist's *History of Economic Doctrines*)[78] since at that time it did not represent any danger and appeared only, as indeed it was, a purely objective and scientific statement. Its value as polemic and as moral and political education, without any loss of objectivity, was to be acquired only with the advent of critical economy. The problem is, furthermore, bound up with the fundamental problem of 'pure' economic science, viz. that of identifying what must be the concept and historically determined fact, independent of the other concepts and facts relevant to other sciences: the fact that is peculiar to modern economic science cannot be anything other than the commodity, the production and distribution of commodities and not a philosophical concept, as Croce would have it; for Croce even love is an economic fact and the whole of 'nature' is reduced to the concept of the economic.

It might also be noted, if one so wishes, that the whole of language is a series of elliptical comparisons, that history is an implicit comparison between the past and the present (historical actuality) or between two distinct moments of the development of the historical process. And why is ellipsis illegitimate if comparison is made with a future hypothesis, while legitimate if made with a past fact (which in this case is assumed exactly as a hypothesis, as a useful reference point for a better understanding of the present)? Croce himself, speaking of predictions, maintains that prediction is none other than a special judgement on the actuality that is the only thing known, since by definition one cannot know the future, since it does not exist and has not existed, and one cannot know the inexistent (cf. *Conversazioni Critiche*, 1st series, pp.150-3). One has the impression that Croce's reasoning is rather that of a literary academic and of one whose phrases are chosen for their effect.

Q10II§41vi.

42 Croce and the Falling Rate of Profit

A fundamental flaw is to be noted in Croce's essay on the tendential fall in the rate of profit. This problem had already been formulated in the first volume of the *Critique of Political Economy*, where relative surplus value and technical progress are spoken of being precisely the cause of relative surplus value;[79] in the same point it is observed how a contradiction arises in this process, i.e. while on the one hand technical progress allows an expansion of relative surplus value, on the other it determines, by means of the

The Philosophy of Benedetto Croce

change it introduces into the composition of capital, a tendential fall in the rate of profit which is then demonstrated in Volume III of the *Critique of Political Economy*. To the theory expounded in Volume III, Croce presents the treatment contained in Volume I as an objection. In other words he expounds as an objection to the tendential law of the fall in the rate of profit the demonstration of the existence of a relative surplus value due to technical progress, without however even once mentioning Volume I, as if the objection had sprung from his brain, or was even the consequence of good sound sense. (However the texts of the *Critique of Political Economy* will have to be looked at again before putting forward this criticism of Croce's objection, a precaution which moreover must be understood for all these notes, which have been written to a very large extent on the basis of memory.)

In any case it must be established that the question of the tendential law of the rate of profit cannot be studied solely on the exposition given in Volume III; this treatment is the contradictory aspect of the treatment expounded in Volume I, from which it cannot be detached. Furthermore, a better determination will perhaps be necessary of the meaning of 'tendential' law. Since any law in political economy cannot but be tendential, given that it is obtained by isolating a certain number of elements and thus by neglecting the counteracting forces, one should perhaps distinguish a greater or lesser degree of tendentiality and, while the adjective 'tendential' is usually understood to be obvious, one must instead insist on it when the tendential nature assumes an organic importance. Such is the case when the falling rate of profit is presented as the contradictory aspect of another law, that of the production of relative surplus value; in this situation, one law tends to cancel the other, with the prediction that the fall in the rate of profit will be the prevailing one. When can one imagine the contradiction reaching a Gordian knot, a normally insoluble pass requiring the intervention of Alexander with his sword? When the whole world economy has become capitalist and reached a certain level of development, i.e. when the 'mobile frontier' of the capitalist economic world has reached its pillars of

Hercules. The counteracting forces of the tendential law, which are summed up in the production of ever greater relative surplus value, have limits that are given, for example, technically by the extension of the elastic resistance of matter and socially by the level of unemployment that a given society can stand. That is to say, the economic contradiction becomes a political contradiction and is resolved politically by overthrowing praxis.[80]

On the subject of the tendency of the rate of profit to fall, bear in mind a work reviewed in the first year of *Nuovi Studi* that was written by a German economist, a dissident pupil of Franz Oppenheimer, and a more recent volume by Grossmann reviewed in the journal *Economia* of Trieste and in *Critique Sociale* by Lucien Laurat.[81]

Q10II§33.

43 Relative Surplus Value and the Falling Rate of Profit

After having noted that, in his essay on the fall in the rate of profit, Croce does nothing other than present as an objection the other contradictory aspect of the process linked to technical progress <i.e. the theory of relative surplus value> that had already been studied in Volume I of the *Critique of Political Economy*, it is also to be noted that in his analysis Croce forgets a fundamental element in the formation of value and profit, i.e. 'socially necessary labour', whose formation cannot be studied and brought out in a single factory or undertaking. Technical progress in reality gives the single firm the molecular chance of raising labour productivity to a level above the social average, thereby realising exceptional profits (as was studied in Volume I), but as soon as this given progress is socialised, this initial position is lost in stages and the law of the social average of labour, which lowers prices and profits through competition, comes into force: at that point one has a fall in the rate of profit, since the organic composition of capital assumes an unfavourable ratio. The entrepreneurs tend to prolong the initial advantage as long as possible even by means of legislative intervention – the defence of patents, of industrial secrets and so on – which however cannot but be limited to some, perhaps secondary, aspects of technical progress but in any case they have their certainly not unimportant weight. The most effective means for individual entrepreneurs to escape the law of the falling rate is that of constantly introducing new forward-looking changes in all aspects of work and production, without neglecting the smallest contributions to progress that in the really vast enterprises, when multiplied on the grand scale, give rise to very appreciable results. Henry Ford's whole industrial activity can be studied from this point of view: a continual, incessant struggle to escape the law of the falling rate of profit by maintaining a position of superiority over his competitors. Ford had to get out of the strictly industrial field of production to organise the transportation and distribution of his goods as well, thereby creating a more favourable distribution of the mass of surplus value for the industrial producer.

Croce commits various types of error. He sets off from the supposition that any technical progress immediately produces, as such, a fall in the rate of profit, which is mistaken because the *Critique of Political Economy* states only that technical progress gives rise to a contradictory process of development, one of whose aspects is the tendential fall. He says he has borne in mind all the theoretical premisses of critical economy and forgets the law of socially necessary labour. He quite forgets the part of the question dealt with in Volume I, which would have spared him this entire series of errors, an oversight so much the more serious in that he himself recognises that the section of Volume III devoted to the law of the tendential fall is incomplete but only sketched out etc., an essential reason for studying everything that this same author has written elsewhere on this subject. (The question of the text of Volume III can be the object of fresh study now that there is available, as I am to believe, the critical edition of all the notes and comments which were to have served for the definitive version. It is not to be excluded that the traditional edition could have left out some passages which, after the polemics that have taken place, could have a much greater importance than might be imagined from the first reordering of the fragmentary material.)

An economic expert would at this point feel obliged to take in hand the general formula of the law of the tendential fall, which fixes the moment at which the law itself comes into play, and define in a critical manner the whole series of passages that tendentially lead to it as a logical conclusion.

The reference to the meaning attached to 'tendential', when applied to the law of the fall in profit, is to be developed. It is obvious that in this case the tendential nature cannot refer just to the counteracting forces in the real situation every time that some isolated elements are abstracted from it to construct a logical hypothesis. Since the law is the contradictory aspect of another law, that of relative surplus value which determines the molecular expansion of the factory system, i.e. the very development of the mode of capitalist production, one cannot deal with such counteracting forces as those of the common economic hypotheses. In this case, the counteracting force is itself studied organically and gives rise to another law, equally organic in nature to that of the fall. It seems that the meaning of 'tendential' must, on this account, be of a real 'historical', and not a methodological, nature: the term serves in fact to indicate this dialectical process by which the molecular progressive thrust leads to a tendentially catastrophic result in the social ensemble, a result from which other individual progressive thrusts set off in a continual overhauling process which cannot however be reckoned as infinite, even if it does break up into a very large number of intermediate stages of different size and importance. For the same reason it is not completely correct to say, as Croce does in the preface to the second edition of his book that if the law regarding the fall in the rate of profit were established exactly, as its author believed, it 'would mean neither more nor less than the automatic and imminent end of capitalist society'. There is nothing automatic and even less imminent about it. This inference of Croce's is in fact due to the error of having examined the law of the falling rate of profit in isolation from the process within which it was conceived; rather than isolating it for the scientific purpose of better exposition, he does so as if it were valid 'absolutely' instead of being a dialectical term in a vaster organic process. That many have interpreted the law in the same way as Croce does not exempt him from a certain scientific responsibility. In this way a 'myth' has been created of many affirmations of critical economy, and one cannot say that such myth formation has not had its immediate practical importance and might not still have one. But this is another aspect of the question, which has but little connection with the scientific formulation of the problem and with logical deduction: it will have to be examined at the level of the critique of political methods and the methods of the culture of politics. It is probable that at that level the political method of arbitrarily forcing a scientific thesis in order to draw from it a vigorous and propulsive popular myth is, in the last analysis, to be demonstrated inept and productive of greater damage than use. The method might be compared to the use of narcotics which create an instant of euphoria as regards physical and psychic forces but which weaken the organism permanently.

Q10II§36.

44 Fordism and the Falling Rate of Profit

On the tendential fall in the rate of profit. This law ought to be studied on the basis of Taylorism and Fordism. Are these not two methods of work and production that represent the progressive attempts to overcome the tendential law, getting around it by multiplying the variables in the conditions of the progressive rise in constant capital? Among the most important variables – though one could compile a complete and very interesting list from Ford's books – are the following: 1) the machines continually being introduced are more perfect and refined; 2) the metals used are more resistant and last longer; 3) the formation of a new type of worker, in whom a monopoly is created through high wages; 4) the reduction of waste in manufacturing materials; 5) the ever wider utilisation of ever more numerous by-products, i.e. the saving of previously unavoidable waste, which the great size of the enterprises makes possible; 6) the utilisation of waste heat energy, e.g. the heat from blast furnaces which previously was dispersed into the atmosphere is now being sent by pipe to heat living environments etc. (Through the Taylorised rationalisation of motion, the selection of a new type of worker allows a relative and absolute production greater than was previously possible with the same workforce.)

With each one of these innovations, the industrialist passes from a period of increasing costs (i.e. one of a falling rate of profit) to a period of decreasing costs, in so far as he comes to enjoy a monopoly of initiative which can last a (relatively) long time. The monopoly is also long-lasting due to the high wages that these progressive industrialists 'are obliged' to pay if they want a first-rate skilled workforce and if they want to contend with their competitors for those workers who, from the psycho-technical point of view, have the best aptitude for the new forms of work and production (recall the similar fact of Senator Agnelli who, in order to absorb the other car firms into Fiat, used the bait of high wages to corner the market in panel beaters; the factories, deprived through this of their specialised mudguard-producing departments, tried to resist by attempting to make plywood mudguards, but the innovation came to nothing and they had to capitulate). The extension of new methods brings about a series of crises, each of which reproposes the same problems of rising costs and whose cycle can be imagined as recurrent until: 1) the extreme limit of resistance of the material being used is reached; 2) the limit is reached in the introduction of new automatic machinery, i.e. the ultimate ratio between men and machines; 3) the saturation limit of world industrialisation is reached, where one has to take account of the rate of increase of population (which, moreover, declines with the spread of industrialism) and of production for the renewal of consumer and capital goods.

The tendential law of the fall in profit would thus be seen to lie at the basis of Americanism, i.e. would be the cause of the accelerated pace observed in the progress of work and production methods and in the modification of the traditional type of worker.

Q10II§41vii.

D CROCE, ACTUALISM AND REFORMISM

45 Past and Present[3]. Political and Civil Society

Political and civil society. Polemic over Ugo Spirito's criticisms of traditional economics. The polemic contains numerous ideological presuppositions and implicit aspects on which discussion, so it seems, has up to now been avoided both by the 'economists' and by Spirito. It is obvious that the economists do not want to discuss Spirito's conception of the state, but it is just here that the nub of the dispute lies. Spirito, furthermore, does not wish, or hesitates, to press and engage them on this ground, since the consequence would be to provoke a general political discussion and show up the existence of several political parties in the same party, one of them closely linked to the so-called non-party people: there would appear to exist a party of science and high culture. The scientists, moreover, would find it easy to demonstrate the whole arbitrary nature of Spirito's propositions and his conception of the state, but they do not want to go beyond certain limits which seldom transcend indulgence and personal courtesy.

What is comic is Spirito's pretension that the economists should construct an economic science for him according to his point of view. But not all Spirito's polemic is to be rejected. There are some real exigencies, submerged amid the farrago of 'speculative' words. The episode is therefore to be noted as one moment of the political-cultural battle. The exposition must in fact start from the conception of the state peculiar to Spirito and to Gentilian idealism, which is quite far removed from the conception held by the 'state' itself, i.e. by the dominant classes and the more active political personnel, in other words it has not at all (indeed, anything but!) become an element of governing political culture. The Concordat is opposed to this (an implicit opposition, it may be added), and Gentile's antagonism to the Concordat, as expressed in 1928, is well known (cf. articles in the *Corriere della Sera* and speeches of the time); one must bear in mind Paolo Orano's speech in the Chamber (compare what he had to say) in 1930, all the more significant if one takes account of the fact that he has often been an 'unofficial' spokesman there.[82] Another thing to take stock of is the brief but violent criticism of Spirito's book *Critica dell'economia liberale* [*Critique of Liberal Economics*] published in the *Rivista di Politica Economica* <December 1930> by A. De Pietri Tonelli, given that this review is an organ of the Italian industrialists (cf. the editorship which was in the past in the hands of the Association of Limited Companies). Again, the noted orthodox economist P. Jannaccone, who tore Spirito to shreds in *Riforma Sociale* <December 1930>,[83] has been elected to the Academy. Cf. also Croce's note in the *Critica* of January 1931. From Spirito's publications that have appeared in *Nuovi Studi* it seems that up to now the only person to have accepted his theses *en bloc* is none other than that well-known political and economic adventurer Massimo Fovel. However, Spirito is allowed to make a fair amount of noise and take on positions of responsibility (given him, I believe, by Minister of State Bottai who founded the *Archive of Corporative Studies* with a broad participation of Spirito and Co.).

Spirito's conception of the state is not very clear and rigorous. Sometimes he even seems to be maintaining that before he became 'philosophy', no one had ever understood anything of the state and the state did not exist or was not a 'real' state and so forth. But since he wants to be historicist, when he bethinks himself he admits that <even> in the past the state existed, but now everything has changed and the state (or the concept of the state) has been enriched and put on 'quite different' speculative bases than in the past and since 'the more speculative a science is the more practical it is', it thus seems that these speculative bases must, *ipso facto*, become practical bases and the whole real

The Philosophy of Benedetto Croce

construction of the state must change because Spirito has changed its speculative bases (not of course the empirical man Spirito, but Ugo Spirito-Philosophy). Compare what is said on p.180 of *Critica dell'economia liberale*: 'My essay on Pareto was intended as an act of faith and goodwill. Faith in that through it I wished to begin to develop the programme of *Nuovi Studi* and thus the rapprochement of and effective collaboration between philosophy and science'. The inferences are then: philosophy = reality, hence also both science and economics, in other words Ugo Spirito = the radiant sun of the whole of philosophy-reality who invites specialist scientists to collaborate with him and bask in the principles of his sunshine, rather to be[84] this radiant sunshine itself so they may become 'true' scientists, in other words 'true' philosophers.

Since scientists do not want to let themselves do this and only a few let themselves be persuaded to enter into correspondence with him, this is why Spirito challenges them on his ground and, if they still do not accept, he smiles his sardonic and triumphant smile – they do not pick up the gauntlet because they are afraid or something of the like. Spirito cannot comprehend that scientists do not want to be bothered with him because he isn't worth the trouble and they have better things to do. Since he is 'philosophy' and philosophy = science and so on, these scientists are not 'true' scientists, or rather 'true' science has never existed and so on and so forth.

Volpicelli and Spirito, the editors of *Nuovi Studi*, the Bouvard and Pécuchet of philosophy, of politics, of economics, of law, of science etc., etc.[85] A fundamental problem: Spirito and Volpicelli's utopia consists in confusing the state with regulated society, a confusion that comes about for a <purely> 'rationalistic' concatenation of concepts: individual = society (the individual is not an 'atom' but the historical individuation of the whole of society), society = state, <therefore> individual = state.[86] The characteristic that differentiates this 'utopia' from the traditional utopias and from, in general, quests for the 'best state' is that Spirito and Volpicelli assume this 'fantasy' being of theirs is <already> in being, existing but not recognised by others than them, in whom the 'true truth' is deposited, while these others (especially the economists and in general the social scientists) understand nothing, are in 'error' and so on. By what 'devilment' it happens that only Spirito and Volpicelli possess this truth, while the others do not want it, has not yet been explained by the pair, but here and there is a glimmer of the means by which the twins maintain that the truth will have to become widespread and part of self-consciousness: it is the police (recall Gentile's speech at Palermo in 1924). For political reasons, it has been said to the masses: 'What you expect and was promised you by the charlatans, here – look! it already exists,' in other words the regulated society, economic equality, etc. Spirito and Volpicelli (behind Gentile who, however, is not as foolish as these two) have broadened this assertion, made it 'speculative', 'philosophised' it, put it in its proper place, and are fighting like stuffed lions against the whole world, which well knows what to think of all this. But a critique of this 'utopia' would require far different criticism, and have far different consequences than the more or less brilliant career of the two Ajaxes of 'actualism'; so it is that we are witnessing the current jousting-match. At any rate, the intellectual world well deserves to be under the heel of these two clowns, as the Milanese aristocracy remained so long under the heel of the triad. (The subscription for the marriage of Donna Franca could be compared with the act of homage to Franz Joseph in 1853; to go from Franz Joseph to Donna Franca indicates the depths plumbed by the Milanese aristocracy.)[87] One would also have to observe that Spirito and Volpicelli's conception is a logical derivation of the most stupid and 'rational' democratic theories. Again, it is linked to the conception of a 'human nature', identical and without development just like this was conceived of before Marx; according to this conception all are fundamentally equal in the realm of the Spirit [Spirito] (in this case the Holy Spirit [Spirito] and God the Father of all men).

This conception is expressed in Benedetto Croce's quotation 'from an old German dissertation' in the chapter 'On Italian Positivism' in *Cultura e Vita Morale* [*Culture and Moral Life*], p.45: 'Omnis enim Philosophia, cum ad communem hominum cogitandi facultatem revocet, per se democratica est; ideoque ab optimatibus non iniuria sibi existimatur perniciosa'.[88] This 'common faculty of thought', become 'human nature', has given rise to lots of utopias <of which> one sees traces in many sciences that begin from the concept of perfect human equality etc.

Q6§82.

46 Identification of Individual and State

To show that the new enunciations of 'speculative economy' of Spirito & Co's group are just sophistry, suffice it to recall that the so-called identification of individual and state is also the identification of state and individual; obviously an identity does not change whichever term comes first or second in the order in which one writes or hears it. On this account, to say that one must identify individual and state is less than nothing, it is sheer twaddle, if affairs really were as claimed. If by individual we mean 'egoism' in the narrow 'sordidly Jewish' sense,[89] the identification would only be a metaphorical way of accentuating the 'social' element of the individual, stating in other words that 'egoism' in the economic sense means something different from 'narrowly egoist'. It seems to me that, in this case, too, the question is that of the absence of a clear statement of the concept of the state and of the distinctions within it between civil society and political society, between dictatorship and hegemony, etc.

Q10II§7.

47 Notes on Italian Culture [1]. Science and Culture

The idealist philosophical currents (Croce and Gentile) have effected a first process of isolation of scientists (the natural or exact sciences) from the cultural world. Philosophy and science have been detached from each other and the scientists have lost much of their prestige. Another process of isolation has come about through the new prestige that has been given to Catholicism and through the formation of the neo-scholastic centre. Thus 'secular' scientists have religion and the most widely-diffused philosophy against them: they cannot but get enveloped in a cocoon and suffer from a 'malnutrition' of their scientific activity, which cannot develop in isolation from the general cultural world. Furthermore: since scientific activity in Italy is intimately linked to the state budget, which is not generous, one cannot, in compensation for the atrophying of scientific 'thought', of theory, even have a development of instrumental and experimental 'technique', for this demands ample means and funding. This disintegration of scientific unity, of general thought, is much felt: attempts have been made to remedy the situation by the development, even in this field, of a scientific 'nationalism', that is to say by upholding the thesis of the 'nationality' of science. But it is apparent that we are dealing with an extrinsic, external construction, good enough for congresses and oratorical celebrations but having no practical effectiveness. And yet Italian scientists are talented and, though having few means at their disposal, make unheard-of sacrifices and obtain admirable results. The greatest danger would seem to come from the neo-scholastic group which is threatening to absorb a great deal of scientific activity by sterilising it, as a reaction against Gentilian idealism. (Look at the organising activity of the National Research Council and the effectiveness it has had in developing scientific and technological activity, together with that of the scientific sections of the Italian Academy.)

Q14§38i.

48 Notes on Italian Culture [2]. Science

The speeches of the Italian scientists at the 1929 History of Science Exhibition have been collected together and may be seen in the volume edited by Gino Bargagli-Petrucci and published by Le Monnier. The volume also includes a speech by Father Gemelli that is a sign of the times as regards the audacity these good-for-nothing priests have taken upon themselves. (See the review of this speech in *Educazione Fascista* in 1932 and the article by Sebastiano Timpanaro in the *Italia Letteraria* of 11 September and 16 October 1931.)[90]

Q14§38iii.

49 Giovanni Gentile

On Gentile's philosophy, compare the article in *Civiltà Cattolica* 'Culture and Philosophy of the Unknown', 16 August 1930, which is of interest for seeing how formal scholastic logic can be appropriate for criticising the banal sophisms of an actual idealism that has pretensions to being the perfection of the dialectic. And in fact, why should 'formal' dialectics be superior to 'formal' logic? One is dealing only with logical instruments and a good, but old, tool may be superior to a more modern, but low quality, one; a good sailing boat is superior to a broken-down motorboat. In any case it is interesting to read the criticisms the neo-scholastics make of Gentile's thought (Fr Chiocchetti's books etc.).

One can say that Gentile, together with his followers Spirito, Volpicelli and their like (see the group that collaborate on the *Giornale critico della filosofia italiana*), have heralded a real and proper literary 'seventeenth centuryism', since in philosophy witticisms and ready-made phrases take the place of thought. However the most acute comparison is that of this group with the Bauers, satirised in the *Holy Family*: it is also the most fruitful in its literary possibilities (the magazine *Nuovi Studi* offers many varied opportunities for this development).

Q11§6.

50 G. Gentile and the Philosophy of Politics

Cf. the article published by G. Gentile in the *Spectator* of 3 November 1928 and then reprinted in *Educazione Fascista*: 'Philosophy that one does not think (!?) but creates and, because of this, philosophy that one states and asserts not through formulas but through action.' Since, from the time that humanity has been in existence, people have always 'created', 'action' has always existed, this philosophy has always existed, it has therefore been the philosophy of ... Nitti and Giolitti. Every state has 'two philosophies': what is stated in formulas and is a simple art of government, and what is asserted through action and is real philosophy, in other words history. The problem is that of seeing to what extent these two philosophies coincide, diverge, are in conflict, are individually and mutually internally consistent. Gentile's 'formula' in reality is merely the sophisticated mask for the political 'philosophy' better known under the name 'opportunism' and empiricism. If Bouvard and Pécuchet had known Gentile, they would have found the correct interpretation of their renovatory and revolutionary activity (in the non-corrupt sense of the term, as one might say) in his philosophy.

Q13§40.

51 Past and Present[4]. Gentile-Gioberti

On the subject of the importance that Gentile attaches to Gioberti for defining a permanent and significant continuity in national philosophy, two studies on Gioberti should be consulted: one by the Catholic writer Palhoriès (*Gioberti*, Paris 1929) and the other by the idealist Ruggero Rinaldi (*Gioberti e il problema religioso del Risorgimento* [*Gioberti and the Religious Question in the Risorgimento*], with a preface by Balbino Giuliano). Although they have different starting points, both arrive at similar demonstrations, viz. that Gioberti is not by any means the Italian Hegel,[91] but rather stays firmly within the field of ontologism and of Catholic orthodoxy. One has to bear in mind the important place – basically an episode of *Kulturkampf*[92] or an attempt at Catholic reform – that the idealist interpretation of Gioberti holds within 'Gentilianism'. Note also Giuliano's introduction to Rinaldi's book, since he seems to put forward some of the cultural problems posed by the

Concordat in Italy, in other words the question of how, once a political agreement has been stipulated between Church and state, there can be an 'agreement' between transcendence and immanence in the field of culture and philosophical thought.

Q7§79.

52 A Judgement on Gentile's 'Actual Idealism'

From Bruno Revel's article 'The VII Congress of Philosophy' in the *Italia Letteraria* of 23 November 1930: '*actual idealism* presents us once again with history as the supreme instance of justification. But pay heed: this *history* is pregnant with all the universal and positive values in themselves that used at one time to be isolated in a transcendent realm of essences and norms. This immanentist idealism, therefore, by making use of such values that in the course of time have been knowingly isolated and absolutised (valid in absolute terms only because they have been asserted as transcendent and pure), may allow itself to preach and teach morals almost ignoring its own incurable relativism and scepticism. And as social evolution, marked by a growing organisation pivoted on the factory, tends to steel-like and well-ordered rational centralisations, so actual idealism only lends a sheen of the absolute, of metaphysical dignity to this evolution in the light of its theory of the state.[93] And it thinks that by so doing it is conferring an absolute ethical character to the contingent industrial necessities of the modern state.' Cobbled together and contorted as may be, the influence of historical materialism is there to be seen.

Q7§11.

53 Past and Present[5]. Gentile's Philosophy

Savage attack on Gentile and his disciples unleashed in the October 1931 number of *Roma fascista*. Gentile is accused of 'high treason', of disloyal and fraudulent practices. A stop was officially put to the attack but it does not seem that the attacker (G.A. Fanelli) has been subject to sanctions, despite the extreme gravity of the charges, obviously not proven since Gentile has remained in the positions he occupied. Recall Paolo Orano's previous attack etc. It appears that Gentile's official position in national culture is not to remain undisputed and strengthen itself to the point of becoming an institution. Gentile's philosophy is not recognised as the official and national one, since this would mean the explicit subordination of Catholicism and its reduction to a subaltern task.

Q8§16.

54 Past and Present[6]. The Crocean Utopia

Cf. the note dealing with Croce's collaboration in 1919-20-21 (see) with Coppola's *Politica*,[94] in contrast with the approach adopted in 1915 in *Italia Nostra* towards Coppola, his ideology and his particular cast of mind. From this one may see and make a judgement of the 'utopian' nature of Croce's theoretical and practical activity, where 'utopian' is said in the sense that the consequences that depend on this stance of his are contrary to his 'intentions' as these latter are shown by his subsequent attitude to the consequences.

Croce thinks that what he does is 'pure science', pure 'history', pure 'philosophy', but in actual fact it is 'ideology'; he offers practical instruments of action to specific political groups. Then he is taken aback when they are not 'understood' as 'pure science' but 'deviated' from their real aim which was purely scientific. Cf., for example, the two chapters 'Philosophical Fixation' on p.296 and 'Political Facts and Historical Interpretations' on p.270 of the volume *Cultura e vita morale*. On p.296, Croce protests against Gentile's famous Palermo speech in 1924:[95] 'But if, at a certain place on our planet, the citizens of a state that previously used to debate their affairs thanks to those "methods of force" defined as criticism and oratory and association and voting and others of the like, have adopted the other usage of recourse to the cudgel and the dagger, and there are amongst them those who regret the old custom and are working to suppress the new modes, which they consider to be savage, what on Earth is the role fulfilled by the philosopher who, intervening in the contest, hands down the judgement that any force, including therefore cudgel and dagger, is a spiritual force?' and so on and so forth (the continuation is interesting and, if such be the case, is to be quoted). But he himself had written on p.270: 'To write poetry is one thing and to set to with one's fists is, in my opinion, another and who does not succeed in the first occupation may yet be very successful in the other, and it is not to be ruled out that the eventual rain of fists might even, in certain cases, be usefully and opportunely administered.' So wrote Croce in 1924 and it is probable that in 1924 Gentile, wishing to put that 'usefully and opportunely' in philosophical terms, had added the cudgel and even the dagger to fists. Nor was Croce to arrive solely at 'fisticuffs' and no further (moreover one can get killed even with fists and there is indeed a public security measure against 'forbidden knuckle fights'). Gentile has put into 'actualist' language Croce's proposition based on the distinction between logic and practice; for Croce this is crude, but meanwhile it is happening all the time and it is a fine excuse to want to be understood to perfection and then to justify oneself for having been misunderstood. One may compare what Croce has written in other chapters[96] on intolerance, the Inquisition, etc. to see his different states of mind – from the exclamation marks, which he said were also one of the means used by the Holy Inquisition to exert pressure on the will of others, he has had to return to the cudgel and dagger that has appeared before our eyes as a means of persuading us of the truth.

Q6§112.

55 The Theoretical Affirmation

Examine again the principle of Croce's (or accepted and developed by him) of the 'volitional nature of the theoretical affirmation' (cf. on this subject the chapter 'Freedom of

Conscience and of Science' in *Cultura e vita morale*, pp.95 et seq.).[97]

Q10II§41xv.

56 Actualism, Ideology and Philosophy

Actual idealism makes ideology and philosophy coincide verbally (this being, in the last analysis, nothing other than one of the aspects it postulates of the superficial unity between real and ideal, between theory and practice etc.) and this represents a degradation of traditional philosophy with respect to the height to which Croce had taken it with the so-called dialectic of 'distincts'. This degradation is exceptionally clear in the developments (or regressions) that actual idealism shows at the hands of Gentile's disciples: the review *Nuovi Studi* of Ugo Spirito and A. Volpicelli is the most conspicuous document of this phenomenon. The unity of ideology and philosophy, when asserted in this form, creates a new form of sociologism, i.e. one which is neither history nor philosophy but a set of abstract verbal schemes, supported by a tedious and parrot-like phraseology. Croce's resistance to this tendency is truly 'heroic': alive within Croce is the knowledge that all the movements of modern thought lead to a triumphal revaluation of the philosophy of praxis, i.e. to the overthrow of the traditional position of philosophical problems[98] and to the dissolution of philosophy as traditionally understood. Croce is resisting the pressure of historical reality with all his strength, having an exceptional awareness of the dangers and of the appropriate means of obviating them. The study of his writings from 1919 to now is, for this reason, of the greatest sigificance. His preoccupation was born with the world war, which he himself stated was the 'war of historical materialism'.[99] His '*au dessus [de la mêlée]*' position was already, in a certain sense, an index of this preoccupation and represented a position of alarm (during the war, philosophy and ideology were joined in frenzied matrimony). Even Croce's attitude towards books such as those of De Man, Zibordi and so on cannot be explained in any other way given that they are in strident contradiction with his pre-war ideological and practical positions.

This shift of Croce's from the 'critical' position to one that is tendentially practical and preparatory to effective political action (within the limits allowed by circumstances and by Croce's social position) is highly significant. What importance can his book on the *History of Italy* have had? Something can be deduced from Bonomi's book on Bissolati, from that by Zibordi quoted above, from Schiavi's preface to the book by De Man. The De Man book, too, serves as a bridge.[100]

One must however recall Orazio Raimondo's letter, quoted by G. Castellano in his *Introduzione allo studio delle opere di Benedetto Croce* [*Introduction to the Study of Croce's Works*].[101] The letter shows the influence that Croce exercised in certain circles, penetrating through channels that remained subject to no control. And this is Raimondo, the freemason, truly soaked in masonic ideology through to the marrow and democratic '*à la française*', as comes out in many of his orations but especially in that of the defence of the Tiepolo woman (who murdered the army batman Polidori [actual name Polimanti]) where masonic theism appears in all its manifest evidence.

Q10II§59iv.

57 Croce on De Man

The judgements passed by Croce on De Man's *Il superamento* [*The Supersession*][102] shows that in his present stance the immediate 'practical' element has complete mastery over his theoretical and scientific interests and preoccupations. De Man represents in fact a derivation from the psychoanalytic current and the whole presumed originality of his research comes from the employment of a psychoanalytic terminology that has been tacked on from the outside. The same observation can be made for De Ruggiero, who has reviewed not only *Il Superamento* but also *La gioia del lavoro* [*The Joy of Labour*] and followed this up with a savage, but somewhat hurried and superficial, attack on Freud and psychoanalysis, without however having pointed out that De Man is strictly dependent on them.

Q10II§26.

58 Henri De Man

From Arturo Masoero's article 'A Non-Hedonist American'[103] in the February 1931 issue of *Economia*, it turns out that many of the ideas expressed by H. De Man in his *Gioia del lavoro* and thence also in other books of his are taken from the theories of Thorstein Veblen, the American economist. Veblen has introduced some sociological principles of positivism, especially those of A. Comte and Spencer, into economic science; in particular he wants to bring evolutionism into economic science. Thus, what in Veblen we find as the 'instinct of workmanship' De Man calls the 'creative instinct'. W. James outlined the notion of an 'instinct of constructiveness' in 1890 and Voltaire had already spoken of a mechanical instinct.[104] (Compare De Man's crude conception of 'instinct' with what Marx wrote on the instinct of the bee, and on what distinguishes the human race from this instinct.)[105]

But it appears that De Man has also taken from Veblen the crude and dumbfounding conception, on which he insists so much in the *Gioia del lavoro*, of an 'animism' in workers. Masoero explains Veblen's conception as follows: 'Among primitive peoples, mythical interpretation ceases to be an obstacle and often becomes an aid as regards the development of the techniques of stock-rearing and agriculture. For it cannot but help this development if plants and animals are thought of as having a soul or even divine characteristics, since from such a consideration come that care and attention that can lead to technical improvements and innovations. An animistic mentality is, on the other hand, decidedly contrary to technical progress in manufacturing, to the deployment of the instinct of the worker on inert matter. Thus Veblen explains how in Denmark agricultural technique was already advanced at the beginning of the neolithic era while manufacturing technique remained non-existent for a long period. At the present time the instinct of the worker, no longer hindered by belief in the intervention of elements of providence and mystery, must be joined to a positive spirit and achieve that progress in the arts of industry that defines the modern era.'

De Man thus seems to have taken from Veblen the idea of an 'animism of the worker' that Veblen believes existed in the neolithic era, but does so no more, and to have rediscovered it, with great originality, in the modern worker.

One may note, given these Spencerian origins of De Man's, the coherence shown by Croce who has seen in him someone who has superseded Marxism etc. Between Spencer and Freud, who goes back to a still more mysterious form of sensationalism than that of the eighteenth century,[106] De Man really has deserved to be exalted by Croce and see himself proposed for study by Italians of intelligence. A translation of Veblen on the initiative of Minister Bottai is being announced. In any case, this article of Masoero's has the essential bibliography attached. As is apparent in the article, there is a certain influence of Marxism in Veblen who, in turn, seems to me to have had an influence on the theorisations of Ford.

Q7§32.

59 Sorel, Proudhon, De Man[1][107]

In certain ways, De Man may be compared to Sorel, but what a difference between the two of them! De Man gets absurdly tangled up in the history of ideas and lets himself get blinded by superficial appearances. If a criticism may be made of Sorel, it is exactly from the opposite direction – that he devotes too minute an analysis to the substance of an idea and often loses his sense of proportion. Sorel finds that a series of post-war events are Proudhonian in nature; Croce finds that De Man marks a return to Proudhon but, typically, De Man does not understand the post-war events singled out by Sorel. For Sorel, what is of a Proudhonian nature is 'spontaneous' creation by the people, while whatever is of bureaucratic origin is 'orthodox' because in front of him there stand like obsessions, on one hand, the bureaucracy of German organisation and, on the other, Jacobinism, both of them phenomena of mechanical centralisation whose levers of command are in the hands of a band of functionaries. De Man remains in reality a typical example of the pedantry of the Belgian Labour bureaucracy; everything of his, even his enthusiasm, is pedantic. He thinks he has made great discoveries because he uses some 'scientific' formula to repeat the description of a series of more or less individual facts. It is the typical manifestation of positivism to repeat the fact, describe it, generalise it in a formula and then make of the formulation of the fact a law of the fact itself. For Sorel, as may be seen from the *Nuova Antologia* essay, what matters in Proudhon is the psychological orientation, not really his practical stance, on which to be truthful Sorel never explicitly commits himself. Proudhon's psychological orientation consists in 'merging' with the popular sentiments (peasants and artisans) that concretely swarm from the real situation that the state-economic set-ups create for the people, in 'immersing' himself in them so as to comprehend and express them in juridical, rational form; this or that interpretation, or all of them taken together, may be wrong, or hare-brained or even ridiculous, but the overall approach is one that produces most in the way of praiseworthy consequences. De Man's attitude is instead 'scientistic': he bows before the people not in order to comprehend them in disinterested fashion, but to 'theorise' their feelings, to construct pseudo-scientific schemes; not to put himself at one with them and extract juridical-educational principles, but to act like the zoologist observing the insect world, like Maeterlinck observing bees and termites.[108]

De Man has the pedantic pretension of highlighting in close up the so-called 'psychological and ethical values' of the workers' movement; but can that, as De Man claims, mean a peremptory and radical refutation of the philosophy of praxis? That would be like saying that underlining the fact that the great majority of people are still at the Ptolemaic stage means refuting the Copernican doctrine, or that folklore should replace science. The philosophy of praxis maintains that people become conscious of their social position on the ideological terrain; has he maybe excluded the people from this way of acquiring consciousness of themselves? But it is an obvious comment that the ideological world is (taken as a whole) backward as compared with the technical relations of production. A negro just arrived from Africa can become one of Ford's employees, while still staying a fetishist for a long time and while still remaining convinced that cannibalism is a normal, justified way of gaining nourishment. After carrying out an investigation on this, what conclusions could De Man draw? That the philosophy of praxis should study objectively what people think of themselves and others on this subject is beyond doubt, but must it supinely accept as eternal this way of thinking? Would this not represent the worst types of mechanicism and fatalism? The task of any historical initiative is to modify the preceding stages of culture, to homogenise culture at a higher level than it was and so on. In reality, the philosophy of praxis has always worked on that terrain that De Man believes he has discovered, but it has worked there to innovate, not to preserve in supine fashion. De Man's 'discovery' is a commonplace and his refutation a not particularly savoury rehash.

It is this 'conservativism' that explains the modest success that De Man has enjoyed in Italy, at least in certain circles (especially among Crocean-revisionists and Catholics). An announcement was made of De Man's main book by Croce in *La Critica* in 1928 and De Ruggiero reviewed it in 1929; reviews in *Civiltà Cattolica* and *Il Leonardo* in 1929; G. Zibordi mentions it in his book on Prampolini; in a note on its forthcoming books the Laterza publishing house highly commended Schiavi's translation while his own preface was lavish in its praise; *I problemi del Lavoro*, which reproduced the book's final theses that the Schiavi translation did not contain, published articles in its support. The *Italia Letteraria* of 11 August 1929 carried a review by Umberto Barbaro, who wrote: '... a critique of Marxism which, if one makes use of the previous "revisions" of an economic nature, is in principle based on a tactical question (*sic*) related to the psychology of the masses of workers'. 'This is certainly not one of the weightier and even less is it one of the more systematic of the many attempts to go "*au delà*" [beyond] Marxism. (The translator, the well-known lawyer Alessandro Schiavi, introduces – quite justifiably moreover (!) – a title modified somewhat in the Crocean sense of "supersession", since De Man himself considers his own position as being a necessary antithesis for reaching a higher synthesis.) Among other things, these reservations regard the critique's being predominantly based precisely on that mysterious and fleeting, although certainly fascinating, pseudo-science of psychology. The book is rather defeatist on the "movement" and at times even supplies arguments to the tendencies it wants to combat: it provides fascism with a number of observations about the states of feelings and "complexes" (in the Freudian sense) of the workers, from which they derive ideas on the "joy of labour" and "artisan" production, while it concedes to communism and fascism together that the arguments in defence of democracy and reformism are of but little effectiveness.'

Paolo Milano's review in the September 1929 *Italia che scrive* singles out two findings in De Man's work: 1) the mass of psychological observations on the stages of development, deviations and contradictory reactions of the workers' and socialist movement of the last few years, in short an intelligent collection of social *data* and *documentation* – according to Milano the analysis of the reformist evolution of the working masses on one hand and the bosses' organisations on the other is rich and satisfactory; and 2) the theoretical discussion from which there should spring the 'supersession of Marxism' (for De Man it is, in precise terms, a 'repudiation' of Marxism). In its *mechanicist* and *rationalistic* base (!) the philosophy of praxis has for De Man been overtaken by the most recent investigations, which have assigned to rational concatenation merely a place – and not even the most important one at that – in the series of causes of human acts. To the mechanical reaction (!) of the Marxist dialectic, modern science (!) has victoriously (!) substituted a *psychological reaction*, whose intensity is not proportional (?) to the causal agent. For Milano, 'It is by now clear that any critique whatsoever of the Marxist conception of history automatically leads us to the formulation of the conflict between the materialist and the idealist interpretations of the world and, in essence, to assign a priority to being or to knowing.' De Man has avoided this problem or, rather, has stopped half way, pronouncing in favour of a conception, put forward by Adler, of human activity as generated by 'psychological agents' and social 'complexes', in other words he is influenced by Freudian psychology, most of all through the applications to social doctrines, as attempted by Adler. (Perhaps the Adler is Max Adler? But in what writings?)[109]

Milano goes on: 'One further knows that psychology is a shifting ground in historical enquiry and is even more equivocal in the type of research of which we are speaking. For psychological phenomena lend themselves to being indicated from time to time either as volitional tendencies or as material factors. De Man too oscillates between these opposing interpretations and thus avoids adopting a position on the crucial point of the conflict. An acute reader will judge the origin of De Man's work indeed to be really psychological; born of a crisis of lack of confidence and the realisation that Marxist doctrines taken in their entirety are insufficient to explain the phenomena offered to the notice of the author during the course of his routine political work. Despite the best of intentions, the tenor of the book does not overcome this documented and agitated realisation, nor does it succeed in a theoretical refutation at an adequate level or with the "necessary" vigour'. He finishes thus: 'Proof is given by the last chapter, where the treatment of the subject would like to conclude by making some recommendation as to practical political conduct. Equidistant from the two extremes of the tactic of the seizure of power and an exclusively idealist apostolate, De Man advises a generic education of the masses and in so doing puts himself outside that socialism of which he had yet declared himself a faithful and enlightened follower.'

The article in *Civiltà Cattolica* (7 September 1929) 'Towards social peace' by Fr Brucculeri, which comments on the famous commendation of the Congregation of the Council in the conflict between Catholic workers and industrialists in the Roubaix-Tourcoing region,[110] contains this extract: 'Marxism, as is demonstrated in the finest pages of De Man, has been a materialising current of the modern working-class world.' In other words, De Man's pages are all praiseworthy, but some even more so. (This stance the Catholics have adopted towards De Man's tendency may explain why Giuseppe Prezzolini, in the *Pégaso* of September 1930, in mentioning Philip's volume on the American working-class movement[111] defines Philip as a 'Christian democrat' even though the book gives neither such a definition nor justification for it.)

The *Civiltà Cattolica* numbers of 5 October and 16 November 1929 publish an extended essay on De Man's book. His work is considered 'despite its deficiencies, the most important and, let it also be said, inspired of all those up to now found in anti-Marxist literature'. Towards the end of the essay there is this overall impression: 'Although the author (De Man) has overcome a crisis of thought, rejecting Marxism with a magnanimous gesture, he is still however wavering and his intelligence, eager for truth, is not satisfied to the full. He is knocking at the door of truth, gathering the rays, but not pushing forward to plunge into the light. Our hopes go out to De Man so that, overcoming his crisis, he may raise himself up, like the great Bishop of Tagaste,[112] from that divine reflection which is the moral law of the soul, to the infinite divine, to the everlasting splendid source of *all that the universe holds scattered through its maze.*'[113]

Q11§66 (excerpt).

60 Sorel, Proudhon, De Man[2]

<Cf. p.78>.[114] The *Nuova Antologia* of 1 December 1928 has published a long essay by Georges Sorel under the title 'Last Reflections (Unpublished Posthumous Essay)'. It is one of his writings of 1920, which should have served as a preface to a collection of articles that he had published in Italian journals from 1910 to 1920 (then published by

Corbaccio, Milan, as *L'Europa sotto la tormenta* [*Storm-Tossed Europe*], edited by Mario Missiroli, with possibly quite different criteria from those that would have been applied in 1920 when the preface was written; it would be useful to see if the volume contains articles like those devoted to Fiat together with some others). The delay in publishing the book is not independent of the ups and downs of Sorel's standing in Italy, which was due to a series of more or less unintentional ambivalences and is now at a very low ebb: there already exists an anti-Sorelian literature.

The essay published by *Nuova Antologia* sums up all Sorel's merits and defects. Though it jumps around and is tortuous, inconsistent, superficial, sybilline and so on, it gives or suggests original points of view, finds unconsidered yet real connections, obliges one to think and enrich the argument.

What is the meaning of the piece? This emerges clearly from the whole article, which was written in 1920; *Nuova Antologia*'s slip of a prefatory note (perhaps penned by this same Missiroli, whose intellectual loyalty is best not trusted) is a patent falsification that ends thus '... a writer, who assigned intellectual and political primacy in Europe to post-war Italy'. But to which Italy? Something explicit on this might either be said by Missiroli or be found in Sorel's letters to him, but in any case may be inferred from numerous articles of Sorel's. (According to what has been announced, the letters should be published, but will not be or at least not in an uncut form.) From this essay it is useful, as an aid to memory, to comment on some of the points, bearing in mind that the whole piece is very important for an understanding of Sorel and his post-war stance.

a) Bernstein has maintained (*Socialismo teorico e social-democrazia pratica*, French translation, pp.53-54) that a superstitious respect for the Hegelian dialectic led Marx to prefer revolutionary theses very close to the Jacobin, Babouvist or Blanquist tradition rather than the constructions of the *utopians*;[115] in that case, however, one does not understand whyever the *Manifesto* makes no mention of the Babouvist literature that Marx was undoubtedly acquainted with. Andler is of the opinion (Vol.II of his edition of the

Manifesto, p.191) that Marx makes a very contemptuous allusion to the Conspiracy of the Equals when he speaks of the crude and universal asceticism noticeable in the earliest proletarian demands made after the French Revolution.

b) It seems that Marx was never able to rid himself completely of the Hegelian idea of history, according to which different epochs succeed one another in humankind, following the order of the development of the spirit which seeks to reach the perfect realisation of universal reason. To the doctrine of his master he adds that of class struggle; although people know only social wars, into which they are thrust by their economic antagonisms, they co-operate unconsciously in a work that only a metaphysician hypothesises. This is a very hazardous hypothesis for Sorel to make and he does not justify it, though it is obviously very dear to him because of both his exaltation of Russia and his prediction regarding Italy's civil function. (Here, on this juxtaposition between Russia and Italy, one must draw attention to D'Annunzio's attitude, almost simultaneously [with Sorel], in the manuscripts he circulated in the spring of 1920.[116] Was Sorel aware of this stance of D'Annunzio's? Only Missiroli could answer this.) According to Sorel, 'Marx had such great confidence in the subordination of history to the laws of the development of the Spirit that he taught that after the fall of capitalism, the evolution towards *perfect Communism* would be produced without the agency of a class struggle (*Letter on the Gotha Programme*). It seems that Marx, like Hegel, believed that the different moments of evolution are manifested in different countries, each of which is especially appropriate to each of these moments (see the Preface of 21 January 1882 to a Russian translation of the *Manifesto*). He never made an explicit statement of his doctrine, so many Marxists are persuaded that all stages of capitalist evolution must be produced in the same form in all modern peoples. These Marxists are not sufficiently Hegelian.'

c) The question: before or after 1848? Sorel does not understand the significance of this problem despite the literature on the subject (albeit of a second-hand stall variety) and mentions the curious (sic) change produced in

Marx's mind at the close of 1850. In March he signed a manifesto of revolutionaries[117] who had taken refuge in London, which outlined the programme of revolutionary agitation to be undertaken in expectation of a new, not far distant, social upheaval – Bernstein finds this worthy of the first thing that comes to the mind of coffee-house revolutionaries (*Socialismo teorico* etc., p.51) – whereas he later convinces himself that the revolution born through the crisis of 1847 finished with that crisis. Now, the years subsequent to 1848 were of an unparalleled prosperity; the first necessary condition for a planned revolution – a proletariat reduced to idleness and ready for combat – was therefore lacking (cf. Andler, I, pp.55-6, but what edition?). In this way the idea is said to have been born among Marxists of increasing poverty which should have served to frighten the workers and induce them to fight, in view of a probable worsening even in a prosperous situation. (An infantile explanation, contradicted by the facts, even if it is true that the theory of increasing impoverishment was made into an instrument of this type, an argument of immediate persuasion: moreover, was this arbitrary? On when the theory of growing impoverishment was born, see the publication by Robert Michels.)[118]

d) On Proudhon. 'Proudhon belonged to that part of the bourgeoisie nearest the proletariat; on account of this, Marxists have been able to accuse him of being a bourgeois, while shrewder writers consider him an admirable prototype for our (i.e. French) peasantry and artisans (cf. Daniel Halévy in the 3 January 1913 number of *Débats*).' This judgement of Sorel's may be accepted. And this is how he explains Proudhon's 'juridical' mentality: 'Because of the weakness of their resources, the peasants, the owners of the smallest factories, the small businessmen are forced into a bitter defence of their interests in the courts. A socialism that aims at protecting the strata in the lower reaches of the economic scale is naturally destined to attach great importance to *legal safeguards* [*sicurezza del diritto*]; and such a tendency is particularly marked among those writers, like Proudhon, whose heads are stuffed with recollections of country life.' And he goes on to make other points to strengthen this not entirely convincing analysis. Proudhon's juridical mentality is linked to his anti-Jacobinism, to literary memories of the French Revolution and to the *Ancien Régime* that is supposed to have led to the Jacobin explosion precisely because of the arbitrary nature of justice. The juridical mentality forms the substance of Proudhon's petty bourgeois reformism and his social origins contributed to forming it for another and 'higher' nexus of concepts and feelings. In this analysis Sorel sinks into the mentality of the 'orthodox' whom he so despises. It is strange that Sorel, having such a conviction regarding Proudhon's social tendency, should then exalt him and at times put him forward as the model or fount of principles for the modern proletariat. If Proudhon's juridical mentality has this origin why should workers be bothered with the question of a 'new legality', of a new set of 'legal safeguards' etc.?

At this point, one has the impression that Sorel's essay has been mutilated and exactly the part that deals with the factory movement in Italy is missing. From the published text, one can imagine that Sorel found in the internal commissions movement (which attempted to control factory regulations and in general an internal factory 'legislation' that was uniquely dependent on the untrammelled will of the entrepreneurs) the agency corresponding to the needs that Proudhon reflected for the peasants and artisans. The essay as published is incoherent and incomplete; as is usual with Sorel its conclusion regarding Italy ('Many reasons had long led me to suppose that it is up to Italy to provide what a Hegelian would term the *Weltgeist* [spirit of the world]. Thanks to Italy, the light of the new times will not be extinguished.') is not demonstrated, not even by hints and allusions. The last note mentions the workers' and peasants' councils in Germany 'that I considered conformed to the spirit of Proudhon' and refers readers to the *Materiali per una teoria*[119] etc. (pp.164 and 394). It would be of interest to know if the essay really has been cut and by whom: whether at first hand by Missiroli or by others.

1st Note. Sorel as a 'revolutionary intellectual' figure[120] cannot be understood except in the context of post-1870 France, just as Proudhon cannot be understood without the 'anti-Jacobin panic' of the age of the Restoration. 1870 <and> 71 saw France suffer two terrible routs – the national defeat that weighed on the bourgeois intellectuals[121] and the popular defeat of the Commune that weighed on the revolutionary intellectuals. The first created types like Clémenceau, the quintessence of French nationalist Jacobinism, while the second created the anti-Jacobin Sorel and the 'apolitical' syndicalist movement. Sorel's curious anti-Jacobinism – sectarian, mean and anti-historical – is a consequence of the popular blood-letting of 1871[122] (see on this subject the 'Lettre à M. Daniel Halévy' in the *Mouvement Socialiste*, 16 August and 15 September 1907) which sheds a strange light on his *Reflections on Violence*.[123] The popular blood-letting of 1871 severed the umbilical cord between the 'new people' and the tradition of 1793; Sorel would have wished to be the representative of this break between people and historic Jacobinism, but did not succeed in so becoming etc.

2nd Note. Sorel's post-war writings have a certain importance for the history of western culture. He attributes a whole series of this period's ideological foundations and standpoints to Proudhon's thought. Why has he been able to do this? Is this judgement of his absolutely arbitrary? And given Sorel's acumen as a historian of ideas which, at least to a great extent, excludes this arbitrariness, from what cultural experiences did he set off, and is all this not of importance for an overall assessment of his work? It is beyond doubt that one must go back to studying Sorel to grasp what, beneath the parasitic incrustations that intellectuals and dilettante admirers have deposited on his thought, it contains of a more a permanent and essential nature. It must be borne in mind that there has been a great deal of exaggeration about Sorel's 'austerity' and intellectual and moral 'seriousness'. It emerges from his letters to Croce that he did not always conquer a tendency towards vanity; this is to be seen, for example, in the embarrassed tone in which he tries to explain to Croce his (hesitant and still platonic) membership of Valois's 'Proudhon Circle' or his flirting with some of the younger elements of the clerical and monarchical tendency.[124] Yet again, there is much of the dilettante, of the 'not wanting ever to be fully engaged', and hence much intrinsic irresponsibility in Sorel's 'political' stances, which were never purely political but 'cultural-political', 'intellectual-political', *au dessus de la mêlée*. Sorel too could be accused of similar things to those contained in the pamphlet of one of his disciples *I misfatti degli intellettuali* [*The Misdeeds of the Intellectuals*].[125] He himself was a 'pure' intellectual and one must therefore, by careful analysis, distinguish between what in his work is brilliant, superficial, accessory, bound to the requirements of extemporary polemics, and the substantial, the 'real meat', so that, when thus defined, it can be admitted to the circle of modern culture.

3rd Note. In 1929, after publication of a letter in which Sorel spoke of Oberdan,[126] articles rained down in protest at the expressions he had used in his letters to Croce and he was subject to scathing criticism (an article at the time written by Arturo Stanghellini in *L'Italia Letteraria* was particularly violent). The correspondence was halted in the subsequent number of *La Critica* and recommenced, without any reference to the incident, with some novelties. Several names were printed only by their initials and one got the impression that a number of letters were not published or carried deletions. From this point journalists began a new evaluation of Sorel and his relations with Italy.

Q11§66 (excerpt).

61 Sorel, Proudhon, De Man [3]

(continuation of p.70a et seq.)[127] In 1932 Corbaccio Editions of Milan published Mario Missiroli's 'announced' selection of articles written by Georges Sorel for Italian newspapers between 1910 and 1921 under the title *L'Europa sotto la tormenta* [*Storm-Tossed Europe*]. Sorel's essay, published in the *Nuova Antologia* of 1 December 1928 under the title 'Last Reflections (Unpublished Posthumous Essay)', is not reproduced in the volume, although by way of preface it had been announced as having been written. Furthermore, the choice of articles reproduced precluded the printing of this preface, which has nothing to do with the book. It is quite obvious that Missiroli has not kept to the guidelines that Sorel must have given him for making the selection and that may be found in the discarded 'preface'. The selection was made for 'use of the uninitiated', taking account of only one of the many lines of Sorel's thought, which one cannot say the author considered the most important one since otherwise the 'preface' would have had quite a different tone. The selection has instead a preface by Missiroli that is one-sided and in strident contrast with the censored one, of which – quite disloyally – no mention is made.

Q11§69.

62 The Movement and the End[128]

Is it possible to keep a movement alive and efficient without the perspective of mediated and non-mediated ends? Under the appearance of an 'orthodox' interpretation of dialectics, Bernstein's claim that the movement is everything and the end nothing hides a mechanicist conception of life and historical movement. The forces of humanity are considered passive and unaware, an element not dissimilar to material things; the vulgar evolutionist concept in its naturalistic sense is here substituted for that of development and dynamic.

This observation is all the more interesting in that Bernstein has taken his weapons from the armoury of idealist revisionism (forgetting the glosses on Feuerbach) that should instead have brought him to the assessment of human intervention (people undertaking activity and therefore pursuing certain mediated and non-mediated ends) as being decisive in the dynamic of history (in the conditions they are given, it must be understood). But on analysing this more deeply, one sees that Bernstein and his followers do not totally exclude human intervention at least implicitly (which really would be too stupid), but rather admit it, though only unilaterally, since it is admitted as the 'thesis' but excluded as the 'antithesis'. While human intervention is considered efficient as thesis, in other words in the moment of resistance and conservation, it is rejected as antithesis, in other words as initiative and as antagonistic progressive thrust. There can exist 'ends' for resistance and conservation (these 'resistance and conservation' factors are ends requiring a special civil and military organisation, active control of the adversary, timely intervention to prevent this enemy reinforcing itself too much and so on), but not for progress and innovatory initiative. We are here dealing with none other than a sophisticated theorisation of passivity, with a 'ruse' (in Vico's sense of a 'ruse of providence') by which the 'thesis' intervenes to weaken the 'antithesis', since it is precisely the antithesis (which presupposes the reawakening of latent and sleeping forces to be spurred on vigorously) that needs to set itself ends, both mediated and non-mediated, in order to strengthen its movement towards supersession. Without the perspective of concrete ends, a movement cannot exist at all.

Q16§26.

E CROCE'S POSITION IN THE INTELLECTUAL WORLD

63 The Party Man

Croce as the party man. Distinction of the concept of a party. 1) The party as the practical organisation (or practical tendency), that is as the instrument for the solution of a problem or a group of problems of national and international life. In this sense Croce has never explicitly belonged to any of the liberal groups; rather, he has explicitly fought against the very idea and against the fact of permanently organised parties. ('The Party as Judge and as Prejudice', in *Cultura e Vita Morale*, an essay published in one of the first numbers of the Florentine *Unità*)[129] and pronounced in favour of political movements that do not give themselves a definite 'dogmatic', permanent, organic 'programme', but work towards the resolution of immediate political problems as they come up. Amongst the various liberal tendencies, it was furthermore the conservative one, represented by the *Giornale d'Italia* that Croce sympathised with. For a long time not only did the *Giornale d'Italia* publish articles from *Critica* before the numbers of the review came out, but it had a 'monopoly' over the letters that Croce wrote from time to time to express his opinions on political issues and cultural policy which were of interest to him and on which he considered it necessary to make a pronouncement. In the post-war period, *La Stampa* too printed pre-publication extracts from *Critica* (or Croce's writings contained in Academic Proceedings), but not the letters which continued to be published first by the *Giornale d'Italia* and which only then were reprinted by *La Stampa* and other newspapers. 2) The party as general ideology, superior to the various more immediate groupings. In actual fact, the liberal party's mode of being in Italy after 1876 was that of presenting itself before the country as an 'extended battle order' of fractions and national and regional groups. All were fractions of political liberalism – the liberal Catholicism represented by the *popolari*[130] as much as the nationalists (Croce was a collaborator on A. Rocco and F. Coppola's *Politica*), the monarchist unions as much as the republican party and a large part of the socialist area, the radical democrats as much as the conservatives, Sonnino-Salandra as much as Giolitti, Orlando, Nitti and Co.[131] Croce was the theoretician of what all these groups and grouplets, cliques and mafias[132] had in common, the head of a central propaganda office which all these groups benefited from and made use of, the national leader of the cultural movements which sprang up to breathe new life into old political forms.

As has been observed elsewhere, Croce shared with Giustino Fortunato this office of national leader of liberal democratic culture. From 1900 to 1914 and even after (but as its resolution) Croce and Fortunato appeared as the inspirers (as the leaven) of every serious new movement among the young that aimed at renewing the overall political 'conduct' and life of the bourgeois parties: thus it was for the

Voce, *Unità*, *Azione Liberale*, the *Patria* (of Bologna) and so on. Piero Gobetti's *Rivoluzione Liberale* marked a fundamental innovation: the term 'liberalism' came to be interpreted in a more 'philosophical' or more abstract sense, and the concept of liberty in the traditional terms of the individual personality went on to that of liberty in terms of the collective personality of the great social groups, and of the competition no longer between individuals but between groups. One must bear in mind this office of national leader of liberalism in order to understand how Croce widened the circle of his guiding influence beyond the shores of Italy, on the basis of one element of his 'propaganda': the revisionist one.

Q10II§59i.

64 Croce in the Intellectual Hierarchy

Croce's relative position in the intellectual hierarchy of the dominant class has changed in the wake of the Concordat and the fusion that has taken place of the two great divisions of that class into one moral unit. Those in charge of affairs now have a double labour of education before them: education of the new leadership personnel who must be 'transformed' and assimilated – and education of the Catholics who have, at least, to be subordinated (in certain conditions, even subordination means education). The mass entry of the Catholics into state life after the Concordat (an entry this time as Catholics and in as much as they are Catholics and, in fact, with cultural privileges) has made the work of the 'transformism' of the new forces of democratic origin much more difficult. That Gentile, unlike Croce, has not understood the problem shows the difference in feeling for and sense of the nation that exists between the two philosophers. That if Gentile has understood the problems then he has, at the least, put himself in a situation of not being able to do anything outside work like that of the Popular University of Cultural Institutes[133] (his disciples' irate articles in *Nuovi Studi* against Catholicism evoke but little response) demonstrates his reduction to a wretched condition of intellectual subalternity. It is not in fact a question of an 'analytical' education, i.e. of an 'instruction', of a stockpiling of notions, but of a 'synthetic' education, of the penetration of a conception of the world that has become a norm of life, of a 'religion' in the Crocean sense. That the Concordat had posed the problem, multiplying and complicating it, had been understood by Croce, as is apparent from his speech to the Senate. Moreoever, it is exactly the Concordat, through its introduction into state life of a great mass of Catholics as such, and as such enjoying certain privileges, that has posed the problem of the education of the ruling class not in terms of the 'ethical state' but in terms of an educative 'civil society', i.e. of an education through 'private' initiative entering into competition with that of the Catholics which now occupies such a great part of civil society and which does so under special conditions.

To understand to just what extent Croce's activity, in all its perseverant inflexibility, is appreciated by the more responsible, far-sighted (and conservative) part of the dominant class, on top of the 'prediction' quoted from Missiroli (and one has to understand what of an implicit critical sense the term 'prediction' may mean in this case), it is useful to recall a series of articles published by Camillo Pellizzi in Mino Maccari's review *Il Selvaggio* (now coming out in Rome in the form of a monthly, but it would be of interest to analyse the whole collection in all its different phases). Here below is an exact copy of the text of an extract, commenting on one of these articles of Pellizzi's in the 29 May 1932 *Italia Letteraria*, taken from the 'Press Review' compiled by Corrado Pavolini: '*Believe in few things*, but believe in them! This very fine maxim may be read in the last number (1 May) of *Il Selvaggio*. I am sorry for Camillo Pellizzi, one of the first fascists, a man of integrity, of real sterling value and of a very acute intellect, but the muddled style of his last open letter to Maccari – "Fascism as Liberty" – makes me doubt whether the concepts he is talking about are very clear in his mind, or, if they are clear whether they are considered too abstractly for any practical application. "Fascism was born as the supreme effort of a civilised people, the most deeply civilised people of all in fact, in order to realise a form of civilised communism. Or in other words, to resolve the problem of communism within the greater problem of civilisation; but since there is no civilisation without the spontaneous manifestation of those ancient and ever renewed individual values of which we have spoken, we conclude that, in its deepest and universal meaning, fascism is a *free communism* in which, to be quite clear, the means, the empirical organism, the instrument of action that responds to the problem of a specific moment of history is communistic or collectivistic, while the real end, the final destination, is civilisation, or, in the sense already stated and repeated, freedom." This is undigested philosophical language. "Believe in few things ..." For example, to believe simplistically that fascism is *not* communism, and never in any sense of the word either concretely or figuratively has been, may turn out to be more "useful" than labouring after the pursuit of definitions which are too clever by half not to be, in the last analysis, ambiguous and harmful. (There is, after all, Spirito's speech at the corporative Congress at Ferrara ...).'[134]

It comes out quite clearly that Pellizzi's series of articles in *Il Selvaggio* has been suggested by Croce's latest book and is an attempt to absorb Croce's position within a new position that Pellizzi considers superior and capable of resolving all the antinomies. In actual fact, Pellizzi moves amongst Counter-Reformation concepts and his painstaking efforts intellectually may give rise to a new *City of the Sun*, and in practice to a construction like that of the Jesuits in Paraguay.[135] But this is of little importance since we are not dealing with practical possibilities, remote or otherwise, for either Pellizzi or Spirito; we are dealing with the fact that these abstract developments of thought keep in being dangerous ideological ferments, and stop the formation of an ethico-political unity in the ruling class and threaten to put off till kingdom come the solution of the problem of 'authority', i.e. that of the re-establishment of the political leadership of the conservative groups through consent. Pellizzi's stance shows that Spirito's position at Ferrara is not some sort of cultural 'eccentricity'; this is also demonstrated by certain of *Critica Fascista*'s articles that exhibit varying degrees of discomfort and ambiguity.

Q10II§14.

65 Croce's International Importance

Why it is necessary to write in the sense outlined in the first paragraph on p.42.[136] One has to convey the sense of the cultural importance that Croce has not only in Italy, but in Europe, and thus of the significance both of the wide readership his most recent books like the histories of Italy and Europe have found and of the speed with which it has been built up. That Croce sets himself the task of educating the ruling classes does not seem to me in doubt. But how, in effect, is his educative work received, to what ideological 'bonds' does it give rise? What positive feelings does it give birth to? It is a commonplace to think that Italy has been through all the political experiences of modern historical development and that in consequence ideologies and institutions conformant to these ideologies would, for the Italian people, be like yesterday's leftovers heated up again and now disgusting. But it is not true that it is yesterday's warmed-up leftovers: the 'leftovers' have been eaten only 'metaphorically' by the intellectuals, and would be warmed up only for them. They are not 'leftovers' that have been reheated and are therefore disgusting for the people (leaving aside the fact that the people, when hungry, eat warmed-up leftovers even two or three times). Despite Croce's fine armoury of sarcasm for equality and fraternity, and his exaltation of liberty – albeit speculative liberty – this will in any case be understood as equality and fraternity, and his books will appear as the expression of and implicit justification for a 'constituentism' that is oozing through the pores of that Italy *'qu'on ne voit pas'* [that one cannot see] which has only been doing its political apprenticeship for ten years.[137]

Look in Croce's books for his references to the function of the head of state. (One reference may be found on p.176 of the Second Series of the *Conversazione Critiche* in the review of Ernesto Masi's book *Asti e gli Alfieri nei ricordi della villa di S. Martino* [*Asti and the Alfieri Family in the Memories of the Villa S. Marino*]: 'Even modern life can have its elevated morality and its simple heroism, albeit on different foundations. And it is history that has laid these different foundations, history which does not allow of the ancient simplistic faith in the king, in the god of one's fathers, in traditional ideas, and which prevents one closing oneself for a long time, as once used to happen, within the narrow circle of family life and the life of one's class.' I seem to recall that D'Andrea, in his review of the *History of Europe* that appeared in *Critica Fascista* rebukes Croce for another of these expressions, considered detrimental by D'Andrea.) (Masi's book dates from 1903 and Croce's review was thus probably published in *Critica* a short while afterwards, in either 1903 or 1904.) May one suppose that Croce, besides the polemical part, also has a reconstructive side to his thought? And might there be a 'jump' from one to the other? From what transpires from his writings, this does not seem the case. But it is exactly this uncertainty that is, I think, one of the reasons for which even a lot of people who think like Croce are seen to be cold or at least worried. Croce's answer would be: let the practical people, the politicians, think about the reconstructive part, and in his system of theoretical distinctions this reply, formally speaking, is apposite. But it is true only 'formally speaking', and this leaves Gentile with a lot of space to carry out his more or less philosophical acts of aggression, which seem to me all the more frenetic in so far as he cannot and does not want to pose the whole problem (the Vatican's position over the book *Una storia e un'idea*),[138] cannot and does not want to speak clearly to Croce and make him see where his position of ideological polemics and of principle[139] may lead. But one would have to see whether Croce is not setting himself this very task in order to get a reformistic activity from above that would weaken the antitheses and reconcile them in a new, 'transformistically' obtained legality. But there cannot be a neo-Malthusianism[140] as Croce wants, the will not to 'get involved' to the hilt, which is the way of 'looking after one's own interests' of the latter-day Guicciardinism[141] typical of many intellectuals for whom it seems it is sufficient simply 'to speak the word' – '*Dixi, et salvavi animam meam*' ['I spake and saved my soul'] – but the soul is not saved just by saying the word. Deeds are needed, and how!

Q10II§22.

66 Croce as a Renaissance Man [1][142]

One could say that Croce is the last Renaissance man and that he expresses international and cosmopolitan exigencies and relationships. This does not mean that he is not a 'national element', even in the modern meaning of the term, it means that even in regard to national relationships and exigencies he expresses in particular those more general ones which coincide with broader nexuses of civilisations than those of the national area: Europe, what is usually called Western civilisation etc. Croce has managed to recreate in his own person and in his position as world cultural leader that role of the cosmopolitan intellectual that was fulfilled collegially by the Italian intellectuals of the Middle Ages right up to the end of the seventeenth century. Moreover, if Croce experiences very keenly his preoccupations with being a world leader, preoccupations which continually induce him to assume evenly balanced, Olympian attitudes without taking on commitments of a temporary and episodic nature that would be too compromising, it is also true that he himself has inculcated the principle that if there is a desire to de-provincialise Italian culture and practices (and provincialism still remains as a residue of political and moral disintegration) then the tone of intellectual life has to be raised through contact and the exchange of ideas with the international world. (This was the programme of renewal of the *Voce* group in Florence.) There is, then, an essentially national principle immanent in his attitude and his role.

Croce's role could be compared with that of the pope in the Catholic world, and one must say that Croce, in his sphere of influence, has sometimes known how to conduct himself more ably than the pope. In his concept of the intellectual, moreover, there is something of the 'Catholic and clerical', as can be seen from his wartime publications and as emerges even now from his reviews and pieces written 'for the occasion'; in a more organic and concise form his conception of the intellectual approximates to that expressed by Julien Benda in the book *The Great Betrayal*.[143]

Q10II§41iv (excerpt).

67 Croce and Julien Benda

One can compare the ideas and position adopted by B. Croce and the flood of Benda's writings on the problem of the intellectuals (as well as Benda's book the *Treason of the Intellectuals*, one should also examine the articles published in the *Nouvelles Littéraires* and perhaps in other reviews). In actual fact, despite certain appearances to the contrary, the agreement between Croce and Benda is only superficial or as regards some particular aspects of the question. Croce's thought is an organic construction, there is a doctrine of the state, of religion and of the function of the intellectuals in the life of the state, which does not exist in Benda, who, more than anything else, is a 'journalist'. One also has to say that the position of the intellectuals in France is very different from that in Italy, both organically and in immediate terms; Croce's politico-ideological preoccupations are not those of Benda for this reason, too. Both are 'liberals', but with quite different national and cultural traditions.

Q10II§47.

68 Croce as a Renaissance Man [2]

From the standpoint of his cultural role it is not so much Croce as a systematic philosopher that is under consideration as certain aspects of his activity: 1) Croce as theoretician of aesthetics and of literary and artistic criticism (the latest edition of the *Encyclopaedia Britannica* entrusted Croce with the entry 'Aesthetics', a treatment published privately in Italy under the title *Aesthetica in nuce*; the *Breviario d'Estetica* [*A Breviary of Aesthetics*] was compiled for the Americans.[144] Germany has many followers of Crocean aesthetics); 2) Croce as critic of the philosophy of praxis and as theoretician of historiography; 3) in particular, Croce as moralist and instructor in life's ways, the constructor of principles of conduct that abstract from every religious faith, showing in fact how one can 'live without religion'.

Croce's is a lordly atheism, an anti-clericalism that detests the crudeness and plebeian roughness of the vulgar anti-clericals, but it is still atheism and anti-clericalism; one asks, then, why Croce has not headed – if not actively then at least sponsoring and lending his name to – an Italian *Kulturkampf* movement,[145] which would have had an enormous historical impact. (For the hypocritical attitude of the Croceans towards clericalism, see G. Prezzolini's article 'The Fear of the Priests' in the volume *Mi pare ...*, published by Delta of Rijeka.) Nor one can say that he has not been involved in the struggle out of considerations of a philistine nature, for personal considerations etc., since he has shown that he does not give two hoots about these worldly vanities, freely living with a very intelligent woman whose salon in Naples was always lively and frequented by Italian and foreign scholars and who knew how to arouse the admiration of these people; this free relationship stopped Croce entering the Senate before 1912, when the lady died and Croce once again became a 'respectable' person in Giolitti's eyes. One may also note, on the subject of religion, Croce's ambiguous stance towards modernism: that he should be anti-modernist could be understood in so far as he is anti-Catholic, but his formulation of the ideological struggle was not this. Objectively, Croce was a precious ally of the Jesuits against modernism (in *Date a Cesare* [*Render unto Caesar*], Missiroli praises, for a Catholic readership, Croce's and Gentile's stance against modernism in this sense) and the reason for this battle – that there can be no ambiguity and equivocation, no suggestion of a third way between transcendental religion and immanentist philosophy – seems a total pretext. In this case, too, he appears as the Renaissance man, like Erasmus, with the same lack of character and civil courage. The modernists, given the mass character they acquired from the contemporary birth of a rural Catholic democracy (linked with the technical revolution that was taking place in the Po Valley with the disappearance of the *corvée* and compulsory labour and the growth of the agricultural day labourer and less servile forms of share-cropping), were religious reformers who came onto the scene not due to the pre-established intellectual schemes dear to Hegelianism, but because of the real and historical conditions of Italian religious life. They represented a second wave of liberal Catholicism, much more widespread and more popular in character than had been neo-Guelphism before '48 and the purer Catholic liberalism subsequent to '48.

Croce and Gentile's attitude (together with their altar boy Prezzolini) isolated the modernists in the cultural world and made it easier for the Jesuits to crush them; indeed it seemed a victory of the papacy against the whole of modern philosophy, although the anti-modernist encyclical[146] is in actual fact against immanence and modern science, and it was in this sense that it was expounded in the seminaries and religious circles. (It is a curious fact how, today, the attitude of the Croceans towards the modernists, or at least the principal ones, but not however towards Buonaiuti, has undergone a big change, as can be seen from the elaborate review by Adolfo Omodeo in the *Critica* of 20 July 1932 of Alfred Loisy's *Mémoires pour servir à l'histoire religieuse de notre temps*.[147])

Q10II§41iv (excerpt).

69 Croce and Modernism

One should compare what Croce says about modernism in his interview on the freemasons (*Cultura e Vita Morale* 2nd edition)[148] with what A. Omodeo writes in the *Critica* of 20 July 1932 in his review of Alfred Loisy's three-volume study (*Mémoires pour servir à l'histoire religieuse*). For example on p.291: 'Pius X's facile non-Catholic allies in the same anti-clerical republic (*and, in Italy, Croce*)[149] are taunted by Loisy for their ignorance of the nature of absolutist Catholicism and the danger represented by this international empire in the hands of the pope; he reproaches them with the damage (already pointed out in his time by Quinet) of letting such a great part of humanity be reduced to a stupid, empty-headed flock, void of moral life and animated solely by a passive acquiescence. In these observations there is undoubtedly a large measure of truth.'

Q10II§47 (excerpt).

70 Croce as a Renaissance Man [3]

Why did Croce not give the same logical explanation of modernism as the one which, in the *History of Europe*, he gave of liberal Catholicism, as if it were a victory of the 'religion of liberty' even managing to get inside the citadel of its bitterest antagonist and enemy etc.?[150] (Look again at the *History of Italy* where it talks of modernism. I have the impression, however, that Croce skates over it, while extolling the victory of liberalism over a socialism that had become reformist due to the scientific activity of Croce himself.)[151]

(The same observation may be made about Missiroli, who also comes from the anti-modernist and anti-popular mould. If the people cannot arrive at the conception of political liberty and the national idea except by having gone through the experience of a religious reform, i.e. after having mastered the notion of liberty in religion, then one cannot understand why Missiroli and the liberals of the *Resto del Carlino*[152] were so fiercely anti-modernist – or perhaps one can understand too well since modernism, politically, meant Christian Democracy,[153] which was particularly strong in Emilia-Romagna and in the whole of the Po Valley, while Missiroli together with his liberals were fighting for agrarian reform.)

One can pose the question of who represents contemporary Italian society more adequately from the theoretical and moral standpoint – the pope, Croce or Gentile? In other words: 1) Who has most influence from the point of view of hegemony as the regulator of the ideology which provides civil society and thus the state with its most intimate cement? 2) Who, in the framework of world culture, is the best representative of Italian influence abroad? It is not an easy problem to resolve, since each one of the three is dominant in different environments and among different social forces. The pope, as head and guide of the majority among the Italian peasantry and among women, and because his authority and influence operate in conjunction with a centralised and well ramified organisation, is a great political force, the most important one in the country after the government, but his is an authority that had become passive and accepted out of inertia, one which even before the Concordat was, in fact, a reflection of state authority. For this reason it is difficult to make a comparison between the influence of the pope and that of a private individual in cultural life. A more rational comparison can be made between Croce and Gentile, and here it is immediately evident that Croce's influence, despite appearances to the contrary, is by far superior to Gentile's. At the same time Gentile's authority is anything but admitted even among his own political supporters (remember Paolo Orano's parliamentary attack on Gentile's philosophy and the personal attack on Gentile and his followers by G.A Fanelli in the weekly magazine *Roma*).[154] To my way of thinking, Gentile's philosophy, actualism, is more national only in the sense that it is closely linked to a primitive stage of the state, to the economic-corporative phase, when all cats seem grey. For this same reason one can believe in the greater importance and influence of this philosophy, in the same way that many believe that in parliament an industrialist is more than just an advocate representing industrial interests (or than a professor or than a leader of the workers' unions), without thinking that, if the entire parliamentary majority were composed of industrialists, parliament would immediately lose its function of political mediation and all its prestige. (For Gentile's corporativism and economics, look at the speech he made in Rome, published in the volume *Cultura e Fascismo* [*Culture and Fascism*]).[155]

The Philosophy of Benedetto Croce

Croce's influence is stealthier than that of Gentile but it goes deeper and is better rooted; Croce is really a sort of secular pope, but his overall ethical stance is too much that of the intellectuals, too much that of a Renaissance type such that it cannot become popular, while the pope and his doctrine influence countless masses of people through their maxims for conduct that refer even to the most elementary things. It is true that Croce claims that these ways of life are, by now, not specifically Christian and religious, since 'after Christ we are all Christians', i.e. Christianity in what is a real exigency of life and not mythology has been absorbed by modern civilisation. (This aphorism of Croce's certainly contains a large measure of truth. Senator Mariano D'Amelio, first president of the Supreme Court of Appeal, rejected the objection that the western codes could not be introduced into non-Christian countries like Japan, Turkey etc., exactly because they have been constructed using many elements introduced from Christianity, by recalling this 'simple truth' of Croce's. Now, in actual reality, the western codes are being introduced in 'pagan' countries as the expression of European civilisation and not of Christianity as such, and good Muslims do not believe they have become Christians and forsworn Islam.)

Q10II§41iv (excerpt).

CONCORDANCE TABLE

The present anthology, like others in the past, relies on the usually more authoritative 'B' and 'C' texts (see p.xx of the General Introduction): any departure from this practice, by inclusion of an earlier 'A' text, is explained in the footnotes to that paragraph. The table that follows lists the paragraphs that comprise each chapter and their dates, as far as it has been possible to establish them, together with any alternative draft that exists: the ones not used are enclosed in round brackets. The collocation of each paragraph (notebook number and, after an oblique stroke, the paragraph number and any sub-division of it) is given for Gerratana's Critical Edition, corresponding to what is listed at the end of each sub-section in the current volume, and cross-referenced to the original Platone-Togliatti thematic edition, published in six volumes by Einaudi and subsequently reprinted with a different pagination by Editori Riuniti; naturally, post-1975 reprints differ somewhat from the first editions because of integration of material from the Gerratana volumes. The abbreviations used for the thematic editions are: MS = *Il materialismo storico e la filosofia di Benedetto Croce* (1948); INT = *Gli intellettuali e l'organizzazione della cultura* (1949): MACH = *Note sul Machiavelli, sulla politica e sullo stato moderno* (1949): RIS = *Il Risorgimento* (1949): LVN = *Letteratura e vita nazionale* (1950): PP = *Passato e Presente* (1951). The dating of the various paragraphs follows the painstaking chronological reconstruction, published in *L'Officina Gramsciana* (*The Gramsci Workshop*), Naples 1984, by Gianni Francioni, whose study of the manuscripts extended

Concordance Table

Gerratana's work. Further useful information, used by Francioni to update his chronology (see the Autumn 1992 number of *Studi Storici*), is found in the letters between Gramsci and his sister-in-law, Tania, his wife, Julka, and children, Delio and Giuliano; between Tania and Piero Sraffa; and between her and her own or Gramsci's family.

In addition to the entries in the Concordance Table, there are a number of other paragraphs from the Notebooks included either in part or in their entirety in the current volume. The 'B' text paragraphs quoted in their entirety are Q15§9 (the autobiographical note found on pp.lxxxiv-lxxxvii at the end of the general introduction to this volume) and Q10II§3 (reproduced in Q10II§2, p.335, as the citation from Sorel's letter to Croce), while the 'A' texts are Q7§28 (footnote 21, p.522), Q8§168 (footnote 13, p.539), Q7§22 (footnote 11, p.542), Q11§68 (in all its essentials as footnote 7, p.555), Q8§189 (footnote 19, p.557-8), Q10II§51 (footnote 38, p.569) and Q7§37 (footnote 32, p.574). The datings of these paragraphs may be obtained by interpolation from the data of the Concordance Table itself.

Concordance Table

I RELIGION: A MOVEMENT AND AN IDEOLOGY

A The Church as an Institution and the Clergy as Intellectuals

	Critical edition B/C text	A text	Platone-Togliatti volume	Einaudi 1948-51 page	Riuniti 1971 page	Date
1 Religion [1]	6/41		MACH	292	377-8	Early '31
2 Clergy and Intellectuals [1]	1/154		INT	39	56	May '30
3 Religion as a Principle and the Clergy as Feudal Class-Order	1/128		MACH	294	381	Feb-Mar '30
4 The Clergy as Intellectuals	1/51		MACH	294-5	381	Feb-Mar '30
5 The Social Origin of the Clergy	1/52		MACH	295	382	Feb-Mar '30
6 The Clergy, Church Property and Analogous Forms of Landed or Non-Landed Property	3/77		MACH	295-6	382-3	Aug '30
7 Religion [2]	8/111		MACH	300	389	Mar '32
8 Past and Present [1]. Fables. Points on Religion	8/155		PP	121	163-4	Apr '32
9 Cultural Questions. Fetishism	15/13		MACH	157-8	204-6	Apr '33
10 The Conception of Organic Centralism and the Priestly Caste	3/56		MACH	294	381	Mid '30
11 Arms and Religion	6/87		MACH	121-2	162	Mid '31

12	Past and Present [2]. *The Spread of Christianity	8/97		PP	120-1	Mar '32
13	Conflict between Church and State as Eternal Historical Category	6/139		MACH	262	Aug '31
14	History of the Intellectuals. Struggle between Church and State	7/104		INT	40	Dec '31
	B Reformation and Counter-Reformation					
15	Development of the Bourgeois Spirit in Italy	5/85		INT	33-5	49-51	Oct-Nov '30
16	History of the Italian Intellectuals. *Galileo and Giordano Bruno	6/152		INT	39	54-5	Oct '31
17	Catholic Action [1]. *Roberto Bellarmino's Canonisation	6/151 17/15		MACH RIS	281 36	364-5 53	Oct '31 Sept '33
18	Humanism and Renaissance					
19	Reformation and Renaissance. Nicholas of Cusa	5/53 26/11	(5/136 & 139)	RIS RIS	34-5 36-7	50-1 53-5	Oct-Nov '30 Mid '35
20	*Formation and Reformation					
21	Past and Present [3]. *Lutheran Reformation – British Calvinism – French Rationalism	4/75		PP	120	162	Nov '30
22	Notes on Italian Culture. On Protestantism in Italy	14/26		INT	43-6	61-4	Jan '33

Concordance Table

C Catholic Social Policy, the Hierarchy and Popular Religion in Italy

	Critical edition B/C text	A text	Platone-Togliatti volume	Einaudi 1948-51 page	Riuniti 1971 page	Date
23 Catholic Action [2]. *Catholic Action's History and Organisation	20/1	(1/38)	MACH	225-9	297-302	'34-early '35
24 Catholic Action and the Franciscan Tertiaries	20/2	(1/139)	MACH	229-30	302-3	'34-early '35
25 On Poverty, Catholicism and the Church Hierarchy	20/3	(1/1)	MACH	230-1	303-4	'34-early '35
26 Catholic Action [3]. *The Pre-History of Catholic Action	6/183		MACH	232	305-6	Dec '31
27 Catholic Action [4]. *Catholic Action's Origins	6/188		MACH	232-4	306-7	Dec '31
28 Catholic Action [5]. *Catholic Action and Neo-Guelphism	7/98		MACH	234-5	307-9	Dec '31
29 The Risorgimento, 1848-49	8/11		RIS	107-8	138-9	Jan '32
30 Catholic Action [6]. The Role of the Catholics in Italy	3/25		MACH	235-6	309-10	1st ½ Jun '30
31 Catholic Action [7]. *Gianforte Suardi	5/47		MACH	236	310-11	Oct-Nov '30
32 Clergy and Intellectuals [2]. *Leo XIII	1/77		MACH	283-4	367-8	Feb-Mar '30

33 Catholic Action [8]. *The Church's Reduced Role in the World	14/55		MACH	236-7	311-2	Feb '33
34 On Catholic 'Social Thought'	5/7		MACH	237-8	312-3	Oct '30
35 Catholic Social Thought	5/18		MACH	238-9	313-4	Oct-Nov '30
36 Catholic Action [9]. The Workers' Retreats	5/133		MACH	231	304-5	Nov-Dec '30
37 Catholic Action [10]. *Catholics and Insurrection	7/78		MACH	240-1	315-6	Dec '31
38 Catholic Action [11]. The Lille Conflict	2/131		MACH	239-40	315	Dec '30
39 Davide Lazzaretti	25/1	(3/12 & 9/81)	RIS	199-203	249-53	Mid-late '34
40 Religion, the Lottery and the Opium of Poverty [1]	16/1	(8/209, 228,230)	MACH	288-91	373-77	Mid-late '34
41 Religion, the Lottery and the Opium of Poverty [2]	16/10		MACH	291-2	377-8	Mid-late '34
D Concordats and Church-State Relations						
42 The Concordat	3/50		MACH	261	340	Jun-Jul '30
43 Nature of the Concordats	5/71		MACH	260-1	339-40	Oct-Nov '30
44 State-Church Relations [1]	16/11i	(1/3 & 5)	MACH	249-57	326-36	Mid-late '34
45 Concordats and International Treaties	16/11ii	(4/53 & 54)				
46 State-Church Relations [2]	16/14		MACH	257/8	336/8	Mid-late '34

	Critical edition		Platone-Togliatti volume	Einaudi 1948-51 page	Riuniti 1971 page	Date
	B/C text	A text				
47 The State is the Church	5/70		MACH	259/60	338-9	Oct-Nov '30
48 Past and Present [4]. Religion in Schools	7/89		PP	122-3	165-6	Dec '31
49 Catholicism and Secularism. Religion and Science etc.	3/140		MACH	300/1	389-90	Sept '30
50 Encyclopaedic Notions [1]. Civil Society	6/24		PP	164-5	217-8	Dec '30
E Integralist Catholics, Jesuits and Modernists						
51 *The Rise of the Integralists	20/4i	(5/1 & 11)	MACH	263-6	343-7	'34-early '35
52 *Action Française and the Integralists	20/4ii	(5/14)	MACH	266-72	347-54	'34-early '35
53 *An Action Française Journalist in Rome	20/4iii	(5/16)	MACH	272	354	'34-early '35
54 *Action Française's Long Crisis	20/4v	(5/141)	MACH	273-6	354-8	'34-early '35
55 *Maurras and Paganism	13/37	(1/106)	MACH	112-3	151-2	Summer '34(?)
56 Maurras and 'Organic Centralism'	13/38	(1/49 & 54)	MACH	113	152	Summer '34(?)
57 The Turmel Case	6/195		MACH	276-8	359-61	Dec '31
58 The Case of Abbé Turmel of Rennes	20/4iv	(5/137)	MACH	276	358-9	'34-early '35
59 *Luigi Salvatorelli and Fr Turmel	14/52		MACH	278-9	361-2	Feb '33

60	Introduction to the Study of Philosophy. *Fr Lippert	10II/28i	MS 290	346 Jun '32
61	*The Encyclicals against Modern Thought	14/20	MACH 280	363-4 Jan '33
62	Past and Present [5]. Papal Encyclicals	6/163	PP 123-4	167 Oct-Nov '31
63	Roberto Bellarmino	7/88	MACH 280-1	364-5 Dec '31

F Organised Religion in the Metropolitan Countries

64	The Italian Risorgimento. *Jewish Culture and Consciousness in Italy	15/41	RIS 166-8	208-10 May '33
65	Integralist Catholics, Jesuits, Modernists. *Spain	6/164	MACH 285-6	370 Nov '31
66	Catholic Action [12]. *France	15/40	MACH 243-4	318-20 May '33
67	Lucien Romier and French Catholic Action [1]	5/9	MACH 244	320-1 Oct '30
68	Lucien Romier and French Catholic Action [2]	5/15	MACH 244-5	321 Oct-Nov '30
69	Catholic Action [13]. *Catholic Action in Germany and Austria	8/129	MACH 245	321-2 Apr '32
70	Relations between the German Centre and the Vatican	2/20	MACH 171-2	224 May-early Jun '30
71	Catholic Action in Germany [1]	5/22	MACH 245-6	322 Oct-Nov '30
72	Catholic Action in Germany [2]	5/59	MACH 246	322-3 Oct-Nov '30

	Critical edition B/C text	A text	Platone-Togliatti volume	Einaudi 1948-51 page	Riuniti 1971 page	Date
73 Catholic Action in the United States [1]	5/57		MACH	246-7	323	Oct-Nov '30
74 Catholic Action in the United States [2]	6/187		MACH	247-8	323-5	Dec '31
75 Catholic Action [14]. *Catholicism and Social Democracy in Britain	7/69		MACH	304	394-5	Oct-Dec '31
76 British Labourism. The Archbishop of Canterbury and Labourism	7/94		RIS	216-7	269-70	Dec '31
77 The Ecumenical Movement	5/17		MACH	241	316-7	Oct-Nov '30
78 Ecumenical Movements	3/164 (excerpt)		MACH	305	396	Oct '30
79 Religious Movements. *The Ecumenical Movement and its Subsidiary Organisation	5/134		MACH	286	371	Nov-Dec '30
80 Religion and Politics	8/131ii		PP	161-2	214	Apr '32
G **Religious Culture in Other Major Countries**						
81 Ecumenicalism and Protestant Propaganda in South America	2/135		MACH	286-7	371-2	Dec '30
82 South American Culture	6/190		INT	79	104-5	Dec '31

83	*Jesuitism in South America	1/107	MACH	296	Feb-Mar '30
84	Catholicism in India	3/164 (excerpt)			
85	*Rebel India	5/89	MACH	301-2	Oct '30
86	*Non-Resistance and Non-Co-operation		PP	212	Oct-Nov '30
87	*Religiosity in India	6/78	RIS	46-7	Mid-lateMar'31
88	Encylopaedic Notions [2].	2/86	MACH	302	Aug-Sept '30
	Theopanism	6/178	PP	166-7	Dec '31
89	Brief Notes on Indian Culture	6/32	INT	82-3	Dec '30
90	Intellectuals. On Indian Culture	7/71	INT	83	Dec '31
91	The Question of the Intellectuals	7/62	INT	67	Oct '30
92	Brief Notes on Chinese Culture [1]	5/23	INT	89-91	Oct-Nov '30
93	Brief Notes on Chinese Culture [2]	5/51	INT	90-1	Oct-Nov '30
94	Brief Notes on Japanese Culture [1]	5/50	INT	91-4	Oct-Nov '30
95	Brief Notes on Japanese Culture [2]	8/87	INT	94	Mar '32
96	The New Evolution of Islam	2/90	INT	80-2	Aug-Sept '30
97	Brief Notes on Islamic Culture	5/90	INT	79-80	Oct-Nov '30
98	The Influence of Arab Culture on Western Civilisation	16/5	(4/92) INT	82	109	Mid-late '34

383-4
391
274-5
65-6
391-2
220
109-10
110
90
116-8
118-20
120-3
123
107-9
105-7

II THE ORIGIN OF MODERN EDUCATIONAL PRINCIPLES

	Critical edition B/C text	A text	Platone-Togliatti volume	Einaudi 1948-51 page	Riuniti 1971 page	Date
1 *Some Problems of Modern Pedagogy	1/123		INT	115-6	149-50	Feb-Mar '30
2 Scholastic Questions [1]	9/119		INT	121-3	156-9	Aug-Sept '32
3 The Professional School	6/179		PP	109-110	149-50	Dec '31
4 Professional Orientation	5/41		INT	123-4	159-60	Oct-Nov '30
5 *Universities and Academies	12/1	(Q4/50)	INT	106-7	136-7	Mid '32
6 The Academies	6/211		INT	125	162	Jan '32
7 Italian and French Culture and Academies	3/145		INT	125-6	162	Sept-Oct '30
8 The Italian Universities	1/15		INT	119-20	154-5	Summer-Aut'29
9 Scholastic Questions [2]	6/206		INT	120-1	155-6	Jan '32
10 Intellectual and Moral Order	15/46		INT	118-9	153-4	May '33
11 The Organisation of Cultural Life	8/188		INT	126-7	163-4	Dec '31
12 Types of Periodical	4/77		INT	149	190	Nov '30
13 Italian Culture	14/56		INT	124	160-1	Feb '93
14 *The Popular Libraries	2/88		INT	124-5	161	Aug-Sept '30
15 Ideological Material	3/49		PP	172-3	226-7	Jun-Jul '30

16 Introduction to the Study of Philosophy. *Pedagogy and Hegemony	10II/44		MS	25-7	29-31	Autumn '32
17 Antonio Labriola [1]	11/1	(Q8/200)	INT	116-8	150-2	1932
18 Antonio Labriola [2]	11/5	(Q8/53)	INT	116(Note)	151 (Note)	1932

III THE NATURE AND HISTORY OF ECONOMIC SCIENCE

1 *Machiavelli as an Economist	8/162		MACH	211	277-8	Apr '32
2 Points to Reflect on for a Study of Economics [1]. *The Beginning of Economic Science	10II/25		MS	264	316-7	Jun '32
3 Points to Reflect on for a Study of Economics [2]. *The Method of Economic Research	10II/37i		MS	265	317-8	Summer '32
4 Brief Notes on Economics [1]. *The Concept of 'Homo Oeconomicus'	10II/15		MS	266-7	319-20	Jun '32
5 Points to Reflect on for a Study of Economics [3]. *On the Subject of the So-Called Homo Oeconomicus	10II/27		MS	267	320	Jun '32
6 Points to Reflect on for a Study of Economics [4]. *Classical Economy and Critical Economy	10II/23		not in pre-1975 editions			Jun '32

	Critical edition B/C text	Critical edition A text	Platone-Togliatti volume	Einaudi 1948-51 page	Riuniti 1971 page	Date
7 Points to Reflect on for a Study of Economics [5]. *Observations on Pantaleoni's *Pure Economics*	10II/30		MS	268-9	321-2	Summer '32
8 Points to Reflect on for a Study of Economics [6]. *Regarding Pantaleoni's *Pure Economics*	10II/32		MS	269-71	322-4	Summer '32
9 Brief Notes on Economics [2]. *Lionel Robbins	15/43		MS	262-3	314-6	May '33
10 Brief Notes on Economics [3]. *Political Economy and Critical Economy	15/45		MS	265-6	318-9	May '33
11 *Outlines of Marxist Economics	10II/37ii		MS	281-3	336-8	Summer '32
12 Freedom and 'Automatism' or Rationality	10II/8		MS	277	331-2	2nd ½ May '32
13 Brief Notes on Economics [4]. Ugo Spirito & Co.	8/216		MS	273-5	328-9	Mar '32
14 Encyclopaedic Notions. Conjuncture [1]	15/16ii		PP	148-9	198	Apr-May '33
15 Encyclopaedic Notions. Conjuncture [2]	6/130		PP	149	198	Summer '31

16	Points for a Study of Economics.				
	*The Einaudi-Spirito Polemic over the State	10II/20	MS	275-6	Jun '32
17	Economic History Studies	8/212	MS	277-8	Feb-Mar '32
18	Graziadei's Land of Cokaygne	7/23	MS	280-1	Feb '31
19	Graziadei and the Land of Cokaygne	7/27	MS	281	Feb '31
20	Graziadei	8/166	not in pre-1975 editions		Nov '31
21	On Graziadei	7/30	MS	278-80	Feb '31
22	Points to Reflect on in Economics.				
	*The Science of Economics	10II/57	MS	261-2	Feb-May '33

IV ECONOMIC TRENDS AND DEVELOPMENTS

	A The Geo-Political Situation				
1	Geo-Politics	2/39	MACH	221	1st half Jun '30
2	World Politics and European Politics	2/24	MACH	175	May-early Jun '30
3	The Atlantic and the Pacific	2/78	MACH	181-2	Aug-Sept '30
4	America and the Mediterranean	5/8	MACH	360	Oct '30
5	*Great Britain and the United States	2/97	not in pre-1975 editions		Aug-Sept '30
6	*Britain, Russia, Germany	2/40	not in pre-1975 editions		1st half Jun '30

Concordance Table

	Critical edition B/C text	A text	Platone-Togliatti volume	Einaudi 1948-51 page	Riuniti 1971 page	Date
7 Encyclopaedic Notions [1]. *The Four Pillars of Europe	6/39		not in pre-1975 editions			Dec '30
8 A Policy for Peace in Europe	2/18		MACH	171	223	Early-mid May '30
9 Augur	2/32		PP	210	272-3	May-early Jun '30
10 *Geo-Political Developments	2/16		MACH	various passages 175-81	229-37	Early-mid May '30
11 America	3/5		MACH	355-6	457-8	Late May '30
12 Past and Present [1]. Otto Kahn	3/55		PP	87	122-3	Jun-July '30
13 Oil, Petrol and Petroleum Products	2/54		MACH	221-2	291-3	1st ½ Jun '30
14 Italy and the Yemen in the New Politics of the Arab World	2/30		MACH	196-8	257-9	May-early Jun '30
15 Britain and the United States after the War	2/16		MACH	176-7	229-31	Early-mid May '30
16 The American Negroes	8/47		PP	211	273-4	Feb '32

B The World Economic Crisis

17 Past and Present [2]. Observations on the World Crisis	6/123	PP	93-4	Spring-Sum '31
18 Past and Present [3]. *The Standard of Living	6/75	PP	22-3	Mar '31
19 Psychology and Politics	6/90	MACH	151	Spring-Sum '31
20 Past and Present [4]. The Crisis	15/5	PP	88-91	Feb '33
21 Past and Present [5]. Elements of the Economic Crisis	14/57	PP	92-3	Feb '33
22 Brief Notes on Political Economy	15/26	MS	273	May '33
23 Points to Reflect on in Economics [1]. *Agnelli's Ideas	10II/55	MS	271-3	Feb '33
24 Points to Reflect on in Economics [2]. *Distribution of the Human Forces of Labour and Consumption	10II/53	MS	267-8	Feb '33

C National Economic Problems and International Relations

25 *Post-War Contradictions	2/122	MACH	188-9	Oct-Nov '30
26 *Inflation and the Domestic Economy	3/160	not in pre-1975 editions		Sept-Oct '30
27 *International Tariffs and Trade	2/125	MACH	179-80	Oct-Nov '30
28 The National Economy	9/32	MACH	185	May-Jun '32

		130-2	
		43-4	
		197-8	
		124-8	
		128-30	
		327	
		324-7	
		320-1	
		246-7	
		234-5	
		241-2	

Concordance Table

	Critical edition B/C text	A text	Platone-Togliatti volume	Einaudi 1948-51 page	Riuniti 1971 page	Date
29 Relations Between City and Countryside	8/193		MACH	218	287	Dec '31
30 City and Countryside	2/137		MACH	144-5	189-91	Dec '30–early '31
31 *Colonies, Capital Flow and the Demographic Question	19/6	(9/105)	MACH	195-6	255-7	Spring 1934(?)
32 *Questions of Hegemony	1/149		RIS	210-1	262-3	Late May '30
33 The Colonies	8/80		PP	210-1	273	Mar '32
34 Robert Michels	7/64		MACH	219	288	Oct '31
35 Past and Present [6]. Studies on the National Economic Structure	15/1		PP	95-6	132-3	Feb '33
36 Nationalisations and State Takeovers	7/40		MACH	220	289-90	Mid-late(?) '31
37 Past and Present [7]. Nationalisations	8/92		PP	96	133-4	Mar '32
38 The Italian Risorgimento. *Savings, Agricultural Protectionism and Industry	15/44		RIS	175-6	218-9	May '33
39 Past and Present [8]. The Error of the Anti-Protectionist Left	8/72		PP	22	42-3	Feb-Mar '32

40 Past and Present [9]. The Individual and the State	6/109	PP	96-7	134	Spring-Sum. '31
41 On the National Economic Structure	19/7 (9/110 & 112)	MACH	185-8	242-6	Spring '34(?)
42 *Humanity-as-Labour and Modern Internationalism	19/5 (9/127)	RIS	66-7	90-1	Spring '34(?)
D American Industrial Culture					
43 America and Europe	3/26	MACH	360	463	1st ½ Jun '30
44 *American Industry	2/138	MACH	358-9	460-1	Dec '30-early '31
45 Past and Present [10]. Fordism	6/135	PP	101-2	140-1	Aug '31
46 Americanism	15/30	MACH	354	455-6	May '33
47 *The Origin of the American Theory	15/53	INT	51-2	71-2	May-Jun '33
48 American Pragmatism	1/34	MACH	162	211	Dec '29-early '30
49 American Philosophy	1/105	MACH	360	463	Feb-Mar '30
50 Vittorio Macchioro and America	4/76	MACH	354-5	456-7	Nov '30
51 Brief Notes on American Culture	8/89	INT	78	103-4	Mar '32
E Britain's Role in the World Economy					
52 Cultural Questions. Disraeli	17/53	PP	209	271-2	Jun '35

Concordance Table

	Critical edition B/C text	A text	Platone-Togliatti volume	Einaudi 1948-51 page	Riuniti 1971 page	Date
53 The British Empire	2/16		MACH	174	227	Early-mid May '30
54 Constitution of the British Empire	2/48		MACH	172	224-5	1st ½ Jun '30
55 Britain	5/86		MACH	174-5	227-8	Oct-Nov '30
56 Paying off the National Debt	2/6		not in pre-1975 editions			Early-mid May '30
57 London's World Role	16/7	(4/60)	PP	208-9	270-1	Mid-late '34
58 Past and Present [11]. The British Government	6/40		PP	124-5	168-9	Dec '30
59 *The Crisis of Parliamentarism	24/3	(1/43)	INT	143	181	Mid-late '34
60 Past and Present [12]. Britain and Germany	9/61		PP	125-6	169-70	July-Aug '32
F The New Society and the New Economic Individual						
61 Cultural Topics. *Conformism and the Collective Man	9/23		PP	187-8	245-6	May '32
62 Reformation and Renaissance. *The Present Process of the Molecular Formation of a New Civilisation	7/44		not in pre-1975 editions			Mid-late(?) '31

63	*The Modern Prince and the Collective Man	(13/6 & 7)	8/52	(MACH	140/83	184/114)	Feb '32
64	*Economic Activity and the Law	(13/11)	8/62	(MACH	88-9	119-20)	Feb '32
65	Freud and the Collective Man	15/74		PP	216-7	280	Aug '33
66	Encyclopaedic Notions [2].						
	*Liberty-Discipline	6/11		PP	154	205	Nov-Dec '30
67	Man as Individual and Man as Mass	7/12		MACH	149-51	195-7	Nov-Dec '30
68	*Passive Revolution in a Planned Economy	(not copied in C text 10I/9)	8/236	not in pre-1975 editions			Apr '32

V SCIENCE, LOGIC AND TRANSLATABILITY

A Preliminary Notions

1	Encyclopaedic Notions [1]. 'Scientific': What is 'Scientific'?	6/180	PP	162-3	215	Dec '31
2	Encyclopaedic Notions [2]. Science and Scientific	6/165	PP	163	216	Nov '31
3	Encyclopaedic Notions [3]. Empiricism	9/59	PP	150	200	July-Aug '32
4	Popular Manual of Sociology. *Objections to Empiricism	17/23	MS	156	185	Sept '33
5	Methodological Criteria [1]	14/5	LVN	33	52-3	Dec '32
6	Methodological Criteria [2]	14/36	PP	173	227	Jan-Feb '33

Concordance Table

	Critical edition B/C text	A text	Platone-Togliatti volume	Einaudi 1948-51 page	Riuniti 1971 page	Date
7 Philosophers-Literati and Philosophers-Scientists	11/61		PP	216	279-80	Late '32-early '33
B Science and Scientific Ideologies						
8 *The New Science and Misconceptions about It	11/36	(8/170 & 176)	MS	50-53	59-63	Late Summer-Aut '32
9 *Science, Humanity, Objectivity	11/37	(4/41)	MS	54-6	63-6	Late Summer-Aut '32
10 *Science as Ideology	11/38	(4/7)	MS	56	66	Late Summer-Aut '32
11 Philosophy-Ideology, Science-Doctrine	4/61		not in pre-1975 editions			Nov '30
12 *Popular Ignorance about Science	11/39	(4/71)	MS	56-7	67	Late Summer-Aut '32
C The Logical Instruments of Thought						
13 *Methodology, Logic, Epistemology	11/40	(8/184)	MS	58/9	68/9	Late Summer-Aut '32
14 Dialectics as Part of Formal Logic and Rhetoric	11/41	(8/183)	MS	59	69-70	Late Summer-Aut '32

15	The Purely Instrumental Value of Formal Logic and Methodology	11/42	(8/189)	MS	59	70	Late Sum-Aut '32
16	*Tobias Dantzig's Book	11/43	(8/194)	MS	294	351	Late Sum-Aut '32
17	The Technique of Thought	11/44	(4/18 & 21)	MS	59-61	70-73	Late Sum-Aut '32
18	Past and Present [1]. Don Ferrante's Logic	14/25		PP	69	101	Jan '33
19	Philosophical and Scientific Esperanto	11/45	(7/3)	MS	61-2	73-4	Late Sum-Aut '32
20	Cultural Topics. Formal Logic and the Scientific Mentality	17/52		PP	182-3	239-40	Jun '35

D The Translatability of Scientific and Philosophical Languages

21	Introduction to the Study of Philosophy [1]. The Translatability of Scientific Languages	10II/6iv		not in pre-1975 editions		2nd ½ May '32
22	Introduction to the Study of Philosophy [2]. The Subjective Conception of Reality and the Philosophy of Praxis	10II/6ii		not in pre-1975 editions		2nd ½ May '32
23	*Lenin and Translation	11/46	(7/2)	MS	63	75	Late Sum-Aut '32

Concordance Table

	Critical edition B/C text	A text	Platone-Togliatti volume	Einaudi 1948-51 page	Riuniti 1971 page	Date
24 *Translation between Different Civilizations	11/47		MS	63	75	Late Sum-Aut '32
25 Giovanni Vailati and the Translatability of Scientific Languages	11/48	(4/42)	MS	63-5	75-8	Late Sum-Aut '32
26 *The Mutual Translatability of National Cultures	11/49	(8/208)	MS	65-7	78-80	Late Sum-Aut '32
27 Introduction to the Study of Philosophy [3]. *Gioberti on French and German Philosophy	17/18iii		MS	292	347-8	Sept '33
28 The Translatability of Different Cultures	15/64		not in pre-1975 editions			Jun-July '33
29 Miscellaneous Notes. The History of Terminology and Metaphors	11/50	(8/207 & 234)	MS	68-70 70-1	81-4 84)	Late Sum-Aut '32
30 The Proposition that One Must 'Put Man Back on his Feet'	10II/60	(1/152 & 155)	(MS 10II/60 not in pre-1975 editions			Feb-May '33
E Machines and Technology						
31 On Ancient Capitalism	6/156		PP	147	196	Oct '31

32 Encyclopaedic Notions [4]. The Machine	8/90	PP	154-5	205-6	Mar '32
33 Political Nomenclature. Artisans and Small, Medium and Big Industry	7/96	PP	143-4	191-2	Dec '31
34 Introduction to the Study of Philosophy [4]. *Technology as Mediator between Science and Reality	15/33	MS	290	345	May '33 Mid '32- Late '33
35 On the Development of Military Technology	13/28 (9/137)	MACH	152-3	199-200	
36 Past and Present [2]. *War	17/36	PP	20	40	Late '33

VI REFERENCE POINTS FOR AN ESSAY ON B. CROCE

*Summary	10I [Summary]	(8/225, 227, 233, 236 & 240: pieces integrated in MS with corresponding note of Q10I)			Apr-May '32 with additional notes mid-'35
1 *Croce's Stance During the World War	10I/1	(8/225)	MS	173-5	206-8	Apr-May '32
2 *Croce as Intellectual Leader of Revisionism	10I/2	(8/225)	MS	176	209	Apr-May '32

Concordance Table

	Critical edition B/C text	A text	Platone-Togliatti volume	Einaudi 1948-51 page	Riuniti 1971 page	Date
3 *Development of the Theory of Ethico-Political History	10I/3	(8/225)	MS	177-8	210-1	Apr-May '32
4 *Croce's Relative Popularity	10I/4	(8/225)	MS	179-80	212-3	Apr-May '32
5 *Croce and Religion	10I/5	(8/225 & 233)	MS	181-3	214-7	Apr-May '32
6 *Croce and Italian Historiography	10I/6	(8/225)	MS	184-6	218-20	Apr-May '32
7 *Definition of Ethico-Political History	10I/7	(8/227 & 233)	MS	187-9	221-4	Apr-May '32
8 *Transcendence-Theology-Speculation	10I/8	(8/224)	MS	190-1	225-7	Apr-May '32
9 *Paradigms of Ethico-Political History	10I/9	(8/236)	MS	192-4	228-30	Apr-May '32
10 *Liberty as Identity of History and Mind and as Ideology	10I/10	(8/112)	MS	195-7	231-4	Apr-May '32
11 *Croce and the Philosophy of Praxis	10I/11		MS	198-200	235-8	Apr-May '32
12 *Ethico-Political History and Hegemony	10I/12		MS	201-2	239-40	Apr-May '32
13 Notes	10I/Notes	(8/223, 226, 227, 240)	MS	203-4	241-4	2nd ½ May '32

VII THE PHILOSOPHY OF BENEDETTO CROCE

A Premiss

1 Some General Methodological Criteria for the Critique of Croce's Philosophy	10II/[Preface]		MS	171-2	203-4	Apr '32
2 *The Central Nucleus of the Essay	10II/29ii		not in pre-1975 editions		Jun-Aug '32
3 *South and North	10II/38ii		MS	292	348-9	Jun-Aug '32
4 *The Man Standing on his Head	10II/1		MS	215-7	257-9	Apr '32

B Crocean Philosophy

5 *The Dialectic of Distincts	10II/59iii		MS	216	258	Spring '33
6 Croce and Hegel	10II/4		not in pre-1975 editions		Apr '32
7 *Ethics and Politics	10II/41iii	(7/9)	MS	188	223	Late Sum-Aut '32
8 Science of Politics	10II/5		MS	255	305-6	Apr '32
9 The 'National' Origins of Crocean Historicism	10II/41xiv	(8/25, 27 & 39)	MS	219-21	261-4	Late Sum-Aut '32
10 *Croce's Historicism	10II/41xvi		MS	221-2	264-5	Late Sum-Aut '32
11 *The Histories of Italy and Europe	10II/29i		MS	246	294	Jun-Aug '32
12 History and anti-History	(10II/28ii)	8/210	(MS	41-2	48-9)	Feb-Mar '32

	Critical edition B/C text	A text	Platone-Togliatti volume	Einaudi 1948-51 page	Riuniti 1971 page	Date
13 *History, Anti-History and Hegel	10II/41ix		MS	206	246	Late Sum-Aut '32
14 Past and Present [1]. *Giolitti and Croce	6/107		PP	25-6	47	Spring-Sum '31
15 Past and Present [2]. *The World is Moving Towards …	15/36		PP	27-9	49-51	May '33
16 Identity of History and Philosophy	10II/2		MS	217-8	259-60	Apr '32
17 *Philosophy, Religion, Ideology	10II/31i	(8/198 & 231: also part of 'B' text 7/44)	MS	231-5	276-81	Jun-Aug '32
18 *Crocean Passion and Sorelian Myth	10II/41v	(7/39)	MS	242-4	289-92	Late Sum-Aut '32
19 Passion and Politics [1]	10II/56		MS	244-5	292-3	Feb-May '33
20 Passion and Politics [2]	10II/58		MS	245-6	293-4	Feb-May '33
21 *Political Ideologies	10II/41xii	(4/15, 20 & 22)	MS	236-9	281-6	Late Sum-Aut '32
22 *The Autonomy of the Politico-Economic Moment	10II/41x	(4/56)	MS	240-2	287-9	Late Sum-Aut '32
23 Appendix. Philosophical Knowledge as a Practical Act, an Act of the Will	10II/42		MS	253-4	303-4	Late Sum-Aut '32
24 Introduction to the Study of Philosophy. Reality of the External World	10II/6iii		MS	140	166	2nd half May '32

C Croce and Historical Materialism

25	*Religion, Philosophy, Politics [1]	10II/41i	(7/1)	MS	222-3	266-7	Aug '32
26	*A Philosophy for Barbarians	10II/41xiii	(4/44)	not in pre 1975 editions		Late Sum-Aut '32
27	*Originality and Popularisation	10II/41ii	(7/8)	MS	223	267	Late Sum-Aut '32
28	*Religion, Philosophy, Politics [2]	10II/41i	(7/1)	MS	223-31	267-76	Aug '32
29	*Croce and the Philosophy of Praxis	10II/34		not in pre-1975 editions		Jun-Aug '32
30	*The Real Development of History	10II/59ii		MS	222	265-6	Late Sum-Aut '32
31	Some Causes of Error	3/33		MACH	161	209-10	Jun-July '30 2nd half
32	Croce in the Second Post-War Period	10II/11		MS	255	305	May '32
33	*The War of Historical Materialism	10II/41xi	(4/15)	MS	175	208	Late Sum-Aut '32
34	*Croce's Four Criticisms of Marxism	10II/41viii		MS	205-6	245-6	Late Sum-Aut '32
35	*The Immediate Practical Element	10II/16		MS	207-8	247-8	Jun '32
36	*Croce, Einaudi and Loria	10II/18	(1/11)	MS	207	247-8	Jun '32
37	*Note on Luigi Einaudi	10II/39	(7/13)	MS	255-6	306-7	Jun-Aug '32
38	Cultural Topics, *Philosophy of Praxis and Historical Economism	17/12		PP	183-4	240	Sept '33
39	*The Crocean Critique of Marxism	10II/31ii		MS	206-7	246-7	Jun-Aug '32
40	*The Theory of Value in Critical					

Concordance Table 503

	Critical edition B/C text	A text	Platone-Togliatti volume	Einaudi 1948-51 page	Riuniti 1971 page	Date
Economy						
41 *The Theory of Value as an Elliptical Comparison	10II/38i	(7/42)	MS	208-9	249-50	Jun-Aug '32 Late Sum-Aut '32
42 *Croce and the Falling Rate of Profit	10II/41vi	(7/42)	MS	209-11	250-1	Jun-Aug '32
43 *Relative Surplus Value and the Falling Rate of Profit	10II/33		MS	211-2	252-3	Jun-Aug '32 Late Sum-Aut '32
44 *Fordism and the Falling Rate of Profit	10II/36		MS	212-4	253-6	
	10II/41vii	(7/34)	MS	214-5	256-7	Late Sum-Aut '32
D Croce, Actualism and Reformism						
45 Past and Present[3]. *Political and Civil Society	6/82		PP	79-82	113-7	Spring-Sum '31
46 Identification of Individual and State	10II/7		MS	276-7	331	2nd half May '32
47 Notes on Italian Culture [1]. Science and Culture	14/38i		INT			
48 Notes on Italian Culture [2]. Science	14/38iii		INT	46-7	64-6	Jan-Feb '33
49 Giovanni Gentile	11/6	(8/178 & 221)	MS	289	343-4	1932

50 G. Gentile and Political Philosophy	13/40	(1/87)	MACH	216	Sum '34(?)
51 *Past and Present [4]. *Gentile-Gioberti	7/79		PP	112-3	Dec '31
52 A Judgement on Gentile's 'Actual Idealism'	7/11		MS	289	Nov '30
53 Past and Present [5]. Gentile's Philosophy	8/16		PP	112	Jan '32
54 Past and Present [6]. The Crocean Utopia	6/112		PP	26-7	Spring-Sum '31
55 *The Theoretical Affirmation	10II/41xv		not in pre-1975 editions		Late Sum-Aut '32
56 *Actualism, Ideology and Philosophy	10II/59iv	(1/132 & 157)	MS	218-9	Feb-May '33
57 *Croce on De Man	10II/26		MS	207	Jun '32
58 Henri De Man	7/32		MS	113-4	Feb '31
59 Sorel, Proudhon, De Man [1]	11/66ii	(4/2, 30, 48; 8/167)	MS	110-13	Aut '32 – Beginning '33
60 Sorel, Proudhon, De Man [2]	11/66i	(4/31, 70 44, 63)	MS	105-10	Aut '32 – Beginning '33
61 Sorel, Proudhon, De Man [3]	11/69		MS	105-6	Aut '32-Beginning '33

Concordance Table

	Critical edition B/C text	Critical edition A text	Platone-Togliatti volume	Einaudi 1948-51 page	Riuniti 1971 page	Date
62 The Movement and the End	16/26	(9/6)	PP	190-1	248-9	Spring-end '34
E Croce's Position in the Intellectual World						
63 *The Party Man	10II/59i		MS	172-3	204-6	Feb-May '33
64 *Croce in the Intellectual Hierarchy	10II/14		MS	250-2	299-301	2nd half May '32
65 *Croce's International Importance	10II/22		MS	252-3	301-3	Jun '32
66 *Croce as a Renaissance Man [1]	10II/41iv	(7/17)	MS	246-7	294-5	Late Sum-Aut '32
67 Croce and Julien Benda	10II/47i		MS	257	307-8	Late Sum-Aut '32
68 *Croce as a Renaissance Man [2]	10II/41iv	(7/17)	MS	247-8	295-6	Late Sum-Aut '32
69 Croce and Modernism	10II/47ii		MS	257-8	308-9	Late Sum-Aut '32
70 *Croce as a Renaissance Man [3]	10II/41iv	(7/17)	MS	248-50	297-9	Late Sum-Aut '32

NOTES AND REFERENCES

Note on the Translation

1. Hamish Henderson (*Gramsci's Prison Letters*, London 1988, p.219) suggests 'market equilibrium' for *mercato determinato*, but this perhaps forces the reading a little too far.
2. D. Ricardo, *On the Principles of Political Economy and Taxation*, (Vol. 1 of the *Works and Correspondence of David Ricardo*), edited P. Sraffa, Cambridge 1951, p.284, quoting A.L.C. Destutt de Tracy's *Elémens d'Ideologie*.
3. Cf. Christine Buci-Glucksmann's fundamentally similar position in her *Gramsci and the State*, trans. David Fernbach, London 1980, pp.273-82 (especially pp.275-6) and footnote 92, p.444; see also Jean-Pierre Potier, *Lectures italiennes de Marx*, Lyon 1986, pp.239-52.
4. Hugues Portelli, *Le bloc historique*, Paris 1972, quoted from p.xii of the Italian translation, Rome and Bari 1976. On p.x Portelli also draws attention to 'the theoretical incorrectness of conceiving the historical bloc as a pure and simple alliance between social classes'.

Introduction

1. The volumes are *Selections from the Prison Notebooks*, edited and translated by Quintin Hoare and Geoffrey Nowell Smith, London 1971; *The Modern Prince and Other Writings*, edited and translated by Louis Marks, London 1957; *Selected Political Writings 1910-20*, edited by Quintin Hoare and translated by John Mathews, London 1977; *Selected Political Writings 1921-26*, edited and translated by Quintin Hoare, London 1978; *Selections from Cultural Writings*, London 1985, edited by Geoffrey Nowell Smith and David Forgacs and translated by William Boelhower; *A Gramsci Reader*, edited by David Forgacs, London 1988; *Gramsci's Prison Letters* edited and translated by Hamish Henderson, London 1988 (first published in the *New Edinburgh Review*, Edinburgh 1974); *Letters from Prison*, edited and translated by Lynne Lawner, London 1979; *Gramsci's Prison Notebooks*, edited and translated by

Joseph Buttigieg, New York 1992 (Vol. 1, covering the miscellaneous notebooks 1 and 2).
2. John Cammett, *Bibliografia Gramsciana*, Rome 1991.
3. Ruggero Grieco, another leading communist, in Amedeo Bordiga's journal, *Il Prometeo*, 15 February 1924, pp.28-30.
4. Books in excess of the limit were kept in a store-room, thus making it easier for the authorities – central as well as local – to keep a watchful eye on 'subversive' ideas. It has recently come to light (Yvon De Begnac, *Taccuini Mussoliniani* [*The Mussolini Notebooks*], edited by Francesco Perfetti, Bologna 1990, p.423) that Mussolini claimed 'I read the notebooks of the people sentenced by the Special Tribunal' but, even if his boast were true, it is not known whether he saw those of Gramsci.
5. Antonio Gramsci, *Quaderni del Carcere* (*Prison Notebooks*), Turin 1975, edited in four volumes by Valentino Gerratana (pp.lxviii + 3369, the last volume of a thousand pages being a critical apparatus but not, on the whole, the type of guide offered by SPN, SCW and the present volume). Gerratana's edition consists of all twenty-nine Notebooks devoted to Gramsci's reflections, ordered numerically according to the date (as far as can be told) when the notebook was begun; at the time the current volume goes to press consideration is being given to the publication of four others, as yet unpublished, that contain various translations Gramsci did in prison.
6. Gustavo Trombetti, impromptu conversation-lecture at the University of Urbino, 5 April 1990, the partial text of which is now available as 'Cell-mate of Detainee 7047' in a special number on Gramsci of the Italian expatriate journal *Emigrazione*, Vol. 23, August-September 1991, pp.18-21.
7. Aldo Natoli, *Antigone e il Prigioniero* (*Antigone and the Prisoner*), Rome 1990; Piero Sraffa, *Lettere a Tania per Gramsci* (*Letters to Tania for Gramsci*), Rome 1991; Tatiana Schucht, *Lettere ai familiari* (*Letters to Her Family*), Rome 1991.
8. The notebooks were smuggled out of Italy in the Soviet diplomatic bag, probably in early 1939, to be handed over to Gramsci's wife Julka (Julia). Togliatti was thus able to see them on his return to Moscow from the Spanish Civil War and they were consigned to him once and for all by the Soviet Embassy in Italy on 3 March 1945 after the Schucht family had, during the war, placed them in the care of the central archive of the Comintern. For a reconstruction of the notebooks' journeyings see Gianni Francioni, 'The English Trunk. Notes for a History of Gramsci's Notebooks' (*Studi Storici*, October-December 1992, pp.713-41, especially pp.716-21); other information published there is freely drawn on for this section of the introduction.
9. Sraffa, op. cit., p.xlviii; Gerratana here paraphrases a remark ('political economy is not a closed text') made by Maurice Dobb in summing up the debate sparked off by Sraffa; see Dobb's *Theories of Value and Distribution since Adam Smith*, London 1973, p.272.
10. K. Marx, *Contribution to a Critique of Hegel's Philosophy of Law. Introduction*, now in *Marx-Engels Collected Works*, Vol. 3, London 1975, p.182.
11. Judith Herrin, *The Formation of Christendom*, Oxford 1987, p.7, a

phrase from which, admirably summing up Gramsci's approach to religion, is borrowed as the heading to this section of the introduction.

12. The first quotation here is from a speech of Togliatti's in parliament (25 March 1947) on enshrining religious freedom in the republican Constitution, recalling a comment of Gramsci's in 1912. The second, from an article 'The Roman Question' (signed Caesar) by the Catholic communist Cesare Seassaro in *L'Ordine Nuovo*, 2 October 1920 (now in the anastatic reprint of the review *Ordine Nuovo 1919-1920, 1924-1925*, Milan 1976), goes on 'Today Christ's scarlet robe flames more dazzlingly, more scarlet, more Bolshevik.' The positions cited are in Tommaso La Rocca's comprehensive survey *Gramsci e la religione* (*Gramsci and Religion*), Brescia 1981, pp.58-60.

13. The statements are now in the anthologies of Gramsci's pre-prison writings *Sotto la Mole (1916-1920)*, (*Under the Tower* – the title of a regular column of his), Turin 1975, p.495, *L'Ordine Nuovo 1919-1920*, Turin 1970, p.476 (*not* to be confused with the reprint of the newspaper cited in note 12) and *La Costruzione del Partito Comunista (1923-1926)* (*Building the Communist Party (1923-1926)*), Turin 1974, p.313, respectively.

14. B. Croce, *The Conduct of Life*, trans. Arthur Livingston, London and New York 1924, pp.320-6 and 27-33 respectively.

15. Fr G.B. Montini, letter to his father (now in the Paul VI Institute, Brescia), cited in part in *L'Unità*, 20 March 1993. Radical Catholics left Montini behind when, after the Second Vatican Council (convened by John XXIII and concluded by Montini himself as Paul VI), they stressed the role of the 'people of God' and, instead of interpreting 'ecclesia' as 'Church' in the sense of a hierarchical institution, restored to it its original Greek meaning of 'assembly' (of the faithful).

16. Gramsci differed in this from the extreme left of the Communist Party, led by Amadeo Bordiga, who favoured a policy of isolating Miglioli in order to win over his followers.

17. Rosario Villari, 'Gramsci and the South' in *Politica e storia in Gramsci* (*Politics and History in Gramsci*), Vol.I, Rome 1977, pp.481-97, especially pp.489-90.

18. K. Marx and F. Engels, *On Religion*, Moscow and London 1955, pp.121 and 123 respectively, taken from Marx's letter to Engels of 2 June 1853; Engels's answer of 6 June 1853 (p.124) concurs. They toyed with the relevance of the idea even for the West for many years; in a letter of 17 February 1870 we find Marx saying that 'communal property [in land] ... is of Indian origin and is therefore to be found among all civilised European peoples in the early stages of their development' (*Letters to Dr Kugelmann*, trans. Jane Tabrisky, Moscow and Leningrad 1934, p.99). Some of Marx's information was however faulty and the idea – an integral part of the highly debatable 'Asiatic mode of production' hypothesis – seems to have been quietly let drop: see Perry Anderson, *Lineages of the Absolutist State*, London 1974, pp.484-95 and Geoffrey de Ste. Croix, *The Class Struggle in the Ancient Greek World*, London 1983, pp.155-7 and 544.

19. Gramsci, letter to Julka of 30 July 1929, now in *Gramsci's Prison Letters*, op.cit., p.101. The Schucht family attachment to Geneva was such that the little extra money that Tania (who was born there) saved was normally put aside to pay off the mortgage that she and Julka's father, Appollon, had taken out on a small house there.
20. Letter to Julka of 30 December 1929 now in *Letters from Prison*, op. cit., p.162. The wording of the letter is as reported here, i.e. 'external' not 'extreme' violence as Harold Entwistle has it (p.58) in his polemical but, on the whole, convincing discussion *Antonio Gramsci: Conservative Schooling for Radical Politics*, London 1979.
21. K. Marx, speech at the General Council of the International held on 17 August 1869 (minuted by J.G. Eccarius) now in *Documents of the First International*, Vol.3, London 1964, p.147.
22. A. Gramsci in *L'Avanti*, 18 December 1917, quoted in his *Scritti Politici*, (*Political Writings*), edited by Paolo Spriano, Rome 1971, pp.90-3.
23. A. Gramsci, letter to G. Lombardo-Radice rediscovered in 1964 and first published in the Communist weekly *Rinascita*, 7 March 1964. Letter and reply are now in the pre-prison *Lettere 1908-1926*, edited by Antonio A. Santucci, Turin 1992, pp.92-4.
24. Unsigned article in *L'Ordine Nuovo*, 1 April 1925, attributed to Gramsci and now in *La Costruzione del Partito Comunista*, op.cit., pp.48-50. The two parts of the course that saw the light, both prepared at least under Gramsci's guidance, are now in Corrado Morgia, *Il rivoluzionario qualificato* (*The Skilled Revolutionary*), Rome 1988, pp.59-209.
25. A. Gramsci, letter to Piero Sraffa of 2 January 1927, in *Lettere dal Carcere*, edited by Sergio Caprioglio and Elsa Fubini, Turin 1965, p.30, not in either English version of the prison letters. Later, when Gramsci was in a prison-approved clinic at Formia (1933-35) and Bordiga was under a type of house arrest in the same town, Gramsci was able, while taking exercise along the sea front, to acknowledge his presence but not to speak to him.
26. A certain imprecision is sometimes apparent in the notes. In particular, on Piero Sraffa's advice, Togliatti and Platone did not publish the note 'Classical Economy and Critical Economy' (pp.168-70 of this volume) in their thematic edition of the Notebooks since it gave 'an impression of superficiality that one does not meet in some of the other economics notes. ... What Gramsci here calls 'classical economy' is contemporary bourgeois economics, as is clear from the whole context, and in particular from the statement that it arrives at the concept of value 'through marginal utility', which – as is well-known – is an invention of the post- and anti-Marxist bourgeois economists.' Sraffa also regarded as inconsistent Gramsci's uses of the term 'comparative costs' (limited in classical economy to international trade) and questioned an apparent discrepancy in Gramsci as to whether 'socially necessary labour' was of interest to bourgeois economics; Sraffa's point was that 'the whole idea of competition is based on this type of concept'. Sraffa's letter to Togliatti,

Notes to pages xxxv–xxxviii

now in the Archives of the Gramsci Institute, may be read in Nicola Badaloni, 'Two Unpublished Manuscripts of Sraffa on Gramsci', *Critica marxista*, No.6 (1992), pp.43-50; see especially pp.44 and 45.

27. Badaloni, op. cit. in footnote 26, p.48.

28. Niccolò Machiavelli, *The Prince and The Discourses*, trans. L. Ricci and E.R.P. Vincent, New York 1950. The passages, from the *Discourses* (on the first ten books of Livy), Book 1, Chapters 10 and 55 (pp.108 and 255 respectively), are both quoted in an article (see Chapter III, footnote 1) on Machiavelli which Gramsci read, as are other fleeting references to the roles of industry and other employments as forming 'the nerve and life of the town' (*The Prince*, Chapters 10 and 21, pp.40 and 85 respectively); Gino Arias, the article's author, was however more concerned with glorifying the fascist state than with evaluating Machiavelli's ideas seriously.

29. Antoin E. Murphy's biography *Richard Cantillon: Entrepreneur and Economist*, Oxford 1986, casts doubt on the accepted story that he was murdered in 1734 and his body burnt; the facts that Cantillon withdrew £10,000 from his private account just before the corpse was found and that a mysterious 'Chevalier' appeared shortly afterwards in Surinam loaded with money, arms and a good number of Cantillon's papers suggest that he may have staged the whole affair and fled to escape criminal charges.

30. W.S. Jevons, *Contemporary Review*, January 1881, reprinted in his *Principles of Political Economy*, London 1924.

31. The Royal Economic Society of London published Henry Higgs's English translation (London 1931) with the French of the first edition of 1755 (reprinted Amsterdam 1756 in the edition Marx knew) while F.A. and Hella Hayek did a German translation (Jena 1931). An English version (*The Analysis of Trade, Commerce etc.*, London 1759) by Richard's (perhaps distant) cousin, Philip Cantillon, purporting to be the original, is highly unreliable.

32. Isaac Ilyich Rubin, *A History of Economic Thought*, trans. Donald Filtzer, London 1989, from the second Russian edition, Moscow and Leningrad 1929; see p.75 on Cantillon.

33. Erich (later Eric) Roll, *A History of Economic Thought* (first edition 1938); see pp.125 and 158-60 respectively of the second (revised) edition, London 1949.

34. Piero Sraffa, letter of 30 October 1948 to Giulio Einaudi, a photostat copy of which is now in the Einaudi publishing houses's celebration volume *Cinquant'anni di un editore* (*Fifty Years of Publishing*), Turin 1983, pp.66-7.

35. Piero Sraffa, *Production of Commodities by Means of Commodities*, Cambridge 1960.

36. See, e.g., Marco Lippi, *Value and Naturalism in Marx*, trans. Hilary Steedman, London 1979, Chapter V (pp.109-19) and postscript (pp.120-33, perhaps especially pp.120-1 and 130-3).

37. In conversation with the Canadian economist Gilles Dostaler, Sraffa said that his model described 'certain aspects of the same reality as that described by Marx', mentioning specifically class conflict and exploitation;

he regarded his 'values' and Marx's production prices as referring 'exactly to the same reality'; see Jean-Pierre Potier, *Un économiste non-conformiste. Piero Sraffa*, Lyon 1987, p.151.

38. Letter of 30 May 1932 to Tania; this part was intended for Sraffa; a slightly different wording is found in *Gramsci's Prison Letters*, op. cit., pp.219-20; the letter also uses the words 'realist, immediately historical "immanence" ' to distinguish between his own concept and the idealist one.

39. Piero Sraffa, letter of 21 June 1932 now in *Lettere a Tania per Gramsci*, op.cit., p.74. Jean-Pierre Potier, *Lectures italiennes de Marx 1883-1983*, Lyon 1986, pp.223-4, states that for the law of tendency Sraffa possibly had in mind Marshall's 1890 *Principles of Economics* which speaks of economic laws as 'statements of economic tendencies'.

40. David Ricardo, *Principles of Political Economy*, edited by Piero Sraffa for the Royal Economic Society, London 1951, p.120; Ricardo uses the words 'tend' and 'tendency' at least a score of times in this volume for both short-term fluctuations and longer-term effects.

41. Credit is due to Maurice A. Finocchiaro, *Gramsci and the History of Dialectical Thought*, Cambridge 1988, p.150, for spotlighting the importance of this passage but his claim that the new concept of immanence is 'synthetically identified' with 'the dialectical reasoning of Hegelianism' seems based on a grammatical misreading. It is rather 'the law of causality of the natural sciences ... purged of its mechanistic character' (*Lettere dal Carcere*, op.cit., p.629) that is identified with such reasoning; the dialectic is used to *arrive* at the realist concept of immanence but immanence and the dialectic are not identical for Gramsci.

42. 'Speculative Immanence and Historicist or Realist Immanence' (Q10II§9), SPN, pp.399-400. Hoare and Nowell Smith's translation is correct whereas a misprint in Gerratana's Critical Edition leads one to suppose that the origin of the philosophy of praxis lies in three cultural 'moments' rather than 'movements'.

43. Sraffa's reply to the letter of 30 May 1932, partially transcribed by Tania in her letter to Antonio of 5 July 1932, did not grasp the point of Gramsci's enquiry about a possible philosophical importance of Ricardo but informs us that he was a 'stockbroker of mediocre culture' whose 'sole cultural element that one can find is derived from the natural sciences'; see Sraffa, *Lettere a Tania per Gramsci*, loc.cit.

44. Rubin, op.cit., pp.242-3.
45. Roll, op.cit., p.177.
46. Ludwig Wittgenstein, *Philosophical Investigations*, Cambridge 1953, preface p.viii.
47. Ray Monk, *Ludwig Wittgenstein. The Duty of Genius*, London 1990, p.261.
48. Brian McGuinness, 'Dear Ludwig, Don't Leave Cambridge', in *Rinascita*, 16 June 1984, pp.16-7.
49. Ferruccio Rossi-Landi, p.21 of Section 4 ('A Few Hypotheses on Sraffa's Influence') of the essay 'Towards a Marxian Use of Wittgenstein'

in *Language as Work and Trade*, trans. Martha Galli Adams et al., South Hadley (Massachusetts) 1983.
50. F. Rossi-Landi, quoted by McGuinness, loc.cit.
51. The first quotation is from Wittgenstein, op.cit., proposition 43, p.20; the second is an aphorism which Norman Malcolm (*Ludwig Wittgenstein: A Memoir*, London 1958, p.93) attributes to Wittgenstein as summing up much of his philosophy; the third is from Rossi-Landi, op.cit., p.22.
52. Rossi-Landi, op.cit., pp.20-3, who cites the last comment from the economist Claudio Napoleoni: see also Fabio Ranchetti and Claudio Napoleoni, *Pensiero economico del novecento* (*Twentieth-Century Economic Thought*), second edition, Turin 1990, p.198.
53. Ranchetti and Napoleoni, op.cit., pp.209-10.
54. Lionel Robbins, *An Essay on the Nature and Significance of Economic Science*, London 1937, p.16 (first published 1932).
55. J.M. Keynes, *The General Theory of Employment, Interest and Money*, London 1936, author's preface, p.vii.
56. Ranchetti and Napoleoni, op.cit., p.xii.
57. This passage, written by Marx in English, is on p.134 of the *Grundrisse* in English (*Marx–Engels Collected Works*, Vol.29, London 1987, first German edition Moscow 1939-41).
58. Jean-Pierre Potier, *Lectures italiennes de Marx*, op.cit. See Chapter 3, 'L'interpretation d'Antonio Gramsci', especially p.261 and p.257 and its footnote, citing Bukharin's highly influential article 'Capitalist Stabilisation and Proletarian Revolution' in *La Correspondance Internationale*, 7 December 1926, and Chapter 4 ('The Sharpening of Contradictions: Rationalisation'), of E.D. Varga, *The Decline of Capitalism. The Economics of the Decline of Capitalism after Stabilisation*, London 1928; Varga's later *The Crisis and its Consequences*, London 1934, seems more nuanced on these arguments.
59. The title – 'On the Capitalist Use of Machines in Neocapitalism' – of Panzieri's most famous article (*Quaderni Rossi*, No.1, 1961, reprinted Rome 1978, pp.53-72) is a programmatic statement in itself; see also his 'Surplus Value and Planning: Notes on the Reading of *Capital*', trans. Julian Bees in Pamphlet No.1 of the Conference of Socialist Economists, London 1976 (first published in *Quaderni Rossi*, No.4, 1964).
60. The criterion adopted was to select notes having a fairly direct bearing on the great powers or on subsequent events. The odd note on internal 'regional' conflicts, then of some importance but now pretty well forgotten, has been omitted.
61. J.M. Keynes, *The Economic Consequences of the Peace*, London 1919, p.254-5, written as a criticism of the decisions of the Paris Peace Conference after his protest resignation from the post of British Treasury representative there.
62. Piero Sraffa, op.cit., p.73, in his letter of 21 June 1932 criticises Rodolfo Morandi for neglecting the function of agricultural areas in providing a market for industry similar 'to the one that, for instance, the overseas territories have in the British case'; Gramsci's discussion of Morandi's book is in 'On the National Economic Structure', pp.248-53.

63. Piero Sraffa, op.cit., pp.33-4, letter of 9 September 1931.
64. The entry headed 'Treatise on Money' in the index to Keynes's classic *General Theory of Employment* (London 1936) offers a reliable guide to the revision of his views. Sraffa, in a letter to Giulio Einaudi of 30 January 1966, cited here by kind permission of the Einaudi publishing house, observed that the *Treatise [on] Money* 'was repudiated by the author and superseded by the General Theory'.
65. Sraffa, letter to Tatiana of 9 September 1931, cited above.
66. J.-P. Potier, op.cit., p.265.
67. H.G. Scheffauer 'On American Naturalism', *Die Literarische Welt*, 14 October 1927, translated by Gramsci on pp.2-2a of Notebook A, one of the four unpublished notebooks that, with the exception of key passages from Marx in Notebook 7, contain the translations he did in prison.
68. Gian Giacomo Migone cites these names in 'Birth of American Hegemony, Seen at the Moment of its Decline' (in Italian), in *Birth of Which Nation? America's Self-Images, 1865-1929*, Perugia 1989; Migone, a leading Italian Americanist, unaware at the time of much of Gramsci's writing on America, reaches a similar standpoint to Gramsci's. In the post-Vietnam period he sees American world hegemony as being superseded by pure domination.
69. The text here reports as faithfully as possible the original wording of the 'C' text (Q13§18, see SPN, pp.158-67). The 'A' text (Q4§38), written before the finalisation of Gramsci's work on Croce and hence before the full incorporation into his vocabulary of terms like 'ethico-political', reads 'since hegemony is political, but also and especially economic, it has its material base in the decisive function exercised by the hegemonic grouping within the decisive core of economic activity'.
70. In a major essay of 1967, now in *Saggi su Gramsci* (*Essays on Gramsci*), Milan 1990, Norberto Bobbio, a critic always to be taken seriously, claims (p.50) that civil society is viewed by Gramsci 'as belonging to the moment of the superstructure and not to that of the structure'. In the 1990 preface he reiterates (p.10) this view: for Gramsci, 'the moment of civil society, closely bound up with the two questions of hegemony and the role of the intellectuals, belongs to the superstructural plane'. The interpretation given here is clearly in conflict with Bobbio's reading, which tends on occasion to be rather schematic and in this case leads to a reductive interpretation of the civil society-economy-hegemony nexus, among other things by introducing into a discussion of Gramsci a rigid division between the structural and superstructural planes, which Gramsci himself was at pains to emphasise was merely one of convenience for the purposes of analysis within the unity of the historical bloc.
71. See the 'Athos Lisa Report', bearing the date 22 March 1933 and made public in *Rinascita*, 12 December 1964, pp.17-21. Lisa took part in discussions among the communists gaoled with Gramsci at Turi di Bari at the end of 1930 and, on release, wrote a memorandum for the Party which included Gramsci's view (repeated in October 1932) that, in the conquest of power, allies had to be won for the proletariat through the intermediate stage of a Constituent Assembly.

72. Paolo Spriano, *Gramsci and the Party: the Prison Years*, London 1979, trans. John Fraser, Chapter IV, and Piero Sraffa, op.cit., p.xlvi; for other divergences between Gramsci and the International see Giuseppe Fiori, *Antonio Gramsci. Life of a Revolutionary*, trans. Tom Nairn, London 1970, pp.251-6.

73. Gramsci, letter dated 14 October 1926 (less than a month before his arrest), now in *La Costruzione del Partito Comunista*, op.cit., p.171. Togliatti, the Italian Party's representative in Moscow, judged it prudent, for the sakes of both the Party and Gramsci personally, not to transmit the letter.

74. See in particular J-P. Potier, *Lectures italiennes de Marx*, op.cit., pp.252-65; the proceedings of the 1987 conference on Gramsci's critique of Americanism *Modern Times: Gramsci e la critica dell'americanismo*, edited by Giorgio Baratta and Andrea Catone, Milan 1989; Derek Boothman, 'Gramsci as an Economist' (in German), *Das Argument*, No.185, pp.57-70, January-February 1991; and Nicola Badaloni, op.cit.

75. P. Sraffa, *Lettere a Tania per Gramsci*, op.cit., pp.23-4; letter of 23 August 1931.

76. Tom Bottomore, *The Frankfurt School*, Chichester, London and New York 1984, p.30, quoting Max Horkheimer, *Critical Theory: Selected Essays*, New York 1972, pp.140-87.

77. Max Horkheimer, 'Observations on Science and Crisis' (in German) in *Zeitschrift für Sozialforschung*, No.1, 1932, p.3, quoted in Phil Slater, *Origin and Significance of the Frankfurt School*, London 1977, p.41.

78. Bottomore, loc.cit.

79. Bottomore, op.cit., p.48, citing especially Chapter 6 ('Technological Rationality and the Logic of Domination') of Marcuse's *One Dimensional Man*, London 1964. The three interrelated elements are the one noted here, the culture industry and aspects of domination present in the ideological influence of science and technology (cf. *Americanism and Fordism*); all parallel the prison writings, while differing on important points.

80. Jürgen Habermas, 'Technology and Science as Ideology' in *Towards a Rational Society*, trans. J.J. Shapiro, London 1971, p.84, summarising Marcuse's views.

81. R.G. Collingwood, *The Idea of Nature*, Oxford 1945, p.176.

82. F.W. Aston, *Isotopes*, London 1922, p.1.

83. Thomas Kuhn, *The Structure of Scientific Revolutions* (second enlarged edition), Chicago 1970, pp.101-2 and 134-5 and 'Reflections on My Critics' in *Criticism and the Growth of Knowledge*, edited by I. Lakatos and A. Musgrave, Cambridge 1970, p.267.

84. Francesco Fistetti, 'Post-Empiricist Philosophy of Science' in *Neurath contro Popper* (*Neurath Against Popper*), Bari 1985, p.42; yet another nail in the coffin of the fact-hypothesis distinction is what he here calls the 'irreducibly metaphorical' (cf. Gramsci) and 'imprecise' nature of scientific language.

85. Franco Selleri, *Quantum Paradoxes and Physical Reality*, Dordrecht 1990, pp.15, 100, 345-7 and 349; see also Silvano Tagliagambe, *L'Epistemologia Moderna*, Rome 1991, pp.259-64.

86. Hoare and Nowell Smith's translation reads 'knowledge', 'specialists' and 'pursuit of knowledge', which is justifiable but does lead to a loss of the more specific and literal 'science', 'scientists' and 'scientific research' respectively.
87. Kuhn, 'Reflections on My Critics', op.cit., pp.252-3.
88. K. Marx,*Economic and Philosophical Manuscripts*, now in *Marx Engels Collected Works*, Vol. 3, London 1975, p.304.
89. Marx, op.cit., p.303.
90. Marx, *Capital*, Vol. 1, London 1967, p.373.
91. Paul Feyerabend, 'Consolations for the Specialist' in *Criticism and the Growth of Knowledge*, op.cit., p.228.
92. Massimo Aloisi, 'Gramsci, Science and Nature as History' in *Società*, Vol. VI, no.3, September 1950, pp.385-410.
93. In 1985 the distinguished physicist Rudolf Peierls (Selleri, op.cit., p.118) asked about the existence and description of quantum phenomena 'Does the observer create the world around him?' His reply was that 'this is a non-question because the word "existing" is undefined. ... Of course if there is no observer to have any knowledge of a system there is no quantum mechanical description of it, since this is in terms of an observer.'
94. Louis de Broglie, quoted in Selleri, op.cit., p.19. Only slightly later than Gramsci, the Marxist physicist Paul Langevin wrote in an essay published in English as 'Modern Physics and Determinism' (*The Modern Quarterly*, Vol.3, July 1939, p.215) that 'Idealist philosophers and those physicists who share their ideas, such as Eddington, Jeans, Jordan, Dirac and others, have once again affirmed that the recent advances in physics prove that there does not exist a real world independent of thought.'
95. A quantum paradox of the realist school, formulated just two years before Gramsci's death and presently again the subject of debate, is that due to Albert Einstein, B. Podolsky and N. Rosen; see the *Physical Review*, Vol.47 (1935), pp.777-81.
96. Valentin N. Voloshinov, *Marxism and the Philosophy of Language* (first published in Russian, Leningrad 1929), trans. L. Matejka and I.R. Titunik, New York and London 1973, especially pp.23-4.
97. Augusto Ponzio, p.6 of the introduction to the Italian translation (*Marxismo e filosofia del linguaggio*) of Voloshinov, op.cit., Bari 1976.
98. W.V.O. Quine, *Word and Object*, Cambridge (Mass.) 1960, especially Chapters 1 and 3. Quine's theory and the Sapir-Whorf hypothesis are subject to criticism from a materialist stance in Len Doyal and Roger Harris, 'The Practical Foundations of Human Understanding', *New Left Review*, No.139 (1983), pp.59-78.
99. Mario Garuglieri's testimony of a prison conversation with Gramsci, 'A Recollection of Gramsci', first published in *Società*, July-December 1946, and now in *Gramsci ritrovato 1937-1947* (*Gramsci Rediscovered 1937-1947*), edited by Enzo Santarelli, Catanzaro 1991, p.213. Cf. the comment in the British Marxist press of the time, made by the Bolshevik literary critic D.S. Mirsky, that Croce represented 'perhaps the most consistent philosophy of the dying bourgeois world' ('Bourgeois History

and Historical Materialism', *The Labour Monthly*, July 1931, p.455). Sraffa drew attention to this article in a letter of 11 July 1931 now in P. Sraffa, op.cit., p.14, observing that the journal's 'articles are uneven in quality but the Notes of the Month, written by the editor, are always very good'.

100. Most Marxist philosophers of the immediate post-fascist period owed more to Gentile than to Croce, who was more influential in the literary, political and historical fields.

101. Antonio Labriola, *Lettere a Benedetto Croce 1885-1904*, edited by Lidia Croce, Naples 1975, letters of 8 January 1900, pp.335-6 and 3 March 1898, pp.267-9 respectively.

102. B. Croce, 'Twenty Years Ago' in *Quaderni della 'Critica'*, No. 10 (1948), footnote on p.110.

103. Federico Chabod, 'Croce as Historian' in *Rivista storica italiana*, No.4 (1952), pp.473-530, especially pp.501-2.

104. R.G. Collingwood, *An Autobiography*, Oxford 1939, p.87 (not to be confused with Collingwood's translation, under the same title, of Croce's *Contributo alla critica di me stesso*, also cited in the current volume).

105. Mirsky, loc.cit. in note 99.

106. G.V. Plekhanov, 'On Croce's Book', a harsh but fair review of the first edition of *Historical Materialism*, in *Selected Philosophical Works Vol. II*, London 1976, pp.658-71.

107. A.I. Tiumeniev, 'Marxism and Bourgeois Historical Thought' in *Marxism and Modern Thought*, trans. Ralph Fox, London 1935, pp.235-319, especially p.276.

108. E.Ya. Egermann, 'The Struggle of the Italian Communists with the Reactionary Philosophy of Croce' (in Russian), *Voprosy Filosofii*, No.2 1951, pp.135-42.

109. Vittorio Foa, *Il cavallo e la torre* (*The Knight and the Rook*), Turin 1991, pp.92-3.

110. A. Gramsci, 'Some Aspects of the Southern Question', SPW 1921-26, pp.454 and 460 respectively.

111. G.J. Whitrow, 'Time' in *Dictionary of the History of Ideas*, New York 1973, Vol. IV, p.394, citing MacTaggart's *Studies in the Hegelian Dialectic*, Cambridge 1922, p.171. The aspects of relative openness and historical dynamic characteristic of Croce's historicist dialectic were features which Gramsci obviously found attractive.

112. Biagio de Giovanni, 'Croce's Revisionism and Gramsci's Critique of State Idealism' in *Lavoro Critico*, No. 1 (1975), pp.131-65.

113. The title appended to the American (but not the British) edition of Ainslie's translation of this book (*History: Its Theory and Practice*, New York 1921), like certain other editorial headings to translations of Croce, is thus misleading as regards the later Croce. As part of his definitive break with any conscious Marxist influence he switched to a rejection of the possibility of a *theory of history*, as is quite clear from the philological evidence of his footnote on p.182 of *Conversazioni Critiche. Serie Prima* (*Critical Conversations. First Series*), Bari 1942 (3rd edition). When he later speaks of a theory or philosophy of history, as in *Historical*

Materialism and the Economics of Karl Marx, trans. C.M. Meredith, London 1966 (reprint), p.116 (see footnote 67 to Chapter VII of this volume), it is normally to refer to someone else's (in this case Marx's), without committing himself to such a concept. When Gramsci speaks of Croce's 'theory of history' (*Gramsci's Prison Letters*, op.cit., London 1988, pp.210 and 215) it is to be understood that such a theory can be constructed and that Croce is wrong in removing everything to the superstructure.

114. Hayden White, p.xvii of his translator's preface to *From History to Sociology*, London 1962, by the Crocean philosopher Carlo Antoni.

115. See, for example, Croce's 'Economico-Political History and Ethico-Political History' in *Politics and Morals*, trans. Salvatore J. Castiglione, New York 1946, pp.67-77, especially p.68: 'Just as I was among the first to recommend the study of the concepts of historical materialism ... so I wish to be among the first to recommend that we rid ourselves of its residual prejudices.' Piero Sraffa, op.cit., p.62, in a letter to Tania of 30 April 1932, quotes an unidentified follower and friend of Croce, who remained unconvinced by his master's switch, to the effect that for Croce 'historical materialism has no value, even as a practical canon of interpretation'. The change in Croce's position also came out fairly clearly in his 1928-29 polemic with Corrado Barbagallo in the *Nuova rivista storica*.

116. Giovanni Gentile, letter to Croce of 17 January 1897 in *Lettere a Benedetto Croce* (*Letters to Benedetto Croce*), edited by S. Giannantoni, Florence 1972, p.21.

117. B. Croce, *Logica come scienza del concetto puro* (*Logic as Science of the Pure Concept*), Bari 1920, p.110.

118. Karl Popper, *The Poverty of Historicism*, London 1961, pp.128 and iii respectively. Some authorities – see Hayden White, p.x of Antoni, op.cit. – maintain that Italian historicism has little in common with the types criticised by Popper who, in any case (and not for the only time), attacks either vulgar Marxism as if it were the genuine article or affirmations of Marx that are far from being central to his theoretical construct.

119. Popper, op.cit., p.130.

120. B. Croce, *Historical Materialism*, op.cit., pp.60-1; in these statements Croce was, of course, following the lead given by the marginalist school of economics.

121. Emilio Agazzi, *Il giovane Croce e il Marxismo* (*The Young Croce and Marxism*), Turin 1962, p.566. David D. Roberts, *Benedetto Croce and the Uses of Historicism*, Berkeley 1987, especially pp.77-8, comes close to this viewpoint but in so doing is nearly alone of Crocean scholars among traditional intellectuals of the English-speaking world with their legendary ignorance of Marx; see also de Giovanni, op.cit., pp.136-8.

122. B. Croce, *La Critica*, November 1930, pp.455-6, review of D.B. Ryazanov's edition of the first four volumes (in German) of *Marx-Engels Collected Works* (or *MEGA*), Moscow 1927-30.

123. Antonio Labriola, op.cit., p.336.

124. H.S. Harris, *The Social Philosophy of Giovanni Gentile*, Urbana and London 1966, p.176 and footnote 43, quoting 'Fascism and Sicily' in Gentile's *Che cosa è il fascismo (What Fascism Is)*, Florence 1925, pp.50-1.
125. N. Bobbio, *Saggi su Gramsci*, op.cit., pp.86-7.
126. Guido Calogero, 'On the So-Called Identity of History and Philosophy' in *Philosophy and History: Essays Presented to Ernst Cassirer*, edited by R. Klibansky and H.J. Paton, New York, Evanston and London 1963, pp.36 and 35 respectively.
127. B. Croce, review of Gramsci's *Lettere del Carcere*, Turin 1947, in *Quaderni della 'Critica'*, No. 8 (1947), pp.86-8.
128. B. Croce, review of *Il materialismo storico e la filosofia di Benedetto Croce* in *Quaderni della 'Critica'*, No. 10 (1948), pp.78-9.
129. P. Sraffa, op.cit., p.72, referring to Gramsci's letters to Tania of the four successive weeks from 18 April to 9 May 1932 and 6 June 1932, now in *Gramsci's Prison Letters*, op.cit., pp.208-17 and 221-3 respectively, but first published in *Lo Stato Operaio*, Nos 5-6 (1937), pp.290-7, where the Communist Party's intention of publishing volumes of Gramsci's letters and other prison writings was first announced. This aspect of Gramsci's work seems to have been the first to appear in English: see issue no.10 of *Science and Society* (1946), pp.283-92.
130. B. Croce, review of *Gli intellettuali e l'organizzazione della cultura*, Turin 1949, in *Quaderni della 'Critica'*, No. 13 (1949), p.95.
131. B. Croce, 'A Game that Has Now Gone on Long Enough', *Quaderni della 'Critica'*, Nos. 17-18 (1950), pp.231-2.
132. He makes a similar comment to this in his notes on 'The Formation of the Intellectuals' (Q12§1) in SPN, p.17, and immediately adds in brackets (in a couple of lines omitted in SPN) 'moreover, all these notes must be considered simply as departure points and *aide-mémoires* that have to be checked on and examined in greater depth'.
133. In conferences in 1991 celebrating the centenary of Gramsci's birth Johanna Borek was responsible for underlining the importance of Gramsci's 'living philology' approach. As well as what is immediately apparent in the text of his writings, this is often shown in the bibliographical detail which, when not in the context of another note, is often either omitted or included as 'scattered notes' even in Italian editions.
134. Joseph Femia, *Gramsci's Political Thought*, Oxford 1981, p.254 for the conclusion cited here on Gramsci and pp.248-52 for the discussion of the other trends in Marxism referred to.
135. Iring Fetscher in Vol.I of *Gramsci e la Cultura Contemporanea (Gramsci and Contemporary Culture)*, edited by Pietro Rossi, Rome 1967, p.164.
136. Some of the sentiments in this note were expressed in a letter to Tania of 6 March 1933, unfortunately not included in either partial version of the prison letters in English. As the present volume goes to press we have news of the publication, by the Columbia University Press, of Frank Rosengarten's two volume edition of the full prison letters, translated by Raymond Rosenthal.

Chapter I Religion: A Movement and an Ideology

1. For *Adversus Colotem* (*Reply to Colotes*), see Vol.XIV of the Loeb Classical Library edition of Plutarch's *Moralia*, trans. B. Einarson and P.H. De Lacy, London and Cambridge, Mass. 1967, p.301. The two additions in brackets are Gramsci's.
2. Reinach's book was published in French in 1909 and translated into English by Florence Simmonds (*Orpheus: A History of Religions*, London 1931). Gramsci here quotes §5 of the Introduction (of which Simmonds omits the word 'taboos'), probably at second hand from Turchi since Reinach does there consider other definitions of religion but rejects them as too narrow.
3. A common distinction between theism and deism is that due to Kant (*Critique of Pure Reason*, 1787 second edn., trans. J.M.D. Meiklejohn, London and New York, 1979 reprint of 1855 original). In Book II, Chapter III, Section VII of the 'Transcendental Dialectic' (pp. 367-8 of edition quoted), Kant states that the cognition of a primal being 'is based either upon reason alone (*theologia rationalis*) or upon revelation (*theologia revelata*)'. The object of the former is cogitated 'either by means of pure transcendental conceptions' (i.e. not determinable by experience) 'and is termed *transcendental theology*; or by means of a conception derived from the nature of our mind, as a supreme intelligence, and must then be entitled *natural theology*. The person who believes in transcendental theology alone is termed a *Deist*; he who acknowledges the possibility of a *natural* theology also, a *Theist*'. ...[While] 'we might, in strict rigour, deny to the *Deist* any belief in God at all, and regard him merely as the maintainer of the existence of a primal being or thing ... it is more correct – as it is less harsh – to say, the Deist believes in a God, the Theist in a *living God* (*summa intelligentia*).' See also 'Religion [2]' pp.13–14 in this Chapter.
4. Q5§78 ('Monasticism and the Feudal Order') discusses this question from a somewhat different angle. The Church 'reproduces and develops the regime of the patrician Roman "villa" '. In the big monasteries, the place of peasant-monks is taken over by the ordinary laity to allow the monks 'to be within the convent at any hour to carry out the rites. Within the monastery, the monks take on different "work" – industrial (artisan) labour and intellectual labour (which contains a manual part in the work of copying). The relation between cultivators and monastery is feudal, with stipulated concessions, and is moreover tied to the internal diversification taking place in the monks' labour, as well as to the expansion of the landed property of the monastery.' There thus grew up a sophisticated division of labour – and concomitant hierarchical decision-making process – within the monastery.
5. 'Action Française and the Integralists' (see especially p.82) also adds what was chronologically the first of these decisive turning points, viz. the East-West schism defined by the advent of Charlemagne's empire.
6. Vincenzo Gioberti was the leading philosopher of the Risorgimento moderates, and introduced Hegelian notions (though in a mutilated form

Notes to pages 11–15   521

– see 'Croce and Italian Historiography', pp.341-3 of this volume) especially in his 1844 four-volume *Introduzione allo studio della filosofia* [*Introduction to the Study of Philosophy*] which (Q10II§43) 'proposed to "revolutionise" a cultural world, in all its complexity'. *Delle cinque piaghe della Chiesa* (a partial English translation by H.P. Liddon, London 1883, has now been replaced by Denis Cleary's full edition, *The Five Wounds of the Church*, Leominster 1987), written by the liberal Catholic priest Antonio Rosmini in 1832-33 but published only in the freer atmosphere of 1848, argued for much needed reforms in Catholicism.

7. *Le problème ouvrier aux Etats-Unis* (*The Working-Class Question in the United States*), Paris 1927; see also 'Sorel, Proudhon, De Man[1]' p.454 in this volume and SPN, especially p.286.

8. Up to here, this passage goes over some of the same ground as the celebrated essay that Gramsci was working on when arrested, 'Alcuni temi della quistione meridionale' ('Some Aspects of the Southern Question'); see SPW 1921-26, especially pp.455-6, point 3.

9. Here Gramsci changed opinion; after having originally written 'only in Sicily' he later put this in brackets and, between the lines, added 'no'.

10. Though there were still impediments to their use of the franchise, many peasants showed a passionate interest in this election. According to Angelo Tasca, of Gramsci's *Ordine Nuovo* group (but later expelled from the Communist Party), this played a large part in turning Gramsci towards socialism (Tasca, *I primi dieci anni del PCI* [*The PCI's First Decade*], Bari 1971, p.88).

11. For Maurras, see the later section of this chapter entitled 'Integralist Catholics, Jesuits and Modernists', pp.76-102.

12. Croce calls Paul Bourget's novel a 'Stendhal-type pastiche, made silly by the introduction of philosophico-moral elements silly in nature' (*Pagine sulla guerra* [*Pages on the War*], Bari 1928, p.188).

13. In the 'Transcendental Dialectic' (Book III, Ch. III, Sections IV to VI of the *Critique of Pure Reason*; see p.372 of edition cited in note 3, above) Kant demonstrates the impossibility of ontological, cosmological and physico-theological proofs of the existence of God, concluding that the objective reality of 'a Supreme Being ... can neither be proved nor disproved by pure reason'. Having thus cleared the way, he argues in Book II, Ch. II, Section V of the later *Critique of Practical Reason* (1788, seven years after the *first* edition of his *Pure Reason*) that 'through the concept of the highest good [*Summum Bonum*, identified with the Kingdom of God and with Morality] as the object and final end of pure practical reason, the moral law leads to religion. Religion is the recognition of all duties as divine commands, not as sanctions, i.e. arbitrary and contingent ordinances of a foreign will, but as essential laws of any free will as such. Even as such, they must be regarded as commands of the Supreme Being ...' (*Critique of Practical Reason*; now in Kant's *Writings in Moral Philosophy*, trans. L. W. Beck, Chicago 1949, p.226).

14. This is discussed mainly in 'Religion, Philosophy, Politics[2]', pp.408-9 of this volume.

15. For the position of Spirito (and other actualist philosophers) on the

state, see in particular 'Political and Civil Society' and 'Identification of Individual and State', pp.435-9 and 'The Einaudi-Spirito Polemic over the State', pp.182-4.

16. See the two chapters on Croce, in particular 'Development of the Theory of Ethico-Political History' (pp.335-6), 'Definition of Ethico-Political History' (pp.343-6), 'Paradigms of Ethico-Political History' (pp.348-50), 'Ethico-Political History and Hegemony' (pp.357-8), 'The Central Nucleus of the Essay' (p.367) and 'Ethics and Politics' (pp.372-3).

17. In Q3§142, Gramsci comments on the way *diritto* (law) has evolved within Christendom. While 'the Romans fashioned the word *jus* to express *diritto* as power of the will ... Christianity, more than the concept of *jus*, elaborated the concept of *directum* [*diritto*] in its tendency to subordinate the will to the norm, in order to transform power into duty. The concept of *diritto* as power refers only to God, whose will becomes a norm of conduct ...'

18. Gramsci seems to use 'discipline' here in the sense not of an imposition but of something self-created and accepted, rather like his polemical use of 'conformism'; see the last section, 'The New Society and the New Economic Individual', of Chap. IV, pp.269-77, *passim*.

19. See 'Civil Society', pp.75-6.

20. In English as 'The Unending Struggle between "Church" and "State" ' in *Politics and Morals*, trans. Salvatore J. Castiglione, London and New York 1946, pp.125-30.

21. Compare this with Q7§28 ('Civil Society and Political Society', here quoted in its entirety): 'Civil society split off from political society. A new problem of hegemony is posed, i.e. the historical basis of the state has shifted. One has an extreme form of political society: either struggle against the new and conserve the tottering old structure, welding it together by coercion, or, as expression of the new, break the resistance that it is meeting in its development, etc.'

22. Albertino Mussato, a contemporary of Dante, is now best remembered as a poet who, like Dante and Petrarch, received the prized laurel wreath as 'poet laureate'. The centenary referred to in the *Nuova Antologia* article is thus the sixth.

23. Roberto Bellarmino (1542-1621, sometimes referred to as Bellarmine) was a Tuscan Jesuit cardinal remembered for his defence of Catholicism against Protestant controversialists, including James VI of Scotland (James I of England), as well as for the Galileo affair. His role in this latter (see next sub-section, pp.21-2) is still far from clear. An interview that, at the Pope's request, he granted Galileo immediately after the 1616 anti-Copernican decree was brought up in the 1633 trial by the prosecution, who maintained Bellarmino had given Galileo a formal and personal injunction to abjure the doctrine of the Earth's motion; Galileo denied this and produced an attestation in his favour drawn up by Bellarmino himself. Though controversy still rages about the exact nature, authenticity and status of the interview and attestation, suffice it to say that once Galileo had broached the matter, the prosecution dropped the injunction question.

24. In *De Controversiis* and *De Potestate*, this latter work (condemned as treasonable in the non-papal atmospheres of the Venetian Republic and Paris) being a reply to William Barclay of Aberdeen.
25. L. von Pastor, *The History of the Popes from the Close of the Middle Ages*, Eng. trans. Wilmington 1977, 40 Vols; the quotation here is found on p.300 of Vol.25 and is slightly rearranged to include the explicit subject of 'damped' (in the previous sentence in the English translation, but as written here in the Italian version). James Bradley (1693-1762), a meticulous observer and former assistant to Edmund Halley (of Comet Halley fame), went on to become Astronomer Royal in 1742.
26. Although in 1616 – 26 years before Galileo's death – the Holy Office (Inquisition) officially condemned heliocentrism and put Copernicus's *De Revolutionibus*, as well as other Copernican works, on the *Index* of banned books, forbidding Galileo to maintain the theory publicly, it is still in doubt whether he was *personally* on trial in the sense that he definitely was in 1633 (which Gramsci considers the second trial).
27. In fact it was the same Council of Basel mentioned just below. It must be borne in mind that Cusanus lived in the century before the Lutheran and then the Calvinist Reformation and a couple of centuries before Galileo; in his time, then, the Roman Catholic Church did not feel itself threatened, so it was easier to put forward advanced views.
28. 'Learned ignorance' and 'identity of opposites' respectively.
29. Gramsci surmised correctly.
30. This piece, Q26§11 (which unites two earlier 'A' texts, Q5§136 and Q5§139), also deals with other matters, not directly pertinent to religious matters, whose nature is specific to Italian history. To provide a smooth opening, the first sentence here is taken from Q5§139, while the rest is the later, more 'finished' version indicated; the major change to note is that the earlier draft does make it more explicit that secular culture had not been 'penetrated' by 'the conviction that the Church had undergone a Reformation'.
31. In Q5§145, again on religion in Britain, Gramsci quotes from an article in *Civiltà Cattolica* 'The New Blessed English Martyrs, Defenders of the Primacy of Rome' attacking the English clergy which 'during Henry VIII's persecutions "*for the main part* ... showed a culpable and illegitimate submission by promising by law ... to have approval of any ecclesiastical law depend on the king". When Henry imposed the "oath of loyalty" and wanted to be recognised as head of the Church "unfortunately many of the clergy, *faced with the threat of the loss of goods* and life, yielded at least as regards appearances, to the great scandal of the faithful".' The wording in double inverted commas is from *Civiltà Cattolica* while the emphasis is Gramsci's.
32. Gramsci uses the term '*totalitaria*', not then as ideologically-loaded as it is now; see also 'Catholic Action's Origins' and 'Catholic Action and Neo-Guelphism', pp.37-9, as well as SPN, footnotes 23 on p.147 and 50 on p.157.
33. Antonio Labriola's essay 'Concerning the Crisis of Marxism', first published in 1899 and now in his *Socialism and Philosophy*, trans. Ernest

Untermann, Chicago 1934 reprint, pp.195-221, is a polemical review of T. G. Masaryk's *Die philosophischen und sociologischen Grundlagen des Marxismus* (*The Philosophical and Sociological Foundation of Marxism*).

34. This second essay was written by Trotsky, not mentioned in the text to avoid censorship problems. The article 'Professor Masaryk on Russia' appeared in German in the December 1914 number of the Social Democratic monthly *Der Kampf*.

35. Rather than *papale* ('papal'), Gramsci here uses (in inverted commas) *papalina*, which often refers specifically to the latter days of the temporal power of the popes in the Papal States (or States of the Church).

36. Gramsci was on Ustica, an island about 50 kilometres north of Palermo, from 7 December 1926 to 20 January 1927. While there he directed the literary-historical section and Amadeo Bordiga, leader of the intransigent left of the Communist Party, the scientific section of a party school among the detainees.

37. The French *manant*, coming from the verb *manoir* ('to dwell or inhabit') and originally referring to an inhabitant of a village, has now, like the change from 'villein' to 'villain' in English, come to take on more the meaning of 'scoundrel'.

38. The CIL (Confederazione Italiana dei Lavoratori) was created in September 1918 from the 'white' (i.e. Catholic) unions, founded in the first decade of the century. The Popular Party (Partito Popolare Italiano) was launched on 18 January 1919 through Don Luigi Sturzo's appeal 'to the strong and the free'. 'Popularist' is used in the translation where the reference is clearly to the PPI or its associated movements; Gramsci in such cases often uses *popolaresco* rather than simply *popolare*, which normally means 'people's' or 'popular' (in all senses), though it too can have a political meaning, as in the name of the party.

39. The *Social Code* was formulated by the International Union of Social Studies (founded at the Belgian city of Malines or Mechelen) in 1920, as a guideline for Catholic social policy, partly to counterbalance socialists 'whose growing activity threatens the total de-Christianisation of our industrial societies' (p.13 of the Introduction to the *Codice sociale*, Rovigo 1927). While the parts of the code on industrial relations and nationalisation come close to positions then held by reformist socialists, others on education, the position of women, the 'unity, stability and fecundity' of the family, or voting rights ('the father could, in addition to his own personal vote, dispose of a number of votes equal or proportional to the importance of the household whose guardian he is', pp.47-8) are highly conservative. On international relations it states that 'colonisation, i.e. the methodical action of one people organised over another whose development is manifestly insufficient, or over a depopulated territory, is legitimate' (p. 81).

40. The Tertiaries, founded in 1221 as a lay accessory to the Franciscan Order, consisted mainly of labourers of different sorts devoting themselves to the social work of the order; they were soon regarded by the hierarchy as a dangerous link with heretical social movements. The distinction Gramsci seems to be drawing is that whereas the early

Franciscans, of whatever tendency, aimed at a global reform of the Church, Catholic Action had and has the more limited scope of work within given sectors.
41. *Totalitaria*; see footnote 32.
42. Translated as 'The Pre-History of Catholic Action', immediately above (pp.35-6); the second part of the article on La Mennais appeared a couple of years after the first, but was not commented on by Gramsci.
43. Cf. 'Catholic Action and the Franciscan Tertiaries' pp.33-4 and n.40 above; 'integralist', similar in concept to *totalitario* in not admitting the legitimacy of other views, is discussed in the section 'Integralist Catholics, Jesuits and Modernists' of this chapter, pp.76-102.
44. In his analysis (1817-25) of the religious indifference of the masses Abbot Hugues-Félicité-Robert de La Mennais (or Lamennais; 1782-1854) concluded that truth could not be reached by individual but only by universal reason, of which the Church was the legitimate interpreter. Continuing this argument in his 1829 book *Les progrès de la révolution et de la guerre contre l'Eglise* ('Progress Made By the Revolution and the War against the Church'), he called for the separation of Church and state on the grounds, it seems, that the state had not been able to guarantee the success of the Church's mission. Instead of the old alliance of Pope and King, he proposed one of Pope and People. Though this was positive in providing a justification for mass organisations such as Catholic Action and in supporting press freedom and adult (male) suffrage, he also laid the basis for another form of Catholic integralism by assigning a privileged position to the Church; his views were however sufficiently radical for him to be the implicit and then explicit target of the encyclicals *Mirari vos* (1832) and *Singulari nos* (1834). The 'La Mennais Mark II' may refer to even later years when he went still further, arriving at republicanism.
45. I.e. 'The Pre-History of Catholic Action' and 'Catholic Action's Origins', above, pp.35-8.
46. The neo-Guelphs wanted the Pope to head a confederation of Italian states, though, as Gramsci says, that would have meant a clash with Austrian Catholics. Despite their temporalist aspirations of a return to the medieval Church (referred to later in this sub-section), they may be regarded as a tendency within liberal Catholicism or Catholic democracy (see 'The Risorgimento. 1848-49', pp.39-40). The Sanfedistas took their name from *Santa Fede* ('Holy Faith'); at the instigation of Cardinal Ruffo, their original bands were instrumental in the overthrow in 1799 of the short-lived, progressive Parthenopean Republic of Naples.
47. It must be remembered that the 'moderates' were the right wing of the national forces of the time, who completely out-manoeuvred the left, formed by the Action Party. In this phrase, then, a 'moderate' has to be understood not in the 'cosy' sense of a 'relative (though not excessive) reactionary' but, quite simply, 'right-wing reactionary'.
48. The *non expedit* was the papal ruling (1871), after the unification of Rome with the rest of the Kingdom of Italy, that it was not expedient (or convenient) for franchised Catholics to vote in political (i.e. general)

elections, since this went against the papacy's temporal claims. It was however accepted right from 1871, and even with some warmth (see Q5§44, in which Pius IX is quoted to this effect in the memoirs of Paolo Campello della Spina) that they could vote in administrative (i.e. local) elections. As Pietro Scoppola points out on p.37 of *Dal neo-guelfismo alla Democrazia cristiana* (*From Neo-Guelphism to Christian Democracy*), 2nd edition (revised), Rome 1963, from the original merely tactical judgement the *non expedit* became for a generation, through the intervention in 1886 of the Holy Office (ex-Inquisition), an obligation of conscience.

49. I.e. the date when the armed forces of the Savoy monarchy entered Rome through the breach of Porta Pia and put an end to the temporal power of the papacy.

50. Thomism (or neo-scholasticism) was the set of doctrines based on the philosophy of the greatest medieval Catholic schoolman, Thomas Aquinas, that tried in part to reconcile modern philosophy with the terms of his schema and in part to lay the basis for Catholic social thought.

51. Leo XIII's encyclical on the social movement, *Rerum Novarum* (*On the Condition of the Working Classes*), was published in 1891; it is included as Appendix III to Mary Mackintosh's translation of F.S. Nitti's *Catholic Socialism*, London and New York 1895, under the title *On New Things*. The Genoa Congress included all the main socialist organisations and tendencies; it broke with anarchism and gave birth to the *Partito dei Lavoratori Italiani* (Italian Working People's Party), which then became the Socialist Party of the Italian Workers and, in 1895, the Italian Socialist Party.

52. In 1898 the government shot down 80 workers in cold blood and imprisoned several of the most prominent socialist leaders. To protect its left flank from attacks by the liberally-inclined bourgeoisie it pandered to the latter's traditional anti-clericalism by simultaneously suspending for a few months (the dissolution that Gramsci refers to) over 3,000 Catholic organisations, in the main linked to the increasingly powerful *Opera dei Congressi*, then the umbrella association – under intransigent and integralist leadership – for Catholics in the social field. This move widened incipient cracks in the *Opera* on socio-economic questions and on whether to form a political movement; the organisation, now seriously weakened, limped along until formally dissolved by the Vatican in 1904.

53. The Austro-Hungarian monarch, Joseph II, abolished serfdom in the Empire in 1781 and introduced other radical social measures. However, the efforts of his state officials and goodwill of many peasants 'were quite insufficient to break the resistance of the outraged Church, nobility, provincial estates and chartered towns ... To save his dominions from disintegration, Joseph and his successor, Leopold II, were compelled to make concessions that virtually destroyed his handiwork' (George Rudé, *Revolutionary Europe*, London 1964, p.39).

54. As among 'the most important measures ... to reinforce [the Church's] internal unity in modern times' Gramsci cites Pius X's 1910 decree laying an '*obligation* on families to have children make their first communion at *seven*. One understands the psychological effect that the

ceremonial trappings ... must have on seven-year-olds ... and what source of terror and hence attachment to the Church it may become.' 'One thus understands the resistance the measure has met in families, worried by the harmful effects this premature mysticism has on the infant mind.' (Q5§58)

55. Though only days after writing this note Gramsci recalls (in 'Catholic Social Thought', pp.46-7) that Napoleon III was termed a man of providence, he cannot but have also had in mind a notorious papal statement. Just after signature of the Treaty and Concordat between Italy and the Roman Catholic Church (see the section of this chapter 'Concordats and Church-State Relations, pp.59-76), Pius XI claimed of Mussolini that 'a man was needed such as he whom Providence has had Us meet ...' (see A.C. Jemolo, *Chiesa e Stato in Italia negli ultimi cento anni* [*Church and State in Italy in the Last Hundred Years*], Turin 1948, pp.640-1).

56. 'Past and Present' is a generic heading that Gramsci gave to many notes; most were collected together under that title as one of the six original thematic volumes of the Notebooks. That the present note is put here with those on Catholic social policy and Catholic Action but could equally well be included with other notes is quite normal.

57. French Catholics were extraneous to the regime that followed the falls of Napoleon III (September 1870) and then of the Paris Commune in 1871. Pope Leo XIII obtained their reinsertion into state life by his call for a rally (*ralliement*) to the Republic.

58. After a colourful history trying to raise revolts in France during the 1830s and early 1840s, Napoleon's nephew and step-grandson Louis Napoleon (1808-73) was elected to the Constituent Assembly in 1848, taking his seat when the law banishing the Bonapartes was repealed. On 10 December 1848 he was elected President, further strengthening his position by the *coup d'état* of 2 December 1851 (which Marx, in Chapter 6 of his *18th Brumaire of Louis Napoleon*, called a 'parody of an imperialist restoration') and by becoming Emperor Napoleon III on 2 December 1852. He died in exile in Chislehurst.

59. Catholic Action was subject to attacks culminating in May 1931 in physical assaults on their local offices, organisers and even priests. On 2 June the government dissolved all 10,000 or so youth organisations not directly affiliated to the Fascist Party or its youth movement, reducing Catholic Action's function to a solely devotional one. Pius XI's encyclical of 5 July voiced opposition to both this and the compulsory oath of allegiance to the regime, but the speed with which matters were smoothed over indicated the opposition was little more than ritual.

60. I.e. a member of the religious order founded by St Philip Neri.

61. When David refused to heed a warning from the Carabinieri to dissolve the peaceful procession he was leading and go back, they opened fire and shot him in the forehead; his daughter's eye-witness account is retold by her step-granddaughter, Anna Innocenti Periccioli, in *David Lazzaretti*, Milan 1985, especially pp.94-105.

62. It should be remembered that political life was fragmentary, the franchise being limited to males from an extremely narrow social

background; this made it easy for individual politicians to dominate affairs in the single-member constituencies, at the expense of a party structure based on alternative programmes.

63. F.S. Nitti, *Il socialismo cattolico*, Turin and Rome 1891. See the English version, *Catholic Socialism*, *op. cit.*, pp.368-70, for Lazzaretti's 'Communism based on fraternity and mysticism' and the Benevento 'bands'. In the latter case, anarchists won over two villages in south-central Italy and proclaimed the Social Revolution; two local priests, later among the 37 tried as ring-leaders 'side by side with Malatesta, Cafiero and other noted internationalists', blessed the insurgents as liberators, calling them 'true apostles of the Lord'. Nitti considers that episodes like this led to Leo XIII's encyclical *Quod Apostolici Muneris* ('*On the Social Question*', dating from 1878, like the trial) that denounced anarchists, socialists and communists; its original text is printed as Appendix to *Catholic Socialism*.

64. In Q6§158, Gramsci takes issue with those who regarded the Lazzarettian, Benevento and similar movements as 'Messianic currents'; like 'the republican and internationalist movements in the Romagna or the South', they were 'single isolated happenings demonstrating more the "passivity" of the great rural masses', which was not helped by a void (due to the lack of 'definite and concrete programmes and goals' of the left) 'capable of being filled by the most disparate thing'. Slightly earlier (Q6§144), though, he did recognise the 'ideological effectiveness of Lazzaretti's death' as exemplified by the 1899-1900 stance of Giovanni Pascoli, the poet and internationalist who however later became a chauvinist.

65. Matilde Serao's *Il Paese di Cuccagna* exists as *The Land of Cockaygne*, (translator unknown), London 1901.

66. H. de Balzac, *A Bachelor's Establishment*, trans. Eithne Wilkins, London 1951, p.50; the English title is a literal rendering of the alternative French one.

67. Marx's famous expression is actually from the *Introduction* to the *Critique* rather than the *Critique* itself: '*Religious* distress is at the same time the *expression* of real distress and also the *protest* against real distress. Religion is the sigh of the oppressed creature, the heart of a heartless world, just as it is the spirit of spiritless conditions. It is the *opium* of the people.' (Marx Engels Collected Works, Vol.3, London 1975, p.175). Paul Lafargue's remark is from his 'Personal Recollection of Karl Marx'; see p.185 of *Karl Marx: Man, Thinker and Revolutionist: A Symposium edited by D.B. Ryazanoff*, London 1927. In his notebook, Gramsci writes 'C.M.', i.e. Carlo Marx, to avoid censorship problems.

68. Engels, letter to Margaret Harkness (April 1888).

69. Lanson quotes word-for-word the first paragraph of §187 ('Order') of Section III ('Of the Necessity of the Wager') of Pascal's *Thoughts*; the English translation here is that of W.F. Trotter, New York 1910.

70. This is not true if Gramsci means the argument surfaced only in the 1840s; despite the mutilated early versions of Pascal's *Pensées*, there is, for example, a discussion of the wager on pp.56-7 of Guillaume Desprez's 1670 Paris edition.

71. 'God has revealed nothing to make us believe in an after-life, and nor does Moses speak of it. Maybe God doesn't even want the faithful to be so firmly convinced they'll survive. In his fatherly goodness, maybe he wants to surprise us with it.' (Heinrich Heine, 'Gedanke und Einfälle', in *Gesammelte Werke*, ed. W. Harich, Vol.VI, p.419, Berlin 1951).

72. In fact the only other note is the one immediately above from the same notebook.

73. 'Order' in this title is to be understood as a juridical order or 'set-up', as in 'Nature of the Concordats', immediately below. Fr Luigi Taparelli (1793-1862, born Prospero Taparelli D'Azeglio), an early Jesuit Thomist, was a son of the Marquis Cesare D'Azeglio of Catholic press fame ('The Pre-History of Catholic Action' and 'Catholic Action's Origins', pp.35-8); though favouring an accord between Catholics and moderate liberals, he upheld the temporal power of the popes (Q2§13). His more famous brother, Massimo, when governor of Milan, refused arms to Garibaldi's Expeditionary Force (1860) during the campaign to unite Italy (Q2§56).

74. The *Kulturkampf* (cultural struggle or struggle for civilisation) was Bismarck's fight (1871-87) to subject Roman Catholicism to state controls in Wilhelmine Germany.

75. The Mensheviks were the majority party in the Georgian government which, in the 7 May 1920 treaty with Soviet Russia, granted Georgian Bolsheviks the right to function legally, though they were, they claimed, subject to harsh persecution. An unsuccessful application was made for admission to the League of Nations (December 1920), then, in a complex political and military situation involving Turkey, Armenia, Azerbaijan and Russia, the fall of Tbilisi to Georgian and Soviet Bolshevik forces led in February 1921 to the proclamation of a Georgian Soviet Republic. Lenin advised concessions to local economic and intellectual forces and the formation of a coalition with the Mensheviks; see E.H. Carr, *The Bolshevik Revolution*, Harmondsworth 1966, Vol.1, pp.347-54.

76. It should be remembered that *laico* is used in Italian for both lay (most of those who have not taken vows or orders) and secular (non-religious). The more appropriate meaning has been selected for each case where the word appears.

77. Milan's private Catholic 'University of the Sacred Heart' was given full state recognition by the Fascist government in October 1924. It had been founded three years earlier by Edoardo Gemelli (1878-1959), a former anti-clerical who, on conversion and entry into the Franciscan Order of Friars Minor as Fr Agostino, became a rigid integralist and, when Rector of the University, was not above denouncing anti-fascist students to the regime.

78. The teacher training schools mentioned are not higher education colleges but secondary schools, granting diplomas allowing people to teach in elementary schools. Luigi Credaro (1860-1939), Minister of Public Instruction in the years 1911-14, was responsible for creating provincial educational councils that, in most municipal areas, put elementary education in the hands of the state, thus angering the Church which had, up to then, had an almost complete monopoly in this sector.

79. Gramsci deals elsewhere with Church-state finances. In Q3§97 he notes with some wonderment that the financial settlement offered the Church in the 1871 'Guarantee Act' (*Legge delle Guarentigie*) contained a clause that, if the Church did not take up the offer within five years – which is exactly what took place – the indemnity would cease, yet the state continued to budget for this item up to 1928. In Q6§23, after citing the papal position that Treaty and Concordat stood or fell together, he claims that if the Treaty fell, the Church would have to repay all the money granted under its terms, nor could it shelter behind the 1871 law.
80. I.e. the preceding sub-section, 'Concordats and International Treaties', pp.61-70.
81. The so-called laws on subversion (*leggi eversive*) were no more than the laws abolishing the special privileges enjoyed by the Church.
82. This is an extract from the papal encyclical 'Rappresentanti in Terra' of 31 December 1929, sometimes cited in English as 'On the Christian Education of Youth'. The translation is found in Anne Fremantle, *The Papal Encyclicals in their Historical Context*, New York 1956, p.225.
83. The *Sodalitium Pianum* or 'Sodality of St Pius V' was founded by Benigni in 1909 as part of his campaign against theological modernism, Catholic liberalism and the attempts to create the first Christian Democrat movements. Though Pius XI endorsed its generic aims, he stopped short of formal approval. The organisation was officially suppressed in November 1921 after the Holy See had been sent the Ghent archive that Gramsci mentions; publicly, it was stated that the Sodality had served its purpose but more probably the ban was imposed for its opposition to the more open discussion favoured by Benedict XV.
84. The *Sillon* (or 'Furrow'), a progressive French Catholic movement founded by Marc Sangnier, was condemned by Pius X in 1910 in his letter to the French bishops 'Notre charge apostolique' (*Acta Apostolicae Sedis*, II, 1910, pp.607-31).
85. *Pascendi dominici gregis* (sometimes called 'Feeding the Lord's Flock') was Pius X's anti-modernist encyclical of 1907; an English translation is included in Buonaiuti's *The Programme of Modernism*, trans. George Tyrrell and A. Leslie Lilley, London 1908.
86. I.e. what was formerly the Inquisition.
87. The Irish Jesuit, George Tyrrell (1861-1909), had a Calvinist upbringing but converted to Catholicism and became a leading modernist; the joint translator of Buonaiuti's 1907 booklet *Il programma dei modernisti* (see note 85), he was subject to the minor excommunication for public criticism of Pius X, who apparently did not appreciate the name 'Losing the Lord's Flock' by which Tyrrell referred to his anti-modernist encyclical.
88. In Italian *ordine sparso*, used metaphorically on a few occasions in the Notebooks. Its nearest equivalent in British Army manuals of the time (e.g. *Infantry Training*, Vol.I, London 1926, p.130) seems the 'extended order' (i.e. an 'open' or 'scattered' order) of battle formation.
89. In Italian *integrismo*. The word is now rarely used and is normally considered a synonym for 'integralism', though some give it a stronger meaning, for which see footnote 93.

90. This is probably the clearest definition Gramsci gives in the Notebooks of what he meant by East and West and should always be borne in mind when he speaks of these concepts; cf. Q7§16 (SPN, p.238): 'in the East, the State was everything, civil society was primordial and gelatinous; in the West there was a proper relation between State and civil society ...', which thus should not be read in the context of merely twentieth century developments. The other principal meaning attached to 'East' in the Notebooks is what is often called the 'Far East'.
91. Benedict XV's *Ad Beatissimi* ('An Appeal for Peace') was published on 1 November 1914; see *Papal Pronouncements on the Political Order*, compiled and edited by Francis J. Powers, Westminster (Maryland) 1952, p.27.
92. Mariano Rampolla del Tindaro, from 1887 Leo XIII's Secretary of State, angered French monarchist and Italian secular opinion when, as part of the hostilities against the Italian state, he paved the way for the French Catholics to 'rally' to the Republic (see 'Catholic Social Thought', pp.46-7), while continuing to keep Italian Catholics aloof from the still new unitary state. A scandal was caused when, though for many Leo's natural successor, his election was blocked by the Cardinal of Krakow's use of the Austro-Hungarian Emperor's right of veto, at the instigation of Giovanni Zanardelli, later Italian Prime Minister.
93. The Spanish 'Integrist' party was founded in 1892 as a nationalist and anti-liberal party of an extreme clerical type, preaching the state's total subordination to the Catholic Church. Any distinction between 'integrist' and 'integralist', as the bishop seems to be making here, would be based on this criterion.
94. For Thomism, see footnote 50 to this chapter.
95. Along with Alfred Loisy (1857-1940), the French priest Joseph Turmel (1859-1943) was on the extreme radical wing of modernism.
96. Anyone who is *excommunicatus vitandus*, i.e. subject to the major excommunication, loses all form of ecclesiastical office and is forbidden to receive the sacraments or attend any type of public divine worship; the faithful are warned to have as little to do with them as possible.
97. Henri Massis, *Défense de l'occident* [*Defence of the West*], Paris 1927; see also p.92 ('*Action Françaises*'s Long Crisis'). Despite their similar extreme rightist views, Massis and Maurras were on occasion in bitter conflict.
98. Emile Combes (1835-1921) trained as a priest but left the Church before ordination and sat with the anti-clerical Radicals when elected to the French Senate. He presided over the separation of Church and state that was responsible for the secularisation of education (1905) and led to the Vatican temporarily breaking off diplomatic relations before Catholics were finally reintegrated into state life through Leo XIII's *ralliement* policy referred to here (see also 'Catholic Social Thought', pp.46-7).
99. This note seems never to have been written. Gramsci was probably finding it more and more difficult to write and never had the strength to return to the subject.
100. In fact Buonaiuti was one of a dozen or so out of about 1,200

university professors who refused the oath of loyalty to the regime and thus lost his post; the others mentioned in this volume are the Southernist economist Antonio De Viti De Marco and the aesthetician Giuseppe Antonio Borgese. After the Second World War Rome University, caving in to Vatican pressure, refused to take him on again.

101. In Q9§30, written nearly a year before this note, Gramsci comments 'Félix Sartiaux's work *Joseph Turmel, prêtre, historien du dogma* was put on the Index on 6 April 1932. The book defends Turmel after the latest stupefying cases regarding this exceptional example of the French clerical world.'

102. After the fascist murder in 1924 of Giacomo Matteotti, parliamentarian and secretary of the reformist Unitary Socialist Party (PSU), a group of dissident Popular Party deputies gave the fascists a helping hand by forming the Italian National Centre to oppose any collaboration between Catholics and Socialists whether of the PSI or the PSU.

103. *Mémoires pour servir à l'histoire religieuse de notre temps*, Paris 1931 (three volumes), by the modernist theologian Alfred Loisy (note 95), for whom see also 'Croce as a Renaissance Man [2]' pp.470-2 and 'Croce and Modernism' pp.472-3, both in Chap. VII.

104. The modernists were frequently accused of having rejected traditional Catholic transcendentalism in favour of an immanentism stemming from Hegel.

105. The 1907 encyclical *Pascendi* (see note 85) was, as Gramsci says, dated 8 September, but the 1864 *Quanta Cura* and the accompanying *Syllabus* of 80 anathematised errors were however dated 8 December. It was *Quanta Cura* (partial translation in Fremantle, op. cit.) that was in fact published on an anniversary, significantly the tenth one, of the pronouncement as dogma of Mary's Immaculate Conception, which thus gave it added weight.

106. The latter of these encyclicals (*Quadragesimo Anno* in Latin, English translation in Fremantle, op. cit.) was published on the fortieth anniversary of the former (for which see note 51, above).

107. I.e. 'Integralist Catholics, Jesuits, Modernists'.

108. See 'Galileo and Giordano Bruno', 'Roberto Bellarmino's Canonisation' and 'Humanism and Renaissance', pp.20-2 of the 'Reformation and Counter-Reformation' section, above.

109. The wording is not exact here; there were *attempts* to promote Bellarmino's cause for beatification and canonisation in the eighteenth century, but they were blocked by fierce factional in-fighting, even though they had the powerful support of Benedict XIV. In the next century it was not judged prudent to support a person like Bellarmino who argued that monarchs should be indirectly subject to the papacy; he had to wait until the twentieth century to be beatified, canonised and declared 'Doctor' of the Church, all in rapid succession.

110. For the Sanfedistas, see 'Catholic Action and Neo-Guelphism' (pp.38-9) in this chapter. Their *éminence grise*, Cardinal Fabrizio Ruffo, led the wild 'mountain-men' from the Aspromonte in the extreme

south to ' "eat out the heart" of the Neapolitan Jacobins. This myth (!) produced and fuelled a large part of the political banditry of the first decade after unification. ... They say that from Paris, where she was exiled, Queen Maria Sophia [last Queen of Naples] sent Musolino a little money so the bandit could keep the rebellion alive in Calabria' (Q7§100, quoting the *Corriere della Sera*, 24 December 1931).

111. The review (and Chap. 6 of Roth's book) specifies that the person Gramsci calls 'the Jew Leone' was Rabbi Leone da Modena, the 'pride and disgrace' of Venetian Jewry according to Roth. A wastrel and inveterate gambler, given to short-lived periods of repentance, he was however immensely gifted and 'probably no Jewish savant has ever represented Hebrew scholarship to the gentile world to anything like the same extent'.

112. In Q19§25, Gramsci does however recount a number of anti-semitic episodes fostered by clerical reaction, as part of the battle against revolutionary forces (1799 and 1847-48) or when counter-revolution was in full flow (e.g. the 1815 expulsion of the Jews from the universities and the professions). Through Antonio's sister-in-law, Tatiana, Piero Sraffa, who was of full Jewish descent, pointed to the anti-semitism shown in the contemporary *de facto* exclusion of Jews from key positions (Tatiana, letter of 2 February 1932 to Antonio, footnote to pp.570-1 of *Lettere dal Carcere*, Turin 1965). In his reply of 8 February, Gramsci did 'not exclude that an anti-semitic tendency may arise later', but noted that after the Concordat Jews were in much the same position as Protestants, while the real social pariahs were unfrocked priests and monks. Sraffa remained unconvinced (Tatiana's letter of 18 March 1932, op. cit.).

113. Niceto Alcalá Zamora, a progressive Catholic and Prime Minister in 1931, was forced to resign from the Constituent Assembly – which had adopted a militant secularist stance – because of negotiations he had entered into with the Vatican. Cardinal Segura, the Spanish Primate, was both brilliant and reactionary enough to be at times an embarrassment to the Vatican.

114. Henry Charles Lea, *A History of the Inquisition of Spain*, 4 vols., New York and London 1906-7; see especially Vol.4, pp.284-9. Gramsci most likely had in mind the mid-seventeenth-century dispute between the Jesuits and the Jansenists, who restated the position of St Augustine, Catholic orthodoxy – and Calvin – on grace, free will and predestination (for which read morals and discipline), all 'intellectual and moral reforms' that Gramsci considered important for the development of capitalism. The Dominican-led Inquisition tended to uphold Augustinianism and thus came into a factional-type conflict with the Jesuits, accused (mainly by the Jansenists) of a relaxed morality and an observance of the merely outward appearance of faith. After about a century, the Jesuits bent the Inquisition to their way of thinking.

115. Though this may now seem non-controversial, it was challenged in some Catholic circles. The 'integralist and ultra-reactionary' Mons. Ugo Mioni, a writer of 'low quality adventures for young people' (see also SCW, p.212) maintained in his text-book *Manuale di Sociologia* (Turin

1932) that 'Christian sociology is *hostile* to any participation of women in public life'; *Civiltà Cattolica* (20 August 1932) upbraided him on this, citing the contrary opinion of 'one of today's most celebrated schools of Christian sociology (the French Social Weeks)' (Q4§90).

116. The German Centre Party (*Zentrumspartei*), founded as the Catholic party in 1870 and for a time the biggest party in the Reichstag, lasted until its dissolution by Hitler.

117. I.e. the one on military matters mentioned in the previous sub-section ('Catholic Action in Germany and Austria') which allowed Bismarck to set military estimates for a seven-year period without reference to parliament.

118. Alfred (Al) Smith, the Democrat Governor of New York, in 1928 became the first Catholic to run for the presidency on behalf of one of the major parties; he was beaten by Herbert Hoover.

119. For these two encyclicals, see notes 106 and 51, above.

120. As with the next sub-section, Gramsci's source was the *Manchester Guardian Weekly*, to which he then subscribed. In the 19 June 1931 issue (pp.481 and 484), the Archbishop of Westminster, Cardinal Bourne, is reported as saying that though in the British Labour Party 'there are some who say they are socialists in the technical sense – a thing which no true Catholic can be ... good sincere Catholics have been ... members of the Labour Party' as well as Conservatives or Liberals. 'No good Catholic can ally himself to any of [the three parties now existing in England] absolutely and entirely,' since when a person's religious faith or conscience 'come into conflict with the claims of the party he must obey his conscience'. The *Manchester Guardian* deduced that the Labour Party's socialism seemed not of 'the pernicious type that falls under the Papal condemnation'.

121. Pius XI's encyclical on 'Religious Unity'; see Powers, op. cit., p.172.

122. Söderblom (1866-1931) is described by his English-language biographer as 'one of the pioneers of the ecumenical movement' (Bengt Sundkler, *Nathan Söderblom: His Life and Work*, Lund 1968, p.9). He showed sympathy for the socialist movement and in his activity tried to illustrate the relevance of Christianity to questions of work, as well as rousing Christian opposition to war; in 1930 he was awarded the Nobel Peace Prize. Following Sundkler, 'catholicity' (i.e. a catholic, or universal, outlook distinct from the Roman variety) is used here for what Gramsci terms simply *cattolicismo*, a synonym for *cattolicesimo* (referring normally to Roman Catholicism).

123. Gabriel García Moreno was actually an important politician in nineteenth-century Ecuador; Daniel O'Connell led the struggle for Catholic (male) emancipation in mid-nineteenth-century Ireland; the Belgian Auguste Beernaert (d. 1912), joint winner of the Nobel Peace Prize in 1909, is compared by Meda to Gladstone; Georg Hertling (d. 1919), elected head of the Bavarian government in 1912, and Ludwig Windthorst (d. 1891), perhaps the most prominent German Catholic politician of the nineteenth century, led the Catholic Centre Party, opposing both Bismarck and the Socialists; Antonio Maura (d. 1925),

several times Spanish Prime Minister between 1903 and 1922, was a conservative with authoritarian leanings who nevertheless opposed the 1923 right-wing *coup d'état* of Primo de Rivera.

124. For the *Kulturkampf* movement see note 74, above.

125. Alvaro Obregón played an important role in the Mexican Revolution sparked off by the revolt of November 1910. He served as President of the country from 1920 to 1924; re-elected in 1928, he was assassinated before he could assume office. Plutarco Elias Callés, President from 1924 to 1928, followed the same generally progressive line as Obregón.

126. A *Sannyasi* (or *Sunnyasee*) is a Brahmin in the fourth stage of his life, a wandering fakir or religious mendicant; *Upadhyaya* is a title meaning simply 'teacher'.

127. The Sadhu, a great admirer of Gandhi, was a former Hindu who converted to Protestantism and came under fierce attack from some Catholics; he died in 1929, still relatively young, while crossing over to Tibet on foot on a missionary trip.

128. The *Ispolcom* was the Executive Committee of the Third International. In this note, Gramsci abbreviates the name of the International itself – in the name of the Genevan grouping formed to combat it – to 'TI'.

129. For Massis and his movement see note 97, above.

130. 'Hegemon' (*egemone*) is used on occasion by Gramsci as the person, force etc. exerting hegemony.

131. The Critical Edition of the Notebooks perpetuates the error, faithfully copied by Gramsci from Viscardi's article, of attributing to King Ezekias or Hezekiah what is in fact a summary and paraphrase of the words of Ezekiel (see Chap. III, especially verses 18 and 20 of the Old Testament book of this prophet). The New English Bible version is here chosen as being closer than most other English ones to the sense of the Italian wording.

132. Gramsci copied the *Nouvelles Littéraires* interview in French.

133. While Brahmins are the 'highest' of the Hindu castes, a Kshatriya or Kshatri (*Chattrya* in the transliteration of the original article) is of the second caste, the military or reigning order.

134. Loria, as quoted in Croce's 'The Historical Theories of Prof. Loria' in *Materialismo Storico ed Economia Marxistica*, 4th (1921) edition, p.28 (not included in the partial translation of the book into English), claims that increasing population and decreasing land productivity would lead to 'the exploiters having partially or wholly to reduce the payments made to their agents, scientists, lawyers, poets and so on. What can be done in this case? Seek another master. And the unproductive workers pass into the service of the exploited, whence the successive historical crises.'

135. This is the second part of a long note by Gramsci on China. The first part deals with the material way in which culture developed in China and with the first serious studies by Rémusat and Julien of Chinese culture using 'scientific methods and not those of the Catholic apostolate, as was the case with the Jesuits'. The starting point is the complex but, for the

intellectuals, unificatory ideographic and 'esperantist' nature of the script. For the common people, given the double difficulty of remembering multiple meanings of ideograms and of acquiring experience in constructing the logical and grammatical thread linking them, oratory remained the most common way of disseminating culture. The adoption of an alphabet using letters would lead to a flowering of popular languages and the possibility of the formation of new groups of intellectuals representing 'national forces' rather then the previous ' "cosmopolitan" type' which Gramsci compares explicitly to the 'Catholic cosmopolitanism' of 'the western and central Europe of the Middle Ages'. Whereas the threat to this part of Europe came on the whole from the technical-military power of Islam, Gramsci says that the threat to China is the military, economic and cultural might of Britain, America and Japan, which could be countered if Sun Yat Sen's right-wing successors in the Kuomintang called an All-China Convention capable of rousing even the traditionally passive masses of the hinterland; such a convocation 'would make the hegemony of the present leading groups difficult unless they brought in a programme of popular reforms, and would force unity to be sought on a federal rather than a bureaucratic-military basis'.

136. In the China of those years Hu Shih was, together with the famous literary figure Lu Hsun, a leader of the New Culture movement (better known as the 4 May movement, which also provided the leadership nucleus of the infant Chinese Communist Party). He studied at Columbia University under John Dewey, and his doctoral dissertation *The Development of the Logical Method in Ancient China* (dating to 1917, but published five years later in Shanghai and London) has a great overlap in content with the book mentioned by Gramsci, which, however, never seems to have been translated into English. During the Second World War, Hu Shih was Chinese Ambassador to the United States.

137. See the section on 'Translatability' in Chapter V of this volume, in particular 'The Translatability of Different National Cultures', pp.314-5.

138. The term tu-chun can be loosely translated as 'war-lords'; they were often the military governors of a province, so 'regional militarist' is also found as a translation of the name.

139. Elsewhere (Q5§122), Gramsci credits the Jesuits operating in China, in particular Fr D'Elia, with various possible translations into a western cultural form of the notion mentioned here, which Gramsci himself interprets as 'the three principles of the national-popular policy of Sun Yat-Sen' (or Sun Wen). His 'Three People's Principles' were *min-tsu chu-i* (nationalism), *min-ch'üan chu-i* (democracy) and *min-sheng chu-i* (socialism or, literally, 'people's livelihood'). The texts of sixteen lectures by Sun Yat-Sen on the three principles are available in book form in English under the title *San Min Chu I – The Three Principles of the People* (trans. Frank W. Price and edited by L.T. Chen), Shanghai 1927.

140. For the Social Code of Malines, see 'Catholic Action's History and Organisation' (pp.28-33) and accompanying note 39; the two papal encyclicals mentioned (1891 and 1885 respectively) form part of Leo XIII's formulation of Catholic social doctrine.

141. Gramsci here uses the word 'Riforma', which may be translated 'Reformation' or 'Reform'. The latter has been chosen here as making a clearer reference to the matters dealt with immediately previously. The fact that 'Riforma' is written with a capital letter indicates that he was probably also thinking of the Protestant Reformation in Europe, which, as is argued in various places in the Notebooks, led both to a secularisation of thinking (analogous to his prediction for Japan in the last lines of the present note and more extensively in the next one, 'Brief Notes on Japanese Culture [2]'), and also, indirectly, to the philosophy of praxis.
142. See the preceding sub-section 'Brief Notes on Japanese Culture [1]'.
143. The Wahabites are the followers of the Muslim religious reformer Abd-el-Wahhab (1691-1787); see also 'Italy and the Yemen in the New Politics of the Arab World', pp.210-13.
144. Sufism originated in the eighth century of the Christian era and developed, especially in modern Iran, into an ascetic sect whose goal was communion with the deity through contemplation and ecstasy.
145. The word used by Gramsci, translated here as 'shock troops', is *arditi*. This term was commonly used in the 1920s to refer to several different types of volunteer force (First World War commandos, the nationalists who tried to annex Rijeka to Italy or workers' self-defence leagues against fascist squads; see also SPN, footnote 25 on p. 230).
146. Levi's work in this field is again briefly mentioned in Q5§42 in relation to the Spanish Arabists and, in Q5§123, as regards both the importance of the Spanish Jews and the reintroduction into Europe of philosophical themes that were to heavily influence medieval Scholasticism. In this latter note, Gramsci singles out Averroes (1126-98), Islam's greatest medieval Aristotelian, as a major influence on the debates of the famous Parisian school of those times.

Chapter II The Origin of Modern Educational Principles

1. As Washburne notes on pp.3-4 of his book (published in 1926, not 1930 as Gramsci copied) Oundle is 'very far from public in the American sense, being a high-priced boarding school for the elite'. The best-known of various studies of the school is H.G. Wells, *Saunderson of Oundle*, London 1924.
2. Rosa Bassett, headmistress of this South London state school, took over ideas such as letting children organise their own programmes for part of the day from the private school at Dalton, Massachusetts – hence the name 'Dalton system' – run by Helen Parkhurst who, in her turn, had met and been influenced by the famous educationalist Maria Montessori.
3. See Washburne, op. cit., pp.53 and 62. Kearsley was a typical cotton-weaving town on the edge of the Lancashire coal field, about 15 kilometres North West of Manchester in the North of England.
4. See Washburne, op. cit., pp.111 and 116 respectively; it is not clear

whether the latter comment was made by Gläser or one of his collaborators.

5. This passage arguing for a close link between the common school and existing and possible future higher educational institutions is from the monographic twelfth notebook, the rest of which is published in its entirety as the first two chapters (pp.5-23 and 26-43) of SPN; it concludes the eight-page sub-section (ending on SPN, p.33) headed 'The Organisation of Education and Culture'.

6. There are scattered references to the Rotary Clubs throughout the notebooks. Gramsci regarded their ideological, practical and organisational aspects as an interesting expression of Americanism. In Q5§2 (headed 'Rotary Club'), he draws attention to the principle, adopted in 1928, that the Rotarian philosophy of life attempts to reconcile the eternal conflict between the wish to earn money and the duty to serve one's neighbour: 'who serves best earns most'. In their statement of aims the Rotarians defined themselves as businessmen and professional workers; for Gramsci, unlike the Freemasons (of a lower social extraction and a petty-bourgeois democratic and anti-clerical outlook), they involved the people only indirectly. He goes on to say (Q5§4) that, of the two, linked indirectly through common roots in positivism, the Rotarians represented 'a modern right-wing form of Saint-Simonism'.

7. As elsewhere in the notebooks, the term is used in the sense of a clique protecting itself by somewhat dubious, though usually not illegal, means; rather than the Sicilian term *mafia* given in the English here, Gramsci uses *camorra*, its equivalent in Campania (the region centred on Naples).

8. J.H. Newman's speech, made in November 1858 at the newly founded Catholic University in Dublin, was first published the following year under the title 'Discipline of Mind' and has been reprinted many times; the extracts quoted here may be found on pp.402 and 404 of his *The Idea of a University Defined and Illustrated*, Oxford 1976. The article from which Gramsci copied (published in *Gerarchia*, March and April 1933) omits a number of phrases or sentences from Newman's original. The last word ('proof') of the second extract is rendered 'arguments' in the Italian translation.

9. I.e. the British Association for the Advancement of Science, founded in 1831.

10. There are a number of references in the Prison Notebooks to the Popular Universities as institutes of working-class education, all disparaging because of the slavish copying, inappropriate for people unused to the habits of formal study, of the 'orthodox' higher educational system (including some of its worst aspects). The *Umanitaria* ('Humanitarian') was a working-class self-help organisation of a wide-ranging scope.

11. Q10II§44 ('Pedagogy and Hegemony') is to be found in its entirety in SPN, pp.348-51, which the extract reproduced here follows. It is included as a necessary link, implicitly referred to in footnote 36 on p.350 of SPN, between pedagogy or educational theory as normally understood at the individual level and the same as an essential part of the hegemonic

relationship between different classes or nations (see also 'Antonio Labriola [1]', that follows immediately after the current sub-section).

12. I.e. 'passion' in a sense taken over from Croce – see the three consecutive sub-sections of Chapter VII, 'Crocean Passion and Sorelian Myth' and 'Passion and Politics', parts [1] and [2] pp.389-94 – and modified to allow for 'passion' becoming a permanent rather than a momentaneous feature of political life.

13. Johann Friedrich Herbart was a founder of modern educational theory. The type of instruction he (or, more exactly, his followers) favoured is now considered too rigid and schematic but many of his positions – pedagogy as an autonomous science, the necessity of providing education with a sound psychological base and the need to stimulate the pupils, taking into account their social experience – are correct and have a bearing on what is discussed here. It may be noted that Gramsci commented in a brief 'A' text (Q8§168, 'Antonio Labriola and Hegelianism'), crossed out as though to be included later (but then never recopied): 'A study should be made of how Labriola, starting off from Herbartian and anti-Hegelian positions, arrived at historical materialism. In a nutshell, the dialectic in Antonio Labriola.'

14. As Gramsci implies, Labriola wrote relatively little for someone of his intellectual stature and even the volume cited, *Scritti vari* (Bari 1906), of speeches, essays, letters and interviews – some published there for the first time and most not available in English – was edited posthumously by Croce. Labriola regarded an Italian occupation of Libya as a move to establish Italy as a world power and as doing no harm since Libya was under-populated and emigration there could only help develop it.

15. The reference is to Marx's sarcasm directed at the historical school of law in Germany: 'A school which legitimates the baseness of today by the baseness of yesterday, a school that declares rebellious every cry of the serf against the knout once that knout is a time-honoured, ancestral, historical one ...' (Introduction to *A Contribution to the Critique of Hegel's Philosophy of Law*, now in *Marx Engels Collected Works*, Vol.3, London 1975, p.177).

16. Presumably referring to ideas (and practices) current in the Soviet Union, though Gramsci opposed Trotsky's post-civil war proposal for the militarisation of labour (see SPN, pp.301-2).

17. This polemic involving colonialism, class relationships and education in general should be read in the light of Gramsci's unsigned article in *L'Ordine Nuovo* of 10 January 1920 (now in the anthology of his writings *L'Ordine Nuovo 1919-1920*, Turin 1975, pp.469-70). He there attacks industrialists and political demagogues who treated workers partly as if they were children and, mirroring the colonialists, partly as if they were 'a mass of negroes easily contented with a few trinkets. Do you want those who yesterday were slaves to become men? Start off by treating them like men all the time, for by so doing you will already have taken the biggest step forward of all.'

18. I.e. the sub-section 'Antonio Labriola [1]', immediately above.

19. See Chapter IV, 'The Error of the Anti-Protectionist Left', pp.246-7.

Chapter III The Nature and History of Economic Science

1. Gino Arias, 'The Political Thought of Niccolò Machiavelli', *Annali di Economia*, Milan 1928; Vincenzo Tangorra, essay of same title as that by Arias in Tangorra's book *Saggi critici di economia politica* (*Critical Essays in Political Economy*), Turin 1900.
2. Briefly speaking, although it is difficult to ascribe any centralised body of doctrine to the mercantilists, they tended towards the accumulation of precious metals as the most desirable form of wealth and thus foreign trade was generally confined and fairly rigidly subordinated to this end. The physiocrats represented the next stage in the development of economic thought: wealth came from the soil (industry being unproductive because it merely combined things already produced) and so productivity of land and more efficient marketing were key issues, thus raising the question of city-countryside relationships. For them, domestic and foreign trade had to be freed from restriction, so their view of the state was radically different from that of the mercantilists. There is thus an overlap of interest between Machiavelli and the physiocrats as regards the city-countryside-state nexus.
3. I.e. Marx's *Theories of Surplus Value*, often referred to by its sub-title, as given here, in its Italian and French translations. The description of Petty opens Karl Kautsky's edition of Marx's manuscript (Stuttgart, 1919 reprint of 1905 first edition).
4. Though *Verbum Sapienti* was written around the date quoted by Gramsci, it was published posthumously in 1691 in an edition prepared by N. Tate, now available either as a facsimile reprint, *The Political Economy of Ireland and Verbum Sapienti*, Shannon 1970, or in T.H. Hull's two-volume edition of *The Economic Writings of Sir. W. Petty*, Cambridge 1899, repr. New York 1964. In a list of his writings Petty himself wrote 1665 beside the title and Hull, basing himself in part on Petty's biographer, Fitzmaurice, cites 1665 or 1666; the contents list of Hull's book gives 1664, presumably due to a typographical error.
5. Richard Cantillon, *Essai sur la nature du commerce en général*, trans. Henry Higgs, London 1931, p.3; Gramsci quotes the French of what is probably the original edition. The statement that the book was written in 1730 finds support in Antoin E. Murphy's biography *Richard Cantillon: Entrepreneur and Economist*, Oxford 1986, p.246; it was however published only in 1755 with a claim that it was 'traduit de l'Anglois'. An early English edition does exist but dates to 1759 and is a corrupt text cobbled together somewhat crudely by Cantillon's cousin, Philip; no copy of the claimed English first edition has ever come to light.
6. See pp.48-9 of Botero's *Treatise, concerning the causes of the Magnificencie and Greatnes of Cities* ... 'done into English by Robert Peterson of Lincolnes Inne Gent', London 1606, repr. Amsterdam and New Jersey 1979.
7. Edwin Cannan, *A Review of Economic Theory*, London 1929.

8. A partial and somewhat unreliable translation by C.M. Meredith of this book of Croce's exists as *Historical Materialism and the Economics of Karl Marx*, London 1914 (repr. London 1966); the quote here is found on p.155. Perhaps the clearest exposition of the reasons for what might be termed the logico-historical method adopted by Marx is that written by Engels for *Das Volk*, 20 August 1859, in his review of Marx's *A Contribution to the Critique of Political Economy*, now included as an appendix to that work (London and Moscow 1981) or, in a slightly different translation, to some editions of Engels's *Ludwig Feuerbach and the End of Classical German Philosophy*: '... the critique of economics could still be arranged in two ways – historically or logically. Since in the course of history, as in its literary reflection, the evolution proceeds by and large from the simplest to the more complex relations, the historical development of political economy constituted a natural clue, which the critique could take as a point of departure, and then the economic categories would appear on the whole in the same order as in the logical exposition. This form seems to have the advantage of greater lucidity, for it traces the *actual* development, but in fact it would thus become, at most, more popular. ... The logical method of approach was therefore the only suitable one. This, however, is indeed nothing but the historical method, only stripped of the historical form and diverting chance occurrences. The point where this history begins must also be the starting point of the train of thought, and its further progress will be simply the reflection, in abstract and theoretically consistent form, of the historical course.' Engels again referred to a similar approach in his very last article, which may now be read as a supplement to *Capital*, Vol.III, New York 1967, p.895: 'we are dealing here not only with a pure logical process but with a historical process and its explanatory reflection in thought, the logical pursuance of its inner connections.' See also Marx's unfinished and posthumously published *Introduction* to *A Contribution to the Critique of Political Economy*, now in the *Grundrisse*, Marx Engels Collected works, Vol.28, London 1986, pp.37-45, especially p.44: 'It would therefore be inexpedient and wrong to present the economic categories successively in the order in which they played the determining role in history. Their order of succession is determined rather by their mutual relation in modern bourgeois society, and this is quite the reverse of what appears to be their natural development or corresponds to the sequence of historical development. The point at issue is not the place the economic relations took relative to each other in the succession of various forms of society in the course of history ... but their position within modern bourgeois society.'

9. Maffeo Pantaleoni (1857-1924, whose influential text book *Pure Economics* is discussed on pp.170-3) was, along with Luigi Einaudi (1874-1961, President of the Republic from 1948 to 1955) and Vilfredo Pareto (1848-1923), among the most representative of Italian liberal economists of Gramsci's time.

10. By 'critical economy' Gramsci means Marxist economics and by 'classical economy' not only the classical school of Adam Smith and

Ricardo but also the marginal utility school that grew up around 1870 and those who worked within and developed this tradition. Thus in this passage we have the reference to 'psychological research' as an indication of the role played by personal preference and, in general subjective factors, in determining value according to what should be called the post-classical, rather than the 'classical' school.

11. Elsewhere (Q7§22), Gramsci adds this brief note headed *Theory of comparative (and decreasing) costs*: 'It is to be seen whether this theory, which occupies such an important position in modern official economics together with the other one of static and dynamic equilibrium is possibly perfectly consistent with (or corresponds in another language to) the Marxist theory of value (and of the falling rate of profit), i.e. whether it is not possibly its scientific equivalent in official and "pure" language (where by "pure" we understand a language stripped of any political clout for the subaltern producing classes).'

12. The book referred to, which Gramsci knew in the French translation *Précis d'économie politique*, is, in its English translation, *An Outline of Political Economy: Political Economy and Soviet Economics* by I. Lapidus and K. Ostrovityanov, London 1929.

13. In other words Gramsci is saying that labour will have to deal with the problems traditionally treated by neo-classical economy such as that of utility in its technical sense of the power of a commodity or service to satisfy a want, particularly the rate at which the satisfaction varies with the quantity of the commodity or service that can be furnished and the additional cost of producing each additional increase in the volume of the commodity or service. Productivity here is one key element, and it is to this that Gramsci is referring when he writes 'competitions', i.e. the 'socialist emulation' movement of the first Five-Year Plan, then in full swing in the Soviet Union as a means of raising productivity; the rather similar Stakhanovite movement came considerably later.

14. The book, first published in Florence in 1889 and sometimes referred to under the slightly different title of *Manuale di Economia Pura*, was translated into English with 'additions and alterations by the author' by T. Boston Bruce and published under the title *Pure Economics*, London 1898. Pantaleoni follows Jevons, Menger and Walras in rejecting the labour theory of value in favour of one based on the 'final degree of utility' or marginal utility (see Parts 2 and 3 and, in particular, pp.215 *et seq.* of the English translation). The hedonistic postulate, as Pantaleoni states it, is that people are moved to act exclusively by the desire to acquire the greatest possible satisfaction of their needs from the least possible individual sacrifice (1st part, Chap. 1 'Of the Subject of Economic Science').

15. Croce held that there were four 'distincts' or eternal values of the human spirit in some sort of dialectical relation one with another. To the three traditional values of the true, the beautiful and the good, he added the economic (with which are associated the useful and its opposite the harmful), rooted in the individual's urge to self-preservation. Economic action is moral or immoral according to whether it is carried out in conformity with or in defiance of social duty. More on the dialectic of

distincts is contained in the section on Croce in the general introduction, pp.lxxvi-lxxix; see also SPN, p.xxiii.).

16. Pure economics (i.e. from Jevons in the 1870s onwards) takes the subjective concept of value as its starting point. As Jevons notes on p.165 of later editions of his *Theory of Political Economy* (repr. New York 1965):

> Cost of production determines supply:
> Supply determines final degree of utility:
> Final degree of utility determines value.

Pantaleoni, in a footnote on p.96 of the Italian edition of his book, comments that the final degree of utility is the cardinal point of any economic and financial doctrine (and thus of his 'pure economics'). The traditional concerns of classical political economy ('economic art' for Pantaleoni) are outside the scope of economic science (pure economics), a discussion of them remaining 'altogether superficial and inconclusive if not based ultimately on theorems of Pure Economics' (preface to English edition of *Pure Economics*). For critical economy, on the other hand, as Gramsci concludes, the basic input data of 'pure economics' appear as 'superstructural' items after having set off from the concept of 'socially necessary labour' in order to arrive at a theory of value (see 'Classical Economy and Critical Economy', pp.168-70).

17. As Robbins writes on p.125 of the book referred to, 'all that part of the theory of Public Finance (graduated income tax vs. non-graduated poll-tax etc.) which deals with "Social Utility" goes by the board. ... It is simply the accidental deposit of the historical association of English Economics with Utilitarianism: and both the utilitarian postulates from which it derives and the analytical Economics with which it has been associated will be the better and the more convincing for the separation.' Early formulations, by Jevons and his followers, of the 'utility theory of value' included the so-called 'hedonistic postulate' or 'pleasure principle', according to which the test of conduct is the pleasure or pain (in a wide sense) involved in a given activity 'including economic activity'. According to Robbins and the modern marginalist school, these 'hedonistic trimmings ... were incidental to the main structure of a theory which ... is capable of being set out and defended in absolutely non-hedonistic terms' (Robbins, op. cit. p.86). It would seem in this sense that there is a difference in the concept of 'utility', as Gramsci conjectures.

18. The citation in this sentence is found in Robbins, op.cit., p.77. Marshall conceived of economic behaviour as a balance between searching for satisfaction and avoiding sacrifice, maintaining that value was determined jointly by utility and production costs. These latter were, as Robbins comments (p.79), the two blades of Marshall's scissors, neither of which is able to cut (i.e. produce value) without the other; the duality was removed by Wieser and his followers who showed, on the basis of these assumptions of the marginalist school, that 'in the end subjective valuations govern costs equally with product prices' (p.80).

19. I.e. Marx's prefaces to the various editions and translations of *Capital* and the celebrated *Preface* to *A Contribution to the Critique of Political*

Economy, where, in one long paragraph, Marx gives a summary of his general doctrine, though studiously avoiding reference to class struggle in order to get round the German censor.
20. I.e. the previous sub-section, headed 'Lionel Robbins'.
21. See footnote 12 (above) to 'Classical Economy and Critical Economy'.
22. The books referred to are Carlo Cafiero, *'Il Capitale' di Carlo Marx brevemente compendiato*, Milan 1879; Gabriel Deville, *Le Capital de Karl Marx résumé et accompagné d'un aperçu sur le socialisme scientifique*, Paris 1883 (It. trans. Cremona, 1893); Karl Kautsky, *Karl Marx Oekonomische Lehren, Gemeinverständlich dargestellt und erläutert*, 1886 (It. trans. Turin 1898), Edward B. Aveling, *The Students' Marx. An Introduction to the Study of Karl Marx's 'Capital'*, London 1892; Ettore Fabietti, *Il capitale, volgarizzato da Ettore Fabietti*, Florence 1902; Julian Borchardt, *Das Kapital. Kritik der politischen Oekonomie*, Berlin 1919 (Eng. trans. *The People's Marx. Abridged popular edition of... 'Capital'*, 1921).
23. For comments on other concepts that, in Gramsci's opinion, were developed or used by Ricardo (such as the law of tendency, the determinate market and 'economic man'), together with his influences on the economic and possibly (at least as regards methodology) the philosophical development of Marx and Engels, see the earlier sub-sections of this chapter and also SPN, pp.399-402 (Q10II§9) and pp.410-414 (Q11§52); further comments on this influence on these and on later thinkers are to be found on pp.xxxviii-xlii of the general introduction to this volume.
24. Ugo Spirito, *La critica dell'economia liberale (The Critique of Liberal Economy)*, Milan 1930. Spirito, a follower of the actualist philosopher Giovanni Gentile, was an exponent of a would-be left current within fascism in his identification of the state's corporative economy with, to use Gramsci's expression, a 'regulated' (i.e. planned) economy. Whereas Gentile was shot in the street by partisans in 1944, Spirito's leftward aspirations eventually led him in the post-war era into the Communist Party.
25. The agitation/propaganda distinction comes from Lenin, *What is to be Done?*, Moscow 1967, pp.67-7 (Section III B of the pamphlet): 'the propagandist ... must present "many ideas", so many, indeed, that they will be understood as an integral whole only by a (comparatively) few persons. The agitator ... will direct his efforts to presenting *a single idea* to the "masses", ... he will strive *to rouse* discontent and indignation among the masses against this crying injustice, leaving a more complete explanation of this contradiction to the propagandist. Consequently, the propagandist operates chiefly by means of the *printed* word; the agitator by means of the *spoken* word.'
26. For further comments on the polemic against Spirito's (and hence Gentile's) concept of the state, see the fourth part of Chap. VI of this volume, devoted to Gramsci's criticisms of actualism and other trends.
27. See the paragraphs on translatability in Chap. IV of this volume, especially 'Giovanni Vailati and the Translatability of Scientific Languages', pp.307-9.
28. In his preface to the third volume of *Capital* (New York 1967, pp.9-10),

Engels quotes part of the criticism made of the second volume of *Capital* by the self-declared 'vulgar economist' Lexis: 'The capitalist sellers ... all make a gain on their transactions by selling at a price higher than the purchase price, thus adding a certain percentage to the price they themselves pay for the commodity. The worker alone is unable to obtain a similar additional value for his commodity; he is compelled by reason of his unfavourable condition *vis-à-vis* the capitalist to sell his labour at the price it costs him, that is to say, for the essential means of his subsistence ... Thus, these additions to prices retain their full impact with regard to the buying worker, and cause the transfer of a part of the value of the total product to the capitalist class.' Engels notes: 'this explanation for the profits of capital, as advanced by "vulgar economy" amounts in practice to the same thing as the Marxian theory of surplus-value; ... it is just as easy to build up an at least equally plausible vulgar socialism on the basis of this theory, as that built in England on the foundation of Jevons's and Menger's theory of use-value and marginal utility ... In reality, however, this theory is merely a paraphrase of the Marxian.'

29. E.R.A. Seligman, *The Economic Interpretation of History*, London 1902.

30. Thierry ('The father of the "class struggle" in French historiography' as Marx described him in his letter to Engels of 27 July 1854), Mignet and Guizot may, as economic materialists, be considered as precursors of the materialist conception of history; see G.V. Plekhanov, *Fundamental Problems of Marxism*, London 1969, p.78. For the later influence on historians such as Pirenne, see Plekhanov's essay 'The Role of the Individual in History' in the same volume, p.153.

31. The references in these two sentences are to Croce's *Historical Materialism and the Economics of Karl Marx, op. cit.*, p.140 in the English translation, and to *Under the Banner of Marxism* (pub. in German and Russian) which, under the editorship of A.M. Deborin, became the leading theoretical journal of the Communist International. After making more or less the same comments and quoting the same bibliographical references, Gramsci goes on to observe in Q28§11: 'The Land of Cokaygne motif that Croce draws attention to in Graziadei is of a certain general interest because it serves to trace a subterranean current of popular romanticism and fantasy that has been fed by the "cult of science", by "the religion of progress" and by nineteenth-century optimism, which is itself a form of opium. In this sense, it is to be seen whether Marx's reaction was perhaps not a legitimate and very important one in that, through the law of the tendency of the rate of profit to fall and his so-called catastrophism, he doused the flames; it is also to be seen to what extent the "opium dependency" has hindered a more accurate analysis of Marx's propositions.'

32. I.e. the question of value – see the passage translated above ('Graziadei's Land of Cokaygne'); for Loria on value, see Engels's comments in his supplement to Vol.III of *Capital* (pp.891-3, New York, 1967).

33. Gramsci quotes the passage from Gide and Rist in the original

French; the English translation given here is a corrected version of that done by R. Richards and E.F. Row (*History of Economic Doctrines*, London 1948, p.425).

34. In the 12 December 1909 number of the magazine *Viandante* Graziadei gave his opinion on socialist participation in the government, stating, among other things: 'I do not at all consider that the participation of socialists in the government conflicts with the spirit and methods of the class struggle. Class struggle and class co-operation are not absolutely incompatible terms ... They are, rather, complementary terms. There exist questions (for example that of national defence, the increase of social wealth, etc.) for which only class co-operation is conceivable. On the other hand, there exist other questions (for example that of the distribution of wealth) for which only class struggle in conceivable.'

35. This particular *obbligato* was a type of land tenure limited to the area around the town of Imola in what is now the region of Emilia Romagna; in return for a set number of days worked each year for the landowner, agricultural workers could build their houses on reclaimed land at favourable rates. By no stretch of the imagination could Graziadei's 'generalisation' therefore be considered well-grounded.

36. Gramsci is here referring to the positivist school of penology (and psychiatry), many of whose adherents passed over from socialism to support of fascism, which favoured the institutionalisation of those considered mentally infirm and tended, in the limit, to the criminalisation of social dissent, based among other things on a racist view of Southerners. There is a pun in the last part: as a synonym for 'Meridionali' ('Southerners') Gramsci writes 'anzi, Sudici' which, instead of meaning 'Southerners' (as the opposite of 'Nordici' – 'Northerners') means 'filthy'.

Chapter IV   Economic Trends and Developments

1. 'The author' referred to is the author of an article signed 'A.M.' in the *Nuova Antologia* of 1 August 1927. Gramsci's note is headed 'The Scandinavian and Baltic Problem' and gives a summary of the original article, one which 'strays off a little and is full of hazy pretentiousness but which is on the whole interesting since, among other things, it deals with a theme not normally considered'. We have selected only the second part; Gramsci's original comments are in parentheses. The first part of the article deals with the different interests, on one hand, of Denmark and Norway (in the British sphere of influence and more or less disarmed – maybe so Britain could 'enter the Baltic without violating any "little Belgiums" ', as Gramsci comments) and, on the other, of the forceful Finland and the industrialised Sweden (the latter being under German influence). Poland could become the great protector state in the Baltic, acting against both Germany and Russia, but, as Gramsci notes, 'Lithuania is averse to this, Finland has great reservations about it and other Baltic states are diffident and suspicious.' With the elimination of

the German fleet, the Baltic in a certain sense was neutralised, but this neutrality, according to 'A.M.' was one under British control.

2. This sub-section is a summary by Gramsci of what Tommasini wrote; Gramsci's own comments are in brackets. It has been included, with the editorial heading, to give an indication of the background against which Gramsci judged the economic crisis that was building up in the 1920s.

3. The words 'two powers standard', which appear twice in this paragraph, are in English in the Notebook.

4. In English in the original.

5. From the middle of the nineteenth century the Catholic Church in Mexico was subject to numerous restrictions, including the confiscation of its property and the state's refusal to recognise religious marriages, to which it retorted by excommunicating all who swore to support the 1857 constitution. For the *Kulturkampf*, see note 74, p.529.

6. Joseph Caillaux (1863-1944) was a French pacifist politician whose moves to bring in income tax were thwarted by the conservative Senate in 1909. He became Prime Minister briefly in 1911 and leader of the Radical and Radical Socialist deputies in 1913; at this time he was generally under attack from the right. Later he supported Daladier's negotiations with Hitler (1938-39) though he never came out in favour of the pro-fascist Vichy regime.

7. Charles E. Hughes was American Secretary of State from 5 March 1921 to 4 April 1925 under Presidents Harding and Coolidge, and subsequently Chief Justice of the Supreme Court for the whole of the 1930s.

8. 'Big Independents' is in English in the original text.

9. Gramsci uses a literal Italian translation (*Arabia felice*, i.e. 'fortunate' or 'happy' Arabia) of the Latin name given here, whose primary sense is 'fertile Arabia', as distinct from the 'Arabia petrea' or 'stony Arabia' to the North.

10. His full name also appears as Yahya Mahmud Al-Mutawakkil.

11. Hussein (or Husayn) ibn Ali, a lineal descendent of the prophet Mohammed, was ruler of Mecca from 1908 to 1916, then from 1916 to 1924 King of Hejaz (the mountainous strip in what is now Saudi Arabia, bordering the Red Sea between Asir in the South and the frontier with Jordan in the North and containing Mecca and Medina); after his defeat by Ibn Saud (see the present sub-section) the British sent him to Cyprus where he lived until 1930, dying the following year in what was then Transjordan.

12. Sidi Mohammed Idris Al-Mahdi As-Sanusi, later first king of Libya until his regime was overthrown in 1969 by Col. Muhammar al-Gadhafi.

13. Asir is the coastal region in the South-West of Saudi Arabia, centred on Abha and bordering, in the South, on (North) Yemen. The Farasan islands are just off shore in the southern Red Sea.

14. The Yemeni port in the Tihamah plain, also known as al-Hudaydah.

15. Or Nejd, the central area of Saudi Arabia, based around the present Saudi capital, Riyadh.

16. Or Wahhabiyah, a puritan sect of Islam, also commented on in 'The New Evolution of Islam', Chapter I, pp.132-4; Ibn Saud died in 1953.

17. For Hejaz, see footnote 11 (above).

18. A region about 600 kilometres up the coast from Aden in the direction of Oman.
19. The *Rivista d'Italia* article clarifies that the Emir of the Asir was el-Hasan ibn-Ali, brother of the future King Idris of Libya, and that the ex-Sanusi (where the term appears to be used to mean a Sanusi leader) was the Emir's cousin, Ahmed-ash-Sherif; the Sanusiyah (or Sennusiya, or, in the Italian here, *Senussi*) were a mystic Sufi brotherhood founded in 1837 by Idris's grandfather.
20. All near the coast of the Arab Gulf, providing an eastern outlet to the sea, and including at least in part relatively fertile agricultural land.
21. The venerated 'black stone' is housed in the sacred edifice (the Kaaba) at Mecca.
22. Or Zaydi, a brand of Shi'ism taking its name from Zeid, a follower of Mohammed's son-in-law, Ali (see the beginning of this sub-section).
23. The Italian *politica* means both 'policy' and 'politics'; the most convincing reading here of what Gramsci considered Russian influence on Britain probably refers to 'policy' towards the Empire but 'politics' domestically.
24. Although Stephen Leacock was Professor of Economics at McGill University, he is now better remembered as a humourist. The article in question (*New York Herald Tribune*, Magazine Section XII, 17 January 1932), though reading like a bad parody of Marcus Garvey's 'back to Africa' ideas, was in fact meant to be taken in all seriousness. The version given here is a translation of De Ritis's *Corriere della Sera* article that follows his paraphrase of the original (with all its additions, deletions and distortions) while attempting to keep close to the wording of Leacock's original article.
25. The publications referred to, sent on to Gramsci by Piero Sraffa, were the *Annuaire Statistique International*, Geneva 1930, of the League of Nations (Section économique et financière), and the *Report Presented to Parliament by the Financial Secretary to the Treasury by Command of His Majesty, June 1931*, London 1931, of the House of Commons Committee on Finance and Industry, the so-called Macmillan Report, 'to a great extent written and wholly inspired by Keynes' (see Piero Sraffa, letter of 9 September 1931 now published in *Lettere a Tania per Gramsci* [*Letters to Tania for Gramsci*], edited and introduced by Valentino Gerratana, Rome 1991, pp.33-4).
26. While the passage can be taken at face value, it may also be read as a comment on capitalism (taking the place of the Roman Empire), the subaltern forces being the modern proletariat; 'the struggle between the social groups' is yet another example of Gramsci's evasion of prison censorship when dealing with the class struggle.
27. The attempt, much vaunted by the regime, at national self-sufficiency, or autarky.
28. The argument here is not all that clear. It may be an allusion to the fact that, in the regime's drive for national self-sufficiency in grain (cf. note 27), peasants, salaried agricultural labourers, share croppers and so on 'cushioned' both the higher rural classes and the urban classes (the

working class as well as the middle and upper classes) by providing them with cheaper staple food while their own conditions were comparatively harsher. Official statistics – see Emilio Sereni, *Vecchio e nuovo nelle campagne italiane* [*Old and New in the Italian Countryside*], Rome 1956, Table XXVII, p.445 – later in fact confirmed that, while agricultural produce cost in 1933-34 little more than half what it did in 1928, the ratio of the agricultural sector's expenditure on essential industrial goods (such as fertilisers and agricultural machinery) to its earnings was about 1.5 – a 'scissors effect' – and continued to remain high. Although urban workers could use the little money saved on necessities to purchase better quality foodstuffs (i.e. there did exist a type of wage 'elasticity', that Gramsci puts in inverted commas to underscore the irony of the poor being pitted against the poor to benefit the relatively better-off), they found themselves worse off relative to 'higher' social classes, especially those he characterises as parasitic. This 'scissors effect' was also a key element in a demagogic ruling-class hegemonic strategy that, under fascism as under the previous liberal regime, attempted to bind industrial workers to the (especially northern) employers.

29. The similarity of concepts and actual wording hints that Gramsci is here implicitly referring to Lenin's position on monopoly: 'Capitalist monopoly, ... like all monopoly engenders a tendency to stagnation and decay' linked to 'a stratum of rentiers, i.e. people who ... take no part in any enterprise whatever, whose profession is idleness. The export of capital ... still more completely isolates the rentiers from production and sets the seal of parasitism on the whole country' (Chapter VIII of Lenin's *Imperialism, the Highest Stage of Capitalism*).

30. 'Boom' and 'run' are in English in the Notebook.

31. In the original English, *Recovery. The Second Effort*, London 1932.

32. The special laws (*leggi eccezionali*) of 5 November 1926, were applied retroactively against the Communist Party and other anti-fascist organisations in a period when, although subject to police harassment, they were certainly legal; despite his parliamentary immunity Gramsci himself was arrested on 8 November 1926 and held in prison for a year and a half before being tried.

33. These figures assume a baseline of 100 for the dollar in 1913.

34. The Sinaia (Romania) and Warsaw agreements attempted to regulate trade in agricultural produce in the developed countries immediately after the First World War.

35. Aristide Briand (1862-1932), winner of the Nobel Peace Prize in 1926, was French Prime Minister eleven times and, from 1925, Foreign Minister in fourteen successive governments. An early advocate of the League of Nations and of collective security, he and the American Secretary of State Frank Kellogg, in the 1928 Pact that bears their name, persuaded sixty nations to outlaw war as an instrument of national policy. The pan-Europeanism mentioned by Gramsci refers to Briand's call in 1930 for a federal union of Europe.

36. See Chapter III, footnote 11.

37. As a response to the crisis following the First World War that led to

the collapse of a number of important firms and jeopardised certain banks, the government created a special medium- and long-term industrial credit institute, the *Istituto Mobiliare Italiano* or IMI, to avoid a dangerous situation in which failure in one sphere might be transferred to another by a 'domino' effect. This measure was carried one stage further in 1933 with the creation of the *Istituto per la Ricostruzione Industriale* (IRI) when, as well as the main heavy industries and three of the most important private banks, the Bank of Italy, too, was threatened. The industrial restructuring division was to sell off the IRI's industrial, agricultural and property holdings to the private sector to repay debts to the Bank of Italy, while the industrial finance division was to collaborate with the IMI to provide industrial credit.

38. The reference is to the celebrated essay which Gramsci was working on when arrested and which he entitled 'Notes on the Southern Question and on the Attitude Taken Towards it by Communists, Socialists and Democrats'. It has, however, always been known by an alternative title, rendered fairly literally into English as 'Some Aspects of the Southern Question'; see SPW 1921-1926, p.450. Pietro Grifone, a Roman Communist then working with his party's clandestine organisation in the capital, claims to have supplied Valitutti with a copy of the essay; Senator Valitutti kindly confirmed by letter that such was the case.

39. *Le vie nuove al socialismo* (*New Roads to Socialism*), Palermo 1907. Ivanoe Bonomi (1873-1952), expelled from the Socialist Party in 1912 as part of the ultra-reformist wing, became Prime Minister in 1921 and was immediately charged by Gramsci with being 'the true organiser of Italian fascism' in the sense that, under him, Gramsci predicted that 'Italian reaction to Communism will become legal rather than illegal' (SPW 1921-1926, pp.54-5). The position of Engels hinted at here is of exceptional interest as foreshadowing the themes later developed by Gramsci of the unfinished revolution, the South, the fiscal regime and the relation of all these to the working-class movement. See Engels, letter to Turati, 26 January 1894, now in V.I. Lenin, *Sul movimento operaio italiano* (*On the Italian Working-Class Movement*), Rome 1962, pp.249-52.

40. For the syndicalists, see the immediately preceding sub-section ('Savings, Agricultural Protectionism and Industry'). *La Voce*, edited by Giuseppe Prezzolini (1882-1982), and *L'Unità*, edited by Gaetano Salvemini *alias* Rerum Scriptor (1873-1957), were influential 'Southernist' organs of the enlightened fractions of the bourgeoisie; Prezzolini played an unobtrusive role under fascism while Salvemini actively opposed the regime from abroad.

41. Rodolfo Morandi (1901-55) was a Marxist socialist economist, sentenced to ten years' imprisonment for anti-fascist activities by the regime. Liberated after the fall of Mussolini, he was nominated President of the National Liberation Committee for Upper Italy (CLNAI) and went on in the post-war era to become one of the leading exponents of a type of workers' control approach. In this sub-section citations from De Viti De Marco's review of Morandi's book are in quotation marks and Gramsci's

comments on them are in brackets. It is to be noted that, once again, one of the major differences between Gramsci and others on the left contemporary with him is in the evaluation of the role of the South in national life.

42. These firms from various key sectors of Italian industry, together with the Discount Bank, all went bankrupt in 1921, forcing the government to intervene (see first sentence of footnote 37, above).

43. I.e. exception being made for the exceptions or 'the exception proving the rule'.

44. This passage is a translation of the conclusions to one of Gramsci's most extended notes (seventeen handwritten pages), entitled 'Interpretations of the Risorgimento', to be found in the lengthy Notebook 19, which runs to some 140 pages. Although untitled, the notebook bears Gramsci's comment at the start that it would contain a double series of researches – on the Risorgimento and on the preceding history that had its repercussions in the Risorgimento. If his comment is taken at face value it is apparent, from this note and from other extracts from Q19 translated for the present volume, that Gramsci's notion of the Risorgimento extended up to the contemporary popular movement, seen as the heir to the classical Risorgimento.

45. The word 'turnover' is in English in the Notebook.

46. The words 'open shop' and 'dumping' in this paragraph are in English in the original. The argument may be compared with pp.307-11 of the 'Americanism and Fordism' chapter of SPN which is a translation, very slightly rearranged, of all but two minor sub-sections of Notebook 22, to which Gramsci himself gave the title 'Americanism and Fordism'.

47. For 'ceto' see the 'Note on the Translation', p.x.

48. This piece, although headed 'Americanism', was (like the previous sub-section 'Past and Present [10]. Fordism') not included by Gramsci in the special monographic Notebook 22.

49. 'What, indeed, is agnosticism but, to use an expressive Lancashire term, "shamefaced" materialism?' Engels asks in his 1892 Introduction to *Socialism: Utopian and Scientific*, London 1932, p.xiv. For more on James's pragmatism, see SPN, pp.372-3.

50. Royce, together with John Dewey and William James, all influenced by the philosopher and semiotician C.S. Peirce, were the dominant philosophers in the United States at that time. While the better-known Dewey and James were very much in the pragmatist-empiricist tradition, Royce was closely tied to European and, more specifically, Hegelian idealism.

51. This sub-section is also to be found in SCW, pp.280-1.

52. Backed by a wide-ranging and somewhat heterogeneous coalition of forces, the Progressive Party contested the 1912 and 1924 US Presidential elections on a platform containing a mixture of socialistic and populistic elements. Though the candidate in 1924, Senator Robert La Follette, won a sixth of the popular vote, the party dissolved following his death the next year.

53. The use of 'particolaristico' rather than the simple 'particolare'

('particular') almost certainly means that what is intended here is in fact 'particularist' in the technical sense of 'leaving each state in an empire or federation free to retain its own government, laws and rights' (*Shorter Oxford English Dictionary*). Gramsci here uses both the Italian and the English wording (in brackets in his text) for the British Commonwealth of Nations, this body's official title from 1931 to 1946. Following (bad) Italian custom, he normally refers to Britain as Inghilterra. The translation however attempts to distinguish, where appropriate, between the two senses, giving for example 'Englishness' in 'Disraeli' (immediately preceding sub-section) since within Britain the ruling class's quality of being English seems of greater importance than its being more generically British; whether Gramsci would have made the same distinctions is an open question.

54. This sub-section is a lengthy, at times word-for-word, summary of an article that Gramsci read on the British Empire in *La Nuova Antologia*. Included here are Gramsci's comments – the notes contained in parentheses – but not his summary, which occupies another two printed pages and deals with the Dominions' autonomy in foreign policy, the question of Governors General and High Commissioners, the UK signature to the 1928 Geneva Security Pact (after having previously consulted with and obtained the approval of the Dominions) and the question of autonomy and voluntary reciprocal obligations as laid down at the November 1926 Imperial Conference. The article concludes: 'British foreign policy cannot but be influenced by the Dominions.'

55. V.I. Lenin, 'The Rights of Nations to Self-Determination', Section 6, in *Collected Works*, Vol.20, London 1964, pp.393-454.

56. By this vague formulation it does not seem clear whether Gramsci is referring to the Labour Party's inability to separate itself off clearly from bourgeois parties or to the lack of an internal differentiation through the creation of left and revolutionary trends.

57. I.e. figures are given in the article that Gramsci was to a great extent merely summarising; the passage translated here consists of about one-sixth of Q2§6, to which Gramsci gave the general title 'Article "Financial Problems" Signed Verax (Tittoni) in the *Nuova Antologia* of 1 June 1927'. Its fifteen-and-a-half manuscript pages, in which Gramsci includes his comments in parentheses, deal predominantly with Italian budgetary policy in the first half of the 1920s. His main preoccupation seems to have been to analyse how various expedients were used to maintain the socio-economic privileges of the rich at the expense of the poor and middle strata (see, in particular, pp.7 and 11 of the manuscript notebook for his explicit comments on this). At the same time, the excerpt reproduced here gives an international comparison of relevance to his paragraphs, also contained to a large extent in the same notebook, on the 'geo-political' situation. We quote, at the end of the extract, his 'conclusion', which in the notebook is then followed by a half-page summary of an article in the successive number of *Nuova Antologia*, ending with the comment 'General criterion: lessen the nominal financial pressure in proportion to monetary revaluation, so as not to make the real financial pressure too heavy.'

58. 'Sinking fund' is in English, followed by its translation ('fondo di ammortamento') into Italian.
59. I.e. after the 'special measures' adopted by the Fascist government that led to all opposition members forfeiting their seats in parliament and to the arrest of Gramsci and others (see footnote 32, above).
60. The statement in fact dealt with 1929 but was that given to the AGM in January 1930 (see the *Bankers' Magazine*, March 1930, pp.501-11).
61. The word 'deficit' is underlined and in English in the original.
62. The reference is to the financial crisis of 1931 when Britain went off the gold standard and, in consequence, those countries whose currencies were linked to sterling had to devalue; this sterling area bloc had the Commonwealth at its core but was joined by many other countries in the 1930s. The original draft of this paragraph (Q4§60, written in November 1930) was of course too early to contain anything about the collapse of sterling. The later version is more cautious in its judgement as regards the free movement of gold, which Gramsci previously considered essential to the British monetary system.
63. Other notes on, broadly speaking, this topic may be found in SPN in the chapter on State and Civil Society, especially pp.242-3, 246-7, 258-9 and 260.
64. The *Economist* of 1 November 1930 carried a special supplement on the Soviet Union that, although critical of some points, was well-balanced and sympathetic towards the regime. Its anonymous author, M.S. Farbman (who also used the name R.B. Rafail), was a correspondent for the *Manchester Guardian* and *Observer* who, after 1917, had been in the 'democratic centralist' tendency of the Bolshevik Party and was later considered by the exiled Trotsky to be one of the real leaders of the anti-Stalinist opposition; an interview of his with Lenin is printed in V.I. Lenin, *Collected Works*, Vol.33, London and Moscow 1965, pp.383-9.
65. I.e. the USSR.
66. T.G. Masaryk, *Russland und Europa. Studien über die geistigen Strömungen in Russland, Erste Folge. Zur russischen Geschichts- und Religionsphilosophie. Soziologische Schizzen*, Jena 1913. It exists in an English translation by Eden and Cedar Paul, *The Spirit of Russia, Studies in History, Literature and Philosophy*, London and New York 1919, reprinted 1955.
67. L.D. Trotsky, 'Professor Masaryk on Russia' (in German), *Der Kampf*, Vienna, December 1914, reprinted by Gramsci in *L'Ordine Nuovo*, 19 June 1920 as well as in the last number (26 October 1918) of *Il Grido del Popolo*.
68. The short extract here on the collective man and the modern Prince gives the paragraphs in reverse order as compared with the text of Q8§52 to underline the argument of the title rather than the meaning of 'political class', of whose use by Mosca Gramsci is very critical. This preliminary 'A' text sub-section was later revised and appears as part of two final 'C' texts (paragraphs 6 and 7 of Q13) now in SPN pp.242-3, an editorial footnote to which contains a shortened version of Q7§12, translated in full in this Chapter (below).

69. English translation, *The Ruling Class*, New York 1939.
70. The text given here is an 'A' text, whose 'C' version, Q13§11, is on pp.246-7 of SPN. While some conceptions of the SPN text are more 'finalised' and polished, Q8§62 contains a more explicit statement of the durable nature of superstructural factors (end of first paragraph). The end of the sub-section reproduced here reads more convincingly than the SPN text; by omitting the words 'of groups and individuals' that appear in the 'C' text, Gramsci's 'A' text makes it clear, both grammatically and semantically, that it is an 'action that rewards' rather than the ' "prize-giving" activities of individuals and groups' (SPN, p.247 and editorial footnote 49) which must be incorporated as a positive aspect into penal law. The present interpretation finds support in Q3§52 (headed *Le pilori de la vertu*) where a planned newspaper column, 'The Pillory of Virtue', is, for Gramsci, to be linked to 'the "criminalist" doctrines expounded in his *Mysteries of Paris* by Eugène Sue, for whom a remunerative justice is contraposed to punitive justice and all its concrete expressions in order to complete it'.
71. Enrico Ferri (1856-1929), founder of the positivist school of criminology that regarded punishment solely as a deterrent and neglected any idea of rehabilitation, explained the differences between southern and northern Italy on the basis of the genetic inferiority of the southerners. After a career as an apparently 'intransigent' left socialist he went over to fascism after 1922.
72. A considerable part of the output of Paul Bourget (1852-1935), a French critic, essayist and novelist very influential among French conservative intellectuals of his time, is devoted to psychological studies, either of his generation (*Essais de psychologie contemporaine*, Paris 1893) or of the (frequently) well-to-do characters who populate his novels. For other comments on Bourget's views, see sub-section 7 ('The Four Pillars of Europe') of this chapter.
73. The quotation is from Giovanni Faccioli's review in *L'Italia letteraria*, 31 August 1930, of René Fülöp-Miller's *Il volto del bolscevismo* (*The Face of Bolshevism*), Milan 1930, which Gramsci had with him in prison. A reprint of this book, originally published in German, exists in English as *The Mind and Spirit of Bolshevism*, trans. F.S. Flint and D.F. Tait, New York and London 1965, with an epilogue written in 1962. The book, although generally hostile to the intellectual life of the Soviet Union, seems to have played a part in Gramsci's idea of the 'collective man' developed in the last notes of this chapter.
74. Gramsci wrote these comments as a preliminary note for that part of his critique of Croce contained in the so-called first part of Notebook 10 (see Chapter VI of this volume, pp.328-61). The full passage compares fascism and nineteenth-century liberalism as forms of passive revolution, while the excerpt given here (*not* recopied in any rewritten 'C' text) is in brackets in his draft as if to detach it somewhat from the rest of the argument; indeed, the reference to the avoidance of 'radical and destructive cataclysms of an exterminatory kind' leads one to suspect that, as well as dealing with changes in a fascist economy, there may possibly

also be an implicit criticism of the then current policies in the USSR. The full version of the passage is in *An Antonio Gramsci Reader*, London 1988, pp.264-5; differences in wording are minor.

Chapter V   Science, Logic and Translatability

1. In fact Turati, the chief spokesman of Italian reformist socialism, appended the subtitle *Rivista quindicinale del socialismo scientifico (Fortnightly Review of Scientific Socialism)* to *Critica Sociale* only from 1893 to May 1898.
2. Gramsci is here referring to the last part of his Q11§26, to be found in translation on p.430 of SPN, which attacks the tautological nature of sociological laws that are really no more than 'a duplicate of the observed fact itself'; the explicit target named in the cross-referenced paragraph is the political sociologist Robert Michels but the remark is of general application.
3. Note that Gramsci uses the same word, *esperienza*, for what is here translated 'experiment' and 'experience'. As in English until the eighteenth century, *esperienza* ('experience') can be used to refer to the external world of objects as well as to the inner world of feelings and subjective knowledge. This terminology also reflects what Italian (and not only Italian) culture defines as science – the whole sphere of human enquiry and investigation, not just what the British tradition and its heirs regard as 'proper' science (i.e. the natural and exact ones). This cultural difference must be borne constantly in mind when reading Gramsci on science.
4. A.S. Eddington, *The Nature of the Physical World*, Cambridge 1928. The sentence quoted by Gramsci from the French translation is to be found on pp.1-2 of the English reprints of this work. In the text, Gramsci gives his own translation into Italian from the French.
5. Giuseppe Antonio Borgese, *Escursione in terre nuove (A Journey into Foreign Lands)*, Milan 1931.
6. Here Gramsci uses the word *rapporti* which can mean either relationships or (mathematical) ratios.
7. Later on in the same notebook (Q11§68), Gramsci comments 'In Jules Verne's novel *From the Earth to the Moon*, Michel Ardan, in outlining his position, makes the lyrical claim that "distance does not exist" since "the solar system is a solid homogeneous body; the planets which compose it press against, touch and adhere to one another, and the space between them is only the space which separates the molecules of the most compact metals, such as silver, iron, gold or platinum." Borgese, following on in Eddington's footsteps, has turned Verne's reasoning upside down, maintaining that "solid matter" does not exist since the vacuum in the atom is such that a human body, reduced to its solid parts, would become a speck visible only under the microscope. This is Verne's "imagination" applied to the science of the scientists rather than schoolboy science.' Verne's novel is quoted from the English translation

by J. and R. Baldick, London and New York, 1970, pp.117-8.
8. Jørgen Jørgensen, p.6 of the *Proceedings 7th International Congress on Philosophy (Oxford 1930)*, ed. G. Ryle, London 1931, in outlining the dominant, phenomenalist interpretation of quantum mechanics developed by the members of the Göttingen-Copenhagen school, states that we 'cannot determine the processes as they are going on "objectively", i.e. as they presumably would run if we had not investigated and thereby disturbed them. And as this, according to the quantum theory, is a matter of principle, it is regarded as a manifestation that the conception of these processes as existing "objectively", i.e. independent of the subject who observes them, is untenable ... In other words: it seems impossible to separate the subjective element in the observation from the objective, and even the very existence of an objective physical world has thus become to a certain degree problematical.'
9. Gramsci's emphasis.
10. See Gösta Ekehorn, 'On the Principls of Renal Function', *Acta Medica Scandinavica Supplementum 36*, Stockholm 1931, especially Chap. 20 (pp.182-9), for the argument outlined here.
11. Under the heading 'Encyclopaedic Notions' Gramsci gives the following definition of the demiurge, or demiurgos: 'From the original meaning of "working for the people, for the community" (artisan) right up to the present meanings of "creator" etc.' (Q8§150).
12. Rutherford's most famous experiment in his investigation of the structure of the atom consisted in firing α-particles at a thin metal foil and observing their scattering through various angles. According to the then current picture of the atom, only small-angle deflections should have been observed, but Rutherford and his student Marsden noted that a small fraction (fewer than one in ten thousand) was scattered through a large angle. This event, Rutherford later commented, 'was almost as incredible as if you had fired a 15-inch shell at a piece of tissue paper and it came back and hit you'. A 'chain' of reasoning then led back to an inverse-square law for the force involved and a nucleus (for gold) of less than 3 million millionths of a centimetre in diameter, compared with an atomic diameter of about 2 hundred millionths of a centimetre.
13. These are references to some of the paradoxes of Zeno of Elea on the subject of motion and plurality. In a race in which Achilles gives the tortoise a start, when Achilles reaches the point where the tortoise started from, the tortoise has already moved on; so also for when Achilles reaches that point, and so on: Achilles can, therefore, never overtake the tortoise. Objects at rest occupy a space equal to their dimensions, as, at any moment, does an arrow in flight; thus an arrow in flight is at rest. In the heap (or 'millet seed') paradox it is stated that one millet seed makes no sound when it falls but a thousand do; a thousand nothings thus become something.
14. Like Vico and Hegel, Gramsci distinguished between 'common' and 'good' sense, the first normally meaning a set of commonly held but often inconsistent notions and the second 'practical empirical common sense in

the English sense of the term' (SPN, pp.322-3 and footnote). In Q11§56 he cites the fanciful notions related in Manzoni's *I promessi sposi* of how the plague was supposed to have been spread and the wiser views that did not dare make themselves heard: 'There was, we see, a secret outlet for the truth – in domestic confidence. Good sense existed; but it was kept hidden for fear of common sense' (*The Betrothed*, trans. Archibald Colquhoun, London and New York 1956, p.446).

15. Mario Missiroli (1886-1974), a leading left-inclined liberal journalist before he caved in to fascism, claimed that science was a 'bourgeois conception and class privilege ... In asserting that its laws are objective and affirming the dualism between being and knowing, [it] upholds the present authoritarian system' (*L'Ordina Nuovo*, 19 July 1919), a position close to Sorel. Like Gramsci here, Togliatti's rejoinder attacked the handing-down of scientific conclusions as articles of faith while comparing scientific development to the laborious achievement of 'mechanical and technical perfection' in the factory so that even the apprentice feels part 'of a single community that has operated across the centuries'; through its liberatory nature, the class struggle represented 'the true science, the true philosophy of the proletariat'. See also 'Religion, Philosophy, Politics [2]', pp.406-15 of this volume, especially p.410.

16. 'The attempt [by Govi to create a neopositivism] may, it seems to me, be compared with those of the mathematical philosophers such as Bertrand Russell; what "mathematics" is for Russell, "methodology" is for Govi ... A methodological hash is made of this clear derivation from Russell. In Russell the reference to mathematics makes the system less cumbersome and confused.' (From the first draft, Q8§184, of the comments on Govi.)

17. Gramsci was using a French translation of Plekhanov's *Fundamental Problems of Marxism* which included, as an appendix, the section referred to here; the subsequent (1946) Italian edition, which followed the French one, did in fact give the title *Dialettica e logica* to this appendix. Not all English language editions of the book carry the appendix, however; in particular the 1969 London edition translated by Julius Katzer and edited by James S. Allen does not. The appendix is however to be found in the other, undated, commonly available English edition, with a preface by V. Fomina and again translated by Julius Katzer (with minor changes in the wording as compared with the other edition). This latter edition comments (p.110) that the appendix is part of Plekhanov's preface to Engels's *Ludwig Feuerbach and the End of Classical German Philosophy* and was included in the German edition of the book *Fundamental Problems* at Plekhanov's express wish.

18. As in 'The Technique of Thought' (pp.298-303 of this volume), this may be compared with Macaulay's essay 'On the Athenian Orators', to which explicit reference is made in 'Oratory, Conversation, Culture', SCW, pp.380-5.

19. Gramsci's first draft of this paragraph, for once, reads quite differently from the final version. In Q8§189, we read (under the title 'Formal Logic and Methodology'): 'Formal logic or abstract methodology

is the "philology" of philosophy [interlinear variant 'of thought'], it is the "erudition" (the erudite method) of history. Aesthetics and philology as dialectics and formal logic. But these similarities do not give an exact concept of the status of formal logic. The best comparison would be that with mathematics, but this is also the cause of infinite errors since it gives rise to an infinite extension of logic and logical or methodological figures. Mathematics has been able to develop enormously in various directions (geometry, algebra, different types of calculus) which cannot happen for formal logic since formal logic must not and cannot develop beyond the limits of immediate necessities (whereas mathematics cannot be limited). (This concept to be gone into in more detail).' These reflections on mathematics stimulated the note headed 'Bibliography, Tobias Dantzig', p.298 of this edition.

20. This much-reprinted book, known only indirectly to Gramsci, presented to non-specialist readers the development of the number concept as a cultural issue at a time when this was still being keenly debated by mathematicians and philosophers. Albert Einstein commented that it was 'beyond doubt the most interesting book on the evolution of mathematics which has ever fallen into my hands'. The first edition was published London and New York in 1930.

21. The wording here is a translation of Croce's paraphrase of Engels, rather than of Engels. The preface to the second edition of *Anti-Dühring* reads 'the art of working with concepts is not inborn and also is not given with ordinary everyday consciousness but requires real thought, and that this thought similarly has a long empirical history, not more and not less than empirical natural science' (Marx Engels Collected Works, Vol.25, London 1987, p.14). Thus Engels does not actually use the expression 'technical work of thought', preferring instead 'real thought'; Italian editions of the book have the more precise 'experimental' rather than the 'empirical' which creeps into the English, although both specify that the limited mode of thought of the natural sciences was 'inherited from English empiricism'. The page number of Croce's book refers to the Italian edition since the quotation is from one of the five chapters not translated for the English edition.

22. See, for example, the passage translated in SCW, pp.380-5, especially p.383.

23. See p.141 of B. Croce, *Saggio sullo Hegel*, Bari 1913; the passage comes in the Conclusion (Chapter XI) to the book's first part (translated into English as *What is Living and What is Dead in the Philosophy of Hegel*, London 1915). See also Engels, *Anti-Dühring*, loc. cit., p.26: 'That which still survives, independently, of all earlier philosophy is the science of thought and its laws – formal logic and dialectics. Everything else is subsumed in the positive science of nature and history.'

24. For the principle of distincts, see the part of the general introduction dealing with Chapters VI and VII on Croce and the relevant footnotes.

25. Loisy's unorthodoxy (see footnotes 95 and 103 to Chapter 1 of this volume) led in 1908 to his excommunication from the Catholic Church after Pius X's encyclical *Pascendi dominici gregis (Feeding the Lord's*

Flock) condemning modernism.
26. See footnote 18 on p.557 of this volume.
27. See Giuseppe Prezzolini (Giuliano il Sofista), *Il linguaggio come causa d'errore. H. Bergson (Language as a Cause of Error. H. Bergson)*, Florence 1904, and V. Pareto, *The Mind and Society*, trans. A. Bongiorno and A. Livingstone, London 1935. In the latter work (*Trattato di sociologia generale* in the original Italian) Pareto distinguishes between the language of the logical-experimental sciences, which he maintains is objective and universal, and that of everyday life, which is subjective and changeable.
28. Interlinear variant: 'logical rigour'.
29. Gramsci, in the Notebooks, gives his own translation of the French edition of Sinclair Lewis's *Babbitt* (Paris 1930, trans. M. Rémon). The quotation here is from p.44 of the original edition (New York 1922). Gramsci's comments on Babbitt as a type and on the difference between the American and European petty bourgeoisie may be read in SCW, pp.278-80. Don Ferrante is one of the incidental characters in Manzoni's *The Betrothed*. In Chapter 27 of this work the description of him and his (for those days) quite considerable library shows him as still wedded to outmoded ways of thinking. Gramsci's comment refers to the closing pages of Chapter 37, in which Don Ferrante's impeccable logic leads him to deny any material cause for the bubonic plague that, in 1630, carried off about three-quarters of the population of Milan (according to the authors quoted by Manzoni), including Don Ferrante himself, swearing to the last that the cause of everything lay in the influence of the stars, in particular the conjunction of Jupiter with Saturn in 1628. For the Tolstoy, see *The Death of Ivan Ilyich* (London 1905, trans. H. Bergen, p.39).
30. The fascist coup d'état came during the preparation of the Theses on Tactics that Bordiga wrote for the Second Congress of the young Community Party. Gramsci wrote a couple of years later that, at that time, the Party's official position was that a military or fascist dictatorship was impossible and 'only with great difficulty did I manage to have this conception taken out of the written theses'; see Togliatti, *La formazione del gruppo dirigente del partito comunista italiano* (*The Formation of the Leadership of the Italian Community Party*), Rome 1962, p.199.
31. i.e. of a transitory nature, subject to constant change.
32. Like Esperanto, Volapük, is an artificial language, invented in the last quarter of the nineteenth century, to aid international communication.
33. For Gramsci's discussion of the 'homo oeconomicus' see especially 'Brief Notes on Economics [1]. The Concept of "Homo Oeconomicus" ' pp.166-7, 'Points to Reflect on for a Study of Economics [3]. On the Subject of the So-Called Homo Oeconomicus' pp.167-8 and 'Points to Reflect on for a Study of Economics [6]. Regarding Pantaleoni's "Pure Economics" ' pp.171-3 of this volume.
34. See G.W.F. Hegel, *Hegel's Philosophy of Right*, trans. T.M. Knox, London 1942, Part III, Section II, paragraph 189. Here, under the general sub-heading 'The System of Needs', Hegel writes 'Political economy is the science which starts from this view of needs and labour but then has the

task of explaining mass-relationships and mass-movements in their complexity and their qualitative and quantitative character.'

35. The year was in fact 1922 and the occasion the Fourth Congress of the Communist International. In referring to the problem of translating the terms of the resolution on organisation at the previous year's Third Congress Lenin commented that, although the motion was excellent, 'it is thoroughly imbued with the Russian spirit ... we have not learnt how to prevent our Russian experience to foreigners.' (V.I. Lenin, *Collected Works*, Vol.33, pp.430-1, London 1966).

36. Giovanni Vailati (1863-1909) was an Italian pragmatist philosopher and distinguished mathematician.

37. The passage from *The Holy Family*, Marx-Engels Collected Works Vol.4, London 1975, p.39, reads: 'If Herr Edgar compares French *equality* with German "self-consciousness" for an instant, he will see that the latter principle expresses *in German*, i.e., in abstract thought, what the former says *in French*, that is, in the language of politics and of thoughtful observation. Self-consciousness is man's equality with himself in pure thought.'

38. Cf. SPN p.395, where the same lines are quoted, in this case in the translation of Q16§9. Hoare and Nowell-Smith's translation accords with the National Edition of Carducci's Collected Works whereas Gramsci, misquoting, said that Kant and Robespierre were 'united in the one faith' rather than having 'opposite faiths'. They were however united in the sense of 'being moved by a common desire for truth', as Croce notes at the beginning of this extract from *Conversazioni Critiche*, Bari 1972 (reprint), pp.292-4, which Gramsci copied at times word-for-word in the first part of this note. The passage referred to from *The Holy Family* is to be found in footnote 37 above.

39. The passage from Heine may be read in the Appendix (p.267) to *Kant's Prolegomena to any Future Metaphysics*, ed. P. Carus, London 1902: 'Mark this, ye proud men of action, ye are nothing but unconscious instruments of the men of thought who, often in the humblest seclusion, have appointed you to your inevitable task. Maximilian Robespierre was merely the hand of Jean-Jacques Rousseau.'

40. G.W.F. Hegel, *Lectures on the History of Philosophy*, trans. E.S. Haldane and F.H. Simson, London 1892; we read in Vol.III, p.409 'In the philosophy of Kant, Fichte and Schelling, the revolution to which in Germany mind has in these latter days advanced, was formally thought out and expressed; ... In this great epoch of the world's history, two nations only have played a part, the German and the French, and this in spite of their absolute opposition, or rather because they are so opposite ... In Germany this principle has burst forth as thought, spirit, Notion; in France, in the form of actuality.'

41. G.W.F. Hegel, *The Philosophy of History*, trans. J. Sibree, New York 1956, p.443; the words 'tranquil theory' are Gramsci's emphasis.

42. This is Gramsci's paraphrase of his own translation of the eleventh thesis on Feuerbach which, elsewhere in the Notebooks (Q7, p.3), he renders from the German original as 'The philosophers have only

interpreted the world in various ways; the point is now to change it.'

43. Here Gramsci quotes from memory Engels's *Ludwig Feuerbach and the End of Classical German Philosophy*. What he puts in quotation marks, presumably to avoid rousing the censor's suspicions, is not 'people' but 'working class movement' in the English translation of Engels's book, *Collected Works of Marx and Engels*, Vol.26, London 1990, p.398 and the equivalent 'movimento operaio' in the standard Italian translation.

44. The passage referred to by Gramsci is not in the *Contribution to the Critique of Hegel's Philosophy of Law* as such but in the more widely-quoted *Introduction* to the *Critique*, which Gramsci had with him in prison: 'The criticism of the *German philosophy of state and law*, which attained its most consistent, richest and final formulation through *Hegel*, is both a critical analysis of the modern state and of the reality connected with it, and the resolute negation of the whole *German political and legal consciousness as practised* hitherto, the most distinguished, most universal expression of which, raised to the level of a *science*, is the *speculative philosophy of law* itself ... In politics the Germans *thought* what other nations *did*' (Marx-Engels Collected Works, Vol.3, p.181, London 1975).

45. See, e.g., Kant's *Critique of Pure Reason*, London and New York, 1979, pp.30-40, 77-81, 85-90 and 126-8 (trans. J.M.D. Meiklejohn).

46. In an extremely condensed form we see here a great deal of Gramsci's estimation of the major forces in the Risorgimento. Liberal 'moderatism' (influenced to a certain extent by the Italian Hegelians) was hegemonic but, being classically rightist in its social policy, rather than 'moderate' in the sense of 'centrist', lacked an appeal to the popular forces, especially the southern peasantry. As a radical democrat De Sanctis thus felt impelled to break with the 'moderates' and pass over to the parliamentary left (as well as, in philosophy, to positivism and, in literature, to *verismo*, the Italian naturalist school) as part of his attempt to build not just a 'national' but a 'national-popular' consciousness that would stem from the union of the cultured and the popular classes: in other words the beginning of a new hegemonic social bloc. In the key essay 'Science and Life' De Sanctis approached very closely, in Gramsci's view, to that 'unity of theory and practice' which is a Marxist ideal. For further comments on all these themes, see SPN pp.55-84 (especially pp.57-60, 65-66 and 76-79) and pp.102-4, SCW pp.22, 93-8, 212-6 and 247-9, and this volume pp.341-3 and 157-9.

47. The extract is in fact from Chapter X, rather than XI, as stated by Gramsci; the emphases are Gramsci's.

48. In various places in the Foreword to *The Holy Family* and in the *Economic and Philosophical Notebooks of 1844*, Marx speaks of communism as '*real humanism*', and as 'fully developed naturalism' equal to 'humanism' or 'fully developed humanism' equal to 'naturalism', being the '*positive* transcendence of *private property* as *human self-estrangement*'; as 'humanism' or 'consistent naturalism'; and as '*positive* humanism' (Marx-Engels Collected Works, London, 1975, Vol.4, p.7 and Vol.3, pp.296, 336 and 342 respectively) but not, apparently as 'neo-humanism'.

49. Note also that in a letter to his sister-in-law, Tatiana (Tania), dated 23 August 1933 (i.e. probably no more than two months at most after Q15§64 was drafted), Gramsci made one of his very rare comments in that particular year on his work: 'As well as its language [*linguaggio*] in the strictly technical sense of the word, every country has a language "of civilisation" of its own which one must first be acquainted with in order to know the former.'

50. Cf. Marx, Preface to *A Contribution to the Critique of Political Economy*, Collected Works of Marx and Engels, London 1987, Vol.29, p.262: 'My enquiry led me to the conclusion that neither legal relations nor political forms could be comprehended whether by themselves or on the basis of a so-called general development of the human mind, but that on the contrary they originate in the material conditions of life, the totality of which Hegel, following the example of English and French thinkers of the eighteenth century, embraces within the term "civil society"; that the anatomy of this civil society, however, has to be sought in political economy.'

51. I.e. type in the sense of something typifying the ideal characteristics to be adopted.

52. Marx, loc. cit., p.263: 'Just as one does not judge an individual by what he thinks about himself, so one cannot judge such a period of transformation by its consciousness, but, on the contrary, this consciousness must be explained from the contradictions of material life, from the conflict existing between the social forces of production and the relations of production.'

53. I.e. Marxist historiography.

54. Gramsci returns to this theme in Q16§20, noting that the change that came about 'in the law relating to trials and in the theoretical discussions on the subject ... in 1859 were still of recent memory. The old procedure, in fact, required a confession by the accused (specially for capital crimes) in order to be able to deliver sentence of condemnation: the "habemus confitentem reum" seemed the crowning point of every judicial proceeding, whence the urgings, the moral pressures and the various degrees of torture (not as punishment but as investigative procedure). In the updated procedure, the interrogation process of the accused becomes just one, sometimes a negligible, element that in any case is of use only for giving direction to the further enquiries of the investigation and trial ... It is to be seen whether ... a comparison has been made between the investigative method that attempts to reconstruct the penal responsibility of single individuals and the critical method, typical of the philosophy of praxis, that attempts to reconstruct the objective "personality" of historical events and their development, and [whether there has been carried out] an examination of the movement for the updating of trial law as one element that "suggested" an updating of the study of history ... [This] updating which had no small importance in the political sphere, bringing about a strengthening of the tendency towards the separation of powers and the independence of the magistracy (hence towards a general reorganisation of the structure [of the apparatus] of government) has been

toned down in many countries, leading back in many cases to the old methods of investigation and even to torture: the systems used by the American police, with third degree interrogations, are quite well-known ...'

55. Lorenzo Stecchetti (1845-1916), the pen name of Olindo Guerrini, was a writer who specialised in rather morbid and even what were regarded at the time as semi-pornographic novels.

56. Hegel's metaphor is the source of Marx's comment in the afterword to the second German edition of *Capital* to the effect that with Hegel the dialectic is upside down and must be turned the right way up if one is to extract its rational kernel. The original metaphor is in Hegel's *Philosophie der Geschichte*, Berlin 1840, p.535; confusingly, the English translator of *The Philosophy of History* gives only the sense of the metaphor but not the metaphor itself (New York 1956, p.446), thus giving rise to notable confusion about the precise origin. The editorial footnote to be found on p.26 of *Anti-Dühring* (London 1947) gives a faithful translation of the original German of Hegel: 'Since the sun had been in the firmament, and the planets circled round him, the sight had never been seen of man standing upon his head – i.e., on the Idea – and building reality after this image. Anaxagoras first said that the Nous, reason, rules the world; but now, for the first time, had man come to recognise that the Idea must rule the mental reality. And this was *a magnificent sunrise*.'

57. I.e. Q11§49, 'The Mutual Translatability of National Cultures' translated above (p.310-3).

58. In the *Nuova Rivista Storica* polemic referred to the thesis upheld by Barbagallo tended to cancel any essential difference between the economic systems of different eras, and this despite the fact that he regarded himself as a historical materialist. This claim drew Gramsci's scorn, and the accusation of 'Lorianism' (the phenomenon due to the 'scanty cultural organisation and thus the absence of any check or criticism' – Q1§25 – especially among those who thought they could 'enrich, correct or go beyond Marxism'). The *tone* of the polemic reminded Gramsci of the eighteenth-century one over the respective merits of the ancients and the moderns which 'was the expression of a developing consciousness that a new historical phase was now underway, one that completely renovated all modes of being and represented a radical overthrow of the past'. But in asking himself what the *meaning* of this modern polemic was, Gramsci provided the reply that 'It is undoubtedly reactionary, tends to spread scepticism, remove any value of development and progress from economic activity; the polemic, however, is limited to small circles of professional and not even very significant scholars and is not an element of culture like the eighteenth-century one' (Q4§60).

59. It should be borne in mind that at the time Gramsci was writing, and still now, though to a lesser extent, the word *tecnica* used in this and the following passage was often used to indicate both 'technology' or 'technological' (which seems the most consistent reading here) and 'technique' or 'technical'.

Chapter VI Reference Points for an Essay on B. Croce

1. The 'Introduction' was added at some later date than points 1 to 12 and thus, like other such additions (see the editorial introduction to this Chapter), is included in angled brackets. The 'first note' to which Gramsci refers is the extended version of the summary he jotted down and with which we begin this part of Notebook 10, while his reference to page 37a corresponds to Croce as 'The Party Man' (see pp.462-4 of this volume).
2. This is the paragraph in brackets at the end of point 11 beginning 'A certain literature' through to 'have to be cleared up' (pp.331-2).
3. Published in English in B. Croce, *The Conduct of Life*, New York and London 1924, pp.27-33; the volume is the translation by Arthur Livingston of Croce's *Frammenti di etica* (*Ethical Fragments*), later included in his *Etica e politica* (*Ethics and Politics*). Francesco De Sanctis (1817-93), the most influential Italian literary critic and aesthetic theorist of his time, became Minister of Public Education after the defeat of the 'Historic Right' (or 'moderates') and the coming to power in 1876 of the 'Left'; for his essay on 'La Nerina' of Giacomo Leopardi's poem 'Le ricordanze' ('Recollections', in English in *Leopardi's Canti*, trans. J.H. Whitfield, Naples 1962), see the general introduction to this volume, p.xxii.
4. The twentieth-century neo-scholastics returned to some of the doctrines of St Thomas Aquinas (i.e. Thomism) for their inspiration. According to the authoritative *Filosofi Università Regime*, T. Gregory, M. Fattori and N. Siciliani De Cumis (eds.), Rome and Naples 1985, Fr Agostino Gemelli, founder of the Catholic University in Milan, was a determined opponent of the teaching of philosophical idealism and therefore philosophically agnostic only within the realms, as Gramsci too emphasises elsewhere, of a certain (at least primitive) realism to which consistent Catholic theology subscribes. Gemelli was also a fervent supporter of fascism and played an important role in advising Catholic professors to swear an oath of loyalty to the regime; see also note 77 to Chapter I of this volume.
5. The particular Caracciolo referred to here is Galeazzo (1517-86), often called the 'Marquis of Vico'. Although a nephew of Pope Paul IV, Galeazzo Caracciolo became the most important Italian Protestant of his time and, in order to escape the Inquisition, fled the country in 1555, becoming a close collaborator of Calvin, who dedicated to him, among other things, the second edition of his commentary on the Epistle to the Corinthians.
6. Everything mentioned in this paragraph serves to place Croce in direct lineal descent from the so-called 'Historic Right' (see footnote 3, above).
7. B. Croce, *Etica e politica*, Bari 1931, p.343 or, in Salvatore J. Castiglione's translation of some of this book's essays, *Politics and Morals*, London and New York 1946, p.129 (in the essay 'The Unending Struggle between "State" and "Church" ') we read a passage which, for

its relevance to the themes discussed by Gramsci, deserves to be quoted at length: 'The term Churchmen must be understood, as in the term Church, in an ideal sense, as including those who, in modern and lay society, are represented by the worshippers of the truth, by those who increase their own and others' understanding, by the custodians of ideals, by all those who, like the ministers of religions, have the care of souls ... When men whose behaviour has been merely utilitarian ... suddenly assume a moral role, expressing ideas not expected of them and accomplishing generous actions, that particular change of occupation is greeted with profound satisfaction. On the contrary, we feel profound disgust when Churchmen, lovers of truth, teachers, custodians of ideals, play the part of politicians, of violent men, of traffickers, of intriguers, of gendarmes and of executioners. In this case the change of role ... reduces to an apostasy, a desertion, a failing in honour.' See also 'Science of Politics', p.373 of this volume.

8. Modernism here of course refers to the trend in Catholicism, for which see Section E of Chapter I in particular.

9. Gramsci here misquotes '*caveant consules*' ('let the consuls beware') for the correct '*provideant consules*' ('let the consuls take measures'). The exact passage may be found on p.132 of *Historical Materialism and the Economics of Karl Marx*, op. cit.; if Labriola is afraid 'that a crisis in Marxism of whatever kind, or the commencement of it, may be used by those whose interest it is to lead astray and scatter the workers' movement, then *provideant consules*' (the original translation, here corrected, gives 'neutralised' for 'used').

10. Amadeo is Amadeo Bordiga, the first, gifted (but ultra-left) leader of the Italian Communist Party; Jacques Mesnil, writing in the French Communist Party daily *L'Humanité* (14 March 1922), claimed that the Theses for the Second Congress of the PCd'I, written by Bordiga, showed the influence of Croce.

11. Lyautey was a French Army Captain who, Gramsci wrote, 'belonged to the big bourgeoisie which was closely allied to the aristocracy' and, although a monarchist, served the Republic, playing an important role in conquering Morocco. He 'was and remained a thoroughgoing nationalist, but conceived of national solidarity as follows. In Rome he had become acquainted with Count von Dillen, a German Captain of Uhlans, and wrote of him to his friend Antoine de Margerie in these terms: "A gentleman, of perfect education and charming manners, sharing our ideas in religion, politics, everything. We speak the same language and understand each other marvellously well. What more do you wish? In my heart reigns a ferocious spirit, that of disorder, of revolution. Without doubt, I feel closer to all fighters, whatever their nationality, than to those of our fellow-countrymen with whom I do not have any ideas in common and whom I consider public enemies." ' (Q6§141, in which Gramsci quotes the original French of Edmond Jaloux's review in *Les Nouvelles Littéraires*, 8 August 1931.)

12. The original French of Sorel's letter is quoted by Gramsci. The same extract is also quoted, again in the original French, as Q10II§3 (not included in the next chapter to avoid repetition).

13. Rather than Castellano's interview (*Cultura e Vita Morale* [*Culture and Moral Life*], Bari 1926, pp.143-50), which deals with the masonic mentality in Italy, the interview that Gramsci was trying to recall is the subsequent one in the same book (pp.150-9, like Castellano's also first published in *La Voce*), appearing under the signature Falea di Calcedonia and entitled 'The Death of Socialism'.
14. *Theory and History of Historiography*, trans. D. Ainslie, London and Sydney 1921; Gramsci had the 1927 third edition with him in prison but the book was first published in 1916.
15. This claim is found on p.283 of Croce's *History of Italy 1871-1915* (trans. C.M. Ady, Oxford 1929), but was made in conversation during the First World War. In this latter form it is quoted by Guido De Ruggiero ('Italian Thought and the War' in *Revue de métaphysique et de morale*, 1916 no. 5, cited by Ady on p.327) and – with Croce's interjection – reads: 'One of our intellectuals (it was I [Croce] who had said this in conversation) summarised this conception scientifically when he remarked that this war seemed to him "the historical materialist war". It is an appropriate turn of phrase and gives food for thought.' See also 'The War of Historical Materialism', p.418 and footnote 65 to Chapter VII of this volume.
16. See, e.g., Croce's article 'Antistoricismo' (in Italian) in the *Proceedings of the VII Congress of Philosophy*, ed. Gilbert Ryle, London 1931 and elsewhere in this volume for Gramsci's critique of this aspect of Crocean philosophy.
17. Where Ivanoe Bonomi – see p.550 of this volume – speaks of Croce in his book *Leonida Bissolati* (Rome 1929, especially pp.12-13 and 17-18), it is to deal with the influence of Marxism on the intellectuals in general and on Croce in particular. Croce's stated position was that 'As for political conceptions, Marxism brought me back to the best traditions of Italian political science, thanks to its firm assertion of the principle of force, of struggle, of power, and its satiric and caustic opposition to the insipidities of natural law, anti-historical and democratic positions, the so-called ideals of 1789.' (From his preface to the 1918 edition of *Historical Materialism*, p.xv, quoted by Bonomi, who goes on to say that Croce outlined the reasons as to why Marxism had had a beneficial effect on the Italian turn-of-the-century intellectuals in his *History of Italy 1871-1915*.) Ignazio (not, as Gramsci says, Orazio) Raimondo, in his letter, pays tribute to Croce's breadth of scholarship and to his having taught a whole generation how to think, rather than just absorb information; see also 'Actualism, Ideology and Philosophy', pp.446-7 of this volume.
18. Now in *The Conduct of Life*, op. cit. in reference 3. The essay 'Religion and Peace of Mind' is to be found on pp.27-33.
19. This last clause seems the most likely interpretation of Gramsci's somewhat elliptical grammar, with '*tra loro*' ('among or between them') referring to the neo-scholastics rather than to Crocean and Gentilian philosophies.
20. Gramsci (Q8§105, not translated here) regarded Papini's article 'Croce and the Cross' as an exercise in pure hypocrisy. Papini lists a

number of newly created religious orders (*La Nuova Antologia*, 1 March 1932) to counter Croce's arguments, but in Gramsci's view these orders were primarily ' "disciplinary" over the "simple" mass, ramifications and tentacles of the Society of Jesus' rather than ones having any great religious significance (Q8§220).

21. The Restoration was the period of political reaction following the end of the Napoleonic Wars in which the predominant forces of conservative liberalism did not really want, however, to go as far as restoring the *Ancien Régime* (see 'Catholic Action's Origins' and 'Catholic Action and Neo-Guelphism' pp.37-9 of this volume); for Gramsci, then, 'restoration is only a metaphorical expression' (SPN p.398).

22. For the neo-Guelphs, a moderate Catholic liberal tendency of rather limited appeal, see footnote 46 to Chapter I as well as 'Croce as a Renaissance Man [2]' pp.470-2 of this volume and SPN pp.58n, 109 and 110.

23. The Parthenopean Republic, founded by Neapolitan liberals who sympathised with the French Revolution, foundered on fanatic religious opposition whipped up among the lower classes; see also footnote 46 on p.525.

24. Hegel's argument was that slavery is the cradle of liberty. Bertrando Spaventa, a leading Hegelian philosopher of the Risorgimento and brother of Silvio, Minister in the government of the Historic Right (1861-76), argued that while this was true, the cradle did not constitute the whole of life, although some would like it to do. Gramsci makes use of this argument in several places, perhaps most notably in the notes on education translated in this book, but also in regard to economic protectionism, which might be useful as a temporary measure but not forever (Q8§53 and its corresponding 'C' text, p.160 of this volume). Croce imbibed the notions of the Historic Right and of Hegelianism, though not at the time that he he lived in the house of Silvio Spaventa, his father's cousin, after the death of his parents in the big earthquake of 1883; he was influenced by these ideas only much later (see *An Autobiography*, Oxford 1927, trans. R.G. Collingwood, pp.28 and 87).

25. A more extended definition of 'catharsis' is in SPN pp.366-7.

26. This sub-section has already been published in SCW pp.104-7, but is also included here for reasons of completeness and continuity of the argument. The only changes of any substance are the preferred readings 'moral consciousness' for 'moral conscience', the alternative meaning 'critical situation' rather than simply 'situation' for *frangente* in this context, 'a "metaphorical" language *appropriate* (rather than *adapted*) to the public for whom it is destined' and the choice of 'superstructural *factors*' rather than '*facts*'.

27. These two volumes, London and New York 1924 and 1946 respectively, together with Collingwood's translation of Croce's *Autobiography* (see note 24, above), include most, but not all, of the enlarged edition of Croce's *Etica e Politica*, Bari 1926.

28. Gramsci had in prison nos. V-VI of the 1928 volume of the *Nuova Rivista Storica*, in which Croce quoted words that had already appeared in

his *Cultura e vita morale*, op. cit. in note 13, pp.24-5: 'The point is to seek in the actual world *where, at a given moment in history, the real state is in fact to be found*; where the ethical force does in fact reside. For if the state is ethical nature made concrete, it is not a foregone conclusion that this is always incarnated in the government, the sovereign, the ministers, the various houses of parliament; on the contrary, it may be found in those who do not take a direct part in government, in the adversaries and enemies of a particular state, in the revolutionaries.'

29. Cf. the closing lines of Croce's 'Unending Struggle between "State" and "Church" ' (*Politics and Morals*, op. cit. p.130): 'it is not possible to write a history of humanity ... except as ethico-political history. Modern historiography has its origin in the *Historia ecclesiastica*, founded by Christianity.'

30. Numa-Denis Fustel de Coulanges, *The Ancient City*, trans. W. Small, New York 1956, published in Italian by Laterza (Croce's publishers) as *La Città Antica*, Bari 1925; Gramsci, however, had seen the slightly earlier Vallecchi version (Florence 1924).

31. *An Autobiography* (op. cit. in footnote 24, above) is the translation of the initial version of the *Contributo alla critica di me stesso* (*Contribution to a Self-Criticism*), now the appendix to *Etica e politica*, op. cit., pp.361-411; significantly, it is prefaced by Goethe's words: 'Why should the historian not do to himself what he has done to others?'

32. This is a reference to Vico's definitions of 'certainty' and 'truth'. In 'The Unending Struggle between "State" and "Church" ' (see note 29, above) Croce draws attention to 'the Vichian conflict between "certain" (in a practical meaning, that is as an assertion of force) and "true" (in a moral meaning)'. This distinction foreshadows the one that he himself makes in the practical, rather than the theoretical, sphere of human activity between the moral (corresponding to Vico's 'truth'), which presupposes the economic and develops this latter within itself, and the economic or utilitarian (corresponding to Vico's 'certain') which does not presuppose the moral.

33. This sub-section together with its summary (see above) has – like its companion piece 'Definition of Ethico-Political History' (pp.343-6, above) – also been previously published in English, with a slightly different wording, in SPN (pp.118-20). It, too, is included here for completeness and continuity of exposition.

34. *Storia del Regno di Napoli*, Bari 1925, trans. Frances Fresnaye, Chicago 1970, as the *History of the Kingdom of Naples* (edited and introduced by H. Stuart Hughes). *The Neapolitan Revolution of 1799* and the *History of the Baroque Era in Italy* were first published in 1897 and 1929 respectively.

35. The Italian word *libertà* may be translated as 'liberty' or as 'freedom'. It has here been translated as 'liberty' if referring to a general concept and sometimes 'freedom' if there is a more specific connotation, especially when there is a contrastive use. The choice of 'liberty' for the general concept also helps focus on the part of Gramsci's argument that draws attention to the common etymological root of 'liberty' and 'liberal'.

36. The square brackets indicate an editorial interpolation *not* to be found in the original notebook, which reads simply: 'Liberty as the identity of history and liberty as religion-superstition ...'. However, in his introductory 'Summary' to Q10I (i.e. the beginning of the current Chapter), Gramsci does in fact explicitly write 'liberty as the identity of history and mind [*spirito*]'. On the identity of history/spirit (or mind) see, for example, Hegel's 'Introduction' to his *Philosophy of History* (trans. J. Sibree, New York 1956 reprint): 'History in general is therefore the development of spirit in *time*' and '... we shall find (this image) symbolising the course of History, the great Day's work of Spirit' (p.103); in Croce's *History of Europe in the Nineteenth Century*, trans. H. Furst, London and New York 1934, p.9, history 'was seen to be the activity of the spirit'.

37. The 'Syllabus of Errors', a list of what the Catholic hierarchy considered the 80 major errors of the time, was drawn up by Cardinal Bilio for Pope Pius IX and published on 8 December 1864; see also footnote 105 to Chapter I of this volume. It represented the ultra-traditionalist line of the Catholic Church, reaffirmed that the separation of Church and state was wrong and condemned any opening to modern society; the accompanying encyclical *Quanta Cura*, among other things, defined Socialism and Communism to be 'most fatal errors'.

38. Gramsci comments further on liberty in Q10II§51: 'On the concept of "liberty". Show that with the exception of the "Catholics", the philosophy of liberty and the realisation of liberty provide the terrain for all other philosophical and practical currents. This demonstration is necessary because it really is the case that a sporting mentality has been created that has turned liberty into a football to be kicked around. "Every churl who would a party lead" imagines himself a dictator and the dictator's job seems easy: give peremptory orders, sign papers and so forth on the assumption that "by the grace of God" everyone will obey, that verbal and written orders will be translated into action – the word will be made flesh. If this does not come about, then we have to keep on waiting until "grace" (in other words, so-called "objective conditions") make this possible.' The phrase quoted by Gramsci (in Italian 'Ogni villan che parteggiando viene') is from the *Purgatory* of Dante's *Divine Comedy* (VI Canto, line 126), trans. Laurence Binyon, London 1979.

39. Croce was Minister of Education in Giovanni Giolitti's 1920-21 administration.

40. See 'The Mutual Translatability of National Cultures', pp.310-3 of Chapter V of this volume.

41. For Gramsci's more detailed discussion of De Man see, in Chapter VII, 'Croce on De Man', 'Henri De Man' and 'Sorel, Proudhon, De Man [1]', pp.447-54.

42. This sub-section also appears in GR, p.195; where in that translation 'tool' (of historical research) has been used to translate *canone*, we have preferred the stronger and more precise 'canon' (i.e. a general rule or law).

43. Leon Battista Alberti (1404-1472), *Il trattato della pittura e I cinque*

ordini architettonici; English translation *On Painting and On Sculpture* by Cecil Grayson, London 1972, p.37. James (Giacomo) Leoni's elegant earlier translation (London 1726, Vol.III, Book I of the three books *Of Painting*) reads: 'for the Mathematician considers the nature and forms of things with the mind only, absolutely distinct from all kind of matter: whereas it being my intention to set things in a manner before the eyes, it will be necessary for me to consider them in a way less refined'.

44. The peasants, historically hostile to their immediate 'superiors', often regarded the liberals, who occupied this position in the social hierarchy, as oppressors rather then liberators and thus – perhaps somewhat paradoxically – found themselves in alliance with the ultra-reactionary 'Church and King' party.

45. Doggerel in Neapolitan dialect praising Francis II (affectionately known as Franceschiello – 'Frankie'), the last of the Bourbons: 'Abbiamo scritto 'n bronte, Evviva Francische seconde'.

46. Giovanni Giolitti, the secret negotiator on behalf of the secular conservatives of the 1913 'Gentiloni pact' that brought Catholics fully into political life, and architect of the alliance between the northern industrialists and workers at the expense of the (particularly) southern peasants, dominated Italian politics in the 30 years prior to the advent of fascism. As Prime Minister Antonio Salandra put down the so-called 'red week' of popular rebellion in July 1914, led by people as disparate as the then Republican (and later Socialist leader) Pietro Nenni, the anarchist Errico Malatesta and the then 'left' Socialist Benito Mussolini.

Chapter VII The Philosophy of Benedetto Croce

1. Due to its nature as a type of premiss to the rest of what Gramsci writes about Croce and its position on the very first page of Q10, this paragraph was not given a number in the Critical Edition of the Notebooks; for this volume it has therefore simply been designated 'Preface'.

2. Giovanni Castellano, *Introduzione allo studio delle opere di B. Croce* [*Introduction to a Study of the Works of B. Croce*], Bari 1920 and Francesco Flora, *Croce*, Milan 1920, are referred to; both later wrote or edited other books on Croce. For the *Autobiography* see note 24 to Chapter VI of this volume.

3. Actualism or 'actual idealism', as Gramsci writes here, was the philosophically idealist trend (the 'philosophy of the pure act') initiated by Giovanni Gentile, the regime's Minister of Education and main philosophical prop. For Gramsci's discussion of Gentile, see in particular Section D of this Chapter.

4. The title used here is Gramsci's original heading, later cancelled. The reference is to the necessity to turn Hegelian (and more in general idealist, including Crocean) dialectics or philosophy the right way up to extract its rational kernel: see the Afterword to the third edition of *Capital*, Vol. I, or the second chapter of Engels's *Ludwig Feuerbach*, often referred to by the editorial title of 'Idealism and Materialism'.

5. There is an error in the 1975 Critical Edition of the *Quaderni*, leading one to suppose that Gramsci is saying, in a contorted grammatical form, that Croce has not succeeded in demonstrating what is dialectical in the dialectic of distincts; the manuscript says, instead, that it is the overall concept whose dialectical nature he has not demonstrated.

6. *Politics and Morals*, op.cit. in note 7 to Chapter VI.

7. See 'Religion, Philosophy, Politics [1]', pp.403-4 of this volume.

8. In reviewing the first two volumes (up to 1844) of Marx's writings and the first two of the Marx-Engels correspondence in D.B. Riazanov's edition of the *Collected Works of the Marx-Engels Archive*, Croce claims that, while Marx's theories no longer have any scientific value, they are kept alive by 'their undoubted practical and political virtue', i.e. in Crocean conceptual terms, they are to be considered 'ideology' (or, as he says in the review, 'pseudo-theories'), not 'philosophy'. According to him the labour theory of value is logically incorrect and the structure/superstructure model reintroduces dualism since it 'once more divides reality into noumenon and phenomenon, and moreover puts the Economy in the place of the *Deus absconditus* [the hidden God]', while history must consist of the explanation of events in terms of ethical and religious motives. All these points form part of Gramsci's polemic against Croce (see this Chapter).

9. This was the first version, read in the form of an academic paper before the *Academy of Moral and Political Sciences of the Royal Society of Naples*, of what subsequently became the first part of the *History of Europe in the Nineteenth Century*, op.cit. in footnote 36 to Chapter VI of this volume. Some of Gramsci's own reflections on the history of Europe, stimulated by a reading of Croce's book are in Q10II§61, now in SPN, pp.114-8.

10. René Fülöp-Miller's *Geist und Gesicht des Bolschewismus* (see 'Man as Individual and Man as Mass', pp.275-7, and footnote 73 to Chapter IV of this volume) was reviewed by Croce in the 20 September 1926 number of *La Critica*.

11. Hegel's celebrated maxim in his Preface to the *Philosophy of Right* (trans. T.M. Knox, Oxford 1952) reads: 'What is rational is actual (*wirklich*') and what is actual is rational'. By 'actual', one should not understand simply what is 'real' (in German *real*) in the sense of mere existence, but 'real' or 'actual' in the sense of embodying the essence of something: in Knox's example (op.cit., p.302), statesmen who accomplish nothing are not 'real statesmen'.

12. 'Sollen', left in German in the notebook, is the verb indicating general and here specifically moral obligation, Kant's categorical imperative.

13. See 'Definition of Ethico-Political History', especially p.345, and footnote 28 to Chapter VI of this volume.

14. Cf. footnote 13, above.

15. Cf. 'Croce and Italian Historiography', p.342 of Chapter VI of this volume. Edgar Quinet (1803-75), a historian and professor of foreign literature at the *Collège de France*, welcomed the 1848 risings that led to the proclamation of the Republic, and took his seat as a deputy for the extreme left of the period. He was one of the foremost proponents of the separation of Church and state.

16. The word used by Gramsci is *sovversivismo*, which does not always bear the same implications as the English 'subversion' (whose Italian equivalent is normally *eversione*); 'rebelliousness', sometimes of a violent nature, perhaps comes closest to the Italian concept.

17. The ideal man of Machiavelli's contemporary, Francesco Guicciardini, stood in relation to Machiavelli's Prince like Cavour's moderates did in relation to the absent 'Jacobin' left that the Action Party should have been. In his famous essay 'Guicciardinian Man' Francesco De Sanctis (see footnote 3 to Chapter VI) defines this man as a morally flaccid being and ironically put the failure to create a unified country in the sixteenth century (and by analogy the failure to carry out an agrarian revolution necessary for the unification on an equal footing of nineteenth-century Italy) down to the fact that 'very few were crazy, while the majority was composed of wise men ... Force was lacking, its place being taken by intrigues, ruses, simulation and two-facedness. And since everyone looked to 'their own interests' [*suo particulare*], in the storm that all were subject to, all were shipwrecked.' Gramsci (see below) carries the argument one step forward to a criticism of reformism.

18. Further on in this paragraph, Gramsci defines 'moderatism' as the 'anti-Jacobin' conservative current of the Risorgimento; it is *not* to be confused with any positively-overtoned 'moderation'.

19. The wording used in this sub-section (*concezione di*) *storia a disegno* or '(conception of) history according to a pattern' has been rendered 'preconceptualised (idea of) history', while 'preconceived pattern' is used for *disegno preconcetto*. What Gramsci took exception to was a major defect of nearly all of idealist philosophy: its attempt, whatever the cost, to fit history into a preconceived framework, to superimpose a philosophy onto history. Almost alone among idealist philosopher-historians Croce ostensibly denied the possibility of such an approach but Gramsci's claim is that Croce too was guilty of just this idealist distortion of history. It is significant that the title of Croce's major work in the field is *Theory and History of Historiography*, an implicit rejection of the possibility of any 'theory *of* history', while on p.1 of Q1 Gramsci writes, as the very first point in his initial listing of subjects to be discussed in the Notebooks, '*Theory of history and of historiography*', in obvious polemic with Croce's title and approach at the same time as being an assertion, against the rest of idealism, of the Marxist concept of the science of history (cf. footnote 67, below).

20. Despite Oriani's weakness of a doctrinaire, abstract kind, he was 'the most honest and enthusiastic proponent of Italy's national-popular greatness among the Italian intellectuals of the old generation'. *La lotta politica* 'seemed like the manifesto for a great popular national democratic movement' but could not achieve its aim since Oriani was 'too steeped in the idealistic philosophy of the type that developed in the Restoration period to be able to speak to the people as a leader and an equal at the same time, or to make the people join in a criticism of themselves and their own weaknesses' (Q8§165 in SCW, p.251).

21. In two minor polemical notes not included here (Q10II§45 and

Q10II§49), Croce's *History of Europe* is subject, in the first case, to Arrigo Cajumi's erudite (but perhaps really rather carping) criticism and, in the second, to a Catholic-reactionary one from Roberto Forges Davanzati. For this latter Croce's political liberalism was a 'bankrupt' and 'cultural, logic-chopping, encyclopaedic monstrosity' that represented the 'antithesis of Poetry, Faith, believing Action, i.e. of militant life. Croce is static, retrospective, analytical even when he seems to be seeking a synthesis.'

22. This is a first draft ('A text') of Q10II§28ii, whose final version (pp.369-70 of SPN) reproduces the above with some modifications and a final short paragraph on Calvinist predestination as the seemingly paradoxical source of 'one of the greatest impulses to practical initiative the world has ever known'.

23. In his essay 'A New Champion of Autocracy' in *Selected Philosophical Works*, Vol.I, London 1977, G.V. Plekhanov (p.375) quotes Hegel's *Science of Logic* (pp.314-5 of Vol. I of the 1812 Nuremberg edition): 'The ordinary notion of the *appearance* or *disappearance* of anything is the notion of a *gradual* appearance and disappearance. Nevertheless, there are transformations of being which are not only changes from one quantity to another, but also changes from the qualitative to the quantitative and vice versa; such a transformation is an *interruption of 'gradual becoming'* and gives rise to a kind of being qualitatively different from the preceding.' This same essay is also to be found in a different translation under the title 'Sudden Changes in Nature and History' in Plekhanov's *Fundamental Problems of Marxism*, London 1937 (see pp.104-5).

24. This essay is in *Eternità e Storicità della Filosofia*, Rieti 1930, op. cit. in 'Croce's Relative Popularity', Chapter VI of this volume.

25. For the proposition from Hegel, see footnote 11 (above), while for 'leaps' in history, see the preceding sub-section 'History and Anti-History', the subject of which is continued in *Philosophy, Religion, Ideology*', pp.383-9 of this volume.

26. Organ of extreme right forces of the time; see also 'The Crocean Utopia' and 'The Party Man', pp.444-5 and 462-4 of this Chapter respectively.

27. Charles-Augustin Saint-Beuve, *Pierre-Joseph Proudhon, sa vie et sa correspondance* [*Pierre-Joseph Proudhon, His Life and Correspondence*], Paris 1872.

28. Marx's *Poverty of Philosophy*.

29. This appears to be Spirito's 'Inside and Outside' in the 1 July 1932 number of *Critica Fascista*; for the 'left-corporativist' views he expressed at the Ferrara Congress see 'Identification of Individual and State', p.439 of this Chapter, and 'The Einaudi-Spirito Polemic over the State', pp.182-4 of Chapter III. Cf. also the arguments Gramsci uses in 'Passive Revolution and the Planned Economy', p.277 of Chapter IV, and the latter part of 'Paradigms of Ethico-Political History', pp.348-50 of Chapter VI.

30. The neologism 'conformant' seems perhaps the best choice to convey

consistency between economic and moral behaviour (see Chapter IV, Section F where 'conformism' is used a dozen times in a polemical but positive sense) or, as here, between one's world view and norm of conduct.
31. Croce, *Historical Materialism*, op. cit., footnote to p.115: 'we might speak like Labriola of historical materialism as a *philosophy of praxis*, i.e. as a particular way of conceiving and resolving, or rather of over-coming, the problem of thought and being' (Meredith's translation corrected).
32. This potentially rather misleading formulation seems to mean that it is from Feuerbach's contemplative materialism, as it is sometimes called, that the philosophy of praxis has deduced the will to change the world. On the roles of contemplation and action, see also the very brief note (Q7§37): 'Find where and in what senses Goethe stated: "How may a man attain to self-Knowledge? By Contemplation? Certainly not, but by Action".' Gramsci saw this in André Maurois's *La vie de Disraëli*; it may be read on p.303 of *Disraeli* (trans. Hamish Miles, London 1927), and refers to a Scottish professor who wrote out maxims of Goethe for Gladstone in the 1879 Midlothian campaign. The passage continues 'Try to do your Duty and you will find what you are fit for. But what is your Duty? The Demand of the Hour.'
33. *L'expérience du bolschevisme* (*The Experience of Bolshevism*), Paris 1931, not referred to explicitly by Gramsci, presumably so as not to alert the censor.
34. This book appears to be what Erazim V. Kohák refers to as *The Making of a State* on the dustjacket of his English edition of *Masaryk on Marx* (Lewisburg 1972, first published in 1898 as *Otázka Sociální*), but we have been unable to trace an English translation. On p.360 of Masaryk's study of Marx we do find the germ of an idea similar to that ascribed to him by Gramsci here: Marxism, like the Renaissance and Reformation (which 'initiated a general transformation' and 'were an attempt at...a new world view, a new religion, politics and ethics'), is also 'one of the attempts at a new world view'.
35. In other words, class conflict.
36. Ophelimity was a term coined by the economist and sociologist Vilfredo Pareto in his *Trattato di Sociologia Generale*, (*The Mind and Society*, trans. Andrew Bongiorno and Arthur Livingston in collaboration with J.H. Rogers, London 1935) in an attempt to distinguish economic 'utility' (seemingly the maximisation of the subject's satisfaction or presently perceived self-interest) from other types of utility. In Vol. IV, §2110, p. 1458, we read 'Pure economics ... has taken a single norm, the individual's satisfaction, and it has further set down that of that satisfaction he is the only judge. So economic "utility" or "ophelimity" came to be defined.'
37. A shortened version of this sub-section is to be found in GR, pp.196-9.
38. The first edition of Friedrich Lange's book *Geschichte des Materialismus und Kritik der seiner Bedeutung in der Gegenwart*, Leipzig 1866, exists in English as *History of Materialism and Criticism of its*

Present Importance, trans. E.C. Thomas (1877, reprinted with introduction by Bertrand Russell, London 1925, for which see also 'Religion, Philosophy, Politics', p.412 of this Chapter). That historical materialism is a 'way of speaking' with 'no essential connection' (with materialism) is said by Croce, citing Lange, on p.8 of *Historical Materialism*; the passage cited in the text is a modified version of Meredith's translation while, in addition, Gramsci substitutes 'philosophy of praxis' for the 'historical materialism' of the original.

39. The passage is on p.93 of *Materialismo Storico*. The first extract cited, in Meredith's translation is, quite simply, wrong and has been corrected; the second has been adjusted.

40. Cf. Croce, *Historical Materialism*, p.118: 'Marx ... teaches us, although it is in propositions approximate in content and paradoxical in form, to penetrate to what society is in its *effective reality*. Indeed, from this point of view, I am surprised that no one has yet thought of giving him the honorary title of the "Machiavelli" of the proletariat.' (Meredith's translation, modified, following the edition of Croce's book that Gramsci had.)

41. Gramsci did, however, regard Giovanni Botero (for whom see 'Machiavelli as an Economist' and 'The Beginning of Economic Science', pp.164-5 of Chapter III), alongside Tommaso Campanella (author of the utopian communist *City of the Sun*), as a figure of European stature (Q3§141 and Q6§145, not translated here) in Counter-Reformation Italy; see also 'Originality and Popularisation', pp.405-6 of the current Chapter. The difference in role between *The Prince* and *The Discourses* is outlined by Gramsci in Q13§5 (partial version in note 3, p.125 of SPN) where he writes that Luigi Russo 'makes *The Prince* into Machiavelli's treatise on dictatorship (moment of authority and of the individual), and *The Discourses* into his treatise on hegemony (moment of the universal and of liberty). Russo's observation is correct, although there are allusions to the moment of hegemony or consent in *The Prince* too, besides those of authority or force.'

42. See the part of the general introduction dealing with Croce for the 'distincts' (or values characterising the human spirit). Note also the view stated by Galvano della Volpe, the Marxist aesthetician of Gentilian formation: 'The formal principle of the distinction of categories of the spirit and their unity of circulation does allow us, in spite of its abstraction, to grasp effectual "reality".' (From the 1960 essay 'Laocoön' in della Volpe's *Critique of Taste*, trans. Michael Caesar, London 1978, p.190.)

43. See 'Economic-Political History and Ethico-Political History', pp.67-77 of *Politics and Morals*, op.cit.

44. The 'A' text (Q4§56) is more explicit in asking whether 'Vico-Spaventa [act as] a link with Hegelianism for Croce and Gentile respectively' and is clearer grammatically in the formulation of the question of Hegel in the context of the French Revolution and Napoleon. In addition where, lower down, the finalised 'C' text asks what historical movement of importance Vico took part in, the earlier 'A' text asks what real historical movement his philosophy shows signs of.

45. G.E. Muller's introduction to the *Encyclopedia of Philosophy*, New

York 1959, reads (p.43) 'In the year 1806 Napoleon defeated the Prussian army in the Battle of Jena. Hegel, at that time professor of philosophy at the University of Jena, interrupted his writing – he was just finishing the last pages of the *Phenomenology of Mind* – in order to watch from his window the French Conqueror riding on his white horse into the surrendered town.' Hegel wrote to his friend Niethammer that Napoleon, victor of this battle that sealed the fate of Prussian feudalism, appeared the incarnation of the spirit of the world (*Weltgeist*) on horseback. It seems an embroidery on the tale (p.18 of J.B. Baillie's introduction to his translation of *The Phenomenology of Mind*, London 1931) that all this happened exactly at the time claimed.

46. While grammatically 'spiritual' applies solely to 'activity' in Gramsci's wording, it may be that it ought also refer to 'facts'.

47. Collected under the title given in Croce's *Philosophy, Poetry, History*, ed. C.J.S. Sprigge, London 1966, pp.749-62.

48. A favourite expression of Gramsci's to indicate an individual considered in isolation from the rest of society and taken, of course, from Defoe's *Robinson Crusoe*.

49. L.N. Tolstoy, *Childhood, Boyhood and Youth*, Ch. XIX of 'Boyhood', in which he tells of turning round suddenly to catch himself unawares and see nothing, not having yet had a chance to create 'reality' (see the section 'The So-Called "Reality of the External World"', Q11§17, pp.440-6 of SPN and in particular the footnote of relevance to the present passage on p.443).

50. In *Eternità e storicita della filosofia*, op.cit.; see 'Croce's Relative popularity', pp.337-8, above, for other comments on this book, regarding Croce's down-to-earth attitude as a philosopher.

51. Croce's speech is published in the *Proceedings of the Seventh International Congress on Philosophy*, op.cit. in footnote 16 to Chapter VI of this volume.

52. Interlinear variant 'art' instead of 'science'.

53. The actual title is *Rinascimento, riforma, controriforma (Renaissance, Reformation, Counter-Reformation)*, Bari 1930.

54. '*Ubicumque regnat lutheranismus, ibi literatum est interitus*' or 'wherever Lutheranism reigns, there is the death of letters'.

55. This would appear to be Gramsci's paraphrase of Croce's *History of Europe in the Nineteenth Century*, op.cit., p.25: 'the old faith was still a way, a mythological one if you will, to soothe and calm suffering and sorrows and to solve the painful problem of life and death, and it was not to be rooted out with violence or insulted with mockery. And it would not be very politic, either, because those beliefs and the consolation derived from them and their teachings were the basis for many men, of the formula and the authority of social duties, and gave rise to foundations and institutions of social welfare, and motives of order and discipline – all forces and capacities to be assimilated and transformed gradually, but not to be struck down without knowing what to set in their places or without replacing them at all.'

56. Generally assumed to be 'Religion and Peace of Mind', pp.27-33 of

The Conduct of Life, op.cit.; it could however also be the less well-known 'The Religious Spirit', pp.320-6 of the same volume, in which some aspects of Gramsci's argument find a parallel and in which Croce explicitly states his view that the 'faith or religion that blossoms and fructifies on the tree of philosophy is the consciousness a man comes to have of his oneness with the All, with true and complete and full Reality.'

57. In the manuscript *L'Ordine Nuovo* is referred to simply as *O.N.* so as not to arouse the suspicions of the censor. For Missiroli's article and Togliatti's rejoinder on behalf of the review, see footnote 15 to 'Science as Ideology' in Chapter V of this volume. Gramsci uses the word *tecnica* ('technology' *or* 'technique') for what has here been translated 'technology' but in 'Science, Humanity, Objectivity', p.292, and again in Q15§33, p.323, both of Chapter V, he specifies that it is in fact 'technology' (*tecnologia*) that is the mediator between humanity and the real world.

58. Although the modern tendency is to abandon the term *gnoseologia* in favour of *epistemologia* a differentiation was often made between the two, gnoseology being the theory of knowledge and epistemology that part of gnoseology that studied the structure, validity and limits of scientific knowledge.

59. For Milan's Catholic University of the Sacred Heart see footnote 77 to Chapter I on p.529.

60. F.A. Lange, *History of Materialism and Criticism of its Present Importance*, op.cit. in footnote 38, above.

61. This position of Croce's formed part of his polemic with the Soviet Commissar for Culture, Anatoly Lunacharsky, at the 1930 Oxford Philosophical Congress discussed in this sub-section.

62. The latter part of this passage, found on p.31 of *Historical Materialism and the Economics of Karl Marx*, op.cit., is also cited at the start of 'Political Ideologies', pp.394-9 of this Chapter. The title given to the essay in Meredith's translation is 'Concerning Historical Materialism Viewed as a Science of Social Economics'. The sentence beginning 'Just as' is, of course, Croce's rather disparaging summary of Stammler's interpretation of Marx, later however to become his own, while the emphasis laid on 'must consist' is Gramsci's.

63. This is not a slip of the pen of Gramsci's or an error of transcription, but his way of indicating the turbulent years of factory occupations and then of fascist reaction as the 'second' war following on the First World War.

64. Cf. end of 'Political and Civil Society, pp.438-9 of this Chapter.

65. Croce, *History of Europe*, op.cit., p.283; cf. footnote 15 to 'Development of the Theory of Ethico-Political History' in Chapter VI of this volume. 'The Liberals of the Right could not accept the view that the war which was being waged was simply a war of ideas between liberal and autocratic régimes; they realised that ideal motives were rare or wholly absent, that industrial or commercial interests were paramount, and that the whole conflict was fed by uncontrolled desire and distorted imagination – that it was in a sense a war of "historical materialism" or "philosophical irrationalism".'

66. The books referred to are *Philosophy of the Practical. Economics and Ethics*, London, 1913 and *What is Living and What is Dead in the Philosophy of Hegel*, London 1915, (both trans. Douglas Ainslie). The latter serves in effect as Croce's introduction to his own 1907 translation of Hegel's *Encyclopaedia of the Philosophical Sciences*; Andler was translator of the *Communist Manifesto* into French.

67. For these four points (Meredith's translation with relatively minor changes) Gramsci had access to the text of the third (1917) edition in which the wording, when compared with the first edition, indicates that Croce's distance from Marxism was increasing considerably. At the end of point two, the first edition continued: 'in which field the programme of Marxism cannot but appear one of the noblest and boldest and also one of those which obtain most support from the objective conditions of existing society'. Gramsci's transcriptions have his normal circumlocutions to avoid the prison censor, but where, at the beginning of point two, Croce says 'the theory of history' in the edition Gramsci had, and 'the philosophy of history' (first edition), Gramsci's notebook reads 'the science of history'.

68. This is from Croce's essay on the Italian economist Achille Loria, not in Meredith's translation; the 'heading' of the first line of this sub-section is Gramsci's generic one for notes on Croce.

69. I.e. 'Croce, Einaudi, Loria', immediately above.

70. This phrase from Marx's first Thesis on Feuerbach refers especially to Chapters XI and XIX of Ludwig Feuerbach's *The Essence of Christianity*, trans. Marian Evans (George Eliot), London 1854. In criticising an alleged 'egoism' in Judaism and its concept of Jehovah as the *ego* of Israel Feuerbach says that miracles (a staff changed into a serpent, a rock into a fountain, the sun standing still, etc.) were held to happen 'for the welfare of Israel, purely at the command of Jehovah, who is nothing but the personified selfishness of the Israelitish people, to the exclusion of all other nations' (New York 1957 reprint, pp.113-4). Thus what is portrayed by later believers (and others) as a noble concept (a universal God) was used by the people whose tribal god he originally was for merely particularist ends, hence Marx's *schmutzig jüdisch*, i.e. 'dirty' or (in many translations of the *Theses on Feuerbach*) 'sordidly Jewish'. See also 'Identification of Individual and State', p.439, below.

71. The work referred to is *Historical Materialism and the Economics of Karl Marx*, op.cit. For the 'final degree of utility', or marginal utility theory of value, see 'The Beginning of Economic Science', pp.164-5 of this volume and relevant footnote. Elsewhere (Q7§18, see SPN pp.402-3), Gramsci states his opinion that, in economics, 'the unitary centre is value, alias the relationship between the worker and the industrial forces of production' and that those who deny the [labour] theory of value 'fall into crass vulgar materialism by posing machines in themselves – as constant or technical capital – as producers of value independent of the operator'.

72. *Historical Materialism*, op.cit.; the first part of the essay is on pp.48-66 of the English translation.

73. The booklet in question is not in fact the one that Gramsci names but Graziadei's *Sindacati e Salari (Unions and Wages)*.

74. Croce's essay was first published in 1897, whereas the three volumes of *Theories of Surplus Value* were edited and published by Karl Kautsky between 1905 and 1910.
75. This essay, 'Marxism and Pure Economics' is not in the English translation of *Historical Materialism*.
76. The surplus in capitalist society being extracted by economic rather than extra-economic means, as for example in a feudal set-up.
77. In English in the text.
78. Op. cit. in 'Graziadei', pp.186-7 and footnote 33, Chapter III of this volume.
79. For the creation of relative surplus value through the agency of relative surplus value, see Section IV of Volume I of Marx's *Capital* ('The Production of Relative Surplus Value'). Gramsci's phrase seems simply to restate succinctly the argument that a technical advance in a single firm produces relative surplus value for that firm, which then becomes generalised when others in the same branch of industry catch up with the innovation.
80. 'Rovesciamento della praxis' in Gramsci's translation (Q7, p.2) of Engels's gloss (*umwälzende Praxis*) of Marx's phrase (*revolutionäre Praxis*) in the third *Thesis on Feuerbach*. This has given problems to translators in both Britain and Italy. Modern German Marxist scholars normally interpret it as 'revolutionary praxis' and not as translated by Gramsci from Engels's version, repeated here and in 'Political Ideologies', p.395.
81. Oppenheimer's pupil, Fritz Sternberg, wrote *Der Imperialismus*, Berlin 1926, while the article by the French socialist Lucien Laurat appeared in *Critique Sociale* in March 1931. Henryk Grossmann's book *Akkumulations- und Zusammenbruchsgesetz des kapitalischen Systems* (*The Law of Accumulation and Collapse in the Capitalist System*), Leipzig 1929, stands out as the first and, until Alfred Sohn-Rethel's much belated recognition, only really *specific* work on economics of what became known as the Frankfurt School. A note on a review of Grossmann's book, not reproduced here since it is essentially a criticism of the review's author rather than a discussion of the book, is the subject of a short paragraph (Q7§41), in which Gramsci said that the book 'must be interesting' and, while promising to return to it, never explicitly did so. Among other things, the book is rare in parallelling to a certain extent Gramsci's own work on the structural modifications introduced into capitalism by rationalisation and Taylorist work methods.
82. Orano (see also 'Croce as a Renaissance Man[3]', p.474, and 'Past and Present[5]. Gentile's Philosophy', pp.443-4) maintained that fascism was not in any way connected with the various currents of Italian idealist philosophy, and indeed Gentile was sometimes subject to attack.
83. Discussed in 'Brief Notes on Economics[4]. Ugo Spirito & Co.', pp.180-1 of Chapter III of this volume.
84. Interlinear variant 'to become'.
85. Flaubert's last (unfinished) novel was entitled *Bouvard et Pécuchet* and dealt with two Parisian clerks of those names who gathered together all the information they could over a whole encyclopaedic range of

subjects, hoping to inform themselves but finding contradictions everywhere.
86. This is also, of course, Gentile's position. In his notorious Palermo speech, referred to directly by Gramsci here and in other paragraphs, he outlined what he called his 'liberalism', which he claimed stemmed from German and Italian thought but which was inherently totalitarian: 'individual and social education make it [liberty] a reality by actuating in the individual the common will which takes the form of law and hence of the state ... The greatest liberty always coincides with the maximum of state force' (G. Gentile, *Cosa è il fascismo* [*What Fascism Is*], Florence 1925, p.50). See also H.S. Harris, *The Social Philosophy of Giovanni Gentile*, Urbana and London 1960, pp.174-5, for this speech.
87. In 1853 some two hundred Milanese aristocrats signed a letter of obeisance to the Austro-Hungarian monarch while his troops were executing Milanese patriots.
88. Seen by Croce in a German university thesis: 'For all philosophy, since it invokes the common faculty of human reasoning is, in itself, democratic; and, by that token, the patricians are not mistaken in considering it a great danger to themselves.' This same position is restated in Q7§38 (SPN, p.362) and, this time not in Latin, in Q10II§35: 'idealism claims that philosophy is the democratic science *par excellence* in so far as it relates to the faculty of reasoning common to all, which explains the hatred that aristocrats nurture for philosophy and the legal bans on its teaching and culture imposed by the classes of the old regime'. Gramsci's fundamental attack on Croce's brand of idealist philosophy is that notwithstanding these pretensions, his outlook was in effect highly élitist, hence anti-democratic, and characterised by a fear of the masses (see, e.g., 'Croce's International Importance' pp.467-9 in this Chapter).
89. See 'Cultural Topics. Philosophy of Praxis and Historical Economism', pp.423-4, and footnote 70 to this Chapter.
90. The author of the article, 'Scientific Actuality. Italy and Science', is, of course Sebastiano Timpanaro, Snr.
91. This may be compared with the judgement Gramsci passes on him in Q10II§43 when he writes that Gioberti's *Introduzione allo studio della Filosofia* (*Introduction to the Study of Philosophy*) aimed at ' "revolutionising" a cultural world ... the philosopher and thinker could not be detached from the politician and party man'. Gioberti was thus comparable to Mazzini though their actions were determined by different ends and different social forces.
92. See footnote 74 to Chapter I of this volume.
93. Gramsci missed out one word (*ferree* or 'steel-like') and transcribed 'sheen' as 'faith'; the original and Gramsci's copy both have 'ordered' in French (*agencées*).
94. This note appears to be 'Past and Present[1]. Giolitti and Croce', written only just before the current one. The nationalists Francesco Coppola and Alfredo Rocco (see also 'The Party Man', pp.462-4), who edited the journal referred to, became leading Fascists; the latter, as Minister of Justice, drew up the regime's legal code under which, among

many other things, the Special Tribunal was set up to try 'political offences', including Gramsci's.

95. This election campaign speech has already been commented on in footnote 86, regarding the identification of individual and state, to 'Past and Present[3]. Political and Civil Society'. Gentile is here making the point that there are those who 'distinguish moral from material force: the force of the law freely voted and accepted, from the force of violence which is rigidly opposed to the will of the citizen. But ... all force is moral, for it is always directed at the will; and whatever method of argument is adopted – from sermon to blackjack – its efficacy cannot be anything but its power to convince men in their hearts and persuade them to agree' (Harris, op.cit., p.176). Gentile tried to defend himself by a comment (added in the version of the speech published only after the election) that the force meant was that of the state but, as Gramsci says here about Croce, 'it is a fine excuse ... to justify oneself for having been misunderstood'. Ironically, in the most debatable act of the war to liberate Italy, Gentile himself was to fall victim to a partisan bullet.

96. In the chapter of *Cultura e vita morale* cited in 'The Theoretical Affirmation', which follows the current sub-section.

97. This cryptic reference is explained thus in the essay cited: 'What are called religious persecutions ... are two different orders of facts interwoven. In the first place, political and social struggles between races, peoples, states or classes ... [and] in the second, struggles having the nature of theoretical affirmations during which, in order to triumph, people had recourse to pressures exerted on the will, as a consequence of the conviction that a person who refused to recognise what is true was maintained in that obstinacy by passions, interests or diabolical spirit. ... all of us, at every moment, exert pressure on the wills of others to induce them to ensure that thought should think in the way that to us seems the Good.'

98. 'Position' is probably here not so much 'stance' as 'way of posing' or 'statement' (elsewhere used unambiguously in this sense by Gramsci).

99. See 'The War of Historical Materialism', p.418, and 'Development of the Theory of Ethico-Political History', Chapter VI, pp.335-6, with relevant footnotes.

100. For Gramsci's more detailed discussion of De Man and his books see 'Croce on De Man', 'Henri De Man' and the three parts of 'Sorel, Proudhon, De Man', which follow directly on the current sub-section. For Bonomi on Bissolati see 'Development of the Theory of Ethico-Political History' (cf. footnote 99).

101. Giovanni Castellano's *Introduction*, Bari 1920, was instrumental in popularising Croce. The letter referred to was in fact by Ignazio Raimondo, a freemason and – when he wrote it – also a socialist, who claimed that Croce had taught a generation how to think; see also 'Development of the Theory of Ethico-Political History' (also cross-referenced in footnotes 99 and 100). However, the lawyer Gramsci refers to was actually Orazio Raimondo, whose denial at Maria Tiepolo's trial for the murder of Quintilio Polimanti (Gramsci wrote 'Fioravante'

and then replaced it with 'Polidori'), her alleged former lover and batman to her army officer husband, of a revealed religion and claims that 'science of man' could prove his client's blamelessness, was perhaps closer to deism than theism (see note 3, p.520 of this volume).

102. The Belgian reformist socialist Henri De Man, later found guilty of collaborating in the Second World War with the Nazi forces occupying his country, wrote *Au delà du Marxisme*, reviewed by Croce in the 20 November 1928 number of *La Critica*. An Italian translation under the title *Il Superamento (The Supersession)*, rather than simply *Beyond Marxism* as in French, came out in 1929.

103. For hedonism in economics see Chapter III of this volume, especially the three consecutive sub-sections 'Observations on Pantaleoni's *Pure Economics*', 'About Pantaleoni's *Pure Economics*' and 'Lionel Robbins', pp.170-5.

104. In the notebook, Gramsci cites the phrases 'instinct of workmanship' and 'instinct of constructiveness' in English, in the first case in inverted commas without translation and in the second one in inverted commas in brackets after the Italian translation *istinto costruttivo*.

105. 'A bee puts to shame many an architect in the construction of its cells, but what distinguishes the worst of architects from the best of bees is namely this. The architect will construct in his imagination that which he will ultimately erect in reality. At the end of every labour process, we get that which existed in the consciousness of the labourer at its commencement.' (Marx, *Capital*, Vol.I, London 1974, p.174.)

106. Sensationalism is the name often given to eighteenth-century French materialism.

107. Parts 1 and 2 of 'Sorel, Proudhon, De Man' represent the editorial division of Q11§66 into two halves, here presented in reverse order as compared with the manuscript in order to maintain the continuity of the discussion of De Man.

108. Maurice Maeterlinck (1862-1949), the Belgian symbolist poet and playwright, also wrote prose works that married philosophical pessimism and a lively interest in the world of nature, as in his 1901 *La Vie des abeilles (The Life of the Bee)*, to which implicit reference is made here.

109. The limits posed on Gramsci's knowledge of contemporary developments in psychology and psychiatry are clear here; the Adler referred to was the Viennese psychiatrist Alfred, pupil and then opponent of Freud, who had nothing to do with the Austro-Marxist school represented by Max and others of his family.

110. This conflict is also discussed in 'Catholic Action[11]. The Lille Conflict', pp.49-50 of this volume.

111. André Philip, *Le Problème ouvrier aux Etats-Unis (The Problem of the Working Class in the United States)*, Paris 1927.

112. The Bishop of Tagaste, the ancient Roman Thagaste and modern Algerian Souk-Ahras, is St Augustine in the sense that it was there that he was born; his see was, however, the nearby Hippo, now Annaba.

113. The quotation 'ciò che per l'universo si squaderna' is line 87 of the final canto (Canto XXXIII) of Dante's *Paradiso*, here reproduced in

Laurence Binyon's translation (London 1979).

114. Gramsci's page reference, added later, is to 'Sorel, Proudhon, De Man[3]', the sub-section immediately following this one, which (see note 107) is actually the *first* part of Q11§66.

115. The English *Evolutionary Socialism*, London 1909 (trans. Edith C. Harvey), does not include the specific chapter cited here. The original states explicitly 'In Germany, Marx and Engels, by basing themselves on the Hegelian dialectic, got as far as working out a completely analogous doctrine to that of Blanqui.' Bernstein maintained that the 'utopian' Proudhon was far more realistic and correct in his estimation of the balance of forces and in his general programme. Blanqui, though totally committed to the proletariat, is universally regarded as erring in his preference for secret revolutionary conspiracies, along the lines of the 1796 Babouvist 'Conspiracy of the Equals', in which, against a background of mounting economic crisis, Gracchus Babeuf aimed at toppling the rightward-moving Directory of the French Revolution and ushering in a communist society.

116. Gabriele D'Annunzio, the poet and adventurer who in 1919 led the nationalist attack on the Croatian port of Rijeka and ruled it as a dictator until December 1920 in an attempt to have it annexed to Italy, privately circulated letters on the wider foreign policy implications of this act in which he argued for friendly relations to be established between Italy and the Soviet Union in defiance of the Entente powers.

117. Here, as elsewhere in the text, terms like this are abbreviated to get round the censor; Sorel's original reads 'communists'.

118. Michels, *La teoria di K. Marx sulla miseria crescente e le sue origini* (*Marx's Theory of Increasing Impoverishment and its Origins*), Turin 1922. This added comment in round brackets is Gramsci's own while the rest of point c) is taken either word for word from Sorel's article or is a faithful summary.

119. *Materiaux pour une théorie du prolétariat* (*Materials for a Theory of the Proletariat*), Paris 1921.

120. In dealing further with Sorel in Q17§20, Gramsci makes the telling points that 'while Sorel may, because of the variety and inconsistency of his points of view, be utilised to justify the most disparate practical attitudes, there is however in him one undeniable, one fundamental and constant, point: his radical 'liberalism' (or theory of spontaneity) that blocks any conservative consequence of his ideas. Bizarre factors, incongruencies, contradictions are to be found everywhere in Sorel, but he cannot be detached from one constant tendency of popular radicalism: his syndicalism is not of an indistinct "association" type, of "all" social elements in the state, but of just one of them, and his "violence" is not the violence of just "anybody" but of one <sole> "element" that democratic pacifism tended to corrupt and so on. The obscure point in Sorel is his anti-Jacobinism and his pure economism...' In Q5§80, Gramsci states that Sorel took this anti-Jacobinism directly from Proudhon, for whom it is 'the application of the absolutism of divine right to popular sovereignty'; it 'proceeds willingly by violent means, summary executions... the Jacobins are the Jesuits of the revolution.'

121. The first draft of this part of the note (Q4§31, autumn 1930) also adds 'and the politicians'.
122. The first draft adds 'it is an anti-Thiers stance' (Adolphe Thiers, as Prime Minister, was responsible for the massacre of the Communards).
123. Sorel's *Reflections on Violence* may be read in J. Roth and T.E. Hulme's translation, New York 1961 (reprint).
124. The 'Cercle Proudhon' was founded by Georges Valois, a right-wing literary-inclined figure, while the others referred to were of Charles Maurras's 'Action Française', for which see 'Action Française and the Integralists', 'An Action Française Journalist in Rome', 'Action Française's Long Crisis', 'Maurras and Paganism' and 'Maurras and "Organic Centralism" ', pp.80-94 of Chapter I of this volume. There was frequent feuding between Valois's and Maurras's groups.
125. Edouard Berth, *Les méfaits des intellectuels*, Paris 1914. Berth later collaborated with Gramsci's friend Piero Gobetti on this latter's journal *Rivoluzione Liberale*.
126. In 1882, when parts of North-East Italy still formed part of the Habsburg Empire, the Austro-Hungarian police arrested the Italian patriot Guglielmo Oberdan, in possession of bombs, while he was travelling to Trieste, where the Emperor Franz Joseph was shortly to arrive. Despite international protests Oberdan was hanged. According to Croce's *History of Italy* (p.120) this ensured that Italy – alliances notwithstanding – would not, 'save in the most exceptional and desperate circumstances', find itself entering the field at the side of the Austro-Hungarian Empire.
127. I.e. 'Sorel, Proudhon, De Man[2]', immediately above.
128. This note criticises further the conception of the dialectic as understood by the reformism of the era. Though the passage does not deal directly with Croce, it may be recalled that, for Gramsci, Bernstein was closely linked with Croce (and Sorel) as providing the intellectual justification for reformist socialism in their respective countries. The letter quoted mentioning all three names together ('Croce as Intellectual Leader of Revisionism', Chapter VI, repeated word for word without additional comment as Q10II§3, not included here) is to be read in this sense (see point 2 of Gramsci's 'Summary' introducing Q10I, pp.328-32 of this volume).
129. The progressive newspaper, founded by Gaetano Salvemini, that aimed at closing the gap between North and South in Italy; not to be confused with the Communist *L'Unità* founded by Gramsci in 1924.
130. One of the very few references in the whole of the notebooks to the Catholic Popular Party, set up after the First World War.
131. It may be recalled that, in the penultimate note of sub-section 13 that ends Q10I, Gramsci points out that both Giolitti and Salandra pay tribute to Croce by concluding their Memoirs with letters of his.
132. 'Mafias' in the sense of closed self-protecting groups, not to be understood here as criminal organisations.
133. See also 'The Popular Libraries', pp.154-5, and footnote 10 to Chapter II of this volume; for more on the potentialities and practical limitations of these institutions see GR, pp.64-7.

134. See also 'The Einaudi-Spirito Polemic over the State' and 'Brief Notes on Economics[4]: Ugo Spirito & Co.' (pp.182-4 and 180-1 of Chapter II) and 'Identification of Individual and State' and 'Political and Civil Society' (pp.439 and 435-9 in Section D of this Chapter) as well as Q6§10 (SPN, pp.270-2) which contain both a discussion of Spirito's (and Gentile's) position – that there is a reciprocal identification between individual and state – and Gramsci's criticism of it.

135. Two Jesuit priests, Frs Cataldini and Maceta, were responsible for introducing a constitution into seventeenth-century Paraguay. Rather than this being an attempt at establishing a primitive communist society along the lines of the utopian experiment of Tommaso Campanella's *City of the Sun*, as claimed by Paul Lafargue, following E. Gothein (*Der christlich-sociale Staat der Jesuiten in Paraguay*, Leipzig 1883), the state merely represented the 'simple accommodation of the Jesuits to the communistic habits of the savage Guarani tribes. The Jesuits instructed the Guarani in how to work in the fields and their pretended Campanella-style communism came down to a wise capitalist exploitation that was a source of great riches for the Order.' (Croce, *Materialismo Storico*, third edition, p.227, citing Karl Kautsky's position; this chapter is not in the partial English translation of the book.)

136. I.e. 'Croce's Stance during the World War', pp.332-4 of Chapter VI of this volume.

137. The ten-year apprenticeship was that under Fascism which had effectively had the upper hand from 1922. What here is termed 'constituentism' was the call for a new Constituent Assembly to decide on an interim state form to replace Fascism (and thus not simply a vague 'constitutionalism'). At the time of writing this note (1932) Gramsci was almost completely isolated from other Communists in raising this demand as a transitional stage on the way to what he still hoped would be a national form of 'dictatorship of the proletariat'. He first expressed the idea in 1930 in a series of educational conversations with other Communist detainees in the prison at Turi di Bari, including Athos Lisa, and repeated it to him in October 1932. Lisa relayed the information as soon as possible (March 1933) to the party leadership, but the 'Athos Lisa report' was made public only thirty years afterwards in *Rinascita*, 12 December 1964. Although a majority of Gramsci's prison comrades approved the general lines of the 'Constituent' proposal, through fears of 'fractional activity' because of the delicate nature of the call (which clearly went against the then current line of the Communist International), the talks were suspended. The other subjects raised in the talks foreshadow some of the most important themes of the notebooks.

138. This book (*A Story and an Idea*, Turin 1926) by Guido Miglioli, leader of the extreme left of the Popular Party, deals with his 1926 trip to the Soviet Union, also mentioned implicitly in Q5§6 (not translated here) which refers to a similar initiative undertaken by another Catholic, Count Carlo Lovera di Castiglione. Miglioli was expelled from the Popular Party for his support of the *Krestintern*, the Communist International's peasant organisation. In Q9§138 Gramsci narrates an anecdote told him by Athos

Lisa (see previous footnote): rather sardonically, the leading conservative Southernist, Giustino Fortunato, told him there were 'two really dangerous men in Italy, one of whom was Miglioli' (left as 'Migl.' in the note to avoid censorship problems); the other, not named, was Gramsci.

139. The translation here follows the wording of the manuscript; the printed version, in omitting the first 'of' is somewhat obscure.

140. (Neo-)Malthusianism is often used by Gramsci to indicate a disparaging attitude towards the people, here an activity limited solely to a small number of 'enlightened' intellectuals that in a 'transformist' manner would keep power in the hands of the rulers and leave many negative aspects of popular life untouched. 'Constituentism' (see earlier in this paragraph), if taken seriously, would potentially have brought about more far reaching changes.

141. See 'The National Origins of Crocean Historicism', pp.373-6, and footnote 17 of this Chapter.

142. For convenience Q10II§41iv is here presented as three separate sub-sections; in between each are the paragraphs (the two parts of Q10II§47) that Gramsci wrote shortly afterwards (on Julien Benda and on Catholic modernism) to add the detail to the argument he is dealing with.

143. *The Great Betrayal*, London 1928, is Richard Aldington's translation of Julien Benda's *La Trahison des Clercs*, the subtitle of the English version and the name by which it appears in Q10II§41iv; in the note 'Croce and Julien Benda' Gramsci uses the wording of the title followed by an Italian translation *Il tradimento degli intellettuali*. The 'clercs' (Chaucer's 'clerks', or 'clerics') were 'those who seek their joy in the practice of an art or a science or metaphysical speculation, in short in the possession of non-material advantages ...' but 'at the end of the nineteenth century, a fundamental change occurred: *the "clerks" began to play the game of political passions*. The men who had acted as a check on the realism of the people began to act as its stimulators' (Benda, pp.30-1). Apart from this tendentially negative judgement, he also says they can fulfil a positive role like 'Zola in the Dreyfus affair ... [as] the officiants of abstract justice'. In Q3§2 (SCW, pp.260-2), Gramsci notes that 'Croce, like Benda, examines the question of the intellectuals abstracting from the class situation of the intellectuals themselves and from their function, which has become more defined with the mass circulation of books and the periodical press. But if this position is explicable in the mediocre writers, how can one explain it in the great personalities? (Perhaps the explanation is coordinated: the great personalities govern the mediocre ones and certain practical prejudices are necessarily involved which are not detrimental to their works.)'

144. The *Encyclopaedia Britannica* entry was translated by R.G. Collingwood for the fourteenth edition; see also *Philosophy, Poetry, History*, ed. C.J.S. Sprigge, London 1966. *The Breviary of Aesthetic* (trans. Douglas Ainslie) appeared as a Rice Institute Pamphlet, Vol.2 No.4, Houston 1915 (repr. in the same series in 1961) and also as *The Essence of Aesthetic*, London 1921.

145. For the *Kulturkampf* see "Gentile-Gioberti', pp.442-3 of this

Chapter and footnote 74 to Chapter I.
146. Pius X's *Pascendi dominici gregis* of 8 December 1907.
147. For Loisy, the theologian generally credited with the origin of modernism, and his book see footnotes 95 and 103 to Chapter I and footnote 25 to Chapter V of this volume.
148. Croce regarded the religious modernists as, at best, noble souls, perplexed by their inner struggle between faith and thought, but more usually as dilettantes caught between religion and philosophy (and in neither case the genuine thing) or merely as people in bad faith using the Church to further their own ends (*Cultura e vita morale*, op.cit., pp.148-9).
149. Note added by Gramsci.
150. On p.122 of his *History of Europe*, op.cit., Croce paints a glowing picture of the Italian liberal Catholics as being 'in agreement with the Mazzinians and the democrats and the anti-clericals' (i.e. the 'classical' continental European liberals) over the 'two aims, Italian independence and political liberty' but not at all wanting to appeal to 'the imaginary people that would rise in the fields and the factories to drive out with their improvised arms the foreigner and domestic tyrant'.
151. The reference in the *History of Italy*, op.cit., appears on p.246 where, in the middle of a long self-eulogy, Croce refers to Gentile, who had 'fought gallantly against the modernists (who had claimed for their little heresy within the bosom of the Catholic Church the character of a great reformation in thought)'.
152. This newspaper was and is published in Bologna, on the southern edge of the Po Valley agricultural plain, where the conflicts between the landowners and the still largely Catholic peasantry were at times particularly sharp.
153. I.e. the first Christian Democrat movement, dating back to the last years of the nineteenth century. Associated most of all with the modernist priest, Don Romolo Murri, it supported the formation of organisations of Catholic workers or peasants rather than unions between these classes and the employers. As such it is arguable that it was closer to the concept of Catholic trade unions than to the post-World War II Christian Democrats, of which it was however also a forerunner.
154. For Orano and Fanelli's attacks on Gentile see 'Past and Present[5]. Gentile's Philosophy', pp.443-4, and footnote 82 to this Chapter.
155. See Gentile's speech on constitutional reforms and fascism on pp.199-218 of *Cultura e Fascismo*, op.cit., Florence 1924. In arguing for an upper chamber of 'corporations' (and an authoritarian one, as transpires from the general tenor of the speech), Gentile claimed that 'eighteenth-century liberalism, which knew nothing other than individuals, has had its day. The individuals remain but are aggregated in common interest groupings, and hence promoted to a higher economic, moral and intellectual power by the very laws inherent in their social activity.' Going on, he stated 'there is no true freedom without a strong state – a state capable of making laws and having them respected ... A strong state in reality above the factions' (pp.215-7).

NAME INDEX

Abd-el-Wahhab, 212
Abdullah (Sultan), 212
Adler, Alfred, 453, 582
Adler, Max, 453, 582
Agazzi, Emilio, 518
Agliardi, (Cardinal) Giuseppe, 41
Agnelli, Giovanni, lxxxi, 226-8, 434
Ahmed ash-Sherif, 211, 548
Ahmed ibn-Idris el-Hasani el-Idrisi, 211
Alberti, Leon Battista, 19-20, 358, 569
Alcalá Zamora, Niceto, 104, 533
Ali (Caliph, son-in-law of Mohammed), 210, 548
Aloisi, Massimo, 516
Althusser, Louis, lxxxiii
'A.M.', 197, 546-7
Ambrosio, Renato, 394
Anaxagoras, 318, 563
Anderson, Perry, 509
Andler, Charles, 419, 455, 457, 578
Antonelli, (Cardinal) Giacomo, 6, 8
Anzilotti, Antonio, 11, 389
Aquinas, (St) Thomas, lxxx, 526, 564
'Argus' (Vittorio Ciampi), 199-200
Arias, Gino, 163-4, 215-6, 511, 540
Aristotle, lxxxi, 125
Arrow, Kenneth, xlii-xliii
Aston, Francis William, lvi-lvii, 515
'Augur', 196, 200

Augustine (St, of Hippo), 101, 454, 533, 582
Aveling, Edward Bibbins, 176, 544
Avenarius, Richard, liv
Avolio, Gennaro, 12
Avveroes (Abu I-Walid Muhammad ibn Rushd), 137

Babeuf, Gracchus, 455, 583
Badaloni, Nicola, xxxv, 510, 515
Baggesen, Jens, 311
Bainville, Jacques, 90
Bakhtin, Mikhail Mikhailovich, lxiii
Balfour, Arthur James, 206
Balzac, Honoré de, xxvii, 55-6
Balzani, Ugo, 19
Banfi, Antonio, 21
Barbagallo, Corrado, 336, 369, 563
Barbaro, Umberto, 451
Barbera, (Fr) Mario, 73-4
Barclay, William, 523
Bargagli-Petrucci, Gino, 440
Barrès, Maurice, 360
Barzellotti, Giacomo, 51-3
Bassett, Rosa, 537
Baudelaire, Charles, 58
Bauer (family), 311, 441
Beaverbrook, Lord, 232
Beernaert, Auguste, 116, 534
Bellarmino, (Cardinal) Roberto, 21, 67, 101-2, 522, 532
Belluzzo, Giuseppe, 72
Benda, Julien, 470, 586
Bendiscioli, Mario, 99

Name Index

Benedict XV (Pope), 7-8, 85-6, 530-2
Benigni, (Fr) Umberto, 8, 76-7, 79-80, 82, 84, 86-8, 530
Benini, Rodolfo, 173, 182-3, 308
Benni, Antonio Stefano, lxxxi
Bergson, Henri, liv
Bernstein, Eduard, lxviii, 328, 335, 364, 455, 457, 461, 583-4
Bertalanffy, Ludwig von, 22
Berth, Edouard, 584
Bertram, (Archbishop) Johannes Adolf, 109
Bilio, (Cardinal) Luigi, 569
Billot, (Cardinal) Louis, 8, 80, 84, 95
Bismarck, Otto von, 69-70, 108, 529, 534,
Bissolati Bergamaschi, Leonida, 336, 447, 566
Blanqui, Louis-Auguste, 455, 583
Bobbio, Norberto, lxxix, 514, 519
Böhm-Bawerk, Eugen von, 424
Bohr, Niels, lviii
Bonomelli, Geremia, 41
Bonomi, Ivanoe, 246, 336, 447, 550, 566
Bonomi, Paolo, 41-2
Boothman, Derek, 515
Borchardt, Julian, 177, 544
Bordiga, Amadeo, xxxiii, 334, 509, 510, 524, 559, 565
Borek, Johanna, 519
Borgese, Giuseppe Antonio, 259, 286-9, 516, 532, 555
Borsa, Mario, 266
Botero, Giovanni, 163-5, 399, 405, 540, 575
Bottai, Giuseppe, 436, 449
Bottomore, Tom, 515
Boulin, Abbé (Roger Duguet), 84
Bourbaki, Nicolas (collective pseudonym), xli
Bourget, Paul, 13, 198, 274, 554
Bourne, (Cardinal) Francis, 112, 534
Bradley, James, 22, 523

Brahmabandhav, Upadhyaya (i.e. 'Teacher'), 117, 535
Briand, Aristide, 233, 549
Brucculeri, (Fr) Angelo, 46, 144, 453
Bruers, Antonio, 22
Bruno, Giordano, lxxx, 20-2
Buci-Glucksmann, Christine, 507
Bukharin, Nikolai Ivanovich, xiv, xxxiii, xxxv, liii, lx, 279, 513
Bulferetti, Domenico, 50-2
Buonaiuti, (Fr) Ernesto, xxvi, 8, 77, 79-80, 96-7, 472, 530-1

Cabiati, Attilio, 251
Cadman, John, 210
Caesar, Caius Julius, 253, 261
Cafiero, Carlo, 176, 528, 544
Caillaux, Joseph, 208-9, 547
Cairnes, John Elliot, 308
Cajumi, Arrigo, 573
Calles, Plutarco Elias, 117, 535
Calogero, Guido, 332, 371, 519
Calvin, John (or Jean), 533, 564
Cambon, Victor, 257
Cameroni, Agostino, 42
Camis, Mario, 218, 287-9, 302
Cammett, John, xiii, 50
Campanella, Tommaso, lxxx, 22, 575, 585
Campello della Spina, Paolo, 526
Canosa, Antonio Capece Minutolo, (Prince of), 38
Cannan, Edwin, 165, 540
Canterbury (Archbishop of, i.e. Randall Thomas Davidson), 112
Cantillon, Philip, 511, 540
Cantillon, Richard, xxxvi-xxxvii, 164-5, 171, 511, 540
Caracciolo, Galeazzo (the 'Marquis of Vico'), 329, 564
Carducci, Giosue, 310-2, 355, 375, 560
Carlyle, Thomas, 257
Carson, Edward, li, 267-8
Cassel, Gustav, 231
Castellani, Alberto, 124-5

Name Index

Castellano, Giovanni, 335-6, 367, 447, 566, 570, 581
Cataldini, (Fr), 585
Cavour, Camillo Benso, Count of, 250, 374, 572
Chabod, Federico, 163, 517
Chamberlain, Austen, 199
Charlemagne (Emperor), 82-3, 520
Chaucer, Geoffrey, 586
Chiocchetti, (Fr) Emilio, 339, 411, 441
Cione, Edmondo, 74-5, 331
Clémenceau, Georges, 404-5, 459
Cocchi, Romano (Adami), xxiv
Collingwood, Robin George, lvi, lxx, 515, 517
Colwyn, Lord, 265
Colyer (in notebook Collyer), William Thomas, 112
Combes, Emile, 531
Comte, Auguste, xxi, 43, 93-4, 448
Condillac, Etienne-Bonnot de, 313
Confucius (Kung-Fu-Tzu), 125-6
Constantine (Emperor), 18
Copernicus, Nicolaus, 22, 523
Coppola, Francesco, 379, 444, 463, 580
Cornaggia Medici Castiglione, Carlo Ottavio (Marquis), 42
Corsi, (Fr) Mario, 297
Costantini, (Mons.) Celso, 127-8
Cousinet, Roger, 143
Credaro, Luigi, 66, 529
Crémieux, Benjamin, 337
Crespi, Angelo, 266
Crispi, Francesco, 250
Crispolti, Filippo, 36
Croce, Benedetto, xiv, xxii, xxxi-xxxii, xxxv, xli, xliii, liii, liv-lvii, lxii, lxvi-lxxxi, 13, 18-9, 26, 44, 55, 75, 149, 157, 162, 165-6, 171, 173-4, 182, 184-5, 281, 283, 299-300, 310-2, 318, **327-61**, **364-475**, 509, 514, 516-9, 522, 535, 541, 545, 554, 558, 560, 566-82, 584-7
Croizier, P., 90

Cuoco, Vincenzo, 329, 341, 375
Cusa (or Cusanus), Nicholas of (Cardinal), 22-3, 523

Daladier, Edouard, 547
D'Amelio, Mariano, 475
D'Andrea, Ugo, 468
D'Annunzio, Gabriele, 412, 456, 583
Dante, Alighieri, lxxx, 20, 254, 522, 569, 582
Dantzig, Tobias, 298, 558
D'Azeglio, Cesare, 35-6, 38, 529
D'Azeglio, Massimo, 529
D'Azeglio, Prospero, see Taparelli, Luigi
Dazzi, Manlio Torquato, 19
De Begnac, Yvon, 508
De Bernardi, Mario, 163-4
Deborin (Ioffe), Abram Moiseievich, 545
Debreu, Gerard, xlii-xliii
De Broglie, Louis, lxi, 516
de Giovanni, Biagio, lxxiii, 517
D'Elia, (Fr) Pasquale 127, 536
della Volpe, Gaetano, 575
De Lollis, Cesare, 379
De Maistre, Joseph, 39
De Man, Henri, 331, 336, 356, 365, 446-54, 582
De Michelis, Giuseppe, 235-6
Denikin, Anton Ivanovich, 529
De Pietri Tonelli, Alfonso, 294, 436
De Ritis, Beniamino, 214, 548
De Ruggiero, Guido, 21, 58, 266, 379, 388-9, 406, 418, 447, 451, 566
de Ste. Croix, Geoffrey, 509
De Sanctis, Francesco, xxii, 312, 329, 368, 374, 378, 561, 564, 572
De Stefani, Alberto, 245
De Stefano, Antonino, 80
Destutt de Tracy, Antoine-Louis-Claude, 507
Deterding, Henry (Hendrik W.A.), 210

Name Index

Deville, Gabriel, 176-7, 544
De Viti De Marco, Antonio, 248, 532, 550
Dewey, John, 259, 536, 551
di Giamberardino, Oscar, 197
Disraeli, Benjamin, 68, 261, 574
Dobb, Maurice, xviii, 508
Donini, Ambrogio, xxvi
Dorso, Guido, 407
Dostaler, Gilles, 511
Dostoievsky, Fëdor Mikhailovich, 271
Doyal, Len, 516
Dreyfus, Alfred, 359, 586
Dubreuil, Henri, 282
Ducati, Bruno, 135-6
Duhamel, Georges, 256
Dutt, Rajani Palme, 517

Eddington, Arthur Stanley, 286-7, 555
Egermann, E. Ya., lxxi, 517
Einaudi, Giulio, xxxvii, 511, 514
Einaudi, Luigi, xxxvii, xlii-xliii, lxxi, 163-5, 172-3, 180-5, 225-7, 266, 308-9, 336, 420-3, 541
Einstein, Albert, 516, 558
Ekehorn, Gösta, 288, 556
el-Hasan ibn-Ali, 211-2, 548
Engels, Frederick, x, lxxii, lxxvii, 56, 183-4, 246, 258, 282, 299-300, 311, 315, 330, 355, 369, 385, 396, 403, 425, 509, 541, 544-5, 550-1, 558, 561, 570-1, 583
Entwistle, Harold, 510
Erasmus, 343, 407-8, 472
Ezekiel, 120, 535

Fabietti, Ettore, 154, 176, 544
Faccioli, Giovanni, 554
Faggi, Adolfo, 126
Faina, Claudio, 144
'Falea di Calcedonia', 566
Fanelli, Giuseppe Attilio, 444, 474
Farbman, Michael S. (R.B. Rafail), xlviii, lii, 271, 553

Fatimah (daughter of Mohammed), 210
Fatini, Giuseppe, 53, 55
Feiler, Arthur, 388
Femia, Joseph V., 519
Ferrabino, Aldo, 329, 340-1
Ferrando, Guido, 140-1
Ferrante, Don (character in Manzoni), 303, 559
Ferri, Enrico, 189, 272, 554
Fetscher, Iring, lxxxiv, 519
Feuerbach, Ludwig, 385-6, 574, 578
Feyerabend, Paul K., 516
Fichte, Johann Gottlieb, 310-1, 313, 560
Findlay, John Niemeyer, lxxiii
Finocchiaro, Maurice, 512
Fiori, Giuseppe, 515
Fistetti, Francesco, 515
Flaubert, Gustave, 579
Flora, Francesco, 367, 570
Foa, Vittorio, lxxi, 517
Fontaine, Nicolas, 80-2, 86, 110
Ford, Henry, 186, 255-7, 288-9, 431, 433, 449, 451
Forges Davanzati, Roberto, 573
Forke, Alfred, 124-5
Fortunato, Giustino, lxxii, 328, 368, 463, 586
Fovel, Massimo, 436
Francioni, Gianni, 476-7, 508
Francis (St, of Assisi), 34, 120
Francis Xavier (St), 129
Francis II (*or* Franceschiello; King of Naples), 359, 570
Franckenstein (in notebook Frankenstein), Georg Eugen Heinrich Arbogast, 108
Francqui (Belgian minister), 265
Franz Joseph (Austro-Hungarian Emperor), 69, 438, 580, 584
Freud, Sigmund, 273, 448-9, 453, 582
Frisella Vella, Giuseppe, 196
Fueter, Eduard, 19
Fülöp-Miller, René, 370, 554, 571

Fustel de Coulanges, Numa-Denis, 346, 568

Gabbrielli, Gabriele, 118
Galileo (Galileo Galilei), 20-2, 101, 337, 410, 522-3
Gandhi, Mohandas Karamchand (Mahatma), 118-9, 535
García Moreno, Gabriel, 116-7, 534
Garibaldi, Giuseppe, 529
Garuglieri, Mario, 516
Garvey, Marcus (Moziah), 548
Gary, Elbert Henry, 208
Gasparri, Cardinal Pietro, 7-8, 59, 106
Gautama (Buddha, the Enlightened One), 125, 129
Gemelli, Edoardo (Fr Agostino), 8, 42, 329, 411, 440, 564
Gentile, Giovanni, xxx-xxxi, xxxii, lxviii, lxxiv, lxxix, 72, 140, 149, 158-9, 300, 309, 339-40, 344, 356, 364, 368-9, 400-1, 409-10, 414, 436, 438-9, 441-5, 464, 468, 471-5, 517-8, 544, 570, 575, 579-81, 587
Gentiloni, Vincenzo Ottorino, 570
Gerratana, Valentino, xvi, xix, 476-7, 508
Giaccardi, Alberto, 242
Giannino (King, of Siena), 53
Gide, Charles, 186, 427, 512, 545
Gioberti, Vincenzo, lxxviii, 11, 313, 342, 373-5, 381, 401, 442, 520, 580
Giolito (Giolito de' Ferrari), 21
Giolitti, Giovanni, xxxi, 334, 360, 379, 409, 442, 463, 471, 569-70, 584
Giretti, Edoardo, 185
Giuliano, Balbino, 442
Gladstone, William Ewart, 574
Gläser (headmaster in Hamburg), 142-3, 538
Gobetti, Piero, 25-6, 407, 423, 464, 584

Goethe, Johann Wolfgang von, 337, 350, 568, 574
Gohier, Urbain, 86
Gompers, Samuel, 254
Gonzales Palencia, Angel, 137
Gothein, Eberhard, 585
Govi, Mario, 295-7, 557
Gramsci, Delio, xviii, xxix, 138, 477
Gramsci, Giuliano, xviii, xxix, 138, 477
Grandi, Dino, 237
Gravina, Manfredi, 199, 209
Graziadei, Antonio, 162, 185-9, 425, 546, 578
Greenway, Charles, 210
Gregory XVI (Pope), xxvi, 5-6, 8, 99
Grieco, Ruggero, 508
Grifone, Pietro, 550
Grossmann, Henryk, 430, 579
Guicciardini, Francesco, 16, 19, 374, 572
Guidi, Michelangelo, 132-3
Guizot, François-Pierre-Guillaume, 184, 545

Habermas, Jürgen, 515
Halecki, Oscar, 105-6
Halévy, Daniel, 457, 459
Hamilton, Robert, 264
Harding, Warren Gamaliel, 204
Harris, Henry Silton, 519, 580
Harris, Roger, 516
Hartmann, Richard, 133
Hauser, Henri, 184
Havard de la Montagne, Robert, 88
Hegel, Georg Wilhelm Friedrich, xiv, lxxii-lxxiii, lxxviii-lxxix, 73, 75, 157, 160, 305, 310-3, 315, 318-9, 330, 351, 355, 371-2, 378, 386, 400, 408, 419, 442, 456, 563, 532, 556, 559-60, 562, 567, 571, 573, 575-6, 578
Heiler, Friedrich, 113

Name Index

Heine, Heinrich, 57, 310-1, 529, 560
Henderson, Hamish, 507
Henry VIII (King of England), 523
Herbart, Johann Friedrich, 157, 539
Héritier, Jean, 95
Herrin, Judith, 508
Herriot, Edouard, 107
Hertling, Georg, 116, 534
Hitler, Adolf, 534, 547
Hoare, Quintin, xiii, xv, 512
Höpker-Aschoff, Hermann, 60
Høffding, Harald, lviii
Hoffmann, Karl, 209
Hoover, Herbert, 534
Horkheimer, Max, lv, 515
Hughes, Charles E., 209, 547
Hull, Cordell, 1
Hu Shih, 125, 536
Hussein (Husayn) ibn Ali (Sherif of Mecca; later King of the Hejaz), 211-2, 547
Huxley, Aldous, 122

Ibn Saud (King of the Hejaz and later of Saudi Arabia), 211-3, 547
Ibrahim (Pasha), 212
Idris (Sidi Mohammed Idris Al-Mahdi As-Sanusi, later King of Libya), 211, 547-8
Ignatius (St, of Loyola), 47, 101
'Ignotus', 72
Ikbal Ali Shah (Sirdar), 132-4
Imperiuzzi, Filippo, 51
Innocenti Periccioli, Anna, 527
Iotti, Nilde (Leonilde), xix
Iturbide (Emperor of Mexico), 202

Jacuzio, Raffaele, 70
Jaloux, Edmond, 565
James, William, 258-9, 448, 551
James VI (King of Scotland; later James I of England), 522
Jannaccone, Pasquale, xlvii, 180, 215-6, 436

Jaurès, Jean, 404
Jemolo, Arturo Carlo, 6, 11, 61, 389, 527
Jesus, 35, 101, 106, 135, 274, 340, 475
Jevons, William Stanley, xxxvi, 511, 542-3
John XXIII (Pope), 509
Joseph II (Austro-Hungarian Emperor), 526
Julien, Stanislas, 535
'Junius', 262

Kahn, Otto, 208, 210
Kaller, (Mons.), 109
Kampffmeyer, Georg, 133
Kant, Immanuel, xxi, lxxvi, 13, 310, 312-3, 330, 355, 520, 521, 560-1
Kaser, Kurt, 11
Kautsky, Karl, 176-7, 540, 544, 579, 585
Kellogg, Frank, 549
Kemal Pasha (Mustafa Kemal, Kemal Atatürk), 134
Kemmerer, Edwin Walter, 231
Kennan, George, 1
Keynes, John Maynard, xliii, xlvi-xlviii, 231, 513-4, 548
Kierkegaard, Søren, lviii
Kjellén, Rudolf, 195
Knox, Thomas Malcolm, 571
Kuhn, Thomas, liv, lvii-lx, lxiv, 515-6

Labanca, Baldassarre, 297
Labriola, Antonio, lxviii, lxxviii, 25, 139, 157-60, 318, 331, 334, 382, 384, 517-8, 523, 539, 565, 574
Lachelier, Jules, 58
Lacointe, Félix, 89
Lafargue, Paul, 56, 528, 585
La Follette, Robert, 551
Lamennais (de La Mennais), (Abbé) Hugues-Félicité-Robert, 8, 37-8, 525

Name Index

Lange, Friedrich Albert, 394, 412, 574-5
Lanino, Pietro, 255
Lanson, Gustave, 56, 528
Lanteri, Abbot Pio Brunone
Lao-Tzu (Lao-Tse), 125-6
Lapidus, Ia. A., xxxvii, 177-8, 542
La Rocca, Tommaso, 509
Laurat, Lucien, 430, 579
Lavedan, André, 108
Lazzaretti, David (Davide), xxiv, 50-5, 527-8
Lea, Henry Charles, 105, 533
Leacock, Stephen, 214, 548
Lenin, Vladimir Ilyich (Ulyanov), xxxii, liv, 262, 306, 357, 544, 549-50, 552-3, 560
Lensi, Alfredo, 20
Leo XIII (Pope), 6, 8, 42-3, 50, 69, 89, 95-6, 108, 526-8, 531
Leone da Modena (Rabbi), 103, 533
Leopardi, Giacomo, xv, xxii, 329, 564
Leopold II (Austro-Hungarian Emperor), 526
Levi, Ezio, 137, 537
Lewis, Sinclair, xlix, 302, 559
Lexis, Wilhelm, 545
Liberatore, (Fr) Matteo, 297
Liénart, (Mons.) Achille, 49
Lippert, (Fr) Peter, 99
Lippi, Marco, 511
Lisa, Athos, 514, 585-6
Lisio, Giuseppe, 19
List, Friedrich, 184
Livy (Titus Livius), 511
Locke, John, 313
Loisy, Alfred, 8, 94, 98, 300, 472-3, 531-2, 558, 587
Lombardo-Radice, Giuseppe, xxxii, 140, 510
Lombroso, Cesare, 50, 189
Loria, Achille, 122, 186, 308, 358, 421-2, 535, 545, 578
Losacco, Michele, 23
Louis XVIII (King of France), 28

Lovera di Castiglione, Carlo (Count), 585
Luciolli, Ludovico, 231
Ludendorff, Erich von, 79
Lugli, Giuseppe, 319
Lu Hsün, 536
Lukács, Georg (György), lxxxiii
Lumbroso, Giacomo, 103
Lunacharsky, Anatoly Vasilievich, 577
Luther, Martin, 407-8
Lyautey, Louis-Hubert-Gonzalve, 334, 565

Macaulay, Thomas Babington, 301, 557
Maccari, Mino, 465
Macchioro, Vittorio, 259
MacDonald, James Ramsay, 208
Maceta, (Fr), 585
McGuinness, Brian, xl, 512
Mach, Ernst, liv
Machiavelli, Niccolò, xxv, xxxv, lxxix, 19-21, 160, 162-4, 188, 325, 333, 399, 405, 414, 511, 540, 572, 575
MacTaggart, John MacTaggart Ellis, lxxii
Maeterlinck, Maurice, 450, 582
Malagodi, Giovanni Francesco, 394
Malatesta, Errico, 53, 528, 570
Malcolm, Norman, 513
Manoilesco, Mihail, 234-5
Manzoni, Alessandro, 36, 57, 303, 337, 557, 559
Marcuse, Herbert, lv-lvi
Marescalchi, Antonio, 57
Maria Sophia (Queen of Naples), 533
Maritain, Jacques, 8, 92
Marsden, Ernest, 556
Marshall, Alfred, 175, 512, 543
Marshall, (General) George, l
Martire, Egilberto, 70
Marx, Karl Heinrich, x, xii, xiv, xx, xxvii-xxviii, xxxii, xxxv-xlv,

Name Index

liv-lv, lvii, lix-lx, lxv-lxvi, lxix-lxxii, lxxiv, lxxvii, 56, 164, 177, 186-7, 280, 308, 311, 313, 315, 318, 330, 339, 341, 355, 369, 384, 396-9, 403-4, 411, 415, 425, 438, 448, 455-7, 508, 509, 510, 511, 513-4, 516, 518, 527-8, 539-41, 543-5, 561-3, 571, 573, 575, 577-8, 582-3
Masaryk, Tomás Garrigue, 25, 271, 388, 524, 553, 574
Masi, Ernesto, 468
Masoero, Arturo, 448-9
Massis, Henri, 92, 95, 118, 531
Mataloni, G.M., 79, 84
Mattalia, Daniele, 373
Matteotti, Giacomo, 532
Matthew (St), 101
Mattioli, Raffaele, xix
Maura, Antonio, 117, 534-5
Maurois, André, 574
Maurras, Charles, 8, 13, 43, 80-1, 83-4, 88-96, 98, 531, 584
Maximilian (Emperor of Mexico), 203
Mazzini, Giuseppe, 580, 587
Meda, Filippo, xxiv, 7, 116
Menger, Carl, 542
Mesnil, Jacques, 334, 565
'Metron', 150, 320-1
Meyer, Robert, 186
Michelangelo (Michelangelo Buonarroti), 360
Michels, Robert (Roberto), 242, 276, 457, 555, 583
Miglioli, Guido, xxiv-xxv, 509, 585-6
Mignet, François-Auguste-Marie, 184, 545
Migone Gian Giacomo, 514
Milano, Paolo, 452-3
Mill, John Stuart, 308
Mioni, (Mons.) Ugo, 533
Mirsky (Sviatopolk-Mirsky), Dmitri Petrovich, lxx-lxxi, 516, 517
Missiroli, Mario (Spectator), lvi, 25-7, 293, 404, 407, 410-1, 417-8, 455-6, 458, 460-1, 465, 471, 473, 557, 577
Mohammed (the Prophet), 135, 210, 212-3, 547
Mohammed Ali, 212
Momigliano, Arnaldo, 102-4
Monk, Ray, xl, 512
Monroe, James, 202
Montessori, Maria, 141, 537
Morandi, Rodolfo, 248-50, 513, 550
Morello, Vincenzo, 70-1
Morgan, John Pierpont, 208
Morgia, Corrado, 510
Mosca, Gaetano, 272, 553
Muir, Ramsay, 267-8
Muller, (Fr) Albert, 46
Murphy, Antoin E., 511, 540
Murri, (Don) Romolo, 587
Musolino, Giuseppe, 533
Mussato, Albertino 19, 522
Mussolini, Benito, 508, 527, 550, 570

Naldi, Filippo (Pippo), 33
Napoleon I, 72, 198, 330, 375, 401, 527, 575-6
Napoleon III, 47, 203, 381, 527
Napoleoni, Claudio, 513
Natoli, Aldo, 508
Negro, Luigi, 186
Nenni, Pietro, 570
Newman, (Cardinal) John Henry, 8, 139, 151-2, 538
Newton, Isaac, 22
Niceforo, Alfredo, 189
Niethammer, Immanuel, 576
Nitti, Francesco Saverio, 53, 442, 463, 526, 528
Nowell Smith, Geoffrey, xiii, xv, 512

Oberdan, Guglielmo, 460, 584
Obregón, Alvaro, 117, 535
O'Connell, Daniel, 116, 534
Ojetti, Ugo, 92, 118

Name Index

Olgiati, (Mons.) Francesco, 339, 411
Omodeo, Alfredo, 300, 472
O'Neill, Edward F., 142
Oppenheimer, Franz, 430, 579
Orano, Paolo, 436, 444, 474, 579
Oriani, Alfredo, 377, 407, 572
Ostrovityanov, Konstantin Vasilievich, xxxvii, 177-8, 542

Palhoriès, (Abbé) Fortuné, 442
Pantaleoni, Maffeo, xlii, 168, 170-1, 541-3
Panzieri, Raniero, xlv, 513
Papini, Giovanni, 47, 186, 329, 340, 567
Paratore, Giuseppe, 230-1
Pareto, Vilfredo, 301, 308, 437, 541, 559, 574
Pascal, Blaise, 56-9, 528
Pascarella, Cesare, 359
Pascoli, Giovanni, 254, 528
Pasqualigo, (Fr), 80
Pastor, Ludwig von, 21-2, 522
Paul IV (Pope), 564
Paul VI (Pope), xxiii, 509
Pavolini, Corrado, 465
Peano, Giuseppe, 282
Peierls, Rudolf, 516
Peirce, Charles Sanders, 551
Pellizzi, Camillo, 465-6
Pestalozzi, Johann Heinrich, 139
Petrarch (Francesco Petrarca), 21, 522
Pettazzoni, Raffaele, 129, 131
Petty, William, xxxvi-xxxvii, 164, 511, 540
Philip, André, 11, 454, 582
Philip Neri (St), 527
Pirenne, Henri, 184, 545
Pirou, Gaëtan, 293-4
Pitt, William (the Younger), 264
Pius V (Pope), 77, 530
Pius VII (Pope), 43
Pius IX (Pope), 6, 84, 99, 526, 569
Pius X (Pope), 6-7, 41-2, 76, 81, 84, 86, 91, 96, 475, 526, 530, 558, 587
Pius XI (Pope), 7-8, 28, 59, 67, 69, 75, 77, 81-2, 84, 99, 101, 106, 109, 112, 527, 530, 534
Plato, lxxxi
Platone, Felice, xvii, 476, 510
Plekhanov, Georgi Valentinovich, lxxi, 297, 378, 412, 517, 545, 557, 573
Plutarch, 9, 520
Podolsky, Boris, 516
Poincaré, Henri, liv
Polimanti (in the manuscript 'Polidori'), Quintilio, 447, 581
Ponzio, Augusto, 516
Popper, Karl, lviii, lxxv, 518
Portelli, Hugues, xii, 507
Potier, Jean-Pierre, xliv, xlviii, 507, 512-5
Prampolini, Camillo, 451
Prato, Giuseppe, 423
Prezzolini, Giuseppe, 301, 308, 454, 471-2, 550, 559
Price, Richard, 264
Primo de Rivera y Orbeneja, Miguel, 535
Proudhon, Pierre-Joseph (Herr Edgar), 26, 307, 311, 329, 341, 365, 381, 449-50, 457-9, 560, 583

Quesnay, François, xxxvii
Quine, Willard van Orman, lxv-lxvi, 516
Quinet, Edgar, 342, 375, 473, 571

Racca, Vittorio, 426
Raimondo, Ignazio, 566, 581
Raimondo, Orazio, 336, 447, 566, 581
Rampolla del Tindaro, (Cardinal) Mariano, 89, 531
Ranchetti, Fabio, xliii, 513
Rasmussen, Emil, 52
Ravà, Adolfo, 311-2
Reinach, Joseph, 404
Reinach, Salomon, 9, 520

Name Index

Reinhold, Karl Leonhard, 311
Rémusat, Abel, 535
Renan, Ernest, 25-6, 404
'Rerum Scriptor', *see* Salvemini, Gaetano
Revel, Bruno, 443
Rezzara, Niccolò, 41-2
Rhees, Rush, xl, xliii
Ricardo, David, xi, xxxv, xxxviii-xl, xlii, 179, 308, 425-7, 507, 511-2, 542, 544
Rice, J.P., 254
Rigola, Rinaldo, 422
Rinaldi, Ruggero, 442
Rist, Charles, 186, 427, 512, 545
Robbins, Lionel, xlii-xliii, 162, 174-5, 513, 543
Roberts, David D., 518
Robespierre, Maximilien, 310, 312, 330, 355, 560
Rocco, Alfredo, 70, 444, 463, 580
Rockefeller, John Davison, 209
Rodbertus, Johann Karl, 186
Rodin, Auguste, 360
Roll, Eric (Erich), xxxvii, xxxix, 511, 512
Rolland, Romain, 118
Romagnosi, Gian Domenico, 184
Romier, Lucien, 107
Roosevelt, Franklin Delano, l
Root, Elihu, 203, 205
Rosa, (Fr) Enrico, 8, 78-9, 82, 84, 86, 92, 96, 118
Rosen, Nathan, 516
Rosenberg, Alfred, 91
Rosmini, Fr Antonio, 8, 11, 521
Rossi-Landi, Ferruccio, xl-xli, 512, 513
Rostagni, Augusto, 314
Roth, Cecil, 102, 533
Rotta, Paolo, 22
Rousseau, Jean-Jacques, xxix, 90, 139, 560
Rovani, Giuseppe, 52
Royce, Josiah, 258, 551
Rubin, Isaac Ilyich, xxxvii, xxxix, 511, 512

Rudas, László, 185
Ruffini, Francesco, 57
Ruffo, Cardinal Fabrizio, 525, 532
Russell, Bertrand, lxiii, 282, 297, 557, 575
Russo, Luigi, 368, 575
Rutherford, Ernest, 290, 556
Ryazanov (Ryazanoff), David Borisovich (Goldenbach), 56, 518, 528

'Saggiatore', 323
Sagot du Vauroux, (Mons.) Charles-Paul, 88, 91, 531
Saint-Beuve, Charles-Augustin, 381, 573
Saitzew, Manuel, 244
Salandra, Antonio, 360, 463, 570, 584
Salata, Francesco, 69-70, 89
Salter, Arthur, 229
Saltet, L., 96
Salvatorelli, Luigi, 97
Salvemini, Gaetano, xxxii, 247, 550, 584
Samuel, Marcus (and brother), 210
Sangnier, Marc, 7, 530
Sapir, Edward, lxv-lxvi, 516
Sartiaux, Félix, 97-8, 532
Sbarretti, (Cardinal) Donato, 49
Schaumann, Johann Christian Gottlieb, 311
Scheffauer, Hermann George (Orchelle R.L.), 514
Schelling, Friedrich, 310, 313, 560
Schiappoli, Domenico, 61
Schiavi, Alessandro, 336, 447, 451-2
Schlund, Erhard, 109
Schopenhauer, Arthur, 386
Schucht, Appollon, 510
Schucht, Julka, xxix, 138, 477, 510
Schucht, Tania (Tatiana), xviii-xix, xxxviii, liv, lxxxi, 477, 508, 512, 514, 519, 533
Scoppola, Pietro, 526
Seassaro, Cesare, 509

Name Index

Segura y Saenz, (Cardinal) Pedro, 104, 533
Seligman, Edwin Robert Anderson, 184, 545
Selleri, Franco, 515
Serao, Matilde, 55, 528
Sergi, Giuseppe, 189
Shakespeare, William, 68
Shylock, 68
Simon (Parisian financier), 85-6
Smith, Adam, xxxvi, xxxvii, xxxix, 308, 541
Smith, Alfred (Al), 534
Söderblom, (Archbishop) Nathan, 113, 534
Soffici, Ardengo, 368
Sohn-Rethel, Alfred, 579
Sombart, Werner, 184
Sonnino, Giorgio Sidney, 463
Sorel, Georges, lxviii, 25-6, 293-4, 328, 335, 365, 389, 397, 403-5, 408, 410, 414, 418, 449-50, 454-61, 557, 565, 583-4
Spaventa, Bertrando, 158, 160, 311, 343, 567, 401
Spaventa, Silvio, lxviii, 25, 567
Spencer, Herbert, 448-9
Speziale, G.C., 319
Spirito, Ugo, xliii, 15, 162, 170, 180, 182-3, 308-9, 381-2, 435-9, 441, 446, 466, 521, 544, 573
Spriano, Paolo, 515
Sraffa, Piero, xviii-xx, xxxv-xxxviii, xl-xlii, xlvii-xlviii, lii, liv-lv, lxxxi, 164, 477, 508, 510-6, 518-9, 533
Stalin, Joseph Vissarionovich, liii
Stammler, Rudolf, 394, 415-6, 577
Stanghellini, Arturo, 460
Stecchetti, Lorenzo (Olindo Guerrini), 317, 563
Stenterello (character of the Commedia dell'Arte), 188, 333
Sternberg, Fritz, 579
Stirner, Max (Johann Caspar Schmidt), 386
Sturzo, (Don) Luigi, 524
Suardi, Gianforte, 40-2
Sue, Eugène, 273, 554
Sundar Singh (Sadhu), 118, 535
Sundkler, Bengt, 534
Sun Yat Sen (Suen Wen, Sun Wen), 127-8, 131, 536

Tagliacozzo, Enzo, 331
Tagliagambe, Silvano, 515
Taine, Hippolyte, 13, 51
Takahira, Kogoro, 203, 205
Talleyrand-Périgord, Charles-Maurice de, 72
Tangorra, Vincenzo, 163, 540
Taparelli, (Fr) Luigi (Prospero Taparelli D'Azeglio), 59, 529
Taramelli, (Fr) Onorio, 53
Tasca, Angelo, xviii, 521
Tennant, R. Hugh (Chairman, Westminster Bank), 266
Terlinden, Charles, 49
Thierry, Jacques-Nicolas-Augustin, 184, 545
Thiers, Marie-Joseph-Louis-Adolphe, 584
Tiepolo, Maria, 447, 581
Timpanaro, Sebastiano (Snr), 441, 580
Tittoni, Tommaso (*or* Verax), 40, 265, 552
Tiumeniev, A.I., lxxi, 517
Togliatti, Palmiro, xvii, lxxxi, 6-7, 410, 476, 509, 510, 515, 557, 559
Tolstoy, Lev (Leo) Nikolaevich, 118-9, 303, 402, 559, 576
Tommasini, Francesco, 201, 207, 547
Trombetti, Gustavo, xvi, 508
Trompeo, Pietro Paolo, 57
Trotsky, Lev Davidovich, 271, 524, 539, 553
Tucci, Giuseppe, 120-1
Turati, Filippo, 282, 550, 555
Turchi, Nicola, 9, 520
Turmel, (Abbé) Joseph, xxvi, 8, 94-8, 531-2

Name Index

Tyrrell, (Fr) George xxvi, 8, 80, 95, 530

Vailati, Giovanni, 183, 307-8, 560
Valitutti, Salvatore, 245-6, 550
Valois, Georges (Alfred-Georges Vessent), 459, 584
Vanini, Giulio Cesare Lucilio, 22
Varga, Eugen (Evgenii, Jeno) D. (*or* Samuilovich), 513
Veblen, Thorstein, 448-9
Vercesi, (Don) Ernesto, 43-4
Verga, Andrea, 50
Verne, Jules, 555
Vialatoux, Joseph, 92-3
Vico, Giambattista, lxviii, lxxx, 157, 349, 401, 462, 556, 568
Vigo, Pietro, 351
Villari, Rosario, 509
Viscardi, Antonio, 120, 535
Vitruvius, (Marcus Vitruvius Pollio), 319
Voloshinov, Valentin Nikolaevich, lxiii-lxiv, 516
Volpi, Giuseppe (Count of Misurata), 208
Volpicelli, Arnaldo, 437-8, 441, 446

Voltaire (François-Marie Arouet), 90, 448
Waldo (Valdo, Valdes) Peter, 120
Walras, Marie-Esprit-Léon, 542
Warburg, Paul, 208
Washburne, Carleton Wolsey, 140, 143, 537
Wells, Herbert George, 537
White, Hayden, 518
Whitrow, Gerald James, 517
Whorf, Benjamin L., lxv-lxvi, 516
Wieser, Friedrich von, 543
William I (King of the Netherlands), 49
Wilson, Woodrow, 1, 204
Windthorst, Ludwig, 109, 116, 534
Wittgenstein, Ludwig, xl-xli, lxiii, 512, 513

Yahya ibn-Mohammed Hamid (Yahya Mahmud Al-Mutawakkil), 210-3, 547

Zanardelli, Giovanni, 89, 531
Zeno (of Elea), 556
Zibordi, Giovanni, 446-7, 451
Zola, Emile, 586

SUBJECT AND KEY CONCEPT INDEX

abstraction, process of, xxxix, lxii, lxxvii, 166-8, 171-3, 293, 299, 304-5, 307, 341, 370, 427, 429, 432, 471
abstract-concrete movement (*see also* Ricardo, method of), xl-xliii, lxxxiii, 170, 313; – and axiomatisation of economics, xlii
academies (of higher education and learning), 145, 147, 440, 538
Action Française, xxvi, 8, 50, 77, 80-94, 98, 584
Action Party (left wing of Risorgimento forces), 40, 525
actualism (Gentilian actual idealism), lxxviii, 15, 63, 67, 301, 309, 331-2, 340, 344-5, 356, 364, 367, 369-70, 418, **435-62**, 474, 566, 570
Africa, 214-5, 262; North –, 136, 157, 539, 565
agriculture and agrarian factors, xxxviii, lxxii, 144, 153, 188, 194, 198, 227, 231-2, 234-7, 245-6, 248-50, 256, 352, 472, 509, 513, 535, 549-50; reform (or revolution), agrarian, 349, 352, 572; share-cropping, 188, 472, 548; *see also* peasantry
America, Central and South, 116-7, 187, 200, 202-4, 207-8, 466, 585
America (North and USA), xxxiv-xxxv, xliv-xlvi, xlviii-l, liii, 145, 195-7, 200-10, 213-4, 216, 219, 228, 230-1, 241-2, **254-60**, 262, 264-5, 434, 536, 563; duties and tariffs in –, 231-2; Monroe doctrine in –, 203; religion in –, 11, 13, 68, 110-2, 115-6, 259; Wall Street, 219, 260
Americanism, xlix, liii, 256-7, 434, 551
anti-clericalism, xxi, 27-8, 117, 208, 403, 409, 411, 418, 471, 473, 587
anti-Croce (and anti-Gentile), lxxii, 356, 365
anti-historicism and anti-history, lxxviii, 198, 270, 299, 336, 342, 374-5, 378-9, 381, 383, 459, 566
anti-semitism, 84, 104, 533
Arab world, xlv-xlvi, 137, 210-3, 293: *see also* civilisation
Aristotelianism, 93, 99, 410, 537
artisans, 12, 65, 236, 256, 321-2, 450, 452, 457-8, 520, 556
Asia, 196-8

base (Marx's metaphor): *see* structure
behaviour, economic, 167, 294; social –, 294
bloc, historical –, xi-xii, xv, liii, lx, lxiv, lxvi, 328, 332, 357, 360, 397, 400; – and structure-superstructure model, 397, 414; social –, xi-xii; *see also* hegemony
Bolsheviks, *see* Communist Party

Subject and Key Concept Index

and communists (Russian or Soviet)
bourgeoisie, xxi, xxxvi, lvi, lxx-lxxii, 19-20, 40, 159, 226, 235, 253, 265-6, 398, 457, 463, 550; petty –, 64, 117, 143, 189, 253, 263, 350, 559
Britain, xxxiii, xlvii-li,112-4, 195-202, 205-14, 257, **261-9**, 536, 546-7; emigration from –, 241-2; finances of –, 213-4, 262-5; industrial decline of –, l, 263; parliamentary politics in –, 267-8; world role of –, 266-7; British Empire, l, 197, 210, 213, 232-3, 261-2; British Association (for the Advancement of Science), 152, 538
Buddhism, 78, 124, 129-31

Calvinism, 11, 24, 91, 329, 389, 408, 523, 530, 533; predestination in –, 389, 573; *see also* grace, doctrine of
capital, xliv, xlvi-xlvii, 188, 208, 215, 218, 224, 230, 238, 242, 250, 263, 350, 429, 545; – goods, 434; – investment 237, 263; – formation, 215, 250; composition of –, 430; constant –, 221, 433; enterprise –, 244; finance –, l, 260; variable (human) –, 230, 240, 253; export of –, 266
capitalism, xlviii, 94, 134, 166, 169, 173, 238, 244, 250, 256, 262, 266, 319, 429, 432, 456, 541, 548, 585
capitalists, 166, 168, 172, 264, 545; *see also* industrialists, bourgeoisie
catharsis, 343-4, 353, 567
Catholic Action (organisation), xxii-xxiii, 28-44, 48-50, 70, 77, 81, 100, 117, 525, 527; – in Austria, 107; – in France, 105-7; – in Germany, 107-10, 533; – in USA, 110-2

Catholic Centre (Popular Party dissidents), 98, 532
Catholic Church or religion and Catholics, xxi, xxv-xxvii, xxxi, 4-8 **8-102**, 104-19, 128-9, 134, 147, 156, 198, 253, 270-1, 339-40, 352, 359, 398, 401, 403, 407, 410-2, 440, 443-4, 451, 454, 464-5, 468-70, 473, 523, 533, 547, 569, 585; – and conservatism, xxi, xxvii, 40-2, 570; – as idolatrous, 55; bishops and hierarchy within –, xxiii, 27, 30, 34, 65-6, 82, 85, 87, 96-7, 108-9, 123, 134, 333; general doctrines of –, 72-4, 97-8, 118, 442; general tendencies in –, xxv-xxvii, 4-5, 37, 44, 80, 98, 120; laity in –, xxiv, 27-8, 33-4, 36, 47-8, 67, 77, 86, 88, 90, 411; role of – in Middle Ages, 10, 76, 119-20, 520; later role of –, 29, 34, 62-3, 93, 523; religious orders in –, 33, 38, 71, 80, 85, 340, 567; right, left and centre in –, **76-102**; Sacred Congregation of the Council of –, 85, 454; social doctrines of –, 6, 31, 35, 45-50, 127-8, 524, 536; structural features of –, 15-6, 65-7, 82-3, 133, 334, 473-4; *see also* Catholicism; Church; Code, Social (of Malines); Index; Jesuitism; integralism; Inquisition; modernism; *non expedit* decree
Catholicism, democratic tendencies in –, 27, 34-5, 40, 50, 65, 77, 90, 472; liberal – (*see also* Guelphs), 27, 37-8, 40-1, 407, 463, 472-3, 525, 567, 587; other tendencies in –, 38-9, 117, 135, 352, 403; – in Belgium, 49, 76; – in Britain, 112; – in China, 127-8; – in France (*see also* Action Française), 22, 46-7, 76, 89, 91, 95-6, 359, 531; – in India,

Subject and Key Concept Index

117; – in Japan, 129; – in South America, 116-7, 207-8, 547; – in USA, 68, 110-2
catholicity, 113, 534
centralism, 'organic', 15-6, 94
Centre Party (*Zentrumspartei*) in Germany, 108-9, 534
China, 123-8, 130, 196, 201, 203, 205-8, 262; national movements and rebellions in –, 126-8, 205, 207, 536
Christian Democrats: – in Italy (at beginning of twentieth century), 7, 35, 473, 587; – elsewhere, 50, 81, 90, 454
Christianity (and Christians or Christendom), 4, 44, 68, 93, 118, 127, 129-35, 290, 293, 340, 475, 522, 568; origins and early spread of –, 18, 119, 130; radical social trends in –, 50-5, 119-20, 528, 534; primitive –, 24, 34, 93, 96, 119-20
Church, – and science, 20-2, 74-5, 410-1, 522; – and state, xx, xxiii,, xxv, 17-9, **59-76**, 106, 117, 127-8, 354, 443, 529-30, 565-6, 569, 571; – as institution, **8-19**; history and teachings of –, 21-2, 43-4, 77, 82, 106; Orthodox –, 113-4
Churchmen, 334, 565
city-countryside relation, xxv, lxvi, 164, 234-7, 540
civilisation(s), lxiii, lxv-lxvi, 55, 122-3, 133, 157-9, 196, 239, 253, 256-8, 273, 276, 307, 309, 344, 401-2, 466, 562; ancient –, 119, 130; Arab –, 137, 293, 537; eastern and western –, 82; economic and industrial –, 226, 241; 'new' –, 270-4; North African –, 136; western, European and modern –, 117, 122-3, 133, 136-7, 199, 340, 355, 361, 469, 475; – and intellectuals, 258; renewal of –, 405;

wars of –, 333; *see also* Greece, Rome
class (social group, mass) and classes: xii, xxxi, xliii, liii, lxiv-lxv, lxxvii, lxxix, 10, 35, 158-9, 179, 183, 219-20, 222, 234, 238-9, 274-5, 348, 350, 352, 375, 386, 402, 412-3, 416, 464, 539, 581, 586; political – (Mosca), 272; *see also* artisans; bourgeoisie; feudal rulers; industrialists; landowners; parasitic classes; peasantry; ruling classes; serfs; subaltern classes
classicism, 373-4
cleavage, spirit of (Sorelian), 156, 389
clergy, xxviii, 4, 9-13, 16, 19, 26, 35, 53, 61, 63-6, 71, 77, 86, 108, 121, 134, 270, 440, 565.; – as caste, 16, 333; – as intellectuals, **8-19**; *see also* Churchmen
Code, Social (of Malines), 31, 35, 46, 48-50, 128, 524
Cokaygne (*or* Cockaygne), Land of, 55, 185, 226, 295, 545
colonies and colonialism, xlvi, 157-9, 198, 202, 214, 234, 237-9, 241-2, 256, 262, 524, 545
commodities and goods, xl-xli, 169, 221-2, 224, 226-7, 229, 233-4, 238, 262-3, 266, 428, 431, 542; labour as –, 183
Commune, medieval Italian –, xxv, 19-20; Paris –, 405, 459, 527, 584
communism and communists, xxi, lxxv, 173, 194, 452, 456, 466, 528, 536, 569, 583, 585
Communist Party and communists (Italian), xviii, xxiii-xxv, xxxiii, lii, lxxxi, lxxxiv, 162, 514-5, 519, 549, 585
Communist Party and communists (Russian or Soviet), lxiv, lii-liii, 529, 553
Concordat, – and Treaty between Vatican and Italy, xxiii, xxxi, 7,

Subject and Key Concept Index 603

59-63, 67, 69-74, 436, 443, 464-5, 474, 530; – in general, xxiii, **59-76**
conformism, cultural –, 301; social –, xi, xxxiv, li-lii, 194, 269-71, 273-6, 522, 574; – between philosophy and mode of conduct, xxii, 383-4, 386, 390, 396, 574
conformity, to ends, 283, 405
Confucianism, 124, 130
consciousness, xv, xx, xxix, lxxx, 15, 102-4, 119, 127, 131, 299, 409, 451, 577, 582; collective –, 16, 156; critical –, 270, 351; Italian national –, 102-4; moral and social –, 345, 348, 567; political and legal –, 561; proletarian – of historic mission, 405; self-consciousness, xlix, 310, 313, 438, 451, 560
consent, lxxix, 16-7, 344, 357, 380, 396, 399, 446, 575
Conservative Party (British), 200, 267, 534
'Conspiracy of the Equals' (of Babeuf), 455-6, 583
consumption, xlvii, 215-6, 224, 226, 229-30, 252
contradictions (in Marxist sense), xliv, 277, 395-6, 416, 426, 428-31, 562
cosmopolitanism, 220, 253, 334, 469, 536; Catholic and religious –, 104, 134, 401, 536; medieval –, 254, 314; Roman –, 83, 254, 314; modern –, 253-4
costs, comparative, 169-70, 234, 510, 542
Councils (of Roman Catholic Church), – of Basel, 23, 523; – of Constance, 6, 23; – of Trent (Trentino), 24, 83, 340; First Vatican –, 6
Counter-Reformation (Catholic), 10, 19-21, 23-4, 270, 466, 575; Counter-Reformation and Reformation, **19-28**
crisis, xxviii, xliv, xlvii-xlviii, 133, 180-2, 217-9, 224, 231, 236, 239, 263, 265, 269, 276-7, 321, 434, 457, 549, 583; – in Marxism, 406; – of authority, 399; – of over-production and under-consumption, 215, 236; general –, 219-21, 234, 237, 535, 547; social –, 121, 216, 218, 231, 263; world economic –, xlvi-xlviii, **215-29**, 193, 237, 241, 268
Crocean aesthetics, lxx, lxxvi, lxxx, 337, 344, 374, 402, 470-1, 586
Crocean concept of religion, xxii, lxx, lxxix, 329, 338-41, 352-3, 377, 383-4, 390, 406-8, 465, 470, 577
Crocean (philosophical) idealism, lxvi-lxvii, lxxii-lxxiv, lxxvii, lxxx-lxxxi, 24, 300, 327-8, 331, 337-40, 344-5, 351, 355-7, 364, 366-7, 369, 396, **370-403**, 408, 412-5, 444, 470, 542, 573, 580; – and reality or realism, lxxii, lxxiv, 331, 337-8, 356, 366, 369, 413; – as methodology of historiography, lxix, lxxix, 300; category of the spirit in –, lxxvi-lxxvii, 171, 174, 186, 371, 389, 400, 575; Gramsci's youthful –, lxxii, 355; Hegelianism and –, lxviii, 372; instrumental value of –, 332, 357; Marxism and –, lxviii, lxx-lxxi, lxxiii-lxxiv, lxxvii, lxxx, 369, 518; origin of –, 370; science in –, 410; *see also* anti-Croce; error, philosophical doctrines of
Croce's general cultural, scientific and philosophical activity, stance, etc., lxix, 149, **328-61**, 328, 333, 340, 375, 395, 399, 418, 444, 447, **462-75**; role as 'secular' pope, 469-70, 475
Croce's economics, lxxvii, 162; – as category of the spirit, lxxvi-

604 Subject and Key Concept Index

lxxvii, 171, 174, 186, 371, 394, 402, 419, 427-8

Croce's ethical and moral position, lxix, lxxvi, 333, 337-8, 352, 372-3, 471, 475

Croce's historiography and concept of history, xxii, lxix-lxx, lxxiii-lxxiv, lxxvi, lxxix, lxxxi, 20, 327, 330, 332, 335-6, 341, 344, 353, 357, 360, 366, 372, 377, 380, 382, 385, 444, 467, 471; concept of liberty in –, lxxiii, 327, 396, 517-8

Croce's literary activity and style, lxix, 328, 333, 337-8, 374, 470

Croce's 'minor writings', lxix, 326, 338, 367, 394, 408, 463, 470

Croce's ideological, political and practical stance, lxvii-lxxii, 327-8, 334, 349, 372-3, 389-90, 418, 444, 447, 463, 468, 470, 573, 580

Croce's revision of Marxism and polemics with the philosophy of praxis (historical materialism), lxix-lxxi, lxxvii, 328, 330-31, 334-6, 347, 352-4, 356-7, 364, 369, 379, 390, 394, **403-35**, 451-2, 464, 471, 578, 584

culture, xiii-xiv, xxx, xlix, lxv-lxvi, 43-4, 105, 123-5, 147, 151, 198, 257, 261, 276, 279, 284, 292, 301, 315-6, 323-4, 330, 332-4, 336, 344-5, 357, 402, 417, 423, 435, 439-41, 443-4, 451, 460, 463, 469-70, 472, 474; eastern –, 137, 535; European or western –, lxxii, 119, 123, 328, 336, 345, 348, 379, 407-8, 459, 474, 536; expansion of – as ethico-political moment of history, 330, 349, 400; integral – (of philosophy of praxis), 355; mass –, 385; national –, 147, 153-4, 307-15, 328, 338, 344, 375, 444, 459, 474; organisation of –, 145-8, 152-7; political –, 436;

popular –, 51, 418; religious, 64, 410; scientific – and speculative –, 368; secular –, 24, 64, 68, 411

currency: *see* money

democracy, lxxi, 10, 82, 84, 90, 92, 98, 132, 404-5, 418, 439, 452, 536, 566, 580, 587

determinism, xxix, 15, 179-80

dialectic, xxxii, xxxix, xliii, lxxviii, 23, 158-9, 271, 299-301, 323, 329, 332, 342-3, 351, 354-5, 357, 371-2, 374, 376-9, 381-2, 388-9, 396, 400, 406, 452, 461-2, 512, 558, 563, 570, 584; – as logic of motion, 297; – as understood by Risorgimento 'moderates', lxxviii-lxxix, 342; – of conservation and innovation (i.e. reformism), 374; Crocean – in general, lxvii, lxxvi, lxxviii, 329, 369, 375, 570; Crocean – and system of distincts, xli, lxxvi-lxxviii, 299-301, 344, 369-71, 399, 414, 446, 468, 543, 571, 575; Hegelian –, 343, 375, 455, 512, 570, 573, 583; idealist –, lxxii-lxxiii, 158-9, 396, 441, 570; – in historical becoming, nature, real systems etc., lxxv, 376, 394, 396, 413, 432-3; *see also* contradictions, unity

discipline, 159, 274, 277, 391, 522; – and order, 17, 576

East, 'Far –', xxviii-xxix, 123, 201, 203, 205-7, 509, 262; 'Middle –', 133-4, 197, 201, 210-3, 262, 475; – and West, lxxxiii, 23, 82, 130, 197-9, 320, 520, 531

economic-corporative aspect (as opposed to hegemonic), 164, 217, 257, 260, 343, 400, 474

economic forces, factors, relations, 277, 345, 358, 373, 388, 399-400, 423-4, 427; – as aspect of hegemony, xxxiv

Subject and Key Concept Index   605

economics, 45, 294, 305, 308, 315, 350, 371, 386, 393-4, 396-7, 402, 415, 419, 423, 426, 428-9, 435, 439, 443, 448, 450; – and the economy, xlv-liii, lxxi, **193-277**; – as economic science, xxxiii-xlv, **162-90**; history of economic science, xxxiv, xxxv-xxxvii, 163-5, 178, 541; methods of –, 165-6, 173-4, 179, 185; national and international trends in –, **230-54**; nature of –, xlii-xliii, 174-5, 179; classical economy, xli, 162, 164, 168-9, 179-80, 186, 196, 198, 234, 315, 350, 370-1, 427, 510, 541, 544, 563; command – ('regulated' or 'planned' –), xi, 180, 237, 277, 350; critical (Marxist) –, xxxiv, xlii, 162, 165-6, 168-9, 171-2, 175-80, 184, 419, 422-3, 425-8, 431, 433, 541, 543; political –, xx, xxxiii-xxxv, xxxix, 184, 305, 429, 559, 562; vulgar (marginalist, liberal, neo-classical, 'political' or 'pure') –, xxxiv, xxxvii-xxxviii, xli-xliii, 166, 168-9, 171-6, 178, 183-4, 225, 308, 426-7, 435-6, 510, 541-3, 574; *see also* capital; costs, comparative; Croce's economics; equilibium, economic; exploitation; fascism, corporativism within; hedonism; mercantilism; ophelimity; physiocrats; structure (as hidden god)

economism, 332, 357-8, 583; historical –, 420, 422-4

ecumenical movement, Christian, 8, 113-6

education, xxix-xxxiv, 19, 72-5, 131, **139-59**, 128, 259, 377, 408, 427, 450, 453, 464-5, 467, 524, 531, 539, 567, 580, 585; – and force, 157; – and hegemony, xxix, 156-7; – and spontaneity, xxix, 140; adult –, xxxii, 138; Church control of –, 63-5, 72-3, 529; class system of – in Italy, 143-4; Dalton (and Montessori) system of –, 141-2, 537; religious –, xxxi, 72-4, 111, 158, 339, 353, 409; *see also* academies, schools, universities

emigration, (and immigration), 117, 203, 205, 224, 230, 235, 238-42, 249, 257

encyclicals, papal, and papal letters, ix, 28, 35-6, 100-1, 110, 527: *Ad beatissimi*, 85, 531; *Immortale Dei*, 128; *Mirari vos*, xxvi, 5, 99, 525; *Mortalium animos*, 113; *Notre charge apostolique*, 530; *Pascendi dominici gregis*, 7, 79, 84, 96, 99, 530, 532, 558-9, 472, 587; *Quadragesimo Anno*, 100, 112, 532; *Quanta cura*, 99, 532, 569; *Quod apostolici muneris*, 528; *Rappresentanti in terra*, 530; *Rerum novarum*, 43, 100, 112, 128, 526; *Singulari nos*, 5, 525

Enlightenment and illuminist trends, 11, 38, 132, 260, 355, 390

epistemology (and gnoseology), lxi, 280, 296, 410, 413, 577

equilibrium, economic, xlii, 169, 215, 221, 308, 542

error, philosophical doctrines of, 331, 339, 342, 353, 356, 411, 413-7, 420-1

ethic, national, 329, 341

ethico-political, – activity, 339, 343; – form and socio-economic content, 360; – historiography, 367, 382; – history, lxvi, lxx, 17, 328-30, 332, 335-6, 343-6, 343, 348-50, 357-8, 360, 399-400, 568, 571; – history as canon of historical research, 332, 357; – principle, 358-9; – unity, 466

ethics (or morals and morality),

124, 277, 300, 308, 329, 333, 337, 345, 352, 366, 383-4, 386, 388, 390, 395-6, 400, 420, 443, 450, 468, 568, 574
Europe (or countries within), 195-201, 203, 214, 216, 232-3, 237, 259, 330, 348-52, 356, 377, 546-7, 549; eastern and south-eastern –, 214, 235, 237, 336; Nordic –, 114, 197, 204, 262, 546-7; *see also* Britain, France, Germany
evolutionism, 158, 293, 411, 420, 448, 461
exploitation, xxxviii, xliv, 234-5, 246, 511, 535, 585

Fabian Society, xxxii
factory, – movement in Turin, xxiv, xxxiii, 40, 458; – system, 237, 276, 321-2, 430-4, 443, 557
facts (data), nature of, liv, lvi-lviii, lxxvii, 283-4, 287-9, 291, 293-4, 316, 394-5, 402, 415, 417, 428, 576
fascism (Italian), xxvii, xxxi, liii, lxix, lxxi, lxxv, 7, 73, 208-9, 349-50, 452, 465-6, 527, 537, 546, 549-50, 553-4, 557, 559, 564, 570, 579-80, 585; corporativism within –, 162, 277, 350, 382, 474, 544, 573, 587
fetishism, 14-5, 17, 282, 403, 451
feudal rulers, 10, 19, 132, 134, 164, 166, 208, 349, 576
Feuerbach, Marx's theses (or 'glosses')on –, 311, 382, 384-5, 414, 424, 439, 461, 560-1, 578-9; *see also* praxis, 'overturning of'
force and forces, – as opposed to consent, lxxix, 17, 399-400, 444-5, 566, 572, 581; – as material factor, xx, 294, 330, 373, 444-5; – as factor of hegemony, lxx; – in physical sciences, lvii; – of innovation, 374-5; – of state, 580-1; coercive –, xxix, liii, 159, 350, 372, 400, 444-5, 580-1; material and moral –, lxxix, 119, 568, 581; physical –, 393, 444-5, 581; political –, 391; social and political –, liii, 39, 75, 234, 349, 377, 393, 427, 462, 464, 474, 583; *see also* economic forces
Fordism, xxxiv, xxxv, xliv-xlv, xlix-li, liii, 256, 433-5, 551
France, xxxix, lxv, 115, 118, 195, 197-9, 201-2, 205-6, 208-9, 232-3, 237, 257, 260, 265-6, 310-3, 330, 334, 342, 349, 356, 359, 547, 560; religion and right-wing politics in –, 76, 80-96; Catholicism or Catholic Action in –, 22-3, 26, 50, 76, 105-7; *see also* Conspiracy of the Equals; Revolution, French
freedom (liberty), lxxi, lxxiii-lxxiv, 17, 49, 142-3, 179, 198-9, 274-5, 277, 310, 312, 327, 330, 350-4, 359, 376, 380, 393-4, 396, 464-7, 473, 567-9, 575, 580, 587; – and authority, 351-2, 354, 358; – of individuals and classes, 464; degrees of – (for Croce), 396
freemasonry, 11, 75, 79, 84, 89, 117, 359, 403, 409, 447, 472, 538, 566, 581-2
Freudianism, 273-4, 448, 452-3

geo-politics, **195-215**
Germany (and German empire and Reich), 60-1, 69, 76, 83, 91, 99, 107-10, 114, 149, 195, 197-9, 201, 204, 213, 233, 237, 240, 242, 257, 268-9, 310-3, 318, 330, 334, 338, 341, 356, 450, 458, 546-7, 560, 583; workers' movement in –, 382, 384, 401, 561; *see also* Hitlerism, *Kulturkampf*
Ghibellines (pro-Emperor faction), 20, 38
goods, *see* commodities

Subject and Key Concept Index   607

governors and governed, 15-16, 154, 157, 218, 333, 359, 395
grace, doctrine of –, 11, 58, 271, 329, 389, 533; – as 'objective conditions', 569
Gramsci, Antonio, *passim*; autobiograpical note of –, lxxxiv-lxxxvii
Greece and Greeks (ancient), 125, 313-5, 355, 536
Guelphs and neo-Guelphs (propapacy faction), 20, 38-40, 341-2, 472, 525-6, 567

hedonism, economic postulate of, 170-1, 173-4, 308, 448, 542-3
Hegelianism, lxvi, lxxii, 258, 313, 318, 339, 341-3, 351, 355, 371-2, 375, 384-7, 409, 419-20, 456, 458, 472, 512, 520, 539, 551, 561, 567, 570; *see also* dialectic; rational and actual
hegemon, xi, 118, 535
hegemony, xii, xv, xxiii, xxv, xxix, xxxi, xxxiv-xxxv, xlvii, li-lii, lxiv, lxvi, lxx, 4, 19-20, 39, 60, 75, 80, 123, 139, 154-60, 208, 232, 247, 253, 255, 276, 306, 328-9, 332, 343, 345, 349-51, 357-9, 395-6, 399, 412, 418, 439, 474, 536, 538, 549, 561, 575; – and civil society, lii, 75, 372, 514; –, consent and the historical bloc, liii, 332, 357; – of Britain, 263; – of Europe, 201; – of finance capital, 208-9; – of northern Italy, 39, 240, 247; – of philosophy of praxis, 418; – of proletariat, liii, 247; – of USA, xlvi, xlix-l, 196-7, 207, 514; – of West, 82; economic aspects of –, li-liii, 266, 514; ethico-political history and –, lxvi, lxx, 329, 343, 345; hegemonic states, 223, 233
Hinduism, 117, 121-2, 535
historicism, xxxviii, lxxiii-lxxiv, 159, 188, 304, 372, 374-5, 381, 401, 436; – of idealists and moderates, 159, 304, 330, 375; Croce's –, lxxiii, 331, 348, 354, 364, 369, 373-7, 381, 436; Gramsci's and realist ('real') –, lxxiv-lxxv, 306, 330, 348, 355, 374
historicity (sense of transience), Crocean –, 396; Gramsci's –, lxxxi; – and philosophy of praxis, 347-8; – of ideology, philosophy and superstructures, 346, 384-6, 395-6, 398, 412-3; – of languages, 304; – of natural sciences, lvi, lviii, 293
Historic Right (in later nineteenth-century Italy), lxviii, lxxix, 250, 349, 564, 567; *see also* moderates
historiography, xxii, xxvi, 316, 332, 335, 341-2, 346, 357, 397, 423, 562; – of the moderates, 342; *see also* Croce's historiography
history (historical life, movement or reality), xxxix, liii, lxxiii-lxxiv, lxxxiii, 17-9, 44-5, 63, 119, 172, 184, 222-3, 239, 294, 300, 305, 308, 318, 323, 325, 327, 329-30, 332, 337-8, 342, 344, 346-50, 353, 357-60, 372, 374-9, 381-3, 385-7, 395, 400-1, 409-10, 413, 416-7, 428, 442-4, 446, 453, 456, 461, 467-8, 541, 558, 562-3, 572; – and mind, 330, 351-4, 569; – and philosophy, 346, 382-3, 385, 387, 401, 441, 446; – and politics, 373, 382-3, 417; as – of hegemonic states, 223; as – of the intellectuals, 370; as – of liberty, lxxiii-lxxiv, 351, 358; as – of ruling classes, 223; – as ensemble of material conditions, 416; – as process, 276, 294, 329, 338, 343-4, 376, 424, 568; – as rationality, lxxiii, 337; – created by ethico-political activity, 339; – of Europe, 330,

348-50, 358, 571; – of ideas, 449, 459; – of philosophy, 310, 313, 385, 401; dialectical process in –, lxxv, 456; forces of –, 317; formal –, 370; laws of –, lxxiii-lxxv, 456; partial or extrinsic – and integral –, 332, 358-9; periods of –, 123, 456; preconceptualised view of –, lxxiv, 342, 376-7, 472, 572; religious –, xxviii, 93, 96, 130, 346, 430, 568, 571; speculative –, 358, 360; theory or science of –, 328, 335, 414, 419, 517-8, 572, 578; *see also* Crocean historiography; economics, history of; ethico-political history; identity (of history and politics); philosophy
Hitlerism, 83, 91, 534
homo oeconomicus (economic man), xli, lxxvii, 166-8, 172, 194, 305, 370, 426-7, 544
humanism, 313-4, 347, 561; *see also* Marxism
humanity (as biological species), xxix-xxx, xxxii, lix-lx, 93, 135, 166, 172, 285, 287, 290-3, 295, 314, 320-1, 343, 351, 387-8, 392, 395-6, 401, 409-10, 414, 438, 442, 456, 461, 473, 577; *see also* man
hypothesis, scientific, lvi-lviii, 166, 168, 293-4, 426-8, 432

idea, absolute –, lxxiii-lxxv, 563
idealism, xxxi, lxvii, lxx, lxxii, lxxiv, 24, 27, 74, 282, 300, 306, 339-40, 388, 408, 443, 564; – and science, lxi, 280, 286-7, 289, 292, 299-300, 329-30, 339-40, 345, 410, 438, 443, 453, 461, 579; – as highest degree of liberty, 396; – as subjective concept of reality, 292,, 306, 345, 347-8, 370, 413; – and superstructures, 413; *see also* actualism, Crocean idealism, philosophy, solipsism
identity, – of history and philosophy, 382-3, 385, 387, 401, 441; – of history and politics, 382-3, 417; – of politics and philosophy, 382; – of philosophy and ideology (or Crocean concept of religion), 383-4; *see also* philosophy; unity (of politics and philosophy)
ideology, xiv, xxix, xxxi, lxiv, lxxix, 15-6, 34, 155-6, 171, 217, 219, 223, 290-1, 293-4, 303, 316, 327, 330, 333, 343, 349-51, 353, 374, 376-7, 382-3, 388-90, 394-9, 407, 413-4, 444, 446-7, 451, 459, 463, 466-7, 471, 474, 528, 571; – and consciousness, 451; – as ensemble of the superstructures, 413; – of capitalism, 271; Catholic social doctrine as –, 46; scientific ideologies, **286-95**; *see also* philosophy, science
immanentism (and immanence), xxii, xxix, xxxix, 74, 99, 323, 347, 371-2, 374, 382, 384, 443, 469, 471-2, 512; – in Hegel, 372, 532
impoverishment, increasing (theory of), 457, 583
Index (Catholic, of Banned Books), 8, 22, 329, 411, 523, 532
India, xxviii, 117-24, 196, 201, 206, 262
industrialists, entrepreneurs etc., xxi, xlvii-xlviii, 35, 49, 122, 168-9, 172, 186, 227-8, 231, 246, 255-6, 264, 398, 430-1, 434, 436, 452, 457-8, 474, 539, 570, 587
industry, industrialism, 13, 145, 153, 198, 201, 221, 224-6, 230-1, 234-7, 240-1, 243, 248, 255-6, 263, 266, 319, 321-2, 434, 513, 550-1; – in northern Italy, 240; big –, 236, 245-6, 249-51, 255-6, 321-2; industrialised nations, 194, 235

Subject and Key Concept Index 609

Inquisition, Catholic (Congregation of the Holy Office), 22, 80, 94-5, 105, 352, 411, 445, 458, 523, 526, 530, 533, 564
instincts, 448-9, 582
integralism (Catholic), xxvi, 5-8, 37, 76-82, 84-9, 91, 94-5, 98, 100, 102, 104, 525-6, 530-1
intellectual and moral factors, xxxii, 28, 64, 151-2, 277, 317-8, 353; – in Croce, 333; – for Gentile, 587
intellectual and moral reform, xxii, lxii, lxiv, lxvi, 24-7, 36, 131-2, 280, 315, 336, 406, 408, 533, 574; *see also* philosophy of praxis
intellectuals, xx, lxvi, lxxii, 4-5, 13, 27, 121-4, 129, 135, 139, 157, 189, 199, 257-8, 260, 276, 300, 314, 317-8, 329, 333-4, 337, 339-40, 343, 352-3, 358, 370, 377, 379-81, 390, 402-3, 405-8, 438, 459-60, 467, 469-70, 514, 535-6, 554, 566, 572, 586; bourgeois –, 459; caste and secular –, 63-4; class position of –, 586; clergy as –, 4, **8-19**, 26, 63-4, 121; cosmopolitan –, 469, 536; French democratic-revolutionary –, 90; Italian Renaissance –, 21-2, 314, 469; new (Marxist) –, 124, 253; organic and technical –, 241, 257; 'pure' –, 460; revolutionary –, 458-9; subaltern –, 65-6; traditional or great –, xlix, 121-4, 141, 253, 257-8, 332, 357, 411, 586; intellectual factors and life, 143, 357
International, First, 351, 528; Third (Communist) –, xxiv, lii, 118, 515, 553, 560, 585; Peasant – (Krestintern, of Third –), xxiv, 585
internationalism, 220, 253-4
inventions, *see* progress, technical

irrationalism and irrationality, 374-5, 577; Bergsonian –, 342
Ireland: Northern –, li, 267-8; sweepstake in –, 58
Islam, xxvii-xxviii, 23, 78, 129, 132-6, 210-3, 475, 536
Islamic movements: Maraboutism, 136; Sanusiya (Sufi brotherhood), 211-2, 548; Sufism, 135-6, 537, 548; Wahabites, 134, 211-2, 537; Zeidi (or Zaydi) Shi'ite sect, 213, 548

Jacobinism and Jacobins, lxiv, 17, 334, 341, 349, 375, 450, 455, 458-9, 572, 583; – as Jesuits of the revolution, 583
Jansenism, 11, 59, 77, 91, 340, 389, 533
Japan, 125, 195, 203, 205-8, 242, 251-2, 475, 536
Jesuits and Jesuitism, lxii, 7, 21, 24, 27-8, 39, 46-8, 59, 79-82, 84-6, 88-91, 94-5, 97-104, 106, 116-7, 121-3, 128-9, 134, 139, 208, 340, 352, 410-1, 466, 471-2, 529, 533, 535-6, 567, 585; – as representative of 'centre' tendency in Catholic Church, 4-5, 7, 77-8, 80, 98
Jews (Jewry or Judaism), 30, 68, 79, 93, 261, 286, 424, 439, 533, 537, 578; – and Italian national consciousness, 102-4; *see also* Feuerbach, Marx's theses on
Josephism, 43, 526
Kulturkampf, 60, 117, 208, 442, 471, 529

labour, – as activity or process, xxxviii-xxxix, lxxvii, 164-5, 169, 171, 183, 185-6, 227-9, 238, 246, 295, 409-10, 419, 433-4, 452, 559, 582; – force and human – power, 183, 238, 240, 253-4, 256, 320-1; compulsory – (*corvée, obbligato* etc.) 188,

472, 546; division and organisation of –, 64, 146, 169, 221, 236, 239, 269, 520; industrial and mental –, 141, 145; productivity of –, 227-8; socially necessary –, xxxviii-xxxix, 169, 430-1, 510-1, 543; surplus –, 185; *see also* workers
Labour Party and labourism (British), xviii, 112-3, 187-8, 209, 263, 534, 552; Belgian –, 450
landowners, 12, 98, 235, 250, 473
language, lxi-lxvi, xl-xliii, 140, 292, 303-4, 312, 428, 516; – as expression of national-popular conception, 147-8, 156; – of civilisations or cultures, 307-8, 313, 562; French political –, 307, 309-13, 560; German philosophical –, 307, 309-13, 560; historicist (i.e. Marxist) –, 343; metaphor and –, lxi-lxiv, 289-90, 315, 346, 426, 567
languages, artificial –, 303, 559; philosophical and/or scientific –, 304, 390; technical/scientific –, 182-3, 308-9; – as descriptions of world, 308; *see also* translation and translatability
law (jurisprudence and justice), 17-18, 46, 71, 75, 220, 225, 245, 272-3, 312, 314, 316, 394, 396-8, 415, 423, 437, 450, 457-8, 475, 522, 530, 549, 554, 561-2, 566, 580, 586-7; divine –, 53-4; 'special' laws, 230, 549, 553, 581
laws (as expression of regularity), 179, 189-90, 275, 284, 290; – of evolution, 94; – of society, 426; – of relative surplus value, 432; – of social average of labour, 430; – of supply and demand, 255; – of tendency of rate of profit to fall, xxxviii, xliii-xlv, liii, lxxiv-lxxv, 419, 425, **428-35**, 542, 545; natural and rational –,

398; 'sociological –', 284, 555; tendential –, xxxviii-xxxix, xliii-xlv, 429, 432, 544
liberal democracy, lxix, 40, 83, 325, 463
liberalism (and liberals), xlvi, lxxi, lxxiv, 12, 27, 29, 36-7, 39-41, 49, 81, 85, 87, 91-2, 98, 159, 224-5, 247, 274, 294, 312, 341, 349, 351-3, 359, 376, 380, 406-7, 415, 423, 462-4, 470, 473, 529, 529, 554, 561, 567, 570, 573, 577, 580, 587; economic and political –, 396; Gobetti's –, 464; radical – (or spontaneity), 583
liberty, *see* freedom
literati, xlix, 285, 301, 407, 428
logic, xxxii, xlii, lv, lxii, lxxvi, 124-5, 166, 173-4, 280, 282, 290, 292, **295-305**, 312-3, 343, 359, 371, 445, 536, 541; – of fields of scientific research, lxxv, 175, 185, 282; – of philosophy, 371, 410; formal –, 296-300, 304-5, 441, 557-8; history of –, 298; popular –, 303, 559; sophist –, 185, 290, 441
'Lorianism', 563
Lutheranism and Lutherans, 10, 23-4, 113, 407-8, 523, 576

machines, **319-22**, 259, 433
Macmillan Report (on Finance and Industry), xlvii, 193, 548
Malthusianism, 89, 468, 586
man, economic –, *see* homo oeconomicus; biological –, *see* nature, human; humanity
man, – as individual, xxix, 43, 402, 437, 439, 464, 580, 587; biological –, 170, 172; collective or social –, xxxiv, li, 156, 194, **269-74**, 276, 439, 464, 554; Guicciardinian –, 374, 469-70, 572
markets, xlii, 169, 181, 183, 231, 249, 251, 256, 513; determinate

Subject and Key Concept Index

–, x-xi, xxxviii, xlii, 163, 171-2, 180, 183, 187, 507, 544; financial and stock –, 228, 252, 260, 265-6; foreign and world –, 163, 232-3, 236, 247, 252, 263, 266

Marxism (and Marxists), xiv, lxx, lxxxiii, 258, 280-1, 294, 404, 419-20, 449, 451-4, 456-7, 519, 541, 563, 565-6, 574; – as humanism, 313-4, 561; – as ideology), 571; as – theory of contradictions, 395; Bukharin's positivist –, xiv, lxvii, 279; Frankfurt School of –, lv-lvi, lxxxiii, 515; Gramsci's –, lxvii; revisionist currents in –, lxviii, 328, 335, 451; western –, lxxxiii, 519; *see also* Croce's revision of Marxism; materialism, historical; philosophy of praxis

materialism, historical –, x, xxxiii, lii, lxxiii-lxxiv, 24, 124, 184, 189, 271, 328, 335, 354, 360, 364, 369, 378, 382, 388, 415, 418, 443, 539, 545, 563, 571, 574-5, 577; – or philosophy of praxis as interpretative canon of history, 335, 358, 419-20, 423-5; war of –, 336, 418, 446, 566, 577; *see also* Marxism, philosophy of praxis

materialism, philosophical, 388, 394, 412, 415, 453; abstract, metaphysical (contemplative) and vulgar –, lx, 134, 171, 316, 373, 385, 395, 574; *see also* philosophy, French materialist

mechanicism, 15, 158, 307, 329, 332, 357, 407, 451-2, 461

mercantilism (economic doctrine), xxxvi, 163-4, 540; modern forms of –, 234

metaphysics, xxix, lxi, lxxiii, 99, 125, 292, 297, 300, 330, 346-8, 369, 398, 410, 443, 456, 586

Middle Ages, 10, 17, 137, 407, 469, 537

middle classes, 66, 122, 226, 240-1, 253, 272, 350, 457, 549, 552

mind, human, 330, 351, 358, 562; *see also* spirit, human

moderates and moderatism (right wing of Risorgimento forces), 39-40, 312, 329, 341-3, 374-5, 520, 561, 572

modernisation, xlviii, 243; economic –, 198

modernism (Catholic), xxv-xxvi, 5-8, 27-8, 77-80, 84-5, 94-100, 102, 334, 340, 471-3, 530-1, 559, 565, 586-7

money, xxxix, xlvi-xlviii, 221-2, 230-1, 252, 263-7, 553

movement and end (in Bernstein), 461-2

Muslims, *see* Islam

myth (in Sorel), 389-90, 433

nationalism, xxviii, 13, 83-4, 93, 116-7, 119, 126-8, 134, 220, 224, 253, 256, 262, 334, 341, 359, 463, 536; – as religion, 359-60; Arab –, 210-3; economic –, 222, 224, 230, 232, 234-5, 238, 245, 548; French –, 253, 359

nationalisation, 244-5, 524

national-popular, 256, 561, 572

naturalism, *see* Marxism as humanism

nature, xxix, liv, lx, 126, 130, 165, 283, 285, 292, 295, 313, 330, 392, 398, 410, 428, 450, 582

nature, human, xxix, x, 167, 170, 172-3, 330, 438-9

necessity, historical (and realm of), 38, 76, 274, 374-5, 378, 405, 485

negation of the negation: *see* dialectic

'negroes', 214-5, 262, 406, 451, 539

neo-scholasticism, *see* Thomism

non expedit decree, 6-7, 41-3, 52, 525-6

notebooks (Gramsci's prison),

approach, nature and structure of, xv-xix, lxxxii, 279-8, 326-7, 364-5, 508, 570; 'A', 'B' and 'C' texts in –, xvi, 476; dating of paragraphs in –, 476-7, **478-506**; first mention of publishing –, 519; journeyings after Gramsci's death xix, 508
noumenon (the Kantian 'unknowable'), lxi, 223, 292, 371-2, 402
objectivity, 291-3, 410; objective as universal subjective, lix, 291, 416; *see also* reality of external world
objectivism, 323, 410
oil, politics of, 209-11
ophelimity, 393, 574
oratory, 223, 298, 301, 404, 406, 440, 444, 447, 536, 557
Ordine Nuovo, xviii, xxi, xxiv, xxxii, 410, 577

paganism, 89, 92-3, 106, 403, 475
pantheism, 121, 313; *see also* theopanism
paradoxes, logical –, lxi-lxii, 290, 556; social –, 359, 570
parasitic (passive) classes, xlvii, 13, 216, 224, 226, 228-9, 234, 238-9, 246, 250, 253, 269, 549
particularism, religious, 104; – in an Empire, 261, 551-2
parties, xxxi, 11, 15, 33, 115, 200, 267, 272, 328, 344, 351-2, 358, 390-1, 435, 462-3, 534, 552, 580; – in USA, 260, 551; revolutionary –, 345, 358, 372, 568; *see also* Centre, Communist, Conservative, Labour, Popular, Socialist Parties
passion, Crocean concept of –, 157, 316, 334, 343-4, 354, 381, 389-93, 400, 462-3, 538, 581; – in Julien Benda, 586
peasantry, xxiv-v, xlvii, lxxii, 10, 12-3, 30, 35, 44, 51-3, 65, 103, 118, 143-4, 194, 198, 235, 237, 246-7, 253, 256, 352, 359, 406, 450, 457-8, 474, 520-1, 548, 561, 570, 587; rural classes, 164, 235
philology, 146, 298, 310, 347, 388, 558; 'living –', lxxxii-lxxxiii, 519
Philosophy Congress (VII World –, of 1929), 67, 287, 369, 379, 403, 412, 443, 577
philosophy and philosophies, xxxv, lv, lxviii-lxxiv, lxxxii, 13, 42-4, 73-4, 92, 121, 124-5, 139, 175, 189, 259, 280, 291, 293-4, 302-4, 306-7, 313-4, 316-7, 337-8, 340, 343, 345-6, 353, 374, 379, 383-8, 396, 400-3, 406-15, 436-44, 446, 471, 526, 537, 557, 572, 577, 580; – and ideology, xiv, lxxix-lxxxi, 327, 333, 343, 352-3, 382-3, 446, 571; – as history, 442; – as history of philosophy, 385, 387; – as methodology of historiography, lxix, 300; – of history, 310; – of liberty, 354, 569; – of practice, 366; – of religion, 42-3, 93, 297; agnosticism, pessimism or scepticism in –, 316-7, 329, 413, 443, 582; Chinese –, 124-5; classical German –, xxxix, lxv-lxvi, lxviii, 24, 132, 307, 310-3, 315, 319, 356, 382-3, 385, 401, 407, 418, 561; democratic nature of –, 438-9, 580; empiricist and pragmatist, 125, 174, 258-9, 297, 301, 308, 560; French seventeenth- and eighteenth-century materialist –, 24, 170, 313, 386, 449, 582; history and development of –, 282, 290, 310, 314; idealist –, 180, 283, 347, 402, 570, 572, 575; Kantian –, 297, 308, 311; modern –, 23, 43, 99, 410, 472; political –, 405, 441-2; speculative –, language and method, 125, 306, 319, 329-30, 337, 341, 343-4, 346-8, 354, 356-7, 367, 368, 385-6, 388,

411, 435-8; *see also* actualism; Crocean idealism; Hegelianism; identity (of history and philosophy; of politics and philosophy; of philosophy and ideology); sciences; Thomism; translation and translatability; unity (of politics and philosophy)

philosophy of praxis, x, xxxviii, lii, lxxv, 179, 182-3, 258, 291-3, 299, 304, 315, 317-9, 323, 329-32, 336, 345-8, 354-8, 361, 367, 370, 382, 384-7, 390, 394-9, 401, 403, 406-7, 412-5, 418-25, 446, 450-2, 471, 537, 562, 574-5; – and doctrine of error (illusion), 413; – and ethics, 420; – and mass or modern culture, 385, 423; – as anthropology, 424; – as 'heresy' of religion of liberty, 361; – as intellectual and moral reform (or cultural movement etc.), xxii, 315, 336, 406, 574; – as modern (or historicist) conception of world, 27, 348; – as 'scientism', 407, 565; – as theory of contradictions, 395; crisis in –, 406; renewal of –, 355; translation and –, lxvi, 306-7, 355; vulgarisation of –, 355; *see also* Croce's revision of Marxism; materialism, historical

philosophy of the pure act: *see* actualism

physics (*properly speaking* chemistry), 354; modern –, lxi-lxii, 280, 286-7, 290, 515-6, 556

physiocrats (economic school), xxxv-xxxvi, xxxvii, 164, 540

pleasure principle (economics), *see* hedonism

Popular Party (Italian) and popularism, xxiv, 7, 12, 30-3, 40, 92, 117, 407, 463, 532, 584-5

positivism, lv, lviii, lxvii, lxxii,

lxxiv-lxxv, 27, 43, 170, 272, 276, 280, 295-7, 304, 329, 339-40, 367, 370, 418, 448, 450, 546, 554, 557, 561

praxis, 'overturning of' (*or* 'revolutionary –'), 395, 430, 579

Prince, modern, *see* parties, revolutionary

production, Asiatic mode of –, 509; economic, industrial or capitalist –, xxxiv, 181, 215, 221, 235-6, 251, 255, 263, 276, 321, 393, 432; forces, means, modes or relations of –, xxxv, 20, 220, 321, 350, 423, 427, 451, 562

profits, xxxviii, 168-9, 185, 216, 227, 245, 350, 428, 430; – from financial operations, 263; *see also* laws

progress, technical, xliv-xlv, 225-9, 428-31, 448, 579

protectionism, 160, 185, 223-4, 230-3, 234-5, 245-9, 252, 256, 567

Protestantism, xxvii-xxviii, 6, 16, 20, 23-7, 58, 93, 109-11, 113-7, 119, 129, 135, 207, 271, 533, 535, 564; *see also* Calvinism; Lutheranism; Reformation

Prussia, *see* Germany

psychology, 170, 172, 174-5, 218, 227, 276, 411, 447-8, 450, 452-3, 539, 582; – of individual, 316-7; – of intellectuals, 187; – of ruling class, 146; of students, 150; – of workers and workers' movement, 217, 322, 411, 450, 452-3, 554; Cartesian –, 313; psychoanalysis, 447-8; *see also* Freudianism

quantity-quality relationships, 275, 321, 383, 560

rational and actual (in Hegel), 310, 312, 372, 379, 560, 571

rationalism, 14, 24, 276, 342, 403,

406, 418, 437-8, 452
rationality, 179, 337, 359, 375; science as –, 283
rationalisation, industrial, xliv, xlviii, li, 145, 226, 236, 255, 273, 276, 322, 434, 579; *see also* Americanism, Fordism, Taylorism
realism, historical and philosophical –, 291, 323, 331, 341, 356-7, 400, 413-4; neo-realism, 297; primitive –, 290-1, 410, 564; *see also* science; translation
reality (external, nature of), lix, lxiv, lxvii, lxxiii-lxxiv, lxxviii, 168, 281, 283, 290-3, 296, 323, 338, 369-71, 383-5, 390, 394-5, 399, 402, 409-10, 413-7, 437, 571, 575-7; concept of – and of becoming, 369-70, 395-6, 437
reason and reasoning, 43, 56-7, 136, 302-3, 318, 392, 439, 456, 520-1, 525, 563, 580; *see also* thought
reform, religious, 388, 406, 472-3; Catholic –, 24-5, 443
Reformation (Protestant), 10, 23-5, 58, 75, 82-3, 131, 270-1, 343, 355, 407-8, 523, 537, 574; Reformation and Counter-Reformation, **19-28**
reformism, xlvii, lxxviii, 98, 155, 187, 343, 349, 374, 376-8, 452, 458, 461, 468, 473, 524, 555, 572, 582, 584; Croce, actualism and –, **435-62**
regularity, *see* laws
relations, social, 330, 349-51, 386-7, 423
religion xx-xxix, **4-137**, 158-9, 211-3, 273, 290, 292-3, 295, 329, 338-41, 347, 403, 406-15, 424, 447, 471-5, 574, 576, 582; – and ideology, 333; – and reason, 56, 582; – and science, 410-1; – and superstition or mythology, lxxx, 330, 352-3, 403, 409, 414; – as ideology or instrument of domination, 290, 359, 383, 414; – as lower form of philosophy, xxii, 73, 158-60, 334, 338-9, 409; – as opium of the people, xxvii, 56, 58, 528, 545; – as organising principle of society, xxi, 13-4; – as wager, 56-9; – of liberty, 352, 359-61, 396, 473; – of fatherland, 359-60; – in Far East, xxviii, 117-32; – in Italy, **28-59**; – in metropolitan countries, **102-15**; – in Middle East, *see* Islam; religious culture in other major countries, **115-37**; arms and – (force and consent), 17; concepts and definition of, – xx-xxi, 9, 78, 124, 520-1; polytheistic –, xxviii, 8-9, 130, 135-6; popular or mythological –, 55-8, 134-6, 403, 409, 414, 448-9, 475; positivist (rationalistic) aspects of –, xxviii, 117, 136; state control of –, 130, 529; *see also* Crocean concept of religion
religious (i.e. people under vows), xxviii, 86, 111, 411
'religious' conception of war, 333
Renaissance (Italian) 22-4, 75, 257, 271, 314, 355, 407-8, 469, 472, 475, 574
Restoration (of monarchy), 23-4, 37-9, 329, 341, 375, 459, 567
Revolution, French –, 5, 10, 17, 26, 38, 83, 94, 103, 198, 310-2, 318, 324, 330, 348-51, 359, 401, 456, 458-9, 533, 566-7, 575, 583; industrial, economic or technical –, 203, 240, 255, 319-20, 472; national –, 126, 342; Parthenopean (Neapolitan) –, 341, 525, 533, 567; passive –, lxiv, 277, 329-30, 341-2, 350, 360, 373-4, 382, 554; permanent –, 357; Russian –, 199, 203; social –, and revolutionaries (*see also* parties), xxiv, xxviii, liii, 121,

Subject and Key Concept Index 615

126, 349, 351-2, 372, 374, 378, 384, 405, 455, 457, 528, 568, 583
revolution-restoration, 330, 342, 349, 373-4, 377, 382
Ricardo, method of –, xxxix, 179; philosophical importance of –, xxxiii-lv, 512, 544; relationship of – to Marx, xxxv, xl, 511, 544
Risorgimento (Italian national movement), xxv, 11, 23, 39-40, 252, 312, 330, 343, 348, 375, 377, 520, 551, 561, 572
'Robinsonades', *see* solipsism
Roman world (ancient), xx, 93, 96, 119, 125, 130-1, 223, 253-4, 259, 261, 275, 314-5, 319, 522, 536, 548
Romanticism, 94, 337
Rotary Club movement, 11, 147, 538
ruling (dominant) class, xlvi, xlix, 10, 12, 19, 64-5, 75, 120, 143, 146, 155-6, 159, 189, 217, 223, 229, 239, 274, 350, 352-3, 395-6, 399, 435, 444, 464-6, 549, 552, 580; owning (boss) –, 159, 235, 250, 272, 452; 'political' class (of Mosca), 272
Russia, tsarist, xxix, 115, 198, 201, 206, 213; *see also* USSR

Saint-Simonism, 93, 186, 538
Sanfedista movement, 38-9, 103, 525
savings, xlvii, 13, 215-8, 231, 239, 246, 250, 252-3
schools, 111, 127-8, 259; active (progressive) –, xxx, 139-43, 157; common –, xxx, 140-1, 145, 147, 157, 538; Church –, 71, 127-8; elementary and primary –, xxxi, 64, 66, 71, 73-4, 122, 142-3, 158-9, 339, 353, 408-9, 529; secondary and high –, xxxi, 46, 64, 66-7, 71, 73-4, 86, 141, 143-4, 147, 409, 529; internal Communist Party –, xxix, xxxiii-xxxiv; *see also* academies, education, universities
science (and scientists), lxxvii, lxxxiv, 13, 22, 43, 68, 74, 125, 146, 148-9, 152-3, 159, 166, 171, 189-90, 280, **281-95**, 296, 304, 308-9, 323-4, 368, 392, 397, 405, 409, 415, 418, 420, 426, 435-7, 451, 472, 557, 582, 586; – as rational project, 283, 287; Croce and –, liv, 283, 444; development of –, 20, 22; doctrines of –, 339; empiricism and/or of –, liv-lv, 283-4, 297, 370, 558; epistemological bases of –, 280, 296; fact-hypothesis distinction in –, lvi-lviii, 293, 515; historical aspect of –, lvi, lix, 153, 292, 298-9, 558; humanity, nature and –, lx, 290-2; idealist philosophy as true –, 396; languages of and in –, 308-9, 426; Marx and –, lix, lxxvii; mentality of –, 305; objectivity of –, lix, 293; popular notions of –, 68, 294-5; positivism, idealism and –, lv, 276; realism (or neo-realism) and –, lxi, 291-2, 297; truth in –, lix, lxxxi, 292, 309, 323: *see also* economic science; hypothesis, scientific; sciences (specific groups thereof); translation and translatability
sciences, humanistic and social (erudite, historical, juridical, moral, political, etc.) –, lv-lvi, lxxv, lxxxii, 146, 189, 276, 305, 315-6, 346, 366, 373-4, 376, 389-90, 392, 396, 399, 405, 437, 439, 452, 473, 561, 572
sciences, natural, biological, exact, physical and mathematical –, xxxi, xxxix, liv-lxii, lxx, lxxv-lxxvi, 22, 43, 137, 171-3, 179, 189, 280-3, 285-9, 292, 298-9, 302, 305, 315-6, 324, 354, 360, 392, 397, 410-1, 410-1, 414, 418,

Subject and Key Concept Index

439-41, 512, 558; ideological nature of –, lvi, 292-3; national trends in –, 287, 440
sciences, philosophical and speculative –, liv, 283, 301, 436-7, 444, 580; method in the –, xxxii, lxxv, 281-5, 294-6, 304, 444
scientism, lv, 117, 407, 450
sensationalism, *see* philosophy, French materialist
sense, common (i.e. popular, unreflected), 15, 166, 290-1, 299, 301, 387, 409-10, 556-7
sense, good (i.e. sound common –), 299, 329, 338, 345, 410, 429, 556-7
serfs, 166
Shintoism, 129-32
Sillon (French Catholic social movement), 7, 77, 90, 92, 530
slavery, 157-60, 166, 539
Social Democracy and socialism, lxxi, 7, 39, 49, 112, 244, 341, 404-5, 452-3, 457, 463, 473, 536, 545-6, 569
Socialist Party and Socialists, in Italy, 33, 41, 43, 187, 246, 463, 473, 526, 546, 554, 570; in England, 534; elsewhere, 49-50, 244
society, lxxvii, 43, 45-6, 75, 106, 142, 314, 348, 397, 437; regulated –, 437
society, civil –, xxxi, 18, 43, 64, 75-6, 167, 276, 323, 344, 357, 427, 435, 439, 465, 474, 514, 531; – and the economy, lii, 562; – as sphere of ethical action (Croce), 372; Church and –, 17, 43; hegemony and –, lii, 75, 372, 514; – and political society, 20, 435, 439, 522; *see also* society, political; state
society, political, 16, 43, 75, 435, 439; *see also* society, civil
sociology and sociologism, 304, 344, 370, 446, 448, 555

solipsism, 289, 345, 402, 576
South, 12, 51, 528; intellectual tradition of –, 364, 368; – and North, 231, 240, 245, 249, 364, 368, 570, 584; Southern question (in Italy), xxv, xlvi-xlvii, lxxii, lxvi, 189, 231, 240, 245-6, 249, 546, 550-1
Spain, 29, 91, 99, 104-5, 137, 202, 204, 208, 533, 537
spirit, human, 313, 316, 438, 456, 561; *see also* mind
standard of living, xlvii, 13, 181, 215-7, 229, 235, 249-50
state, xxi, xxiii, xxxi, 17-9, 44-6, 59-76, 93, 117, 130-2, 144, 160, 163, 167, 182-3, 198, 207-8, 217, 222, 238, 241-3, 247-9, 252, 260, 270, 272-3, 276, 318, 323, 330, 332, 341, 344-5, 350, 357-8, 393, 435-7, 439, 443-4, 464-5, 467, 470, 474, 531, 561, 568, 580-1, 583, 585, 587; – and the economy, xlviii, 182-3, 220, 222, 225, 247-8, 308, 427, 450, 551; – and the individual, 15, 437, 439, 581; – as rule of law, lxxix; – as authority or force, lxxix, 352, 357, 372, 580-1; – as sphere of political action (Croce), 372; ethical – (especially in Gentile), lxxix, 443, 465, 568, 687; hegemonic and subaltern –, 223; liberal –, 39, 376; *see also* society, civil; society, political
structure (economic, of society), 167, 273, 277, 312, 317, 329-30, 400, 416, 514; – as claimed 'hidden God', 330, 347, 414, 571, 577; – as ensemble of social relations, 347; – as real past, 416; Marxian –, lii, 293
structure and superstructure, xii, 312, 315, 398, 400, 414-5, 514, 562; Croce and –, lxxiii, 414, 571
struggle, class –, xxv, xxxviii, lxiv,

Subject and Key Concept Index

222, 390, 392, 456, 464, 511, 545-6, 548, 557, 574; cultural –, 357; social and political –, 158, 330, 343, 349, 355, 357, 376-7, 380, 391-2, 396, 400-1, 456, 581
subaltern (popular) classes (masses), 10, 14, 35, 58, 64-7, 98, 117, 119-24, 146, 217, 238, 247, 260, 274-5, 300, 314-5, 333-4, 349, 353, 359, 373, 379-80, 390, 392, 396, 398, 404-6, 409-10, 453, 457, 552, 580, 587; – allied to workers, 156
subjectivism (subjective conception of reality), 286-7, 292, 306, 330, 345, 347-8, 370, 413; *see also* idealism; philosophy, idealist; solipsism
superstructures, liii, 172, 212, 273, 306, 312, 316-8, 330, 345-6, 394-8, 400, 412-3, 416, 514, 543, 554, 567; Gramsci as theorist of –, liii; science and –, lvi, 293; – and appearance, 133, 346, 394, 398, 412-3, 415-6
Syllabus of Errors (of Catholic Church), 6, 84, 99-100, 351-2, 361, 569
syndicalism, 246, 389, 459, 583

Taoism, 124-6
Taylorism, 255, 273, 276, 433-4, 579
technology, lvi, lix-lx, 251, 255, 281, 293, **319-25**, 410, 440, 577; military –, 323-4; – as mediation between reality and science, 281, 323; – as mediator between humanity and nature (reality), 292, 410
tertiaries (Franciscan), 33-4, 78, 524
theology, xxv, 19, 43, 77, 135, 172, 300, 329-30, 346-8, 369, 403, 410-1, 564: *see also* grace, doctrine of

theopanism, 121; *see also* pantheism
Thomism and neo-Thomism (scholasticism and neo-scholasticism), 42-4, 67, 94, 297, 329, 339-40, 367, 411, 418, 440, 526, 531, 537, 564, 566
thought, lxvii, 18, 23, 43, 74-5, 124, 159, 298-9, 301-4, 310, 323, 332, 338, 346-8, 370-1, 376, 439-41, 558, 580-1; – and action, lxxviii, 441-2; – and being, 574; abstract – (Gentile), 410; economic and/or political –, 24, 163; philosophical –, 286, 346, 443; scientific –, 22, 440
trade unions, xxiii, xliv, 15, 30-3, 35, 49-50, 187, 207, 223, 225, 254, 302-3, 427, 474, 524, 587; open shop, 256
transcendence and transcendentalism, xxix, 14, 273, 313, 330, 346-8, 369, 371-2, 403, 443, 471, 520, 532; *see also* immanentism
transformism, 360, 464, 586
translation and translatability, lxii-lxvii, lxxxiii-lxxiv, 183, 280-1, **306-19**, 329, 339; – and Gramsci's 'open Marxism', lxvi, lxxxii-lxxxiv; – of Crocean, speculative and national philosophies into Marxist concepts, lxvi-lxvii, lxxi, 344, 355, 385, 413; – of philosophy of praxis into speculative or transcendental terms, lxxxii, 355, 367, 385, 403
truth, lviii-lix, lxxx, 23, 43, 292, 309, 323, 347, 390, 396, 398, 402, 410, 525, 568, 581; *see also* science

United States, *see* America (USA); Americanism
unity, – of opposites, 371; – of process of reality, 371, 414; – of society, 156, 348, 385; – of the

spirit, 344, 400, 575; – of theory and practice (ideal and real, philosophy and politics), 311, 323, 355, 384, 400, 446, 561; *see also* dialectic; identity (of politics and philosophy)
universities, xxxii, 64-6, 122, 138-9, 142, 145, 147-52; Catholic and other ecclesiastical –, 64-5, 67, 135, 411, 529; popular –, xxxii, 155, 464, 538
USSR, xlvi, xlviii, lii, lxxi, 195, 197-200, 207, 213, 271, 330, 456, 529, 539, 542, 546, 553, 555, 560, 583, 585
utility, 170, 175, 248, 308, 371, 393, 542-3, 574; marginal or final degree of –, 168, 172, 424, 510, 542-3, 545, 578

Vatican, *see* Catholic Church
value, xxxv, xxxviii-xxxix, 172, 187, 430, 542; Marxist and labour theories of –, xxxvi, xxxviii, 168, 185-6, 419, 424-6, 542, 545, 571, 578; Marxist theory of – as elliptical comparison, 424-8; other (especially marginalist) theories of –, xxxvi-xxxviii, 174-5, 184-5, 308, 424, 542-3, 545; exchange –, 172; surplus –, xliv-xlv, 168, 425-6, 431, 579; relative surplus –, xliv, 428-30, 579; use –, 172
verismo (Italian naturalist literary school), 312

wages, 145, 215-7, 222, 227, 230, 235, 239, 249-50, 255-6, 433-4
wars of manoeuvre and position, lxxxiii, 324, 350
wealth, lxxvii, 164-5, 171, 405; labour theory of –, 165, 171
will (volition), acts of, 374-5, 402; human (collective) – and – of individual, lxxix, 17, 126, 156, 179, 190, 274, 276, 310, 323, 375, 378, 383-5, 391, 445, 453, 574, 580-1; moral –, 383; political –, 391
women, 317, 397; social position of –, 107, 118, 524, 534; – and Catholicism, 44, 474
workers, industrial (proletariat), and workforce, xxi, xxiv, xxxv, xlvii, 7, 34, 43, 47-9, 143, 145, 166, 185-6, 207, 216, 224, 227-8, 234-5, 237, 241, 248, 250, 253-6, 262, 264, 269, 320-1, 399, 405, 419, 427, 433-5, 448-50, 452, 454, 457-8, 526, 535, 539, 542, 545, 548, 550, 565, 575, 587; – as innovatory class, 156; French workers' movement, 342; German workers' movement, 382, 384-5, 401, 561